WITHDRAWN
UTSA Libraries

The SAGE
Handbook of
Case-Based Methods

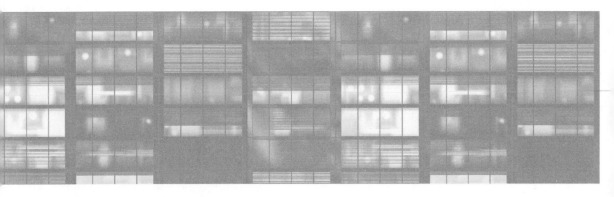

The SAGE
Handbook of
Case-Based Methods

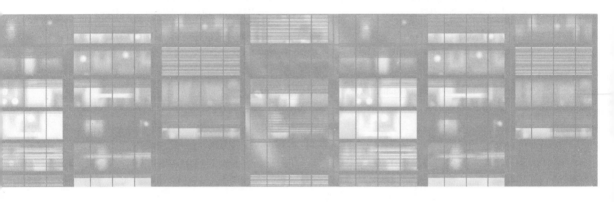

Edited by
David Byrne
and Charles C. Ragin

Los Angeles | London | New Delhi
Singapore | Washington DC

Introduction and editorial arrangement © David Byrne and Charles C. Ragin 2009

Chapter 1 © David L. Harvey 2009

Chapter 2 © Lars Mjøset 2009

Chapter 3 © Bob Carter and Alison Sealey 2009

Chapter 4 © Malcolm Williams and Wendy Dyer 2009

Chapter 5 © David Byrne 2009

Chapter 6 © Colin Elman 2009

Chapter 7 © Emma Uprichard 2009

Chapter 8 © Dianne Phillips and John Phillips 2009

Chapter 9 © Emma Whelan 2009

Chapter 10 © Ray Kent 2009

Chapter 11 © Gisèle De Meur and Alain Gottcheiner 2009

Chapter 12 © Benoît Rihoux and Bojana Lobe 2009

Chapter 13 © Ronald L. Breiger 2009

Chapter 14 © David Byrne 2009

Chapter 15 © Nigel Fielding and Richard Warnes 2009

Chapter 16 © Seán Ó Riain 2009

Chapter 17 © Gary Goertz and James Mahoney 2009

Chapter 18 © Nick Emmel and Kahryn Hughes 2009

Chapter 19 © Fred Carden 2009

Chapter 20 © Edwin Amenta 2009

Chapter 21© John Walton 2009

Chapter 22 © Albert J. Bergesen 2009

Chapter 23 © Paul Downward and Joseph Riordan 2009

Chapter 24 © James Mahoney and P. Larkin Terrie 2009

Chapter 25 © Peer C. Fiss 2009

Chapter 26 © Frances Griffiths 2009

Chapter 27 © Sue Dopson, Ewan Ferlie, Louise Fitzgerald and Louise Locock 2009

Chapter 28 © Philippa Bevan 2009

Chapter 29 © Wendy Olsen 2009

Chapter 30 © David Byrne, Wendy Olsen and Sandra Duggan 2009

Chapter 31 © Charles C.Ragin 2009

First published 2009

Apart from any fair dealing for the purposes of research or private study, or criticism or review, as permitted under the Copyright, Designs and Patents Act, 1988, this publication may be reproduced, stored or transmitted in any form, or by any means, only with the prior permission in writing of the publishers, or in the case of reprographic reproduction, in accordance with the terms of licences issued by the Copyright Licensing Agency. Enquiries concerning reproduction outside those terms should be sent to the publishers.

SAGE Publications Ltd
1 Oliver's Yard
55 City Road
London EC1Y 1SP

SAGE Publications Inc.
2455 Teller Road
Thousand Oaks, California 91320

SAGE Publications India Pvt Ltd
B 1/I 1 Mohan Cooperative Industrial Area
Mathura Road
New Delhi 110 044

SAGE Publications Asia-Pacific Pte Ltd
33 Pekin Street #02-01
Far East Square
Singapore 048763

Library of Congress Control Number: 2008931584

British Library Cataloguing in Publication data

A catalogue record for this book is available from the British Library

ISBN 978-1-4129-3051-2

Typeset by CEPHA Imaging Pvt. Ltd., Bangalore, India
Printed in India at Replika Press Pvt Ltd
Printed on paper from sustainable resources

**Library
University of Texas
at San Antonio**

Contents

Acknowledgements

All intellectual projects are the resultant of the work of lots of individuals and indeed often of many institutions. That is particularly true of a collective effort like this Handbook. Many people have helped us in many ways. Some of them are contributors here, some are not. First, to institutions. The UK's Economic and Social Research Council (ESRC) funded a seminar series 'Realising the potential: realist social theory and empirical research' in 1999–2001 organized by Caroline New of Bath Spa University and Bob Carter of the University of Warwick which played an important role in developing methodological arguments for many of our UK contributors. Second, the British Academy funded a very useful workshop organized by Wendy Olsen 'Quantitative Social Science – Challenges and Possibilities' in September 2004 which enabled us to bring Charles Ragin to the UK and start the dialogue which resulted in this Handbook. In 2004–2005, the ESRC under its Research Methods programme funded a series of workshops/research events under the title 'Focusing on the Case' which enabled us to develop the issues raised in the original British Academy event. Several of the chapters in this Handbook have been written by participants in this series and the chapter on 'Causality and Interpretation in Policy Related Research' in Section Three is a direct product of them. We would like to acknowledge the work of Sandra Duggan and Linda Campbell at Durham in organizing these workshops and of Angela Dale, Director of the ESRC Research Methods programme and Ruth Durrell, the administrator for that programme, all of whom were always supportive and helpful in making that series work as well as it did. Wendy Olsen was the co-director of that series and she has always been a source of intellectual stimulation as well as a colleague whose administrative competence more than compensates for David Byrne's deficiencies in that respect. The ESRC Research Methods festivals in Oxford, originally organized by Angela and Ruth, provided us with a venue for developing arguments, locating more contributors, and generally have served as a fantastic base for the development of methodology and methods in recent years. They will be an important element in the history of methodological progress in the social sciences.

The suggestion that we should produce this book was originally made by Chris Rojek at SAGE and he has always been supportive and helpful. Jai Seaman at SAGE held our hands through the process of assembling chapters and calmed us down when things were a bit sticky – and to the credit of our contributors that did not happen very often. She has been an exemplary editor and an enormous help.

At the personal level our families provided us with support, criticism and a sense of balance so we are grateful to them. Not only did they provide important reality checks, they also knew not to call in the medics when this project left us either staring blindly into space or working maniacally through a new argument or idea. The completion of this project provides testimony to their patience and good humour.

Notes on Contributors

Edwin Amenta is Professor of Sociology and History at the University of California, Irvine. He is the author, most recently, of *When Movements Matter: The Townsend Plan and the Rise of Social Security* (Princeton NJ: Princeton University Press. 2006) and *Professor Baseball: Searching for Redemption and the Perfect Lineup on the Softball Diamonds of Central Park* (Chicago: University of Chicago Press, 2007).

Albert J. Bergesen is Professor and Head of the Department of Sociology at the University of Arizona. His research on culture includes studies of popular culture (*The Depth of Shallow Culture: The High Art of Shoes, Movies, Novels, Monsters and Toys*. Boulder: Paradigm Publishers, 2006; paper 2007) and (*God in the Movies*. New Brunswick, NJ: Transaction Publications. With Andrew M. Greeley. (2000); paperback edition: Transaction Publications, 2003). His work on cultural theory includes (*Cultural Analysis: The Work of Peter Berger, Mary Douglas, Michel Foucault, and Jurgen Habermas*. With Robert Wuthnow, James D. Hunter and Edith Kurtzweil. London: Routledge and Kegan Paul Ltd., 1984), and more recent efforts to generate a transformational grammar of art styles can be found in, 'Culture and Cognition'. pp. 35–47, in M. Jacobs and N. Hanrahan (Eds.) *The Blackwell Companion to the Sociology of Culture*. New York: Basil Blackwell, 2005; and, 'A Linguistic Model of Art History'. *Poetics, 2000*, 28, 73–90.

Philippa Bevan is an independent researcher in the sociology of development who has worked at the universities of Oxford and Bath. Between 2002 and 2006 she was a member of the Bath-based Research Group 'Wellbeing in Developing Countries' (WeD). Her main role was as Country Co-ordinator of the Ethiopia WeD study (see www.wed-ethiopia.org) and she is currently engaged in writing two books out of that experience; one on power and life quality in Ethiopia and the other on the complexity science methodology which she developed during the research programme. She and a colleague have also been using the WeD data to produce commissioned policy-related research papers and briefings on Ethiopia.

Ronald L. Breiger is Professor of Sociology and a member of the Graduate Interdisciplinary Program in Statistics at the University of Arizona. He is currently Chair-Elect of the Section on Mathematical Sociology of the American Sociological Association. His interests include social networks, stratification, mathematical models, theory and measurement issues in cultural and institutional analysis.

David Byrne is Professor of Sociology and Social Policy at Durham University. Previously he has worked as both an academic and in community development. His books include *Complexity Theory and the Social Sciences* 1998 and *Interpreting Quantitative Data* 2002. His major empirical research interest is in the consequences of deindustrialization for places and people and in the nature of social exclusion on a global basis. He is also keenly interested in the development of methodological perspectives and methods as tools which can be used in the application of social science to real social problems and sees case-based methods as having enormous potential in this context.

Fred Carden is Director of Evaluation at the International Development Research Centre (Canada). He holds a PhD from the University of Montreal and was Research Fellow in Sustainability Science at Harvard University (2007–2008). He has written in the areas of evaluation, international cooperation and environmental management, and has co-published *Outcome Mapping*, *Enhancing Organizational Performance*, among others. His most recent publication is *Knowledge to Policy: Making the Most of Development Research*, (London: Sage, 2009).

Bob Carter is Associate Professor in Sociology, University of Warwick, UK. He has published widely on the politics of racism and immigration and on social theory and sociolinguistics. He is the author of *Realism and Racism: Concepts of Race in Sociological Research* (New York: Routledge, 2000) and the co-author (with Alison Sealey) of *Applied Linguistics as Social Science* (London: Continuum, 2004). He also co-edited (with Caroline New) *Making Realism Work* (New York: Routledge, 2004).

Gisèle De Meur (BELGIUM) is Professor of Mathematics at the Université Libre de Bruxelles. Her research theme began with pure geometry, then mathematical anthropology and mathematics related to political science (electoral systems, theory of democracy, gender studies…). Her more recent works concern methodology of the small-N studies, and in particular 'qulali-quantitative comparative analysis.

Sue Dopson is Rhodes Trust Professor of Organisational Behaviour at Oxford University, and a Governing Body Fellow of Green Templeton College, formerly Vice-President of Templeton College. She is also Director of Research Degrees at the Oxford Said Business School. She acts as an advisor, consultant, referee and editorial board member in a variety of settings. Her research involvements lie principally in the area of health care management, built over the past 18 years. This has included the evaluation of government policy, and reviews of managerial change and organizational interventions. She has published several books and articles on changes in the management of the NHS, the changing nature of middle management, management careers and developments in public sector management. Sue worked as a Personnel Manager in the NHS before pursuing a research and academic career at the University.

Paul Downward is Director of the Institute of Sport and Leisure Policy, University of Loughborough. Along with Alistair Dawson, he is the author of the textbook *The Economics of Professional Team Sports* (Routledge, 2000) and the author of a forthcoming book *The Economics of Sport: Theory, Evidence and Policy* with Alistair Dawson and Trudo Dejonghe (Butterworth Heinemann). He is the editor of a book for the Office for National Statistics on the Use of Official Data in understanding Sports, Leisure and Tourism markets and the author of numerous articles on the economics of sport. He has recently undertaken consultancy work for Sport England on participation, volunteering in sports clubs, and performance management; and UK Sport on Volunteering at the Manchester Commonwealth Games. He is a member of the International Association of Sports Economics, a founding member of the editorial board of the Journal of Sports Economics, and member of the British Philosophy of

Sport Association. Paul is currently playing veteran's rugby and coaches a junior side at his local club.

Sandra Duggan has experience in a wide variety of research areas with an underlying theme of effectiveness i.e 'What works?'. She was involved in the ESRC-funded project, Focusing on the Case in Quantitative and Qualitative Research, with Dave Byrne and Wendy Olsen. The project involved a series of workshops aimed at helping researchers to develop their thinking about case-based methods using a dialogical learning approach. Sandra is now working at the University of Teesside.

Wendy Dyer is Senior Lecturer in Criminology at Northumbria University. She worked with the Cleveland Diversion Team for Mentally Disordered Offenders as an Action Research Worker until 1997. She was awarded ESRC funding for her PhD at the University of Durham, Department of Sociology and Social Policy (1997–2001). Following completion of her PhD Wendy worked for two years on a project with the Centre for Public Mental Health and in 2004 she was awarded funding by the NHS National R&D Programme on Forensic Mental Health (along with Professor John Carpenter). She was then appointed Senior Research Associate, Department of Psychiatry, University of Oxford working on a project to evaluate the Dangerous and Severe Personality Disorder (DSPD) programme. In 2005 Wendy, along with two colleagues from HMP Durham and the Care Services Improvement Partnership (CSIP), set up the Prison and Offender Research in Social Care and Health – North East, Yorkshire and Humberside network (PORSCH-NEYH). The network has been awarded funding by the Home Office and Department of Health. She acts as coordinator for the networks activities. Wendy was appointed as Senior Lecturer in Criminology at Northumbria University in January 2008.

Colin Elman is Associate Professor of Political Science in the Maxwell School of Syracuse University. He is currently engaged on a book project investigating America's rise to dominance in the Western Hemisphere. He is also working on other book and article projects on realist international relations theory, qualitative methods and the diffusion of unconventional conflict practices. Elman is (with Miriam Fendius Elman) the co-editor of *Progress in International Relations Theory: Appraising the Field* (MIT Press, 2003); and *Bridges and Boundaries: Historians, Political Scientists, and the Study of International Relations* (MIT Press, 2001); and (with John Vasquez) of *Realism and the Balancing of Power: A New Debate* (Prentice Hall, 2003). Elman has published articles in *International Studies Quarterly*, *International History Review*, *American Political Science Review*, *International Organization*, *International Security* and *Security Studies*. He is a co-founder and Secretary-Treasurer of both the International History and Politics and the Qualitative and Multi-method Research organized sections of the American Political Science Association, and a co-founder and Executive Director of the Consortium for Qualitative Research Methods.

Nick Emmel is a Senior Lecturer in the Sociology and Social Policy of Health and Development at the University of Leeds. His research interests include inequalities in health, social exclusion and poverty. Recent methodological research includes identifying methodologies for accessing socially excluded individuals and groups and Connected Lives, a qualitatively driven, mixed-method investigation of networks, neighbourhoods and communities. Currently he is using qualitative longitudinal methods to investigate the role of grandparents in supporting their grandchildren out of social exclusion in low-income communities. In all of these research projects a case-based methodology is being used to manage data and facilitate theorization and abstraction within and between cases.

Ewan Ferlie is Professor of Public Services Management and Head of the Department of Management at King's College London. He has published widely in the field of organizational studies in health care, and has been co-editor of the *Oxford Handbook of Public Management*. Much of his work uses the comparative case method, including a co authored paper in Academy of Management Journal (best paper award, 2005).

Nigel Fielding is Professor of Sociology and Associate Dean of Arts and Human Sciences at the University of Surrey. With Ray Lee, he co-directs the CAQDAS Networking Project, which provides training and support in the use of computers in qualitative data analysis, and which has latterly become a 'node' of the ESRC National Centre for Research Methods. His research interests are in new technologies for social research, qualitative research methods, mixed method research design and criminology. He has authored or edited 20 books, over 50 journal articles and over 200 other publications. In research methodology his books include a study of methodological integration (*Linking Data*, 1986, Sage; with Jane Fielding), an influential book on qualitative software (*Using Computers in Qualitative Research*, 1991, Sage; editor and contributor, with Ray Lee), a study of the role of computer technology in qualitative research (*Computer Analysis and Qualitative Research*, 1998, Sage; with Ray Lee), a four-volume set, *Interviewing* (2002, Sage; editor and contributor), the *Sage Handbook of Online Research Methods* (2008; editor and contributor) and a further four-volume set on *Interviewing* (forthcoming). He is presently researching the application of high performance computing applications to qualitative methods.

Peer C. Fiss is an Assistant Professor of Strategy at the Marshall School of Business, University of Southern California. He works in the areas of corporate governance, framing, the spread and adaptation of corporate practices and the use of set-theoretic methods, particularly in management and strategy. His research has appeared in journals such as the *Academy of Management Journal, Academy of Management Review, Administrative Science Quarterly, American Sociological Review* and *Strategic Management Journal*. He is the recipient of the 2008 Marshall Dean's Award for Research and serves on the editorial boards of the *Academy of Management Journal, Journal of International Business Studies* and *Business Research*. Peer received his PhD jointly from the Departments of Sociology and Management & Organization at Northwestern University.

Louise Fitzgerald is Professor of Organization Development, Department of HRM, De Montfort University. Her research centres on the management of innovation and change in professional, complex organizations and the restructuring of professional roles. She is currently working on a major, empirical project on the management of organizational networks in health care. She has published in a range of journals, such as *Academy of Management Journal* and *Human Relations*, and has co-authored a number of books, such as *Knowledge to Action? Evidence-Based Health Care in Context*, (Oxford University Press, 2005) and *The Sustainability and Spread of Organizational Change*, (Routledge, 2007). She has previously worked at City University Warwick University, and Salford University.

Gary Goertz teaches Political Science at the University of Arizona. He is the author or co-author of eight books and over 50 articles and chapters on issues of international conflict, institutions and methodology. His books include *Social Science Concepts: A User's Guide* (Princeton 2006) *Contexts of International Politics* (1994), *International Norms and Decision Making: A Punctuated Equilibrium Model* (2003) and with Paul Diehl *War and Peace in International Rivalry* (2000). He is currently working on a book on the evolution of regional economic institutions and their involvement in conflict management.

Alain Gottcheiner is Assistant Lecturer in Applied Mathematics and Computer Science at the Université Libre de Bruxelles, Brussels, Belgium. His main areas of interest are mathematical models as applied to decision-making, to human sciences and to linguistics. He has also studied the mathematical methods (operational research, combinatorial mathematics, groups) and computer science methods which allow the data modeling in administrative sciences, social anthropology, cultural anthropology, comparative linguistics, and phonology, with particular emphasis on the transfer of these methods to non-mathematicians. Alain has reviewed current methods of research in mathematics, physics, astronomy and cosmology, linguistics, etc. all in light of theories of proof of Popper and Lakatos, and positivists' theories of truth.

Frances Griffiths trained in medicine at University of Cambridge and Kings College Hospital, London and went on to become a general practitioner in Stockton-on-Tees. While working as a GP she undertook her PhD at the University of Durham, Department of Sociology and Social Policy and was a founder member of the Northern Primary Care Research Network. Frances joined the University of Warwick in 1998 and became founding Director of the Warwick West-Midlands Primary Care Research Network and developed her research interest in the impact of technology on perceptions of health. In 2003 she was awarded a Department of Health National Career Scientist Award for developing a programme of research on Complexity and Health. Frances undertakes her research with interdisciplinary research teams both within the University and internationally. Although her research mainly links social science and medicine, her research programme related to complexity now includes research collaboration with physical sciences and the humanities.

David L. Harvey is Professor Emeritus of Sociology at the University of Nevada, Reno. He has written on such topics as: poverty and the subculture of poverty; social alienation and the social psychological measurement of reified consciousness; and Critical Marxist sociology. More recently, he has attempted to apply the Critical Realist perspective and the Chaos/Complexity paradigm of non-equilibrium systems to sociological subject matters. His essay in this Handbook reflects these dual interests as they pertain to the understanding of qualitative case studies. Finally, Professor Harvey is currently completing a social history of a poor, Southern–white community located in the American Midwest. It is entitled *Potter Addition: The Social History of a 'Hillbilly Slum'*. When completed, it will be a companion volume to an earlier ethnographic investigation, *Potter Addition: Poverty, Family and Kinship in a Heartland Community*.

Kahryn Hughes is a Senior Research Fellow, and Co-Director of Families Lifecourse and Generations Research Centre (FlaG), at the University of Leeds. Her main theoretical interests are theorizing time, space and relational identity constitution. Thematically, she is interested in exploring inter-generational experiences and meanings of social exclusion; practices of addiction; and theorizing social networks in the context of low-income communities.

Ray Kent is currently Senior Lecturer in the Department of Marketing at the University of Stirling. He has published several books in sociology, media audience measurement, data analysis and marketing research. He is currently exploring alternative methods of data analysis including the use of fuzzy-set analysis, chaos theory and neural network analysis.

Bojana Lobe completed her PhD in Social Sciences Methodology at the University of Ljubljana. She is a researcher at Centre for Methodology and Informatics, and teaching methodological courses at Faculty of Social Sciences. She is a member of editorial board of International Journal of Multiple Research Approaches. She is involved in Eu Kids Online project. Her current research activities and interests are: methodological issues in mixed methods research, new technologies in social science data collection (virtual ethnography, online focus groups, online qualitative interviews), systematic comparative methods, methodological aspects of researching children's experience.

Louise Locock is a Qualitative Researcher interested in personal experiences of health and illness, evidence-based medicine, quality improvement and organizational change in health care. Since 2003 she has been a senior researcher with the DIPEx Health Experiences Research Group at the University of Oxford.

James Mahoney (PhD 1997, University of California, Berkeley) is a Professor of political science and sociology at Northwestern University. He is the author of *The Legacies of Liberalism: Path Dependence and Political Regimes in Central America* (Johns Hopkins University Press, 2001) and co-editor of *Comparative Historical Analysis in the Social Sciences* (Cambridge University Press, 2003). His work also includes articles on political and socioeconomic development in Latin America, path dependence in historical sociology and causal inference in small-N analysis. Mahoney's most recent book is *Colonialism and Development: Spanish America in Comparative Perspective* (Cambridge University Press, forthcoming).

Lars Mjøset (b. 1954) is Professor at the Department of Sociology and Human Geography, and Director of The Oslo Summer School for Comparative Social Science Studies, both at the University of Oslo, Norway. His main fields of interest are the philosophy of the social sciences and comparative political economy with special reference to the Nordic countries and the integration of small countries in the world economy. Besides books in Norwegian, he published *The Irish Economy in a Comparative Institutional Perspective* (Dublin: NESC 1992), and recently co-edited and contributed to two special issues of *Comparative Social Research: Vol. 20* with Stephen van Holde, *The Comparative Study of Conscription in the Armed Forces* (Amsterdam: Elsevier Science, 2002), and *Vol. 24* with Tommy H. Clausen, *Capitalisms Compared* (Amsterdam, London, New York: Elsevier Science, 2007).

Wendy Olsen works as a Senior Lecturer in Socioeconomic Research at University of Manchester. Her research covers UK labour markets, global economic development and research methods. Her specialist areas include the regulation of labour markets; feminist analyses of labour relations; gendered labour force participation in India; global patterns of gendered human development; and methodological pluralism (especially across the qualitative–quantitative 'divide'). Her publications include *Rural Indian Social Relations* (Delhi: Oxford University Press, 1996); *The Politics of Money* (2002); *Modelling Gender Pay Gaps* (with S. Walby, Equal Opportunities Commission, 2004). She is currently working on fuzzy-set causal analysis, causes of gender pay gaps, habitus and moral reasoning strategies about economic policy.

Seán Ó Riain is Professor of Sociology at the National University of Ireland, Maynooth. He has carried out a range of case study research, including ethnographic studies of software workplaces and transnational studies of high technology growth and development. Publications include *Global Ethnography* (2000, co-edited) and *The Politics of High Tech Growth* (2004). Current projects include a study of Silicon Valley and Ireland as a case study of a transnational system of work and employment and a life history study of social change in twentieth century Ireland that mixes qualitative and quantitative methods.

Dianne Phillips (b. 1940), BA (Econ) MA (Econ), and PhD, in Sociology at the University of Manchester. Postgraduate diploma in Mathematical Statistics, University of Manchester. Former Principal Lecturer in Social Research Methodology and Social Statistics in the Faculty of

Humanities and Social Science at the Manchester Metropolitan University in the UK. Currently independent consultant, providing support for social research and evaluation. In addition to commissioned research and evaluation reports, publications include contributions to a number of books on methodological topics and to other social research oriented publications. Also an occasional reviewer for Sociology, Social Science Computer Review, Sociological Research Online and the Royal Statistical Society (Social Statistics). Current interests in evaluation methodologies and 'measurement' of soft outcomes.

John Phillips (b. 1939), Degrees Oxford, Psychology, Philosophy; London, Economics; Salford, Sociology. Lectured in Social Theory, Manchester Polytechnic, 1969–1992. After retirement, varied consultancy work. Publications in Social Theory. Current interests in Artificial Intelligence, Dialectics and Sociology.

Charles C. Ragin holds a joint appointment as Professor of Sociology and Political Science at the University of Arizona. In 2000–2001 he was a Fellow at the Center for Advanced Study in the Behavioral Sciences at Stanford University, and before that he was Professor of Sociology and Political Science at Northwestern University. His substantive research interests include such topics as the welfare state, ethnic political mobilization and international political economy. However, for the past two decades his work has focused primarily on broad issues in social science methodology, especially the challenge of bringing some of the logic and spirit of small-N case-oriented research to the study of medium-sized and large Ns. Central to this effort is the use of set-theoretic methods of analysis and the treatment of cases of bundles of interpretable combinations of aspects and not simply as raw material for the assessment of the net effects of 'independent' variables. His most recent books are *Redesigning Social Inquiry: Fuzzy Sets and Beyond*, published by University of Chicago Press in 2008 and *Configurational Comparative Methods: Qualitative Comparative Analysis and Related Techniques* (co-edited with Benoît Rihoux), also published in 2008 (Sage). He is the author of more than 100 articles in research journals and edited books, and he has developed two software packages for set-theoretic analysis of social data, *Qualitative Comparative Analysis* (QCA) and *Fuzzy-Set/Qualitative Comparative Analysis* (fsQCA).

Benoît Rihoux is Professor of Political Science at the Centre de Politique Comparée of the Université catholique de Louvain (Belgium). His substantive research interests include political parties, new social movements, organizational studies, political change, environmental politics and policy processes. He is Co-ordinator of the COMPASSS international research group (http://www.compasss.org) and oversees the management of its linked Web pages, databases and archives. He is also joint convener of international initiatives around methods more generally, such as the ECPR Standing Group on Political Methodology, the ECPR Summer School in Methods and Techniques and the ECPR Research Methods book series (Palgrave; co-editor with B. Kittel). He has recently published *Innovative Comparative Methods for Policy Analysis: Beyond the Quantitative–Qualitative Divide* (Springer/Kluwer, co-editor with H. Grimm, 2006) and *Configurational Comparative Methods: Qualitative Comparative Analysis (QCA) and Related Techniques* (Sage, co-editor with Charles C. Ragin, 2008).

Joseph Riordan is a Senior Lecturer in Economics at the University of Hertfordshire. He is a member of the International Association of Sports Economics (IASE) and the European Association of Sports Management (EASM) and recently presented a paper on the effect of participation in sport on people's self-reported health at the EASM conference in 2008. He has acted as a referee for academic journals on sports and economics including the Journal of Sports Economics and European Sport Management Quarterly. With Dr Paul Downward, he is currently examining sports participation in the UK using a variety of official datasets. Joe is a keen runner and regularly participates in the London Marathon, despite his weight!

Alison Sealey is a Senior Lecturer in Modern English Language, University of Birmingham, UK. She has published extensively on various aspects of sociolinguistics, applied linguistics and discourse analysis. She is the author of *Childly Language: Children, Language and the Social World* (Longman, 2000) and the co-author (with Bob Carter) of *Applied Linguistics as Social Science* (Continuum, 2004).

P. Larkin Terrie is a Doctoral candidate in Political Science at Northwestern University. His dissertation project focuses on state development in Latin America. His interests also include qualitative and quantitative methodology.

Emma Uprichard is a Lecturer in Social Research methods at the Department of Sociology, University of York. Her research interests revolve around the methodological challenge involved in studying the complex social world, and include the sociology of children and childhood, cities and urban change, time and space, and complexity theory. Her current research extends her previous doctoral study of cities as complex systems by focusing specifically on the changing patterns of food and eating throughout the life course in York and the UK since the post-war period.

John Walton is Research Professor of Sociology at the University of California, Davis. He was Distinguished Professor of Sociology at UCD, 1978–2004, and previously Professor of Sociology and Urban Affairs at Northwestern University, 1966–1978. He has been a fellow at the Center for Urban Affairs at Northwestern University and the Woodrow Wilson International Center for Scholars in Washington, DC. In 2001 he was a Leverhulme Trust Fellow in the UK. He has held offices in both the American Sociological Association and the International Sociological Association. In 2005 he received the Robert and Helen Lynn Award for Distinguished Career Achievement in Community and Urban Sociology from the American Sociological Association. John is author and editor of twelve books and he has also written some two hundred articles, chapters, essays and reviews in the areas of historical sociology, international development, social movements and collective action, and environmental sociology.

Richard Warnes is an Analyst at RAND Europe, Cambridge UK and his interests lie in the fields of Policing and Counter-terrorism. He joined RAND in early 2007 after serving for nine years as an Officer with the Metropolitan Police Service in London and earlier service in the British Army. Between completing his first degree and military service he worked for seven years in international relief and human rights, travelling extensively to Eastern Europe, the Middle East and South East Asia. He is currently a part time PhD candidate with the University of Surrey where he is carrying out doctoral research on counter-terrorist responses in seven countries. This research is supported by both an Airey Neave Trust Fellowship, and a Bramshill (National Police Staff College) Fellowship. He holds an MA in Criminal Justice Studies from Brunel University and a BSc (Honours) in International Politics from the University of Portsmouth.

Emma Whelan is an Associate Professor of Sociology in the Department of Sociology and Social Anthropology, Dalhousie University, Halifax, Canada. Her research and publications are concerned with claims-making, standardization and credibility struggles in health, illness and medicine. She has particular interests in pain medicine, endometriosis, expert-lay relations and disease classification.

Malcolm Williams is Professor of Social Research Methodology and Head of the School of Law and Social Science at the University of Plymouth. His main area of interest is methodological issues in social science, in particular probability, causality and objectivity, and he has published extensively in these areas. His empirical research is in the area of housing need, counter-urbanization and household change. Malcolm is the author/editor of six books/edited collections including *Philosophical Foundations of Social Research* (Sage, four volumes 2006); *Making Sense of Social Research* (Sage, 2003); *Science and Social Science* (Routledge, 2000); *Knowing the Social World* (with Tim May, Open University Press, 1998).

Introduction

Case-Based Methods: Why We Need Them; What They Are; How to Do Them

David Byrne

Science studies cases. It examines – to use one of the more than ten dictionary definitions of the multi-faceted word 'case' – instances of a particular situation or set of circumstances. A plethora of methods use the term 'case' in some way to describe approach and focus. The purpose of this collection is to present an account of those methods in their range and variety of application. However, and this qualification has the most emphatic of emphases, the focus on cases here is much more than a way of demarcating a set of methods understood merely as techniques of investigation. The 'turn to the case' represents a fundamental break with a tradition of explanation that has dominated the physical sciences, been understood (although not without challenge) as representing a model for the biological sciences and has been much contested in the social sciences. We – the editors of this book – start from the proposition that the central project of any science is the elucidation of causes that extend beyond the

unique specific instance. Danermark et al. (2002, p. 1) have firmly stated:

> ... first, that science should have generalizing claims. Second, the explanation of social phenomena by revealing the causal mechanisms which produce them is the fundamental task of research.

We agree, and have considerable sympathy with the turn to critical realism as a basic meta-theoretical foundation for social research practice that is proposed by those authors. However, we want to qualify and elaborate somewhat on these fundamental premises. First, we want to make it clear that for us generalizing is not the same as universalizing. It is important to be able to develop an understanding of causation that goes beyond the unique instance – the object of ideographic inquiry. However, it is just as important to be able to specify the limits of that generalization. We cannot establish universal laws in the social sciences. There is no valid nomothetic project. We hope to demonstrate here that case-based methods help us both to elucidate causation *and* to specify the range of applicability of our account of causal mechanisms. The emphasis on the plural form of mechanism in the preceding sentence is very important. It is not just that different mechanisms operate to produce, contingently in context, different outcomes. It is rather that different mechanisms may produce the same outcome – the complete antithesis of the form of understanding that is implicit in, and foundational to, traditional statistical modelling's search for *the* – that is to say the universal, always and everywhere, nomothetic – model that fits the data.

The traditional mode through which science has sought to determine causality has centred on the notion of the variable as the causal agent in the world with real entities – cases – understood as the determined consequences of the operation of relationships among variables. Another way of saying this is that the conventional view is to see cases simply as sites for observing and measuring variables. Cross-case analysis of these variables, once measured via 'cases' (as instances of generic processes) is then seen as the primary 'source' of scientific knowledge established in the form of causal models derived from the description of associations among variables. This analytic strategy, derived from the programme of Newtonian physics, has come to dominate the quantitative programme across science as a whole and has a far greater influence on qualitative social science than is often recognized. Against the method of explanation that centres on variables and works through analysis has been set a tradition operating under a range of related labels – interpretation, thick description, the phenomenological programme. Insofar as this alternative project – perhaps best understood as that of the human sciences as defined by Dilthey – has worked with cases, it has tended to understand them as specific and unique instances to be understood in their own terms – the ideographic project – rather than explained by general covering laws – the nomothetic project. We might see this approach as analogous to explaining each individual landslide in terms of unique context and conditions, without reference to general geological principles.

We want to get beyond this. As always in science, this can be achieved not only by a radical set of technical innovations but also by recognizing that many of our existing scientific practices are implicitly, and to an increasing extent explicitly, founded around a 'focus on the case'. So the purpose of this collection will be to present the methods that can be employed by case-focused researchers, certainly in such a way as to enable people to employ them in practice, but also as the foundation for a practical social science – and indeed for a practical biological and particularly biomedical science – which gets beyond the dichotomies of quantitative/qualitative – explanation/interpretation. A number of streams come together in this project. In particular, the synthesis of complexity theory and critical realism proposed by Reed and Harvey (1992, 1996) resonates very strongly with the idea that cases are central to proper social scientific understanding. One answer, although by no means the only one, to the important question: 'What is a case?' (Ragin and Becker 1992) is that cases are complex systems – a position that transcends the holistic/analytic dichotomy by recognizing that in complex systems (far from equilbric systems), trajectories and transformations depend on all of the whole, the parts, the interactions among parts and whole, and the interactions of any system with other complex systems among which it is nested and with which it intersects. Moreover, complexity theory's mode of understanding the causal determination of the trajectories of cases and ensembles of cases resonates with critical realism's understanding of causality as complex and contingent, and both correspond in essence with the configurational conception of causality that underpins Ragin's (2000) assertion that what matters for social scientists are set-theoretic relationships rather than causal models couched in terms of descriptions of associations among abstracted variables.

Issues of methodology and social research practice informed by methodological argument have a particular contemporary saliency. This is not just a matter of arguments in the academy about the constitution of knowledge, although those arguments do matter. It is also about knowledge as it is deployed in more or less democratic societies where political differences founded on overt differences of material and cultural interest have tended to be replaced by competing claims to competence in political administration. This is especially true of post-ideological and post-interest politics in that most scientized and administered of societies, the United Kingdom, where programme and policy outcomes as measured by statistical indicators are the basis of political claims to competence, and hence electability. Simultaneously, the translation of such indices into performance indicators sustains an audit culture that has largely displaced effective local democracy and replaced it with an apparently neutral and technical political administration that is target driven. However, although most developed in the UK, these are general tendencies in democratic capitalist societies where voters are perceived – it may well be wrongly – essentially as consumers, and 'evidence' is supposed to be the basis of policy and practice.

We will return to the issues of the relationship between social research and political administration – the domain of applied social research – but let us begin in the academy itself. Hedström (2005, p. 1) has remarked, in our view correctly, that:

> ... much sociological theory has evolved into a form of metatheory without any specific empirical referent and ... much sociological research has developed into a rather shallow form of variable analysis with only limited explanatory power.

Again we agree, although our solution to unlocking this logjam is diametrically opposed to Hedström's turn to analytical sociology coupled with agent-based modelling. Likewise, we have some sympathy with Flyvbjerg's desire to make 'social science matter' (2001), although rather less

with his assertion of *phronesis* – virtuous judgement we might say – as a practice that can be distinguished from both *episteme* and *techne* – from abstract knowledge and applied skill. When Flyvbjerg (2001, p. 57) asserts that:

> *Phronesis* is that intellectual activity most relevant to praxis. It focuses on what is variable, on that which cannot be encapsulated by universal rules, on specific cases. *Phronesis* requires an interaction between the general and the concrete; it requires consideration, judgment and choice.

we see the second sentence as in fact a general statement to science as a whole, and the third as the first part of the application of science in social practice. The second part of that application in practice, of social science as praxis, is the requirement that social scientists as experts, for expertise we do indeed possess, have to deploy that expertise in *dialogue* with other people in the social contexts in which that knowledge is applied.[1] Flyvberg does turn to the case study in arguing for 'the power of example' and we agree with his endorsement of the explanatory power of case-based narratives, especially in relation to the formulation of policy interventions. However, we want to go further here because we are firmly asserting what Flyvberg's rather tentatively suggests – that case studies of different kinds, and in particular multiple case studies founded on systematic comparison – are the foundations of useful theoretical descriptions of the social world.

This position has a good deal in common with Pawson's argument after Merton for the saliency of 'theories of the middle range'. Pawson deployed two quotations from Merton to illustrate what this term means and we draw on his usage here. Theories of the middle range are:

> Theories that lie between the minor but necessary working hypotheses that evolve in abundance in day to day research and the all inclusive systematic efforts to develop a unified theory that will explain all the observed uniformities of social behaviour, social organization and social change. (Merton 1968, p. 39)

Moreover:

> The middle range orientation involves the spec-
> ification of ignorance. Rather than pretend to
> knowledge where in fact it is absent, it expressly
> recognizes what still must be learned in order to
> lay the foundations for more knowledge. (Merton
> 1968, p. 68)

Perhaps we go further than Merton because
our position really rejects the notion of any
grand unifying social theory, seeing this as not
only impossible in terms of difficulty but in
fact as quite incommensurate with the nature
and character of the emergent world. Indeed,
the use of that word – emergence – implies that
our view of the impossibility/undesirability of
grand unifying theory also applies to much
of the natural world, and with particular
force to intersections between the natural and
the social.

Something needs to be said now, and to
be said with a good deal of force. The turn
to case methods is predicated on an explicit
rejection of the utility of causal modelling
based on variables. Abbott has delivered an
intellectual coup-de-grace to that approach in
his imagining of the reflections of a scholar of
the future, which bears repeating here:

> The people who called themselves sociologists
> believed that society looked the way it did because
> social forces and properties did things to other
> social forces and properties. Sometimes the forces
> and properties were individual characteristics like
> race and gender, sometimes they were truly
> social properties like population density or social
> disorganization. Sociologists called these forces
> and properties "variables". Hypothesizing which
> of these variables affected which others was
> called "causal analysis". The relation between
> the variables (what these sociologists called the
> "model") was taken as forcible, determining. In this
> view, narratives of human actions might provide
> "mechanisms" that justified proposing a model,
> but what made social science *science* was the
> discovering of these "casual relationships". (Abbott
> 2001, p. 97)

As Abbott remarks, can that really be
what sociologists thought? Well, some did,
some still do, and more importantly other
social scientists, and in particular social
statisticians, quantitative political scientists

and economists, not only believe this and
carry out academic work on that basis, but
have a major influence on policy through
the magic of numerically based accounts
of the working of reality. That said, we
want to make it absolutely clear that our
conception of how case-based methods work
explicitly rejects any fundamental distinction
between the quantitative and the qualitative.
We think Hedström is flat wrong when he
asserts that: 'Although qualitative research
can be important for the development of
explanatory theory, it lacks the reliability and
generalisability of quantitative research ....'
(2005, p. 101) whilst agreeing absolutely with
his preceding statement that: '… quantitative
research is essential for sociology' (2005,
p. 101). Our rejection is of the disembodied
variable, not of quantitative measurement,
description, and systematic exploration.

In the social sciences it is often contended
that quantitative work is concerned with cause
whereas qualitative work is concerned with
meaning. This is characteristically accompanied by an explicit citation of Weber's
dictum that explanation must be adequate
at both the levels of cause and meaning.
However, the separation of qualitative work
from the investigation of causes is miscon-
ceived. Indeed, Weber was to a considerable
degree engaged with the interpretation of
meaning precisely because he understood
meanings as causal to social actions. Pawson
and Tilley (1997, p. 21) correctly identify
the traditional interpretative programme of
social research – what they call hermeneutics
I – as concerned with the establishment of
a true representation, which must include
an account of the causal processes in the
context and actions being interpreted. We
regard Geertz's (1975) commitment to 'thick
description', with its emphasis on the specific
and the contextual, as wholly compatible with
this traditional conception of the hermeneutic
programme and with complexity science's
emphasis on the inherent localism but
nonetheless achievable reality of scientific
knowledge. This has to be distinguished from
the radical relativism of contemporary postmodernism, which, in contrast with the project

represented by the different contributions to this handbook, denies the possibility of any knowledge. Of course, knowledge is socially constructed, as is the social itself, but reality has a say in that construction as well as the acts, agency and social character of the knowledge makers. We make a bold contention here – it is by thinking about cases that a proper and explicitly dialectical synthesis can be achieved between cause and meaning/interpretation in order to achieve explanation.

When we think about cases we have to think not just conceptually but also in relation to the actual tools we use for describing, classifying, explaining and understanding cases. Hayles (1999) and Cilliers (1998) have in different ways commented on how the availability of computing technology has given us access to domains of reality in a fashion that is radically different from that of the traditional conception of scientific practice. We have become cyborgs – able to do with technology what we cannot do with 'science'. This has much in common with actor-network theory's notion of 'actants' but differs in that the tool and user become one.[2] We do have very important tools here: the numerical taxonomy techniques of cluster analysis, the configurational approaches developed on the basis of Boolean algebra by Ragin and others, the potential of neural networks in social research and the availability of computer-based methods of what is usually miscalled 'qualitative analysis' (although there are analytic components) but would be better described as systematically structured qualitative interpretation. All of these are important for case-based work and will be dealt with here. We want to integrate the discussion of modes of thought and modes of practice as research as a process necessarily depends on this synthesis.

At this point we want to make something explicit that has thus far been implicit. Although we will include consideration of individual cases and methods for understanding them, the comparative method in its different forms is central to case-based understanding. We see this in terms both

of classification on the basis of comparison and in the exploration of complex and multiple causality. Classification compares to distinguish like from not like. Systematic comparison based on interpretation of a range of cases – with its origins in eighteenth century German *Kameralwissenschaft* – seeks to establish distinctive characteristics of particular cases or sets (ensembles) of cases and to explore how those characteristics taken together are causal to the current condition of cases. There is always at least an implicit and usually explicit process of categorization in which cases are grouped into categories and there is a qualitative examination of historical trajectories in order to ascertain which trajectories produced which outcomes. Classification and comparison are central to any case-based method that attempts any sort of generalization. To reinforce this point, let us refer first to Linnaeus on classification and then to my co-editor on comparison:

> All the real knowledge which we possess, depends on methods by which we distinguish the similar from the dissimilar. The greater number of natural distinctions this method comprehends, the clearer becomes our idea of things. The more numerous the objects which employ our attention, the more difficult it becomes to form such a method and the more necessary. (*General Plantarum* quoted by Everitt 1993, p. 2)
>
> Implicit in most social scientific notions of case analysis is the idea that the objects of investigation are similar enough and separate enough to permit treating them as instances of the same general phenomenon. At a minimum, most social scientists believe that their methods are powerful enough to overwhelm the uniqueness inherent in objects and events in the social world. ... The audiences for social science expect the results of social scientific investigation to be based on systematic appraisal of empirical evidence. Use of evidence that is repetitious and extensive in form, as when based on observations of many cases or of varied cases, has proved to be a dependable way for social scientists to substantiate their arguments. (Ragin 1992, p. 2)

A central theme of the collection is the importance of demonstrating how case-based methods work in practice. Here, by practice we mean both disciplinary application and application to the resolution of central problems of social practice. We note that case-focused methods are of particular importance for interdisciplinary studies at a time when social science is increasingly 'post-disciplinary' both in conceptualization and in practical application. They are also a central part of the repertoire of applied social research. These two areas of interest intersect, particularly in the domains of the applied area academic fields exemplified by health studies, urban studies, education, policy studies, social policy, environmental studies, development studies, science studies and others. It may well be that it is in the applied areas that the social sciences will 'open' as the Gulbenkian Commission (Wallerstein 1996) on their future suggested they should. Case-focused methods and understanding will be a crucial tool in this process.

One final methodological point has to be made now. Ragin and Becker (1992) asked 'What is a case?', and in his introduction to that seminal collection Ragin began precisely by questioning the very idea of case itself and noting that all the contributors to the collection and participants in the workshops from which it derived agreed that case analysis is fundamental to social science and: '… has a special, unexamined status' (1992, p. 8). Ragin's solution to the dilemmas this posed has been to propose that we focus on 'casing' and the process of social inquiry – to quote the title of his concluding chapter to *What is a Case?* He urged us to examine precisely the tactic that social scientists engage in when they delimit or declare cases, and gave this a name – casing. As we shall see, several of the contributions to this Handbook address this idea, and it resonates very much with Cilliers' (2001) discussion of the ways in which we might specify complex systems. Here it is important to make some preliminary comments about how casing works in applied social research and what issues emerge from this.

Typically, applied social researchers work with what appear to be given cases. This is particularly the case when they start, as I (Byrne) have in many research projects, from a statistical array of data arranged in typical spreadsheet style with the cases forming the rows in the matrix and 'variate traces' forming the columns. In other words, we start with the products of surveys and it is worth remembering that Marsh (1982) defined the social survey precisely as something that generated just such a case/variable matrix. Here, we should remember that much of the data that we might use comes not from dedicated research exercises, including official exercises such as the census, but from administrative processes. However, once it is arranged as a case–variate trace matrix, we have a survey. So statistical work takes its cases as given – as the entities presented in the data array. Note that the phrase here is statistical work, not quantitative work. Quantitative data construction involves specification of cases. A very simple example is provided by the question 'Is the case for a social survey, the individual or the household, composed of varying numbers of individuals and having emergent properties beyond those of the individuals constituting it?' Actually, multi-level modelling techniques designed to pursue causality across levels (see Goldstein 1995) do address the issue of casing by trying to take account of the ways in which multiple levels in a hierarchical dataset (as Goldstein correctly remarks, such datasets have the form they do because that is the form of the reality from which they are constructed) work together to produce outcomes. In general, when we engage in causal modelling, the data have been cased for us.

Sometimes this makes good sense. However, even as simple a social phenomenon as the household has a distinct fuzziness, which we can appreciate very well when we pursue the trajectories of households through time using longitudinal panel datasets such as the British Household Panel Survey. In other words, policy researchers have to pay as much attention to the constitution of their cases as they do to processes of operationalization in the construction of measures. This applies with particular force to the evaluation of social intervention programmes but it has general application. An example is appropriate. One of my graduate students, Katie Dunstan, is working on and around an evaluation of an intervention programme in 'depressed' (the depression is contestable) local housing markets, with the 'local' defined as relatively small areas within a city region. It rapidly became apparent that sense could only be made of the trajectories of these localities if they were understood in relation first to the city region of which they were part and the dynamics of housing markets throughout that region. And then came the sub-prime issue, the collapse of Northern Rock and a global or at least British–US collapse in housing markets generally. What is the case here for which causes can be established?

Indeed, the problem of boundaries in spatial studies illustrates the issues of casing in relation to applied research very well. My own work on the trajectories of former industrial city regions into a post-industrial future requires me to think very carefully about the changing spatial boundaries of the regions, and indeed to consider equally carefully temporal boundaries in relation to the exploration of major qualitative changes. This is a relatively pure intellectual problem, although it can have profound policy consequences at a local level when municipal boundaries that do have a reality bear very little relationship to patterns of living and working *and revenue raising* in complex metropolises. It can take on a more extreme character when administrative boundaries taken as cases form the basis of applied policy research and consequent policy implementation with very significant outcomes for local populations. Ruane's (2007) examination of the reconfiguration of emergency and maternity services in Greater Manchester demonstrated that by taking the administrative health region as the case, there was a marked tendency for policy research to argue for services to be moved towards the centre of the region. As this was also happening in adjacent regions, the peripheries were losing key services as it were in both directions – in the case of the Pennine towns towards both Leeds and Manchester. The case was given as the city region but that was not the significant health-care system for people in the periphery.

We have here entered into discussion of the 'boundaries between nested and overlapping cases', in which it might be regarded as a great abyss (Charles Ragin's suggested term) of social science. We are not claiming to have an immediate practical solution to the issues posed by this abyss, although the content of this Handbook is intended to offer us approaches to dealing with it. Rather, our intention is to problematize in a way that shows the knowledge and theory dependence of social research, and the consequent need for close connection to/understanding of empirical cases, however defined or constructed. The reality of the abyss might be what drives many researchers to go micro and focus on the individual as the one true case. We are arguing very firmly that we can do more than that.

So the methodological principles and issues have been laid out before you. Let us now turn to the objectives and organization of the Handbook as a whole. Our intention in assembling these chapters was to cover three interrelated domains of knowledge: (1) the methodological status of case-based methods; (2) the sets of techniques that can be deployed in case-based investigation; and (3) actual examples of the use of the methods in the fields and disciplines that constitute the territory of the social sciences, both in the academy and applied in practice. Of course, these three domains are remarkably fuzzy sets. Contributions in all three sections of this book draw on concepts, methodological programmes and actual examples of empirical research in practice. This is exactly as it should be but there is a heuristic value in the sectioning we have deployed. Each section is introduced by a guide to that section, which essentially presents a brief editor's exposition of the contents of the chapters within that section.

First, we thought it essential to have a set of arguments that relate to the actual methodological status of case-based methods. We wanted to set them in the historical context of the development of social science as an interwoven project of understanding the social that requires both the empirical investigation of the world as it is, as it has become what it is and as it represents a potential for the future;

and the formulation of coherent accounts – theories – of the causal processes that generate becoming, presence and future potential. To a considerable degree we return to some of the central issues raised when Ragin and Becker asked 'What is a case?' but do so more explicitly in relation to arguments about the nature of social science's methodological programme as a whole. The first half of this introduction started this account. It is developed in the first section of the book through a set of five chapters that engage with the way in which contemporary social science handles causality. These pieces develop a set of overlapping themes, which include the historical development of causal reasoning in social explanation, the resonances among complexity theory, critical realism and config- urational approaches to identifying complex and contingent causes, and the ways in which method, methodology and meta-theoretical reasoning about the nature of the world and how it may be known to interact with each other in forming the character of science – note no apologetic confining of this to the social sciences. Implicit in this discussion is a theme that emerges in the succeeding sections: how does how we know engage with how we act in shaping the social world itself?

The second section of this Handbook includes a set of chapters that deal with the methods and techniques of case based research. We begin with a subset that addresses the range of issues associated with classification. The four papers here combine in varying degrees the outlining of methods for classifying with methodologically focused discussions of just what we are doing when we classify and how classification shapes our ways of understanding. Two explicit developed accounts emerge here. One is essentially a classification located repetition of the ontological position which is common to the chapters in section one. The other represents the major coherent rival to the concern with causality that underpins that style of work and draws on actor-network theory (ANT). ANT represents the most sophisticated version of a conventionalist account of the nature of scientific knowledge

and, moreover, one that is firmly grounded in careful consideration of scientific practices themselves. It is important that this different way of thinking is represented here.

The next subset comprises a set of chapters that deal in different ways with quantitative, and especially configurational, approaches. These contain elements of tech- nical discussion and demonstration but are primarily concerned with the underlying logic of explanation that informs configurational techniques. Again, it is absolutely essential to reiterate that the relationship between logic of explanation and actual technique is not unidirectional. It is true that the general principle of a shift from variable-centred views of causality to the proposition that what matters is set-theoretic relationships is fundamental and foundational to qualitative comparative analysis and related configura- tional techniques, but we see here that the actual use of these techniques in practice leads to the development of methodological arguments themselves.

The final subset of section 2 takes a turn to the qualitative. The classification and configurational approaches reviewed in the preceding subsections have a strong but not exclusively quantitative character. Here again we see how the actual processes of doing research and the development of techniques and procedures for that 'doing' interact with our approaches to describing and explaining how the world works. What these chapters demonstrate is that the issues of explanation transcend the false and – let it be bluntly said now – really rather silly false dichotomy between quantitative and qualitative approaches to understanding the social world. Rather, we have a set of unifying issues that include those of generalization, the need to consider relationships as just as real and socially significant as entities and implications for science as description, explanation and practice that flow from the agentic potential of human beings. It is not that these issues do not emerge in relation to quantitative modes of work, and indeed several of the chapters in the two preceding sections address them specifically.

It is just that they are absolutely forefronted in qualitative modes of social research and we get a sharp reminder of their significance here.

Part 2 of the book is by no means just a set of demonstration of case-based methods, although it does include very substantial demonstration of case-based methods. Rather, it mixes demonstration, empirical example and methodological discussion. It is fuzzy but focused – the central principle underlying case-based understanding and consequent methods themselves. This approach continues in part 3, where eleven chapters address the issues of deploying case-based methods in disciplines and fields. Again, we find a constant engagement with methodological issues and with the interrelationship between those arguments and the actual deployment of methods in practice. The areas covered in these chapters include historical account, political science, organizational studies, economics, medicine as both medical practice and biomedical science, health policy, development studies, cultural studies and the general deployment of case methods in applied social research as understood by applied social researchers. The focus of these chapters is on how methods can be understood and used, with the argument often illustrated by a specific empirical example or examples of research, explanation and interpretation in the discipline or field. So we begin with a justification of case-based methods and move through an account of the character of such methods into a discussion of how they work in the practice of knowledge construction both in the academy and in applied research, which is intended to inform policy development and practice.

The Handbook concludes with an overview of the themes emerging in it by my co-editor, but even here it is worth mentioning some points of agreement and disagreement that emerge from reading over the contributions as a whole:

- Agreement: case-based methods are useful and represent, among other things, a way of moving beyond a useless and destructive tradition in the social sciences that have set quantitative and qualitative modes of exploration, interpretation and explanation against each other.
- Agreement: generalization matters, but that generalization is best understood as involving careful attention to the setting of scope. In other words, we cannot generate nomothetic laws that are applicable always and everywhere in the social sciences. No method can construct theories with that character. However, comparative case-based methods do enable us to give accounts that have more than unique ideographic range and individual case studies can contribute to this. The scoping requirement is to pay careful attention to the limitations of our knowledge claims in time and space.
- Disagreement: some contributors consider that the whole logic of case-based methods requires an ontological position that necessarily rejects the value of abstracted variable-based analyses in explanation in the social sciences. Others do not go so far and simply see case-based methods, and in particular set-theoretic methods, as representing an important alternative approach whilst allowing variable-based modelling a role in social explanation.
- Case-based methods are a way of making social science useful: they always have been and they continue to be so.

And so to the meat of the matter …

NOTES

1. The ideas and practice of Paolo Freire in relation to participatory research and dialogical learning are of enormous importance for us here.
2. We must also note that our endorsement of critical realism's deep ontology means that we accept that the real in the form of generative mechanisms and the actual as the contingent consequence of those generative mechanisms have form before we shape that form as the empirical in our construction of knowledge from the materials of reality. Actor-network theory, in contrast, has a shallow ontology in which form is wholly constructed by the practices of science. In essence, we allow reality a role in representations of reality. Representations are made from something, not reified from nothing.

REFERENCES

Abbott, A. 2001 *Time Matters*. Chicago: University of Chicago Press.

Cilliers, p. 1998 *Complexity and Postmodernism.* London: Routledge.

Cilliers, p. 2001 'Boundaries, hierarchies and networks in complex systems' *International Journal of Innovation Management* 5(2): 135–147.

Danermark, B., Ekström, M., Jakobsen, L. and Karlson, J.C. 2002 *Explaining Society.* London: Routledge.

Everitt, B.S. 1993 *Cluster Analysis.* London: Edward Arnold.

Flyvbjerg, B. 2001 *Making Social Science Matter.* Cambridge: Cambridge University Press.

Geertz, C. 1975 *The Interpretation of Cultures.* London: Hutchinson.

Goldstein, H. 1995 *Multilevel Statistical Models.* London: Edward Arnold.

Hayles, K. 1999 *How We Became Posthuman.* Chicago: University of Chicago Press.

Hedström, P. 2005 *Dissecting the Social.* Cambridge: Cambridge University Press.

Marsh, C. 1982 *The Survey Method.* London: Allen and Unwin.

Merton, R. 1968 *Social Theory and Social Structure* (enlarged edition). New York: Free Press.

Pawson, R. 'Middle range theory and programme theory evaluation: from provenance to practice' in F. Leuuw (Ed.) *Evaluation and the Disciplines* (in press).

Pawson, R. and Tilley, N. 1997 *Realistic Evaluation.* London: Sage.

Ragin, C. 1992 'Introduction' in C. Ragin and H. Becker (Eds) *What Is a Case?* Cambridge: Cambridge University Press, pp. 1–19.

Ragin, C. 2000 *Fuzzy Set Social Science.* Chicago: University of Chicago Press.

Ragin, C. and Becker, H. 1992 *What Is a Case?* Cambridge: Cambridge University Press.

Reed, M. and Harvey, D.L. 1992 'The new science and the old: complexity and realism in the social sciences' *Journal for the Theory of Social Behaviour* 22: 356–379.

Reed, M. and Harvey, D.L. 1996 'Social science as the study of complex systems' in L.D. Kiel, and E. Elliott (Eds) *Chaos Theory in the Social Sciences.* Ann Arbor, MI: University of Michigan Press, pp. 295–324.

Ruane, S. 2007 *Report Commissioned by Rochdale Borough Council Re: The Healthy Futures and Making It Better Proposals for Health Services in Rochdale* Leicester: Health Policy Research Unit, De Montfort University.

Wallerstein, I. (Chair of Gulbenkian Commission) 1996 *Open the Social Sciences.* Stanford, CA: Stanford University Press.

PART ONE

The Methodological Context of Case-Based Methods

This Part of the book comprises five papers that locate case-based methods in their methodological context. The first, by David Harvey, sets case-based approaches in relation to the methodological programme of the history of social science in general, but sociology in particular. Harvey's core argument is that debates about the scientific status of case studies have been conducted in methodological and epistemological terms, whereas issues of ontology have either scarcely been considered or have been conflated with 'epistemological presuppositions'. He develops a critique founded in the synthesis of critical realism and complexity frames of reference, which he has proposed in a range of earlier work and proceeds by identifying first 'the anti-ontological bias' of the empirical social sciences and then proposing a complex realist alternative position. He then proceeds to delineate a complex realist standpoint – a position adopted explicitly by several other contributors to the Handbook, and delivers a historical narrative of the 'ambivalent sociological status' case studies have held in American sociology through the twentieth century, concluding with an elaboration of a complex realist model of the case object.

Lars Mjøset takes up Harvey's issue in contemporary terms. He presents an account of 'the contextualist approach to social science methodology' beginning with a specification of the role of methodologists as mediators between professional philosophy of science and the actual technical apparatuses of the practice of social research. As he puts it, for methodologists the: '… task is to produce *practical philosophies of social science*, methodologies that provide concrete guidelines in research practice, and criteria as to what knowledge shall count as science' (see p. 40). There is an interesting argument to be had with the notion that the professional philosophy of science should have any privileged position in adjudicating on the adequacy of practice here, but it is generally held and Mjøset does articulate clearly that methodologies are the product of a two-way dialogue between philosophical orientation and the methods themselves in practice. He develops his argument by identifying three practical philosophies of social science. First is the standard attitude that emerges from some sort of synthesis of logical positivism, the work of Popper and Lakatos, and analytical philosophy. This tends to what we might call scientism – privileging quantification, experiments including thought experiments and statistical analyses. Second is the social–philosophical practical philosophy of social science for which the leading question is 'how is social science possible?' In very crude summary, we might say that the positions here are those that tend to hold that the 'human sciences' are different. Mjøset shows that this position is itself bifurcated with, on the one hand, a transcendental or reconstructionist programme of establishing the general basis for social theory and, on the other, a deconstructionist tradition asserting that no such programme is possible. Finally, we have the contextualist practical philosophy of social science – in effect an approach founded on and displayed in the actual distinctively social methods of social science research as practised. Mjøset demonstrates the relationship of this programme with pragmatism and emphasizes that in contrast with the two preceding positions, those who endorse/practise it, see social science as concerned with intervention rather than representation. Plainly, case-based methods resonate particularly with this style, a style of work as much as a style of thinking, or perhaps it is best to say a style of thinking while working and working while thinking.

Mjøset's chapter proceeds through a five-fold specification of the essentials of each attitude in terms of explanatory logic, popularization of fundamental metaphysical questions, explanatory priorities given to the autonomy of social science, implied sociology of knowledge and assumptions about relationships between the sciences. Mjøset demonstrates how the positions become visible in episodic struggles on methodology but also notes that methodological camps generally 'keep to themselves' and that this is the case between 'mechanism scholars' and 'case scholars'. Essentially, his chapter demarcates the issues and develops a full account of their implications for both the construction of social theory and the practice of social research.

Bob Carter and Alison Sealey develop themes introduced by Harvey and Mjøset with specific reference to the central issues of defining and using cases. Drawing on realist social theory, they follow Ragin in emphasizing the importance of 'casing'

and suggest that: 'because of its explicit social ontology, realism provides the means for making the process of casing a more fastidious one' (see p. 69). These authors put considerable emphasis on the significance of reflexivity in the practices of researching the social in terms of which could be described using the Freirean conception of dialogue, but also insist that social reality is not exhausted by either actors' or researchers' accounts and that we must pay serious attention to realism's stratified social ontology, which has important implications for methodological research.

Malcolm Williams and Wendy Dyer take the idea of the case into engagement with probability as the basis of causal claims in social science. They outline the three different interpretations of probability that have been variously deployed, viz. the frequency interpretations that underpin conventional statistical modelling, the propensity interpretation following on from the work of Popper and subjectivist interpretation, noting that this last is not generally associated with causal explanation but focuses more on personal beliefs about the probability of an event. By taking up Popper's discussion of single case probability, these authors seek to work out a technical approach to the causal exploration of large datasets describing the trajectories of cases through time and interpreting these trajectories in terms of the propensities inherent in individual cases as described in the dataset. The example employed is that of cases moving through experience in a large 'custody diversion' project (a project intended to divert offenders and potential offenders with mental health problems from imprisonment). This chapter combines all of a methodological synthesis of realism, complexity and a propensity view of probability; a developed demonstration of a set of practical techniques using databases, cluster analysis approaches and the mapping of clusters through time; and an account of the experience of an actual research project. For Williams and Dyer: 'What is important and useful is to be able to talk about the probabilities of antecedent conditions that led to specific outcomes and to use this knowledge to produce explanations (and thus predictions) of phenomena' (see p. 98).

This Part concludes with a piece by David Byrne attempting to synthesize complex realist (very much after Harvey as modified by engagement with Cilliers) with configurational approaches to cases. This was originally identified by the author as a rant – and to a considerable extent it continues to be one, but it is a rant to a purpose. That purpose is to respond to the resonance between complex realism as a meta theoretical account of social reality and case-based methods in general, but configurational approaches in particular, as modes of understanding complex causal processes in social reality. By paying particular attention to the idea of control parameters and seeking to understand how such control parameters might be identified using case-based methods, the chapter seeks to initiate methods that can be applied in practice to social purposes.

1

Complexity and Case

David L. Harvey

Case studies have long kindled the sociological imagination. Yet their scientific status has been contested almost from the moment sociology was christened an academic discipline. Avatars of 'hard science' regard case studies as 'too impressionistic' in the interpretive liberties they take and as too aggressive in the range of subjects they presume to address. The legitimacy of case studies has been contested largely, therefore, on *methodological* and *epistemological* grounds, while fundamental issues of *social ontology* seldom attract the same attention. This chapter addresses this oversight as it bears on case-based social research. As such, it has two goals. First, it complements the current discussion of case methods by exploring the ontological requirements of case research; and second, it uses a complex realist paradigm to illuminate the structure of the *case-object* (Byrne 2002, pp. 5–6; Byrne and Harvey 2007, pp. 64–66).

Christopher Norris (2007) defines ontology's intellectual niche and the type of entities that occupy that space as follows:

> Traditionally, … [ontology] … is the field of philosophic inquiry that has to do with things … or with real world objects and their intrinsic structures, properties, causal powers, and so forth. That is to say, it treats of them just in so far as they are taken to exist and to exert such powers quite apart from the scope and limits of human knowledge. (Norris 2007, p. 335)

Norris's realist definition provides a feel for the complexity and dynamic powers of the entities with which this chapter deals. It also anticipates the predicaments that ontological considerations introduce into social scientific discourse.

Three levels of ontological interest are germane to sociological inquiry: (1) *philosophical ontology*; (2) *scientific ontology*; and (3) *social ontology*. Philosophical ontology deduces from the structure of speculative thought the fundamental nature of the entities that constitute our everyday world. Scientific ontologies are nested within philosophical ontologies to the extent they flesh out the local details of a terrain in a way philosophical ontology cannot. They are more narrowly focused because they deal with the existential constitution of the entities scientists investigate. Finally, social ontologies are nested within scientific ontologies in that they deal with the elemental entities and dynamics sociohistorical formations must exhibit if they are to sustain themselves over time.

A clear understanding of *'casing'*, to use Ragin's (1992, pp. 219–220) suggestive term, requires a full explication of a case-object's ontology at all three of these levels. Moreover, in keeping with the complex realist paradigm, we assume that case-objects are *ontologically real,* i.e. they exist prior to the research act itself. Of course, the *conceptual imagery* of the case-object is undoubtedly a product of operationist research strategies. The case-object, however, is not a wholly nominalist invention. Casing does not create the case-object, but only a *construct of the case-object.* Consequently, there is always an aspect of the case-object that eludes or stands over and against casing and its epistemology. For this reason, the ontological autonomy of the case-object imbues social inquiry with a self–referential dialectical tension, akin to T.W. Adorno's (1973, p. 5) 'negative dialectic'. Paraphrasing one of Adorno's most powerful maxims, we can say the relation between casing and its object is such that *whenever a casing construct goes into its case-object, some aspect of the object is left over.* When not trivialized, this 'material remainder' prevents premature closures of inquiry.

Hence, the natural attitude associated with complex realism insists that some part of the case-object's ontology resides in its obdurate properties. Accordingly, if the ontological autonomy of the case-object offers a fresh set of checks and counter-checks for critically evaluating case research in general, it also forces a re-examination of those casing strategies that epistemologically gloss the case-object's autonomy. As we will see, this glossing of ontological issues has been justified by an axiomatic aversion on the part of social scientists to metaphysical speculation. Today, however, there is a growing realization that any science deserving of the name must eventually attend to the ontological underpinnings of its subject matter. Indeed, there is a growing awareness among social scientists of the need to explicate all three ontological moments in framing their research.

In what follows, we first examine how and why it is that sociology gives such short shrift to ontological considerations. In the latter portion of this chapter, we follow up that critique by constructing an ideal typical model of the case-object and its ontological structure.

THE ANTINOMIES OF CASE-BASED RESEARCH

The neo-Kantians and the social sciences

The current casing debate is due in large part to American sociology's long-standing debt to neo-Kantian philosophy. Even now, neo-Kantianism, with its axiomatic aversion to metaphysics and its avoidance of objectivist or realist ontologies limits the forms sociological *praxis* takes. Although few still use its argot, its canonical reduction of ontology to problems of method are at the heart of what we will call *sociology sans social ontology.*

The neo-Kantian movement emerged among German intellectuals in the last half of the nineteenth century, a period of industrial crises and class realignments. These crises were accompanied (in some instances, preceded) by the ascent of the neo-Hegelian and the Positivist worldviews in the academy (Iggers 1968, Ringer 1969, 1997, 2004, Burger 1976). A century before, Kant had developed a watershed subjective idealist philosophy with which he deflected David Hume's withering empirical attack on Newtonian science and its constitutive categories. Under the duress of Modernist thought, the neo-Kantians sought to resuscitate Kantian humanism and, in doing so, to protect nineteenth century historiography from the disenchantment of an aggressive utilitarianism bent upon 'reducing cattle to tallow and men to 'profits'.

This defense was accomplished by a self-conscious 'return to Kant'. That is, the neo-Kantians attempted to revive philosophically the formative role individual subjectivity and morality played in shaping human history and culture. Hence, the neo-Kantians momentarily repelled the various *fin-de-sicle* challenges to Kant's subjective idealism. Ironically, their triumph over Positivism, on the one hand, and neo-Hegelianism on the other, was compromised on two important fronts. First, they made a fateful concession to Kantian orthodoxy by retaining Kant's insurmountable firewall that separated the sensate world of phenomenal experience from the noumenal world of ideas and values. The same partition also segregated the constructive logics of scientific discovery from metaphysical speculation, and, finally, the deterministic world of nature from human agency's willfully constructed social and moral orders.

Their second point of compromise was more serious. In 'vanquishing' neo-Hegelianism, a great many neo-Kantians inadvertently incorporated elements of Hegelian realism into their own philosophical framework. Consequently, as Lewis White Beck (1967, pp. 468–473) observes, the 'neo-Kantian' label actually designated:

> … a group of somewhat similar movements that prevailed in Germany between 1870 and 1920 but had little in common beyond a strong reaction against irrationalism and speculative materialism and a conviction that philosophy could be a 'science' only if it returned to the method and spirit of Kant. …
>
> Because of the complexity and internal tensions in Kant's philosophy, not all the neo-Kantians brought the same message from the Sage of Königsberg, and the diversity of their teachings was as great as their quarrels were notorious. At the end of the nineteenth century the neo-Kantians were as widely separated as the first generation Kantians had been at its beginning, and the various neo-Kantian movements developed in directions further characterized by such terms as neo-Hegelian and neo-Fichtean. (Beck 1967, p. 468)

Sociologists are familiar with the Marburg School of neo-Kantianism led by Paul Natrop and Hermann Cohen, and the Baden or Southwestern School led by Wilhelm Windelband and Heinrich Rickert. To these, Beck adds a third 'Sociological School', which centered on the works of Wilhelm Dilthey and Georg Simmel.

Dilthey's so-called *Lebensphilosophie* established what would soon become a standard distinction between *Naturwissenschaft* and *Geisteswissenschaft*. This division was grounded in a *substantive partition* of experience into objects of nature and historically situated human productions (Tapper 1925, Holborn 1950, Masur 1952, Rickman 1960). These two ontological domains also prescribed two radically different approaches to knowledge. *Naturwissenschaft* remained, in essence, the system Kant had defended. *Geisteswissenschaft* was a science of the human mind, a moral science based on the scholar's imaginative reconstruction of past *Weltanschauungen*. Hence, the *Geisteswissenschaften* could plumb human history and motives with a depth the *Naturwissenschaften* could not.

Windelband (1894/1980) accepted the wisdom of Dilthey's 'two sciences' but offered an alternative theory of what divided them from each other. Dilthey's reply to *Lebensphilosophie* sought to purge the distinction between the two sciences of any ontological residues. Windelband's partition was predicated not in diverging ontologies but in the contrasting logics of procedures the two deployed. Man and society could be understood using both the generalizing methods of the natural science and the particularizing modes of understanding practiced by historians.

Hence, *nomothetic inquiries* could seek universal laws of human nature just as readily as *ideographic inquiry* might pursue and grasp the historical particularity of a distant era and its culture. All that was required was to keep the two logics of investigation and their respective operational lines of thought separated. Moreover, by 'de-ontologizing' the differences between the two, metaphysical entanglements could be avoided. There was, of course, a price to be paid for Windelband's 'epistemological end around', and that price would become evident in Chicago Sociology's attempt to construct a coherent sociology using Windelband's philosophical distinctions.

The paradox of methodological complementarity

Both Simmel and Windelband had profoundly influenced Robert Ezra Park during his doctoral studies in Germany – Simmel at Berlin and Windelband at Strasbourg and Heidelberg (Baker 1973, pp. 256–257). Hence, it should be of little surprise that a neo-Kantian worldview dominated the Chicago School's sociological outlook during the interwar decades of the 1920s and 1930s. This neo-Kantian dualism is most evident in the fact that both nomothetic and ideographic studies were pursued during this era, although at times unevenly so.

Much of this unevenness was related to the unequal value the Progressive Movement placed on nomothetic and ideographic research. During the Progressive Era, historians and social scientists alike were increasingly expected to produce instrumental knowledge that could facilitate the 'Americanizing' of immigrants and the 'dangerous classes'. This emphasis on scientific prediction and programmatic control undoubtedly tended to marginalize ideographic research. Whereas case studies were still to be valued for their anecdotal insights and aesthetic immediacies, their emotion-laden ambience relegated them in some Progressive circles to a status similar to the ethereal programs of Christian uplift, the pleadings of muck-raking novelists, and the sensationalist huckstering of yellow journalism (Bulmer 1984, pp. 1–45, Matthews 1977, pp. 85–120).

This predicament was soon translated into a methodological conundrum for Park and Burgess (1921/1969), as they labored to construct an ostensibly disinterested scientific sociology, while simultaneously preserving the dual heritages of the nomothetic and ideographic traditions. Their task was made incrementally more difficult by the fact that the public reputation of Chicago Sociology's scientific surveys often hinged upon the benchmark participant observer studies, urban ethnographies, and autobiographies it was producing – works whose power flowed directly from their inner sense of verisimilitude (Bulmer 1984, pp. 151–171).

By then, Thomas and Znaniecki's *The Polish Peasant in Europe and America* (1918/1958) had provided a venerated template for Chicago Sociology's case-base studies. Park and Burgess (1921/1969) drew on this masterpiece with stunning effect, although in later years – especially after Park's retirement – it fell to Burgess and his co-workers at the Local Community Research Committee (LCRC) to work out the everyday nuts and bolts of designing a comparative framework for conducting case-based researches and integrating them into the Committee's overall agenda (Burgess 1941, Bulmer 1984, pp. 129–150). Aware of the encroaching power of the new statistical techniques then sweeping the social sciences, Burgess nonetheless continued to navigate between the quantitative social sciences and the lived substance of the field studies being gathered under his supervision (Burgess 1945, Burgess 1974, pp. 367–373, 386–392).

Some notion of the practical difficulty of reconciling these methodological complementarities can be garnered from Burgess's 1927 article, *Statistics and Case Studies as Methods of Sociological Research*. Here we find Burgess looking forward to 'the emancipation of case studies from the domination of statistics' (Burgess 1974, p. 370) even as he underscored the intractable tensions between the two. Hence, Burgess traces the role this methodological tension played in predicting marital adjustment outcomes.

It is in revealing the dynamic factors in human relationships that the distinctive value of case studies exists. An intimate personal document discloses the organic relationship between factors, which, more than the mere presence of the factors, is often significant for marital adjustment.

In order, therefore, to improve prediction, case-study analysis should be employed in combination with statistical procedure. In larger part, case study and statistical methods can be profitably used in close interrelation, but in considerable part the case-study method must be employed in relative independence of statistical procedure in order to derive from it its highest value for prevision. The fact is that they are closely and inextricably interrelated. Obviously, all statistics ultimately come from 'cases'. A schedule is constructed on the basis of data derived from the examination of individual cases. From the examination and analysis of cases come insights, clues, and leads, on the basis of which new items may be introduced into the schedule and their average significance determined. Correspondingly, an unexpected statistical finding may require exploration by interview to determine its meaning and significance for [marital] adjustment. Furthermore, the analysis of ideal types of dynamic and organic relationships derived from case studies may suggest reorganization of predictive items under more significant categories (Burgess 1939/1972, pp. 386–388).

It is not untoward to suggest that Burgess saw the relation between case studies and survey research as a tension-ridden dialectical unity of opposites. He may have even regarded the interdependence of the two techniques as somehow paralleling the symbiotic processes of 'cooperative competition' he saw operating in his dynamic modeling of urban ecology.

Despite the methodological hiatus separating them, when set side by side, the nomothetic and the ideographic studies combined to illuminate the complex moral texture of Chicago's 'natural areas' and ethnic neighborhoods; they were also indispensable tools for mapping the city's centrifugal ecology and concentric structuration (Burgess 1925/1967, pp. 47–63). Hence, no matter how one judges the Chicago School's efforts at nomothetically squaring the ideographic circle, this much is evident: the logical contradictions between the two methods were never resolved. This unabated 'benign neglect' of methodological schisms may have been in all likelihood a constant source of intellectual tension during the interwar period. At the same time, the Chicago School's neo-Kantianism undoubtedly remained a wellspring of sociological creativity, even as it served as a leavening source of departmental ambivalence. In any case, it was no mean trick to negotiate the intractable logics of social scientific surveys and case-based narratives without glossing their differences or submerging the premises of the one into the other. In fact,

the genius of Chicago Sociology resided not in the unification of these antinomies but, rather, in their pragmatic, often piecemeal amalgamations. It was this dialectical ambivalence that sustained Chicago Sociology's watershed scholarship of the 1920s and 1930s.

The rise of methodological factionalism

Just how well Chicago Sociology managed the nomothetic/ideographic split can be gleaned from what happened to it and to the profession after the Second World War. A powerful 'second Chicago School' formed around 'Symbolic Interactionist' social psychology. The Symbolic Interactionist contingent soon set itself off from the survey researchers (Fine 1995, Gusfield 1995, Abbott 1999, 2001, Becker 1999).

Homologous schisms erupted elsewhere in the profession so that by the mid-1950s the language of the earlier neo-Kantian antinomies would be supplanted by an alternative oppositional vocabulary, e.g. variable-oriented, *quantitative* versus *qualitative research and its narrative productions*. At one level, the substantive parameters of the new controversy paralleled the old: only the vocabularies changed. It terms of professional consequences, though, the formal disputes that had been held in relative abeyance now tightened into a Gordian knot. When that knot was finally cut, the former dialectical ambivalence gave way to a viral, profession-wide internecine struggle.

This mutual alienation between the two self-interested factions hardened to such an extent that the position of the former was reduced to what C. Wright Mills (1959, pp. 50–75) deprecated as 'abstracted empiricism': fact-mongering in search of a working hypothesis. Returning the favor, 'positivists' showed contempt for 'grand theory' (again a Millsian epithet) and the extended narratives associated with case research. Indeed, more than one cutting-edge positivist suggested, only half-mockingly, that such sociology be banished to English Departments, American

Studies Programs, or other academic dens of antiquity.

Renegotiating old faits accomplis

Given the progressive anomie that ensued, it should not be surprising that the renewed debate over casing appeared upon first reading to be little more than another counter-hegemonic call for a radical makeover of the discipline. A second reading, however, revealed a series of restorative motifs underlying these polemical appearances. Moreover, this call for restorative self-clarification came from both sides of the quantitative/qualitative divide, resembling what mathematicians call a 'squeezing theorem' tactic. That is, the re-vindication of the proper place of case studies in the social sciences was not analytically deduced from first principles but, instead, was pragmatically pieced together by the practical interests and experiences of both camps.

This ameliorative strategy is at the heart of Ragin and Becker's synoptic work *What Is a Case? Exploring the Foundations of Social Inquiry* (1992). The volume is a wide-ranging 'taking of stock', a momentary pause designed to assess the current status of case research. It reports the proceedings of a symposium that attempted to codify the methodological bounds of case studies. As an exercise in *methodological self-clarification*, the symposium accomplished two tasks: (1) it established the methodological bounds between casing and survey research techniques; and (2) it constructed an interpretive typology for classifying the manifold forms casing strategies might take.

As to the first goal, symposium participants established a rough consensus on the proscriptive limits of casing methods:

- Methodological individualism, in and of itself, did not provide an adequate framework for grasping case processes, '... nor the idea that social life can be understood only from the perspective of individual actors' (Ragin and Becker 1992, p. 7).
- Cases were not purely given as social entities to be defined just as they were, nor were they solely

the product of the interpretations the researcher brought to the problem being investigated (Ragin and Becker 1992, p. 7).
- Whereas theoretical or interpretively selective samplings of case elements were deemed permissible, case analysis could seldom, if ever, ground itself in random samplings of a population (Ragin and Becker 1992, p. 7).
- Finally, in a carefully stated adumbration of the use of multivariate techniques in directly delineating the domain of case studies, it was concluded that the '... concept of "the case" is logically prior both to the concept of "the population" and the concept of "the variable"'. In a context where the concept of 'the case was made problematic, the other concepts appear impenetrable' (Ragin and Becker 1992, p. 7).

The second goal of the symposium was more formidable. Using as his 'sample' the eight invited papers that provided the focus of the symposium's discussions', Ragin developed a four-fold typology of *conceptions of case* to categorize different styles of casing.

Ragin's typology was generated from two dichotomies. The first pertained to the researcher's assumptions concerning the nature of casing: did the researcher conceptualize the case as being an *empirical unit* or was it approached as a *theoretical construct*. The second dichotomy centered on whether the case in question was treated as a 'one-of-a-kind' sociohistorical interpretation or if it was seen as belonging to an already existing class of cases. When Ragin cross-referenced the two dichotomies, a four-fold table (stochastically represented in Figure 1.1) resulted. His synthetic classification generated four cells: (1) '*Cases as Found*', presumptively real, social entities not unlike other 'natural phenomena' given to experience; (2) '*Cases as Objects*', social entities posited to be both phenomenally bounded and conforming empirically to conceptually validated categories already in use; (3) '*Cases as Made*', a conceptually mediated category in which the case in question is defined as a product of the specific unfolding of field research, one that has no parallel or comparative equivalent in the literature; and (4) '*Cases as Conventions*', specific

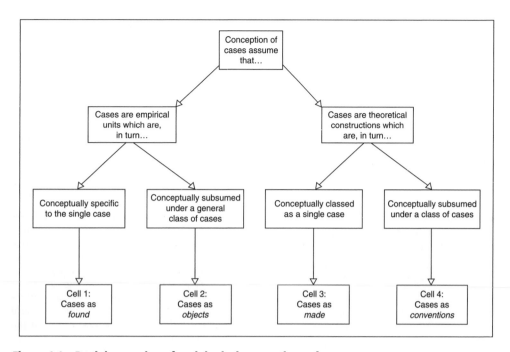

Figure 1.1   Ragin's mapping of sociological conceptions of case.

conceptual constructions whose full meaning emerges only when placed in the context of existing research.

Ragin concludes by noting that these four conceptions of case could be interpreted as pragmatic strategies available to researchers for resolving various problems that arise in the concrete research setting itself. The pragmatic and eclectic tone of his conclusions are underscored when Ragin writes:

> This four-fold division of case conceptions is not absolute. A researcher could both use conventionalized empirical units, accepting them as empirically valid (Cell 2), and try to generate new theoretical categories or case constructs (Cell 3) in the course of his or her research. Frustrations with conventional case definitions and practices (Cell 4) could lead researchers to intensify their empirical efforts and to define cases and their boundaries in a more inductive manner (Cell 1). In fact, most research involves multiple uses of cases, as specific or general theoretical categories and as specific or general empirical units. These multiple uses occur because research combines theoretical and empirical analysis, and the two kinds of analyses need not use parallel cases or units. The

> point of ... [Figure 1.1] ... is not to establish boundaries between different kinds of research, but to establish a conceptual map for linking different approaches to the question of cases. (Ragin and Becker 1992/2005, p. 11)

In keeping with the methodological focus of Ragin and Becker's work, what began ostensibly as a collation of methodological presuppositions has become a 'conceptual map' for finessing possible 'conceptual map' 'blockages' encountered in field research or later interpretive dilemmas.

Notice, however, that although *What Is a Case?* deals adequately with the subjective conceptions the researcher transports to the casing milieu, it never directly addresses the social ontology of the case-object itself, i.e. the possibility that the case-object is, in and of itself, a complex entity with autonomous claims of its own. Instead, the act of casing and its case-object are both approached as if they were social constructions posited during the research act. The typology thus focuses on the *intensive logic* of various *conceptions of casing,* while only tangentially touching on the case-objects's *extensive ontology.* Hence, *What Is a Case?*, for all its theoretical sophistication, never breaks free of the neo-Kantian circle of epistemological concerns.

METHODOLOGICAL WARS OF POSITION

The results reported in *What Is a Case?* give us a fair index of the current thinking of those involved in case-based research. Furthermore, its conceptual tone and conclusions are firmly fixed in the profession's post-war schismatics. Although reasoned in its claims and moderate in its goals, *What Is a Case?* none the less bears the marks of those virulent wars of position that have marked the profession for more than six decades. Waged in a blunt, no-quarters-given style, these seemingly endless struggles have been carried out in the name of building a 'unified social science'. Fought to the point of stalemate, both sides of the controversy have been reduced to encroaching upon the other's 'turf' and attempting to supplant it methodologically. Despite this impasse, there are still those who believe that these 'border raids' will eventually produce closure on the issue of what is or what is not 'scientific sociology'.

Andrew Abbott (1999, 2001), by contrast, promotes a contrarian view concerning the inevitability of methodological and epistemological closure. Although working from differing initial premises than those employed here, he similarly argues that sociology's methodological dualism is deeply rooted in the history of the profession, if not its thought, and is likely to remain so for some time.

Abbott's stance is exemplified by his deconstruction of the molar oppositions of quantitative versus qualitative methodologies into *a series of paired oppositional 'affinities'* (Figure 1.2). When combined, this ensemble of opposed pairings spans what Abbott calls a *methodological manifold* that ultimately sets quantitative sociology and qualitative sociology at loggerheads with one another:

> Perhaps the strongest of these affinities is what we might call the methodological manifold: an affiliation of four or five separate distinctions generally labeled by the distinction of qualitative versus quantitative. At the heart of this manifold is the nearly absolute association of positivism with analysis and of narrative with interpretation. So strongly linked are these two dichotomies that the other way of lining them up – narrative with positivism and analysis with interpretation – is nearly nonsensical to most sociologists. ... Analytic positivism is nearly always realist rather than constructivist in its epistemology, generally concerns social structure rather than culture, and usually has a strongly individual rather than emergent cast. Most of its proponents are strong believers in transcendent social knowledge. By contrast, narrative interpretation usually invokes culture (perhaps social structure as well), is willingly emergent, and nearly always follows a constructionist epistemology. Most members of this school – from Blumer to Foucault – believe social knowledge ultimately to be situated, not transcendent. (Abbott 2001, p. 28)

Abbott's manifold is schematized in the lower portion of Figure 1.2. The lower rows are taken directly from Abbott's work (2001, p. 28). The reversible arrows have been added to represent the dynamics of paradigmatic interaction and the fact that the paired elements of each affinity are antinomies. The upper two rows of Figure 1.2, *Naturwissenschaft* versus *Geisteswissenschaft* and *nomothetic methods* versus *ideographic methods* have been superimposed to underscore our contention that the quantitative versus qualitative methodological dispute is a finely grained duplication of the original neo-Kantian antinomies. Consequently, the reproductive dynamics of these various 'wars of methodological position' parallel those of so-called 'stationary waves', e.g. they are configurations that sustain their relative position and structural patterning *vis-à-vis* their immediate milieu, even as new materials and media traverse it.

By our account, then, the continuing century-long imbroglio over the scientific legitimacy of case research finds a common root in a permutating neo-Kantianism

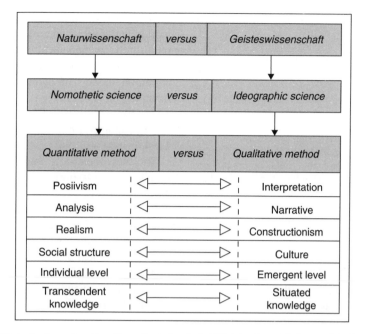

Naturwissenschaft	versus	Geisteswissenschaft
Nomothetic science	versus	Ideographic science
Quantitative method	versus	Qualitative method

Posiivism	◁——————▷	Interpretation
Analysis	◁——————▷	Narrative
Realism	◁——————▷	Constructionism
Social structure	◁——————▷	Culture
Individual level	◁——————▷	Emergent level
Transcendent knowledge	◁——————▷	Situated knowledge

Figure 1.2   Historical continuity of methodological affinities in sociology. This figure is a reconstruction of Abbott, i.e. lots added to Abbott's original.

that, even now, shapes the methodological controversies between 'positivist' sociology and its 'humanist' counterpart. According to our reconstruction, the history of that controversy began with *Lebensphilosophie* and Dilthey's seminal distinction between the *Naturwissenschaften* and the *Geisteswissenschaften*. This problematic was countered with Windelband's division between the *nomothetic sciences* and the *ideographic sciences*. Chicago Sociology's singular philosophical achievement was that it internalized these elements without resolving the antinomical ambiguities inherent in Windelband's and Dilthey's work. After the Second World War, the neo-Kantian hegemony remained intact, but was externally reconfigured to flow along lines of intense professional factionalism. The newly defined struggle emerged in an ideological space in which quantitative research commitments occupied one methodological pole, while the qualitative commitments of a 'humanist sociology' and its narrative traditions defended the other. Although a powerful force for the next five decades, Logical positivism's arrival

in the United States did not become, as first thought, the triggering mechanism of a Kuhnian revolution. Quite the contrary, while profoundly altering social science practice positivism never transcended its own neo-Kantian horizon and the former's tendency to 'discard' ontological questions as unscientific (Freidman 2000).

COMPLEX REALISM AND SOCIAL ONTOLOGY

It is neither unfair nor alarmist to say that the current methodological debate over the scientific status of case research is at an impasse. Nor is it out of order to suggest that the source of that impasse resides in the anti-ontological stance in which not only sociology, but modern science in general, is steeped. The British philosopher Roy Bhaskar has suggested as much when he asks:

How did it come about that ontology was a virtually taboo subject? What was it that made ontology so difficult or even impossible? Although the philosophical doctrines of, say, Hume or Kant are familiar, it is important to appreciate a phenomenological or practical basis for them. This is in a kind of natural attitude to the world in which we do not distinguish between knowledge and objects, in which we don't distinguish ontology from epistemology … in which we just talk about a *known world*. When science is doing normal science, when things are going well, epistemically it is natural to adopt what I call this *'natural attitude'* in which you don't posit ontology on the one side and epistemology on the other: you just have knowledge and you take it that that knowledge is of the world. Ontology really only becomes relevant when you are not satisfied with knowledge, when what passes for knowledge is patently wrong or absurd. (Bhaskar 2007, p. 192)

Bhaskar seems to have described the current attitude of many sociologists toward their work. Their anti-ontological stance is manifested in the failure of social scientific discourse systematically to '… distinguish between knowledge and objects, in which we don't distinguish ontology from epistemology …'. Moreover, such systematic glosses lead to a premature closure of self-critical possibilities. Most immediately, this truncation is magnified by the idea that Humean Empiricism, to the exclusion of more complex models of causation, forms a sufficient basis for scientific explanations. Consequently, when confronted with issues of philosophical or social ontology, the scientist too often falls into a certain obtuseness, insisting that '… you just have knowledge and you take it that [this] knowledge is of the world'. We believe that a complex realist framework of sociological analysis can correct this anti-ontological bias.

As for complex realism proper, it emerged rather haphazardly during the social and political ferment of the 1960s. Responding to the implausible *Weltanschauung* of the era, it navigated between the exhausted claims of Logical positivism and the exaggerated promises of Culutral Hermeneutics. Situating itself between an empiricism that had been dismissive of ontology and a phenomenological method that was verging on solipsism,

complex realism fashioned a social scientific worldview from elements of a resurgent realist philosophy, mathematical chaos theory, non-equilibrium thermodynamics, and punctuated equilibria models of evolutionary development (Sayer 1984, Prigogine and Stengers 1984, Eldredge 1985, Gleick 1987, Gould 1989, Waldrop 1992, Arthur 1994, Collier 1994, Prigogine 1996).

The new science's name reflected the intellectual hurly-burly from which it grew. That is, 'complex realism' was a colloquial compression of two terms: *complexity theory* and *critical realism*. The label *critical realism* had, in turn, been formed from an elision of two philosophical conceptions, e.g. *transcendental realism* and *critical naturalism*. Four fundamental principles subsequently charted the development of complex realism:

- *Transcendental realism*: Complex realism holds that if the sciences are to remain coherent enterprises, their explanatory protocols must embrace, *a priori*, a realist ontology, i.e. they must of necessity assume the existence of an objective moment of experience, some part of which stands over and against our attempts to understand and manipulate our world.
- *Critical naturalism*: Complex realism assumes the possibility of a 'natural science of society' but if, and only if, that science is properly qualified so as to allow active human agency a role in 'co-producing' its everyday institutional forms.
- *The ontological and hierarchical stratification of the world*: The world is ontologically stratified. Hence, the objects of scientific inquiry (either naturally occurring or as products of social construction) form a loosely integrated hierarchy of openly structured, evolving systems, which are themselves ontologically layered and hierarchically nested.
- *The asymptotic predictability of open-system outcomes*: Because of this ontological layering, actual causal processes operating in non-laboratory settings are contingently structured and temporally staggered. They seldom rival the regularity of causal conjunctions elicited in controlled experiments. Consequently, 'causal laws' in complex natural systems are tendential and are best expressed in normic statements or in counter-factual propositions.

Critical realism

The philosophical core of the complex realist perspective originates in the works of Roy Bhaskar (1975/1997, 1979/1989, 1993). Bhaskar's transcendental realist deduction of the world forms the Archimedean point of his critical philosophy. The best way to grasp the logic of his deduction is to note that Bhaskar takes his lead from the critical method of Immanuel Kant.

Just as Kant stood Humean Empiricism on its head, Bhaskar stands Kant's philosophy on its head to arrive at his ontologically real conception of the world. Recall that Kant's 'Copernican revolution' hinged on an 'epistemological turn'. That is, Kant ironically accepted Hume's empiricist epistemology, but only as a preparatory ploy for reconstructing his subjective idealist defense of Newtonian science and its categorical infrastructure. By contrast, Bhaskar's Transcendental Realism begins with an *ontological turn*. While Kant began his demonstration of the validity of scientific knowledge with an 'epistemological feint', Bhaskar's ontological turn accepts science's account of the world in order to deduce from it the world's ontological structure. Hence, he asks, 'Given the unparalleled success of the physical sciences in describing and explaining events in the natural world (the social sciences being another matter altogether), what do the patterns and historical sequencing of significant scientific discoveries tell us about the structure and dynamics of nature itself?' By accepting science's successful methods and epistemological presuppositions of how best to study the world, Bhaskar attempts to tease from method the ontological structure of reality.

Having posed the question, Bhaskar moves post-haste to critically examine the paragon of scientific methodology, e.g. the modern laboratory experiment. In doing so, he demonstrates that if experimentally derived descriptions of natural laws are to remain logically coherent, then they must be justified by appealing to the existence of a reality outside the laboratory. It is here, however, that a paradox emerges: the 'world outside' seldom comports itself with the same causal regularity and predictability reproduced in the laboratory. In nature's open milieu, the constancy of causal sequences – the empiricist's guarantor of nature's 'iron-clad laws' – breaks down. If the scientific method is to be vindicated, the difference between replicating natural laws in the laboratory and their erratic actualization in everyday life demands a new accounting. For critical realism, that vindication begins with the recognition that the constant conjunction of cause and effect engineered in the laboratory is an ideal approximation of natural processes. This is because natural causation is the result of a complex knitting together of a plurality of entities and their powers. This joint production is further complicated by the fact that these causal powers are often 'temporally staggered' in their 'causal firings'. Hence, the ontological complexity of joint causal inputs and their actual timing seldom match the consistency of outcomes produced in the laboratory.

A cursory inspection of the historical patterns of significant scientific discovery suggests that the historical sequencing of significant scientific discoveries involves a 'deepening' across time of already existing knowledge. This deepening points to the possibility that these complex causal entities are arranged in a series of *hierarchically arranged ontological layerings*. Hence, the ontological stratification of natural entities is both nested and hierarchically ordered *vis-à-vis* one another. Moreover, this 'onion-like layering' is structured so that more complex orders tend to emerge from more simply composed strata. In their turn, these newly emerged complexities form the seedbed from which even more complex unities are built. As importantly, despite this common generative chain, each successive stratum possesses an 'organizational surplus' that makes it and its powers ontologically autonomous of the strata from which it has emerged. The generality of this ontological complexity and its hierarchical ordering is summarized by the Nobel Laureate P.W. Anderson:

> The ability to reduce everything to simple fundamental laws does not imply the ability to start from those laws and reconstruct the universe. In fact, the more the elementary particle physicists tell us about the nature of the fundamental laws, the less relevance they seem to have to the very real problems of the rest of science, much less to those of society.
>
> The constructionist hypothesis breaks down when confronted with the twin difficulties of scale and complexity. The behavior of large and complex aggregates of elementary particles, it turns out, is not to be understood in terms of a simple extrapolation of the properties of a few particles. Instead, at each level of complexity entirely new properties appear, and the understanding of the new behaviors requires research which I think is as fundamental in its nature as any other. That is, it seems to me, that one may array the sciences roughly linearly in a hierarchy …
>
> But this hierarchy does not imply that science X is 'just applied Y'. At each stage entirely new laws, concepts and generalizations are necessary, … [thereby] … requiring inspirations and creativity to just as great a degree as in the previous one. Psychology is not applied biology, nor is biology applied chemistry. (Anderson 1972, p. 393)

Using this image of the world as an open, evolving system of ontologically stratified entities, complex realism now moves to distinguish between: (1) what scientists say about the world; and (2) the world as it exists, i.e. the constellation of obdurate entities and dynamic mechanisms that stand over and against human accounts of them. Bhaskar labels these domains the *transitive* and the *intransitive dimensions* of science.

There is a close correspondence between the intransitive domain and the ontological structure of science's investigative object and the transitive domain's focus on scientific method and epistemology. Of the two, the intransitive dimension enjoys an autonomy not allotted to the transitive domain. This is because intransitivity is the fundamental precondition upon which the transitive production of scientific knowledge is predicated. Intransitivity thus provides scientific understanding not only with its ontological object of investigation, but also with its *raison d'être*.

The transitive dimension, by contrast consists of the historically shifting modes of scientific understanding, viz. its theories, its craft-based esoterica, and its technologies of discovery. Unlike its intransitive counterpart, science's transitive domain is neither immune to the distorting effects of ruling ideologies nor free of the technological limitations imposed upon human understanding at any given historical moment. It is, instead, a collectively constructed instrument of social action that bears the material imprint of an epoch's social division of labor and its intellectual mode of production.

This *transitivity of scientific praxis* resides in the paramount fact that scientific problematics are conditioned by the communities that certify the investigator's credentials and functions. The productive principles of science and its investigative 'tricks of the trade' are embedded in the folklore of the profession. Acting as a court of last resort, this community of adepts establishes the *esoteric significance* of individual programs and discoveries. Hence, while this 'collegium' cannot create science's intransitive object, it can control the means of legitimating the expenditure of society's collective labor and resources on one project as opposed to another.

The scientific ontology of complex systems

Critical realism's deduction of the world's stratified ontology and its distinction between the transitive and intransitive domains of science form a suitable launching point for discussing the social ontology of complex social formations. What is needed, though, is a *scientific ontology* that bridges the two. Complexity theory is just such a vehicle: it is a general systems theory, i.e. a science of open-ended, peripatetic entities capable of material and structural evolution (Bertalanffy 1969, pp. 30–53, 120–154).

Complexity's ontological foundations begin with Rosen's distinction between *simple systems* and *complex systems* (Rosen 1991, pp. 314–327). Western science has long been drawn to mechanist metatheories and it seems still to be the hegemonic preference in sociology. Classical Newtonian mechanics is prototypical of simple system problematics. Such a science is predicated upon five assumptions:

(1) Classical systems are *closed systems* in the sense that exogenous forces are either controlled or are analytically excluded from causal consideration.
(2) Once the *initial conditions* of a system's location relative to a fixed set of spatio-temporal coordinates are known; and
(3) Once the researcher has access to the *universal laws* governing such systems; then
(4) Precise predictions of future system states can be made, and these predictions can be tested empirically.
(5) Finally, this explanatory template is sustainable if and only if the combined causal forces driving the developmental dynamics are mechanically related, viz. *they do not interact significantly among themselves.*

Given these constraints, the dynamics of simple systems can be expressed in terms of *linear* and *reductive* formats. They are 'linear' in the sense that the system's dynamics can be causally expressed by a simple summing over the independent vectors driving the system. Sometimes called '*superposition*', the resulting linear combination of causal factors entails the reductive assumption that simple systems as a class are analytically equal to the sum of their parts. When these conditions are met, simple systems are said to be '*conservative*'. Underpinning this conservative designation, though, is the axiomatic assumption that the spatio-temporal nexus framing the system's movements are fixed, viz. the referential framework cannot, in-and-of-itself, evolve during the analytic span of the system.

In contrast to the linear dynamics of simple systems, complex systems roughly conform to realism's ontological deductions. Complex systems are composed of internally stratified elements whose causal powers reciprocally reinforce one another so as to generate a structurally coherent skein. Moreover, the actual sequencing of their causal capacities are often staggered and uneven. Whether natural entities or sociohistorical formations (case-objects not excepted), this asynchronous sequencing of causal inputs confounds most linear explanations. Little wonder, then, that when sociologists confront complex social formations, they resort to 'super-organic' analogies, rather than to the classical, clockwork allusions celebrating Nature's inherent parsimony. Differing sharply from simple systems, the organization of complexity is so tightly knotted by reciprocal causation and stabilizing redundancies that their adaptive integration approximates what Abbott (1999, pp. 196–205) has called a spatio-temporal *interaction field*.

The most significant difference between simple and complex systems, however, is found in the latter's evolutionary capacities. Under propitious circumstances, complex systems can undergo irreversible *phase transitions*. Such sudden perturbations not only induce changes in the material and structural composition of the system itself but, on occasion, such changes actually entail the qualitative transformations of the evolutionary phase space itself. Put more succinctly, the conditions under which complexity's evolution occurs often requires the *evolution of evolution* itself.

Finally, complexity's evolution can be radically disjunctive. The crux of this discontinuity resides in complexity's *sensitive dependence on initial conditions*. Such sensitivity expresses itself when incremental shifts in the system's initial conditions give rise to disproportionately large differences in its final state. Moreover, these small differences and their non-linear amplifications often originate as simple errors in iterative replication or some other series of accidental occurrences.

Dissipative social systems and dissipative social theory

Dissipative systems are complexly structured, material constellations whose growth and evolution are regulated by non-linear processes of evolution. Complex social systems (including case-objects) are considered a subset of dissipative systems because of the open interchange of matter and energy with their environment, as well as the role material production and ecological adaptation play in sustaining their livelihood.

As it presently stands, *dissipative systems theory* provides the social scientist with a valuable heuristic for grasping the dynamics and long-term fate of social formations. It can aid sociologists in their understanding of social atrophy and the anomic disorganization of social institutions, as well as their subsequent renewal.

Dissipative systems theory was originally grounded in the Second Law of Thermodynamics and was the provenance of the relatively new discipline of non-equilibrium thermodynamics. Unlike the First Law of Thermodynamics, which posits the conservation of matter and energy and their continual transformation of one into the other, the Second Law makes no such conservative assumption. Quite the contrary, it posits that, under certain conditions, thermodynamic systems inevitably descend into a state of structural disorder (entropy). For example, closed systems, by definition, have no access to environments in which free energy or assimilable matter is available. With no resources by which they could renew and extend themselves, they will undergo organizational degradation. In the jargon of thermodynamics, this progressive disorganization is due to an irreversible 'accumulation of positive entropy'.

One need only touch a hot tea-kettle to appreciate the point of the Second Law. As we know, only a fraction of the heat summoned from the flame of a gas stove to heat the water in the kettle is transferred to the kettle; and only a portion of that energy actually heats the water. The energy not working to heat the water is radiated into the ambient air as 'wasted energy': the heat is 'dissipated'. But more than wasted heat and working efficiency are lost in the process. The complexity

of the molecular structure of the natural gas being used to heat the water is itself structurally degraded into the combustible by-products of oxidation. Hence, if the stove/tea-kettle/ambient air were a 'closed system' then, along with the mechanical loss due to heat transfer, positive entropy would also have accumulated via oxidation. And as the system was 'closed' – bereft of renewable resources – the growth of positive entropy would be irreversible. That is, the system would have moved itself a step closer toward being a homogeneous milieu devoid of structural form. In such instances, that spatially homogeneous distribution of energies would be called 'thermal equilibrium'.

When dissipative systems are transported to an 'open milieu', the implications of the Second Law shift dramatically. In open-system settings, dissipative organizations have hypothetical access to environmental stores of assimilable matter and free energy: these materials can be used as potential resources for fostering dissipative system development. As they increase their structural complexity, they secure, *ceteris paribus*, the means for staving off their immanent descent into thermal equilibrium. And, in special cases, certain open system milieus may be rich enough and robust enough to set into motion a countervailing dynamic that can blunt, or even temporarily reverse, the system's descent into entropic equilibrium.

Evolution is just such a counter-tendency. Its ascendant tendency toward increased complexification represents the natural possibility that new levels of order and novelty can offset extant levels of immanent disorder. Positive entropy's nemesis, so to speak, takes the form of an *increasing accumulation of negative entropy* or 'negantropy'. Whether as organisms, symbiotically integrated ecologies, or sociocultural structures, dissipative systems are material embodiments of organizational complexity. Taken as systemic totalities, dissipative formations are concrete, spatio-temporal sites in which the dialectics of entropic decay and negantropic structuration constantly play off one another.

Recognizing the analytic potential of this dialectical process, Ilya Prigogine and his collaborators in the Brussels School (Prigogine and Stingers 1984, Nicolis and Prigogine 1989) constructed a general, four-part paradigm for investigating the dissipative dialectics inherent in complex systems. The model posits: (1) a bounded dissipative system whose developmental complexity is driven by the dialectically tensed accumulations of positive entropy and negantropy; (2) the system's immediate environment, from which matter and energy transfers flow back and forth across the system's boundaries; (3) the systemic 'metabolism' of that 'free-energy' to generate structural growth and, occasionally, give way to evolutionary complexity; and (4) the capacity of the dissipative system to slough off the 'waste by-products' (positive entropy) of system complexification into its immediate environment.

Under the assumptions of this model, *open, complex systems* are able to appropriate environmental resources and, in varying degrees, to convert them into increased structural complexity (negantropic accumulation). When sufficient accumulations of negantropic complexity outweigh the dissipative system's ability to slough off its positive entropy, a possible take-off point toward emergent evolutionary development is possible. Such dissipative entities are then said to be in a *far-from-equilibrate state*. When, on the other hand, positive entropy accumulations outstrip negantropic growth, then the dissipative system tends toward a *steady-state thermal equilibrium*. A third possibility, *near-to-equilibrate systems,* enables a dissipative system to sustain itself in a state of homeostatic equilibrium. Unable to evolve to a far-from-equilibrate regime, they nonetheless are able to stave off descent into thermal equilibrium. The hallmark of these near-to-equilibrate systems is their ability to settle into cycles in which they regularly oscillate between two or more fixed reference states.

We now possess a heuristic for modeling the dissipative dialectics of structural order and disorder in complex social systems. More to the point, we have a plausible scientific ontology for reconnoitering the presumed structure and dynamics of case-objects. Of the three dissipative possibilities just listed, far-from-equilibrate, dissipative systems are of greatest interest to sociology. Case-objects may be provisionally likened to ontologically complex entities that live off their material and social environments and thereby risk entropically degrading their relations with each. As dissipative entities, case-objects are 'unstable' in the sense that they are driven by boundary-testing engines that perpetually explore their evolutionary options. When the case-object evolves, this shift may be precipitated as much from within as from without. Consequently, much of the anomic disorder encountered in social formations, case-objects included, is the price exacted for continually seeking transitory adaptations. This anomie is itself a sign of institutional entropy. It exacerbates the case-object's far-from-equilibrate tendencies and, as such, sets in motion new adaptive quests.

TRANSITIVE AND INTRANSITIVE CASE

Two implications concerning the social ontology of case-objects flow from the foregoing discussion of dissipative systems and their scientific ontology. First, case-objects are best approached as if they were complex, dissipative systems, as opposed to simple mechanical ensembles. Second, the transformational dynamics of case-objects follow the regimen associated with far-from-equilibrate, dissipative systems. *They are, in short, evolving, sociohistorical entities* and should be treated as such. Ontologically, case-objects are minimally bounded, complex, dissipative systems that interact with their material and social environments. Moreover, as we will argue below, they are the joint product of the intentional activities of historical actors as well as of inertial institutions. Taken together, the contradictory 'push and pull' of agency and social structure form the sociological source of the case-object's proactive innovations.

The social ontology of the case-object

When approached from the combined perspectives of complex realism's assumptions concerning the ontology of the case-object and the epistemological bracketing of casing developed in *What Is a Case?*, four aspects of casing and the case-object can be used to map the intransitive domain of case research. They are:

(1) *The case-object must support a self-standing narrative*: The case-object must be a sufficiently self-contained entity that it can provide, *prima facie,* meaningful analytic closure. The case-object must also be ontologically complex enough to sustain a *relatively well-formed explanatory narrative.*

(2) *The case-object must be a minimally integrated social system*: The case-object should be a well-bounded, internally nested set of ontologically layered structures that form a minimally integrated constellation. This social integration usually occurs via structural redundancies and 'backups' or functioning reciprocities. It need not, of necessity, be consensually integrated. Indeed, such stabilization could just as readily result from systematic class coercion, a transitory truce or cooptation between competing ethnic or racial factions, or a hegemonic stalemate between symmetrically empowered social or cultural elites.

(3) *Case-objects are open, historically evolving systems*: As a nested, ontologically stratified, entity, the case-object must be in continual exchange with its material habitat and its variegated social environments. As an emergently organized entity, case-objects are *historically constituted* and *reconstituted* in social space and social time. They have the self-directed capacity to evolve, albeit at uneven rates of transformation.

(4) *Case-objects are dialectically reproduced by human intentionality and by institutional stasis*: If the sociological investigation of the case-object is to remain scientifically viable, the intentionality of human agency must be granted equal recognition to that given to the ability of social institutions to coercively channel or exploit the self-directed motives of human agents. Moreover, the chaos that inheres in everyday life is often due to as much as to burgled efforts at institutional control as it does

because of the anarchic 'perversity' authored by human agency.

In the final analysis, though, just as these four characteristics of case-objects are irreducible to one another, so the case-object as an emergent totality is itself an irreducible entity in its own right.

A complex realist paradigm

At this point, Bhaskar's critical naturalism provides a way for plumbing the ontological complexity of the case-object. In this context, the term 'naturalism' denotes the positivist presupposition that social facts may be investigated using the same methods as those employed in the physical sciences. This naive naturalism becomes *critical naturalism* when the constitutive paradox of sociology as a science is confronted. That is, any science of society worthy of the name must reconcile the fact that the coercive powers of historically situated social institutions are always effectuated by human agents and their discretionary conduct. Within limits, agents intentionally interpret (or misinterpret) institutional missions and thereby filter society's 'objective powers' through their situated understandings. Add to the contingencies the serendipitous errors of applying institutional edicts or of anomie that is induced by lingering institutions whose powers no longer produce taken-for-granted outcomes give a a fair sense of the ontological complexity social scientists face when pursuing their craft.

In sorting out these complications, complex realists follow Bhaskar's (1979/1989, pp. 31–37) lead. He begins by selecting two classic, but diametrically opposed, accounts of social life, what he calls the '*Durkheimian*' and the '*Weberian stereotypes*'. Playing off their inverted but mutually exclusive accounts, he develops his own realist conception of sociology's intransitive domain.

In this analytic context, the term 'stereotype' denotes the partial nature of the scientific truths the Durkheimian and Weberian paradigms express. From these one-sided abstractions, Bhaskar then develops

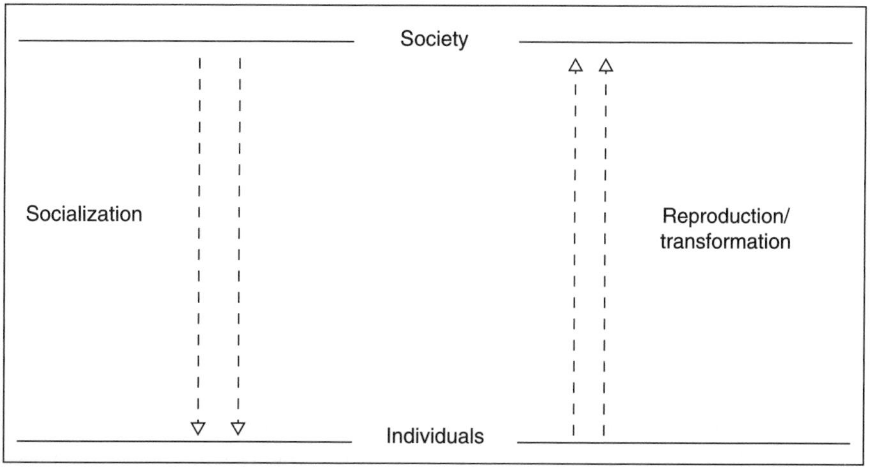

Figure 1.3 **The transformational model of social action (TMSA).**

a dialectically framed naturalism by sublating the contradictory presuppositions of each stereotype into an integrated sociological whole. The results of his reconnaissance are shown in Figure 1.3. The Durkheimian stereotype consists of the triad ≪Society → Socialization Processes → Individual≫. In accordance with Durkheimian positivism, the downward-directed arrows represent the coercive power of Durkheimian 'social facts', which morally constrain the destructive 'appetites' of atomized individuals during periods of social and cultural breakdown. The one-sided, Weberian stereotype reads, ≪Individuals → Production/Transformation → Society≫; it is located on the right side of Figure 1.3. The inverse flow of the Weberian causal vectors signifies the weight Weberian action theory places on human subjectivity and its cultural productions. It should be noted in passing that the TMSA's opposed triads and their dispositional flows conceptually parallel or overlap several of the dualisms already discussed in this paper, viz. nomothetic versus ideographic modes of enquiry, positivist versus social constructivist accounts of social life, and quantitative versus qualitative methodologies.

At this point, Peter Berger's duality of 'Society creates Man' versus 'Man creates Society' can be added (Berger and Luckmann 1966, Bhaskar 1979/1989, pp. 31–33).

Bhaskar uses Berger's unmediated dualism as a foil for completing his dialectical conception of society. Within the context of the TMSA, man no more 'creates' society than society 'creates' man. Instead, both are *ontologically irreducible* to one another. As different as their respective *modus vivendi* are, their powers are complementary, so much so that they form the necessary preconditions for each other's existence. Hence, humans are intentional agents whose self-directed activities:

> ... *reproduce* or *transform* [society]. That is, if society is always already made, then any concrete human praxis, or, if you like, act of objectivation can only modify it; and the totality of such acts sustain and change it. It is not the product of their activity (any more, I shall argue, than human action is completely determined by it). Society stands to individuals, then, as something that they never make, but that exists only in virtue of their activity. (Bhaskar 1979/1989, p. 34)

By contrast, society, for all its power to induce social conformity, is at best an abstract potentiality. Its very real but slumbering powers remain virtually inert without the productive intercession of human agency, individual or collective. Hence:

> Society, then, is an articulated ensemble of tendencies and powers which, unlike natural ones, exist only as long as they (or at least some of them) are

being exercised; are exercised in the last instance via the intentional activity of human beings; and are not necessarily space–time invariant. (Bhaskar 1979/1989, p. 39)

In short, the TMSA has built into it a radical irreducibility between society and human agency that is sustained by an 'ontological hiatus'. Standing by themselves, both are relatively feckless abstractions, unable to fully realize their respective powers. Agency requires an institutional field of action in order to realize its reproductive or transformational potential: the ensemble of institutions lack the material means (human agency) by which to convert an otherwise vapid moralism into a regulative system of ethics. Together, though, the material presence of its other is the *sine qua non* for realizing its own essential powers.

Society in its fullest sense, then, emerges as the material nexus in which the symbiotic interplay of structure and agency takes place. At this point, critical naturalism can hold that society and man are each open, irreducible complexes. Ontologically, they are different types of entities, only when productively combined do they constitute a system of mutual reproduction and transformation.

To the extent the Durkheimian stereo-type excludes human intentionality from its account, its naive positivism assumes its method can be applied unchanged across the physical and the social sciences. Likewise, to the extent that the Weberian stance excludes knowledge of objective society *a priori*, it embraces an errant, at times ethereal, constructivism. In everyday practice, the more the one claims explanatory self-sufficiency, the more it requires the intercession of its opposite to bring credible closure to its accounting.

By contrast, the dialectical amelioration of the two stereotypes sublates the 'flawed' presumptions of each approach, thereby forging a tensed 'synthetic unity of ontological opposites'. The dialectical formulation of sociological laws now becomes possible. Hence, Durkheimian social facts materi-ally constrain human conduct, but only to

the extent that the moral force of social institutions hinges upon the discretionary latitude allotted agency. Similarly, while agents exercise interpretive discretion in deciding when, where, why, how, and to whom institutional controls are to be relaxed or strictly tightened, such decisions are made within the limits of cultural conventions and constraints. Thus, both institutions and agents make their own history, but neither does so from the whole cloth of their unchecked possibilities.

Society is thus possible only as an emergent social space in which the co-respective powers of structure and agency realize their respective potentials by harnessing and transforming the powers inherent in their opposite. The societal and agentive halves of the TMSA are thus 'symbiotically bound' to one another. And if researchers are prone to insisting upon using biological analogies, they are better advised to draw upon the conflict ecology of the biotic community or the urban milieu with their structured dialectic of cooperative competition, rather than the prosaic organicism of an earlier era.

This symbiotic reading of society as an intersection of dialectical forces invites the question as to what mediates between and thereby unifies structure and agency. To answer this question we must return to Figure 1.3 and examine its middle terms: 'socialization' and 'reproduction/transfor-mation'. Under the aegis of complex real-ist social theory, these middle terms are 'mediating thirds'. Each set of mediations simultaneously enables and inhibits, on the one hand, the capacity of social structures to channel the discretionary activities of agency, while, on the other hand, the discretionary powers of human intentionality are allotted a limited freedom to either reproduce insti-tutional histories or to revolutionize them as they see fit.

By transforming these productive media-tions into vehicles of reflexive unification, an *Expanded TMSA* introduces concrete ele-ments of material production and social repro-duction hither-to-fore absent from Bhaskar's original TMSA. Suddenly the TMSA is given a substantive deepening that converts the previously abstract triads into fused productive unities of action. Bhaskar tells us that these fused triads allow us to speak of *dualities of reproduction*:

> ... Now if, following Durkheim, one regards society as providing the material causes of human action, and following Weber, one refuses to reify it, it is easy to see that both society and human *praxis* must possess a *dual character*. Society is both the ever-present *condition* (material cause) and the continually reproduced *outcome* of human agency. And *praxis* is both work, that is, conscious *production*, and (normally unconscious) *reproduction* of the conditions of production, that is society. One could refer to the former as the *duality of structure*, and the latter as the *duality of praxis*. (Bhaskar 1979/1989, pp. 34–35)

By underscoring the emergent duality of structure and duality of *praxis*, their unification, always implicit in the society/agency stereotypes, is now rendered explicit. They are shown to be what they always were, dialectical moments of a single reproductive act.

By invoking these fused dualities, the last step is taken through which critical realist philosophy yields up a complex realist sociological theory. With Bhaskar having demonstrated the possibility of a natural science of society, one that takes into account the differences between the objects natural scientists study and those investigated by social scientists, a complex realist ontology emerges that can situate the material nexus in which sociology's intransitive domain operates:

> ... social structures ... [are] ... (a) continually reproduced (or transformed) and (b) exist only in virtue of, and are exercised only in, human agency (in short, that they require active 'functionaries'). Combining these desiderata, it is evident that we need a system of mediating concepts, encompassing both aspects of the duality of praxis, designating the 'slots', as it were, in the social structure into which active subjects must slip in order to reproduce it; that is, a system of concepts designating the 'point of contact' between human agency and social structures. Such a point, linking action to structure, must *both* endure and be immediately occupied by individuals. It is clear that the mediating system we need is that of the *positions* (places, functions,

rules, tasks, duties, rights, etc.) occupied (filled, assumed, enacted, etc.) by individuals, and of the *practices* (activities, etc.) in which, in virtue of their occupancy of these positions (and vice versa), they engage. I shall call this mediating system the position-practice system. Now such positions and practices, if they are to be individuated at all, can only be done *relationally*.... Thus the transformational model implies a relational interest for sociology. And it suggests in terms of that interest a way of differentiating sociology from the other social sciences (such as linguistics, economics, etc.), which, however, logically presuppose it. (Bhaskar 1979/1989, pp. 40–41)

Here Bhaskar critically deploys Marxian materialism and its grounding in a narrative of productive modes to unify the former abstractions of Durkheimian positivism and Weberian voluntarism. Moreover, by theoretically designating the paired triads as irreducible unities of *positioned practice*, the TMSA becomes a critical tool for minimizing the *social* reifications inherent in Durkheimian positivism, just as it 'naturalistically' exposes the autopoetic excesses implicit in Weberian interpretive sociology.

These extrapolations from the original TMSA can be used to construct a revised TMSA (Harvey 2002), one that fully expresses the dialectical premises of complex realism itself. That revision is schematized in Figure 1.4. The revised TMSA now takes into account both the relational system of positioned practices mentioned above, and the crucial dualities of structure and of praxis by which the dialectical implications of the original TMSA is sustained. The schematic in Figure 1.4 can be visualized as lying in the first quadrant of a system of Cartesian coordinates. Located in social space and social time, we find arrayed along the vertical axis the spatially differentiated systems of positioned practices. The horizontal axis is aligned along the path of an irreversible temporal flow, which designates the TMSA's complex historical movement. The four 'corner boxes' of the schematic represent, as before, the Durkheimian and Weberian stereotypes with which Bhaskar began. As grounding premises of the revised TMSA, they are still ontologically distinct coproducers of society.

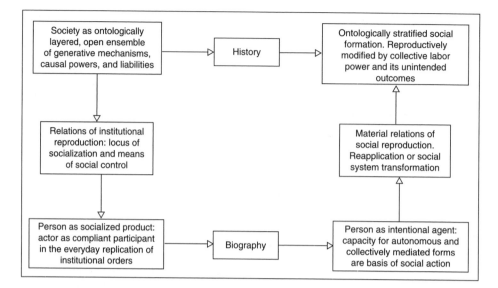

Figure 1.4   Bhaskar's transformational model of social action (TMSA) revised to show material nexus of spatial/temporal action.

At the same time, the dialectical nature of that coproduction is underscored by the alternating 'subject/object' role both structure and agency play successively in this historically driven process.

The remaining four cells – socialization and social control, the reproduction and/or transformation of institutional structures, history, and biography – are material forces that govern the contingencies of societal reproduction. Bhaskar (see above) subsumes the first two complexes under the rubric of positioned practices. He is careful to note that the relational articulation of positioned practices makes them the proper domain of sociological inquiry. History and biography, by contrast, are the irreversible, time-sensitive integuments in which positioned practices and their generative activities are enmeshed. When taken together, these four moments of the Revised TMSA form a provisional paradigm for staking out the social ontology of the case-object.

Finally, the ontological possibilities of the case-object must deal with agency's desire to posit and realize its own identity. Figure 1.5 reconfigures the Revised TMSA of Figure 1.4 to take into account this contingency. It posits

a material nexus of community in which history and biography converge. While both history and biography as previously defined are preserved, they have become elements of a concrete conjuncture in which agentive self-formation and the needs of the community meet. At this level of generality, it matters little whether the community is an ecological constellation or a group integrated around a common set of values, for both formations possess valuable resources, symbolic and material, which stimulate the dialectical exchanges schematized in Figure 1.5.

Hence, the community imposes specific constraints on its members as to their aspirations and the differentially distributed opportunities for self-realization that will be available to each individual person or group. The opportunity structures of the community thus constitute a field in which the agent, now treated as a biographical entity, is given selective access to certain material and cultural resources by which to achieve his or her discretionary self-development. The communal resources in this instance are categorized in terms of the 'historical forms' inherent in the particular community. The agent – acting alone or

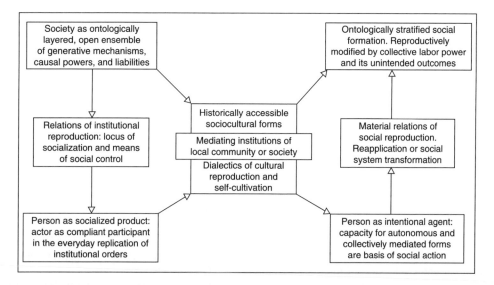

Figure 1.5 Transformational mode of social action (TMSA) showing material nexus of social action, including mechanism of agent's reproductive intervention.

in concert with others – thus seeks a self-realization that secures a series of identities over a lifetime. In return, the agent contributes to the community's welfare by producing or elaborating upon a growing pool of sedimented culture forms.

The reciprocities struck between agency and community are not, however, free of conflict or mutual alienation. The schematic in Figure 1.5 is patterned after Georg Simmel's essay 'On the Concept and Tragedy of Culture' (Etzkorn 1968, pp. 27–46), in which he traces the subjective and personal origins of objective cultural formations, and their subsequent alienation as the agent's existential projects – once realized and publicly objectivated – are ineluctably appropriated and made part of the collective property of the community's 'objective culture'.

It is noteworthy that the revised TMSA in Figure 1.5 is thus constructed from within the horizon of Simmel's *Lebensphilosophie* and the dialectic he describes – i.e., a dialectic that endlessly sets *Life's* subjective content against the cultural forms it constantly produces and then discards, as it searches for more refined expressions of self-hood. And it is no mean irony that in completing our complex

realist mapping of the case-object's social ontology and its agent-based reproduction, we have returned to the neo-Kantian antinomies that drove Park and Burgess's search for a scientific sociology. We have come full circle, but with a difference: in using the revised TMSA to flesh out the social ontology of the case-object, we have discovered a plausible venue for reintroducing social ontology into social science discourse.

CONCLUSION: SOCIAL ONTOLOGY AS SOCIOLOGICAL UNDER-LABORING

This chapter has critiqued case research from the standpoint of complex realism. In the course of that critique, we have found little with which to argue concerning the technical scope or depth to which sociological methodology and its epistemological foundations have been deployed during the casing debate. The main thrust of our comments has been elsewhere – viz. toward the fact that methodological considerations have seldom led to a concurrent consideration of the intransitive infrastructure of social inquiry. We believe that this relative neglect of social ontology is due to a pervasive anti-ontological bias among social researchers. We also believe that a major source of this bias is to be found in the neo-Kantian foundations from which academic sociology first emerged. Indeed, much of this chapter has been devoted to tracing the various incarnations neo-Kantianism has assumed in the history of our discipline.

In opposition to neo-Kantian presuppositions, we have assumed throughout that matters of epistemology and methodology normally recapitulate the contours of ontology. Admittedly, in the concrete research setting, any one of several nuanced methodologies could fruitfully be coupled to a given ontology and could yield significant insights in the process. The degrees of freedom with which an 'eclecticism' is feasible is limited. In the last analysis there is an elective affinity between the nature of the social entity being investigated and the sociohistorical nexus that shapes the posing of scientific questions. For example, our critical vetting of the case-object's ontology has been predicated upon the assumption that when investigating an ontologically complex, stratified social formation, classical forms of linear analysis are far less tractable than, say, the working assumptions of dissipative systems theory.

Testing such assumptions cannot be fully resolved by methodological disputations alone: such resolutions often entail 'speculative discussions' that touch on the ontological bounds of the subject matter under investigation. The revised TMSA developed here is but one possible approach for mapping the ontological contours of the social entities studied by sociologists. It is an idealized construction and, as such, must be judged pragmatically, i.e. in terms of its usefulness in guiding empirical research, or in sifting and sorting through the empirical thicket with which researchers are confronted.

As for doing sociology *sans* social ontology, Bhaskar (1989, pp. vii, 1–2) suggests how we might exit this paradox. He advocates that the philosopher of science becomes an 'under-laborer' to the sciences, working much as the rough-out man does on construction sites or on the factory floor. The under-laborer readies the tools and materials before the other workers begin their tasks. Following this metaphor, far from being an alien task for sociologists, the explication of social ontology is an intellectual under-laboring of the first order. It is the necessary propaedeutic for doing sociology.

REFERENCES

Abbott, A. 1999 *Department and Discipline: Chicago Sociology at One Hundred.* Chicago: The University of Chicago Press.

Abbott, A. 2001 *Chaos of Disciplines.* Chicago: The University of Chicago Press.

Adorno, T.W. 1973 *Negative Dialectics.* New York: The Seabury Press.

Anderson, P.W. 1972. 'More is different' *Science New Series* Vol. 177, No. 2 (4047) 393–396.

Arthur, B. 1996 *Increasing Returns and Path Dependence in the Economy.* Ann Arbor, MI: The University of Michigan Press.

Baker, P.J. 1973 'The life histories of W.I. Thomas and Robert E. Park'. *American Journal of Sociology* 79: 243–260.

Beck, L.W. 1967 'Neo-Kantianism' in P. Edwards (Ed.) *The Encyclopedia of Philosophy, Volumes 5 and 6.* New York: Macmillan/Free Press, pp. 468–473.

Becker, H.S. 1999 'The Chicago School, so-called' *Qualitative Sociology* 22: 3–12.

Berger, P. and Luckmann, T. 1966 *The Social Construction of Reality: A Treatise in the Sociology of Knowledge.* Garden City, New York: Doubleday and Company.

Bertalanffy, L. 1969 *General Systems Theory: Foundations, Development, Applications* (revised edition). New York: George Braziller.

Bhaskar, R. 1975/1997 *A Realist Theory of Science.* New York: Verso.

Bhaskar, R. 1979/1989 *The Possibility of Naturalism: A Philosophical Critique of the Contemporary Human Sciences* (2nd edition). New York: Routledge.

Bhaskar, R. 1989 *Reclaiming Reality: A Critical Introduction to Contemporary Philosophy.* London: Verso.

Bhaskar, R. 1993 *Dialectic: The Pulse of Freedom.* London: Verso.

Bhaskar, R. 2007 'Theorizing ontology' in C. Lawson, J. Latsis and N. Martins (Eds) *Contributions to Social Ontology.* London: Routledge, pp. 192–204.

Bulmer, M. 1984 *The Chicago School of Sociology: Institutionalization, Diversity, and the Rise of Sociological Research*. Chicago: The University of Chicago Press.

Burger, T. 1976 *Max Weber's Theory of Concept Formation: History, Laws and Ideal Types*. Durham, NC: Duke University Press.

Burgess, E.W. 1925/1967 'The growth of the city: an introduction to a research project' in R.E. Park and E. W. Burgess, R.D. McKenzie (Eds.) *The City*. Chicago: The University of Chicago Press, pp 47–62.

Burgess, E.W. 1927 'Statistics and case studies as methods of sociological research' *Sociology and Social Research* 12: 103–120. Reprinted in D.J. Bogue (Ed.) 1974 *The Basic Writings of Ernest W. Burgess*. Chicago: Community and Family Study Center, University of Chicago, pp. 367–373.

Burgess, E.W. 1939 'The distinctive value of the case study'in E.W. Burgess and L.S. Cottrell. *Predicting Success of Failure in Marriage*. New York: Prentice Hall, pp. 332–339. Reprinted in D.J. Bogue (Ed.) 1974 *The Basic Writings of Ernest W. Burgess*. Chicago: Community and Family Study Center, University of Chicago, pp. 386–392.

Burgess, E.W. 1941 'An experiment in the standardization of the case-study method' *Sociometry* 4(4): 329–348.

Burgess, E.W. 1945 'Sociological research methods' *The American Journal of Sociology* 50(6): 474–482.

Burgess, E.W. 1974 *The Basic Writings of Ernest W. Burgess* (D.J. Bogue, Ed.) Chicago: Community and Family Study Center, University of Chicago.

Byrne, D. 2002 *Interpreting Quantitative Data*. Thousand Oaks, CA: Sage Publications.

Byrne, D. and Harvey, D.L. 2007 'Chaos/complexity theory' in M. Hertwig (Ed.) *Dictionary of Critical Realism*. New York: Routledge, pp. 64–66.

Collier, A. 1994 *Critical Realism: An Introduction to Roy Bhaskar's Philosophy*. London: Verso.

Eldredge, N. 1985 *Unfinished Synthesis: Biological Hierarchies and Modern Evolutionary Theory*. Oxford: Oxford University Press.

Etzkorn, P. 1968 *Georg Simmel: The Conflict in Modern Culture and Other Essays*. Teachers College, Columbia University, New York: Teachers College Press.

Freidman, M. 2000 A *Parting of the Ways: Carnap, Cassirer, and Heidegger*. Chicago: Open Court.

Fine, G.A. (Ed.) 1995 *A Second Chicago School? The Development of a Postwar American Sociology*. Chicago: The University of Chicago Press.

Gleick, J. 1987 *Chaos: Making a New Science*. Harmondsworth, UK: Penguin Books.

Gould, S.J. 1989 *Wonderful Life: The Burgess Shale and the Nature of History*. New York: W. W. Norton.

Gusfield, J.R. 1995 'Preface: the second Chicago School?' in G.A. Fine (Ed.) *A Second Chicago School? The Development of a Postwar American Sociology*. Chicago: The University of Chicago Press, pp. ix–xvi.

Harvey, D.L. 2002 'Agency and community: a critical realist paradigm' *Journal for the Theory of Social Behavior* 32(2): 163–195.

Holborn, H. 1950 'Wilhelm Dilthey and the critique of historical reason' *Journal of the History of Ideas* 11(1): 93–118.

Iggers, G.G. 1968 *The German Conception of History: The National Tradition of Historical Thought from Herder to the Present*. Middletown, CT: Wesleyan University Press.

Masur, G. 1952 'Wilhelm Dilthey and the history of ideas' *Journal of the History of Ideas* 13(1): 94–107.

Matthews, F.H. 1977 *Quest for an American Sociology: Robert E. Park and the Chicago School*. Montreal: McGill–Queens University Press.

Mills, C.W. 1961 *The Sociological Imagination*. New York: Grove Press.

Nicolis, G. and Prigogine, I. 1989 *Exploring Complexity: An Introduction*. New York: W. H. Freeman.

Norris, C. 2007 'Ontology' in M. Hertwig (Ed.) *Dictionary of Critical Realism*. New York: Routledge, pp. 334–338.

Park, R.E. and Burgess, E.W. 1921/1969. *Introduction to the Science of Sociology, including the Original Index and to Basic Sociological Concepts* (3rd revised edition). Chicago: The University of Chicago Press.

Prigogine, I. 1996 *The End of Certainty: Time, Chaos and the New Laws of Nature*. New York: The Free Press.

Prigogine, I. and Stengers, I. 1984 *Order Out of Chaos: Man's New Dialogue with Nature*. Boulder, CO: New Science Library.

Ragin, C. and Becker, H.S. (Eds.) 1992 *What Is a Case?: Exploring the Foundations of Social Inquiry*. Cambridge: Cambridge University Press.

Rickman, H.P. 1960 'The reaction against positivism and Dilthey's concept of understanding' *The British Journal of Sociology* 11: 307–318.

Ringer, F. 2004 *Max Weber: An Intellectual Biography*. Chicago: The University of Chicago Press.

Ringer, F.K. 1969 *The Decline of the German Mandarins: The German Academic Community, 1890–1933*. Cambridge, MA: Harvard University Press.

Ringer, F.K. 1997 *Max Weber's Methodology: The Unification of the Cultural and Social Sciences*. Cambridge, MA: Harvard University Press.

Rosen, R. 1991 'Some epistemological issues in physics and biology' in B.J. Hilley and F.D. Peat (Eds.) *Quantum Implications: Essays in Honor of David Bohm*. London: Routledge, pp. 314–327.

Sayer, A. 1984 *Method in Social Science: A Realist Approach* (2nd edition). London: Routledge.

Tapper, B. 1925 'Dilthey's methodology of the Geisteswissenschaften.' *The Philosophical Review* 34: 333–349.

Thomas, W.I. and Znaniecki, F. 1918/1958 *The Polish Peasant in Europe and America.* New York: Dover Publications.

Waldrop, M.M. 1992 *Complexity: The Emerging Science at the Edge of Order and Chaos.* New York: Simon and Schuster.

Windelband, W. 1894/1980 'Rectorial address: Strasbourg' *History and Theory* 19(2): 169–185.

2

The Contextualist Approach to Social Science Methodology

Lars Mjøset

When delimiting a case, we start from a problem, then select a process towards an outcome and define a context in which it takes place. We finally explain by tracing the process within the context. These are the three basic operations of a contextualist methodology. This chapter provides a detailed comparison of this methodology with two other – the standard and the social-philosophical – methodologies. This comparison emphasizes how important it is that researchers in the qualitative tradition do not simply subordinate their reflection on the conduct of case studies to either of the other two methodologies. It also generates more general lessons on how we should think about methodologies, theory and accumulated knowledge in social science.

THE METHODOLOGIST'S DILEMMA

Methodologists are scholars who draw on the professional philosophy of science to develop general methodological guidelines based on experience with certain kinds of research method. They direct students to selected professional philosophical literatures about what science is, and spell out how the main research methods produce results that confirm these principles. Methodologists mediate between the professional philosophy of science and specific technical routines of empirical analysis. Methodologists mostly come in disciplinary varieties. Their role is very authoritative and clear-cut, as they play a crucial role in the socialization of upcoming scholars.

Methodologists face a dilemma. In the following, we present this dilemma with specific reference to social science methodologists, who present methodologies in which their experience in using certain types of social science method is generalized with reference to selected philosophical principles. These methodologies have to appear highly consistent, as they reflect and influence views on what should pass as science in various disciplines. But they can never be highly consistent because they are formulated by social scientists who are not professional philosophers but are specialized in specific research methods and related notions of theory.

The methodologist's mediating role between philosophy and empirical research is the key to this dilemma: Philosophical discussions draw towards fundamental, eternal questions, whether they are called questions of metaphysics, ontology, epistemology or just 'meta-theory'. However, any piece of empirical research must be carried out, reported and defended here and now. Methodologists cannot match the professional philosophers. Rather, their task is to produce *practical philosophies of social science* – methodologies that provide concrete guidelines in research practice and criteria as to what knowledge shall count as science. Such practical demands require methodologies to appear as clear-cut and consistent as possible. However, if the link with philosophy were to be pursued systematically, all kinds of reservations, reflections and conceptual specifications would threaten any clarity whatsoever. In the end, most core methodological concepts become vague, with many proximate, even contradictory definitions.

We should not think about methodology as a question of one set of impeccable normative principles. Instead, we will take for granted that a community of social scientists exists, and that this community does not allow just any kind of knowledge to pass as science. Still, the fact that there are several schools of philosophy and various research techniques in social science, makes it likely that there is more than one practical philosophy of social science. As any methodology is an uneasy balancing act, it is not easy to single out sets of preconceptions that define families of methodologies in recent social science. Still, we make an empirically based attempt, claiming that these methodological standards are shared by broad groups of contemporary social science methodologists.

THREE PRACTICAL PHILOSOPHIES OF SOCIAL SCIENCE

Methodological controversies are clues to different methodological frameworks. Scanning older and recent controversies, we find three broad clusters of methodologies (Mjøset 2006b). However, we also need to rely on sociology of science concepts. We have defined the concept of a methodologist, and others concern disciplinary communities, methods communities, local research frontiers and the external and internal relations of science. Whereas our preferred technical term for what methodologists do is 'practical philosophies of social science', we also use other, shorter labels, such as 'methodological frameworks', 'views', 'positions', 'approaches', 'researcher attitudes' or – following Veblen (1919) – 'preconceptions'. We also use personalized terms, such as 'standard scholars', 'social philosophers' and 'contextualists'.

The three practical philosophies of social science are determined 'from above' by philosophical orientations and 'from below' by the actual research methods their proponents employ. Looking 'upwards', methodologists can orient in three different directions: towards the professional philosophies of natural science, social science and the humanities, respectively. Looking 'downwards' to the everyday practices of social research, the methodologist will basically be familiar with either one of the clusters of empirical methods indicated in the lower part of Table 2.1. Our main claim, then, is that electoral affinities between the downward and upward orientations constitute the three practical philosophies of social science.

The practical philosophies are not 'fundamental' positions taken by professional philosophers, they are loose summaries of the views promoted by three types of methodologist. There may be both internal debates within each cluster, as well as typical debates between them. Our three-fold distinction forms an empirical sociology of knowledge-based framework that might be useful as a meta-perspective on earlier and contemporary methodological debates in social science.

Table 2.1 The three practical philosophies of social science

The philosophy of the natural sciences: twentieth-century traditions emerging from logical positivism, Popper's critical rationalism, Lakatos' research programmes, Kuhn/Popper debate, analytical philosophy	The philosophy of the social sciences: US pragmatism, European critical theory, standpoint epistemologies	The philosophy of the humanities, phenomenology, hermeneutics, structuralism, post-structuralism
The standard attitude	*The contextualist attitude*	*The social-philosophical attitude*
Mathematical modelling. Thought experiments/simulation. Statistical analysis of large data sets. These methods indicate a methods community with the natural sciences	Qualitative methods implying direct or indirect involvement with the cases studied; ranging from long-term participant observation, more or less structured interviewing, comparative work on distinct case histories. These are methods that are distinct to the social sciences	Interpretative analysis of texts: formal, linguistic and narrative analysis, discourse analysis, history of concepts, content analysis, less formal methods of textual exegesis, use of classical texts in social theory to build broad 'philosophy of history'-like interpretation of the present. These methods indicate a methods community with the humanities

Two of these three clusters have become visible from time to time in 'struggles on methodology', such as the critique of positivism in 1960s sociology, the science wars in 1990s science studies or the 'perestroika' debate in recent US political science. The third (contextualist) alternative has mostly appeared as a less obvious third position.

Methodological debates have been imminent since the birth of modern social science. Historically, these controversies display a pattern of recurrence: most of the topics debated today have appeared, disappeared and reappeared many times since the formation of modern social science more than one hundred years ago. In some periods, one methodological approach has held a dominant position, gaining normative status. In other periods, some kind of dualism has prevailed, namely a dualism between generalizing ('nomothetic') natural sciences, and specifying ('ideographic') social/human sciences.[1] Our contextualist third position has been less frequently identified and discussed in its own right. One of the aims of this chapter is to argue that it is a most important one for social science.

The question here is not *just* the difference between methods used, neither is it solely about fundamental philosophical differences.

As the combination of philosophical positions and research methods defines each practical philosophy, the relation between any pair of these cannot be reduced to conventional dichotomies. For instance, the distinction between standard and contextualist attitudes is *not* identical to the distinction between quantitative and qualitative methods, nor to the philosophical distinction between realism and nominalism (constructionism). Rather, such traditional dichotomies are interpreted in specific ways within each framework. More than consistency, each framework has a certain logic in terms of how various famous dichotomies (realism/constructionism, realism/empiricism, explanation/understanding, etc.) are discussed.

The philosophical inputs to a methodology, as well as the mere intellectual energy required to master specific social science methods, make it hard for one researcher simply to switch between practical philosophies. In everyday academic life, methodological clusters mostly remain self-contained, especially in disciplines largely dominated by just one framework. Even in multi-methodology social sciences (sociology, above all) the methodological camps mostly keep to themselves. Sometimes, this results in a situation in which scholars with different attitudes grapple with very similar problems without ever discussing (at least not in a serious manner) the arguments of those who belong to other clusters.

We now turn to a more detailed overview, first sketching the standard and social-philosophical methodologies. We then introduce the third, contextualist attitude, defining its specificity in comparison with the other two. We specify five aspects of each practical philosophy:[2] (1) their master example of explanatory logic; (2) their popularization of fundamental metaphysical questions; (3) their explanatory priorities given the autonomy of social science; (4) their implied sociology of knowledge; and (5) their assumptions about the relationship between the sciences. Furthermore, we define (6) *two* notions of theory within each methodology, showing how each of these notions imply distinct strategies of specification and generalization, thus questioning any unspecified generalization/ specification dualism.

THE STANDARD PRACTICAL PHILOSOPHY OF SOCIAL SCIENCE

In earlier incarnations, the standard attitude was entirely dominant in the early postwar period; it still seems to be the dominant framework. It emerges when practical experiences from mathematical modelling and statistical analysis of large datasets are combined with selected items from the professional philosophy of the natural sciences.[3] Its five characteristics are:

Master example of explanatory logic

There is one logic of explanation. The most direct version of this logic is found in natural science experiments. Natural scientists treat 'nature' as something that can be rearranged for experimental purposes. But in social science, the object ('nature') is a society of humans, into which experimental intervention is mostly undoable. Whereas social science knowledge does not – in any significant sense – grow as a result of

actual experiments and modelling related to experiments, experimental logic is still held to be the best example of the kind of explanatory logic pursued. Thus, standard methodology regards statistical analyses of non-experimental data to be quasi-experiments, considers mathematical modelling as thought experiments, or – as a minimum – employs concepts originating from the conduct of experiments: dependent and independent variables. The experiment becomes the paradigm for reasoning both about past events that were never produced as experimental outcomes and about ongoing processes into which experimental intervention is impossible. It is nearly always implied that the experimental benchmark applies in indirect and modified ways. A sequence of internal methodological debates revolve around the modification of this ideal; these concern the epistemological status of thought experiments, and how statistical analysis of non-experimental data can emulate real experiments (e.g. Lieberson 1985).

Popularization of fundamental metaphysical questions

The standard attitude is based on a broad set of convictions that gained dominance in the early postwar period. It later went through several revisionist interpretations. One of its early roots was interwar logical positivism, which clearly pursued an anti-realist programme (Hacking 1983), aimed at abolishing any metaphysics (any notion of unobservables and causality). But this purely syntactic definition of theory was philosophically hard to defend. As philosophers turned to semantic notions of theory, the question of representation could not be avoided. The main thrust since the late 1950s has been towards secularized approaches to core metaphysical questions, mostly labelled *scientific realism*. Currently, there is something close to a consensus on this view. Scientific theories represent inherent structures, unobservables that lie below or beneath the flow of empirical events. The basic entities of this structure are referred to as the elementary particles or 'atoms' of social science. Internal disagreements relate to the nature of such a generative structure, for instance, whether it is based on individual beliefs and desires, or rather on systems of unintended consequences that cannot be derived from individual intentions.

Explanatory priorities given autonomy of the social science realm

Social science theory represents the inherent structures of the realm of action and interaction. Reductionism (whereby all of society would be made part of nature only) is out of the question, at least in practical terms (Elster 1989, p. 74). The social sphere is, or must be treated as, marked by emergent properties *vis-à-vis* the realm of natural science. Neither concepts of utility (beliefs and desires) nor concepts of generative processes need to be further reduced to entities studied by neuroscience, biology or chemistry. The internal discussion concerns the kinds of explanatory reduction – to individual or non-individual entities – one can pursue within the sciences that cover the realm of the social.

Sociology of knowledge

Scientific beliefs are stabilized only from inside the scientific community, and this is enough to demarcate science from non-science. As a research community, social scientists are driven by the urge to illuminate ever more of the underlying structures behind social events and regularities. Influences from outside this community can certainly be found, but they are not relevant to the growth of social scientific knowledge. A sociology of (scientific) knowledge is irrelevant in this respect. 'The context of discovery' is no topic for the philosophy of science, and only logic matters in the 'context of justification'. Most statements of the standard programme emphasize that its ambitious theoretical ideals have not yet been realized in actual empirical research. Worries about this gap between theory and empirical research have haunted

spokesmen of the standard framework since the early twentieth century.

Assumptions about the relation between the sciences

Compared with the natural sciences, social science is still young and immature, encountering several kinds of barrier in its efforts to mature. A sociology of scientific knowledge may be invoked to explain this. Disagreements revolve around how this is explained, whether it is simply due to younger age of the social sciences or due to the nature of their subject matter.

Notions of theory

These five features do not go together in a consistent system. Still, they appear again and again in the writings of methodologists with a standard conviction. The preconditions can be specified historically. For instance, the nominalistic inclinations were obvious in early postwar operationalism, when Vienna school logical positivism was still broadly influential. Although one can distinguish different varieties of the programme, the above specification is sufficient for our purpose.

Within the standard approach, we find at least two distinct types of theory (Mjøset 2005). The *idealizing notion* conceives theory as thought experiments using mathematical equation systems, investigating the implications (in terms of equilibrium or disequilibrium) of assumptions on actors and their interaction. The *law-oriented notion* emerges from attempts to find law-like regularities in datasets or from the use of qualitative data in ways that allow the researcher to investigate hypotheses about such regularities. One version of the law-oriented notion is a regression equation calculated from a large dataset, yielding the net effects of the relevant independent variables on the chosen dependent variable. Another version is what Merton (1968) called middle-range theory.

Throughout the 1990s, many syntheses (e.g. Goldthorpe 2000) were suggested between the law-oriented and the idealizing notions of theory. But recently, more emphasis has been placed on problems in both of these components. These internal debates have led to what we shall call a *revisionist* standard position, for example, Hedström's (2005) programme of analytical sociology and Pawson's (2000) programme on middle-range realism.

The notion of causal mechanisms is crucial to this revisionist position, which develops further the ambivalence towards high theory that was already built into Merton's notion of middle-range theory (Mjøset 2006b, p. 339f). Given the autonomy of the realm of social interaction, mechanisms define the inherent structure, and representation of this is counted as a satisfactory explanation. Mechanisms are related to elementary particles or to driving forces. Elster (1989, cf. Elster 2007, p. 32, Hedström 2005, p. 25) conceived mechanisms as 'a continuous and contiguous chain of causal or intentional links' between initial conditions and an outcome. Hedström (2005, p. 23) states that we 'explain an observed phenomenon by referring to the social mechanism by which such phenomena are regularly brought about'. As we will see, this standard concept of mechanisms addresses some of the same challenges as the contextualist notion of a process tracing.

THE SOCIAL-PHILOSOPHICAL PRACTICAL PHILOSOPHY OF SOCIAL SCIENCE

Historically, the social-philosophical position was the first one to challenge the standard view in postwar debates. In Germany, second-generation Frankfurt school philosophers challenged Popper's attempt to transcend logical positivism. In Britain, philosophers concerned about Wittgenstein's 'linguistic turn' introduced the continental hermeneutic and phenomenological traditions into English-language methodological debates. Around Western Europe and the US, local varieties of this effort countered the dominant standard methodology, which was seen as an improper projection of natural science principles on to the sciences of man. The leading figures

belonged mostly to the humanities (especially philosophy), but through the 1960s and 1970s, social science and the humanities were often close allies in pursuing these arguments.

Social-philosophical methodology can be drawn from overview works presenting various personal contributions to *social theory*.[4] To the extent explicit methodologies are produced, they are treatises on the methodology of discourse analysis, of conceptual history, etc (see Table 2.1). In the following, we present a stylized account, using the same five properties as in the standard case.

Master example of explanatory logic

Interpreting the standard view as a logic of mechanical, causal explanation, social philosophers emphasize that in human interaction the element of meaning cannot be ignored. Social actors are reflexive. Explanations in social science must therefore be based on a logic of understanding *meaning*. Disagreements revolve around how common these intersubjective meanings are: do they relate to small communities or are they broad discourses that the researcher can tap into in her capacity of being a participant in (e.g. Western) society or culture at large?

Popularization of fundamental metaphysical questions

Whereas the standard position today in broad terms converges on scientific realism, the social-philosophical position has a similar realism/nominalism debate, but with no full convergence around a constructionist/nominalist position. The social-philosophical approach specializes in fundamental questions. The leading question is how social science is possible. Transcendental notions of action, interaction, knowledge and structure are necessarily assumed by anyone who conducts empirical social research. The philosophical discussions about conditions of possibility are linked to empirical questions by means of broad concepts characterizing the state of the present social world: the most frequent core concept is *modernity* (cf. e.g. Habermas 1981, Giddens 1990), but other periodizing labels are also invoked. Modernity is mostly interpreted as a regime of knowledge. There is, however, also a materialist interpretation in which the core of present-day society is seen as an underlying structure of unintended consequences. These driving forces can be conceived in line with, for example, Marx's analysis of the cycles and trends of the capitalist mode of production. Still, there is a sense in which even the materialist interpretation requires an 'understanding' of capitalism in its totality.

Explanatory priority given the autonomy of the social science realm

The exploration of transcendental conditions of social science is social philosophy's demonstration that the study of the social realm must be considered in its own terms. Contrary to the standard reduction to basic social entities, the social-philosophical attitude mostly implies a holistic position. What drives modernity is either a regime of knowledge (e.g. the rationalizing logic of modernization) or underlying driving forces (e.g. capitalist mode of production), which implies specific ideological patterns. Thus, a 'macro to micro'-connection is mostly emphasized. For instance, cases are studied as 'expressions' of a regime of knowledge (see Table 2.2, p. 52), just as the work of an artist synthesizes elements of the contemporary existential situation of mankind or some social group. The idea of individually rational action – whether it is defended or criticized – is a consequence of this regime, and thus not the elementary particle of explanations. Again, there is a more materialist version of this argument: the real forces of technological and economic rationality in a modern (e.g. capitalist) society produce ideologies that influence the growth of social science knowledge on this society. These forces must be the basis of any explanation. Internal debates revolve around the link between 'real structures' and 'regimes of knowledge'.

Sociology of knowledge

In the social-philosophical view, the fundamental processes, *modernity* above all, supply a sociology of knowledge. Modernity is mostly interpreted as a knowledge regime. One can trace its impact in all social spheres, as well as in social science. In such a meta-perspective, the standard position expresses the fascination with natural science's instrumental rationality in the modern world, specifically in Western academic culture. Alternatively, this rationality and the accompanying ideas of 'enlightenment' are linked – via ideologies or cognitive structures – to the underlying driving forces. In both versions of the argument, the sociology of knowledge is an external one: the preconditions implied by social research communities are seen as expressions of more encompassing regimes of knowledge and/or ideologies.

The relationship between the sciences

There is an inclination to consider science as a disguise. The varying maturity of the disciplines is not interesting. Rather, most disciplines play practical roles, they are part of a larger machinery of standardization that imposes discipline. Empirical research is often seen as purely instrumental (as is sectional divisions, the many 'partial sociologies' within sociology). Empiricist instrumentalism is overcome, either by existential accounts or by transcendental arguments about the conditions of social science. In the social-philosophical vision, social science shows its maturity and its superiority over natural science by being able to provide citizens with comprehensive understandings of their present predicament.

Notions of theory

We can distinguish two social-philosophical notions of theory (Mjøset 2006b, pp. 347–349), with corresponding strategies of specification and generalization. *Transcendental* or *reconstructionist theory* is about the transcendental conditions of social science: basic notions of action, interaction, knowledge and structure (Habermas 1981, Giddens 1985). This notion is general at the outset, as it concerns pre-empirical general conditions. With such a starting point, considerations about modernity must be considered *a specification* (see Table 2.2, p. 52). The *deconstructionist notion of theory* is its opposite, aiming to show that no transcendental conditions can be established (Foucault 1969, 1975, Seidman 1991). This implies a far-reaching sociology of knowledge assessment, denying any accumulation of knowledge whatsoever in social science. That approach has a periodization of modernity as its *most general* (see Table 2.2, p. 52) feature (as it doubts any transcendental foundations) and it suggests an exceptionalist strategy of specification close to the one we find within the discipline of history.

Most historians tend to claim exceptional status for their single cases. Their disciplinary socialization does not require them to conduct the explicit comparisons along several properties that might tell them in which respects their case is specific. The predominant view that there are no 'cases of the same', leads historians to avoid the comparisons that would have allowed them to see their cases in different lights. Their perspective changes only when the 'spirit of the time' shifts. At that point, revisionist interpretations crop up, only to be challenged at a later point by post-revisionists. Each period's historians, so goes the old saying, writes the national history anew.

It is true that many of the – at least Western European and American – communities of historians have absorbed a lot of social science inspiration since the student revolt of the late 1960s. However, since the 1980s, many of these communities have been inspired by the methodology of denationalized humanities, developed by the French post-structuralists. Thus, many contemporary historians converge with the deconstructionist branch of social-philosophy. Both groups of scholars are socialized into a style of research typical of the humanities: their focus on archives and written sources leads to a non-comparative focus on the single case. Applied to history, the deconstructionist position would claim that the sequence of revisionisms and post-revisionisms shows that there can be no research frontiers.

THE CONTEXTUALIST PRACTICAL PHILOSOPHY OF SOCIAL SCIENCE

The contextualist framework is a third methodological framework in social science.[5] As outlined in Table 2.1, it differs from the two others in terms of philosophical references and through its reference to styles of social science craftwork that lacks methodological community with either natural science or the humanities.[6] In the following, we define this attitude with reference to the same five aspects as the two attitudes discussed above.

The contextualist approach is closely connected to the conduct of case studies. Before we turn to the five properties of practical philosophies of social science, let us consider some common sense understandings of a 'case'. If you are involved in a case in court, you are attentive to the specificities of the singular case, rather than any general features. You and your lawyer are interested in how your case fits a taxonomy of legal regulations. You are interested in how a specific institution (court) within a legal system will classify your case in the light of the specificities emerging from documents and testimonies presented in court. Certain types of court case require judges/juries to decide on personal responsibility or contextual determination (cf. the discussion in Barnes 2001). Ahead of some court cases lies police work on cases. Turning to other examples, the daily activities of therapists and social workers are work on *cases*. Whereas cases in court refer to conflicting parties, cases here refer to single persons, persons whose life history has led to problems that may be eased through a participatory relation.

The common feature is that we isolate sequences of events towards an outcome as a case because we have an interest in the outcome and thus also in the process. In everyday life, the importance of the case might be quite personal, we make cases out of particularly important chains of events in individual life histories. When social actors become involved with cases (e.g. in court cases, police investigations, therapy), they need to be sensitive to the process leading to the outcome, either because exact understanding of why the outcome came about is needed, or because the interest is in influencing the outcome.

Master example of explanatory logic

The contextualist framework is based on sensitivity to cases. (This is implied in the term '*qualitative* research'). In the highly simplified representation of Figure 2.1, a case is an outcome preceded by a process that unfolds in time. Delimiting cases in social science investigations, we imply a three-fold logic of empirical research. First, we relate to our research problems, selecting the process and/or outcome to be studied. Second, we define the context, the elements that we treat as the environment of the process singled out. Third, we trace the specific links in the process we have selected.

Depending on the quality of our knowledge about the case, we arrive at an explanation of the case.

Sensitivity is necessary because investigators or therapists interact with their own kind. Standard preconceptions tempts scholars to approach experimental logic as closely as possible. The case study, in contrast, can be depicted as the opposite of the experiment. In an experiment, the production of a predicted outcome is just a means to arrive at general statements on the process. In case studies, outcome and process are significant in and of themselves. A case cannot be replicated at any time by any researcher anywhere. Some cases were the case in a particular context and will not necessarily ever happen the same way again. Other cases are produced again and again by an ongoing process, but we are then either interested in its specific cultural significance, or eager to evaluate it and possibly change it.

In an experiment, 'similar context' implies similar experimental set-ups. The fact that the processes studied are driven by humans largely precludes the exact engineering of experimental controls and shielding in social science. We cannot build context, so we cannot produce the isolated workings of particular mechanisms. Instead, we either have to reconstruct both context and process *ex post*, or we intervene in an ongoing process in an existing context. Figure 2.1

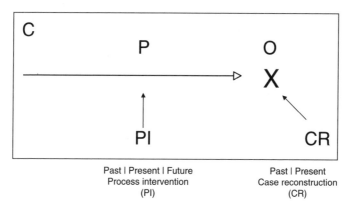

Figure 2.1   Two varieties of case study.
Note: C, context; O, outcome; P, process.

represents these two varieties of case study; both are related to contemporary problems. In case reconstruction, the research problem determines the selection of an outcome. In process intervention, the research problem leads the observer/analyst into (actual or potential) participation in the production of an outcome.

In *case reconstructions*, the researcher reconstructs the process towards an outcome that has occurred in the past – once or several times. In social science, we often make cases out of historically individual and highly significant events in the development of a smaller or larger community. In an indirect sense, case reconstructions are also participatory.[7] For instance, case reconstructions of significant macro-events can contribute to the self-understanding of a community (9/11 in the US). There are many examples of this, for example, in the literature on the politics of ethnic identity. This is particularly the case if the outcome is not just significant but also remains controversial.

In *process interventions*, the researcher takes part in a process and the outcome is in the future. This might be a once-off outcome or, just as likely, a repeated outcome that has occurred many times before. Observation here requires participation (interview, fieldwork, participant observation). Participation differs from experimental manipulation. In many cases, the observer wants to play a passive role, as the interest is in tracing the process as it would be without intervention. Anthropological and ethnographic case studies might not be interested in particular outcomes, but sensitivity relates to the historical and cultural specificity of daily life routines and cultural understandings. Participation, however, inevitably makes the researcher part of the creation of the case. This generates delicate problems of method. Still, these problems differ from problems of process intervention in cases that are inherently very controversial. These are more closely related to the ethics of research, and they might even lead the researcher to become part of mobilization to change the outcome, given the ethical judgement voiced by a social

movement. Below, we define this as critical theory.

We can consider these two varieties *without* sensitivity to case particularities. *Process intervention* would then be an experiment, the production of an outcome predicted by a theory as general as possible. *Case reconstruction* would be the selection of a critical case that can test a high-level theory, even without manipulation by the researcher. Both varieties are well known from the natural sciences.

The interest in the specificity of cases goes together with a focus on learning and intervention. The philosophical background here is in pragmatist (mainly US) and standpoint (originally European) philosophies (Skagestad 1978, Horkheimer 1937). Therefore, unlike the discipline of history, the contextualist position is committed to the explanation of single cases by means of comparison with other cases. The dual purpose is better specification of the original case *and* development of contextual generalizations. But these generalizations emerge through the analysis of specificities. They are important for learning. Learning establishes an important link between process intervention and case reconstruction: in many situations, case reconstructions explaining past outcomes by means of comparisons might be important for the intervention in present-day problems.

Popularization of fundamental metaphysical questions

Pragmatist philosophy is distinguished by its critique of the spectator theory of knowledge. Standpoint philosophies, such as early European critical theory (developing Marx's 'scientific socialism') and postwar feminist philosophy and social science (Smith 1999) particularly emphasize the epistemological consequences of social movements claiming equal rights in the development of society. In Hacking's (1983) terms, both treat science as intervention rather than as representation. Judgements about the real and the constructed are made with reference to local settings. The pragmatist tradition has been invoked by both realists (pointing to Peircian process realism) and by constructionists (there is even an old empirical tradition studying social problems construction, closely connected to the broader interactionist tradition that started with Chicago interwar sociology).

What unifies both realist and constructionist interpretations is the view that accumulation of knowledge is linked to participation, intervention and learning. Pragmatism differs from the far-reaching empiricism of both Hume and the early twentieth-century positivists who counterposed experience-based science to religion and philosophy. The pragmatists instead tried to bridge this gap, aiming both to redefine the area of science and to bring philosophy and religion into line with modern science. Acceptance of the Darwinian revolution was crucial to their efforts to reconcile scientific reasoning and religious belief (Skagestad 1978, pp. 21, 34f). Darwin transcended the Cartesian subject/object dualism because he saw man as an organism that is part of the world it develops knowledge about. Referring to this interaction between the organism and the environment, Dewey (1920/1950, p. 83) wrote that knowledge:

> … is not something separate and self-sufficing, but is involved in the process by which life is sustained and evolved. The senses lose their place as gateways of knowing to take their rightful place as stimuli to action.

The contextualist position implies scepticism towards generalizing statements on fundamental features, whether they are about cultural deep structures or material 'driving forces'. Rather, it holds that statements on such properties must be linked by means of the sociology of knowledge to some participatory, interventionist and/or learning purpose. Like social philosophy, the contextualist position is committed to the analysis of a totality, but the totality of a case, thus not sharing the social-philosophical focus on the totality of driving forces or cognitive deep structures.

Explanatory priorities given autonomy of the social science realm

As for reduction, the emphasis is on emergent properties and the practical context of scientific knowledge. In contrast to the largely theory-driven standard programme of explanatory reduction (cf. Hedström 2005, pp. 26–28, 36), contextualist research is problem driven. Explanations are related to the context relevant to the research question at hand.[8] There is no programme of reduction, not even within social science. The idea of representing inherent structures between social science elementary particles is absent. There may be many layers between the very micro- and macro-levels, but these distinctions are drawn with reference to the research question, not to principal declarations about elementary particles. Explanation might require analysis at lower levels than the outcome, but there is no general micro-to-macro problem. With contextualization as an independent element in the explanatory strategy, the problem of micro-reduction does not emerge. Research may relate to various locations on a micro–macro continuum. A case may be singled out at *any* level of aggregation: therapists deal with single clients as cases, whereas macro-historians deal with nation states, macro-regions or even historical epochs. Statements about inherent structures are always contextualized and depend on the research question being asked. Scholars committed to the standard framework sometimes discuss – and disagree on – what outcomes social scientists should be concerned to explain. Goldthorpe (2000, p. 203) insists on regularities, Hedström (2005, p. 67) on macro-level phenomena and Elster (2007, p. 13) on events. In the contextualist framework, such disagreements seem odd. The problem at hand defines the outcome(s) to be explained, whether events or regularities. Explanatory ventures can be plotted into a space, depending on where they are located on the micro-/macro-continuum, whether the researcher prefers a passive or active position, and whether the process/outcome studied is controversial or non-controversial.[9]

Sociology of knowledge

The cluster of methods involving various kinds of participantion define the contextualist framework 'from below' (see Table 2.1). Gaining knowledge by participation implies that, in principle (although not always in practice), we interact with what we study. Sensitivity to cases implies that we acknowledge the knowledge of actors who are 'in' the cases. Standard researchers tend to judge this just as a source of bias. But given seemingly insurmountable problems of getting sound data on beliefs (Elster 2007, p. 465), the ethnographic pride in 'being there' has its merits. Specific to research into society is that we can enter into the very sphere where the 'mechanisms' (even 'elementary particles') are supposed to be. The basic fact that we study something that we are (or could be) ourselves, implies that there must be some relationship between the way that we gather knowledge and the ways in which people learn. Researchers may pursue knowledge more systematically, but not in a qualitatively different way.

According to the standard spectator theory of knowledge, the scientific community represents 'nature'. In contrast, the contextualist view considers the scientific community as a society (the internal perspective), embedded in society at large (the external perspective). As internal and external factors influence the way researchers represent their research topics, not only the context of justification but also the context of discovery (from biases in funding institutions, to the cultural problems addressed in the public sphere) is important to understand why we get the knowledge we get. This combined focus separates the contextualist sociology of knowledge from the predominantly external perspective of social philosophy. Research collectives with a high degree of (relative) autonomy can pursue strong programmes of basic research. Research collectives have their own internal processes, even fads and fashions. Still, even these collectives relate to current problems,

often as defined by the agenda of funding institutions.

Assumptions about the relationship between the sciences

Although the social sciences are junior partners compared to the natural sciences, to contextualists they are not immature. Rather, the view is that both are related to pockets of relatively robust, problem-related knowledge (local research frontiers). Such knowledge does not converge in one high research frontier. There is no methods community with the natural sciences. Doing case studies, one need not feel bothered by 'immaturity' *vis-à-vis* the natural sciences, there is no commitment to some modified experimental master example. Social science is full of well-crafted and successful case studies, many of which also serve as a basis for learning.

Notions of theory

The contextualist notions of theory are two ways in which knowledge is drawn from and related to our ability to be sensitive to cases.

Explanation-based theory is knowledge of contextual regularities accumulated from explanations of singular cases. These explanations are sharpened by means of comparisons and further cases are sampled with reference to the theory so far developed. Several programmes in social science (e.g. network theory, Granovetter 1985) may be counted as explanation-based theory, but in this chapter, we limit our discussion to the programme of grounded theory (Glaser and Strauss 1967) as a specification of such a notion.

We define *critical theory* as a special case of explanation-based theory (Mjøset 2006a, p. 761). This definition is narrower than the broad definition implied by many social philosophers. The impulse towards critical theory emerges when social researchers participate closely with social groups that have legitimate claims to social change. Some of these groups are organized as social movements, others might be marginalized groups with few capacities to organize. In such cases, the position of the social researcher in a relatively autonomous research community may become problematic. In ethical terms (as argued, for example, in Habermas 1981) it might be untenable just to report research on contextual regularities; moral imperatives lead the researcher to become part of the relevant social movement to change these regularities.

The researcher then joins a movement whose collective action might fail or succeed. In the latter case, it feeds back on the single case. The researcher does not simply reconstruct an outcome but takes part in broader efforts to change an outcome. This is process intervention, but outside the confines of the research community. The kind of outcome differs depending on the kind of social movement. The most prominent examples are movements that have even given name to social science theories, such as 'scientific socialism' (Marxism) and feminism. The kind or permanent structures they point to and want to change differ: capitalist oppression of workers in classical Marxism, the position of women at work and at home in the feminist movement. Critical theory need not be linked to the macro-level: there are concepts of action

research relating especially to firms and in psychology there is therapy relating to groups of persons. Not all such process interventions, however, are critical theory. The line of division between critical and explanation-based theory is a question of both ethical judgement and the social position of the researcher. Our discussion below, however, is mainly focused on explanation-based theory.

Figure 2.2 is the map we use for orientation in contemporary social science. It locates the three methodologies and the six notions of theory at different levels, and judges their potential for accumulation of knowledge. In the following, we use this map to discuss a number of principal questions of relevance to the conduct of case studies.

CASE STUDIES AND GENERALIZATION

How can the study of cases contribute to general knowledge? The question is a classical one in debates on qualitative methodology. In the following, we deal with it in the light of the map in Figure 2.2. Generalization takes

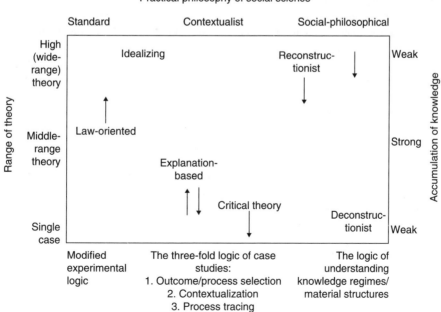

Figure 2.2   Practical philosophies of social science and notions of theory.

Table 2.2   Notions of theory and strategies of generalization and specification

Notion of theory	Strategy of generalization	Strategy of specification
Law-oriented	Segmenting	Cases are analyzed as the locus of selected dependent variables, which are explained by the net effects of selected independent variables
Idealizing	Insulating	Cases as illustrations
Explanation-based	Formal grounded theory (process tracing, mechanisms). Substantive grounded theory (contextualization by means of typologies and periodization)	In combination, substantive and formal grounded theories secure sensitivity to specific cases (this is most properly described as a joint strategy of specification and generalization)
Critical theory	Efforts to promote their world view, challenging the 'model monopoly' of present 'regimes of knowledge'	Contributing to social change
Reconstructionist (transcendental)	Pre-empirical fundamentals	Periodization referring to modernity or some phase thereof. Cases as expressions of such 'logics of the present'
Deconstructionist	Periodization referring to modernity or some phase thereof	Exceptionalist strategy reminiscent of that found in the discipline of history

on different meanings depending on what notion of theory we refer to; not all of these meanings can be equated with 'universal'. Table 2.2 relates one strategy to each of the six notions of theory. The social-philosophical strategies of generalization were defined above, and are summarized in Table 2.2. As the discussions on case studies and generalization mainly concern standard and contextualist methodologies, we do not relate to the social-philosophical framework in this section.

As for the standard notions of theory, the probability-based, statistical version of the law-oriented notion implies a *segmenting* strategy of generalization: the aim is to extract general relations within a specified field of research particularly relying on large datasets. These datasets are special purpose ones: the Organization for Economic Cooperation and Development (OECD) makes datasets on growth available to the econometrician, research on innovation has its patent data and innovation surveys, sociology has its datasets on social mobility, political science has its electoral surveys and so on. The strategy of generalization is to establish general knowledge related to the social segment from which the data on a large

number of cases are gathered: the theory of economic growth, theories of innovative upgrading of mature economies, the theory of social mobility in industrial societies, the theory of voting behaviour and so on. The large number of cases contained in the datasets allows the use of statistical methods of generalization. However, the security of this method comes at the cost of segmentation, and findings based on patterns of correlation are not easy to translate back into a world that seldom is structured so that it gives rise to natural experiments. Given that the purpose of the law-oriented theories is the establishment of 'as general regularities as possible', there is little concern for cases, they are only the raw materials of large datasets. To the extent, however, that Merton-type middle-range theories are derived from other empirical sources than large datasets, another strategy of generalization may be involved. We return to this later.

The idealizing notion of theory implies an *insulating* strategy of generalization. Rational choice theory claims relevance for all social segments. It is based on a general theory of interaction, practised as thought experiments. Cases may here serve to illustrate patterns of interaction modelled in thought experiments. Strong interpretations of the idealizing notion would see game theory, etc. as the source of such patterns, whereas softer interpretations would analyze patterns with reference to a number of empirical sources, including folk wisdom, well-crafted case studies, etc. However, the attitude is still the standard one, and thus a strategy of specification is not considered important: the focus is on the thought experiments as generalized, widely applicable knowledge, and often the 'parsimonious' nature of such knowledge is emphasized. In extreme cases, the aesthetic legitimation sometimes found in mathematics (the 'beauty of a proof') is simply taken over.

The contextualist strategy of generalization is to generalize only within specified contexts (Mjøset 2006a). In this view, specification and generalization are not opposites. Specification is only possible through more general knowledge. For instance, the exact features of Norway as a welfare state must be assessed with comparative reference to other cases of the same (in grounded theory, this is called theoretical sampling). As specifications are made in this way, the results also feed back into more general knowledge: denser and broader typologies, concepts and models of contextualized social interaction patterns. The use of comparison is the main alternative to subsumption under as general as possible concepts and theories in the standard conception, and also an alternative to the use of cases as 'expressions' of broad periodizing notions (e.g. modernity) in the social-philosophical view.

It is not a contradiction to talk about general theory in the contextualist framework, but then it must be distinguished from universal range theory. Generalizations that retain grounding cannot be taken further than the middle range, but we can have more or less general theories within the middle range. Universal range theory must necessarily be ungrounded. Theories can be established at a case level but should not be 'overgrounded', as in the case of the exceptionalist strategy of specification (see above).

Whereas the interwar Chicago school of sociology mainly practised its ethnographic case studies, its second generation in the 1950s launched a criticism of variables as concepts (see, in particular, Blumer, 1969). Blumer's criticism favoured case sensitivity, but the sensitizing concepts he promoted as an alternative to 'definite concepts' alienated quantitative research altogether. A later generation of critics reflected the spread of statistical inference, regression analysis in particular. Ragin (1986, 2008 chapter 10) claimed that the estimation of net effects across the whole population leads to notions of causal analysis that are at odds with the sense of causation we get from tracing processes that leads to outcomes in cases. In contrast to Blumer's social psychological orientation, the later generation was more concerned with macro-studies, especially historical sociology. Their criticism pointed in two directions: to concern with the methodology of macro-comparative social science (Ragin 1986, Mjøset 2000, referring particularly to Rokkan's work in the 1970s, cf. Rokkan 1999), or more generally to exploration of various kinds of process tracing and network models (Abbott 1999, 2001). These contributions generally agreed that Skocpol's (1984) attempts at methodological synthesis in historical sociology did not sufficiently cut the ties with standard preconceptions (Mjøset 2006b).

The other direction was towards alternative quantitative methods. One example is Ragin's (2000) qualitative comparative analysis (QCA), based on set-theory instead of probability. Not relying on correlations, this technique can also analyze small populations. Abbott (2001) proposed models based on the logic of genetic sequencing. More broadly, Shalev (2007) urges scholars to rely on less high-tech statistical methods. The contextualist orientation is more than just a legitimation of qualitative methods, it has recently also led to development of types of quantitative studies that are designed to increase sensitivity to cases even among those who work with large datasets.

In the contextualist approach, the challenge of generalization is the investigation of smaller numbers of cases explained by concepts with high internal validity. The work on qualitative macro-studies, and also on non-probabilistic quantitative approaches, indicates that substantive generalization and comparative specification can go hand in hand. The next two sections present some conceptual and methodological specifications of such a strategy of generalization.

SUBSTANTIVE AND FORMAL GROUNDED THEORY

The distinction between substantive and formal grounded theory, as well as the emphasis on the operation of comparing, makes Glaser and Strauss's (1967) programme of grounded theory – rooted in interwar Chicago sociology – a particularly rich source for investigations of explanation-based notions of theory. In this section, we show how this programme provides further insight into the relation between types of theory and strategies of generalization. We can start from what might seem an inductionist credo:

> Both substantive and formal theories must be grounded in data. Substantive theory faithful to the empirical situation cannot, we believe, be formulated merely by applying a few ideas from an established formal theory to the substantive area. To be sure one goes out and studies an area with a particular sociological perspective, and with a focus, a general question, or a problem in mind. But he can (and we believe should) also study an area without any preconceived theory that dictates, prior to the research, 'relevancies' in concepts and hypotheses. Indeed it is presumptuous to assume that one begins to know the relevant categories and hypotheses until the 'first days in the field', at least, are over. A substantive theory generated from the data must first be formulated, in order to see which diverse formal theories are, perhaps, applicable for furthering additional substantive formulations. (Glaser and Strauss 1967, p. 33f)

This is a statement in favour of substantive *theory,* defined as theory developed 'for a substantive, or empirical, area of sociological inquiry' (e.g. race relations, delinquency, research organizations). The opposite is formal theory, which is 'developed for a formal,

or conceptual, area of sociological inquiry' (e.g. stigma, deviance, formal organization, social mobility). Glaser and Strauss (1967, p. 32f) emphasize that both types of theory are 'middle range' in Merton's sense. However, towards the end of this section, we shall specify differences (see Figure 2.2) between middle-range and explanation-based theories.

Strauss (1970) emphasized that the statement 'without preconceived theory' did not exclude reliance on earlier substantive theory, directly related to the field studied. Let us call this the *principle of substantive primacy*; 'discovering substantive theory relevant to a given substantive area (...), allowing substantive concepts and hypotheses to emerge first, on their own' (Glaser and Strauss 1967, p. 34).

We hold that this is a basic principle in any explanation-based theory. However, Glaser and Strauss never seem to discuss how it relates to the distinction (grounded/ungrounded) that appear in their book title. We make this connection in Table 2.3, considering grounded/ungrounded as an account of how theory is discovered and substantive/formal as a classification of theory that has been discovered (whether it is explanatory or not; its contribution to accumulation of knowledge).

Glaser and Strauss's programmatic formula – theory as grounded in data – refers to qualitative data emerging as researchers exercise sensitivity to cases. Such grounded theory is based on systematic work that codes data to establish core concepts and samples new cases to extend and develop earlier findings. Glaser and Strauss also use the term 'ungrounded theory', indicating theories that are not grounded in this way (see Table 2.3). Both notions can be differentiated in line with the substantive/formal distinction. In the following, we discuss some results of such a differentiation, relating to our typology of theories (see Figure 2.2).

We argue throughout this chapter against the frequent accusation that grounded theory is inductive or descriptive only. In Table 2.3, we can locate description as substantive ungrounded 'theory'. A pure description of the flow of events is impossible, and thus

Table 2.3 Taxonomy of grounded and ungrounded theories

		How knowledge was discovered	
		Grounded	Ungrounded
Types of accumulated knowledge	Formal	Stylized interaction patterns recurring in explanations across various substantive research fields (internal analogies)	Explanatory patterns drawn not from social science but from other domains of science (external analogies, e.g. mechanical, organistic)
	Substantive	Case studies: case reconstruction/process intervention in various fields of society in specified periods. Bounded generalization developed through comparison of cases within an area of research, using typologies and periodization to specify context	Transcendental notions of theory Methods-driven empirical analyses (e.g. net effects, axiomatization) 'Journalistic' generalizations Exceptionalist specifications Examples selected from various fields put forward as illustrations of (formal) theoretical claims Empirical cases as expressions of trends emphasized in broad interpretations of the present

'unconscious' principles of selection must be involved in any description. Moral panics and other forms of 'journalistic' generalization of singular cases are good examples. This is not theory in any proper sense. The exceptionalist strategy of specification (see Table 2.2 and 'The social-philosophical practical philosophy of social science', above), which studies single cases independently of any comparison with other cases of the same, is also an example of substantive but ungrounded knowledge.

The relation between the two divisions of the ungrounded column in Table 2.3 illustrates the gap in the standard framework between theory and empirical research (see 'The standard practical philosophy of social science', above). We can distinguish four attempts to bridge this gap. Two of these *bridging attempts* try to close the gap going 'downwards' from formal ungrounded theory, thus producing substantive ungrounded theory. The other two attempt to find formal theory with some reference to empirical research, let us say they try to move 'upwards'.

As for the relationship between high theories and empirical substance, there is a standard and a social-philosophical version (see Figure 2.2). The standard position implies the idealizing notion of theory, thought experiments in which the researcher establishes

the context via definitions that suits an axiomatic system. The social-philosophical position implies reconstructive theory, which is formal in the philosophical sense of claiming transcendental status. The first downwards bridging attempt implies the quoting of illustrative examples to substantiate idealizing theory. For instance, the works of Jon Elster (e.g. Elster 2007) are avalanches of such examples, used as raw materials for speculations around his increasingly soft version of rational choice theory. The second downwards bridging attempt implies reconstructive theory approaching the study of modernity by linking transcendental notions *either* to selected examples claimed to be expressions of the core concepts (modernity, globalization) in their interpretations of the present, *or* to selected quotes drawn from older or more recent classics who tried to grasp the spirit of their age ('iron cage of rationality', 'anomie').

As for the upward bridging attempts, one is what we earlier discussed as the segmenting strategy of generalization, yielding explanations in terms of net effects. The contextualist criticism summarized above (in 'Case studies and generalization') would consider this methods-driven research, and in that sense *formal* (cf. Abbott's criticism of 'general linear reality', and Ragin's 2008 chapter 10 criticism of 'net effects thinking', which yields 'vague theory').

The second upward bridging attempt would be the Mertonian concept of middle-range theory. As noted (in 'Three practical philosophies of social science'), the revisionist standard notion of mechanisms can be seen as a contemporary update of this programme. It has emerged from frustration with the two standard strategies of generalization (insulating and segmenting), as none of these have been able to close the theory/explanation gap. Their proposed bridging solution lies in explanation by mechanisms; however, before we consider it more closely, we need to discuss the purely formal, ungrounded theories in Table 2.3.

The history of social science has many examples of formal theories 'ungrounded' by 'external analogies'. A theory-driven programme such as Parsons' structural functionalism of the 1950s and 1960s, relied on the analogy of an organic system to develop wide-ranging formal typologies. Despite a standard point of departure, Parsons' theory of action actually ended up quite close to the transcendental position of reconstructive social-philosophy (see Figure 2.2). This kind of 'grand theory' was the main contrast against which Glaser and Strauss developed grounded theory in the 1960s. There was no broad contextualist breakthrough, however, as Parsons' theory was challenged simultaneously by economics-inspired rational choice and by game theory. Here, 'external' formalism was not from another field of science but from mathematical notions of theory as an axiomatic system, 'interpreted' for action theory, thus requiring particularly strongly idealizing assumptions (cf. the economics notion of 'caricature models', Mjøset and Cappelen 2009). The rational choice programme, which can also be considered to be methods-driven, attracted a lot of intellectual energy for several decades, but recent standard revisionism rejects this attempt to close the gap (Hedström 2005, Elster 2007).

This critical stance points in the direction of a contextualist perspective. Ignorance of the principle of substantive primacy, wrote Glaser and Strauss (1967, p. 34), is in most instances the result of:

> ... believing that formal theories can be applied directly to a substantive area, and will supply most or all of the necessary concepts and hypotheses. The consequence is often a forcing of data, as well as a neglect of relevant concepts and hypotheses that may emerge.

The rational choice criticism of functionalism was only about replacing one ungrounded formal theory with another. Both differ from the contextualist, interactionist tradition from Simmel, through Goffman and into contemporary interactionist thinking, which we can conceive as formal grounded theory. This tradition was always close to and partly overlapping with the empirical ethnographic orientation of the Chicago School, which we can count as substantive grounded theory. Can we relate the revisionist notion of mechanisms to these notions?

Let us turn to the grounded column of Table 2.3. The distinction between formal and substantive grounded theory decouples generality and explanatory power. Substantive grounded theory is the basis of the contextual generalization described above. Formal grounded theory leads to formal generalization that recognizes similarities between patterns of social interaction in many fields of study. Such generalization must be grounded. It respects the requirement of *internal* analogies (see Table 2.3), because these must be derived from substantive studies in several fields of social research. It is not indexed to specific contexts, thus it is formal. It is general, but it explains nothing before it is inserted into a context. In terms of the three-fold contextualist logic of explanation (see 'The contextualist practical philosophy of social science'), a formal grounded theory is an appendix to the third step, as it isolates formal patterns visible in several process tracings in different lines of study. These formal patterns can be useful as 'components' of explanations: they are explanatory 'modules', which results from researchers' efforts to spell out in some detail the formal properties of selected interaction patterns.

Glaser and Strauss (1967, p. 34) note that the principle of substantive primacy:

> ... enables the analyst to ascertain which, if any, existing formal theory may help him generate his substantive theories. He can then be more faithful to his data, rather than forcing it to fit a theory. He can be more objective and less theoretically biased.

As an example, they note that it would be wrong to apply Parsonian or Mertonian categories at the start, it is crucial to 'wait to see whether they are linked to the emergent substantive theory concerning the issue in focus'. Formal generalization is not simply an alternative strategy of generalization. Context can be specified only by means of substantive grounded theory. Formal grounded theory does not relieve the scholar of doing the comparative craftwork: exploring categories, core categories, properties and subproperties, devising typologies and periodizations.

This line of argument allows us to conclude on the second upwards bridging attempt, the revisionist standard notion of mechanisms. This can be seen as an attempt to make formal theory substantive, without the problem-related choice of outcome/process and contextualization. This kind of formal theory *isolates one part* of the three-fold logic of contextualist analysis, namely the process-tracing logic. The revisionist notion of explanation by mechanisms requires tracing of the chain of causal and intentional links (Elster 1989). Whether this formal theory is grounded or ungrounded, however, depends on the source of the mechanisms. We have argued that if they rely on external analogies they are ungrounded, but if they rely on internal analogies drawn from social science studies, they are grounded. In the latter case, they rely on earlier substantive grounded theory in the form of explanations of causal processes, as in Elster's 1989 understanding.

Interestingly, Elster in 1998 suggested a revised definition. The old definition he now calls 'causal chain', while according to the new definition, mechanisms 'are frequently

occurring and easily recognizable causal patterns that are triggered under generally unknown conditions' (Elster 2007, pp. 32, 36). With his two successive definitions, it seems, Elster rediscovered Glaser and Strauss's distinction between substantive and formal grounded theory! If we trace a causal chain we need to include the context, and thus, we have substantive grounded theory, the earliest definition. If we recognize patterns in interaction across 'conditions' (contexts), we have formal grounded theory, the most recent definition, in which conditions are unknown, that is, unspecified. Elster has, however, not noted the parallel, because he recognizes no other methodological frameworks than the standard one.

MECHANISMS AND PROCESS TRACING IN THE CONTEXTUALIST FRAMEWORK

By considering the components of grounded theory, we can define a notion of mechanisms within the contextualist framework. Glaser and Strauss (1967, p. 36) define categories and their properties as elements of a theory. A category 'stands by itself as a conceptual element' and a property is a 'conceptual aspect' of a category. The two notions are relative, thus an overall category might have many properties and each of these properties can be seen as categories that have further properties. This can be simplified into a three-level terminology of categories – properties – subproperties.

Let us start from a simple example of typology construction. Size, flavour, juiciness and type of production are properties of the category fruit. Adding a question, specifying the dimensions along which the properties vary and aggregating the two vertical rows, we get a two-fold typology (Table 2.4). The typology is related to the core category that emerges when empirical data are scrutinized with the research question in mind (cf. the various types of coding and sampling in grounded theory; Glaser and Strauss 1967).

Table 2.4 An example of typology construction

Question	Category	Properties	Dimensions
Why different prices?	Fruit, specifically oranges	Size	Large ↔ Small
		Flavour	Sweet ↔ Less sweet
		Juiciness	High ↔ Low
		Production	Ecological ↔ Traditional
Types of orange			*High-price ↔ Low-price*

Within this framework, a mechanism can be defined as *the pattern of social interaction involved as the properties of a category produce outcomes along a dimension*. We can further define *causal chain* or *causal process* with reference to conjunctions of mechanisms involved as social interaction on the dimensions of several (or ideally all) properties create overall outcomes. Thus, process tracing links mechanisms pertaining to the various properties of the core category we see our cases as cases of. The contextualist approach explains by means of many mechanisms linked in causal processes.[10] Furthermore, once we consider causal processes that generate recurrent outcomes, we must also pay attention to the possibility that cumulative change occurs as the processes recur. These changes might originate in contradictory dynamics or in small contextual changes, and cumulative processes might lead to more significant changes in context, either through slow change or through more sudden critical junctures (turning points). In the changed context, new processes might evolve.

In our simple example in Table 2.4, the mechanisms stems from biology and agro-science: specific species of oranges, fertilization, etc. But we can consider a more complex example from comparative political economy. Senghaas's (1985) large project on what developing countries can learn from European development experiences can be reconstructed as a discovery of explanation-based theory (Mjøset 2007). With reference to this research question, Senghaas established the core category of *auto-centred development*, which is understood as the combination of economic growth and improvement in living standards for broad

masses of the population. Relying on a large selection of relevant literature on economic development – theoretical, quantitative and monographic – Senghaas ended up with a table that specifies properties and subproperties of this core category. Table 2.5 is a simplified version.

Given the research problem, it is obviously necessary to close the explanatory chain (to establish context) way 'above' what would be Hedström's (2005) fundamental level (beliefs, desires, opportunities). The number of subproperties is, however, true to the middle-range realist view about stratified reality (Pawson 2000). Each subproperty can be dimensionalized, some in quantitative terms, others just in qualitative terms. This example also allows us to see how a change from dichotomization to more nuanced typologies will increase the detail of the processes traced. The more distinctions we allow into the dimensionalization, that is, in Ragin's (2000) terminology, we turn from crisp to fuzzy sets, the more historical context is allowed for. The same is the case if we increase the number of properties and subproperties involved.

Systematic comparison led Senghaas to emphasize empirical indicators of the egalitarian distribution of farmland and agrarian incomes, postulating a mechanism whereby cash income in the agrarian sector accrued to a large share of the families in the that sector. The context is one in which the majority of the population is in the agrarian sector. With egalitarian agrarian distribution, staple export incomes are spread broadly. This creates broad-based domestic demand that stimulates small, but innovation-oriented manufacturing activities, the simple

Table 2.5   Properties, subproperties and dimensions of the core category auto-centred development

Properties	Subproperties	Dimensions
Agrarian property/ social structure	Distribution Innovation-orientation Cooperative movement	Egalitarian ↔ Skewed High ↔ Low Strong ↔ Weak
Distributional patterns	Income Income distribution/savings Wages and salaries' share in net national product	Egalitarian ↔ Skewed Promote ↔ Block innovation High ↔ Low
Economic institutions	Firms (risk/innovation-orientation) Supportive banking system Nature of national system of innovation Education – training (literacy)	Strong ↔ Low Yes ↔ No Strong ↔Weak High ↔ Low
Social mobilization	Mobilization of farmers Mobilization of workers (unions)	Strong ↔ Weak Strong ↔ Weak
Political mobilization	Democratization (replacement of old elites) Nation-building – sovereignty Clientilism in political parties	Strong ↔ Weak Early ↔ Late Low ↔ High
State	Administrative reform State provision of infrastructure	Yes ↔ No Considerable ↔ Low

Source: Mjøset (2007), synthesized from Senghaas (1985).

products of which are bought mainly by farmers.

Explanations of the development experience of particular cases, however, requires us to look at causal chains connecting several such mechanisms (or explanatory factors). The farmers joined in cooperatives that assisted both with sales and with investments in agricultural equipment. There are many mechanisms here, and one would never reach a conclusion if one were to trace them all the way 'up' from the level of beliefs, desires and opportunities. Instead, they are cut off by means of contextualization. The institutions or social structures that form the context are the results of processes not further traced: agrarian mobilization, church/state relations, colonial history, etc.

The factors that have been deemed important by earlier substantive research are listed in Table 2.5. For each of the subproperties, the dimensionalization creates a scale or a specified typology. These set the context for the mechanisms. But taken as such – at any level – mechanisms are patterns of social interaction, routine behaviour and so on. Mechanisms are formal grounded theories that cannot explain without context. The interesting

feature is how various mechanisms connect in specific contexts defined by typologies related to properties/subproperties. This specifies how reality is layered (Pawson 2000): the various cases of more or less successful overall outcomes in terms of auto-centred development, are produced and reproduced thanks to *conjunctures* (Ragin 1986) of such mechanisms in specific contexts.

The analysis is often in terms of 'stylized facts', which in such an analysis can be specified as typical processes. For instance, Senghaas refers to Hirschman's (1977) notion of linkage effects, which can be specified as various stylized constellations of early manufacturing development and social structure. As Glaser and Strauss (1967, p. 32) emphasize, substantive and formal theory differ only 'in terms of degree'. The theory of linkage effects can be seen as substantive grounded theory, based on explanatory, monographic case studies of economic development. However, it can also be developed towards a more formal grounded theory in the form of network models. However, if the networks are modelled starting from checkerboard structures, as in Hedström (2005), we are in the realm of ungrounded formal theory and it is an open question as to whether a homogenous action rule derived from a regression equation with certain controls will actually ever lead us to such stylized processes.

To the extent that processes are cumulative, there will be change. This illustrates how typologies are not just specific to research questions, but also to historical periods. They must also be revised with reference to major contextual changes, conceived as turning points or more gradual change. However, the formal grounded theory of linkages can be used to trace the impact of manufacturing sector transformations through several periods, whereas the contextual specifications varies.

An important implication of this contextualist principle of substantive priority is that we cannot have accumulation of knowledge at the high level. In terms of accumulation of knowledge (cf. Figure 2.2), high-level formal theory in and of itself is as weak as ungrounded descriptions of the flow of events. Another implication, of equal relevance to the philosophy of the social sciences, is that we cannot have competing formal theories, only competing explanations. If explanations are to compete, substantive theories must be involved. Competition between theories – in other words – requires agreement on problems (outcome or process selection) and on context; it requires all three elements of the contextualist logic of research.

LOCAL RESEARCH FRONTIERS

The claim that contextualist approaches violate the principle that any observation is theory loaded is partly inspired by Popper's philosophy of natural science. As with any broad principle, scrutiny by new generations of professional philosophers (Hacking 1983, p. 171ff) leaves it in dire need of specification. Note that with reference to Figure 2.2, we face at least six different interpretations of what 'theory-loaded' might mean.

In the contextualist framework 'theory-loaded' means that discovery of new theory

relates to earlier substantive grounded theory (Strauss 1970). We shall specify this relationship by means of the notion of *local research frontiers* (Mjøset 2006a). It specifies how explanation-based theory leads to accumulation of knowledge just because it remains in the middle range. Social science knowledge is developed with reference to the various areas of society. The main argument of the pragmatist philosophers was always that accumulation of knowledge takes place because it is important for the community. If many researchers ask the same research questions with reference to similar sets of data and other empirical investigations, we get a local research frontier. Such frontiers develop with reference to problems that are crucial to the community.[11] Rather than believing that we 'observe' in the light of some high theory, we must realize that a problem area requires the definition of a small number of core categories. These categories have many properties, and for each there might be subfrontiers of research, and thus, different types of explanation-based theories.

Local research frontiers synthesize existing analyses of relevant core categories and their properties. It also includes stylized facts, either quantitative (e.g. based on agreement on major indicators) or qualitative (e.g. as in certain commonly used typologies and periodizations). All these components are related to what the community of researchers accept as good explanations of relevant cases. The principle of substantive primacy applies, substantive grounded theory is the basis of local research frontiers. Substantive theory without a local research frontier becomes ungrounded substantive theory, unless the topic/field is entirely unexplored, which is seldom the case. Only when substantive work is done can one check whether existing formal (grounded) theory might be useful in the consolidation of the research.

We have shown (see 'Case studies and generalization') that contextualist researchers have ways of accumulating knowledge that transcends the engrained generalization/specification dichotomy. Even a single case analysis can contribute to growth of knowledge when it is developed with reference to knowledge already accumulated in one or more local research frontiers (Mjøset 2006a). Such analyses can also rely on monographs. Their empirical material might be 'overgrounded' due to the influence of ideas of exceptionalist specification (see 'The social-philosophical practical philosophy of social science'), but they can be regeneralized with due attention to context. The specification of one or more new cases feeds back into the local research frontiers, adding to the generality of knowledge, even though its ties to the context are not cut.

In the standard framework, one imagines 'basic' theory – solving general problems in a high level research frontier – being 'applied' to local problems. The social-philosophical emphasis is on cultural problems that have an existential kind of generality. In the contextualist perspective, one sees all problems as specific and local, emphasizing how social science *theory* is cumulative only in local research frontiers. Local research frontiers should not be confused with exceptionalist specifications, which would narrow down a research frontier to what we know from earlier research on a particular case. Local research frontiers synthesize research on many cases.

Here is a contextualist notion of growth of knowledge: with richer dimensionalization of properties or subproperties, research frontiers become increasingly mature. This should not be conceived as ever more 'correct' representations of basic features of reality, but rather as a growing consensus within a broad social science research collective concerning accumulated knowledge on social structures and processes in local, problem-related research frontiers. Even if some degree of maturity has been reached, it might not last forever, as underlying problems can change. The knowledge might grow further, be transformed in the light of new problems or wither away. Social science today possesses knowledge in several such local research frontiers, but this knowledge is *not* converging into higher level knowledge (see 'Mechanisms and

process tracing in the contextualist framework').

The accumulation of knowledge in local research frontiers has its own sociology of knowledge. If the study relates to uncontroversial cases, few researchers will return to it, the public will not address it and researchers will not judge this knowledge. However, real and persistent problems of social development lead to so much attention that local research frontiers develop and persist. A well-consolidated local research frontier requires funding enough to sustain a research collective over significant periods of time. Certain clusters of problems are better suited than others as a basis for durable collective and even interdisciplinary social science. In some cases, disciplinary idiosyncrasies might lead different disciplines to study the same problems in relative independence of each other. In other cases, the nature of the problems is such that even economists can work fruitfully with non-economist social scientists.

Research into the welfare state is a good example. In the Western world, many interests converge to sustain a local research frontier on this topic. The collective of social researchers now has at its disposal a literature addressing the same cluster of questions by means of carefully maintained and updated databases, frequently used typologies, stylized facts, comparative case studies, models of explanation and converging discussions on historical backgrounds. Whatever a researcher might hold in terms of high theory, he or she will have to rely on this complex of middle-level knowledge, which is based on the best explanations so far provided. This judgement is passed in the local research frontier, within which researchers judge knowledge by drawing on it in further research. This knowledge is not insulated from broader discussions in the public sphere on matters of policy and strategy.

Local research frontiers can cluster and might relate to each other in hierarchies. For instance, research into socioeconomic development patterns in the Nordic countries (which might be relevant for policy learning by poor countries), the welfare state and the position of women in Nordic society are different research frontiers in terms of outcomes analyzed. All can be related to policy learning in several respects. They require us to trace different processes, but they might draw on overlapping contextual knowledge. We can imagine typological maps in a hierarchy, where the highest ones contain general substantive knowledge that might be relevant for several local research frontiers. This is the notion of substantive generalization. Such general knowledge is still specific to certain areas, even geographically. Let us consider this further with reference to Rokkan's political sociology.

Rokkan's contribution to political sociology was based on his contributions to subfrontiers such as nation-building, state-formation, electoral behaviour and the structure of party systems. In his last contributions (in the 1970s, collected in Rokkan 1999), however, he developed a framework that integrated several such research frontiers. It remains substantive, though, because it is valid only for Western Europe. The main outcome to be explained is the structure of the Western European party systems in the postwar period (1950s and 1960s).

Rokkan developed a basic sequential model as well as a multitude of typological maps. As grounded theory (Mjøset 2000), Rokkan's theory draws on historical monographs, studies comparing political institutions and on his continuous work on electoral statistics. His study of Western Europe yields no general formal theory to be applied directly (e.g. to Asia). But by doing a similar craftwork of contextualization, relying on many of the same properties, one could establish new substantive theory in the form of typological maps of, say, the Asian region. This might yield new formal theory, but some of the formal theories developed from Western European developments would surely be useful, provided due attention is given to the different contexts. We see the principle of substantive primacy at work.

Given the clustering of research frontiers at different levels, the three elements in the case-study logic often interact. Within each period given in his sequential model, Rokkan traces economy – territory – culture 'variables'. These broad *contextualizations* allow *choice of a number of more specified outcomes* to be explained, for example, breakdowns of democratic regimes, the structuring of party systems, patterns of political mobilization. Specified typological maps then provide more specified contexts. The resulting explanations lead to successive refinements, both to the specified typological maps and the more basic sequence models.

Rokkan's work also illustrates the combination of formal and substantive theory. Although his main strength was contextualization, process tracing was also involved. However, his formal theories were grounded. They were interaction patterns generalized across research on political and social history: patterns of mobilization, alliance formation, revolts in situations of scarcity, organization building, social movement formation. He also drew on the formal theories of others, for example, Hirschman's 'exit, voice, loyalty' triad and even Parsons's AGIL-scheme, trying to make them serve him as formal grounded theory. He dealt with these formal theories only to the extent he could put them to work together with his substantive arsenal of typologies, periodizations and field-specific processes and mechanisms.

A comparison of (perhaps) the two most quoted Norwegians in international social science gives a striking result: Rokkan follows the principle of substantive primacy and hardly ever uses empirical material as mere examples; Elster, by contrast, pursues formal theory only, and examples are all he has in terms of empirical content. As their implied practical philosophies of social science diverge in this way, it is not surprising that Elster hardly ever finds it interesting to refer to Rokkan's work – so far.

Rokkan provided social science with accumulated knowledge, not just in the form of mechanisms, not as insulated relations between variables, but in the form of contextualizing maps that might be useful to several subfrontiers of research on

European political developments. These were substantive generalizations: they allow later researchers to contextualize also with reference to other significant outcomes, *and* they can be improved and extended. His work has no trace of idealizing models and no interest in connecting his arguments back to elementary particles (beliefs, desires and opportunities). Compared with social-philosophy, Rokkan's work is too disaggregated: it is 'below' the level of modernity.

Besides Weber's wide-ranging typological work in *Economy and Society,* Rokkan's model and maps are some of the most worked out examples we have in the social science of substantive generalization. Within the contextualist framework, we can understand Weber's various 'sociologies' as typological discussions of the properties (law, domination, religion, economy) of 'Western development'. These 'sociologies' are subfrontiers related to a broad local research frontier. The overall explanation, as among others suggested by Collins (1986), ties the various properties together in a complex cumulative process, one that is singular and relevant to many. The explanation traces processes that tie the various properties together. This interpretation challenges both standard and social-philosophical interpretations of Weber.[12] Social philosophers are very fond of Max Weber's few paragraphs on the 'iron cage' nature of modernity. But contextualists are more interested in the main contents of Weber's work, namely his enormous web of typologies contained in each of his sociologies. These various typologies, he wrote in *Economy and Society*, serve to 'create conceptual points of orientation for particular purposes'. There was no intention of completeness, no intention of 'forcing historical reality into schemes' (Weber 1922, p. 154). Like the pragmatists, Weber clearly considered social science knowledge to be problem oriented.

Both from the vantage point of the standard near-consensus about scientific realism, and with reference to the social-philosophical preference for deep structures (real or cognitive), one might claim that processes are too often traced at the event level, 'real science' is to unveil more fundamental processes. Returning to the Senghaas project, for instance, one might claim that an analysis of several development experiences could be reduced to a common deep structural process: the development of capitalism. The typology of different kinds of development outcomes would disappear, being rejected as 'empiricism', and there would be *one* deep structural driving force. Alternatively, one might refer to the Nordic development pattern, claiming that it did not result from specified cumulative processes but that deep-down demography/family structure predetermined the role of women in the Nordic area (Todd 1985, 1987).

Both would bring us closer to or even into 'philosophy of history' kind of modernization approaches. The contextualist approach, however, is sceptical of such statements of deep structures, suggesting instead a sociology of knowledge reflection: different research communities converge on certain stylized processes that seem to be the best answers to their research questions. With a variety of research questions, we also have a variety of claims about 'fundamental' forces.

Typologies should not be turned into *essential* features of reality. Although they are empirically grounded, typologies are still constructions. The degree to which they 'represent' is up for discussion, at least if there is a well developed local research frontier. They most probably have to be changed, as Weber emphasized, if we turn to a new set of research questions.

A more conventional term for local research frontier is 'the literature'. But given the quest for high theory in the standard framework, this concept plays no important role in that methodology: in particular there is no reflection on the fact that it is local, that is, limited to substantive areas. As we have shown, within the standard framework, research frontiers are defined with reference to formal theory only. Elster's notion of a 'toolbox' is adequate, but such a toolbox is irrelevant without the substantive elements contained in local research frontiers.[13] In the contextualist framework, a research frontier consisting of formal theory only is not possible. This also ties in with the pragmatist emphasis on knowledge as problem driven.

Here we reach a conclusion for the practical social research: we need more emphasis on substantive types of accumulated knowledge. We have implied that a basic weakness of both standard and social-philosophical high-level notions of theory is the denial of contextualization as a research craftwork. Typology construction by means of comparison is a main way of specifying context. Typologies synthesize available knowledge in a form that allows further comparison with reference to a set of research questions. They are maintained, revised and improved by updating of cases and addition of new cases. A social scientist must command a repertoire of typologies (logic of contextualization) as much as they need a repertoire of formal theories (logic of process tracing).

The kind of research craftwork that yields substantive theory is underrated in the community of social scientists. The pursuit of typologies – or substantive theory more generally – is weakly institutionalized. Most typologies are sketchy and hard to find; and they give low status publication wise! Many scholars regard typologies as static. But they need not be. They become static if they are not maintained, upgraded, revised and indexed to periods. Whereas statistics and econometric models are well taken care of in economists' research institutions and statistical offices, and large databases in similar institutions, typologies are not cared for in the same way; they should be!

We can here specify our first implication for the philosophy of the social sciences (see the end of 'Mechanisms and process tracing in the contextualist framework'): social science today possesses knowledge in several local research frontiers, but this knowledge is *not* converging into high theoretical knowledge. Neither substantive nor formal grounded theory converge in one overarching research frontier; the former because it is tied to

specific research fields, the latter because it is formal only. Substantive general theory in the contextualist sense is also *not* converging, at least so as long as we require that high theory be explanatory. The highest theory that is still explanatory might very well be typological maps such as Rokkan's, which are applicable to several outcomes that can be chosen for explanation. But even this theory is clearly delimited to a context. There might, as we have seen, be several general theories. Researchers must learn to manoeuvre and know how various frontiers emerge as relevant depending on the research question asked.[14]

But even if there is no high-level convergence, there might be relations of aggregation and overlap between local research frontiers. Topics can rise to dominance and then fade, but certain clusters might emerge and there might be synergies. There is no way for substantive generalizations in a local research frontier to be replaced by formal theory. A logic of falsification is not of much help: rather, substantive generalizations fasten as parts of a local research frontier because they are used and improved in the research collective.

CONCLUSION

No drawing of distinctions is innocent! One might object that our linking of the methodological frameworks to natural science, the humanities and social science implies the conclusion that only the contextualist framework is adequate for social science. Admittedly, our discussion has focused on strong features of the contextualist framework *vis-à-vis* the other two.

However, this chapter is also the work of a methodologist, and the starting point was, after all, that a methodology cannot be consistent! Although we are inclined to claim that contextualism has less of a gap between ideal and reality, theory and explanations, than the standard perspective, and that it avoids the personal, social-philosophical preoccupation with fundamental or existential problems that deflect attention from thorough empirical research, we do not claim that contextualism is without problems or that it can be taken as entirely consistent in philosophical terms.

If we want to make a plea for contextualism, then, it must be consistent with our introductory discussion of the methodologist's dilemma! Our claim, therefore, is that if one wants to understand the social sciences, a three-fold division is better than any of the conventional dualisms. It is a major strength of the contextualist position that it falls between the two others: it is empirically oriented, as are many scholars within the standard approach. It can engage seriously with discussions on empirical methods, comparing the different logics of qualitative and quantitative empirical research: but it is also capable of reflecting in sociology of knowledge terms and of discussing various kinds of contextualization. It is thus it is on speaking terms with social-philosophers.

We have tried to map, as thoroughly as possible, the comparative specificity of the contextualist framework. This is important, as it is so often rejected or embraced as being part of either one or the other two. The third position must guard against polarization between natural science and humanities, which all too frequently degenerate into mutual parodies that serve only to bolster self-righteous identities. Intervening to undermine such methodological polarization, the contextualist position can temper each of the extremes. It has the potential to inspire more fruitful approaches to triangulation of methods and cooperative interdisciplinary work in an era when disciplinary divisions are challenged.

There is, then, first a contextualist lesson concerning the *relation between empirically oriented fellow social scientists:* Triangulation of methods should be performed with reference to real differences in the way researchers work and how they legitimate their research strategies. The message to social scientists who employ qualitative methods is that they should think twice before they buy into either a standard or a social-philosophical methodological style.

Second, there is a contextualist message to *professional philosophers of social science.* The contextualist methodological account, unlike the standard and the social-philosophical, gives professional philosophers of social science impressions of the variety of social science procedures.

Although this chapter was not written to prove that all social science methodology must converge on a contextualist framework, it presupposes a contextualist methodology. The framework we have used to discern three methodologies and six notions of theory has been a contextualist one. The three methodologies have been compared as cases of the same: mediation between methods and selected philosophical elements. By contrast, a standard methodology would be based on normative arguments in favour of one framework, while a social-philosophical methodology would be ripe with accounts of personalized theories. Neither normative, nor personalized, our account traces what researchers do when they conduct research and when they argue about what they do. By means of typologies, contextualized interaction patterns, and sociology of knowledge we contextualize the case of social science in the early twenty-first century.

The research behind this chapter is – at least implicitly – based on a coding of properties of academic social science research, reflecting the author's 'participant observation' in Norwegian, Nordic, European and US academic spheres over more than 25 years. The author maps the contemporary situation in social science, clearly accepting a role as participant in this research community. Social science concepts, we know, are 'interactive kinds' (Hacking 1999); it does matter how we classify ourselves and our fellows. Hopefully, an increasing number of social scientists will find it useful to think of themselves as being guided by a contextualist methodology.

NOTES

1. The dualism was coined by German Neo-Kantian philosophers (cf. Collins 1998 chapter 13),

but later appeared in other academic cultures (cf. e.g. Snow 1959).

2. Some of these can be traced back to Hacking (1999 chapter 3), but we rely more strongly on the sociology of knowledge.

3. This definition partially converges with the definition of the 'received view' in Hands (2001). Examples of standard methodology: Friedman (1953) in economics; King, Keohane and Verba (1994), Geddes (2003) in political science; Stinchcombe (1968), Goldthorpe (2000) in sociology; Pelto and Pelto (1978) in anthropology; Shadish, Cook and Campbell (2002) in psychology.

4. Such as Lyotard (1979), Habermas (1981), Giddens (1985), Alexander (1983). One out of many overviews is Best and Kellner (1991).

5. Abbott (1999 pp. 196ff) uses the term 'contextualist paradigm' in his plea for a return to the programme of the interwar Chicago school of sociology. Even in the 1940s, Stephen Pepper (1942 pp. 232ff) distinguished contextualism as one out of four 'world hypotheses', referring mainly to US pragmatist philosophy. I earlier used the terms 'pragmatist' and/or 'participationist' (Mjøset 2005, 2006a, 2006b), but the term 'contextualist' is a more neutral label and avoids the identification with any particular philosophical school.

6. Examples of this position: Hands (2001), Hoover (2001), Mirowski (2002) in economics; Barnes (2001), Abbott (2001), Ragin (2000), Mjøset (2006a, 2006b) in sociology; Cicchetti and Rogosch (1996), Gottlieb and Halpern (2002), Biglan (2004) in psychology. In much recent political science, one often finds strong elements of contextualism within frameworks that try to retain standard features. Examples are Pierson (2004), Goertz (2006), George and Bennett (2005), and several contributions (e.g. McKeown 2004) in Brady and Collier (Eds) 2004. Unfortunately, a closer discussion of these various combinations is beyond the scope of this chapter.

7. This is a way to state the 'Thomas theorem'; cf. Merton (1968, chapter XIII).

8. In contrast to Hedström, Coleman (1990 p. 5) explicitly denies that 'for a given purpose an explanation must be taken all the way to the individual level to be satisfactory'. He instead invokes a 'pragmatic' criterion: 'The explanation is satisfactory if it is useful for the particular kinds of intervention for which it is intended', In that case, the whole debate on methodological individualism versus methodological collectivism must be judged a rather uninteresting polarization between the standard vision of elementary particles and the social-philosophical totalizing orientation. Standard formulations are ripe with reservations accepting that the ideal of methodological individualism can seldom be realized. Contextualism simply accepts this.

9. We have no space to pursue this further here, but the controversial/non-controversial distinction is implied in our discussion of both critical theory and local research frontiers below.

10. This should fit Ragin's (1986) notion of multiple, conjunctural causation, as well as notions of equifinality and multifinality in the open-systems literature (Cicchetti and Rogosch 1996), but there is no space to expand on this hunch further here. Note that in standard accounts (Hedström 2005), the inclination is often to talk about mechanisms in singular.

11. Although we have no space to pursue it here, the discussion of various types of problem (problems of social engineering, conflict-related problems, existential problems, theoretical problems, etc.) would be a fruitful specification.

12. The standard interpretation is, for instance, Coleman's (1990, chapter 1) model of explanation in social science, and the social-philosophical interpretation is in terms of collective belief systems, civilizations, etc.

13. Elster (1989, 2007) suggests a toolbox of formal mechanisms. We suggest a tool-shed of grounded theories. In this shed there are many shelves for substantive theories: typologies, periodizations, stylized facts. There is also a place for Elster's toolbox, but these mechanisms can only provide explanations in contexts established by substantive theory. Elster tends to leave the tool-shed carrying the toolbox, forgetting to bring any of the substantive theories along. In this way, he retains the standard preoccupation with formal theory, although he often displays an unhappy consciousness that something important has been left behind.

14. Social philosophers are more interested in the conditions of knowledge than in the actual accumulation of knowledge in local research frontiers. Transcendental theory is personal, and so are the resulting interpretations of modernity. This is the position of the literary intellectual, the ability to express the deepest concerns of a generation (or some other unit – a nation, a people, etc.) in an individual synthesis (the work of art). It is interesting here to consider Flyvbjerg's (2001) programme of phronetic social science. This parallels contextualist social science in that both are problem driven. However, thanks to its notion of local research frontiers, the contextualist approach avoids a major dilemma in Flyvbjerg's account, namely that only the high-theory ideal of the standard approach is considered to be *theory*. Flyvbjerg claims that because of 'context-dependence', 'cumulative' and 'stable' research is not possible in the social sciences. The contextualist framework outlined here does not imply that analysis of context precludes theory. One should not grant the standard position a monopoly on notions such as science and theory, but rather define these with reference to local research frontiers. This note is relevant given Laitin's (2003) use of Flyvbjerg as a proxy for the unknown 'Mr Perestroika' in recent controversies within US political science. The result

was yet another polarization (Flyvbjerg 2003 was the response) between standard and social-philosophical positions, in which the real merits of a contextualist position gets lost.

REFERENCES

Abbott, A. 1999 *Department and Discipline.* Chicago: University of Chicago Press.

Abbott, A. 2001 *Time Matters.* Chicago: University of Chicago Press.

Alexander, J.C. 1983 *Theoretical Logic in Sociology* (4. volumes). Berkeley, CA: University of California Press.

Barnes, B. 2001 *On Agency.* London, Sage.

Best, S. and Kellner, D. 1991 *Postmodern Theory: Critical Interrogations.* New York: Guilford Press.

Biglan, A. 2004 'Contextualism and the development of effective prevention practices' *Prevention Science* 5(1): 15–21.

Blumer, H. 1969 *Symbolic Interactionism.* Englewood Cliffs, NJ: Prentice Hall.

Brady, H.E. and Collier, D. (Eds) 2004 *Rethinking Social Inquiry.* Lanham, MD: Rowman & Littlefield.

Cicchetti, D. and Rogosch, F.A. 1996 'Equifinality and multifinality in developmental psychopathology' *Development and Psychopathology* 8: 597–600.

Coleman, J.S. 1990 *Foundations of Social Theory.* Cambridge, MA: Harvard University Press.

Collins, R. 1986 *Weberian Sociological Theory.* Cambridge, Cambridge University Press.

Collins, R. 1998 *The Sociology of Philosophies.* Cambridge, MA: Belknap.

Dewey, J. 1920/1950 *Reconstruction in Philosophy* (1950 edition). New York: Mentor.

Elster, J. 1989 *Nuts and Bolts for the Social Sciences.* Cambridge: Cambridge University Press.

Elster, J. 2007 *Explaining Social Behavior.* Cambridge: Cambridge University Press.

Flyvbjerg, B. 2001 *Making Social Science Matter.* Cambridge: Cambridge University Press.

Flyvbjerg, B. 2003 'A perestroikan straw man answers back' *Politics and Society* 32(3): 389–416.

Foucault, M. 1969 *L'archéologie du Savoir.* Paris: Gallimard.

Foucault, M. 1975 *Surveiller et Punir.* Paris: Gallimard.

Friedman, M. 1953 'The methodology of positive economics' in M. Friedman (Ed.) *Essays in Positive Economics.* Chicago: University of Chicago Press, pp. 3–43.

Geddes, B. 2003 *Paradigms and Sand Castles.* Ann Arbor, MI: University of Michigan Press.

George, A.L. and Bennett A. 2005 *Case Studies and Theory Development in the Social Sciences.* Cambridge, MA: MIT Press.

Giddens, A. 1985 *The Constitution of Society.* Cambridge: Polity Press.

Giddens, A. 1990 *The Consequences of Modernity.* Cambridge: Polity Press.

Glaser, B.G. and. Strauss, A.L. 1967 *The Discovery of Grounded Theory.* New York: Aldine de Gruyter.

Goertz, G. 2006 *Social Science Concepts. A User's Guide.* Princeton, NJ: Princeton University Press.

Goldthorpe, J. 2000 *On Sociology.* Oxford: Oxford University Press.

Gottlieb, G. and Halpern, C.T. 2002 'A relational view of causality in normal and abnormal development' *Development and Psychopathology* 14: 421–435.

Granovetter, M. 1985 'Economic action and economic structure. The problem of embeddedness' *American Journal of Sociology* 78: 1360–1380.

Habermas, J. 1981 *Theorie des kommunikativen Handelns.* Frankfurt am Main: Suhrkamp.

Hacking, I. 1983 *Representing and Intervening.* Cambridge: Cambridge University Press.

Hacking, I. 1999 *The Social Construction of What?* Cambridge, MA: Harvard University Press.

Hands, D.W. 2001 *Reflection without Rules, Economic Methodology and Contemporary Science Theory.* Cambridge: Cambridge University Press.

Hedström, P. 2005 *Dissecting the Social.* Cambridge: Cambridge University Press.

Hirschman, A.O. 1977 'A generalized linkage approach to deveopment, with special reference to staples' *Economic Development and Cultural Change,* 25 (supplement) (Festschrift for Bert F. Hoselitz).

Hoover, K. 2001 *The Methodology of Empirical Macroeconomics.* Cambridge: Cambridge University Press.

Horkheimer, M. 1937 'Traditionelle und kritische theorie' *Zeitschrift für Sozialforschung* VI(2): 245–292.

King, G., Keohane, R.P. and Verba, S. 1994 *Designing Social Inquiry. Scientific Inference in Qualitative Research.* Princeton, NJ: Princeton University Press.

Laitin, D. 2003 'The perestroikan challenge to social science' *Politics and Society* 31(1): 163–184.

Lieberson, S. 1985 *Making It Count: The Improvement of Social Research and Theory.* Berkeley, CA: University of California Press.

Lyotard, J.-F. 1979 *The Postmodern Condition* (English translation, 1984). Minneapolis, MN: University of Minnesota Press.

McKeown, T.J. 2004 'Case studies and the limits of the quantitative worldview' in H.E. Brady and D. Collier (Eds) *Rethinking Social Inquiry.* Lanham, MD: Rowman & Littlefield, pp. 139–167.

Merton, R.K. 1968 *Social Theory and Social Structure.* New York: Free Press.

Mirowski, P. 2002 *Machine Dreams.* Cambridge: Cambridge Unversity Press.

Mjøset, L. 2000 'Stein Rokkan's thick comparisons' *Acta Sociologica* 43: 4.

Mjøset, L. 2005 'Can grounded theory solve the problems of its critics?' *Sosiologisk Tidsskrift* 13(4): 379–408.

Mjøset, L. 2006a 'A case study of a case study. Strategies of generalization and specification in the study of Israel as a single case' *International Sociology* 21(5): 735–766.

Mjøset, L. 2006b 'No fear of comparisons or context: on the foundations of historical sociology' *Comparative Education* 4(5): 337–362.

Mjøset, L. 2007 'An early approach to the varieties of world capitalism: methodological and substantive lessons from the Senghaas/Menzel-project' *Comparative Social Research* 24: 123–176.

Mjøset, L. and Cappelen Å. 2009 'Economics and the others' *Nordic Journal of Political Economy* (in press).

Pawson, R. 2000 'Middle range realism' *Archives Europeennes de Sociologie* 41(2): 283–325.

Pelto, P.J. and Pelto, G.H. 1978 *Anthropological Research. The Structure of Inquiry.* Cambridge: Cambridge University Press.

Pepper, S.C. 1942 *World Hypotheses.* Berkeley, CA: University of California Press.

Pierson, P. 2004 *Politics in Time.* Princeton, NJ: Princeton University Press.

Ragin, C.C. 1986 *The Comparative Method.* Berkeley, CA: University of California Press.

Ragin, C.C. 2000 *Fuzzy-set Social Science.* Chicago: University of Chicago Press.

Ragin, C.C. 2008 *Redesigning Social Inquiry: Fuzzy Sets and Beyond.* Chicago: University of Chicago Press.

Rokkan, S. 1999 *State Formation, Nation-Building, and Mass Politics in Europe.* Oxford: Oxford University Press.

Seidman, S. 1991 'The end of sociological theory: the postmodern hope' *Sociological Theory* 9: 131–146.

Senghaas, D. 1985 *The European Experience.* Leamington Spa, UK: Berg.

Shadish, W.R., Cook, T.D. and Campbell. D.T. 2002 *Experimental and Quasi-experimental Designs for Generalized Causal Inference.* Boston: Houghton Mifflin.

Shalev, M. 2007 'Limits and alternatives to multiple regression in comparative research' *Comparative Social Research* 24: 261–308.

Skagestad, P. 1978 *Vitenskap og Menneskebilde. Charles Peirce og Amerikansk Pragmatisme.* Oslo: Universitetsforlaget.

Skocpol, T. 1984 'Emerging agendas and recurrent strategies in historical sociology' in T. Skocpol (Ed.) *Vision and Method in Historical Sociology.* Cambridge: Cambridge University Press, pp. 356--391.

Smith, D. 1999 *Writing the Social.* Toronto: University of Toronto Press.

Snow, C.P. 1959 *The Two Cultures.* Cambridge: Cambridge University Press.

Stinchcombe, A.L. 1968 *Constructing Social Theories.* New York: Harcourt, Brace, Jovanovitch.

Strauss, A.L. 1970 'Discovering new theory from previous theory' in. T. Shibutani (Ed.) *Human Natures and Collective Behavior. Papers in Honor of Herbert Blumer.* Englewood Cliffs, NJ: Prentice Hall.

Todd, E. 1985 *The Explanation of Ideology: Family Structures and Social Systems.* Oxford: Blackwell.

Todd, E. 1987 *The Causes of Progress: Culture, Authority and Change.* Oxford: Blackwell.

Veblen, T. 1919 *The Place of Science in Modern Civilization.* New York: Viking.

Weber, M. 1922 *Wirtschaft und Gesellschaft.* Tübingen: J.C.B. Mohr.

3

Reflexivity, Realism and the Process of Casing

Bob Carter and Alison Sealey

INTRODUCTION

It is routine in discussions of case-study research to begin with an acknowledgement that the term is used to refer to a wide range of different things, and the current volume is no exception (see also Gomm et al. 2000, Gerring 2007; note that Ragin and Becker [1992] adopts as its title the question *What Is a Case?*). Gerring (2007, p. 13) suggests that 'the defining question of all case study research [is] what is this a case of?' Following in this tradition, we consider in this chapter one of the key problems with cases, namely, how is the case to be defined? Attached to this problem are issues of boundedness and coherence: what are the extents and limits of any given object of study designated as a case? Gerring (2007, p. 53) points out that the question, 'Where do like cases end and unlike cases begin?' is an ontological, rather than an empirical one. However, whereas he opines that 'it seems odd to bring ontological issues into a discussion of social science methodology', we maintain that consideration of the constituents of the social world and their

properties and powers is essential to making principled decisions about (social) scientific method.

We argue that the coherence and boundaries of a 'case' are not self-evident, although empirical social research always involves cases in some sense. Therefore, following Ragin (1992), we suggest that researchers be explicit about the processes of 'casing' involved in determining what is to count as a case. In our discussion, we draw on the contributions to realist social theory of Archer, Layder, Pawson, Sayer and others, suggesting that, because of its explicit social ontology, realism provides the means for making the process of casing a more fastidious one. Identification of the 'domains' of reality, and of the distinctive properties and powers of structure, culture and agency, facilitates a more self-aware approach towards the epistemological machinery that generates the methodological process of casing.

The chapter begins by drawing attention to the distinctive features of researching both the social and the physical world. We contend that the central difference between the two is the human property of reflexivity, in the sense that the relationship between social action and the descriptions of that action employed by researchers is an interactive and dynamic one. Realism entails the recognition not only of reflexivity and the role of meanings in social action, but also of the fact that social reality is not exhausted by either actors' or researchers' accounts of what they do. We therefore discuss the notion of a stratified social ontology, in which the empirical domain is conceived as only one element of social reality. Such an ontology has important methodological implications for case-study research, which are then explored in the next section of the chapter. We conclude by arguing that a modest realism can provide greater methodological self-awareness in the practice of case-study research.

THE NATURAL, THE SOCIAL AND REFLEXIVITY

Researching the physical world

Phenomena and processes researched by physicists, chemists or geographers are sometimes susceptible to a case-study method. With due acknowledgement that the following examples are well outside our own fields of expertise, we cite them merely as illustrations of one way of conceptualising the 'case study', where the case is 'thought of as a constituent member of a target population' (Stake 2000, p. 23). Thus, if there is a class of techniques of 'chemical vapour deposition' called 'atomic layer deposition (ALD)', then an 'in-depth summary of the surface chemistry of *one representative* ALD process' can 'provide a view on the current status of understanding the surface chemistry of ALD, *in general*' (Riikka and Puurunen 2005, emphasis added).

In order to come to conclusions about 'gas-to-particle conversion' in general, Leaitch et al. (1999) conducted a case study of one particular forest over one period of time so as to 'provide evidence of nucleation

and condensation of products related to the oxidation of different biogenic emissions'.

In both examples (and there are numerous others we might have chosen), an object of study has been identified and investigated on the understanding that it will provide useful information about similar objects.

In this chapter we consider differences between the identification of objects of study in the natural and social sciences. However, we should stress that we do not wish to exaggerate the distinction between types of discipline. There has been extensive discussion in the literature about both the ways in which the natural and physical sciences are not as 'uncontaminated' by values, discursive choices and interpretive method as caricatured depictions suggest, as well as a recognition that the social sciences routinely draw on assumptions and methods found widely in the natural and physical sciences. As Sayer (2000, p. 2) concedes, the realist position, to which we also subscribe, 'must acknowledge that the world can only be known under particular descriptions, in terms of available discourses, though it does not follow from this that no description or explanation is better than any other'.

As social scientists, we acknowledge the materiality of human beings and the world we inhabit. A key distinction we discuss in this chapter concerns the degree to which the phenomenon or process that is the focus of study involves, at least potentially, reflexivity. Drawing on Archer's (2003, p. 26) definition, reflexivity is conceived as an 'activity in which the subject deliberates upon how some item, such as a belief, desire or state of affairs pertains or relates to itself'. This process, Archer (2003, p. 34) maintains, is not passive or unremittingly inward-looking, '… but an active process in which we continuously converse with ourselves, precisely in order to define what we do believe, do desire and do intend to do'. It is a significant contribution to the way in which, while the social context in which they operate is shaped by structure and culture, people simultaneously deploy their capacity to respond to these objective features of society.

We propose here not a rigid dichotomy between reflexive and non-reflexive objects of study, but rather a continuum. The material objects and processes studied by physicists and chemists are the least likely to require that reflexivity (as defined above) is taken into account. That is to say, 'atomic layer deposition' (or 'ALD') might be engineered by human beings. In terms of the realist ontology explained in more detail below, this is an example of the scientist bringing about the conditions under which the particular event that is of interest will occur: 'experimental *context* is created by isolating a known *mechanism* to produce a given *regularity*' (Pawson 1989, p. 202). Human intervention has an important part to play, but within certain parameters. The gases and solids involved in the 'gas–solid reactions' entertain no notion that this is how scientists have identified them, contribute no ideas of their own to the process, and should behave in predictable ways no matter when, where or by whom the process is conducted. They are 'indifferent kinds', or, as Hacking (1992, p. 189) puts it:

> ... in the case of natural kinds, classifying in itself does not make any difference to the thing classified. Thinking of things as a kind, and giving a name to that class of things, does not of itself make any difference to the things so distinguished.

In other words, the epistemological consequences of identifying specific particles or chemical reactions as representative cases of such phenomena in general are negligible: describing them in this way does not alter their nature as objects for study, since particles and the like are indifferent to their epistemological description.

At the other end of the continuum are phenomena and processes that are so bound up with the language in which they are described, so inherently intersubjective, that they are, in a limited sense, *constituted* by processes of reflexivity. At intermediate points along this continuum are other phenomena and processes that vary in the degree to which people's understanding of them influences the way they behave.

Researching the social world

Many physical processes, then, can be regarded as 'cases' that are largely indifferent to human enterprise. By contrast, study of the social world includes, among other things, study of material and physical processes that, because they are accessible to human understanding, are also susceptible to human intervention. As we give some examples, we draw on the realist philosophy that seeks to identify both the *real*, 'the structures and powers of objects', and the *actual*, which refers to 'what happens if and when those powers are activated' (Sayer 2000, p. 12). We elaborate on this distinction below.

Underlying our experience as embodied beings – who need to eat, sleep and exercise, and whose bodies grow, change and age – are certain 'structures and powers of objects' in the form of interactions of the molecules that constitute human DNA. Some combinations of genes in the DNA sequence render some human beings vulnerable to particular diseases (sickle-cell anaemia, Tay–Sachs disease, breast cancer and so on). Because the structure of human DNA has been mapped and can be represented, it has become possible for people to intervene and modify some aspects of these hitherto inaccessible processes. Particular genes can be targeted and their actualisation suppressed, while genetic structures can be artificially reproduced (using stem cells to grow various organs, for example). The fact that we are, physically, the product, amongst other things, of a particular organisation of genetic processes is not altered by our knowledge of that fact. However, this knowledge does allow us to significantly modify certain aspects of these mechanisms, in that it becomes possible to inhibit their actualisation. For example, once it was understood that conception resulted from the fertilisation of an egg by a sperm, human beings practised contraception, with increasingly accurate application as knowledge of the process developed – and increased understanding of a whole range of mechanisms involved in health and disease can influence people's decisions about extensive aspects of their behaviour. Indeed, matters of health and illness are aspects of experience about which people do tend to have – and to need – theories and causal accounts, whether metaphysical, alchemical or medical. Developments in human knowledge can, to some extent, be 'fed back' into the mechanisms – of procreation, ageing and disease – in efforts to manage them, so that human behaviour is affected in various ways. (Two potential parents who are carriers of the Tay–Sachs gene might decide to act on that knowledge by choosing not to have children, for example).

Some aspects of the social world are further along the continuum from human-knowledge-impervious to human-knowledge-dependent processes. As human beings are physically embodied, they interact, as Archer (1995, p. 175) points out, with physical resources 'such as land, food, weapons or factories', and sociological realism maintains that these resources are, in a substantive sense, independent of people's perceptions or descriptions of them. Thus some social processes, like many material processes, and the outcomes of those processes, are operative regardless of how they are perceived empirically.

An example of a phenomenon that is partially independent of human understanding, yet partially responsive to it, would be economic relations. Using both large-scale analysis and examination of exceptional cases, economists have identified 'macroeconomic factors' to demonstrate that 'growth is negatively associated with inflation, large budget deficits, and distorted foreign exchange markets' (Fischer 1993). The mechanisms that bring about inflation (and that are not necessarily actualised, because, as is also true in the natural world, powers often remain unrealised) can lead to events that people experience without having access to their (unobservable) causes. So it is that:

.... policies intended to fight inflation tend to lead to higher unemployment and so on. ... In addition, as social realists like to point out, collective action tends to have unintended consequences that are not very well understood by the agents but that are central for an adequate theoretical grasp of the social realm. (Stueber 2006, p. 101)

Furthermore, the effects of inflation on those with a fixed income will be felt irrespective of any theory they might hold about the causes of inflation.

As social actors, our immediate, empirical experience of labour relations and markets – and our explanations of how they operate – might extend only as far as our own job prospects and buying power. Our knowledge and understanding of the structural mechanisms underlying those experiences may be very limited. However, as we have noted, it is a distinctive property of human beings that they communicate about their experiences, name them, reflect on them and seek to change them. Thus, changing perceptions among, for example, workers, house-buyers and borrowers about the stability of the market can lead to actions that directly contribute to its destabilisation. Such was the case with the United States economy during the 1930s, when savers in large numbers – fearing the loss of their savings and the collapse of the banks – tried to withdraw their deposits, leading to these panic withdrawals themselves threatening to bring about the very collapse they feared.

DOMAINS OF REALITY

The empirical, the actual and the real

Emerging from these examples is the distinction alluded to above, between different 'domains' of reality. We have already referred to the notion that objects and structures have properties and powers, and that these are often not empirically observable. We also maintain that particular circumstances are needed to 'actualise' these. The further recognition that empirical reality can sometimes be misleading is linked, in our argument, with the identification of 'cases'. This can be illustrated by the example of two patients ('cases') who present with similar symptoms (empirical reality, described in everyday language); these may turn out to be attributable to different causes (mechanisms operating at the level of the real, described with reference to networks of scientific propositions).

A similar line of argument can be used about other dimensions of human experience. For example, the influential branch of linguistics associated with Chomsky argues that understanding *language* means understanding *how the brain can compute language*. The quest then is for identification of universal, unobservable structures in the cognitive apparatus that underlie all languages. One individual speaker may perceive utterances in, say, Swedish as unintelligible while understanding utterances in, say, French; a Swedish speaker processes the same utterances in exactly the obverse way. Although a linguistic scientist may explain this with reference to 'universal grammar' and the deep structures of the language capacity, to the speakers themselves this is likely to be of little help in boosting comprehension. Their empirical experience is almost certainly accompanied by beliefs and attitudes about 'French' and 'Swedish'; language varieties are shored up by their representation in writing, by grammars, dictionaries and by systems of schooling and assessment. The 'performance' of speakers when they produce utterances cannot, as a dimension of social experience, be readily dismissed as epiphenomenal to their underlying linguistic 'competence'. That is to say, even though researchers accept that empirical evidence can be misleading, it does not follow that it should be disregarded altogether, in favour of exclusive investigation of the 'real', underlying processes generative of the empirical world. These 'domains' of reality are all relevant in the context of social scientific case-study research.

In its basic form, the stratified ontology associated with Bhaskar (1978) proposes a three-part distinction between the empirical, the actual and the real (Figure 3.1). The original typology is represented as a combination of mechanisms, events and experiences.

Figure 3.1   A three-part distinction between the empirical, the actual and the real

	Domain of real	Domain of actual	Domain of empirical
Mechanisms	X		
Events	X	X	
Experiences	X	X	X

Exemplification of the distinction is conventionally provided with reference to phenomena and properties that would, in our terms, be instances of 'indifferent kinds', such as crystals and gravitation. Thus, the *empirical* experience of the sun rising and setting is related to the *actual* 'event' of the earth's orbit around the sun. Both in turn are explicable by the unobservable 'mechanism' of gravitational force – the manifestation, if Einstein's theory of general relativity is correct,[1] of the curvature of space and time. The presence of bodies such as planets *actualise* the mechanism via the 'geodetic' effect, warping space and time so that 'gravity' exerts a force whose effects, again, are *experienced empirically* whenever we drop something and it falls towards the ground. The experience is real, but is not exhaustive, and we might conceptualise it in the following way. Note that we have reversed the canonical order of the columns, because our starting point in the discussion of social research, as will be explained below, is empirically experienced reality (Figure 3.2).

Figure 3.2   Exemplification of the three-part distinction between the empirical, the actual and the real

Domain of the empirical	Domain of the actual	Domain of the real
Experiences	As before, but including also events	As before, but including also mechanisms
Appearance of the sun rising in the east Dropping objects and seeing them fall	Planetary movement and gravitational influence; geodetic effect of the earth	Bodies' warping of space and time

This example of a stratified ontology is of a physical process largely unaffected by human reflexivity: neither the agent of the process, nor the phenomenal outcome of it, is dependent on human knowledge. Our knowledge neither affects the operative mechanisms nor allows any significant intervention in their operation: the earth will orbit the sun irrespective of our understanding of how or why this happens. Nor, for the purposes of managing everyday social life, do people need a theory of relativity: indeed possession of that knowledge has little effect on our phenomenal experience of sunrise, sunset or falling objects.

Pursuing the idea of a 'reflexivity-independent' to 'reflexivity-dependent' continuum, proposed above, we can depict our other examples schematically in a similar way (Figure 3.3).

Structure, culture, agency and reflexivity

It is our contention, then, that social researchers need to be cognisant both of structural phenomena and of the ideas that people might, and frequently do, draw on to legitimate (or indeed to challenge) material relations. '[S]tructural emergent properties' are 'irreducible to people and relatively enduring'. They 'are specifically defined as those internal and necessary relationships which entail material resources, whether physical or human …' (Archer 1995, p. 177). They are 'necessary' in the sense that employees are such in relation to employers, tenants in relation to landowners and so on; this is another indication of the 'reflexivity-independent'

quality of these relations, in the terms outlined above. Structural properties are also anterior to those of other strata, and operate on a longer timescale. Layder (1998, p. 94) draws the distinction in terms of '… behavioural (or action) concepts and systemic (social-cultural) concepts'. Systemic dimensions of the social world include social settings and contextual resources, about which he observes:

> The reproduced character of relations, powers and practices refers to the fact that they have been stretched through time and space away from the face-to-face activities which ultimately feed into their continuity and reproduction. (Layder 1998, p. 97)

Now, as we have already indicated, and as both Archer and Layder acknowledge, these distinctions do not provide us with two fully separated categories of phenomena, although structural emergent properties do retain some autonomy from their constituent elements. Acting as a link between structure and agency is the reflexivity to which we have repeatedly referred: the distinctly human '… capacity for interpreting the same material conditions, cultural elements, circumstances and situations in different ways and hence for introducing novel patterns or courses of action in response to them' (Archer 1995, p. 70). At the same time, however, the fact that people do routinely reflect on and interpret their empirical experience, and that cultural descriptions and systems emerge as they do so, does not override the material quality of structural relations. It is not *necessary* that structural relations be legitimated, understood or accepted, because

Figure 3.3 Schematic depiction of the examples in Figure 3.2

Domain of the empirical	Domain of the actual	Domain of the real
Experience of disease*; ageing, etc.	Particular configurations of genetic relations	Internal genetic relations/ combinations – DNA
Price rises	Inflation	Economic relations
Mutual incomprehensibility of speech produced by speakers of different language varieties	Interaction among some speakers rather than others	Human capacity for language

*Often, the mechanisms involved are actualised only in particular circumstances – if both parents are carriers of specific genes, for example. For a fuller discussion of this argument see Sealey and Carter (2004).

they can also 'be sustained by coercion and manipulation' (Archer 1995, p. 175).

The differential distribution of power implied by this extends also to the ability to produce *effective* 'novel interpretations' or 'courses of action'. People may interpret their 'material conditions, cultural elements, circumstances and situations' with reference to their membership of various kinds of social group. But those who self-identify as members of one kind of group will not necessarily be so identified by others; legislative regimes might well endorse one set of category descriptions while disregarding others – as in apartheid South Africa, for example, or Afghanistan under the Taliban – not to mention many other times and places when people's self-identifications as, say, 'artist' or 'healer' have not been ratified by those with more practical power. Furthermore, there are differences between the identification of groups on the part of: (1) those responsible for the provision and distribution of resources (e.g. the makers of health or education policy); (2) researchers and analysts of the social world; (3) commentators such as media and culture producers; and (4) social actors engaged in the business of 'getting on' in the world (e.g. the implementers and recipients of policies).

The utility – and limits – of the empirical

Let us return to the empirical domain. It is – by definition – the one that is most apparent to us, and the one where our senses inform us about what is going on. As researchers, social scientists investigating social problems may well begin by identifying what seem to be, in empirical terms, cases of the particular social problem in which they are interested. Research that starts with the case, we would argue, takes account of the experiential, of 'emic' categories, and begins, therefore, at the level of the empirical. This orientation is alluded to by Gerring (2007, p. 41) when he observes of the single case that the relationships among its different elements '... have a *prima facie* causal connection: they

are all at the scene of the crime. This is revelatory when one is at an early stage of analysis, for at that point there is no identifiable suspect and the crime itself may be difficult to discern'. Even the single-case ethnography, however, is evidently not isomorphic, as a study, with the experiences of those observed, because for participants the experiences are in-and-of themselves, while for the researcher they become data for analysis. From a realist perspective, things both are and are not what they seem. As Callinicos (2006, p. 180) notes:

> Marx famously wrote that 'all science would be superfluous if the form of appearance of things directly coincided with their essence'. Social critique would not just be redundant, but impossible, if the real and the empirical coincided.

Unsurprisingly, accounts of case-driven/case-based research reveal instances when the very process of investigating collections of apparently comparable cases have led to redefinitions of the characteristics of the problem at issue. For example, Becker (1992) explains how Cressey (1953, pp. 19–22) came to reject the legal definition of 'embezzlement' as accurately descriptive of the cases in his data that shared features in common, substituting as a label 'the criminal violation of financial trust'. Wieviorka (1992, p. 162) draws attention to an equivalent problem in his discussion of the extent of the scope that researchers may adopt in delineating cases. His examples are of social conflicts and he begins, as we would want to do, with an 'empirical' 'notion of conflict – referring to such concrete experiences as students on strike or anti-nuclear activists organizing a demonstration'. He points out that, once 'cases' are viewed in conjunction with other cases, and comparison becomes part of the research process, there is the possibility that this comparison may either 'help deconstruct what common sense takes to be unique or unified [or] ... may construct the unity of what seems to be broken up into practical categories' (Wieviorka 1992, p. 170).

As soon as any such process of (conceptual) construction or deconstruction comes into play, we suggest that analysis has moved beyond the empirical, although we would want to argue for the retention of a connection to this level of reality at all stages of analysis. It has been observed (Ragin 1997) that the '... researcher's specification of relevant cases at the start of an investigation is really nothing more than a working hypothesis that the cases initially selected are in fact alike enough to permit comparisons'. We would argue that this provisionality arises in part because the analyst is obliged to take account both of people's perceptions and of the social relations operating in the domains of the actual and the real, as well as the interplay between them.

Case-study research for the realist, then, involves not simply an acceptance of some given and transparent category of 'cases', but an engagement with theories about which kinds of things in the social world share properties in common. This is made explicit by Ragin (1992, pp. 217–220) when he suggests that, as 'the term "case" is used in so many different ways', it is more helpful to think in terms of the dynamic, productive process of 'casing', 'a methodological step [that] can occur at any stage of the research process'. Ragin represents this process as a response to some 'problematic relation between theory and data', recognising that 'casing often creates objects', in the sense that it foregrounds the features shared by the members of a putative group and 'hides' or 'washes [out]' their singularity. A crucial challenge, we would argue, is to identify the criteria by which the casing process may be justified. Layder (1998, p. 98) proposes that validity and adequacy should be sought 'within connected chains of reasoning as the analyst seeks to place the empirical phenomenon in a wider, more generalized and abstract context of ideas and research'. Where explanation requires recourse to unobserved properties, and to systemic concepts, these will be identified by the observer or analyst, '... because they require more precise, consistent and technical definitions which are typically not available in lay or colloquial usage'.

Let us summarise the claims made so far. We are writing from a realist perspective, but one that accommodates the realm of the empirical and recognises the centrality of human agency in the social world. We suggest that 'cases' in social research are identified initially with reference to empirical experience, but that it is important to remain mindful of the realms of the actual and the real, where processes and mechanisms may be operating in ways that are not readily observable. Scientific enquiry, we suggest, makes possible increasing knowledge of such processes, some of which, such as those governed by the 'laws' of physics, are relatively unaffected by human understandings and descriptions, while others are more bound up with the accounts and propositions which make up the 'cultural system.' (Archer 1988) In these dimensions of the social world, people's perceptions of, and beliefs about, their experiences become, in an important sense, constitutive of social reality. When this happens, the casing process has to come to terms with phenomena that are, in significant ways, interactive and knowledge-dependent. This raises epistemological questions with significant methodological implications. Let us illustrate with some examples.

CASING AND THE SOCIAL WORLD

Interactive kinds and making up cases

It is unavoidable that, for the purposes of research, subgroups of the human population at large are established. Any process of sampling relies on a belief that the subset in the sample is representative of groups to be found in the larger population, and, if the purpose of a statistical sample is to reveal elements of a broader population, then '[i]n this respect, the function of a sample is no different from the function of a case study' (Gerring 2007, p. 11).

However, the identification of groups from the human population can, in a particular sense, bring those groups into being. As Hacking (2002) expresses it, 'Sometimes, our sciences create kinds of people that in a certain sense did not exist before. I call this "making up people"'. In other words, all 'groups' are a product of descriptions of some kind, and one of the consequences of this process is the valourisation of particular kinds of human difference, thus making these differences 'matter'. By making things matter, we mean bringing them into the purview of enquiry as scientific objects, accessible to other researchers – as well as to policy makers, media commentators and so on. As Daston (2000, p. 13) puts it, while 'scientific objects' will 'grow more richly real as they become entangled in webs of cultural significance, material practices, and theoretical derivations', nevertheless, they 'may not be invented'. This last point is crucial, and we (unlike many social constructionists) would want to insist on a link between any candidate description and some property or characteristic to which the description can be shown to refer. One can (indeed, often, one must) mark out populations in particular ways in order to do research, but one must also recognise that this is what one is doing: 'making up people' for a particular purpose. This 'self-aware' approach entails a methodological justification that openly appeals to social scientific criteria of consistency and appropriateness of the researcher's social categories to the task of explanation.

As Hacking has pointed out, as people are 'reactive' – not 'indifferent' – kinds, the labels and descriptions deployed (be it by policy makers, the media or by analysts) tend to be applied to a 'moving target'. 'We think of these kinds of people as definite classes defined by definite properties', writes Hacking, '... But it's not quite like that. They are moving targets because our investigations interact with them, and change them. And since they are changed, they are not quite the same kind of people as before. The target has moved. I call this the "looping effect"'. Hacking's own examples include groups affected by various conditions identified by the medical profession. Gee, similarly, (2000, p. 104) draws attention to the

way in which adults who are candidates for the label 'ADHD' ('attention deficit hyperactivity disorder') 'have actively redefined their behaviors in positive terms – as examples of fluid and dynamic attentional processes and creative proactivity'. Gee distinguishes those characteristics that people are born with from the meanings attached to them, and to other characteristics they acquire, as individuals and through the roles and positions they occupy:

There are people today who view and orient to ADHD in terms of their affiliations within shared practices with others, including others who do not have ADHD as an N-('nature') identity or I-('institution') identity. Such people engage in joint experiences with others – for example, attending groups and events, engaging in political action, creating and participating in internet sites, sharing information and new procedures and practices, and so forth. One need only type 'ADHD' into any search engine and some of the resources for constructing an A-('affiliation') identity will be readily apparent. (Gee 2000, p. 106)

This account highlights an issue that is very relevant to the casing process. Suppose a case-study approach is being deployed to answer questions about different schools' responses to 'children with ADHD', and that the researcher plans to study in detail a small number of relevant sites. How does this researcher decide on the boundaries and coherence of the cases? Does there need to be a medical or institutional diagnosis, or is subjective affiliation sufficient?

In some respects, Gee's account of the different ways of taking on an 'identity' echoes Greenwood's discussion (1994; see also Archer 2003, Sealey and Carter 2001) of aggregates and collectivities. Key to the distinction between these two kinds of group is the presence or absence of 'joint commitments by members to arrangements, conventions, and agreements' (Greenwood 1994, p. 129). Gee's examples illustrate a particular manifestation of the 'looping effect' identified by Hacking: groups whose constitution does not initially rely on shared meanings or commitments might choose, or be encouraged, to develop such resources. In this way, at least some of their members may convert institutionally derived identities into group affiliations:

> For example, businesses try to create a specific sort of affinity group out of their employees or customers. The business creates (socially engineers) certain practices that ensure that employees or customers gain certain experiences, that they experience themselves and others in certain ways, and that they behave and value in certain ways. The business hopes to create a bonding among the employees or customers, as well as to the business, through the employees' or customers' participation in and allegiance to these practices. (Gee 2000, p. 106)

The ability and readiness of social actors to engage with the potentials of group and category membership is, we would argue, evidence of the reflexivity that we explored above, and that is an ontological property of human beings.

'Ethnic conflict': a case of casing?

Ragin (1997) describes case-oriented studies as typically starting 'with the seemingly simple idea that social phenomena in like settings (such as organizations, neighbourhoods, cities, countries, regions, cultures, and so on) ... may parallel each other sufficiently to permit comparing and contrasting them'. In other words, these similarities are empirically apparent. Ragin goes on to stress the importance of his formulation, 'may parallel each other sufficiently', because of the possibility that, '[i]n the course of the research, the investigator may decide otherwise and drop some cases, or even whole categories of cases'.

Gerring (2007) provides an impressive typology of types of case-study research, and supports the would-be case researcher by identifying principles and criteria to help in decisions about the optimal approach to a particular problem. Among the many illustrations he cites are several that in our view are likely to be entangled in the kind of feedback loops discussed above. For example, Gerring's chapter on 'techniques for choosing cases' includes the following in its explanation of the 'diverse case' method (Gerring 2007,

p. 98): 'Where the individual variable of interest is categorical (on/off, red/black/blue, Jewish/Protestant/Catholic), the identification of diversity is readily apparent. The investigator simply chooses one case from each category'.

The reader who has been following our argument sympathetically will notice that the first two of the parenthetical option sets are more likely to be relevant in studies of 'indifferent' kinds, whereas the third is, in our view, not only much less 'categorical' but also of an 'interactive' kind. This is illustrated by an analysis (Sealey 2006) of an extensive set of 140 oral life-history interviews, where a pattern emerges of some respondents reporting at length on their changing perceptions of their own religious affiliation. For example, one woman explains how her marriage in a Catholic church was a solution to a complicated conflict among members of her own and her fiancé's families. This is an extract from her interview:

> ... that was the trauma of our wedding and I don't know whether you would like me to go on about religion but oh, and I go back because of having this wedding in the Catholic church and our own church I had to be baptised because I hadn't been baptised, and of course, once you are baptised then the Bishop wants you then to be confirmed, so I had to go through a confirmation as well, and it was all ridiculous, I mean you can laugh about it now in this day and age, but you had to go through all that to get married ... (Sealey 2006, 007MB)

Should the investigator categorise this speaker as 'Catholic' or not? Another respondent reflects on the category, 'Jewish':

> ... apparently my grandmother was, her father was a Jew, so that made my grandmother half Jew, so I find that the Jewish line run through us. My granddaughter at the moment, her mother is quite white and so is the father but my granddaughter has almost black skin with curly hair ... (Sealey 2006, 005MB)

This speaker's self-identification may or may not satisfy criteria proposed by the researcher, but how flexible should such categories be? More sobering evidence of the way in which such labels are made to 'matter' is provided by

Callil (2006, pp. 222–225). In her account of the Nazi occupation of France, she notes that:

> To the Germans, a Jew was a Jew if he practised or had practised the religion, or had more than two Jewish grandparents. ... [By contrast,] Vichy's first *Statut des Juifs* (Statute on the Jews) ... defined a Jew by race, not religion: three Jewish grandparents, or two Jewish grandparents if the spouse was also Jewish, were sufficient.

One objector at the time thought that 'French Israelites', that is '"well-born" Jews who had been French for generations' should be regarded differently (Callil 2006). Examples of politically motivated interpretations of religious categories are legion, making such putative groupings of human beings particularly suspect as candidates for causal explanations. Among problems of this kind that face the case-study researcher, the concept of 'ethnicity' is particularly salient, so we use this focus here as an illustration of the methodological implications for case-study research of the realist position we have been outlining.

Another example cited by Gerring (2007), this time in the context of testing causal propositions, is Reilly's 'crucial case' of Papua New Guinea (PNG). The theories he seeks to test are those 'that postulate a causal link between ethnic fragmentation and democratic performance', in the belief that:

> ... the PNG case functions as what Harry Eckstein called a 'crucial case study' for [such] theories – in other words, a case study that provides the key test of a theory's validity, and sometimes a more rigorous assessment than even a large-N comparative study. (Reilly 2000–01, pp. 167–168)

We suggest that there are at least three kinds of methodological difficulty involved in undertaking research which relies on a notion of ethnicity – including research about 'ethnic conflict'. These are: (1) the identification and definition of the group; (2) the assumption of 'group-ness'; and (3) the implied explanatory framework. That is, we argue that predictable problems will beset any study located in a notion of ethnicity that assumes: (1) that ethnic differences are meaningful and sufficiently stable to allow for the identification of ethnic groups; (2) that researchers' sampling criteria can be used to define groups for the purposes of research; and (3) that the differences putatively identified as 'ethnic' (such as religion, language, country of origin, various cultural practices and so on – they are many, varied and usually inconsistent) are explanatorily significant.

On the epistemological relations of production

When researchers use concepts of an interactive kind without a relevant degree of methodological self-awareness, it is likely that the concepts employed will conceal their epistemological relations of production. At this point, researchers themselves become an element in the feedback loop of 'making up people'. An illustration of the practical consequences of this kind of process is provided by a study of antenatal screening for sickle-cell disease and thalassaemia (Dyson et al. 2007). These conditions are unevenly distributed in the human population and are frequently described as together affecting disproportionately people who are 'in origin' 'Afro-Caribbean', 'sub-Saharan', 'Arab', 'Mediterranean', 'Indian' and 'Pakistani'. In terms of the argument outlined above, the biological mechanisms responsible for these diseases (molecular defects, in particular genes, resulting from mutations) are physical processes that do not depend for their actualisation on human understandings or beliefs.

Social intervention in the spread of these diseases, however, involves engagement with perceptions about which categories of people are at risk. This is where the process of 'casing' comes into play, when ideas about both 'families' and 'ethnic groups' are utilised in a screening programme carried out by midwives to assess the relative risk to the babies of various mothers. As Ragin (1992, pp. 219–220) notes:

> When the members of a generic category (e.g., families) are declared to be the relevant objects for a theoretical idea and thus 'cased,' researchers

can manipulate them to address the theory's broad claims. ... To collect a sample of 'families,' for example, is to ... close off discussion of 'What is a family?'

Dyson et al.'s study (2007, p. 40) demonstrates that the mismatch between competing concepts of the family, in contexts such as this, may be particularly significant. This is because the meaning for clients of 'family origins' is not 'coterminous with the strict meaning of family for clinical genetics purposes'. In other words, the clients may choose to 'define their family links in social, rather than biological terms'. In relation to ethnicity, this study also found that some midwives (with responsibility for assessing haemoglobinopathy risk) 'hold lay notions of ethnicity at odds with social science concepts of ethnicity', with the result that they 'rely on erroneous conceptions of distinct "races", misunderstand the relationship between ethnic/family origins and risk and inadvertently mislead the client'.

At play here are three kinds of description of a phenomenon (although they are likely to overlap in some respects). First, there are descriptions derived from clinical science, concerning genes, mutations and the genetic inheritance of risk. 'Casing' will have taken place when, for example, the researchers decided how instances of the phenomenon should be classified (given that subtly different molecular defects are associated with the same symptoms). Second, there are social scientific – and applied social policy – descriptions of families and ethnic groups. The classification process here has long been recognised as problematic, and indeed unsatisfactory.

In British health studies, ethnicity has often been indexed by country of birth because of the availability of this information in the census. This is clearly problematic for, say, people born in Britain but of Caribbean family background (or people of British family background born on the Indian subcontinent). (Davey Smith 2000, p. 1695)

Contrasting the questions on ethnicity in the censuses of 1991 and 2001, Davey Smith observes that the larger number of pre-coded choices in the latter, 'will lead to a marked change in the official description of the ethnic composition of Britain'. He continues, 'This demonstrates the way in which methods of data collection construct ethnicity, and this relationship is equally true of the treatment of ethnicity in studies of health status'. Thus it is apparent that the categories required for the health screening to be effective are at odds with those used in social research and policy.

Finally, there are the descriptions used by clients (expectant mothers) and health professionals (midwives). As has been demonstrated, Dyson et al. (2007) found in these a lack of precision, with discrepancies between them and not only the clinical but also the sociological categories relevant to the screening programme.

We would go further than this, however, and argue that ethnicity is an unreliable criterion for casing, because of the assumptions about 'group-ness' that inevitably underlie *any* concept of ethnicity. For example, in an exploration of the Human Genome Diversity Project, Reardon (2005, p. 16) points out that even those involved in this ostensibly anti-racist scientific endeavour necessarily, '... presumed the prior existence of groups in nature and society. Further they presupposed the existence of expertise needed to discern and represent these groups'. The pertinent questions that Reardon identifies are: 'What is the proper role and meaning of systems for classifying humans?' and 'How should human differences be defined and for what purposes?' (Reardon 2005, p. 43). This is not to argue that the quest should be for a 'scientific' definition of ethnicity that will be more 'reliable' than other definitions. Rather, clarity is needed about which human differences 'matter', that is, which are relevant for the purposes of any particular study.

Those engaged in any casing process would thus seek to grasp the historical ontology of the actual and the empirical, the ways in which actual and empirical social forms and objects (such as 'ethnic relations' and 'ethnic groups') come into being. Take, for example, the fact that an online search on 'Google Scholar' generates over 20,000 hits for the phrase 'ethnic conflict'. The process we are suggesting would recognise that, in a case study of any particular conflict, one salient aspect of its analysis would be that, in common with other types of conflict, it has come to be regarded, in both lay and research terms, as within the purview of 'ethnic conflict'. A further methodological point is that being regarded in this way subtly alters the phenomenon itself: such conflicts become, amongst other things, 'cases of ethnic conflict'; they are thus steered into particular analytical frameworks; the likelihood of funding to research them is enhanced or diminished; researchers themselves come to be placed within particular disciplinary and institutional spaces.

This approach leaves open the possibility of identifying more precisely how conflicts or unequal outcomes are caused, not by the 'factor' or 'variable' of ethnicity, but by particular configurations of structure, agency and culture. In one 'case', an unequal distribution of resources, together with the identification by social actors of their needs and interests as in conflict with those of certain others, provides the right conditions for an 'ethnic' interpretation of the conflict or inequality. In a parallel 'case', neither internal nor external interpretations favour the mobilisation of ideas about ethnicity, and the conflict is not represented in these terms.

The 'semiotic layer'

Our realist perspective, then, identifies structure, culture and agency as fundamental components and universal components of the social world. Mediating between them are the 'internal conversations' in which we all engage, and the 'semiotic layer' of the medium through which we all – as actors and as researchers – communicate, most obviously language:

> ... the identification of an 'event' and its constitutive elements (persons, objects, places, etc.) from the ongoing flow of social action and social processes necessarily requires some act of

> semiotic interpretation, even if what happens is totally non-semiotic (i.e. purely material, physical action). ... Semiosis is a condition of the existence of social actors, including acting on reasons, whether these come from public communication or inner conversations, developing identities, interests, motives, reasons, and goals for actions and acting on these in ways that others can understand. (Fairclough et al. 2001, pp. 10–11)

Language affords us the range of labels available to 'make up people'. Our plea, once again, is for case-study research to be particularly self-aware about these processes. We are not proposing that scientists, including social scientists, have a direct line to more accurate systems of labelling than the common-sense descriptions that circulate in the social world. Pawson describes more accurately the distinction between the part played by language in social action and actors' everyday descriptions, and the criteria by which scientific descriptions are assessed:

> Scientists are confident in their usage of particular terms, not because they have some once-and-for-all conceptual anchorage, but because they are entrenched in a formal network of concepts. (Pawson 1989, p. 236)

CONCLUSION

We are persuaded by Ragin's notion of casing in preference to 'the case study'. In our view, the latter often obscures the epistemological work necessary to produce the relevant categories associated with cases; in short, it runs the risk of reifying the case itself. The notion of 'casing', however, properly emphasises the central role played by the researcher's own descriptions in constituting the cases under study. Epistemological work, however, always entails ontological claims and commitments and we have argued that a stratified social ontology provides the most reliable basis for the casing process because it throws a distinctive light on the central problems associated with case-study research, namely boundedness and coherence.

Recognition of the central role of reflexivity in the research of 'interactive kinds' such as human populations entails a greater degree of methodological awareness; cases are important instances of making up people and social objects. Our approach encourages the development of historical ontologies that incorporate the realms of the actual and the real. This approach allows us to examine what sorts of social objects and human populations come into being, and in which ways, and what their effects are in shaping subsequent social action, including social research. Finally, the realist notion of a stratified social ontology rests on the belief that social action and the social world are explicable in terms of causally adequate sociological accounts capable of linking structure, culture and agency.

NOTE

1. Gerring (2007, p. 117) cites Einstein in his discussion of 'the confirmatory (least-likely) crucial case: '… the first important empirical demonstration of the theory of relativity, which took the form of a single-event prediction on the occasion of the May 29, 1919 solar eclipse'.

REFERENCES

Archer, M. 1988 *Culture and Agency: The Place of Culture in Social Theory*. Cambridge: Cambridge University Press.

Archer, M. 1995 *Realist Social Theory: The Morphogenetic Approach*. Cambridge: Cambridge University Press.

Archer, M. 2003 *Structure, Agency and the Internal Conversation*. Cambridge: Cambridge University Press.

Becker, H.S. 1992 'Cases, causes, conjunctures, stories and imagery' in H.S. Becker and C.C. Ragin (Eds) *What Is a Case? Exploring the Foundations of Social Inquiry*. Cambridge: Cambridge University Press.

Bhaskar, R. 1978 *A Realist Theory of Science*. Sussex: Harvester Press.

Callil, C. 2006 *Bad Faith: A Forgotten History of Family and Fatherland*. London: Jonathan Cape.

Callinicos, A. 2006 *The Resources of Critique*. Cambridge: Polity Press.

Cressey, D.R. 1953 *Other People's Money*. New York: Free Press.

Daston, L.J. (Ed.) 2000 *Biographies of Scientific Objects*. Chicago: University of Chicago Press.

Davey Smith, G. 2000 'Learning to live with complexity: ethnicity, socioeconomic position, and health in Britain and the United States' *American Journal of Public Health* 90(11): 1694–1698.

Dyson, S.M., Cochran, F., Culley, L., Dyson, S.E., Kennefick, A., Kirkham, M., Morris, P., Sutton, F. and Squire, P. 2007 'Ethnicity questions and antenatal screening for sickle cell/thalassaemia (EQUANS) in England: observation and interview study' *Journal of Critical Public Health* 17(1): 31–43.

Fairclough, N., Jessop, B. and Sayer, A. 2001 'Critical realism and semiosis'. Paper presented at the International Association for Critical Realism Annual Conference, Roskilde, Denmark. Online, available: http://www.raggedclaws.com/criticalrealism/archive/iacr_conference_2001/nfairclough_scsrt.pdf.

Fischer, S. 1993 'The role of macroeconomic factors in growth' *Journal of Monetary Economics* 32(3): 485–512.

Gee, J.P. 2000 'Identity as an analytic lens for research in education' *Review of Research in Education* 25: 99–125.

Gerring, J. 2007 *Case Study Research: Principles and Practices*. Cambridge: Cambridge University Press.

Gomm, R., Hammersley, M. and Foster, P. (Eds) 2000 *Case Study Method*. London: Sage.

Greenwood, J.D. 1994 *Realism, Identity and Emotion: Reclaiming Social Psychology*. London: Sage.

Hacking, I. 1992 'World making by kind making: child abuse as an example' in M. Douglas and D. Hull (Eds) *How Classification Works*. Edinburgh: Edinburgh University Press.

Hacking, I. 2002 *Historical Ontology*. Cambridge, MA: Harvard University Press.

Layder, D. 1998 'The reality of social domains: implications for theory and method' in T. May and M. Williams (Eds) *Knowing the Social World*. Buckingham, UK: Open University Press.

Leaitch, W.R., Bottenheim, J.W., Biesenthal, T.A., Li, S.-M., Liu, P.S.K., Asalian, K., Dryfhout-Clark, H., Hopper, F. and Brechtel, F. 1999 'A case study of gas-to-particle conversion in an eastern Canadian forest' *Journal of Geophysical Research* 104 (D7), 8095–8112.

Pawson, R. 1989 *A Measure for Measures: A Manifesto for Empirical Sociology*. London: Routledge.

Ragin, C.C. 1992 '"Casing" and the processes of social inquiry' in C.C. Ragin and H.S. Becker (Eds) *What Is a Case? Exploring the Foundations of Social Inquiry*. Cambridge: Cambridge University Press.

Ragin, C.C. 1997 'Turning the tables: how case-oriented research challenges variable-oriented research' *Comparative Social Research* 16, 27–42.

Ragin, C.C. and Becker, H.S. (Eds) 1992 *What Is a Case? Exploring the Foundations of Social Inquiry.* Cambridge: Cambridge University Press.

Reardon, J. 2005 *Race to the Finish: Identity and Governance in an age of Genomics.* Princeton, NJ: Princeton University Press.

Reilly, B. 2000–01 'Democracy, ethnic fragmentation, and internal conflict: confused theories, faulty data, and the "crucial case" of Papua New Guinea' *International Security* 25(3), 162–185.

Riikka, A. and Puurunen, L. 2005 'Surface chemistry of atomic layer deposition: a case study for the trimethylaluminum/water process' *Journal of Applied Physics* 97(12).

Sayer, A. 2000 *Realism and Social Science.* London: Sage.

Sealey, A. 2006 'Are they who we think they are? Using corpus methods in the analysis of self-representation'. Paper presented at the joint international conference of the British Association for Applied Linguistics and the Irish Association for Applied Linguistics at University College, Cork, Ireland, 7–9 September 2006.

Sealey, A. and Carter, B. 2001 'Social categories and sociolinguistics: applying a realist approach' *International Journal of the Sociology of Language* 152: 1–19.

Sealey, A. and Carter, B. 2004 *Applied Linguistics as Social Science.* London: Continuum.

Stake, R.E. 2000 'The case study method in social inquiry' in R. Gomm, M. Hammersley and P. Foster (Eds) *Case Study Method.* London: Sage.

Stueber, K.R. 2006 'How to structure a social theory?: a critical response to Anthony King's *The Structure of Social Theory*' *Philosophy of the Social Sciences* 36(1): 95–104.

Wieviorka, M. 1992 'Case studies: history or sociology?' in C.C. Ragin and H.S. Becker (Eds) *What Is a Case? Exploring the Foundations of Social Inquiry.* Cambridge: Cambridge University Press.

4

Single-Case Probabilities

Malcolm Williams and Wendy Dyer

INTRODUCTION

The history of probability can be thought of as a history of frustrated causality. Humans have always wanted to answer 'why' questions, but since the advent of modern science this desire has taken the form of a quest for law-like explanation – a desire to demonstrate what it is that determines something should happen under particular circumstances. That is, an instance of a phenomenon X should be explained by a covering law appropriate to an explanation of all instances of the x kind. This chapter claims to offer a limited easement of that frustration by beginning from a different place, both in causal and probabilistic thinking. It is an argument for causal explanation, but one based on the measurable probabilities of the single case. This, we maintain, can provide explanations of underlying structures, rather than leading to causal laws.

The quest for regularity and causal explanations of such regularities has lain at the heart of modern science, including social science. In the social sciences and also in the natural sciences, outside of physics and chemistry, what are termed causal laws have been the exception rather than the rule. In social science there has long been an anti-causal tradition, running from the hermeneutics of Vico down to the various 'post-critique' epistemologies of the present day, which denies the legitimacy of the search for causal explanations of the social world. Nevertheless, historically, the social science mainstream has pursued causal explanations. Physics has long had the luxury of laws, such as motion or thermodynamics, in which phenomena will, under given circumstances, behave in a regular apparently deterministic ways: heavy objects will fall to earth. In an isolated system there will be a net energy loss. There may be local exceptions to this determinism, but these are known and can be accounted for. In biology and social science, such deterministic behaviour is unknown[1] or at least as yet undiscovered. Causality in these sciences has long been expressed probabilistically. Put simply, if the certainty of an event is 1 and the impossibility of that event is 0, then the closer the odds of that event happening are to 1, the greater our reasons to believe that the prior phenomena associated with that event are causal. Whilst probabilistic explanation has the advantage of providing a specification of the likelihood of an event, its possibility or impossibility in the classic causal sense can never be determined. Causal explanation is frustrated.

Probabilistic explanation in the social sciences does not always claim to be causal and indeed in the period of its introduction in the late nineteenth and early twentieth century, was overtly anti-causal (Goldthorpe 2001, p. 1). This reflected a more widespread influential view in science that causal language was superfluous to explanation (Russell 1919). However, although at various times a non-causal probabilistic explanation has been prominent, for most part probability has formed the basis of causal claims in social science (Abbot 1998). Probabilistic explanation in social science, both causal and non-causal, has been based on three different interpretations of probability: the frequency interpretation, the propensity interpretation and the subjectivist interpretation. The latter is much less commonly associated with causal explanation (although see Spohn 2001) and its reasoning resides in the ability to measure personal beliefs about the probability of an event. Both the frequency and propensity interpretations are derived from the actual or observed objective properties of a situation, although their individual reasoning is somewhat different. The frequency interpretation has dominated, and only very recently have propensity interpretations found support in social science. Generally, and we will say more about this presently, frequency interpretations derive their probabilities from the relative frequency of an event in a known sequence, whereas the propensity interpretation is based on the dispositions or tendencies of a particular situation. In the version of the latter that we set out here, reasoning begins from the individual case rather than the frequency.

Our argument is not to dismiss the utility of the frequency interpretation to macro-level explanation, but to argue that the propensity interpretation of probability has superior properties in respect of the explanation of the relationship of micro- or meso-level events to those at a macro level.[2]

We begin the chapter with a brief description of the frequency interpretation as utilised in causal models in survey research, its most common manifestation in social science. We argue that such models can only deliver probabilistic inference at a macro level and crucially treat specific events (the frequency) as 'ideal' events in contrast to single-case probability (derived from the propensity interpretation), which treats them and their probabilistic relationship to other events as real properties of the world.

In the second part of the chapter, we illustrate our argument with an empirical example of the derivation of single-case probabilities. This example comes from research by one of us (W.D.) on Custody Diversion Teams, in the North East of England.

CAUSAL EXPLANATION IN SURVEY RESEARCH

Social science students are always told that association does not mean causation. What is usually meant by this is that, however strongly two variables are correlated, it is illegitimate to claim that one variable causes another, even when it can be shown that variable A precedes variable B in time. Causal analysis in surveys proceeds on the basis of the identification of third and subsequent variables that might causally contribute to an outcome.

The principle of causal analysis is simple: suppose an association between parental income and university entrance is observed. If this relationship remains, even after we have controlled for other variables, such as the existence of bursaries, parental participation in higher education, etc., then we might claim that low participation is caused by low parental income. If it does not, the association is artefactual and other possibilities are explored, such as low participation and low income being caused by a third or subsequent variable(s). In such a simple model there will be a good number of students from low-income households who do participate, so other variables must be added to the model to explain them. Some models will adopt procedures, such as logistic regression, that add in variables and attempt to produce the best 'fit' to explain more and more of the variance in the model. On this basis, it is claimed, we get closer and closer to an accurate specification of causes.

The language of causal analysis implies necessity but the relationships remain probabilistic – that the relationships are measured in terms of statistical significance and association (Winship and Sobel 2004, pp. 485–486). Although models can be very sophisticated, it is impossible to move beyond an intricate web of probabilistic relationships. The level and kind of inference made in causal models will vary enormously. The relatively simple version we outline is usually associated with *post hoc* survey analysis, but different kinds of causal claims can arise in the use of true longitudinal models where causal direction at least is more readily identified. Similarly manipulation through experiment emulates much more closely the necessary relationships of singular causation, although its possibilities and efficacies are challenged both on the grounds of external validity and on the issue of 'violation of assumptions', such as those made in treatment assignment (to experimental or control groups makes) (Heckman 1997, Byrne 2002, pp. 84–90). However, without exception, causal analysis – even sophisticated manipulation methods such as counterfactual analysis (Winship and Sobel 2004) – must rely on the identification of sufficient conditions expressed as probabilities.

This inescapable conclusion was realised by Hubert Blalock, who is often credited as a founder of modern non-experimental causal analysis. In *Causal Inference in Nonexperimental Research* (1961), Blalock makes clear at the beginning that the identification of the necessity,[3] of causes is not achievable and that 'causal' relationships can only be inferred. Consequently, he advocated the development of models of social reality, which were not representations of the reality

itself, but heuristics[4] to help us infer how reality might work:

> One admits that causal thinking belongs completely on the theoretical level and that causal laws can never be demonstrated empirically. But this does not mean that it is not helpful to *think* causally and to develop causal models that have implications that are indirectly testable. (Blalock 1961, p. 6 emphasis in original)

Blalock discusses the various difficulties that arise in constructing 'realistic' models of reality and in particular those incorporating all of the variables that might provide an explanation and the mathematical representation of those variables. Ultimately, however sophisticated a model, certain simplifying assumptions must be made and '*at some point we must assume that the effects of confounding factors are negligible*' (Blalock 1961, p. 26 emphasis in original) and causes can be inferred.

As a tool to explain and predict macro-level phenomena, causal inference is undoubtedly useful. However, social science is more often than not concerned to explain the processes at work that lie between the individual and the meso-or macro level. In social science (and specifically in social theory) it is maintained that the actions of individuals produce the social and that the social will influence, enable or constrain individuals in their actions. Yet frequencies allow us to say nothing in respect of these relationships in either direction about an individual agent, or event. We can talk about a location having an offender rate of 5% amongst 18- to 25-year-old males, but we know that this does not mean that a given individual 20-year-old male will have a 5% chance of offending; his chances might be very much less or very much more. The 5% is an average or 'ideal' for 18- to 25-year-old males. This problem is also found in physical systems, which can rarely be explained through deterministic laws and must be explained probabilistically. Thus many physical laws are probabilistic or 'ideal' laws (e.g. Boyle's Law), but the difference is that such laws require only macro-level explanation, no one asks for a causal explanation in relation to (say) an individual molecule of a gas. In social science, individual and meso-level explanation is a legitimate and necessary task.

WHAT SHOULD WE EXPECT FROM A CAUSAL EXPLANATION?

The philosophy of causality has a long history and, for our purposes, some drastic simplification is required. In twentieth-century social science, one could discern three versions of causality: necessary, probabilistic and realist.

The first of these – the necessary – is closest to the common-sense version of causality and can be specified as A caused B, if A preceded B in time and no other causal agents, such as C or D, were involved.[5] It is what Aristotle termed an 'efficient cause', and Mill 'method of agreement'. It is also impossible to establish and the closest we can get is to witness causality as a single event. There are two reasons for this. The first is that causes are always underdetermined. A car jumps the lights and another car collides with it. In this case, we can say that the cause of the crash was that the first car jumped the lights. But we cannot generalise beyond the instance to make any kind of law-like statement about lights and car crashes. Cars jump lights and there are no crashes and there are plenty of crashes when cars don't jump lights. The second reason is that causal sequences exhibit a version of Zeno's paradox. We might see a watch fall to the ground and smash; the common-sense explanation is that it was the impact with the ground that caused the watch to smash but, as a physicist would point out, there were several – possibly an infinite number – of 'links' in the 'causal chain' between the watch hitting the ground and its breaking apart. To specify these would take us on a journey into the subatomic level. Versions of necessary causality have nevertheless found their supporters in (for example) analytic induction and in the work of Robert McIver (1964/1942).

Probabilistic causality attempts resolve the problems of necessary causality through the observation of many instances of A → B under a range of circumstances and derives the probability of a directional relationship holding. As we have noted, a causal explanation is when A → B holds under most circumstances C...n. Often, this is defined as a probabilistic relationship when the advent of variable(s) A raises the probability of B occurring. Probabilistic versions of causality are by far the most common in both natural and social science. Several variants on them offer alternative ways of manipulating or interpreting the data in models (see the papers in Galavotti et al. 2001 for various discussions of these).

Realist causality is epistemologically between the two of these and has been articulated explicitly only in the last two decades or so. In its most common contemporary version (first suggested by Roy Bhaskar 1978, 1998), it seeks the necessity of a causal connection, but like probabilistic causality it allows that all necessary and specific conditions will not be manifested and that the nature of a causal connection must be theorised from incomplete data. However, unlike probabilistic causality it asserts the necessity of a mechanism in the final instance to produce a given causal outcome (see, for example, Sayer 1992, pp. 110–116). The problem for realist causality is the empirical identification of necessity, what Ray Pawson has termed 'realist closure' (Pawson 1989, pp. 197–224, Williams 2003), which – ontologically – makes them identical to the first version of causality. Consequently, realists such as Pawson have attempted to use the tools of probabilistic causal models to reveal the existence of underlying mechanisms and the circumstances under which the mechanisms operate.

These very brief sketches confirm the limitation of causal claims: that they can only refer to classes of object or event, and not to specific objects or events, because these events and objects will retain either unique properties and/or unique connectives with other events or objects. To specify all of the events and objects and their connectives would be to realise Laplace's conjecture of knowing the present state of the universe completely and predicting all of its future states (Williams 2000, p. 17).

In his later work, Karl Popper came to realise this paradox: that we need to establish causal patterns in the world, but apparently we can only ever know the world probabilistically. This led him to a version of causality that was probabilistic but, like the realist version described above, was grounded in the 'dispositions' or 'properties' not just of a single event or object but of the whole situation in which outcomes are realised (Popper 1995). Popper's theory of 'single-case probabilities' is at the same time a theory of probability and a theory of causality. In the earlier iterations of this theory (Popper 1957, 1959), the emphasis lies with probability, but in what was his last published work he explicitly advances his theory as a causal one (Popper 1995). This historic detail is worth noting, because his theory – unlike virtually all other theories of probability and causality – is a unified theory that sees them as two sides of the same coin.

Frequency theories of probability stand in for causality, rather than expressing it.[6] They are essentially heuristics (as Blalock conceded) and have their origins in an empiricist epistemology that is sceptical about the nature of existence, claiming only that we can observe the properties of phenomenon and the logical connectives between them.

POPPER'S SINGLE-CASE PROBABILITIES

Popper regarded causality as a special case of probability, where 1 is the certainty of an outcome and 0 is its impossibility. Thus 1 is when something must be caused and 0 is when it cannot be; all else is probability tending towards 0 or 1. Where Popper differs from the 'frequentists' is that for him this is an ontological and not an epistemological issue. That is, probabilities are properties of situations themselves and not just an expression of our apparent knowledge of them. This is easily illustrated. However, in the social world, prior statements about zeros and ones are all but impossible to make; a physical example must suffice: there is a zero probability of an individual flying unaided to the moon, but a slight yet nevertheless non-zero, probability of that person flying there in a spacecraft.

In the social world, zeros and ones are constantly realised, but they have a uniqueness that we have already described and from them it is very hard to predict the kind of necessity apparently entailed in some physical examples. However, some situations have probabilities very close to 1 and others very close to 0. Crucially, these probabilities change as a result of the realisation (as zeros or ones) of other connected events. The probability of offending for young black male growing up in an impoverished inner city is not just an actuarial calculation but a characteristic of that person that derives from his objective situation. That probability will change as a result of his interaction with the changing situation, whereby he will move closer to a '1' (he offends), or closer to '0',[7] when his circumstances so change as to reduce his propensity to offend.

What is important in Popper's theory is that probability lies not just in the individual case but in the situation in which the case is located. Probabilities (as real properties) are nested in other probabilities. As a metaphysical statement this has a feel of intuitive authenticity and historically prefigured much of the reasoning underlying theories of complexity (see Chapter 1). Empirically, however, it is hard to see how one can make claims about the probability of the single case without knowing the probabilities of the events in the nested situation. Which of course in Popper's definition of the single-case probability is the probability of the total situation; it is the same thing. Although we know that every situation has an inherent ontological probability, to know this we need to know the probability of every other situation that could change the probability of the first.

Popper's theory actually combines a concept of the 'case' as a realised outcome and a propensity interpretation of probability.

Others separate these: Ian Hacking (1965) and Donald Gillies (2000) retain the concept of propensity but maintain that those propensities can only be known in the long run through the observation of frequencies. Thus, the throw of a fair die will, in the long run, produce a frequency of 1 : 6 for the throw of each side. Theoretically, one could apply this to results from a social survey, although the sample size would need to approximate the population and the properties of that population would be probabilistic outcomes of other situations. Empirically, long-run (non-case) propensity theories could deliver no more than their frequency counterparts and would differ only in their statistical reasoning.

MEASURING THE SINGLE CASE

Whilst it would be empirically impossible to know all of the prior probabilities in the realisation of an event, patterns of antecedents can be described taxonomically. That is, causal outcome C1 can be differentiated from causal outcome C2 if we know the antecedent outcomes. All outcomes are zeros or ones, but the aim is to (initially) discover the differing antecedent outcomes (themselves zeros and ones) amongst cases. Once a taxonomic analysis has been conducted, it then seems possible to identify causes as predictors of future states. In this section, we describe in some detail an attempt to operationalise single-case probabilities in empirical research.

Our exemplar research was a two-stage analysis of referrals to a Custody Diversion Team (CDT) in the North East of England. The first stage used cluster analysis of data in a relational database to identify a number of psychiatric and criminal 'career types' experienced by mentally disordered offenders referred to a CDT. In the second stage, discriminant analysis was used to elucidate which variate traces[8] describing the cases and the nature of the intervention interventions were operating as control parameters in determining the trajectories of cases towards different future states.

Health and Social Service CDTs were introduced in England at the beginning of the 1990s because of concerns about the prevalence of psychiatric disorders in the prison population (Gunn, et al. 1991) and the possibility that the latter might be increasing as a result of a process of transcarceration/criminalisation (Weller and Weller 1988). The aim of these teams was to divert mentally disordered offenders away from the criminal justice system and prison and into care and treatment by the health and social services. The claim was that a policy of diversion was a positive step because it avoided the stigma attached to a prison sentence and the development of a long and perhaps notorious criminal career by ensuring people received the care and treatment they required. The question was: did the people referred to CDTs exhibit evidence of exposure to a transcarceration/criminalisation process; and what impact did it have on the psychiatric and criminal careers of those referred?

Relational database

To explore single-case probabilities one need access to data describing a sufficiently large number of cases. Relational databases offer one such example and are now the conventional tools of administrative record keeping by organisations in general and by those organisations concerned with the handling of 'cases' in particular. Medical records take this form, as do those of other human services agencies, including social work and criminal justice institutions. It is important to note that cases are not necessarily individual people. They might be households, extended families, neighbourhoods, localities, regions, schools, hospitals, penal institutions – indeed any set of entities that might be the 'cases' in the case variable (or variate trace) matrix that is generated by any form of survey process.[9]

The example we use here is a relational database individually designed and developed to meet the needs of a highly specialised CDT. At the time the research was undertaken, 1011 individuals had been referred to the team.

The most obvious design that would meet all three of these needs was one that traced the case trajectories of the people referred to the service. For example, it began with a detailed description of the criminal and psychiatric history of an individual, followed by the reasons behind the current referral (including current psychiatric status and any current offences), what actions the team took and, finally, the outcomes. If this person was re-referred to the team at a later date these administrative steps would be repeated: the history would be updated and a second referral record created, beginning with the reasons behind this second referral and so on. The database played a central role in the functioning of the CDT.

In a relational data model, the database is conceptualised as a number of tables (called relations or relational tables). The object type (which in this case was the mentally disordered offender) in the infological model is represented by one table for each cluster of information (Figure 4.1) where a history of criminal convictions is stored in the Previous Convictions table, current demographic information is stored in the Clients table, and details pertaining to each client's current referral to the CDT is held in the Referrals table.

Each table contains one column for each referral variable. The Clients table contains one row for each individual person referred to the CDT. This, however, does not hold for all other tables. One individual might be referred to the team many times, and might have many previous convictions; that person might have committed a number of current offences and have more than one 'social care need' identified by the team. Each piece of

Previous convictions

RecordID	ClientID	Court_Date	Offence_category	Result
37	52	05/07/93	Violence	Probation > 12 Months
46	53	14/04/87	Theft	Youth custody < 12 months
47	53	16/12/87	Burglary	Prob.ord.wthcond>12 months
48	53	03/02/89	Burglary	CSO
49	53	28/07/89	Theft	Youth custody < 12 months
50	53	29/01/90	Theft	Not known
51	53	23/08/93	Motoring	Prob.ord.withcond<12 months
52	53	13/01/95	Motoring	Prob.ord.wthcond>12 months
53	53	22/03/95	Motoring	Fine
54	53	28/07/95	Violence	Probation > 12 Months
55	53	13/11/95	Property/non-violent	Not known
56	53	13/11/95	Theft	Probation > 12 Months
57	53	29/02/96	Motoring	Prob.ord.wthcond>12 months
58	53	29/02/96	Motoring	Prob.ord.wthcond>12 months
59	53	29/02/96	Motoring	Prob.ord.wthcond>12 months
1276	53	29/02/96	Motoring	Prob.ord.wthcond>12 months

Referrals

RecordID	ClientID	Referral reason	Agency	Referral receipt date
45	52	Advice	Police	01/08/95
46	52	Advice	CJS	08/08/95
47	53	Advice	Probation	07/06/95
46	53	Assessment	Probation	31/01/96
48	54	Information	Health	22/05/95
49	55	Advice	Police	09/08/95

Clients

RecordID	Surname	Sex	Age	RecordID
52	Alias	Male	32	52
53	Smith	Male	26	53
54	Orr	Male	19	54
55	Jones	Female	40	55

Figure 4.1   Relational data model of the custody diversion team.

information is stored in one row, so for those with a number of previous convictions for instance there will be a number of rows within the table containing information about them. In Figure 4.1, for example, Mr Alias has one previous conviction for violence and has been referred to the team twice, whereas Mr Smith has 15 various previous convictions and has also been referred to the team twice.

Cluster analysis

The research aimed at identifying underlying structures or mechanisms and cluster analysis was initially chosen for its very practical advantages in identifying and mapping the different psychiatric and criminal careers experienced by people referred to the CDT, and the divergent paths their careers took as a consequence of the team's actions. The processing of cases by the diversion team was observed through time in terms of a series of classifications of the cases at stages in their 'career' within the system. The temporal dimension was not calendar time but rather a stage in the process. The CDT, like other systems of this kind, 'processed' cases and what was interesting and important was what difference the processing made to the outcome for the case. It was possible to describe this using stage-ordered classificatory procedures. Categories of entry could be distinguished (i.e. distinctions among original cases), categories of processing (differences in what was done to individual cases) and categories of outcome (what happened to the cases at the end of the process). Movement could then be mapped throughout the intervention process.

Cluster analysis is essentially a classificatory procedure and its explanatory and predictive power lies in the ability to construct a model of social reality, which might then be seen as a realistic scenario for future similar situations. Unsurprisingly, advocates of cluster analysis have noted its methodological connections and possibilities in terms of neural networks and simulation analyses (Byrne 2002).

Unlike variable-driven approaches, which begin from a sample of individuals, each bearing measurable characteristics, cluster analysis begins from the case, not the variable, and determines whether given categories of a particular case are similar enough to fall into groups or clusters. Cluster analyses are taxonomic and originally developed in biology to 'gather all possible data on organisms of interest, estimate the degree of similarity among these organisms, and use a clustering method to place relatively similar organisms into the same groups' (Aldenderfer and Blashfield 1984, p. 8). In a social setting, the 'case', usually an individual agent, will at any given point in his or her life possess characteristics that can be classified to show where these are held in common with other agents. Unlike variable analysis, one begins from the case and seeks characteristics held in common, rather than beginning with the characteristics and seeking their association with cases.

Clearly, every individual will have a unique biography and there must be some prior notion of what will count as a classification, but this is not necessarily arbitrary, as the case study below will show, and is usually driven by a particular contextual concern – here offending behaviour. Each offender will have a history of prior events that have shaped his or her current situation. Some offenders with the same characteristics will have similar antecedent states, some different. Conversely, offenders with different characteristics might at some point in the past have shared characteristics. At a number of measurable points there will be bifurcations where things happen to an individual, or they make particular choices based on beliefs and desires. Many of the things that happen to individuals will be evidence of structures, where propensities become realised.

Clusters represent these bifurcations, Popper's 'zero' and 'one' outcome states. Each case is first put into its own 'cluster', so in a dataset of 1000, there will be 1000 clusters. At each level of analysis, the clusters are combined, which allows us to trace antecedent conditions and their bifurcations

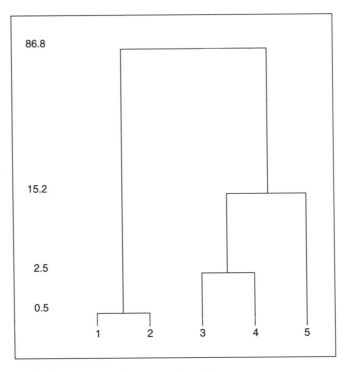

Figure 4.2   Clustering dendogram (Everitt 1993, p. 15).

into current states. The technique is therefore hierarchical. It can be visually represented as a dendogram (Figure 4.2). The usual form of graphic output from a hierarchical cluster analysis is a tree (dendogram). The tree provides a visual representation of the cluster structure of the hierarchy.

Cluster analysis is based on the premise that the most accurate information is available when each case constitutes a group. Consequently, as the number of clusters is systematically reduced from k, k-1, k-2, … 1, the grouping of increasingly dissimilar cases yields less precise information. At each stage in the procedure, the goal is to form a group such that the sum of squared within-group deviations about the group mean of each profile variable is minimised for all profile variables at the same time. The value of the objective function is expressed as the sum of the within-group sum of squares (called the error sum of squares, ESS).[10]

The research project employed a two-stage cluster analysis. Three datasets were created representing the three career stages: (1) History; (2) First Referral; and (3) First Referral Outcomes.

First-stage cluster

Cluster analysis was undertaken within each of these quite separate datasets, thereby describing the state of the system at discrete periods of time. Each emergent cluster was a slice through the psychiatric/criminal career of an individual case, bringing into high relief each discrete time period used to describe careers but losing an overall portrait of longitudinal careers that was necessary to evaluate the impact of the actions of the team. Researching the careers of mentally disordered offenders rendered inadequate any simple focus on clearly delineated and significant episodes. What was needed was a technique that uncovered the complex ways in which some individuals experienced one type of institutional career and others experienced another type, depending on different

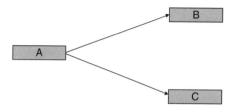

Figure 4.3 Nested probability within a Markov chain.

circumstances and the actions of others. In other words, a method that could be used to trace the movements of cases from one state to another through a process of bifurcation, which was dependent on key changes in the magnitude of underlying causal variables. The process of bifurcation implied neither simple linear determination (constant conjunction where if A happened then B happened) nor random process where anything could happen. Instead, what was implied was complex change, so that in the first bifurcation if A happened then B *or* C happened, depending on small initial variations in the form of A. The observed states can therefore be seen as nested probabilities within a Markov chain[11] (Figure 4.3).

The link between the discrete periods or slices through a criminal/psychiatric career was provided by the individual or the case referred to the team.

Second-stage cluster

Following first-stage cluster analysis, each individual was located in one cluster at the History stage, then in another cluster at the First Referral stage and finally in a last cluster at the First Referral Outcomes stage. The next step, which involved mapping or tracing the movement of people from one set of clusters in a discrete time period to the next, using further cluster analysis and cross-tabulations, brought into focus each complete career structure.

Five different types of career were identified (Figure 4.4). Careers One and Two describe experiences of medicalisation – violent offenders with no psychiatric history who were referred, assessed and diagnosed

but had no health or social care needs identified and were not referred again. Careers Three and Four describe experiences of criminalisation – violent offenders with a psychiatric history, half of whom (Career Three) were referred, assessed and diagnosed, had health or social care needs identified and were not referred again; the remainder (Career Four) were not assessed or diagnosed, nor did they have needs identified and consequently all were re-referred repeatedly. Career Five represents neither medicalisation or criminalisation – individuals referred for information and for whom little else is known.

This two-stage cluster analysis uncovered and mapped the different psychiatric and criminal careers experienced by separate individuals and the different paths their careers took as a consequence of the team's actions; and then identified the shared experiences or types of career that could be used to group people together to generalise which actions had a positive or negative impact on which types of people. Changes could be mapped over time so that it became possible not to predict as such, but to act so that some things happened and others did not.

Supporters of the frequency interpretation of probability are 'deeply uneasy about clustering methods because in general they are not constructed around a central concern with inference from samples to universes' (Byrne 2002, p. 100), although the classifications produced are robust and, if the underlying taxonomy is real, different clustering methods will produce similar classifications. However, as we noted, they are slices through the lifeworld. We can classify and produce stable classifications at different stages but we also want to know what happens between those stages. What is the probability of nesting in the clusters? We need this information to fully understand the mechanism and the causal processes therein. Cluster analysis can tell us a lot about the case, and how the case compares with other cases, but it cannot tell us what the comparative objective probability is of that case being associated with any given characteristic, or the characteristics in

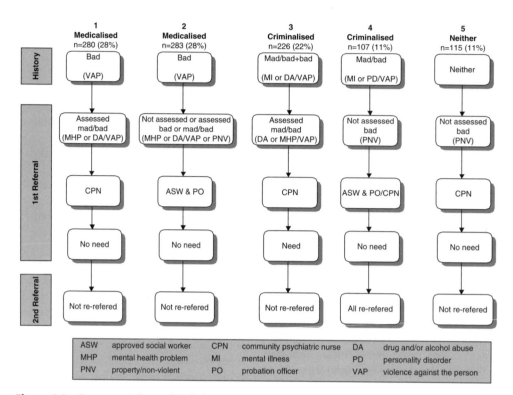

Figure 4.4   Career typology of individuals referred to the custody diversion team (CDT) for mentally disordered offenders (n = 1011).

total that make up the antecedent nesting of characteristics.

Rather simplistically, we could simply work out the comparative odds ratios of cases to variables, but this is little different to variable analysis, just in reverse! At one point, this was our reluctant conclusion, but a second-stage analysis after cluster classifications does indeed seem possible through the use of discriminant analysis.

Discriminant analysis

Discriminant analysis (DA), also known as Discriminant Function Analysis has some similarities with cluster analysis in that it is, or can be used as, a classificatory tool. It allows the researcher to classify cases into groups and to test theoretical assumptions through observing whether cases are classified as predicted. The independent variate traces (or variables) should be at least at interval level. DA builds a linear

discriminant function, which is used to classify observations. The overall fit is assessed by looking at the degree of difference in group means using Wilkes lambda or by calculating the Mahalanobis distance. The calculation of the Mahalanobis distance in the classification permits the derivation of the single-case probabilities. The procedure described here has two stages.

First-stage discriminant analysis

A model is built using data from cases for whom we know the outcome we are interested in predicting. Using the data described in the cluster analysis above, this would be whether people were re-referred to the CDT or not following discharge. The dataset is divided into two parts: one-half or two-thirds can be designated as belonging to learning sample (in similar fashion to training data in neural networks) and the model can be developed using these. The remaining cases can be designated as belonging to the test sample against which the predictive accuracy of the model can be assessed later.

In order to build the model using the learning sample, first, the dependent variable is selected, which in this case is Referral Outcome, where cases could either be: (1) not re-referred – a positive outcome indicating that this person had not gone on to re-offend or otherwise become part of the 'psychiatric revolving door'; or (2) re-referred – a negative outcome indicating that a person had gone on to re-offend or had become part of the revolving door of psychiatric care. Second, all of the independent variables (psychiatric history and previous convictions, demographic details, current offence, CDT actions, outcomes from needs assessments, Court hearings, etc.) that might have an impact on outcome are selected. The stepwise method is employed and the output listing includes details of which variables are included in the functions and which functions are significant.

Second-stage discriminant analysis

When the model has been finalised and the discriminant functions have been derived using the learning sample of data, how well can we predict to which group a particular case belongs from the test sample? Here classification functions are used (these are *not* to be confused with the discriminant functions). The classification functions can be used to determine to which group each case most likely belongs. Each function allows us to compute classification scores for each case for each group in the model (learning sample), by applying a formula and then we can use the classification functions to directly compute classification scores for new cases (in the test sample). The classification functions are calculated using Mahalanobis distances. For each group in the model, we can determine the location of the point that represents the means for all variables in the multivariate space defined by the variables in the model. These points are called group *centroids*. For each test sample case we can then compute the Mahalanobis distances (of the respective case) from each of the

group centroids. The case can be classified as belonging to the group to which it is closest, that is, where the Mahalanobis distance is smallest.

The use of the Mahalanobis distances to produce the classification permits us to derive the case probabilities. The probability that a case belongs to a particular group is basically proportional to the Mahalanobis distance from that group centroid (it is not exactly proportional because a multivariate normal distribution around each centroid is assumed). Because the location of each case is computed from our prior knowledge of the values for that case on the variables in the model, these probabilities must be termed *posterior* probabilities. In other words, the posterior probability is the probability, based on our knowledge of the values of other variate traces, that the respective case belongs to a particular group.

The output from our first preliminary uses of discriminant analysis look very promising.

Classification functions

As described above, discriminant analysis has two sets of techniques based on the purpose of the analysis: descriptive discriminant analysis (DDA) and predictive discriminant analysis (PDA). As Huberty (1994) describes, 'where groups of units are known in advance and the purpose of the research is either to describe group differences [DDA] or to predict group membership [PDA] on the basis of response variable measures, discriminant analysis techniques are appropriate'. Stevens (1996) emphasises the distinction as follows, 'in predictive discriminant analysis the focus is on classifying subjects into one of several groups, whereas in descriptive discriminant analysis the focus is on revealing major differences among the groups'. Whitaker (1997) argues that that each type of discriminant analysis has a different purpose and, as such, it is unlikely that both types are relevant to the research question(s). However, our purpose is both to determine which of the variables we used to identify the five psychiatric/criminal careers discriminated between the groups (using the test sample), that is, which variable(s) were the best predictors of a negative (re-referral to the CDT) or positive (not re-referred) outcome; and to assign new cases (our test sample) to groups based on the composite scores of our predictor variables (i.e. Mahalanobis distance).

There are three types of DA: direct, hierarchical and stepwise. In direct DA, all of the variables enter the equations at once; in hierarchical DA they enter according to a schedule set by the researcher; and in stepwise DA, statistical criteria alone determine the order of entry. The third method is the most popular and therefore is the one used in our initial explorations. As we had five groups we needed to estimate 5 − 1 (i.e. 4) discriminant functions (where the first function provides the most overall discrimination between groups, the second provides second most and so on). Within the first function, the variable with the largest standardised canonical discriminant function coefficient (where the larger the coefficient, the greater the contribution of the respective variable to the discrimination between groups) was the outcome of the first referral 'need' (Figure 4.4), that is, where referral to the CDT resulted in the identification of an individual's health and/or social care needs. The standardised discriminant function coefficient of the variable '1st referral outcome = need' was 0.970, which, bearing in mind that these coefficients

vary between ±1, means that this variable makes a large contribution, that is, it is important. This finding is emphasised by the output from the factor structure matrix (where the factor structure coefficients are the correlations between the variables in the model and the discriminant functions). Here the variable '1st referral outcome = need' has a value 0.777 and the variable '1st referral outcome = no need' has a value of −0.777. The fact that one has a positive correlation whereas the other has a negative one indicates that group separation is determined by the difference between these two variables.

The summary table (Table 4.1) provides an indication of the success rate for the predictions of membership of the grouping variable's categories using the discriminant functions developed in the analysis. The table indicates the overall success rate is 94.8%. It shows that 'Criminalised 3' was most accurately classified, with 100% of cases correct. Note that incorrectly classified 'Medicalised 1' were more likely to be classified as 'Criminalised 4', and that incorrectly classified 'Criminalised 4' were more likely to be classified as 'Neither 5'.

The next problem is whether knowledge of the people referred to the CDT, and the subsequent actions taken by the team, could be used to predict the likelihood of someone going on to be re-referred to the service (a negative outcome indicating that this person would probably go on to re-offend or become

Table 4.1 Classification results[a]

	CLUSTER maximum, variable clusters (history to 6th referral)		Predicted group membership					Total
			1	2	3	4	5	
Original	Count	1	97	3	0	6	1	107
		2	3	269	3	2	3	280
		3	0	0	115	0	0	115
		4	7	1	0	259	16	283
		5	5	3	0	0	218	226
	%	1	90.7	2.8	.0	5.6	.9	100.0
		2	1.1	96.1	1.1	.7	1.1	100.0
		3	.0	.0	100.0	.0	.0	100.0
		4	2.5	.4	.0	91.5	5.7	100.0
		5	2.2	1.3	.0	.0	96.5	100.0

[a]94.8% of original grouped cases correctly classified.

part of the revolving door of psychiatric care) or not going on to be re-referred (a positive outcome indicating that this person probably would not go on to re-offend or otherwise become part of the 'psychiatric revolving). The preliminary analysis has shown that four discriminant functions can be generated, and that these can predict 94.8% of the cases correctly (Table 4.1). However, what about future clients for whom only the data on the predicting variables are known? Again, in our explorations we used the third of our dataset aside as the test sample to assess the predictive accuracy of our model. The probabilities of membership in each of the five clusters was calculated based on discriminate scores and each case was allocated to the group for which it had the largest probability (Table 4.2). Again, the output from our preliminary uses of discriminate analysis to predict future cluster membership looks promising as the predictions offered look reasonable and can be readily explained.

DISCUSSION AND CONCLUSION

We do not claim to have resolved either the issue of causality or that of probability in our advocacy of analyses aimed at deriving single-case probabilities. Nor is it our claim that the method (and research in which it was applied) is the last word in single-case probability analysis. Indeed, the above is offered in the spirit of a Popperian conjecture!

Throughout this chapter (and indeed in Popper's version of single-case probability), there is an implicit commitment to realism. That is the belief in the existence of, and the desire to uncover, the real properties of the world. This is not the same as saying one can or will demonstrate what those properties are (and of course how would we know if we were right!). In Popper this takes the form of verisimilitude (or truth likeness) through the elimination of error (Popper 1979, pp. 47–48). Popper's advocacy of single-case probabilities, and our attempt to translate

Table 4.2 Predicting group membership using the training sample

PTID	Predicted group membership	Probabilities group 1[a]	Probabilities group 2[b]	Probabilities group 3[c]	Probabilities group 4[d]	Probabilities group 5[e]
52	1	0.974	0	0	0.026	0
53	5	0	0	0	0	1
54	3	0	0.008	0.992	0	0
55	4	0	0	0.013	0.987	0
56	2	0	0.998	0.002	0	0
57	2	0	0.998	0.001	0.001	0
58	4	0	0	0.016	0.984	0
60	5	0	0	0	0	1
61	1	1	0	0	0	0
62	4	0	0	0.013	0.987	0
63	3	0	0.008	0.992	0	0
64	2	0	0.998	0.001	0.001	0
65	2	0	0.999	0.001	0	0
66	4	0	0	0.013	0.987	0
67	1	1	0	0	0	0
68	2	0	0.999	0.001	0	0
69	4	0	0.001	0	0.999	0
70	5	0	0	0	0	1
71	1	0.963	0	0	0.036	0
72	3	0	0.008	0.992	0	0

[a] Probabilities of membership in group 1 for analysis 1
[b] Probabilities of membership in group 2 for analysis 1
[c] Probabilities of membership in group 3 for analysis 1
[d] Probabilities of membership in group 4 for analysis 1
[e] Probabilities of membership in group 5 for analysis 1

this empirically, is a fundamentally realist approach because it is aimed at uncovering the 'real' properties of the world.

The frequency interpretation of probability and its emergent probabilistic causal analysis treats cases as 'ideal' and the probability of the case is a function of the frequency distribution. In this approach, the reality of the *case* and its causal characteristics are not relevant. Whereas social scientists such as Blalock did not deny a reality to the social world, in practice they saw this as an unobtainable metaphysical ideal and opted instead for the heuristic of variable-based probabilistic causal models.

Realists in the Bhaskarian tradition, whilst rejecting this scepticism, offer no programme to demonstrate causality except a theoretical one. The method we describe here, in its first stage, uses a taxonomic method to show the causal patterns manifested in the bifurcations in case histories. In its second stage, it attaches probabilities to these outcomes. A crucial feature of the method is its hierarchical nature, which allows us to estimate the single-case probabilities as outcomes of prior nesting. Essentially, these must remain estimates because, as we noted above, the metaphysical problem of knowing the probability of causal outcome for a single case is insoluble.[12]

The issue of causality remains a tricky one. If there can be no necessity beyond the single case, then causal outcomes for the single case are always unique. The method we describe, because it begins with a taxonomy of the case, gets closer to identifying a 'cause' (in the efficient sense) than frequency-based causal analysis, yet we submit that this is not its most important feature. What is important and useful is to be able to talk about the probabilities of antecedent conditions that led to specific outcomes and to use this knowledge to produce explanations (and thus predictions) of phenomena. Of course one could use the language of 'causal powers' or 'mechanisms' in the regularities demonstrated, and this might have value, but to claim causes beyond individual outcomes is to rely on an unwarranted necessity.

The use of single-case probability analysis is in its very early stages. That it is not further advanced is probably mostly due to the long-term historic development of statistical tools to support methods of frequency-based methods within a methodological tradition of empiricism. These were most certainly not historically inevitable. Indeed, in the middle of the twentieth century von Mises (1951, p. 11) recognised the ontological limitations of the frequency distribution, but his commitment to the dominant (logical) empiricism of the time led him to deny the empirical possibility of deriving the probabilities attached to a single case. In the later years of the twentieth century, the alternative (yet nevertheless scientific approach) of realism gained its supporters. Causation is central to realism, but the frequency-based causal analysis does not suit realism well because it is derived from epistemological reasoning and either denies or ignores the possibility of knowing ontological characteristics. So, whereas single-case probability analysis might have some way to go to rival (or supplement) frequency approaches, it is our view that its principles at least should be embraced by realists as a very practical tool to uncover structures or mechanisms. Although, of course, this would require realists to mind their language when it comes to 'causal' claims!

NOTES

1. One could cite the death of an organism as a biologically determined outcome, but this outcome is reducible to explanation through thermodynamics, that is, living organisms are entropic systems.

2. We are using the terms 'micro', 'meso' and 'macro' as indicative of levels of society approximating to: interpersonal social contact; levels of association, such as trade unions, political parties, universities, large enterprises; structures at a national or international level, such as states or supra national formations. As Smelser (1997) has argued these boundaries are far from sharp and probably subject to historical revision.

3. Whilst the word 'determinism' illustrates well the apparent outcomes of classical laws of physics, in the following discussions of causality we use the term 'necessity' to avoid confusion with metaphysical versions of determinism.

4. I am using the term 'heuristic' here to indicate a problem-solving method where no algorithm exists. Thus, a heuristic method of analysis aims to construct a model of reality that is as close to that reality as possible.

5. The aforementioned manipuable and counterfactual theories of causality perhaps come closest to this (see Woodward 2001).

6. Both the frequency and propensity interpretations of probability are referred to as 'objective' probability, because each refers to an objective situation that exists independently of the observer's appraisal of it, whereas the prior odds in subjective probability are derived from observer estimation. Carnap (1950) distinguished the two kinds of objective probability as probability$_1$ and probability$_2$.

7. Zero would presumably be logically impossible for the young male because he would always have a propensity to offend, however small that is. In fact, zero could be achieved only as a logical impossibility when he was deemed no longer to be a 'young' man. This point is not entirely trivial and demonstrates that the logical outcomes of one and zero in the social world might be subject to local social construction.

8. We use the term 'variate trace' here after Byrne (2002), rather than 'variable'. Here, 'variate trace' refers to an evidential property of the single case, rather than 'ideal' case of frequency-based variable analysis.

9. Although we do not pursue this here, relational databases offer us the possibility of relating cases at one level to other 'containing levels' in a hierarchical data system, for example, of individuals to household membership and neighbourhood residence.

10. This can be expressed formally as ESS = $x_i^2 - 1/n \left(\sum \times i\right)^2$

11. A Markov chain is a time-series model (although not necessarily calendar time) in which a given probability is dependent only on the immediate preceding event. However, the approach described here differs from Markov methods, which usually take a 'black box' approach to preceding states of a system and are simply interested in prediction (see Byrne 2002, p. 122).

12. However, the use of a test sample and training sample allows us to test these estimates.

REFERENCES

Abbot, A. 1998 'The causal devolution' *Sociological Methods and Research* 27(2): 148–181.

Aldenderfer, M. and Blashfield, R. 1984 'Cluster analysis' Sage University Paper 44. Newbury Park, CA: Sage.

Bhaskar, R. 1978 *A Realist Theory of Science, 2nd edition*. Hemel Hempstead, UK: Harvester.

Bhaskar, R. 1998 *The Possibility of Naturalism, 2nd edition*. Brighton, UK: Harvester.

Blalock, H. 1961 *Causal Inference in Nonexperimental Research*. Chapel Hill, NC: University of North Carolina Press.

Byrne, D. 2002 *Interpreting Quantitative Data*. London: Sage.

Carnap, R. 1950 *Logical Foundations of Probability*. Chicago: Chicago University Press.

Everitt, B. 1993 *Cluster Analysis*. London: Heinemann.

Galavotti, M., Suppes, P. and Costantini, D. (Eds) 2001 *Stochastic Causality*. Stanford, CA: CSLI Publications.

Gillies, D. 2000 *Philosophical Theories of Probability*. London: Routledge.

Goldthorpe, J. 2001 'Causation, statistics and sociology' *European Sociological Review* 17(1): 1–20.

Gunn, J., Maden, A. and Swinton, M. 1991 'Treatment needs of prisoners with psychiatric disorders' *British Medical Journal* 303: 338–341.

Hacking, I. 1965 *The Logic of Statistical Inference*. Cambridge: Cambridge University Press.

Heckman, J. 1997 'Instrumental variables: a study of implicit behavioral assumptions used in making program evaluations' *Journal of Human Resources* 32: 441–462.

Huberty, C.J. 1994 *Applied Discriminant Analysis*. New York: Wiley and Sons.

McIver, R. 1964/1942 *Social Causation*. New York: Harper.

Pawson, R. 1989 *A Measure for Measures: A Manifesto for Empirical Sociology*. London: Routledge.

Popper, K. 1957 'The propensity interpretation of the calculus of probability, and the quantum theory' in S. Körner (Ed.) *Observation and Interpretation*, London: Butterworth Scientific.

Popper, K. 1959 'The propensity interpretation of probability' *British Journal for the Philosophy of Science* 10: 25–42.

Popper, K. 1979 *Objective Knowledge: An Evolutionary Approach, 2nd edition*. Oxford: Oxford University Press.

Popper, K. 1995 *A World of Propensities*. Bristol: Thoemmes.

Russell, B. 1919 'On the notion of a cause' *Proceedings of the Aristotelian Society* 13: 1–26.

Sayer, A. 1992 *Method in Social Science: A Realist Approach, 2nd edition*. London: Routledge.

Smelser, N. 1997 *Problematics of Sociology: The Georg Simmel Lectures, 1995*. Berkeley, CA: University of California Press.

Spohn, W. 2001 'Bayesian nets are all there is to causal dependence' in M. Galavotti, P. Suppes and D. Costantini (Eds) *Stochastic Causality*. Stanford, CA: CSLI Publications.

Stevens J. 1996 *Applied Multivariate Statistics for the Social Sciences, 3rd edition.* Mahwah, NJ: Lawrence Erlbaum Associates.

von Mises, R. 1951 *Probability, Statistics and Truth, 2nd edition.* London: George, Allen and Unwin.

Weller, M.P.I. and Weller, B.G.A. 1988 'Crime and mental illness' *Medicine, Science and Law* 28: 38.

Whittaker, J 1997 'Use of stepwise methodology in discriminant analysis'. Paper presented at the South West Educational Research Association, Austin, Texas, 23–25 January 1997.

Williams, M. 2000 *Science and Social Science: An Introduction.* London: Routledge.

Williams, M. 2003 'The problem of representation: realism and operationalism in survey research' *Sociological Research* 8(1). Online, available: http://www.socresonline.org.uk/8/1/williams.html.

Winship, C. and Sobel, M. 2004 'Causal inference in sociological studies' in M. Hardy and A. Bryman (Eds) *Handbook of Data Analysis.* London: Sage.

Woodward, J. 2001 'Probabilistic causality, direct causes and counterfactual dependence' in M. Galavotti, P. Suppes and D. Costantini (Eds) *Stochastic Causality.* Stanford, CA: CSLI Publications.

5

Complex Realist and Configurational Approaches to Cases: A Radical Synthesis

David Byrne

This chapter is intended to be deliberately provocative. It is not meant to be prescriptive in relation to the content of other chapters in this Handbook but rather is an expression of the position of one of the editors in relation to our understanding of the nature of cases and the ways in which we might explore social causality using case-based methods.

Note the emphasis on the establishment of causality as the proper project of social science. I endorse absolutely the centrality of interpretation in all modes of social scientific practice. However, for me, interpretation through quantitative exploration and modelling, through qualitative work generating narratives and through any synthesis of these approaches – but particularly through the systematic synthesis of qualitative comparative analysis (QCA) – is directed towards the achievement of Dannermark et al.'s (2002, p. 1) prescription:

> The explanation of social phenomena by revealing the causal mechanisms that produce them is the fundamental task of social research.

Let me immediately assert a position on the form of causation that matters in the social world. Generally, such causation is complex. That is to say, what happens is not the product of any single cause but rather of the interaction of multiple causes, which causes are not 'variables' external to cases but rather embodied aspects of cases.[1] Moreover, a crucial element in causation is context. If we think of generative mechanisms as systems of embodied complex causes then, as Pawson and Tilley (1997) remind us, such mechanisms are always contingent and operate in interaction with context. In other words, although we can hope to establish causation, our accounts will never be universal covering laws. That is not to say that they are necessarily ideographic accounts of specific and unique instances. They may well be generalizable, especially when we establish causation through comparison across numbers of cases – as Charles Ragin (2000, p. 332) puts it we are dealing with: '… an idea widely shared by social scientists – that it is possible to derive useful empirical generalizations from the examination of multiple instances of social phenomena (i.e. from comparable cases)', but the generalizability is always limited and specification of its limits is one of the key tasks of the social researcher. One other thing needs to be said about the implications of thinking of causation as complex. My co-editor, Charles Ragin, has repeatedly pointed out that causation is not only complex, but also it is multiple. In other words the same outcome (what I, employing the terminology of complexity theory, am going to call attractor state) might be generated by different complex causal generative mechanisms or, to use his useful and precise phrase, different causal configurations. There is more than one way in which a system state can come to be in existence.

That reference to my co-editor enables me to make another point about this chapter. It is profoundly influenced by the body of his work since he published *The Comparative Method* in 1987. This chapter is described as an attempt at synthesis. The elements it will seek to synthesize are: Ragin's understanding of configurational causation and his use of systematic comparative method to elucidate such causation, the general critical realist ontology of the social world and 'complex' complexity theory's (especially as represented by the work of Paul Cilliers) understanding of complex systems and account of how we might seek to understand and shape the trajectories of such systems. It seems to me that these three approaches resonate in harmony with each other and my task here is to demonstrate that resonance and draw out the implications of it for the practice of social scientific research in general and case-based methods in particular. An inevitable corollary of that argument is that case-based methods are not only superior to the tradition of quantitative explanation using derivatives of the linear model but that serious consideration of the underlying ontological basis of case-based methods fundamentally challenges the legitimacy of linear variable-based accounts of social causation.

Ragin and Becker's edited collection *What Is a Case?* (1992) poses a crucial question and answered it in a range of different ways. Here, I want to prescribe the nature of 'cases', although if that word is used in different, and entirely legitimate, ways then my prescription will not apply. Let me present a string of quotations that, to varying degrees, correspond to my understanding of the nature of cases:

A case is a bounded system. (Stake, quoting Smith – original not cited – 1995, p. xi)

... cases – meaningful but complex configurations of events and structures – singular whole entities purposefully selected ... not homogeneous observations drawn at random from a pool of equally plausible selections. (Ragin 2004, p. 125)

Implicit in most social scientific notions of case analysis is the idea that the objects of investigation are similar enough and separate enough to permit treating them as comparable instances of the same general phenomenon. (Ragin and Becker 1992, p. 1)

... cases are viewed as configurations – as combinations of characteristics. Comparison in the qualitative tradition thus involves comparing configurations. This holism contradicts the radically analytic approach of most quantitative work. (Ragin 1987, p. 3)

The move from population/analytic approach to case/narrative approach is thus a move first to a new way of regarding cases – as fuzzy realities with autonomously defined complex properties – and a move second to seeing cases as engaged in perpetual dialogue with their environment, a dialogue of action an constraint that we call plot. (Abbott 1992, p. 65)

... consider cases not as empirical units or theoretical categories, but as the product of basic research operations. (Ragin – in imperative mode – 1992, p. 218)

Now let me draw on what I consider to be a seminal article by Cilliers *Boundaries, Hierarchies and Networks in Complex Systems* (2001, p. 141):

Boundaries [of complex systems] are simultaneously a function of the activity of the system itself, and a product of the strategy of description involved. In other words, we frame the system by describing it in a certain way (for a certain purpose) but we are constrained in where the frame can be drawn. The boundary of the system is therefore neither a function of our description, nor is it a purely natural thing.

Replace the word 'system' by the word 'case' (and in a moment I am going to argue that the cases that are of primary interest to us are complex systems) and you have something very like a synthesis of the definitions of case listed above. I use the word 'synthesis' here in an explicitly dialectical sense. Some of the definitions listed contradict each other – we have theses and anti-theses, not least in the four quotations from Ragin, three of which assert the empirical existence of cases and the fourth that describes them as the product of our research processes. Of course, the point is that all four statements are true, precisely in the way that Cilliers identifies the nature of complex systems as we engage with them as researchers.

My take on social constructionism in social research is a version of what I understand to be the critical realist position on social epistemology. Of course, the elements of our scientific practice are social constructions, in any science of any kind, but they are not made out of nothing; they are shaped from reality. Let me quote the most coherent of all phenomenologists on precisely this point. As Merleau-Ponty (1945, 2002) said: '... the world is "already there" before reflection begins – as an inalienable presence' (p. vii) and again: '... the world ceaselessly assails and beleaguers subjectivity as waves wash around a wreck on the shore' (pp. 240–241). So we certainly construct, and construct not only to understand but in relation to specific objectives to be achieved through social action, but our constructions are shaped not just by us but by the reality of the world itself.

CASES AS COMPLEX SYSTEMS

What does it mean to say that cases are complex systems? First, let us establish the nature of complex systems:

> ... a simple system is one to which a notion of state can be assigned once and for all, or more generally, one in which Aristotelian causal categories can be independently segregated from one another. Any system for which such a description cannot be provided I will call *complex*. Thus, in a complex

system, the causal categories become intertwined in such a way that no dualistic language of state plus dynamic laws can completely describe it. Complex systems must then process mathematical images different from, and irreducible to, the generalized dynamic systems which have been considered universal. (Rosen 1987, p. 324)

The implication of this definition is that a reductionist programme of analysis cannot inform us as to the nature or potential trajectory of any complex system. This is not to say that we are turning from simplistic analysis to simplistic holism:

> '... General systems theory focuses on the totality rather than its constituent parts. Thus, it adheres to the holism in the conventional sense of the word. Complexity theory views this type of holism as just as problematic as the reductionism it nominally opposes – the conventional theory holism is reductionism to the whole. Holism typically overlooks the interactions and the organization, whereas complexity theory pays attention to them. (Price 1997, p. 10)

Complex systems are not the same as linear systems in which changes in any parameter value – the values of some component of the system – generates proportionate change in that aspect of the system. Neither are they the same as chaotic systems in which very small changes in key parameter values are always liable to generate radical non-linear changes in the state of the system. Likewise, in general they have the potential to be different from close to equilibric systems in which changes in any parameter or parameters, and/or changes in the external environment of the system that are likely to destabilize it are met by negative feedback, which damps out that disturbance. That said, given that complex systems are robust, for much of the time they do appear like close to equilibric systems – in the terminology of complexity dynamics their trajectory lies within a torus attractor. They do not stay the same but they do not change in any fundamental, qualitative fashion. The crucial point is that complex systems – also described as far from equilibric systems or dissipative systems – have the potential to change in such a fundamental qualitative fashion. Changes in internal parameters and/or changes in external environment can trigger positive feedback, which engenders qualitative change in the system. It is important to emphasize that, usually, this does not mean that the system ceases to exist but rather than it becomes very different, while remaining coherent. The biological process of metamorphosis by which a caterpillar changes into a butterfly provides us with a good metaphor for this process, although of course metamorphosis is precisely a qualitative change in the complex system of an organism. Parsons picked up the distinction between close to equilbric stable systems and far from equilbric complex systems in his work:

> Parsons makes a distinction between what might be called developmental processes and what might be called phase-shift processes. The former consist in a continuous and incremental elaboration and separation of sub-systems, which does not alter the general overall pattern of society. By contrast, phase-shift processes are fundamental differential leaps or evolutionary breakthroughs, typically caused outside the social realm (e.g. in the realms of culture or personality) which reorient the social pattern. (Crooke et al. 1992, p. 5)

Reed and Harvey (1996, pp. 390–391) point out the implications of recognizing the potential for qualitative change in complex systems:

> The dissipative social systems paradigm assumes social order is not always possible, nor is it necessarily desirable. It does not begin, as does the Parsonian project, by asking the Hobbesian question, 'How is order possible ?' Instead it addresses the more perplexing question, 'How do the mechanisms producing social order, periodically produce chaos and pave the way for radical social transformations ?'

Two key terms that we can usefully bring into play from the complexity vocabulary are 'trajectory' and 'attractor'. Both derive from dynamics, the branch of applied mathematics that seeks to describe the state of systems and how those systems change. Trajectory is simply the path through time of a system, usually described in mathematical terms by the co-ordinates of the system at different time points in a multi-dimensional state space, the dimensions of which are the variate measures describing the system. An attractor is a domain within that state space within which systems tend to be located. This can be the torus (doughnut) attractor, which describes close to equilibric systems and complex systems in stable state; or it can be the Lorenz or butterfly attractor, in which there are two possible relatively stable states for the system but in which it can flip from one to the other. However, for our purposes, it is best to think of attractors not in relation to single systems but in relation to whole sets of systems – ensembles of systems. If we think in this way then we have a link between complexity theory and classification because attractor states are basically in qualitative terms, the kind of thing something is, the category to which it belongs.

Why do I assert that cases are complex systems? Because the empirically founded (although socially constructed from that foundation through our research processes) entities with which we deal at any social level – whether micro (in the form of single individuals), any meso level (from household through institution or urban system) to the macro level of nation states or indeed the world order as a whole – have all the properties of complex systems in terms of their inherent nature and potential for change.

Let me illustrate by using the example of the depressed individual. Clinical depression is a long-enduring sense of lack of self-worth and sadness that is inappropriate to the social situation of an individual (e.g. it is not associated with a recent bereavement) and which disables that person, preventing him or her from carrying out normal social functions and obligations. People who are not depressed become depressed and depressed people cease to be depressed. This is not a matter of incremental change. Particularly in relation to the ability to function at a social level, to enter or leave what Parsons called 'the sick role' there is a qualitative change in action and self-regard. It should go without saying that such changes are seldom the product of single factors, and certainly not of drug therapies, but rather are the result of complex and contingent causal processes.

Let me integrate the themes of classification of systems in terms of types,[2] – which in complexity terms can be understood as presence in the attractor space of the ensemble with is a particular category – and the specification of significant change in systems as involving phase shifts – which involves a trajectory to a new attractor space. This way of thinking about types and change indicates that significant change for a system is a change of category, the system becomes not just something different in a unique fashion, but a different sort of thing. It changes kind. Rihoux and Ragin (2004, p. 18) make exactly this point with specific reference to policy:

> ... policy researchers, especially those concerned with social as opposed to economic policy, are often more interested in different kinds of cases and their different fates than they are in the extent of the net causal effect of a variable across a large encompassing population of observations. After all, a common goal of social policy is to make decisive interventions, not to move average levels or rates up or down by some minuscule fraction.[3]

So much for the general character of complex systems. On what basis can I contend that cases are complex systems? Let me specify that I am dealing with cases in the sense specified by Abbott above (1992, p. 65), that is as: '... fuzzy realities with autonomously defined complex properties'. This is an explicitly realist view of cases. They exist prior to our social construction of them, they are autonomous and their properties are complex. This, of course, corresponds pretty well exactly to a preliminary specification of the characteristics of complex systems. Let us add in Ragin's notion of configurations of causes. Inherent in this conception (indeed, Ragin often explicitly develops this point) is a rejection of the notion that causality in relation to the state – present kind – of a case can be understood by the partial decomposition of the case into a set of variables with independent or indeed interactive effects. Of course, the statistical treatment of interaction in causal models is the grudging and incomplete tribute

that statistical procedures based on the general linear model pay to complexity, but Ragin's approach is radically different to that mode of understanding. As Ragin (2004, p. 124) puts it:

> ... case oriented research is not a primitive form of variable-oriented research that can be improved through stricter adherence to variable oriented standards. Rather, the case-oriented approach is better understood as a different mode of inquiry with different operating assumptions.'

The variates that Ragin uses as the basis of his comparative method are a mixture of descriptions of the internal characteristics of the cases and of the environment within which they are located.[4] Ragin and other exponents of QCA never seek to decompose their causal configurations and thereby to assign proportionate causality to any of the variates in a specific configuration. They have no analogue of a partial correlation coefficient. For them, causation is the result of the whole configuration. Although this is not the way QCA researchers usually express their understanding, we can see causation as represented by a configuration as representing the complex product of the components of a complex system, the complex system itself, components of the environment of the complex system and that environment itself. Moreover, the set of cases that correspond to a particular configuration can be understood in complexity terms as the ensemble of cases with trajectories that have located them in a particular attractor space in the overall state space.

The resonance of figurational understandings of complex and multiple causality and the general approach of complexity theory to complex systems is enormous. We can treat real cases as complex systems. Moreover, we can do so at every level of case. The micro level of the social individual is a case. Indeed, medical and social practitioners are generally engaged precisely with single cases.

Let me illustrate by reference to a professional engaging in cognitive behavioural therapy (CBT) with a patient suffering from clinically significant depression. CBT is a 'talking therapy', but it is a talking therapy addressed to changing the behaviour of the patient in the here and now rather than elucidating causes for present state in previous life experience. However, in practice, practitioners of CBT[5] do address the specific characteristics and social context of the actual patient with whom they are dealing. Indeed, even the core of CBT is contextual in that it addresses the specific issues of that specific patient. The objective is to change the state of the case from a non-functioning to a functioning individual, from ill to well – to change the kind of person the patient is. Although CBT has been 'validated' by randomized controlled trials, it is by no means a simple intervention. Rather, it is a complex social process tuned by the individual practitioner in the context of the specific case. CBT is not conducted in the mode of a call centre agent working to a script!

It is important to return to the issue of the nature of boundaries of cases when we consider cases as complex systems. Cilliers (2001, p. 141), drawing on Zeleny (1996), asserts that we should not consider boundaries as:

> ... something that separates one thing from another. We should rather think of a boundary as something that *constitutes* (original emphasis) that which is bounded. This shift will enable us to see the boundary as enabling, rather than as confining.

Zeleny (1996, p. 133) argues that boundaries connect rather than separate, in the sense that they connect systems with their environment. Understood in this way they are: '... not "perimeters" but functional constitutive components of a given system'.

It is interesting to develop the idea of cases as complex systems at the micro level in relation to the very important micro level longitudinal datasets, typified by the British Household Panel Survey (BHPS; http://www.iser.essex.ac.uk/ulsc/bhps/). These studies chart the trajectories of micro level cases – for the BHPS households – across time. The households are rather precise cases

although they do have a fuzzy character in that the composition of particular cases changes over time, new cases are formed by the splitting of existing cases and some cases cease to exist. Although QCA is usually thought of as a small N procedure, it can be applied to very large datasets and the exploration of the complex trajectories of micro cases in the form of households through time is just one example of the potential of the method. This, of course, illustrates the complex nature of households and the complex and multiple causation of their trajectories.

Cases at meso levels – levels that are aggregates of micro cases but which have an emergent reality that is more than simply the sum of the micro effects – and at macro levels (conventionally taken to be nation states, although contemporary views on world systems could be taken to assert there is only one macro system) can be addressed in the same way. There is an increasing body of classificatory and comparative case-based research and examples of it will be included here. Levels include city region, schools and neighbourhood policy interventions. Indeed, any social level could constitute a case in this sense.

This raises the important question of the relationship among levels of cases. Again, Cilliers provides us with a way of thinking through this issue. He takes on the notions of hierarchy and of nested systems. Let us begin by thinking about the implications of these two approaches in terms of the content of the word 'hierarchy' and the phrase 'nested systems'. Hierarchy implies that higher levels have more importance than lower levels. In terms of causation, the implication is that causal processes run downwards. Multi-level models in education provide a good illustration of this. In general, these work with the levels of individual pupil, class and school. Although researchers working in this tradition are perfectly aware that the characteristics of classes and schools are in part determined by the characteristics of the individual pupils (in terms of behaviour) and cohorts of pupils (in terms of overall social characteristics) within them, their models of explanation are all about how the 'higher' levels, taken together with characteristics of the population at the micro level of pupil, determine educational outcomes for pupils. We have to challenge the notion that causation in such instances runs only in one direction.

The phrase 'nested systems' carries less of an etymological burden than hierarchy. However, it does imply that 'contained' systems are somehow bounded within 'containing' systems; for example, households are bounded within neighbourhoods, which are bounded within city regions, which are bounded within nation states, which are bounded within blocks, which are bounded within the world system. In part, this carries a relatively weak implication of 'downward' determination, but more importantly it does not recognize the multiple connections of any system. For example, a household certainly lives within a neighbourhood within a city region and so on. However, a household is quite likely to have extra local, even global, connections in terms of family ties, cultural connections, economic relations (especially for employees of transnational corporations), and so on. I have siblings with whom I have regular contact who live in Australia, family ties to small farming communities in Ireland and Wales, friends in the United States, Libya, Poland, Germany, etc. Some of these ties are mediated by face-to-face interaction but some are now mediated purely through the world wide web.

What does all this amount to in terms of relations among levels of cases? Cilliers (2001, pp. 143–144) gives us the answer. He points out that systems do contain hierarchies; indeed, this is central to the constitution of their structure. However, hierarchies within systems, and by implication among systems, are not nested, are not permanent, are characterized by inter-penetration and are capable of transformation. So, for example, a neighbourhood might be transformed by the actions of a small minority of residents, usually but not invariably in a negative direction. There is good evidence for exactly this in social housing areas and the rather inane

programme of 'respect' enforced by anti-social behaviour orders[6] is directed at dealing with this issue. Likewise, global forces can change the situation of neighbourhoods as was the case with the residualization of many areas of United Kingdom social housing with the transition of the city regions within which they were located from industrial to post-industrial and Fordist to post-Fordist status.[7]

So, we have established something about the nature of cases. The remainder of this chapter is concerned with the actual ways in which social scientists can determine, or perhaps 'explore' is a better term, processes of causation in cases considered as complex systems.

RESEARCHING CASES

Let me continue in assertive mode. The issues that arise in researching causality in relation to cases have little to do with the divide between qualitative and quantitative modes of research. However, they do have rather a lot to do with a particular mode of using the products of quantitative research – the application of procedures within the framework of the general linear model to the products of the measurement processes that are the essence of quantitative research procedures. Linear modelling as a way of representing causality in reality should not be confused with measurement as a way of describing reality. It is very useful to make a distinction between ways of describing reality and representing causality in reality. This has been done in Figure 5.1. We can describe reality through words, sound, images and numbers. Indeed, we often use all three methods and their derivatives – for numbers, descriptive statistics, graphs and classifications – in a single composite description. Moreover, we can use any or all of these methods to describe single cases or multiple cases.

When we turn to causality, the specifically qualitative approach has one method – the narrative – that tells the story, or multiple stories, of causation. The single narrative can only

Modes of description		Mode of causal representation			
Quantitative	Qualitative	Quantitative		Qualitative	
Measurement	Text and / or images – sound	Variable based	Case based	Single narrative – ideographic account	Multiple narratives – text-based comparison
Descriptive statistics, graphs and classifications		Linear models	Multiple causal configurations		

Figure 5.1 Modes of description and causal representation of the social.

offer us an ideographic causal representation of causation in that unique instance. Multiple stories can enable us to tease out comparable elements and absences and thereby create a narrative that is a general account of more than one instance. By contrast, there are two very different approaches to the representation of causality through quantitative methods. These are the variable-based and probabilistic methods of linear modelling and the case-focused and deterministic (at least in terms of retrodiction – account of past causality – and potential – causal accounts are not always fully resolved but they might be by the addition of more knowledge) techniques based on configurational approaches. These approaches are very different and fundamentally incompatible. If one is a way of representing causality in social reality then the other is not.

It is rather important here to sort out the two different ways in which probability is used in linear modelling, although they are very often confused in accounts of the results of such modelling and are often inter-related in particular techniques. Probability theory has a fundamental role in statistical inference – in making statements about populations on the basis of samples from those cases.[8] Techniques derived from inference have been carried over into linear modelling as convenient devices for quantifying the extent to which the model – for example in a binomial regression – fits the data. Here 'fits the data' means the extent to which a model that is more parsimonious than the saturated model, in which all variables and all possible interactions among variables are considered to operate, can reproduce the pattern of data.[9]

Typically, a good model will improve on the specification that the majority outcome is the only outcome. However, such a model tells us about what will happen across a range of cases. It tells us nothing about what will happen with a particular case. As Blalock (1979, pp. 115–116) put it, we can only, '… use the term probability not to refer to single events … but to a large number of events to what happens in the long run'. We work as if the probability across the whole set of cases, the frequentist probability, applied as odds to the single case, but this is not a logically valid way of proceeding. Of course, all our knowledge from data is retrodictive. It tells us what has happened, not what will happen, but it is what we have to work with and we use it as a predictive tool. Note that linear modelling techniques are meant to generate 'the model' – the single model – that fits the data. There is no sense of multiple causation.

Let us compare this with configurational approaches. A configuration of causal components can be resolved. All cases with the same configuration can have the same outcome. However, often configurations in a truth table are contradictory. At a fundamental and necessary level, this suggests that something else is going on, at least one something else, and we should look for it (or them). Often, we have high – but not total – resolutions of a configuration. If, for example, 90% of English schools with a given configuration belong to a 'high-achieving' category, then we can – and do – work in a probabilistic fashion and say that schools with that configuration have a 90% chance of being high achieving in just the same way as we might say that a model generated a 90% accuracy rate in a logistic regression. At this point, our knowledge is probabilistic. However, we can go further to find the other components. We can move to total resolution. This opens up the possibility of deterministic, if retrodictive, knowledge.

The differences between configurational and linear modelling techniques can be summarized in bullet point form:

- Configurational approaches allow for multiple causation, whereas linear modelling does not.
- Configurational approaches see cases as complex systems, whereas linear modelling can only admit complexity through the concession of interaction terms.
- Configurational approaches can achieve deterministic retrodictive knowledge, *which can be applied to the single case*. Linear modelling approaches cannot.

Finally in this discussion, let me make explicit something that has been implicit. I have discussed configurational techniques as if they comprised only the kind of variate specifications that are the elements of a truth table in QCA and related techniques. *Multi-case comparative qualitative work is always configurational when it engages with causes.* The configurations may be rendered as numbers as in QCA or they may be expressed in terms of text, but configurations is what they are.

Configurations say cases are not reducible to variables or event to variables plus interactions. But this leaves us with a dilemma. If cases are not reducible to any sort of component, and causal accounts based on comparison and expressed in text form identify components just as much as measurement-based techniques like QCA, how can we attempt to explain the trajectories of complex systems? Let us turn to a term from complexity theory to help us here.

CONTROL PARAMETERS

At first sight, the idea of control parameters – of aspects of complex systems that have a governing influence on the trajectories of the systems – might seem to contradict the anti-reductionist character of complexity theory as a whole. However, this is not the case. First and simply, control parameters are generally themselves complex. In some instances, a single factor internal or external to the system might induce a phase shift, but far more often we are dealing with multiple and inter-lined internal and/or external aspects. Configuration is in fact a very good term to describe such complexes. Configurations, whether expressed as sets of variates or in textual description, are models of control parameters, but they are models that are simultaneously incomplete and necessary. Cilliers (2001, p. 138) addresses this issue through a discussion of models that, whereas they can never be perfect representations of complex systems, might still be useful to us:

... models have to reduce the complexity of the phenomena being described, they have to leave something out. However, we have no way of predicting the importance of that which is not considered. In a non-linear world where we cannot track a clear causal chain, something that may appear to be unimportant now may turn out to be vitally important later. Or *vice versa* of course. Our models have to "frame" the problem in a certain way and this framing will inevitably introduce distortions. ... This is not an argument against the construction of models. We have no choice but to make models if we want to understand the world. It is just an argument that models of complex systems will always be flawed in principle and that we have to acknowledge these limitations.[10]

If we think of configurations, with that term covering both quantitative and qualitative representation of configurations, as models, then we can proceed further following Cilliers (2001, p. 139) and understand that our models are attempts, '... to grasp the *structure* (original emphasis) of complex systems'. Here, structure is *not* a static arrangement, a meaning that the common usage of the word can only too easily imply. It is the whole dynamic system in action, with potential for radical change being part of the character of that system. Moreover, complex systems are structured in hierarchies not of strictly defined and separate sub-units but, as Cilliers (2001, p. 143) puts it, of messy (with the messiness being indispensable), interpenetrating and mutable (although robust) hierarchical orders of components. Of particular significance is that these hierarchies are context-dependent. In general, they are inherently mutable entities.

The implication of this for case-based research, whether the ideographic investigation of the specific instance or comparative investigation of multiple instances, is that what we are trying to do is to identify, however incompletely, temporarily and locally, the nature of the structure of control parameters *and* the potential of those parameters for bringing about a given state of the system – a qualitative condition of the case. That is what we can do in terms of establishing causality on the basis of cases, and we can do so without falling into the trap of reification of variables outwith cases, which has been the false road of quantitative social science for so long and has led to a wholly artificial and disabling separation of the quantitative and qualitative modes of social research.

NOTES

1. Thus case-based approaches endorse the central demand of the phenomenological programme – that we go back to the things themselves.

2. This means that methods of classification – of assigning cases to categories – are of great importance for case-based research. In this Handbook, processes of classification will be examined in some detail.

3. To which I will add that this applies with equal force to practitioners in all forms of medical and social intervention. There is enormous emphasis these days on evidence-based practice, but most of the evidence is based precisely on the frequentist statistical analysis of linear cause across 'large encompassing populations', which evidence cannot be applied to the single case with which the practitioner is at any one time engaged.

4. This distinction between variates that describe internal characteristics of the case and variates that describe the external environment is not generally made explicit in qualitative comparative analyses, perhaps because so many of the actual studies are based on whole nation states or other high-level political entities. It is rather useful here to think about the notion of multi-levels of data and hierarchical data analysis. Goldstein (1995), an important pioneer in the use of multi-level modelling, explicitly recognized

that multi-level data structures were not merely the product of convenient sampling strategies, but actually reflected the reality of the social world itself. Of course, regression-based multi-level models revert rapidly to linear variable-based accounts of the determination of trajectories of the micro level case (see Byrne 1998, pp. 120–122) but thinking about multiple levels, which are not in any way simply hierarchical in terms of processes of determination, is very useful.

5. In the contemporary UK, such practitioners are far more likely to be clinical psychologists, psychiatric nurses, social workers or occupational therapists than psychiatrists. Psychiatrists are still essentially pill pushers. There is interesting anecdotal evidence (which means systematic investigation is required) to suggest that the non-psychologists using CBT are far more flexible and context-oriented in their approach than psychologists, who retain a positivist notion of an exact protocol.

6. These are a bizarre 'New Labour' innovation whereby civil proceedings can be taken against individuals or families to restrict their behaviour but the penalty for breach of the orders can be substantial terms of imprisonment. So actions that are not themselves criminal offences, e.g. in the case of one young woman in Scotland being visible through her window in her underclothes (one wonders why the neighbours were not charged with some peeping tom offence), can lead to imprisonment.

7. Although national policies under the Thatcher government, and nationally determined but locally implemented planning policies from the 1980s, were also crucial to this transformation.

8. And here it is worth noting that a good deal of the criticism of small N methods, for example Goldthorpe (1997), does not grasp that small Ns are frequently, indeed usually, *not samples* but all the cases in a population. Indeed, increasingly, we have large Ns that are complete (with some missing data) sets of a population. The implication of this is that the concern with estimates parameters from sample values that underpins much of that critique is wholly misplaced.

9. Of course, as Sayer (1992) has reminded us a pattern of data is not an effect, and certainly not an effect in complexity theory terms.

10. For me, the additional factor in our modelling is the potential for purposeful action to achieve a possible outcome. In other words, models plus action can enable determination.

REFERENCES

Abbott, A. 1992 'What do cases do? Some notes on activity in sociological analysis' in C. Ragin and H. Becker (Eds) *What Is a Case?* Cambridge: Cambridge University Press, pp. 53–82.

Blalock, H. 1979 *Social Statistics*. London: McGraw-Hill.

Byrne, D.S. 1998 *Complexity Theory and the Social Sciences*. London: Routledge.

Cilliers, P. 1998 *Complexity and Postmodernism*. London: Routledge.

Cilliers, p. 2001 'Boundaries, hierarchies and networks in complex systems' *International Journal of Innovation Management* 5(2): 135–147.

Crooke, S., Pakulski, J. and Waaters, M. 1992 *Postmodernization*. London: Sage.

Dannermark, B., Ekstrom, M., Jakobsen, L. and Karlsson, J.C. 2002 *Explaining Society*. London: Routledge.

Goldstein, H. 1995 *Multilevel Statistical Models*. London: Edward Arnold.

Goldthorpe, J. 1997 'Current issues in comparative macrosociology' *Comparative Social Research* 16: 1–26.

Merleau-Ponty, M. 1945, 2002 *Phenomenology of Perception*. London: Routledge.

Pawson, R. and Tilley, N. 1997 *Realistic Evaluation*. London: Sage.

Price, B. 1997 'The myth of postmodern science' in R.A. Eve, S. Horsfall and M.E. Lee (Eds) *Chaos, Complexity and Sociology*. London: Sage.

Ragin, C. 1987 *The Comparative Method*. Berkley, CA: University of California Press.

Ragin, C. 1992 'Casing and the process of social inquiry' in C. Ragin and H. Becker (Eds) *What Is a Case?* Cambridge: Cambridge University Press, pp. 217–226.

Ragin, C. 2000 *Fuzzy Set Social Science*. Chicago: University of Chicago Press.

Ragin, C. 2004 'Turning the tables: how case-oriented research challenges variable-oriented research' in H.E. Brady and D. Collier (Eds) *Rethinking Social Inquiry*. Lanham, MD: Rowman and Littlefield, pp. 123–168.

Ragin, C. and Becker, H. (Eds) 1992 *What Is a Case? Exploring the Foundations of Social Inquiry*. Cambridge: Cambridge University Press.

Reed, M. and Harvey, D.L. 1996 'Social science as the study of complex systems' in L.D. Kiel and E. Elliott (Eds) *Chaos Theory in the Social Sciences*. Ann Arbor, MI: University of Michigan Press, pp. 295–324.

Rihoux, B. and Ragin, C. 2004 'Qualitative comparative analysis (QCA): state of the art and prospects'. Paper presented at the APSA 2004 Annual Meeting, Panel 47-9, Chicago, IL.

Rosen, R. 1987 'Some epistemological issues in physics and biology' in B.J. Hiley and F.D. Peat (Eds) *Quantum Implications: Essays in Honour of David Bohm*. London: Routledge, pp. 314–327.

Sayer, A. 1992 *Method in Social Science*. London: Routledge.

Stake, R.E. 1995 *The Arts of Case Study Research*. London: Sage.

Zeleny, M. 1996 'On the social nature of autopoietic systems' in E.L. Khalil and K. Boulding (Eds) *Evolution, Order and Complexity*. London: Routledge, pp. 122–143.

PART TWO

Methods and Techniques of Case-Based Research

This second part of the Handbook comprises a set of chapters that develop arguments about the nature and utility of case-based research in relation to discussions of the actual research procedures of the social sciences. They work through the territories of classification, configurational approaches and qualitative methods, not by opposing these as in some way radically distinctive and incommensurate but rather as complementary ways of understanding social reality.

Elman begins the review of classification by delineating the issues that arise in developing 'Explanatory Typologies in Qualitative Analysis'. Working in a tradition derived from Lazarsfeld, he works through the ways in which we can develop typologies taking the form of multi-dimensional contingency tables or, to use an alternative terminology, high N polythetic classifications. As they stand, such typologies are descriptive. Moving from description to explanation has to be based on explicit theoretical foci, but development of theory-based explanation might require substantial modification of the property space (dimensionality) represented by the contingency table. The chapter demonstrates how researchers might compress or expand typologies to this end.

Uprichard deals with the important quantitative technique of cluster analysis as a case-based method. The chapter has two aims. First, it deals with the actual nature of cluster analyses as a multiple set of techniques in which quantitative information is used to construct typologies of cases. Second, it moves from the actual set of techniques to a consideration of the crucial methodological question – what can cluster analysis, as a case-based set of methods, teach us about the case? In other words, to use Ragin's terminology, what does cluster analysis tell us about casing and, recursively, what issues does thinking about casing raise for considerations of the nature and utility of numerical taxonomy typified by cluster analysis techniques. So the chapter serves both a practical purpose – as an introduction to an important and useful set of practical procedures – and a meta-theoretical purpose in exploring the epistemological issues involved in knowing the case. Uprichard synthesizes these two elements in her discussion and concludes that cluster analyses serve as a useful tool in the methodological kit through which we seek to conceptualize, and increasingly visualize, the whole case and its relationships with other similar and different cases in the world.

There is an importance if implicit distinction between the contingency table-derived approaches described by Elman and cluster analyses. The former fit with the Aristotelian polythetic approach to classification – to belong to a class, an entity must possess all the discrete characteristic of members of that class. By contrast, cluster analyses generate something much more akin to the prototypical notion of classification, which works with a more holistic conception of a class and does not require identity on all aspects as a condition of class membership.

Next, Phillips and Phillips present an account of correspondence analysis understood as an approach to visualizing types.[1] This chapter lays out the essentials of correspondence analysis as a technique and provides an example-based guide to the employment of the method and of the interpretation of the results of that employment. The essential character of the method is that it takes categorical data arranged in the form of a contingency table and represents it as a dimensional map. This makes possible a visualization of the relationships among variables and categories of variables. The authors argue that correspondence analysis can be built into most methodological positions and can serve inductive, testable theory, ideographic and case-comparative approaches to social science. They emphasize the 'preliminary character' of the approach in a way that resonates with Uprichard's insistence on the exploratory character of cluster analyses. Interestingly, their entirely accurate assertion at the end of the chapter that the effective practice of correspondence analysis 'shatters that most pervasive of social science methodological myths – that social statistics belongs solely to a "natural science" method, characterized by hypothesis, theory and test' (see p. 166) can equally justifiably be applied to cluster analysis and to the qualitative comparative analysis (QCA) methods described in this Handbook by De Meur and Gottcheiner, and Rihoux and Lobe.

The typological subsection concludes with Whelan's discussion of 'How Classification Works, or Doesn't', which is illustrated by the case of chronic pain. We were eager to include a chapter in this Handbook that illustrated the arguments about the nature of classification that have been developed on the basis of the employment of Actor Network Theory in science and technology studies. This approach always works through grounding the discussion in relation to real examples and this is precisely what Whelan does here. She conducts: '... a case study of the making of one professional classification system and the network of experts that created, resisted, and eventually accepted (partly, anyway) the system' (see p. 170). It is important to recognize that this is not just a matter of the production of scientific knowledge. Classifications act in the world – as Whelan puts it: 'Classification creates a kind of Pain Cosmology, laying out the rules of pain's being, and hence the rules for engaging with pain' (see p. 170). Whelan presents us with a fascinating case study but she also draws some important and general lessons from it. She demonstrates how: 'When pain experts use the IASP Classification, they make a world that is not the same as the world of the people they are classifying, just as when social scientists use etic categories, the world they make is not the world of those they study' (see p. 180). Indeed, her respectful acknowledgement of the good sense of those she studied is worth quoting precisely for its transferability to social science as a whole:

> Those in the pain medicine community, or at least in the IASP's Subcommittee on Taxonomy, are quite epistemologically modest and reflexive. Their goal is not to capture patients' reality, but to impose an order they know full well is artificial on a problem they acknowledge they do not really understand, in the hopes of creating order at some future point through coordination of activity towards common goals. Are we social scientists always so acutely aware of the artificiality of the categories we use, and the limits of their fit with the worlds, people, and experiences they attempt to represent? (see p. 180)

Of course, there is a realist argument to be had with that statement, and the preceding discussions of classification all take a realist position on these issues. For realists, reality is not a passive recipient of our knowledge making. It beats on our making – as Merleau Ponty said it beat on our perception – like waves beating on a wreck on the shore. And waves shape that which they beat upon. However, Whelan spells out in the most clear way a contrary position that must always inform an ongoing argument in engagement with the realities of other actors in the social world.

Next comes a subset of five papers dealing explicitly with quantitative approaches to case-centred methods. The first, by Kent, begins with a critical assessment of traditional frequentist statistical approaches that have dominated variable-based analyses. Alternative approaches, including Baysian methods, neural net techniques, tipping point accounts and configurational approaches, are then outlined and reviewed. Kent takes a quantitative approach to configurational methods including QCA and fuzzy-set QCA and argues that both Baysian and configurational approaches are superior tools for evaluating arguments about necessary and sufficient causation. In particular, configurational approaches move our discussion away from thinking about causation in terms of specific instances of temporal ordering – if X then Y – to set theoretic inclusion based on comparative examination of numbers of cases. In Kent's view, and we agree, researchers need to be aware of the whole range of methods of engaging with quantitative data as different approaches have differing capacities for revealing patterns of association in social reality. He notes (see Byrne, Chapter 14) that configurational methods can be used with large N datasets to considerable advantage and offer a real alternative to frequentist approaches in exploring causality on the basis of such datasets.

The next four chapters deal with the techniques involved in configurational approaches. De Meur and Gottcheiner outline the logic and assumptions of MDSO–MSDO designs (**most different** cases, **similar outcomes/ most similar** cases, **different outcomes**). These are methods of processing comparison when we have available lots of information about a set of cases and need to reduce the complexity of that information as a basis for comparison without losing relevant information. These approaches are ground-clearing exercises that enable us to proceed to efficient analyses. The chapter works through the methods using an abstract example to demonstrate how to achieve data reduction in order to clarify the actual comparative process. Rihoux and Lobe demonstrate 'The Case for Qualitative Comparative Analysis' by 'adding leverage for thick cross-case comparison'. They do so by addressing two central issues: first, should QCA be understood as a case-centred method or as a middle way between case-oriented and variable-oriented analysis? Second, can QCA be deployed only in relation to a specific conception of the nature of the case or is it appropriately used with a wide and different range of conceptions of the nature of the case? In answering these questions, Rihoux and Lobe note that the strengths of QCA-style methods lie in the combination of a holistic conception of the case as a complex entity with the ability to explore complex causality across multiple cases. Because it permits the examination of multiple cases, it allows for both generalization and replication and so incorporates analytic elements without losing the holistic dimension of phenomena. The chapter includes a worked-through account of the actual procedures involved in QCA, which provides a useful guide to the employment of the methods.

Breiger's chapter addresses the 'Duality of Cases and Variables' and develops a discussion that combines synthesis of techniques with concrete illustration. The chapter resonates with Phillips and Phillips' discussion of correspondence analysis because Breiger shows how QCA can be used to 'tailor correspondence analysis' (see p. 255). Simultaneously, he demonstrates how the visualization capacities of correspondence analysis can be deployed to illuminate the forms of explanation generated by QCA. Breiger lays down his methodological position by asserting that we should understand cases as configurations of variables and variables as configurations of cases. His discussion shows that he regards interactions as components of the set of variables, a position that resonates with a complexity-founded understanding of the nature of cases themselves. The Barycentric form of correspondence analysis, which Breiger outlines in the appendix to his chapter, is shown to provide: '… a very useful guide towards visualizing the cases as intersections and/or unions of the causal conditions' (see p. 249). Breiger re-works two QCA studies by Ragin, the first a crisp-set approach to Ethnic Political Mobilization, and the second a fuzzy-set approach to Democracy in inter-war Europe. In his discussion, he notes that this form of dual working of QCA and correspondence analysis brings the dependent variable, and hence issues of causality, into correspondence analysis, which traditionally appears as a descriptive approach. The argument for synthesis and complementarity of these methods is wholly persuasive.

The last paper in this subset, by Byrne, provides a demonstration of using crisp-set (i.e. with binarized variables) QCA to explore causality in a relatively large N dataset. It demonstrates how to move from the development of a truth table through a further qualitative exploration using the logic of MSDO (as outlined by De Meur and Gottcheiner), i.e. by looking at a deviant case in an almost fully resolved configuration in order to find out what is different about that case. The dataset relates to the performance of secondary schools in the north-east of England in 2006 in terms of the examination achievements of cohorts of pupils, and establishes for one set the importance of fully structured staff-led mentoring schemes – in Ragin's useful phrase a possible intervention – in changing outcomes. A contrast is drawn with the way in which a binary logistic regression using the same data inputs enables us to understand causality. This approach gives a good overall prediction of outcome but offers minimal clues as to complex path-dependent causation for specific cases. The approach demonstrates the validity of Kent's views as to the value of configurational

approaches in exploring causality in large N quantitative datasets shows how we can move from quantitative to qualitative using computer-based qualitative tools, and offers a model for the use of these approaches in trying, in context and with path dependency recognized, to find out what works.

The last subset in this part of the book comprises five chapters that address different aspects of the qualitative exploration and interpretation of case-based materials. Fielding and Warnes provide an overview of the way in which CAQDAS (computer-based qualitative data analysis) can be used in relation to case-based work. They appositely note that:

> The case study field may benefit from a closer engagement with qualitative software, and users of qualitative software may benefit from widening their horizons to include software developed with case study analysis in mind. (see p. 270)

In developing this argument, Fielding and Warnes take us through the nature of CAQDAS and point out how closely the logic of enquiry that underpins many of the actual packages – code and retrieve – is associated with grounded theoretical methodological principles. They outline the resources available in packages and note that whereas these are modelled on code-based rather than case-based approaches, they can be deployed in a case-based fashion. The case-based researcher has to: '… translate but not invent anew' (see p. 273). A particularly useful feature of many packages is the ability to generate quantitative material from the qualitative and export it to packages, including QCA, which require quantitative input. Byrne includes a simple example of this in Chapter 14, and Fielding and Warne include a developed example based on moving from qualitative data in the form of interviews with counter-terrorist experts though comparative textual analysis on a grounded theory basis to a causal analysis using QCAS. As they say, this is a multi-case, multi-method and multi-analytical research model with considerable general potential in identifying 'best practice'. Whereas Byrne (Chapter 14) started with quantitative data and then moved to qualitative exploration, Fielding and Warnes start with the qualitative and move to the quantitative. This contrast shows the flexibility of 'machine shop' use of these methods in practice.

Ó Riain's chapter is concerned with 'Extending the Ethnographic Case Study'. His argument is developed in relation to:

> ... a classic example of the intimate tie between the ethnographic method and the case study, of an ethnographer burrowing into the social relationships of a specific social world and revealing at least some of its internal dynamics and layers of meaning. (see p. 289)

However, it was more complex than that! Ó Riain shows that as the particular project was completed the local world of solidarity broke down and he realized that whereas software work was highly socialized, software careers were highly individualized. In effect, to understand the world of his co-workers in an IT project, Ó Riain had to grasp the whole historical trajectory of the educated Irish middle class at the end of the twentieth century. Drawing on Abbott and Burawoy, Ó Riain shows how ethnographic work is central to the idea of case-based work but considers how we can move, as his example demonstrates we must, beyond the specific. He identifies three modes of extension: the personal founded on individual reflexivity, the theoretical by engagement with macro-social theory and the empirical by extending the empirical boundaries of the ethnographic case. His chapter works through each of these modes in turn and, in his discussion of empirical extension, shows how ethnography is particularly well situated to tackling the problematization of the boundaries of cases in all aspects, but especially in relation to space and time. As he concludes:

> The de- and re-construction of the case that so many have seen as the death knell of ethnography instead places ethnography at the centre of a resurgent contextualist paradigm of social inquiry, a paradigm that is increasingly self-consciously exploring its own theoretical and methodological foundations. (see p. 304)

Goertz and Mahoney address the issue of scope, taking up an issue identified in both the preceding chapters – how can generalizations be made on the basis of case studies? The project of this chapter is making clear how analysts, and especially case-study analysts, understand scope and make choices about the scope of their theories. Their definition of scope is appropriate and important, and concords with the overarching argument about the local character of knowledge and our need to specify the limits of knowledge claims which informs the editors approach to case methods in general: 'A scope statement sets empirical and theoretical limits on the extent to which an inference can be generalized' (see p. 307). That said, whereas we (the editors) would agree with a weak version of the argument that: 'In terms of conceptual homogeneity, researchers need to make sure that measurement stability holds across all units and all key variables of a theory' (see p. 308), by contrast, the whole logic of complex and contingent causation that we (the editors) endorse means that we do not agree with a simple interpretation of the statement that: 'In terms of causal homogeneity, researchers need to make sure that posited causal observations are stable across all observations' (see p. 308).

Goertz and Mahoney illustrate their argument with reference to how scope is discussed in contemporary political science, and their discussion of heterogeneity of observations is particularly significant. They illustrate this with reference to codings of democracy at the level of nation states. Bluntly put, and in very crude summary, it all depends on what you mean by democracy. In relation to causality these authors do accept multiple causation but argue that this is stable causality in relation to that configuration of cases. This raises an interesting question about generalization. In traditional statistical modelling, a causal model established on the basis of a sample drawn from a population is considered to be general for that population and therefore applicable to cases beyond the sample. In not so much small N as in all N studies[2] generalization takes a different form. With real all N then what we find for a configuration is the case for all cases in that configuration and that is our generalization for fully determined configurations, whereas we have to explore further for contradictory configurations. With 'added N' – for example the database developed by Dyer (see Chapter 4) of cases passing through a custody diversion system – we can project outcomes to a new case entering the system on the basis of our projection for the existing configuration to which that case belongs *but* we must enter outcome data for that case as it becomes available and modify our configuration set as necessary. So projection becomes an iterative process.

Emmel and Hughes describe a project that, at first glance, might seem to be a micro-sociological contrast to the kind of macro-social work described by Goertz and Mahoney. They start their discussion by observing that case studies, small N studies and the semi-autonomous development of social theory are the three core activities of social science, and set out to describe what they have learned about these three core activities in developing an application to a methodological strategy for recruiting and researching socially excluded people. The key element in their approach is the idea of the access case – a case that both provides an organizational structure for larger datasets and enables the researchers to identify bounded units, 'to case' in Ragin's terminology, which set limits to the range of both the research process and theory formulated on the basis of that process. Access cases are constituted by more than descriptions of the attributes of people. They include: '… all data on every interaction involved in an attempt to access a socially excluded individual or group' (see p. 319). This means that they are accounts of process as well as accounts of people. This approach enabled the researchers to do three things. First, in a way that corresponds to, for example, the use of the idea of a case node in NVIVO (see Fielding and Warne, Chapter 15) they were able to organize the material in their dataset. Second, they were able to use the access case to track relational flows and all research processes, in particular the relations among research participants and gate-keepers. Essentially, the approach enabled the researchers to construct the kind of database that is necessary for the development of a relational social science as proposed by Emirbayer (1997). Finally, this relational foundation facilitated the continued development of theorization of the social world of the socially excluded. This was a small N study of people with relationships and some of those relationships were with each other. Networks differed and networks mattered. Emmel and Hughes shows us how we can marry attention to networks and relations in a theoretically sophisticated way with case studies in practice.

The last chapter in this part of the book does not deal with a study that was solely qualitative. Rather, in it Carden describes how the International Development Research Centre (Canada) carried out a multi-method set of case studies with the explicit intention of making cross-case comparisons in order to understand how the research the centre supported influenced policy. The 24 cases reviewed were diverse both in location and in field of interest, but this very diversity was understood as valuable in that it reinforced confidence in the applicability of common findings.

Carden takes us through the actual process of execution by the researcher, emphasizing both the need to employ reviewers from the countries in which the research was located and the engagement of programme staff and partners in all aspects of the collective analysis. This was in no way a naïve policy study but, rather, was firmly grounded in relation to substantive methodological debates. Flyvberg (2001) is cited as validating the claim that 'context counts', which, as we have seen, is a crucial common ground among complexity theory, critical realism and set theoretic methods. The crucial point is that cases deliver context. As Carden puts it, they deal in how and why – essentially in the specific histories of cases in relation to outcomes with an eye always to what common knowledge can be generated from careful systematic review of those specific histories. So here we have a chapter that is methodologically informed, deals with an issue of great substantive importance, but particularly shows us how actual policy focused comparative case studies might be conducted to a purpose.

Again, there is a degree of fuzziness around a focus to the chapters in Part Two. All are primarily concerned with how we do social research but, in developing accounts of practice, all deploy illustrative examples and all, either (in the majority of cases) explicitly but sometimes implicitly, engage with fundamental methodological debates in developing the rationale for the techniques which they deploy.

NOTES

1. The significance of visualization in relation to case-based methods should be noted. Increasingly, both our quantitative and qualitative techniques generate visual images of entities, their context, their relationships and, even, of possible underlying generative mechanisms. We are moving increasingly from logocentric discussion to pictorial representation.

2. And all N can be large. Byrne, for example, has worked with a dataset describing all English secondary schools that has more than 4000 cases.

REFERENCES

Emirbayer, M. 1997 'Manifesto for a relational Sociology' *American Journal of Sociology* 103(2): 281–317

Flyvberg, B. 2001 *Making Social Science Matter: Why Social Inquiry Fails and How It Can Succeed Again.* Cambridge: Cambridge University Press

Typologies – Ways of Sorting Things Out

6

Explanatory Typologies in Qualitative Analysis[1]

Colin Elman

Classifications and typologies, together with the shared understandings and standards that they generate, are ever present, important, and indispensable.[2] In addition to their ubiquity in everyday life, typologies constitute a vital tool in scientific inquiry. Accordingly, typologies have a distinguished history in the social and natural sciences, and discussions of what they are and how they work have generated a large body of literature.[3] This chapter focuses on what I will call explanatory typologies, by which I mean multidimensional conceptual classifications based on an explicitly stated theory.[4]

Explanatory typologies are likely to be most valuable for qualitative analysis when scholars systematically apply shared techniques.[5] This chapter provides a brief account of steps used in working with typologies, and an accessible vocabulary to describe them. Two groups of techniques are of particular interest when refining typologies: compression and expansion.[6]

Compression facilitates working with multi-variable explanatory typologies that would otherwise be too large and complex to be helpful. Five forms of cell compression are considered:

(1) *Rescaling compression*: reducing the number of codings for one or more of the typology's dimensions.

(2) *Indexing*: treating equal totals of additive causal variables as equivalent.

(3) *Logical compression*: deleting cells that are the product of impossible or highly improbable combinations of variables.

(4) *Empirical compression*: deleting empty cells.

(5) *Pragmatic compression*: collapsing contiguous cells if their division serves no useful theoretical purpose.

The expansion of a partial typology allows for the rediscovery of deleted cells. This permits the analyst to discover missed combinations and suppressed assumptions, and to identify important cases.

Finally, the chapter considers the potential drawbacks of a typological approach and argues that scholars must be mindful of the risks of reification and of relabeling anomalies.

Explanatory typologies are prone to a form of reification whereby the labels given to a typology's categories displace the underlying theory from which the typology was derived. A second problem is that empirical puzzles for a theory can sometimes be disguised by adding cells that name, but do not explain, the aberrant predictions. This amounts to the semantic relabeling of anomalies, not the development of better theory.

EXPLANATORY TYPOLOGIES

Explanatory typologies invoke both the descriptive and classificatory roles of typologies albeit, as noted in Table 6.1, in a way that incorporates their theoretical focus. At its most straightforward, the descriptive role builds types from the 'compounds of attributes' of concepts.[7] Each unique combination of the attributes of the included concepts provides a separate compound concept. Conventional usage arrays the component attributes in rows and columns to construct an associated property space. Every cell in that space captures a possible grouping of the attributes of the concepts being organized.[8]

In an explanatory typology, the descriptive function follows the conventional usage, but in a way that is heavily modified by its theoretical purposes.[9] The constituent attributes are extracted from the variables

of a preexisting theory. The dimensions of the property space (its rows and columns) reflect alternative values of the theory's independent variables, so each cell in the space is associated with predicted values of the theory's intervening or dependent variables.[10] This association changes the descriptive question being answered from 'What constitutes this type?' to 'If my theory is correct, what do I expect to see?'

The classificatory function of typologies determines to which 'type' a case can be characterized as belonging. Beginning with a typology, empirical data are coded as falling into one cell or another, guiding scholars to answer the question 'What is this a case of?' The property space can be used to map, and compare, a population of cases by their respective scores on the component attributes of the typology.

In explanatory typologies, the classificatory function focuses exclusively on evidence that can arbitrate the theoretical claims being made. For example, analysts may investigate a case to determine whether there is the anticipated congruence between its scores on the typology's dimensions, and the predictions made in the cell in which the case is expected to belong. In addition, the analyst can use the location of cases in different cells as a guide to making the most productive comparisons for testing the underlying theory.

The focus in this chapter is on how explanatory typologies can be helpful to

Table 6.1 Goals of typologies

	Descriptive	Classificatory	Explanatory
Analytic move(s)	Defines compound concepts (types) to use as descriptive characterizations	Assigns cases to types	Makes predictions based on combinations of different values of a theory's variables. Places data in relevant cells for congruence testing and comparisons to determine whether data is consistent with the theory
Question(s) answered	What constitutes this type?	What is this a case of?	If my theory is correct, what do I expect to see? Do I see it?
Example	What is a parliamentary democracy as opposed to a presidential democracy?	Are Britain and Germany parliamentary or presidential democracies?	According to the normative variant of the democratic peace theory, what foreign policy behavior is predicted from a dyad of two mature parliamentary democracies? Do the bilateral foreign policies of Britain and Germany agree with that prediction?

qualitative scholars, who have traditionally combined ordinary language theorizing with the intensive study of a small number of cases using comparative case, process-tracing, and congruence-testing methods. Qualitative scholars can enhance both the development and testing of their theories with a more self-conscious application of typological procedures. With respect to theory development, typologies are complementary to specifiying configurative or conjunctive causation,[11] describing equifinality or multiple sufficient causation,[12] and building in temporal effects and other complexities.[13] With respect to theory testing, typologies help scholars to identify the degree of casual homogeneity between cells,[14] and to engage in counterfactual reasoning.[15]

Explanatory typologies are likely to be most valuable when scholars self-consciously employ typological techniques. This chapter provides an account of what analytical moves are available, an accessible vocabulary to describe them, and concrete examples of how these techniques can be applied. The next two sections of this chapter draw on Lazarsfeld and Barton to develop procedures for manipulating explanatory typologies, looking first at techniques for compression, and then for expansion.

COMPRESSING THE NUMBER OF CELLS IN A PROPERTY SPACE

Lazarsfeld (1937), building on Hempel and Oppenheim (1936), provided the seminal discussion of the different techniques for compressing a property space, later developing them further with Allen Barton.[16] Lazarsfeld and Barton (1965, p. 173) define a 'reduction' (what I am calling a 'compression') as 'any classification as a result of which different combinations fall into one class.' As shown in Table 6.2, available compression procedures include the following.

Rescaling

The number of cells can be reduced by lowering the number of attributes for one or more of the theory's variables represented in the property space. For example, changing a four-variable model from trichotomous to dichotomous measurement reduces the number of cells from 81 to 16.[17] One thing to keep in mind when reducing the number of attributes is that each cell in the typology becomes more inclusive, hence potentially grouping cases that might not fit comfortably together.[18]

Table 6.2   Techniques for compressing property space

Kind of compression	Operation	Examples
Rescaling	Reduce the number of codings on one or more of the typology's dimensions	Rescaling Walt's four-variable balance of threat concept from trichotomous to dichotomous dimensions reduces the number of cells from 81 to 16 cells (Elman 2005, p. 302)
Indexing	Weigh different variables to combine them into a composite index where the same scores are treated as being equivalent	Equality of different combinations of Walt's threat constituents (Elman 2005, pp. 302–303)
Logical compression	Eliminate cells produced by impossible or highly improbable combinations of variables	If regional hegemons reliably balance against rising states in other regions, there cannot be two regional hegemons (Elman 2004, p. 567) Small states and mid-powers cannot be unlimited-aims revisionists (Schweller 1998, p. 85)
Empirical compression	Eliminate empty cells, i.e. cells which are empirically empty	Absence of two multipolar regions, or a multipolar region without an insular state (Elman 2004, p. 312)
Pragmatic compression	Collapse contiguous cells if their division serves no useful theoretical purpose	Deleting proximity as a threat element when using balance of threat theory to analyze the connection between revolution and war (Walt 1987)

Indexing

Barton (1955, p. 46) observes that where multiple attributes 'express essentially the same underlying characteristic or have their effects in the same direction' we can 'give each category on each dimension a certain weight, and add these together to get index scores for each cell.' Indexing treats all combinations that receive the same score as equivalent, in effect 'folding over the typology thus rendering formerly distant types equal.'[19] This technique presents more complex difficulties than its seeming simplicity would suggest, requiring arbitrary decisions on the appropriate weight for the high mid-low rank on each attribute. It should also be noted that indexing presupposes that equal scores are equivalent. It is possible that interaction effects between the different variables render this assumption problematic.

Logical compression

There might be a connection between two or more of the typology's dimensions such that some combinations are logically impossible or highly improbable. If so, we can delete these cells.[20] It should be noted that logical compression is a characteristic of the underlying theory, and it will almost always be an option to add an auxiliary assumption that will render an otherwise unfeasible prediction possible.

Empirical compression

Some combinations of variables might be logically possible, or not highly improbable, but there might nevertheless be no empirical examples of those combinations. If so, we might be able to delete these cells from the typology.[21] This method of reduction raises a number of concerns. First, the analyst would need to have complete knowledge of the population of cases to make a determination that some cells were empty, and could be dispensed with. Second, each cell represents a combination of codings on a number of dimensions. A mistake coding just one

of those dimensions would depopulate an otherwise occupied cell. Third, the technique conflicts with one of the benefits of using property space that derives from its representation of causal possibility: the discovery of counterfactual propositions. Reducing the space to empirically present cells undercuts that possibility. Finally, it is worth mentioning that empirical compression does not imply a direct relationship between cell population and the utility of a cell in a typology. An outlier cell, with a single case, might provide a severe test of the theory.

Pragmatic compression

Scholars can collapse contiguous cells if their division serves no useful theoretical purpose. Using pragmatic compression, 'certain groups of combinations are contracted to one class in view of the research purpose.'[22]

EXPANDING PROPERTY SPACE

Explanatory typologies can be constructed directly from a theoretical statement. They can also be rebuilt from analyses that already use a typology that has previously been minimized. This section considers the technique of expanding a property space from such a partial typology.

Expansion (what Lazarsfeld 1937, p. 132 calls 'substruction') takes an underspecified typology, or one that is implied from the use of a subpopulation of its types, and provides a full account of the associated property space by 'reverse engineering' the classification. The analyst works backward to lay out the property space from which the partial typology is derived, and the type of reduction technique that was used to produce it. As Lazarsfeld (1937, p. 132) notes, the procedure does not assume 'that the creator of the types really had such a procedure in mind. It is only claimed that, no matter how he actually found the types, he could have found them logically by such [an expansion].'

Typological expansion allows analysts to spot important combinations of attributes that were overlooked in the partial typology, and to draw attention to cases that need further attention.[23] The procedure might also help theorists to make explicit the assumptions that were used by the original analyst to suppress particular combinations.[24] The technique can be used to draw out the implications of a theorist employing outstanding 'types' with different attribute clusters, or to expand a formal but reduced typology back to its complete specification.

For example, John Mearsheimer's *The Tragedy of Great Power Politics* (2001) argues that the best strategy for states to ensure their survival is sophisticated maximization of relative power.[25] This prediction is modified by geographical context, especially the stopping power of water. Noting that distance makes global hegemony virtually impossible, Mearsheimer moves his focus to the regional level. The best that a state can reasonably hope for is: (1) to be a regional hegemon; and (2) to be the only regional hegemon.[26] The stopping power of water also makes island states like the United Kingdom relatively safe, and allows them to take a less interventionist role. Accordingly, whereas the theory applies to great powers in general,[27] Mearsheimer distinguishes between different kinds of great power: continental great powers acting in their own region (e.g., France and Germany); insular great powers acting in their own region (e.g., the United Kingdom); and regional hegemons acting in other regions (e.g., the United States).

Expanding the explanatory typology implicit in *The Tragedy of Great Power Politics* demonstrates a lacuna in Mearsheimer's theory, and provides an opportunity for additional analytic moves.[28] As displayed in Table 6.3, the kinds of state are represented in the rows, and the columns show whether the state is acting in its own or another region: the content of the cells are the states' predicted intra- and extra-regional behavior. Continental great powers like Germany from 1862 to 1945 will seek regional hegemony in their own neighborhoods when the distribution of capabilities makes such ambitions feasible.[29] When they are unable to achieve this dominance, such states will still maximize their relative power to the extent possible by appropriating resources from other great powers while blocking other states' similar ambitions.

The second kind of great power is an insular state – 'the only great power on a large body of land that is surrounded on all sides by water.'[30] Where located in a region containing other great powers that are vying for regional dominance, such island states will balance against the rising states rather than trying to be regional hegemons themselves. Accordingly, states such as the United Kingdom act as offshore balancers, intervening only when a continental power is near to achieving primacy.[31]

The third kind of great power in Mearsheimer's theory is one that has already achieved regional hegemony. Such great powers are status quo states that seek to defend the current favorable distribution of capabilities.[32] The only example in the last 200 years is the United State's dominance of the North American continent.[33]

The expansion of the implicit typology draws attention to a key omission in Mearsheimer's discussion of extra-regional

Table 6.3   Typology implicit in Mearsheimer's *Tragedy of Great Power Politics*

Type of great power	Exemplar	In-regional behavior	Extra-regional behavior
Continental great powers	Germany	Attempt regional hegemony while balancing against other states	Unclear. Case studies suggest balance against any would-be regional hegemons
Island great powers	Great Britain	Balance against any would-be regional hegemons	Unclear. Case studies suggest balance against any would-be regional hegemons
Regional hegemons	United States	Balance against other states to maintain regional hegemony	Balance against any would-be regional hegemons

behavior. While plainly predicting that regional hegemons will be robust offshore balancers, Mearsheimer is much less clear on whether the same holds true for continental and island great powers. While suggesting (Mearsheimer, 2001, p.141) that great powers 'strive to prevent rivals in other regions from gaining hegemony,' the discussion following that statement focuses almost exclusively on the behavior of regional hegemons. Elsewhere (Mearsheimer, 2001, p. 251), the volume suggests that great powers at least try to balance against rising hegemons in other regions. The unclear treatment of extra-regional great power behavior is more than just a footnote for Mearsheimer's theory. The sole success story of the last 200 years is the United States. The only plausible balancers that might have prevented its rise were the European great powers. Without explicitly addressing the reasons for their failure to contain the United States, the theory is unable to determine whether its achievement of regional hegemony is evidence that supports sophisticated power maximization as a sensible policy prescription.

PITFALLS IN PROPERTY SPACE: REIFICATION AND PUZZLE RELABELING

The cells in an explanatory typology are best seen as 'containers' of predictions made by the underlying theory. Users of explanatory typologies have to avoid a form of reification,[34] where cell labels themselves become free-standing 'explanations,' rather than the theory from which the property space was derived. To put it another way, in the context of an explanatory typology, reification occurs when a case is 'explained' because we attach a name to it, not because a theory we have deemed valid is seen as being applicable to it. This is less likely to be a problem for the original developer of an explanatory typology, but may well be an issue for scholars who read and use the typology at one remove.

A second challenge is whether a typology is really explanatory, or is instead a form of semantic relabeling that displaces questions without really answering them.[35] Although framed here in the context of increasing the number of cells in a property space, this issue arises whenever theories are amended to cover known anomalies.[36] Philosophers of science worry that an amendment to a theory designed to address a puzzle might just be a move to protect it from falsification, and not real scientific progress.[37] Typically, a concept is redefined, or an auxiliary hypothesis is added, to allow the theory to predict the anomaly.

One way of addressing this problem is to adopt a form of what Alan Musgrave (1974, pp. 3 and 7) calls the historical approach to confirmation of a scientific theory.[38] The historical approach suggests that we cannot determine whether evidence supports a theory solely on the basis of whether it 'fits' the current iteration of the theory. It is not enough to ask whether the theory covers known anomalies. It is also necessary to track the trajectory of a theory as it develops, and ask whether amendments did more than just relabeling empirical puzzles. The question would be whether the new categories provide additional value, signaled by the prediction of novel facts.[39]

CONCLUSION

Social scientists commonly employ explanatory typologies in their analyses; however, it would be helpful if more attention could be paid to the logic that underlies and justifies that usage, as well as to the different techniques that are available for expanding and compressing property space. Although the procedures described in this chapter might seem habitual, even intuitive, explanatory typologies are at their most powerful when they are used self-consciously. A more grounded approach will encourage rigor, enhance transparency, and increase the likelihood of producing cumulative results.

NOTES

1. This chapter draws from Elman (2005). The article from which this chapter was drawn benefited greatly from extensive critiques of several drafts by David Collier. Stephen G. Walker, Miriam Fendius Elman, James Mahoney, Gary Goertz, Reilly O'Neal, John Gerring, Bear Braumoeller, Lisa Martin, two anonymous reviewers, and the participants at the January 2004 Institute for Qualitative Research Methods provided valuable comments.

2. Bowker and Star (1999).

3. For overviews and reviews see, for example, Capecchi (1968), Nowotny (1971), Marradi (1990), Bailey (1972, 1973, 1992, 1994), and Tiryakian (1968). Mastering this literature is made difficult by the proliferation of labels for different kinds of types, including extreme, polar, ideal, pure, empirical, classificatory, constructed, and heuristic. In addition, methodologists tend to invent new terms for the different components in their 'typology of typologies,' and then to compare their approach with previous treatments of other scholars. As a result, the choice of labels for describing the subset of typologies and typological procedures discussed in this chapter is somewhat arbitrary.

4. The approach to typologies taken partly parallels J.W.N. Watkins' (1953) reading of Max Weber's 'individualistic' ideal types (see also McIntosh 1977, p. 267, n. 11 and Lindbekk 1992, pp. 292–295). For different interpretations of ideal types, see Albrow (1990), Burger (1987, pp. 160–167, 2001), Clarke (2001), Hekman (1983), and Rogers (1969). It is also sympathetic to, but goes beyond, Arthur Stinchcombe's (1987, pp. 43–47) description of type concepts and typologies. The approach is also consistent with that taken by Charles Ragin (2000, pp. 76–87) but without adopting his Boolean data-analytic strategy of qualitative comparative analysis (QCA) or fuzzy sets (Ragin 1987, 2000, pp. 120–145). The closest alternate treatment is offered by George and Bennett (2005, pp. 233–262) in their discussion of 'typological theories.'

5. The author of this chapter is a political scientist, a discipline that has benefited from several recent innovative treatments of qualitative methods, including King, Keohane and Verba (1994), Gerring (2001, 2007), Brady and Collier (2004), George and Bennett (2005), and Goertz (2006). For recent reviews and overviews, see Bennett and Elman (2006a, 2006b, 2007a, 2007b, 2007c), Mahoney (2007), Pierson (2007), and Levy (2007). For recent discussions explicitly focused on multi-method aspects of this 'renaissance,' see Lieberman (2005) and Collier and Elman (2008).

6. Lazarsfeld (1937), Lazarsfeld and Barton (1965), and Barton (1955) prefer the labels 'reduction' and 'substruction' to 'compression' and 'expansion.'

7. Lazarsfeld (1937, p. 120).

8. Lazarsfeld and Barton (1965, p. 169).

9. See Collier, LaPorte and Seawright (2008) for an outstanding discussion of descriptive typologies.

10. See McKinney (1950, p.238 and 1954, pp. 164–169) on the relationship between theories and typologies. Note, however, that McKinney's 'constructive typologies' are not always, or perhaps not even usually, theoretical in the sense used in this article. For example, whereas McKinney (1954, p. 195, 1966, p. 63) acknowledges that typologies can be derived from theories, he also suggests (McKinney, 1966, p. 63) that they can most usefully be constructed directly from the particularities of a historical situation.

11. Ragin (2000, pp. 67–82). See Brady (2002) for an outstanding review of different models of causal inference.

12. Bennett (1999, p. 9). See also Bennett and George (2001, p. 138).

13. On such phenomena, see Pierson (2000, 2003, and 2004), Bennett and Elman (2006b), Mahoney (2000), Buthe (2002), Thelen (2003), and Aminzade (1992). On typologies and time, see Nowotny (1971).

14. See Munck (2004, p. 111), Nowotny (1971, pp. 6–11), Rogowski (2004, p. 7), McKeown (2004, p.13), Eckstein (1975, pp. 117–120), and Przeworski and Teune (1970, pp. 32–39).

15. Goertz and Levy (2007). See also Tetlock and Belkin (1996, p. 4), Hempel (1965b, pp. 164–165).

16. Lazarsfeld and Barton (1965, Barton, 1955).

17. Such a compression might, but need not, be associated with a change in the level of measurement. See Stevens (1946, 1951, pp. 23–30, 1959).

18. For discussions of the closely related issues of conceptual differentiation and stretching. See Sartori (1970), Collier and Mahon (1993), Collier and Levitsky (1997), Collier and Adcock (1999), Sartori (1984), and Gerring (1999). On the connection between concepts and classification, see Hempel (1965a, pp. 138–139, 146–148).

19. Bailey (1994, p. 28).

20. Lazarsfeld (1937, p. 126), Lazarsfeld and Barton (1965, p. 173).

21. Bailey (1994, p. 27), Barton (1955, p. 46, 49),and Marradi (1990, p. 144).

22. Bailey (1994, p. 27), Barton (1955, p. 46, 49), and Marradi (1990, p. 144).

23. Barton (1955, p. 53).

24. Barton (1955, p. 50).

25. Mearsheimer (2001, pp. 32–36).

26. Mearsheimer (2001, pp. 140–145).

27. Mearsheimer (2001, pp. 5, 403, n. 5).

28. Note that this redacted discussion only addresses an initial substruction of Mearsheimer's typology. Elman (2004, 2005) includes additional analytical moves and the expansion of a more complex explanatory typology.

29. Mearsheimer (2001, pp. 181–209).

30. Mearsheimer (2001, p. 126).

31. Mearsheimer (2001, pp. 126–128, 261–264).
32. Mearsheimer (2001, p. 42).
33. Mearsheimer (2001, p. 141).
34. On the dangers of reification see Bailey (1994, p. 15), Tiryakian (1968, p. 179), McKinney (1954, pp. 148–149).
35. Vasquez (1997) makes a similar critique.
36. This kind of 'iteration' between theory and evidence is often prescribed (see, for example, Bates et al. [1998, p. 16] and Morrow [2002, pp. 187–188]) and hence the problem is likely to arise often.
37. The best-known discussion of this issue is Lakatos (1970).
38. See also Worrall (1978b, p. 321) and Mayo (1996, pp. 254–256). It should be noted that the historical approach to confirmation looks for different categories of prediction, not evidence that predicted values of the same dependent variable are repeated in additional cases. To be sure, recurring tests of the same proposition are valuable because they offer evidence about whether a prediction is empirically accurate. As Robert Jervis (1985, p. 146) notes, 'Scholars often look at many cases to see if a proposed generalization fits the data. [But t]his is a form of confirmation, not the discovery of new facts.'
39. Philosophers of science disagree on which standard of novelty to apply, i.e. they differ on the answer to the question: 'novel compared to what?' Potential answers to this question include: strict temporal novelty (Lakatos [1970, p. 118], Zahar [1973, p. 101], Worrall [1978a, p. 46 and p. 66, n. 7], Frankel [1979, p. 24], Gardner [1982, p. 2], Nunan [1984, p. 275], and Hands [1991, p. 96]), new interpretation novelty (Lakatos [1970, p. 188], Koertge [1971, p. 171, n. 5], Musgrave [1974, p. 11], Nunan [1984, p. 275], Carrier [1988, p. 207]), heuristic novelty (Zahar [1973, p. 101], Lakatos and Zahar [1975, p. 376, n. 65]), and background theory novelty (Musgrave [1974, pp. 15–16], Worral [1978b, pp. 321–322], Mayo [1996, p. 208]).

REFERENCES

Albrow, M. 1990 *Max Weber's Construction of Social Theory*. New York: St. Martin's Press.
Aminzade, R. 1992 'Historical sociology and time' *Sociological Methods and Research* 20(4): 456–480.
Bailey, K.D. 1972 'Polythetic reduction of monothetic property space' *Sociological Methodology* 4: 83–111.
Bailey, K.D. 1973 'Monothetic and polythetic typologies and their relation to conceptualization measurement, and scaling' *American Sociological Review* 38(1): 18–33.
Bailey, K.D. 1992 'Typologies' in E.F. Borgatta and M.L. Borgatta (Eds) *Encyclopedia of Sociology*. New York: Macmillan, pp. 2188–2194.
Bailey, K.D. 1994 *Typologies and Taxonomies: An Introduction to Classification Techniques*. Thousand Oaks, CA: Sage Publications.
Barton, A.H. 1955 'The concept of property-space in social research' in P.F. Lazarsfeld and M. Rosenberg (Eds) *Language of Social Research*. Glencoe, IL: Free Press, pp. 40–53.
Bates, R.H., Greif, A., Levi, M., Rosenthal, J-L. and Weingast, B.R. 1998 *Analytic Narratives*. Princeton, NJ: Princeton University Press.
Bennett, A. 1999 'Causal inference in case studies: from Mill's methods to causal mechanisms.' Paper presented at the 96th Annual Meeting of the American Political Science Association, September, Atlanta, GA.
Bennett, A. and Elman, C. 2006a 'Qualitative research: recent developments in case study methods' *Annual Review of Political Science* 9: 455–476.
Bennett, A. and Elman, C. 2006b 'Complex causal relations and case study methods: the example of path dependence' *Political Analysis* 14(3): 250–267.
Bennett, A. and Elman, C. 2007a 'Qualitative methods: the view from the subfields' *Comparative Political Studies* 40(2): 111–121.
Bennett, A. and Elman, C. 2007b 'Case study methods in the international relations subfield' *Comparative Political Studies* 40(2): 170–195.
Bennett, A. and Elman, C. 2007c 'Case study methods in the study of international relations' in C. Reus-Smit and D. Snidal (Eds) *Oxford Handbook of International Relations*. Oxford: Oxford University Press.
Bennett, A. and George, A. 2001 'Case studies and process tracing in history and political science: similar strokes for different foci' in C. Elman and M.F. Elman (Eds) *Bridges and Boundaries: Historians, Political Scientists and the Study of International Relations*. Cambridge, MA: MIT Press, pp. 137–166.
Bowker, G.C. and Star, S.L. 1999 *Sorting Things Out: Classification and Its Consequences*. Cambridge, MA: The MIT Press.
Brady, H.E. 2002 'Models of causal inference: going beyond the Neyman-Rubin-Holland theory.' Paper presented at the 16th Annual Meeting of the Political Methodology Group, July, Seattle, WA.
Brady, H. and Collier, D. 2004 *Rethinking Social Inquiry: Diverse Tools, Shared Standards*. Lanham, MD: Rowman and Littlefield.
Burger, T. 1987 *Max Weber's Theory of Concept Formation*. Durham, NC: Duke University Press.

Burger, T. 2001 'Ideal Types: Conceptions in the Social Sciences' in Neil J. Smelser and Paul B. Baltes (Eds), *International Encyclopedia of the Social and Behavioral Sciences*. New York: Elsevier, pp. 7139–42.

Buthe, T. 2002 'Taking temporality seriously: modeling history and the use of narrative as evidence' *American Political Science Review* 96(3): 481–493.

Capecchi, V. 1968 'On the definition of typology and classification in sociology' *Quality and Quantity* 2(1–2): 9–30.

Carrier, M. 1988 'On novel facts: a discussion of criteria for non-ad-hoc-ness in the methodology of scientific research programmes' *Zeitschrift fur allgemaine Wissenschaftstheorie* 19(2): 205–231.

Clarke, S. 2001 'Idealization, abstraction and ideal types' in N.J. Smelser and P.B. Bales (Eds) *International Encyclopedia of the Social and Behavioral Sciences*. New York: Elsevier, pp. 7142–7148.

Collier, D. and Adcock, R. 1999 'Democracy and dichotomies: a pragmatic approach to choices about concepts' *Annual Review of Political Science* 2: 537–565.

Collier, D. and Elman, C. 2008 'Qualitative and multi-method research: organizations, publication, and reflections on integration' in J.M. Box-Steffensmeier, H.E. Brady and D. Collier (Eds) *The Oxford Handbook of Political Methodology*. New York: Oxford University Press.

Collier, D and Levitsky, S. 1997 'Democracy with adjectives: conceptual innovation in comparative research' *World Politics* 49(3): 430–451.

Collier, D. and Mahon, J.E. 1993 'Conceptual 'stretching' revisited: adapting categories in comparative analysis' *American Political Science Review* 87(4): 845–855.

Collier, D., LaPorte, J and Seawright, J. 2008 'Typologies: forming concepts and creating categorical variables' in J.M. Box-Steffensmeier, H.E. Brady and D. Collier (Eds) *The Oxford Handbook of Political Methodology*. New York: Oxford University Press.

Eckstein, H. 1975 'Case study and theory in political science' in F. Greenstein and N. Polsby (Eds) *Handbook of Political Science*. Reading, MA: Addison-Wesley, pp.79–137.

Elman, C. 2004 'Extending offensive realism: the Louisiana Purchase and America's rise to regional hegemony' *American Political Science Review* 98(4): 563–576.

Elman, C. 2005 'Explanatory typologies in qualitative studies of international politics' *International Organization* Spring 59: 293–326.

Frankel, H. 1979 'The career of continental drift theory: an application of Imre Lakatos' analysis of scientific growth to the rise of drift theory' *Studies in History and Philosophy of Science* 10(1): 21–66.

Gardner, M.R. 1982 'Predicting novel facts' *British Journal for the Philosophy of Science* 33(1): 1–15.

George, A.L. and Bennett, A. 2005 *Case Studies and Theory Development in the Social Sciences*. Cambridge, MA: MIT Press.

Gerring, J. 1999 'What makes a concept good? A criterial framework for understanding concept formation in the social sciences' *Polity* 31(3): 357–393.

Gerring, J. 2001 *Social Science Methodology: A Criterial Framework*. Cambridge, MA: Cambridge University Press.

Gerring, J. 2007 *Case Study Research: Principles and Practices*. Cambridge: Cambridge University Press.

Goertz, G. 2006 *Social Science Concepts: A User's Guide*. Princeton, NJ: Princeton University Press.

Goertz, G. and Levy, J.S. (Eds) 2007 *Explaining War and Peace: Case Studies and Necessary Condition Counterfactuals*. New York: Routledge.

Hands, D.W. 1991 'Reply to Hamminga and Maki' in N. de Marchi and M. Blaug (Eds) *Appraising Economic Theories: Studies in the Methodology of Research Programs*. Brookfield, VT: Edward Elgar, pp. 91–102.

Hekman, S.J. 1983 'Weber's ideal type: a contemporary reassessment' *Polity* 16(1): 119–137.

Hempel, C.G. 1965a 'Fundamentals of taxonomy' in C.G. Hempel (Ed.) *Aspects of Scientific Explanation and Other Essays in the Philosophy of Science*. New York: The Free Press, pp. 137–154.

Hempel, C.G. 1965b 'Typological methods in the natural and social sciences' in C.G. Hempel (Ed.) *Aspects of Scientific Explanation and Other Essays in the Philosophy of Science*. New York: The Free Press, pp. 155–171.

Hempel, C.G. and Oppenheim, P. 1936 *Der Typusbegriff im Lichte der Nuen Logik*. Leiden, Netherlands: A. W, Siythoff.

Jervis, R. 1985 'Pluralistic rigor: a comment on Bueno de Mesquita' *International Studies Quarterly* 29(2): 145–149.

King, G.,Keohane, R.O. and Verba, S. 1994 *Designing Social Inquiry: Scientific Inference in Qualitative Research*. Princeton, NJ: Princeton University Press.

Koertge, N. 1971 'Inter-theoretic criticism and the growth of science' in R.C. Buck and R.S. Cohen (Eds) *Boston Studies in the Philosophy of Science, Volume 8: PSA 1970*. Dordrecht, The Netherlands: D. Reidel, pp. 160–173.

Lakatos, I. 1970 'Falsification and the methodology of scientific research programmes' in I. Lakatos and A. Musgrave (Eds) *Criticism and the Growth of*

Knowledge. New York: Cambridge University Press, pp. 91–196.

Lakatos, I. and Zahar, E. 1975 'Why did Copernicus' research programme supersede Ptolemy's?' in R.S. Westman (Ed.) *The Copernican Achievement.* Berkeley, CA: University of California Press, pp. 354–383.

Lazarsfeld, P.F. 1937 'Some remarks on the typological procedures in social research' *Zeitschrift fur Sozialforschung* 6: 119–139.

Lazarsfeld, P.F. and Barton, A.H. 1965 'Qualitative measurement in the social sciences: classification, typologies, and indices' in D. Lerner and H.D. Lasswell (Eds) *The Policy Sciences.* Stanford, CA: Stanford University Press, pp. 155–192.

Levy, J.S. 2007 'Qualitative methods and cross-method dialogue in political science' *Comparative Political Studies* 40(2): 196–214.

Lieberman, E. 2005 'Nested analysis as a mixed-method strategy for comparative research' *American Political Science Review* 99(3): 435–452.

Lindbekk, T. 1992 'The Weberian ideal-type: development and continuities' *Acta Sociologica* 35(4): 285–297.

Mahoney, J. 2000 'Path dependence in historical sociology' *Theory and Society* 29(4): 507–548.

Mahoney, J. 2007 'Qualitative methodology and comparative politics' *Comparative Political Studies* 40(2): 122–144.

Marradi, A. 1990 'Classification, typology, taxonomy' *Quality and Quantity* 24(2): 129–157.

Mayo, D.G. 1996 *Error and the Growth of Experimental Knowledge.* Chicago, IL: The University of Chicago Press.

McIntosh, D. 1977 'The objective bases of Max Weber's ideal types' *History and Theory* 16(3): 265–279.

McKeown, T.J. 2004 'Case studies and the limits of the statistical worldview' in H.E. Brady and D. Collier (Eds) *Rethinking Social Inquiry: Diverse Tools, Shared Standards.* Lanham, MD: Rowman and Littlefield, pp. 139–167.

McKinney, J.C. 1950 'The role of constructive typology in scientific sociological analysis' *Social Forces* 28(3): 235–240.

McKinney, J.C. 1954 'Constructive typology and social research' in J.T. Doby (Ed.) *An Introduction to Social Research.* Harrisburg, PA: The Stackpole Company, pp. 139–198.

McKinney, J.C. 1966 *Constructive Typology and Social Theory.* New York: Appleton-Century-Crofts.

Mearsheimer, J.J. 2001 *The Tragedy of Great Power Politics.* New York: Norton and Company.

Morrow, J.D. 2002 'International conflict: assessing the democratic peace and offense-defense theory' in

Katznelson, I. and Milner, H.V. (Eds) *Political Science: State of the Discipline.* New York: W.W. Norton, pp. 172–196.

Munck, G. 2004 'Tools for qualitative research' in H.E. Brady and D. Collier (Eds) *Rethinking Social Inquiry: Diverse Tools, Shared Standards.* Lanham, MD: Rowman and Littlefield, pp. 105–121.

Musgrave, A. 1974 'Logical versus historical theories of confirmation' *British Journal for the Philosophy of Science* 25(1): 1–23.

Nowotny, H. 1971 'The uses of typological procedures in qualitative macrosociological studies' *Quality and Quantity* 6(1): 3–37.

Nunan, R. 1984 'Novel facts, Bayesian rationality, and the history of continental drift' *Studies in History and Philosophy of Science* 15(4): 267–307.

Pierson, P. 2000 'Increasing returns, path dependence, and the study of politics' *American Political Science Review* 94(2): 251–267.

Pierson, P. 2003 'Big, slow-moving, and … invisible: macro-social processes in the study of comparative politics' in J. Mahoney and D. Rueschemeyer (Eds) *Comparative Historical Analysis in the Social Sciences.* Cambridge, MA: Cambridge University Press, pp. 177–207.

Pierson, P. 2004 *Politics in Time: History, Institutions, and Social Analysis.* Princeton, NJ: Princeton University Press.

Pierson, P. 2007 'The costs of marginalization: qualitative methods in the study of American politics' *Comparative Political Studies* 40(2): 145–169.

Przeworksi, A. and Teune, H. 1970 *The Logic of Comparative Social Inquiry.* New York: Wiley Interscience.

Ragin, C.C. 1987 *The Comparative Method: Moving beyond Qualitative and Quantitative Strategies.* Berkeley, CA: University of California Press.

Ragin, C. 2000 *Fuzzy Set Social Science.* Chicago, IL: University of Chicago Press.

Rogers, R.E. 1969 *Max Weber's Ideal Type Theory.* New York: Philosophical Library, Inc.

Rogowski, R. 2004 'How inference in the social (but not the physical) sciences neglects theoretical anomaly,' in H.E. Brady and D. Collier, (Eds) *Rethinking Social Inquiry: Diverse Tools, Shared Standards.* Lanham, MD: Rowman and Littlefield, pp. 75–83.

Sartori, G. 1970 'Concept misformation in comparative politics' *American Political Science Review* 64(4): 1033–1053.

Sartori, G. 1984 'Guidelines for concept analysis' in G. Sartori (Ed.) *Social Science Concepts: A Systematic Analysis.* Beverly Hills, CA: Sage, pp. 15–85.

Schweller, R.L. 1998 *Deadly Imbalances: Tripolarity and Hitler's Strategy of World Conquest.* New York: Columbia University Press.

Stevens, S.S. 1946 'On the theory of scales of measurement' *Science* 103(2684): 677–680.

Stevens, S.S. 1951 'Mathematics, measurement, and psychophysics' in S.S. Stevens (Ed.) *Handbook of Experimental Psychology.* New York: John Wiley, pp. 1–49.

Stevens, S.S. 1959 'Measurement, psychophysics, and utility' in C.W. Churchman and P. Ratoosh (Eds) *Measurement: Definitions and Theories.* New York: John Wiley, pp. 18–63.

Stinchecombe, A.L. 1987 *Constructing Social Theories.* Chicago, IL: University of Chicago Press. Originally published 1968 by Harcourt, Brace & World.

Tetlock P.E. and Belkin, A. 1996 'Counterfactual thought experiments in world politics: logical, methodological and psychological perspectives' in P.E. Tetlock and A. Belkin (Eds) *Counterfactual Thought Experiments in World Politics.* Princeton, NJ: Princeton University Press, pp. 1–38.

Thelen, K. 2003 'How institutions evolve: insights from comparative-historical analysis' in J. Mahoney and D. Rueschemeyer (Eds) *Comparative Historical Analysis in the Social Sciences.* Cambridge, MA: Cambridge University Press, pp. 208–240.

Tiryakian, E.A. 1968 'Typologies' in D.L. Sills (Ed.) *International Encyclopedia of the Social Sciences.* New York: Macmillan, pp. 177–186.

Vasquez, J.A. 1997 'The realist paradigm and degenerative versus progressive research programs: an appraisal of neotraditional research on Waltz's balancing proposition' *American Political Science Review* 91(4): 899–912.

Walt, S.M. 1987 *The Origins of Alliances.* Ithaca, NY: Cornell University Press.

Watkins, J.W.N. 1953 'Ideal types and historical explanation' in H. Feigl and M. Brodbeck (Eds) *Readings in the Philosophy of Science.* New York: Appleton-Century-Crofts, pp. 723–743.

Worrall, J. 1978a 'The ways in which the methodology of scientific research programmes improves on Popper's methodology' in G. Radnitzky and G. Andersson (Eds) *Progress and Rationality in Science.* Dordrecht, The Netherlands: D. Reidel, pp. 45–70.

Worrall, J. 1978b 'Research programmes, empirical support and the Duhem problem: replies to criticism' in G. Radnitzky and G. Andersson (Eds) *Progress and Rationality in Science.* Dordrecht, The Netherlands: D. Reidel, pp. 321–338.

Zahar, E. 1973 'Why did Einstein's programme supersede Lorentz's?' *British Journal for the Philosophy of Science* 24(2): 95–123.

7

Introducing Cluster Analysis: What Can It Teach Us about the Case?

Emma Uprichard

INTRODUCTION

This chapter introduces cluster analysis as a case-based method. Its aim is twofold. First, it introduces two key issues that are key to the practice of cluster analysis, and are extensively referred to within the related literature: (1) the aims and uses of cluster analysis; and (2) the types of cluster analysis. Second, I ask a more general question about the notion of the case: What can cluster analysis, as a case-based method, teach us about the case? What questions are raised in thinking about some of the key issues that are encountered in cluster analysis? To what extent are some of the difficulties associated with the method in fact a reflection of the difficulties of conceptualising the 'case' in the first place? And to what extent might we learn about ways of thinking about the case, and groups of cases, through reflexively considering the difficulties involved in sorting out multiple cases?

On the one hand, then, the chapter acts as a brief introduction to cluster analysis as a case-based method and some key aspects involved in its practice. On the other hand, and forming the larger part of the chapter, it reflexively argues that the method itself reflects, to some extent at least, the ontology of the 'case' more generally. Here, I ask about cluster analysis and the particular points of contention and unresolved difficulties associated with this method. From these particular issues, I explore what it is about the case that might help to explain some of the on-going, seemingly constant, irresolvable issues associated with cluster analysis. Although I do not claim to fully answer this grand ontological question about the nature of the case, I nevertheless consider it in relation to this particular methodological approach that is used to learn more about cases and their properties more generally. Overall, then, this chapter touches on the epistemological issues involved in knowing the case through the use of a particular case-based method, i.e. cluster analysis, and asks what the ontological issues of the case might be, given these epistemological issues. A good starting point, then, towards achieving this goal is to simply think about the aims and uses of the method in question.

AIMS AND USES

Kettenring's (2006) recent review of the practice of cluster analysis ranks this approach as one of the leading methods being used in the past ten years to explore and analyse large complex quantitative databases. Although the term 'cluster analysis' is often attributed to Tryon (1939) who classified *variables*, the same techniques are used to classify *cases,* and have been used in this way increasingly ever since his publication. Today, unless otherwise specified, the terms 'clustering', 'numerical taxonomy' and 'classification' are used interchangeably. Here, for consistency, the term 'cluster analysis' will be used predominantly throughout the chapter. Similarly, this chapter uses the term 'case' as a convenient way to refer to all taxa, and is used synonymously with the term 'operational taxonomic units', or OTUs, which is used predominantly in literature relating to cluster analysis. The terms 'cluster', 'group' and 'type' are also used interchangeably.

Put simply, the term 'cluster analysis' is used to refer to a branch of descriptive and exploratory (and not inferential) statistical techniques. The method sorts out *cases* (rather than variables, although it is still plausible that variables are considered as cases) into groups of similar cases, whereby the cases within each cluster are more alike than those outside the cluster. The basic principle of all cluster-analysis methods is the same – each case is assigned to a particular cluster based on how similar or dissimilar it is relative to other cases. More recently, authors have extended clustering methods to multi-level classification whereby aggregate attributes (e.g. neighbourhood classifications) are used as just another set of attributes

known about particular individuals or types of individuals (Alsberg 1999, Webber and Farr 2001, Webber 2004, Williamson et al. 2005). Similarly, authors have proposed the use of clustering methods to classify trajectories of dynamic cases, thus extending cross-sectional approaches to cluster analysis to longitudinal, multi-level explorations (Cape et al. 2000, Byrne and Uprichard 2007).

Note that cluster analysis differs from other methods that assign cases to previously defined categories or clusters (e.g. discriminant analysis), which are sometimes referred to as 'identification' methods. Instead, in clustering methods, previously *unknown* clusters emerge out the assortment of configurations of attributes associated with the whole case. More specifically still, these various configurations are used to: (1) establish how the cases relate to one another with regards to their relative similarity and/or dissimilarity to one another, and in so doing; and (2) classify whole cases into types of clusters of cases. Hence, clustering methods are considered to be case-based methods primarily due to the way that they focus on understanding the *relationships between the cases*, and *not*, as with most variable based statistical analyses, on the *relationships between the variables*. This important point will be reiterated throughout this discussion.

Cluster analysis is used for a variety of purposes. Lorr (1983) describes six of them: identification of 'natural' clusters; construction of a useful conceptual scheme for classifying entities; data reduction; generating hypotheses; testing hypothesised classes believed to be present; identification of homogeneous subgroups characterised, which may be useful for prediction. Another five purposes are provided by Good (1965 cited in Cormack 1971, p. 322): mental clarification and communication; discovery of new fields of research; planning an organisational structure; a checklist; for fun. Clatworthy et al. (2005) add an important twelfth purpose, which was previously suggested by Zubin (1936): bridging the gap between nomothetic and idiographic approaches, such that limited knowledge of the individual entity is transcended when its relation to other similar entities is established.

Of the twelve key purposes, Aldenderfer and Blashfield (1984) comment that, although many are combined within any particular study, the 'creation of classifications' probably remains the most frequent use of clustering methods. Sometimes, the creation of classifications might be a first step, main step within a project. As Everitt et al. (2001) point out, 'a classification scheme may simply represent a convenient method for organising a large dataset', after which the variation within and between one or more clusters using more traditional statistical analyses might be modelled. Other times, the creation of classifications is a goal in and of itself. It depends, of course, on the overall aims and objectives of the research project, rather than the potential or purpose of cluster analysis *per se*.

Already, then, in terms of what cluster analysis might teach us about the case, we can say that knowledge about multiple cases helps us know more about the single case (Zubin 1936, Clatworthy et al. 2005). Vice versa, and more accurately according to the 'mechanics' of the method itself, knowledge about many individual cases helps us know more about multiple cases. This is not a new feature *per se*; quantitative research has been founded upon it. Note, however, the important difference: what we are talking about in cluster analysis is knowledge of the *multiple* and not, as is the case in variable focused-analyses, about knowledge of the *aggregate*. Of course, knowledge of the aggregate comes from knowledge about the multiple, but knowledge of the multiple does not necessarily come from knowledge of the aggregate. However, classifications in cluster analysis emerge *not* from aggregate *data* or aggregate *measures per se*, which are derived from many, or combinations of many, individual measures, even where aggregate level knowledge is used as just another 'attribute' of the individual case (Webber 2004); classifications are *not* based on a percentage of those cases that have or do not have this or that particular attribute. Instead, each case is assigned to a cluster,

on a case-by-case basis, according to whether that particular case has or does not have this or that attribute. This difference is important because although knowledge of multiple cases is derived from knowledge of single cases, the nature of that ideographic knowledge is not the same; it is based on the knowledge of the *whole* case, and not on knowledge of one or more *aspects* of the case.

Indeed, the methodological use of the 'variable' is arguably cluster analysis' point of departure from other multivariate methods such as correspondence analysis (see Chapter 8). Both cluster analysis and correspondence analysis are numerical taxonomy techniques that, ultimately, inductively 'find' clusters within the dataset. One might be tempted to conclude, therefore, that both methods should 'find' similar 'types' of cluster within the same dataset, if 'types' are an ontological feature of the cases themselves, but this is not always the case and the reason is epistemological. That is, the way that 'types' are 'created' has much to do with the way that 'distance' is measured in Euclidean space. More specifically, at the heart of both techniques, and indeed of all taxonomic procedures, is the concept of homology – a concept that dates back to pre-Darwinian times and is still troublesome today (see Sneath and Sokal 1973). Sneath and Sokal explain it as follows:

> Homology may be loosely described as compositional and structural correspondence. By *compositional correspondence* we mean a qualitative resemblance in terms of ... constituents; by *structural correspondence* we refer to similarity in terms of (spatial or temporal) arrangement of parts ... (Sneath and Sokal 1973, p. 77)

An additional difficulty in operationalising homology, however, Sneath and Sokal continue (1973, p. 79), is that 'some homology statements are made about unit characters, others about sets of unit characters'. Whilst all taxonomic approaches need to wrestle with these fundamental problems, the ways in which they tackle them also distinguish them. Thus, for example, considering cluster analysis and correspondence analysis together, we might say that they are different in so far as cluster analysis approaches these issues by focusing on the case, correspondence analysis does so by focusing on the variable. Whereas cluster analysis produces 'types' through operationalising and measuring homology between cases, correspondence analysis does this by operationalising and measuring homology between variables. To this extent, whilst both approaches identify 'types', they differ primarily in the way that they 'trust' the summary values of the variables to 'position' each case. There are advantages and disadvantages to both, and so there is some sense in using both (see Guinot et al. 2001), although the time cost involved in doing this will be vastly increased.

ONE APPROACH – MANY METHODS

As already implied, the term 'cluster analysis' embraces a plurality of procedures. Just as the term 'interviews' is used to refer to a family of interview methods (e.g. 'semi-structured', 'structured'), so too are there many kinds of 'cluster analysis'. Exactly how many types of cluster analysis there are depends on the ways in which authors have classified them, and many authors have (reflexively) classified them in a remarkable variety of ways. For the purposes this chapter, and in my own spirit of trying to synthesise and, when necessary, simplify complex ideas as far as possible, but not to the point of error, I draw on the work, or part of the work, of several authors in order to depict a classification of the myriad of main approaches. That said, a few words of caution about how to interpret this depiction are necessary.

First, the methods here are not to be taken as an exhaustive list of the various possible types of clustering methods, but rather as an indication of the main ways of thinking about them and that are also most frequently discussed in the published literature associated with clustering methods. There are many more that are not even referred to and they may or may not sit easily within this classification. Second, whilst this

depiction follows the majority of authors in thinking about cluster analysis as referring to a range of clustering *methods* (Cormack 1971, Sneath and Sokal 1973, Aldenderfer and Blashfield 1984, Everitt et al. 2001, Kettenring 2006), some authors argue that it is more accurate to think of these ways of sorting out cases as the classification of clustering *algorithms* (e.g. Jardine and Sibson 1971), of which there are literally hundreds that use one, more or none of the various combinations of techniques described below. Third, even though I have represented the main approaches as a flow graph of 'crisp' categories, it is probably more accurate to think of these as 'fuzzy sets', which may overlap with one another, to a greater or lesser extent, depending on the specific algorithms that are employed to obtain the final set of clusters. Furthermore, even as 'crisp' methods, they are often used iteratively and interactively together, as a part of a process of 'experimentation' and 'exploration' rather than alone as 'single methods'. Fourth, although I have provided some alternative 'names' for some of the methods, there are many additional alternatives that are not depicted in the diagram. 'The literature on cluster analysis' (see Blashfield and Aldenderfer 1978) is riddled with jargon, so much so that, over two decades ago, Blashfield and Aldender (1978, p. 286) make the point that for iterative partitioning methods, 'it is not even possible to create an organisational table of jargon'. Blashfield and Aldender (1978, p. 85) are particularly sympathetic to the need to clarify this 'jargon' and provide what I consider to be the most helpful list of 'equivalent terms' to those listed here. Given these four points, the classification depicted here should only be used loosely, and as a 'rough guide' or 'way into' the different clustering procedures rather than a fixed, finished framework.

To begin, then, we can think of clustering methods as falling into two main groups (Mezzich 1982): *finished* and *unfinished* clustering methods. Finished clustering methods are those methods that are more typically associated with the terms 'cluster analysis', 'classification' and 'numerical taxonomy', whereby the end product of the analysis are set clusters with specified membership. Unfinished clustering methods require additional work in order to obtain a final set of clusters, e.g. further allocation of cases to clusters. In practice, many researchers will use a combination of both (Kettering 2006). This chapter, however, focuses only on 'finished' clustering methods since 'unfinished' ones are often adaptations of the various 'finished' ones.

There are two main ways of thinking about finished clustering methods: *hierarchical* and *non-hierarchical* methods. There are several kinds of hierarchical method, just as there are non-hierarchical ones. As their names suggest, hierarchical clustering methods generate hierarchical or nested clusters, whereas non-hierarchical methods produce a single-level 'string' of different clusters. Within hierarchical clustering, the two main ones include agglomerative and divisive methods. They differ primarily in the way that they sort out the cases. *Agglomerative methods* construct clusters by treating each case as

a separate entity and then 'fusing' the most similar ones, until all cases are 'agglomerated' within a specific structure. Examples include: single linkage, complete linkage, average linkage and many others. *Divisive methods* construct clusters the other way round, starting from one cluster of all the cases and then 'dividing' off the most different cases, until all cases are 'divided' into appropriate clusters. There are two main types of divisive method: monothetic, which establishes clusters on the basis of (usually the absence or presence of) one attribute; and polythetic, which establishes clusters on the basis of more than one (usually several) attributes. In terms of thinking of these two approaches as hierarchical trees, agglomerative methods begin with the cases as branches and ends when they are fused into a single trunk, whereas divisive methods begin at the trunk and work towards the branches.

Deciding when to use hierarchical or non-hierarchical methods depends on both the nature of the dataset and what is already

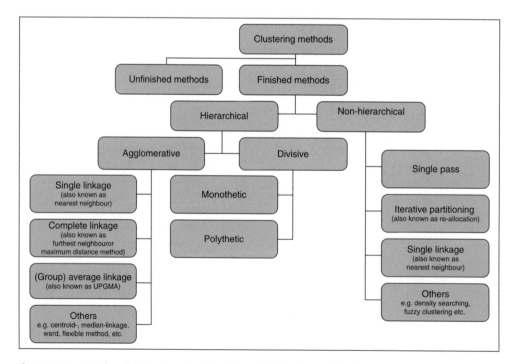

Figure 7.1 Rough guide to the classification of clustering methods.

known about the inter-structure of the cases themselves. Another key difference between these two broad groups of cluster approaches is that, in hierarchical methods, once a case has been assigned to a cluster there is no going back; it remains in that cluster regardless of the subsequent overall formation of the final clusters. Whereas a similar 'single pass' method is available in non-hierarchical clustering, researchers usually prefer to use a more iterative procedure, in which cases are allocated and then re-allocated, until they are in the 'best' cluster, both with respect to the final clusters that are available and the other cases with which it has been compared.

Because of these differences, in many instances, it may be appropriate to combine both approaches. For example, non-hierarchical clustering might be used in the initial stages as a data-reduction technique to classify particular wards, and then hierarchical clustering might be subsequently used to reveal 'major clusters' of types of neighbourhood areas in which several other 'minor clusters' of individuals exist (Webber and Farr 2001). Conversely, Milligan (1980) suggests using a hierarchical cluster analysis to obtain an approximate number of existing clusters within the data, and then to use an iterative non-hierarchical procedures (e.g. k means cluster analysis) to improve, refine and, ultimately, optimise the cluster results.

Within both hierarchical and non-hierarchical approaches, there are literally dozens of methods, and within each one of them, there are even more 'options' relating to which similarity/dissimilarity measure(s) to use. For instance, Sokal and Sneath (1963) consider fifteen main types, Hartigan (1967) lists twelve, which Cormack (1971) suggests are better thought of as fifteen types of indices. Everitt et al. (2001) refer to over twenty, which they mention are only some of the 'main' ones, and (helpfully) organise according to the levels of measurement of the variables used within the analysis. However, they accurately sum up that despite their efforts to classify the 'main ones', in fact 'an almost endless number of similarity and

dissimilarity coefficients exist' (Everitt et al. 2001, p. 52). As result, this chapter only touches the 'tip of the iceberg' of the available approaches to cluster analysis.

It is worth noting, however, that although similarity and dissimilarity measures play a key part, arguably *the* key part, in cluster analysis, there are philosophical issues relating to the concept of similarity that are not explicitly, but are implicitly, incorporated within cluster analysis, regardless of the exact type, which basically concern the issue of homology touched on above. Most measures of similarity/dissimilarity conceptually treat similarity as a symmetric relation. However, as Tversky (1977) has argued, this is not necessarily accurate. His argument is that we say '*a* is like *b*', where *a* is the subject and *b* is the referent, or 'the portrait resembles the person' rather than 'the person resembles the portrait'. His point is summed up in the following:

> In the interpretation of similes, one assumes a resemblance between the subject and the referent and searches for an interpretation of the space that would maximise the quality of the match. The same pair of objects, therefore, can be viewed as similar or different depending on the choice of a frame of reference. (Tversky 1977, p. 349)

In cluster analysis, cases are deemed to be 'similar' or 'dissimilar' compared to another case, or other cases, that are selected *in some way* (of which there are many). Which case(s) become(s) the subject(s) or referent(s) is as much an accident of the method as it is a deliberate step of the method. The issue of how to measure 'resemblance' (whether it be with use of a similarity measure of a dissimilarity measure, or both) is, therefore, not a trivial matter, and ultimately plays a significant role within any cluster analysis.

Hence, whilst 'measurement' is a key issue in any quantitative analysis (see, e.g. Cicourel 1964, Blalock 1982, Sayer 1984, Byrne 2002), measurement issues are compounded in clustering methods because they operate in three ways: (1) the usual issues involved in the operationalisation of the object of study, i.e. the case, in the form of variables (or, as Byrne [2002] puts it, 'variate traces'); (2) the different scales or magnitudes of those variables, e.g. the quantitative difference (i.e. standard deviation) within a particular measurement may be of qualitative import – various methods of standardisation help rectify this issue to some extent, although there are divisions among authors regarding whether this should be done from the outset or only within particular clusters (Aldenderfer and Blashfield 1984); both (1) and (2) also occur at the level of (3): the operationalisation of the notions of 'similarity' and, by implication, 'dissimilarity'. This third 'subset' of measurement issues relating to notions of 'similarity'/'dissimilarity' are necessarily involved in sorting out cases into appropriate clusters, and impact therefore on any interpretation of cluster analyses in general. 'The choice of similarity measure, then', Aldenderfer and Blashfield (1984, p. 19) sum up, 'should be embedded ultimately within the design of research, which is itself determined by the theoretical, practical, and philosophical context of the classification problem'.

Because 'similarity' and 'dissimilarity' measures ultimately dictate the results of any cluster analysis, the question of 'what is a cluster?' becomes problematic as well. Once again, authors have answered this in numerous ways, but the answer tends to remain, necessarily, somewhat vague (May 1982). Cormack argues that despite the lack of formal definitions and the disparity between the different definitions or descriptions, two basic ideas are involved: internal cohesion and external isolation. Isolation refers to the idea that similar entities should be placed together such that a discontinuity between the clusters needs to be observable. Cohesion refers to the idea that an entity is accepted into a group if it is deemed to be 'close enough' in resemblance, the measure of 'close enough' being set by a particular threshold. Cormack (1971, p. 329) argues that sometimes isolation is stressed, sometimes cohesion is stressed, but more usually, both are included. Regardless of the criteria, however, defining clusters remains contentious and needs to be

guided by the dataset itself, and of course the purpose of the research.

FROM METHODOLOGY TO EPISTEMOLOGY AND ONTOLOGY

So far, I have simply described some key aspects of cluster analysis as a general method. I now turn to consider what we might learn about the case, epistemologically and ontologically, given this particular methodological approach. In taking this dialectical approach to both the method and the nature of the object of the method, I explicitly adopt a Bhaskarian approach to cluster analysis as a case-based method (Bhaskar 1975, 1978, 1979, 1997). Just as Bhaskar's critical realist thesis developed from an initial ontological question (about societies and people) that he then goes on to answer, so too is there a key ontological question underpinning this chapter: 'What is the case?' Bhaskar explains:

> … it is because sticks and stones are solid that they can be picked up and thrown, not because they can be picked up and thrown that they are solid (though that they can be handled in this sort of way may be a contingent necessary condition for our *knowledge* of their solidity). (Bhaskar 1979, p. 31, original emphasis)

Similarly, I ask what it might be about the case that might help to explain the pros, cons, issues and controversies of cluster analysis as a method.

There are, of course, issues involved in moving from the methodological, to the epistemological and ontological, not least because of the assumptions we might have about the ontological and because, from a critical realist perspective, all knowledge is fallible (Bhaskar 1979, Collier, 1979, 1994, Archer et al. 1998). There is a need to avoid, what Bhaskar (1979, 1986, 1997) calls, the 'epistemic' and 'ontic' fallacies, whereby the epistemological and ontological are conflated with one another, such that statements about being are interpreted as statements about knowledge (Bhaskar 1986, p. 6) (i.e. the epistemic fallacy) or knowledge is taken as a direct unmediated relation between a subject and being (the ontic fallacy) (Bhaskar 1986, p. 253). Yet the widespread use of classification methods across the disciplines relating to all kinds of cases suggests at least the possibility of 'generic attributes' about cases. This is not to say that the local, specific and contingent nature of the case is unimportant; it certainly is (see the following on this point: Prigogine 1980, Prigogine and Stengers 1984, Gould 1992, Waldrop 1992, Byrne 1998, 2002). As will be suggested, the specific (ontological) details of what the cases actually are become a key factor to refining and increasing the (epistemological) validity and reliability of any cluster analysis. Rather, it is to say that we need to continue to consider the ways in which all methods shape our knowledge about the world (Latour and Woolgar 1986/1979, Mulkay 1990, Collins and Pinch 1993, Law 2004), whilst at the same time recognising that the specific choice of methodology depends on what one wants to learn about the object of study (Sayer 2000), and that every piece of research calls for its own unique methodology (Crotty 1998). However, cluster analysis falls into a particularly precarious niche with respect to the representations of the world that it necessarily 'crafts'. This 'precarious niche' stems partly from the power of its utility, the outcome(s) of which will feedback into (re)constructions and (re)presentations of the world, and also partly due to the 'mechanical and interpretative processes' involved in the method itself. I will briefly consider four of these inter-related issues before concluding.

Methodological paradox – ontological complexity

There are two inevitable paradoxes that play important roles in this particular case-based method. The first is that, whilst cluster analysis is structure seeking, the procedure itself is structure imposing (Aldenderfer and Blashfield 1984). There is no way of completely resolving this dilemma, except to use a cluster method that also reflects the structure of the data. Herein lies the second

paradox, which is well explained by Everitt et al:

> The problem is, of course, that since in most cases the investigator does not know a *priori* the structure of the data (cluster analysis is, after all, intended to help to uncover the structure), there is a danger of interpreting *all* clustering solutions in terms of the existence of distinct (natural) clusters. The investigator may then conveniently 'ignore' the possibility that the classification produced by a cluster analysis is an artefact of the method and that actually she is *imposing* the structure on her data rather than discovering something about the actual structure. (Everitt et al. 2001, pp. 7–8)

Yet as Tukey (1997, p. 21) correctly points out, 'no data set is large enough to provide complete information about how it should be analysed!' Put simply, then, we face the following problem: cluster analysis is structure imposing; this is problematic because obviously the researcher does not want to *impose* the structure on the data, but instead, wants to learn about the *actual* structure of the data; therefore, the researcher needs to use the cluster method that best reflects the structure of the data; but the structure of the data is unknown *a priori*. So where does that leave us?

One way to resolve this predicament is to avoid using the method altogether! Yet it is clearly being used, and used a lot and by many; it is used across many disciplines to explore many different datasets of many types of cases. It is used because it is, despite the intrinsic paradoxes within it, both useful and meaningful. This is mainly because whilst imposing a structure on the data might first appear too problematic, and this should not go unquestioned, the series of steps and decisions to be made about *which* specific structure is imposed on the data are all *data driven*. To this extent, just as the choice of variables to include in cluster analysis needs to be theoretically informed (Aldenderfer and Blashfield 1984), so too the interpretation and construction of clusters need to be case driven – 'case driven' in the sense that prior theoretical and empirical knowledge about the case need be incorporated for any adequate construction and interpretation of the clusters.

This is not to say that prior knowledge of the cases is necessary to construct adequate cluster results (see Sneath and Sokal 1973), but it helps in terms of increasing the internal validity and, hence, confidence. It also helps because the optimal clustering method seeks the structure that is already present among the cases in the dataset, and does so by also imposing *that* particular structure on the data as well (Sokal and Sneath 1963, Jardine and Sibson 1971, Aldenderfer and Blashfield 1984, Milligan 1996, Everitt et al. 2001). If we think about this further, and we look more generally at the structure that is imposed on the data by all cluster methods, then we discover an important assumption about the structural properties of cases in general.

Structure seeking – structure imposing

Research methods are generally viewed as 'good' methods for a particular object study within a particular research design precisely because they allow what is seen as a meaningful interpretation of that object of study. By implication, any 'strengths' or 'improvements' to a particular method may offer insights into that particular object of study. One of the key strengths of the method made by a number of authors is that it serves as a data-reduction technique of moving from millions of cases to a much small number of self-similar 'types' of cases. More specifically, by using knowledge of the whole case and how the whole case relates to many other cases, we can generate a classification of single and multiple cases through creating clusters of self-similar cases; this is the general principal behind cluster analysis. Similarly, whatever the 'improvements' to cluster analysis are, the aim is always to produce 'better' self-similar clusters (see below for issues of reliability and validity of cluster results).

What is interesting is that it is never the notion that cases generally co-exist in self-similar clusters that is questioned in cluster-based methodological developments; nor is it questioned that it is possible to know about those clusters. On the contrary, the assumption within the clustering methods, and the developments of these methods, is that clustering methods are necessary because they are both useful and reflect something that is intrinsic to the cases themselves. As Webber (2004, p. 227) writes about the usefulness of neighbourhood classifications: 'When people discuss the reasons why neighbourhood classifications usually "work", the conventional answer with which they typically satisfy themselves is that "birds of a feather flock together"'. As he suggests, we need to consider *why* they work.

One suggestion is that they work because that is how *cases* work. The method imposes self-similar structures but these structures tend to be present in large datasets anyway. In other words, following Bhaskar's point above about the solidity of sticks and stones being what makes them be able to be picked up, what is being suggested here is that it is because cases of a similar sort or taxa are generally self-similar, but never identical, that similarity and dissimilarity measures are both meaningful and useful when it comes to sorting them out into clusters of cases that are more alike or dislike one another. It is because cases tend to co-exist in self-similar clusters that they can also be known in this way, and not because they can be known in this way that they are arranged as such (although that they can be handled in this sort of way might be a contingent necessary condition of our knowledge of their nested, multi-dimensional complexity). It is also because cases of a similar sort or taxa are generally self-similar, but never identical, that similarity and dissimilarity measures are both meaningful and useful when it comes to sorting them out into clusters of cases that are more alike or dislike one another.

This proposition has been suggested by a number of researchers working on self-similarity and complexity, who argue that certain observations, specifically relating self-similar cluster formation, might be applied *across* taxa (Hughes et al. 1981, Harte et al. 1999, Carlson and Doyle 2002, Turcotte et al. 2002, Martín and Goldenfeld 2006). Indeed, Barbará and Chen (2003) argue that there are variations of self-similarity over a range of scales within many large datasets, as cases within a cluster have a greater degree of self-similarity among them (and a much less degree of self-similarity with respect to cases in other clusters), and propose a specific method (the 'fractal clustering method') that is based precisely on this property of cases. The notion that cases *can* be classified according to variations in self-similarity is, rightly or wrongly, therefore, an implicit part of the method. What we see in the literature on cluster analysis is that, rather than questioning whether or not seeking self-similar cluster is viable, most of the debates revolve instead around determining the 'best' clustering approach relative to the data it is used with, which leads us onto a third issue about the method and what it might also tell us about the case.

Different methods – different clusters

Although all cluster methods imply self-similar structures of cases, there many variations in how this is achieved. This is not a problem *per se*, but what is peculiar to this method is that different cluster methods and different similarity/dissimilarity measures *can*, and *do*, generate different clustering solutions to the same dataset (see, e.g. Cormack 1971, Sneath and Sokal 1973, Mezzich 1982, Lorr 1983, Aldenderfer and Blashfield 1984, Everitt et al. 2001). The trouble with this, as Hudson and associates (1982, p. 1) put it, is that unless the data are artificially constructed, there is no answer at the back of the book. The point being that there is no definitive 'right' or 'wrong' method, but instead a spectrum of 'better' or 'worse' ones. Similarly, there is no definitive 'right' or 'wrong' set of emergent clusters, just ones that are interpreted, for a variety of reasons, as being 'better' or 'worse' representations of the cases in the dataset.

The sheer diversity of ways of classifying the different clustering methods, and the abundance of seemingly different, but actually synonymous, labelling that is associated with these different classifications, are issues that a number of authors have criticised, primarily because of the subsequent confusion created (Cormack 1971, Aldenderfer and Blashfield 1984, Clatworthy et al. 2005, Kettering 2006). Despite the difficulty and confusion caused, it is difficult to see a solution. Some authors (e.g. Aldenderfer and Blashfield 1984, Clatworthy et al. 2005) have suggested that in writing up work that has used cluster analysis, authors should include a particular set of criteria that make their methodological procedures transparent to readers (e.g. details of type of classification method, specifics about the dissimilarity or similarity measures used). Whereas this would certainly be very helpful, it is unlikely that this will fully resolve the problem. This is mainly because the use and continuous adaptation of these different methods and associated algorithms lie not so much with the *inter-* and *intra*-disciplinary biases, although this is certainly an indirect effect of the problem. Instead, the myriad of clustering methods and algorithms is the emergent effect of researchers grappling with *the case*.

However frustrating it might be to researchers venturing into the world of cluster analysis, it is difficult to see a way of settling on a definite 'best' way of sorting out cases, even within any discipline, because the 'exact' nature of the case is, of course, slightly different depending on what *that* case is. Because every case is different, ontologically if not epistemologically, any case-based method needs to grapple continuously with the ever present, yet ever changing, possibilities of clusters of cases. This issue is further accentuated because every case is situated in time and space, and is therefore also subject to change and continuity. However, from a *trans*-disciplinary perspective, what unites the different kinds of cases, regardless of the discipline, is that all cases are complex and multi-dimensional objects of study. Furthermore, all cases are situated in time and space, as are the disciplines within which they are might be situated. Arguably, therefore, all cases, as objects of study, *need to* be described in an ever-increasing and changing variety of ways, and each of those ways may in fact be representing something 'real' about that object of study as well (see Law 2004). This is more than simply a matter of methodological triangulation, where the 'the use of multiple methods or perspectives for the collection and interpretation of data about a phenomenon, in order to obtain an accurate representation of reality' (Polit and Hungler 1999, p. 1). Here, each possible way of classifying cases is simple – one – *possible* way. The question, then, is how to assess *which* classification is the 'better' representation of that particular set of data?

Cluster abstraction – cluster construction

There is no getting away from the fact that cluster analysis is an extremely powerful tool, precisely because it reduces hundreds, thousands or even millions of cases into a more manageable set of categories. Of course, classifying cases is only useful if the classifications are meaningful, and they are only meaningful if: (1) they are useful; and (2) they represent something that is already a feature of the organisation of the cases. The trouble is, there is no way of knowing for sure whether the emergent clusters are an artefact of the method or are an intrinsic part of the data, although there are ways of increasing our confidence of the latter. Consequently, the results of cluster analysis are largely to be judged on its usefulness, rather than in terms of whether it is 'true' or 'false' (Everitt et al. 2001). However, the problem is a recursive one, as Sayer points out:

> Much rests upon the nature of our abstractions, that is, our conceptions of particular one-sided components of the concrete object; if they divide what is in practice indivisible, or if they conflate what are different and separable components, then problems are likely to result. So much depends on the modes of abstraction we use, the way of carving up and defining our objects of study. (Sayer 2000, p. 19)

Hence, it is possible to critique all clustering methods on the basis that classifications

will, to some extent always and necessarily, be abstractions of the cases they represent. It is easier still to be sceptical about the nature of the abstractions intrinsic to cluster analysis precisely because of their inherent paradox of abstracting classifications whilst also imposing the structure of those classifications methodologically. As Aldenderfer and Blashfield (1984, p. 16) comment, 'The key to using cluster analysis is knowing when these groups are "real" and not merely imposed on the data by the method'. There are, of course, a vast number of ways of trying to validate the cluster results (Gower 1967, Milligan 1981, 1996, Blashfield et al. 1982, Mezzich 1982, Fraley and Raftery 1998, Handl et al. 2005, Milligan and Cooper 1986, Milligan and Mahajan 1980, Siegmund et al. 2004), ranging from analysis of variance or multivariate analysis (preferably using variables that were not used in the cluster analysis; see Morey et al. 1983), testing the statistical significance of the matrix correlation coefficient (Lapointe and Legendre 1992), replication using different samples from the same dataset (Breckenridge 1989, Overall and Magee 1992), to comparing different visualisation of the clusters (Lapointe and Legendre 1995, Schonlau 2004, Rehm et al. 2006, Feil et al. 2007). Despite these and other techniques, it remains impossible to be completely confident of the validity of the resulting clusters. As Morey et al. sum up:

> Until more is known about the specific characteristics of the many different clustering techniques, researchers in applied areas must use similar designs to validate clustering solutions. Without extensive validation, the robustness of any obtained classification must remain in doubt. (Morey et al. 1983, p. 327)

Although the results of cluster analysis tell us nothing about the causality of the resulting clusters, when it comes to *social* classifications, people – individually and collectively – recursively act upon those classifications (Burrows et al. 2005, Burrows and Gane 2006, Ellison and Burrows 2007). This particular dialectic inevitably creates further complications in terms of judging the interpretations of social classifications. There is, however, an important advantage that the social scientist has in using cluster analysis: it is possible to approach the individuals to reflexively verify the extent to which the emergent clusters are meaningful representations.

Nevertheless, because of the social dialectic between what 'is' and what is 'useful', when it comes to clustering *social* data, positive and negative feedback dynamics need to be incorporated in our understanding of the emergent clusters. For instance, cluster analysis is increasingly used as a data mining technique to strategically target particular groups in the population for commercial purposes (see, e.g. Kinsey 2000, Lawrence et al. 2001, Webber 2004, Maenpaa 2006). Moreover, whereas results from cluster analysis may be judged by how 'useful' or 'real' they are, what is seen as 'useful' or 'real' might have as much to do with issues relating to the institutionalisation and commercialisation of those 'real' clusters as any possibility of *a priori* ontological clustering *per se*. There is, then, an increasing urgency to reflexively consider both the potential *and* the risk of 'self-sorting' clusters (Burrows 2006), ontologically, epistemologically and methodologically. As Hammersley (2002) has argued, it is important to critically engage with the 'findings' of social science (even if, given the fallibility of all reasoning, we can never be absolutely confident of the validity of our 'findings'). Increasingly, when it comes to the classification of large *social* datasets, it will become important to question *who* is classifying and for what *purposes* classifications are being conducted, alongside *who* decides what is 'useful' or 'real'. In other words, as with all social research, it is important to remain 'ethically aware' in cluster analysis also.

CONCLUSION

Because of the above issues involved in the method, the cluster analyst is forced into a research journey that involves a mixture of exploratory, confirmatory exercises to find the 'best' method that will impose the 'best' structure. Ideally, the researcher is in practice involved in an iterative process of to-ing and fro-ing between a consideration of the specific nature of the cases, based on extant theoretical and empirical knowledge, and the results of a number of particular clustering methods. Conversely, malpractice of cluster analysis would run through just *one* cluster analysis and then just stop there. Instead, authors argue that a series of cluster analyses need to be conducted, each with slight variations, which together help to explore the data and progressively confirm the structure of the data. The idea is that through exploring and experimenting with several cluster methods and similarity/dissimilarity algorithms, researchers can to learn, and eventually confirm, which combination is the 'best' one relative to the dataset (Sokal and Sneath 1963, Jardine and Sibson 1971, Sneath and Sokal 1973, Aldenderfer and Blashfield 1984, Breckenridge 1989, Milligan 1996, Everitt et al. 2001, Handl et al. 2005). Thus, it is through trial and error, iteration, and comparative analysis of the different methods themselves that the 'optimal' cluster method is 'found'.

Although I have deliberately focused on some of the key unresolved, paradoxical and problematic issues of cluster analysis, and suggested that these offer insights into studying cases in general, the need for both exploratory and confirmatory statistical methods was repeatedly advocated by Tukey (1969, 1980, 1986a), who is well known for 'exploratory data analysis' (EDA). He explains:

> Data analysis needs to be both exploratory and confirmatory. In exploratory data analysis there can be no substitute for flexibility, for adapting what is calculated – and, we hope, plotted – both to the needs of the situation and the clues that the data have already provided. In this mode, data analysis is detective work – almost an ideal example of seeking what might be relevant. Confirmatory analysis has its place, too. Well used, its importance may even equal that of exploratory data analysis. (Tukey 1969, p. 90)

Tukey goes as far as saying that 'To concentrate on confirmation, to the exclusion or submergence of exploration, is an obvious mistake' (1969, p. 83). Elsewhere (Tukey 1986b, p. 822), he argues that, '(a) *both* exploration and confirmation are important, (b) exploration comes *first,* (c) any given study can, and usually should, combine *both*'.

Byrne (2002) also argues for this kind of 'detective work' in suggesting that we can 'track' the traces that our cases leave behind, equating the researcher to the 'Indian' tracker in the Western movie. Although Tukey and Byrne both advocate an exploratory attitude to the interpretation of quantitative data, they both stress that the ultimate aim is to trace or reveal patterns that are already present and 'real' to the data itself. In other words, it is exploration for a purpose; the purpose is to know the data; the data is a representation of real cases in the world.

Although Byrne is certainly more case orientated (see in particular, Byrne 2002) than Tukey, Tukey is clear about using variables to learn about real cases (this is seen perhaps most explicitly in Tukey [1969, 1980], where he also refers to classification). The idea behind this exploratory process in cluster analysis is to 'learn to get to know the cases'. It is in this methodical, yet exploratory, way of 'getting to know the cases in the dataset' that the cluster analyst becomes a better 'interpreter' of the results produced by the methods themselves. 'Interpreting quantitative data', for Byrne, involves, among other things, an acknowledgement of the 'complexity' of the social world (see Byrne 1998, 2002). Similarly, for Tukey, it also involves recognising that 'We live in a paradoxical world, where the only true safety, true though limited, comes from admitting both our uncertainty and the incompleteness with which we are able to meet it' (Tukey 1997, p. 23). Both, then, argue that data interpretation about the world takes place in the world, even if our interpretations remain more 'messy' than we might like them to be.

Cluster analysis is arguably a methodological approach that epitomises the exploratory data analysis 'attitude'. After all, the goal is essentially to discover patterns and structures (of clusters) in data. The role of the researcher is 'to listen to the data in as many ways as possible until a plausible "story" of the data is apparent, even if such a description would not be borne our in subsequent samples' (Behrens 1997, p. 132). Like a detective, the researcher looks for clues in the data, and explores different ways of detecting clusters in an attempt to find further clues. In conducting cluster analysis, the researcher is involved in a continual process of careful 'cross-validation' (see Mosteller and Tukey 1977) of the results in order to learn which patterns or structures to trust.

As *critical* social scientists, we need to accept the complexity and paradoxical nature of the world. We need to grapple with the need to think creatively about how to study this world empirically. Equally, we need to accept that studying the case, whatever the case may be, is likely to involve an acknowledgement of the multi-dimensionality of the case in the this world. Furthermore, as is suggested, it is possible that we need to consider ways of learning about the ontological nature of the case, through tentative, yet serious, retrodictive explorations about contentious methodological issues in studying cases in the world, and to consider what it might be about the case that is echoed in those methodological tensions. Also, we need to be reflexive in our explorations and interpretations and we need to situate our explorations in time in the hope that longitudinal patterns will alert us to 'detect' or 'track' traces that help us to learn more about the cases we study. Cluster analysis is but one approach to do this, and despite problematising the method here, it is potentially a very useful method with which to do this. There are many other methods and many other methodological approaches, and we should be willing to try all of them if they offer meaningful representations of the cases we study, and they may *all* do. Like the layers of a holographic image, the representations from different methods potentially facilitate access to a 'fuller' picture of the multi-dimensional case, even if the image remains incomplete.

The challenge will be to conceptualise, and probably increasingly, to visualise, the whole case and its relationship(s) with other similar and different cases in the world. Cluster analysis is one way of tackling this challenge, and should remain an important part of the methodological repertoire involved in knowing the case.

REFERENCES

Aldenderfer, M. and Blashfield, R. 1984 *Cluster Analysis*. London: Sage.

Alsberg, B.K. 1999 'Multiscale cluster analysis' *Analytical Chemistry* 71(15): 3092–3100.

Archer, M., Bhaskar, R., Collier, A., Lawson, T. and Norrie, A. (Eds) 1998 *Critical Realism: Essential Readings*. London: Routledge.

Barbará, D. and Chen, P. 2003 'Using self-similarity to cluster large data sets' *Data Mining and Knowledge Discovery* 7(2): 123–152.

Behrens, J.T. 1997 'Principles and procedures of exploratory data analysis' *Psychological Methods* 2(2): 131–160.

Bhaskar, R. 1975 *A Realist Theory of Science*. Leeds, UK: Leeds Books.

Bhaskar, R. 1978 'On the possibility of social scientific knowledge and the limits of naturalism' *Journal for the Theory of Social Behavior* 8: 1–28.

Bhaskar, R. 1979 *The Possibility of Naturalism: A Philosophical Critique of the Contemporary Human Sciences*. Brighton, UK: Harvester.

Bhaskar, R. 1986 *Scientific Realism and Human Emancipation*. London: Verso.

Bhaskar, R. 1997 *A Realist Theory of Science*. London: Verso.

Blalock, H.M. 1982 *Conceptualization and Measurement in the Social Sciences*. London: Sage.

Blashfield, R.K. and Aldenderfer, M.S. 1978 'Literature on cluster-analysis' *Multivariate Behavioral Research* 13(3): 271–295.

Blashfield, R., Aldenderfer, M. and Morey, L.C. 1982 'Validating a cluster analytic solution' in H.A.H. Hudson (Ed.) *Classifying Social Data*. San Francisco, CA: Jossey-Bass, pp. 167–176.

Breckenridge, J.N. 1989 'Replicating cluster-analysis – method, consistency, and validity' *Multivariate Behavioral Research* 24(2): 147–161.

Burrows, R. 2006 'The self-sorting tendency' *Science and Public Affairs* June (25): 25.

Burrows, R. and Gane, N. 2006 'Geodemographics, software and class' *Sociology* 40(5): 793–812.

Burrows, R., Ellison, N. and Woods, B. 2005 *Neighbourhoods on the Net: Internet-Based Neighbourhood Information Systems and Their Consequences*. Bristol, UK: The Policy Press.

Byrne, D. 1998 *Complexity Theory and the Social Sciences: An Introduction*. London: Routledge.

Byrne, D. 2002 *Interpreting Quantitative Data*. London: Sage.

Byrne, D. and Uprichard, E. 2007 'Crossing levels: the potential for numerical taxonomy and fuzzy set approaches to studying multi-level longitudinal change' *Methodological Innovations Online* 2(2).

Cape, J.N., Methven, J. and Hudson, L.E. 2000 'The use of trajectory cluster analysis to interpret trace gas measurements at Mace Head, Ireland' *Atmospheric Environment* 34(22): 3651–3663.

Carlson, M. and Doyle, J. 2002 'Complexity and robustness' *Proceedings of the National Academy of Sciences of the United States of America (PNAS)* 99: 2538–2545.

Cicourel, A. 1964 *Method and Measurement in Sociology*. New York: Free Press.

Clatworthy, J., Buick, D., Hankins, M., Weinman, J. and Horne, R. 2005 'The use and reporting of cluster analysis in health psychology: a review' *British Journal of Health Psychology* 10: 329–358.

Collier, A. 1979 'In defence of epistemology' *Radical Philosophy* 20: 8–21.

Collier, A. 1994 *Critical Realism: An Introduction to Roy Bhaskar's Philosophy*. London: Verso.

Collins, H. and Pinch, T. 1993 *The Golem: What Everyone Should Know about Science* Cambridge: Cambridge University Press.

Cormack, R. 1971 'A review of classification' *Journal of the Royal Statistical Society A* 134(3): 321–367.

Crotty, M. 1998 *The Foundations of Social Research: Meaning and Perspective in the Research Process*. London: Sage Publications.

Ellison, N. and Burrows, R. 2007 'New spaces of (dis)engagement? Social politics, urban technologies and the rezoning of the city' *Housing Studies* 22(3): 295–312.

Everitt, B., Landau, S. and Leese, M. 2001 *Cluster Analysis*. London: Arnold.

Feil, B., Balasko, B. and Abonyi, J. 2007 'Visualization of fuzzy clusters by fuzzy sammon mapping projection: application to the analysis of phase space trajectories' *Soft Computing* 11(5): 479–488.

Fraley, C. and Raftery, A.E. 1998 'How many clusters? Which clustering method? Answers via model-based cluster analysis' *Computer Journal* 41(8): 578–588.

Good, I.J. 1965 'Categorization of classification' in *Mathematics and Computer Science in Medicine and Biology*. London: HMSO, pp. 115–128.

Gould, S.J. 1992 *The Panda's Thumb*. New York: Norton.

Gower, J.C. 1967 'A comparison of some methods of cluster analysis' *Biometrics*. 23(4): 623.

Guinot, C., Latreille, J., Malvy, D., Preziosi, P., Galan, P., Hercberg, S. and Tenenhaus, M. 2001 'Use of multiple correspondence analysis and cluster analysis to study dietary behaviour: food consumption questionnaire in the Su.Vi.Max. cohort' *European Journal of Epidemiology* 17(6): 505–516.

Hammersley, M. 2002 'Research as emancipatory: the case of Bharskar's critical realism' *Journal of Critical Realism* 1: 49–66.

Handl, J., Knowles, J. and Kell, D.B. 2005 'Computational cluster validation in post-genomic data analysis' *Bioinformatics* 21(15): 3201–3212.

Harte, J., Kinzig, A. and Green, J. 1999 'Self-similarity in the distribution and abundance of species' *Science* 284(5412): 334–336.

Hartigan, J.A. 1967 'Representation of similarity matrices by trees' *Journal of the American Statistical Association* 62: 1140–1158.

Hudson, H. and Associates 1982 *Classifying Social Data*. San Francisco, CA: Jossey-Bass.

Hughes, B., Shlesinger, F. and Montroll, E. 1981 'Random walks with self-similar clusters' *Proceedings of the National Academy of Sciences of the United States of America (PNAS)* 78(6): 3287–3291.

Jardine, N. and Sibson, R. 1971 *Mathematical Taxonomy*. London: John Wiley.

Kettering, J. 2006 'The practice of cluster analysis' *Journal of Classification* 23: 3–30.

Kinsey, J.D. 2000 'Clusters of food consumers: Where do they buy? Where do they eat?' *Cereal Foods World* 45(4): 178–179.

Lapointe, F.-J. and Legendre, P. 1992 'Statistical significance of the matrix correlation coefficient for comparing independent phylogenic trees' *Systematic Biology* 41: 378–384.

Lapointe, F.-J. and Legendre, P. 1995 'Comparison tests for dendrograms: a comparative evaluation' *Journal of Classification* 12(22): 265–282.

Latour, B. and Woolgar, S. 1986/1979 *Laboratory Life: The Construction of Scientific Facts* (2nd edition). Princeton, NJ: Princeton University Press.

Law, J. 2004 *After Method: Mess in Social Science Research*. London: Routledge.

Lawrence, R.D., Almasi, G.S., Kotlyar, V., Viveros, M.S. and Duri, S. 2001 'Personalization of supermarket product recommendations' *Data Mining and Knowledge Discovery* 5(1–2): 11–32.

Lorr, M. 1983 *Cluster Analysis for Social Sciences*. San Francisco: Jossey-Bass.

Maenpaa, K. 2006 'Clustering the consumers on the basis of their perceptions of the internet banking services' *Internet Research* 16(3): 304–322.

Martín, G.H. and Goldenfeld, N. 2006 'On the origin and robustness of power-law species–area relationships in ecology' *Proceedings of the National Academy of Sciences of the United States of America (PNAS)* 103: 10310–10315.

May, R. 1982 'Discriminant analysis is cluster analysis' in H.A.H. Hudson (Ed.) *Classifying Social Data*. San Francisco: Jossey-Bass, pp. 39–55.

Mezzich, J. 1982 'Comparing cluster analytic methods' in H.A.H. Hudson (Ed.) *Classifying Social Data*. San Francisco: Jossey-Bass, pp. 152–166.

Milligan, G.W. 1980 'An examination of the effect of six types of error perturbation on fifteen clustering algorithms' *Psychometrika* 45: 325–342.

Milligan, G.W. 1981 'A Monte-Carlo study of 30 internal criterion measures for cluster-analysis' *Psychometrika* 46(2): 187–199.

Milligan, G.W. 1996 'Clustering validation: results and implications for applied analysis' in P. Arabie, L.J. Hubert and G. de Soete (Eds) *Clustering and Classification*. Singapore: World Scientific, pp. 341–375.

Milligan, G.W. and Cooper, M.C. 1986 'A study of the comparability of external criteria for hierarchical cluster-analysis' *Multivariate Behavioral Research* 21(4): 441–458.

Milligan, G.W. and Mahajan, V. 1980 'A note on procedures for testing the quality of a clustering of a set of objects' *Decision Science* 11: 669–677.

Morey, L.C., Blashfield, R.K. and Skinner, H.A. 1983 'A comparison of cluster-analysis techniques within a sequential validation framework' *Multivariate Behavioral Research* 18(3): 309–329.

Mosteller, F. and Tukey, J. 1977 *Data Analysis and Regression: A Second Course in Statistics*. Reading, MA: Addison-Wesley.

Mulkay, M. 1990 *Sociology of Science*. Bloomington, IN: Indiana University Press.

Overall, J.E. and Magee, K.N. 1992 'Replication as a rule for determining the number of clusters in hierarchical cluster-analysis' *Applied Psychological Measurement* 16(2): 119–128.

Polit, D.F. and Hungler, B.D. 1999 *Nursing Research* (6th edition). New York: Lippicott.

Prigogine, I. 1980 *From Being to Becoming: Time and Complexity in the Physical Sciences*. San Francisco: W.H. Freeman.

Prigogine, I. and Stengers, I. 1984 *Order out of Chaos*. New York: Bantam.

Rehm, F., Klawonn, F. and Kruse, R. 2006 'Visualization of single clusters' *Lecture Notes in Computer Science* 4029: 663–671.

Sayer, A. 1984 *Method in Social Science: A Realist Approach*. London: Hutchinson.

Sayer, A. 2000 *Realism and Social Science*. London: Sage.

Schonlau, M. 2004 'Visualizing hierarchical and non-hierarchical cluster analyses with clustergrams' *Computational Statistics* 19(1): 95–111.

Siegmund, K.D., Laird, P.W. and Laird-Offringa, I.A. 2004 'A comparison of cluster analysis methods using DNA methylation data' *Bioinformatics* 20(12): 1896–1904.

Sneath, P. and Sokal, R. 1973 *Numerical Taxonomy: The Principles and Practice of Numerical Classification*. San Francisco: W.H. Freeman.

Sokal, R. and Sneath, P. 1963 *Principles of Numerical Taxonomy*. San Francisco: W.H. Freeman.

Tryon, R. 1939 *Cluster Analysis: Correlation Profile and Orthometric Analysis for the Isolation of Unities of Mind Personality*. Ann Arbor, MI: Edward Brothers.

Tukey, J. 1969 'Analyzing data: sanctification or detective work?' *American Psychologist* 24: 83–91.

Tukey, J. 1980 'We need both exploratory and confirmatory' *The American Statistician* 34: 23–25.

Tukey, J. 1986a *The Collected Works of John W. Tukey. Volume 3. Philosophy and Principles of Data Analysis: 1949–1964*. Belmont, CA: Wadsworth.

Tukey, J. 1986b 'Methodological comments focused on opportunities' in V.L. Jones (Ed.) *The Collected Works of John W. Tukey. Volume 4. Philosophy and Principles of Data Analysis: 1965–1986*. Belmont, CA: Wadsworth, pp. 819–867.

Tukey, J. 1997 'More honest foundation for data analysis' *Journal of Statistical Planning and Inference* 57: 21–28.

Turcotte, D., Malamud, B., Guzzetti, F. and Reichenbach, P. 2002 'Self-organization, the cascade model, and natural hazards' *Proceedings of the National Academy of Sciences of the United States of America (PNAS)* 99: 2530–2537.

Tversky, A. 1977 'Features of similarity' *Psychological Review* 84(4): 327–352.

Waldrop, M. 1992 *Complexity: The Emerging Science at the Edge of Order and Chaos*. New York: Simon and Schuster.

Webber, R. 2004 'Designing geodemographic classifications to meet contemporary business needs' *Interactive Marketing* 5(3): 219–237.

Webber, R. and Farr, M. 2001 'Mosaic: from an area classification system to individual classification' *Journal of Targeting, Measurement and Analysis for Marketing* 10(1): 55–65.

Williamson, T., Ashby, D. and Webber, R. 2005 'Young offenders, schools and the neighbourhood: a new approach to data-analysis for community policing' *Journal of Community and Applied Social Psychology* 15: 203–228.

Zubin, J. 1936 'A technique for measuring likemindedness' *Journal of Abnormal and Social Psychology* 33, 508–516.

8

Visualising Types: The Potential of Correspondence Analysis

Dianne Phillips and John Phillips

INTRODUCTION

Correspondence analysis is a multivariate technique for use with categorical data. The context in which it works best is exploration rather than justification. It has affinities with case studies and comparative studies aiming at rich interpretation, but this needs careful specification.

Correspondence analysis usually takes data in the form of a contingency table, and re-presents it in a two-dimensional map. This transformation of information permits a clarifying visualisation of relationships between variables and categories of variables. The maps are intuitive and interesting indicators of scores on variables and categories 'going together', for counted populations. On the basis of what goes with what, the maps suggest the most powerful descriptions (and potentially explanations) of multivariate correlations, and what 'types' predominate. These can be surprising. The axes of the maps are specified in relation to the data, and not by preconceptions.

Figure 8.1 is a simple map of data from the 1994 Social Attitudes Survey, relating attitudes to the NHS to categories of income. It is read by seeing how close, geometrically, points representing attitudes ('satisfied', 'dissatisfied') are to categories of income, ('high', 'medium', 'low'). Closer points 'correspond' to one another.

It is presumed that there would be a broad relation between income and attitude, satisfaction with the NHS rising with lower income. Something like this is reflected in the map, with 'satisfied' categories on the left, but with the surprising outcome that 'very dissatisfied' is further from 'high income' than 'quite dissatisfied'. As a working definition, a 'type' would be, for example, the correspondence (closeness) of 'low income' and 'very satisfied'. There is interpretation involved in this 'type', although it follows the initial suspicions about the relationships; it is noting and thinking about the correspondences.

Correspondence analysis, Greenacre and Hastie[1] remark, is principal component analysis for categorical data. Its development

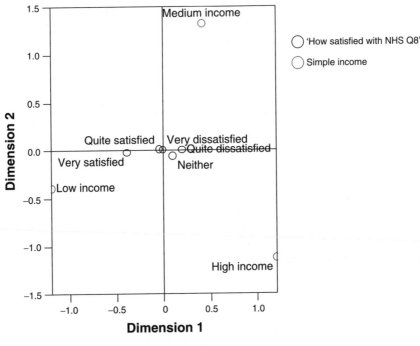

Row and column scores

○ 'How satisfied with NHS Q8'

○ Simple income

Row principal normalisation

Figure 8.1   Correspondence map of attitude to NHS and income.

enables social scientists to use principal component-like analyses in tasks like visualising types. Correspondence maps mean that the availability of principal component analysis comes with an intuitive sense and familiarity. 'Understanding' and 'relevance' crowd in, as with 'low income' and 'very satisfied'.

A review of the procedure in the next section shows how a version of the simple map in Figure 8.1 (and hence of a kind of principal component analysis) can be produced from data using little mathematics or statistics. Then the production of this map using a computer package is examined. This enables attention to 'types' as they are handled in the process. Next, two 'real' examples of correspondence analysis are reviewed. Finally, the place of correspondence analysis in case study method is investigated, conceived according to leading methodological positions.

Input to correspondence analysis is usually from datasets deriving from surveys or equivalent large-N work. Hence, there needs to be an argument for its relevance to case study methods. The relation of typologies to case studies is itself an open set of issues.

Simplified historical sketch: 1

The most sustained discussion of types in sociology is the assessment of Max Weber's ideas about 'ideal types'. (It is less often noticed that Weber's own discussion is also a discussion of case method.) Consideration of Weber's work has taken two opposed routes. Both assessments think that Weber leaves essential matters unresolved, and needs further elaboration. On the one hand, Parsons thinks that Weber's idealisations need to be built into systematic and scientific theory. The theory has to be general, deductive and testable. Types in social science yield the elements of theory.[2]

On the other hand, Schutz[3] thinks there is a foundation lacking in Weber's work, which can be found in Husserl. The origin of types lies in deep experience, including necessary intersubjectivity. Social science typification derives from everyday typification, which becomes, largely, the subject matter of social science. This encourages ever more thorough description, opening the (meaning) horizons of the world and the researcher, with quasi-scientific laws and theory a mistaken direction.

Much of the history of sociological methodology has been to reject these extremes and to recombine the opposed insights – although rarely with a focus on 'types'. For example, recent work on case studies with postponed but serious causal possibilities,[4] and 'transcendental realism'[5] both try new ways of reconciling these dilemmas, and are well represented in the current volume.

Simplified historical sketch: 2

Early in the last century, Scotland Yard was attempting to identify criminals by reference to systematic bodily measurements, a 'criminal type'.[6] This involved twelve measures, e.g. of head length and left foot. Galton suggested that as some of these were highly correlated, there was redundancy in the measures. Edgeworth tried replacing the observed measurements with hypothetical variates that would be uncorrelated, and hence efficient summaries derived from the data. They would recombine the measures, and weight them, so that a new variate might combine '0.16 stature + 0.51 forearm + 0.39 leg length'. Maxwell calls this a purely 'internal' analysis, 'obtained without reference to any outside criterion'.[7]

W.R. Macdonell added the idea of selecting a few minimally correlated organs to '… provide a reliable index to the criminal population'.[8] He invented the correlation matrix for this task, with seven variables correlated with each other. Taking it that the correlation matrix provides a seven-dimensional cloud of points, he is quoted as saying, 'Professor Pearson has pointed out to me that the ideal index characters would be given if we calculated the seven directions of uncorrelated variables, that is, the principal axes of the correlation ellipsoid'.

Pearson's 1901 paper[9] is a relatively simple and geometric solution to finding such principal axes in terms of least squares. Over half a century, it was turned into usable procedures for multiple variables, and principal component analysis became routine with the availability of computation. The development included work on categorical data. While a number of procedures like correspondence analysis have been pursued, e.g. in psychometrics,[10] the term itself and its recent popularity are due to the work of J-P. Benzécri and his colleagues.[11]

Benzécri regards the incorporation of these techniques into the conventional statistical repertoire as a loss, suggesting instead a development of the geometric elements from Pearson. He is uninterested in statistics enabling the formulation of strict models in relation to pre-existing theory, and their testing against the data. He proposes a strikingly inductive alternative, where the models emerge to fit the data, and are not presupposed. The transformation of interval data to categorical organisation can be an advantage in understanding and control, not a loss. He avoids notions of probability, and inference based in probability.

Michael Greenacre suggests that, in work influenced by Benzécri, data description assumes supreme importance, e.g. when the sampling units are the whole population (notice the relevance to 'case study'). Where methodology concentrates on data fitting, and comparison to a postulated model, there is '… little attention to enlightening ways of describing data'.[12] With Benzécri, an alternative to the dominant ideas about the role of statistics is in play.

There is some similarity between our two historical sketches. In each case, there is an alternative that presses to theory and test. There is a second alternative that postpones or even rejects this, emphasising instead something like elaborate description. It is interesting for the development of case studies that at least one influential school of statistics wishes to control the move to general theory.

It must be emphasised that wholly 'standard' versions of correspondence analysis are now in the textbooks, and it is not necessary to take a line on induction or the importance of description to use the procedure. In each case, 'ideal types' or statistical representation, it remains possible to consign 'description', however elaborated, to the 'context of discovery', and to see developed science as moving to the 'context of justification'.

However, not only are there developments in descriptive statistics but there are arguments that there need be no rush to inferential work. Maps do not represent causal relations. They have a manifest 'simultaneity'. We may add this possibility to the emerging production of statistics for case study, and other 'idiographic' or contexted work.[13]

WHAT CORRESPONDENCE ANALYSIS DOES

Among the excellent texts available, both Benzécri[14] and Greenacre[15] use a geometric approach to the explanation of correspondence analysis, which allows a grasp of the concepts without relying on familiarity with statistical techniques. Greenacre's account is used as a continuous resource throughout the following section. (A technical version using related material and a geometric approach is Greenacre and Hastie 1987.)

Data and types

Early in data exploration comes tentative aggregation, which, for categorical data, usually involves a contingency table. Correlation and chi-square procedures are needed to suggest that there is some association between the variables. (There is little point in conducting correspondence analysis if there is no evidence of this.)

Table 8.1 shows the contingency table for income and satisfaction with the National Health Service. Note that income has been

Table 8.1   Cross-tabulation of satisfaction with the National Health Service by income group

| 'How satisfied with NHS' | Income | | | |
	High	Medium	Low	Row total
Very satisfied	38	71	146	255
Quite satisfied	220	301	359	880
Neither	143	148	159	450
Quite dissatisfied	187	211	168	566
Very dissatisfied	106	138	156	400
Total	694	869	988	2551

recoded into three categories: high, medium and low. (The single variable in the survey has been divided into these three elements. This allows categories within the variables to be related to one another.)

The values for correlation and chi-square suggest the existence of a low, but highly significant, association between the two variables.

The list of questions in the survey was, presumably, constructed with some notion of the relationship between structural variables (income) and attitudes (satisfaction with the National Health Service). So there is inbuilt into the cross-tabulation a preliminary orientation to 'types'. The process of constructing the correspondence maps provides the spaces in which 'types' can appear and their relationships be assessed.

Plotting data

A visualisation of the relationship between variables and categories of variables is an attractive concept. Maps are accessible, powerful and enable the reader to interpret the distances between points in a meaningful way. The most simple and familiar device is the scatterplot. Given two sets of similar interval level variables, both on the same scale, distances between the points can be interpreted as showing similarities and differences. Clusters can emerge. The plot can be truly a map, if rarely in social research. In many scatterplots the variables are measured on different scales and are limited in the amount of data they can usefully display.

Given two categorical variables, their use is very limited. We need something like a scatterplot for categorical variables.

Row and column profiles

The first steps towards such a map, are the row and column profiles, i.e. the relative frequencies. Table 8.2 shows the relative frequencies (row profiles) of attitudes across the income groups, Table 8.3 (column profiles), income groups across attitudes.

For each row, the frequency of each cell has been divided by the row total. In the first row of 255 of respondents who reported they were very satisfied, 38 were in the high-income group, that is, 0.149 (or 14.9%). This can be contrasted with the 0.573 (57.3%) in the low-income group.

The last row is the average profile, calculated by dividing each column total in Table 8.1 by the grand total. The row masses are the totals of the rows from Table 8.1,

divided by the grand total, e.g. for the 'very satisfied' row, 255/2551.

Assuming we are most interested in different attitude profiles here, we use the row profiles. The procedures are the same when column profiles are used.

Plotting the profiles

It is possible to represent the row profiles as a triangle (Figure 8.2).[16] In this triangular coordinate system, each side has a length of 1 (the total of the row proportions.) The three sides represent the three categories of the income variable. The row profile for each satisfaction category is plotted as a single point in the equilateral triangle. So proportions in categories of satisfaction are placed in a space defined by the categories of income.

The vertices represent the extreme cases. If all the 'very satisfied' respondents were in the low-income group, their profile point would be in the corner. Having a low income and responding 'very satisfied' would be identical. If a particular frequency is relatively high, then the point will be pulled towards the relevant vertex.

The very satisfied profile is:

	High	Medium	Low
Very satisfied	.149	.278	.573

To plot this, you move from 0 down to .278 on the medium axis, then sketch in a line parallel to the low axis. A similar line is sketched

Table 8.2   Profiles of attitude across income groups: row profile

'How satisfied with NHS Q8'	Income			Row mass
	High	Medium	Low	
Very satisfied	.149	.278	.573	.100
Quite satisfied	.250	.342	.408	.345
Neither	.318	.329	.353	.176
Quite dissatisfied	.330	.373	.297	.222
Very dissatisfied	.265	.345	.390	.157
Average row profile	.272	.341	.387	

Table 8.3   Income groups across the categories of attitude: column profiles

'How satisfied with NHS Q8'	Income			
	High income	Medium Income	Low income	Average column profile
Very satisfied	.055	.082	.148	.100
Quite satisfied	.317	.346	.363	.345
Neither	.206	.170	.161	.176
Quite dissatisfied	.269	.243	.170	.222
Very dissatisfied	.153	.159	.158	.157
Column mass	.272	.341	.387	

The average column profile is in the right-hand column. Average profile and masses are calculated in the same way as for the row table.

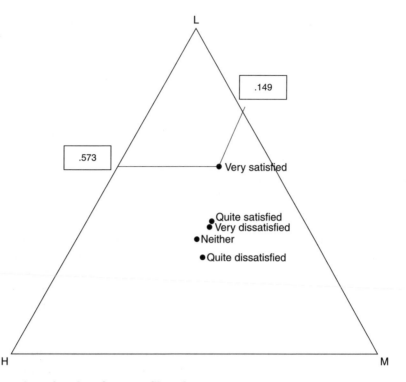

Figure 8.2   Triangular plot of row profile points.

from .573 on the low axis, parallel to the high axis. Where they cross will also be where a line sketched from .149 on the high axis, parallel to the medium axis, intersects. (Two are enough to define the point.) Each point hence combines three values, it is an average of the three values plotted on the sides.

0.573 of the 'very satisfied' respondents are in the low-income group. This relatively high frequency, compared with the relative frequencies in the other two income groups, pulls the point towards the low-income vertex.

Despite the three dimensions, it is possible to specify the distance between the points arithmetically, by subtracting each score from its corresponding one. To get an absolute distance we square the three differences, add them and take the square root.[17] This gives a result in our familiar idea of distance, the 'Euclidean', the distance separating the points.

The graphic has some of the virtues of a scatterplot. It separates the categories of each dimension in a common space, as vertices and as profile points. It tends to associate profiles (e.g. high satisfaction/low income) as our initial review of types would anticipate. However, it is inadequate for purpose. A drawback is that it contains no representation of the size of the population segment in each cell.

The 'very satisfied' profile position is determined by an averaging, in three dimensions, of .149, .278 and .573. Together, they add up to 1.0, which is the whole of the 'very satisfied' subset of the population. This says, however, nothing about how big a proportion of the population is very satisfied.

Weight and mass

The figure we need to build in the size of groups is the mass. This is the proportion of the whole population of the whole of each row or column (depending on our interest). Then figures for particular segments can be weighted by this value.

A chi-square triangular graphic

Each of the income categories ranged from 0 to 1, with an equilateral triangle. This space must change to reflect the size of the categories in relation to the whole population – here, the masses of the income categories.

This is the number of people in each income category as a whole as a proportion of the total population. For the high-income category, $694/2551 = .272$. So the mass figures for weighting we need are the values of the average row profile. (Rather confusing, as the columns of the column profile are the income categories, these are the same as the column masses, and vice versa. Average row profile is the same as column mass; average column profile is the same as row mass.)

So we change the length of the vertices, to reflect the number of people, the size of the income categories. The way correspondence analysis builds in the mass, is to use a chi-square distance measure.[18]

The chi-square stretching factor is division of the original length (presently 1) by the square root of the appropriate element of the average profile. That is, a reworking in chi-squared terms. As the value for the average row profile is a proportion of 1, the effect is to lengthen each vertex. So the new length of the high-income vertex is $1/\sqrt{.272}$, and so on for the others (Figure 8.3).

We mark off sections of each side as before, keeping the existing values. They will be automatically stretched by the new length of each side. The points in the stretched space will change, weighted by their mass. (This is a demonstration, rather than how the weighting would normally be done.)

The scales on each side of the triangles are now different. Points are determined as before by constructing for each profile three lines parallel to the sides, from the appropriate scale point. Hence, a chi-squared distance, e.g. that between any two points, is represented in a space that we can visualise, a Euclidean space. Each point is now a 'weighted average' of the three vertices. The centroid, the row average, must be their average. It must also be the average of the triangle as a whole, with the stretched sides. The interpretation is

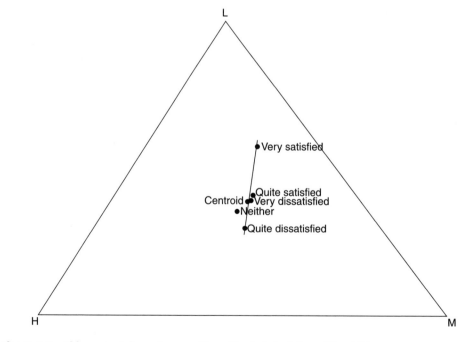

Figure 8.3   Chi-square triangular graphic, with sketched line of best fit.

changed, in this example, only by becoming more precise.

Changing the axes

The graphic now is a plot for nominal data, indicating relationships, distances between points, and between points and centroid. Correspondence maps are based on the centroid, and on axes not derived directly from the original variables.[19] It is easy to sketch a single line of best fit through the centroid of the diagram. This is equivalent to a rough least-squares procedure. To do anything like least-squares procedure in the present case requires an application of matrix algebra, but nevertheless remains easy to see on the graphic.

So, there is a sketched single line, fitted to the graphic so that it runs in the main direction in which the points tend. The structure and the points are rotated with the new line becoming a new horizontal axis. The points do not lie on the line. A second line, at right angles to the first, crossing at the origin (the centroid) would permit a further estimate, in a second dimension, of where the points lie – we could compare their position relative to both axes (Figure 8.4).

The new axes are the closest fit to the data in two dimensions that we can achieve by eye and freehand. The new axes make possible the best available graphic summary of the relations in the data.

We chose the axes to fit the row profile points. So the categories and types dictate how they appear, suggesting what makes them appear that way. Not only do 'types' suggest themselves, but a new 'space' for them to relate in – here, the income/satisfaction space. This is constructed with the new axes.[20]

The new axes require new labels. To label them is a contribution to the interpretation of the map. They are not the axes whose labels derived from any original survey, or the simplified data. Rather, they force the

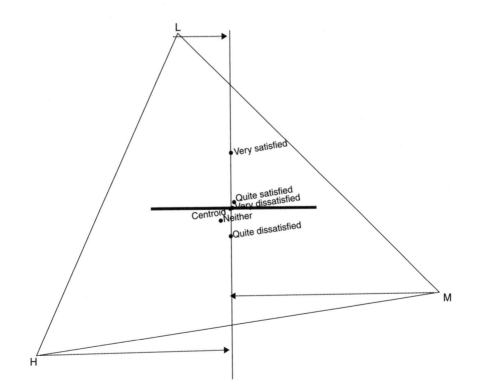

Figure 8.4   Chi-square triangular graphic, axes rotated, with single-dimension solution.

researcher to ask: what is it that separates the types as they now appear? Here on the primary axis, it is satisfaction; on the second, income. But it is clear that something else is operating in the case of the primary axis (which we shall not pursue further).

Although the mathematics required to achieve a full version of this best fit is relatively complex, it is still a least-squares best fit procedure. It becomes complex, and for practicality has to be computed, when there are more dimensions involved, but the basic idea is familiar and accessible.

Accounting for the inertia

The graphs indicate that variation along the first axis is the primary and most important separation of our points. So, this is an underlying description of the relations between the profiles. In the correspondence analysis vocabulary, it accounts for most of the inertia, or dispersion of the points around the centroid. A measure of the inertia, e.g. by summing the distances on the maps from the centroid, would be possible and we could even try to separate left-to-right and top-to-bottom components of this dispersion. For the purposes of this demonstration, it is enough to do the relative assessment.

Contribution of points

Each profile point can be examined for how it is affecting the inertia. The further they are from the centroid, the greater their contribution to the inertia. The links to total inertia and the point contribution to total inertia are given in correspondence analysis output.

Reducing the dimensions

Given that the 'satisfaction' dimension is accounting for most of the inertia, is a still simpler diagram available? This would be the single 'satisfaction' line, with the profile points extended to it. Without the triangle, and without the second axis, this would be a one-dimensional analysis. The single line is a part

of the two-dimensional analysis – the simpler analysis is a part of, and implied by, the more complex one (they are 'nested').

In the present case, the single dimension would account for the greater part of the inertia (we are able to see this in the dispersion of points); so it is an acceptable approximation. Although we cannot visualise more dimensions than three, the same reasoning holds for situations where the dimensions run beyond three. It is possible to get good approximations in reduced dimensionality, like our one-dimensional one. The reduction of dimensions is central to correspondence analysis, enabling a two-dimensional plot to be presented as a useful summary of multiple dimensions. The greater the reduction, the less the precision, but this is more than balanced by the increase in clarity.

Sketched on the diagram is an extension of the line beyond the triangle to allow the vertex points to be put on the line. These are the potential extremes of the satisfaction scores. So they set the limits to the satisfaction scores, which are necessarily 'within' these limits. It is as possible as before to come up with the 'correspondence' interpretation. Profile points are closest to the vertex points that express their greatest weighting. So 'most satisfied' is close to 'low income'. This gives a one-dimensional analysis. It also illustrates further points. The column analysis – asking about income scores in a space defined by attitude – could also be presented in a simple one-dimensional display. The vertex points could again be included; this time they would be the vertices defined by the extremes of the attitude possibilities. So they would be outside, and include, the income profile positions.

The income profiles are scaled to produce the vertices for the attitude analysis. In the column analysis, the attitude profiles would be scaled to produce the vertices for the income analysis. As the scaling is a simple multiplication, the relationships remain the same. This is as far as we can reasonably go in an introduction, using graphics alone. It remains to see how these ideas show up in a full computational output.

Computer programs for correspondence analysis

The tables of row and column profiles are treated as matrices and analysed using the resources of matrix computation. Correspondence analysis shares its treatments and analyses with other multivariate procedures, like factor analysis and principal component analysis, and is close to the latter. In analysing matrices, computer programs have rendered the regular use of the procedures on complex datasets plausible – only simple examples are worked out by hand. The summary below only seeks to follow the general treatment of social types and typifications through the analysis.

Computer programs for correspondence analysis calculate the distances between the points, in chi-squared terms, and then perform a principal components analysis on the distance matrix. The effect is a 'best fit' analysis. It is achieved by decomposing matrices. For those with limited matrix algebra, an idea of what this involves comes by recognising that matrices might be added, subtracted and multiplied – and that there is an operation rather like factorising. A complex matrix may hence be 'decomposed' into simpler ones, or into single lines of figures with a direction, vectors.

The data matrix is taken as complex, and decomposed, this being the precise version of geometric line fitting (to the ellipsoid, or cloud, of data points.) The idea is to express the original matrix in terms of a limited series of further matrices (or vectors) which combine to produce the original one. These underlying matrices can express underlying dimensions, which contribute in different degrees to the shape of the original data.

The principal line is often termed the eigenvector, and this is like the line of best fit, turned into the principal dimension and axis in our triangle. A matrix defines a set of points, for example, in Cartesian geometry. If you seek to turn one matrix into another, you require a direction (the eigenvector) and a scalar value (the eigenvalue). In principle, it can be seen that you can take a complex matrix and reverse the process, visualising the matrices that could turn into the original one.

The program will also rotate the axes. The correspondence map (Figure 8.1) is produced by this procedure. Its close relations to the triangular graphics are obvious. Matrix decomposition is sophisticated 'best fit', but that is what it is here. Chi-squared measures allow this decomposition, and also the calculations of inertia contribution.

Example of correspondence analysis output using SPSS on the present data

First, a summary table, which includes a chi-square value of 68.074 for the table. Significance is .000 with 8 degrees of freedom (Table 8.4).

Two dimensions have been identified in the procedure. The first dimension is always the most important and will have the highest eigenvalue. The SPSS summary gives the singular values, which are the square roots of the eigenvalues. The inertia, or explained variance, at .027, is extremely low – because

Table 8.4   Summary

Dimension	Singular value	Inertia	Chi-square	Sig.	Proportion of inertia		Confidence singular value	
					Accounted for	Cumulative	Standard deviation	Correlation
1	.161	.026			.973	.973	.019	.033
2	.027	.001			.027	1.000	.020	
Total		.027	68.074	.000[a]	1.000	1.000		

[a] Eight degrees of freedom.

there is only a low correlation between income and opinion.

In the proportion of inertia column, the left-hand column gives the proportion of the variance explained by each dimension. Here, the first dimension explains 97.3% of the 2.7% explained by the model. The standard deviation of the singular values contributes to the assessment of the precision of the dimensions.

Table 8.5 shows the mass, the scores that are used as the coordinates for the points on the map, the inertia for each category, the contribution of the points to the dimension and the contribution of the dimension to the inertia of each point.

The contribution of the points to the dimension shows the extent to which the point has contributed to the direction of the relevant dimension. Points with relatively large contributions are the most important, and guide the choice of the label for the dimension. The contribution of the dimension to the inertia indicates how well the model is describing the individual categories. (A similar output table can be obtained for the column variable.)

In computed correspondence analysis, an overlain map is referred to as a biplot, and the idea is to bring the two sets of points (profiles and vertices) close together. The possibility of biplots rests on the relation between profiles and vertices, and the simple scaling between them. Whatever the number of categories in the cross-tabulation, the number of dimensions is the same. Further, the total inertia of row and column is the

same. The biplot correspondence map is Figure 8.1.

It should be remembered that the distances mean different things. Within the groups of profiles on a row or column base, the distances on the maps represent real values. Between the groups, the distances are uninterpretable. However, the position of one point relative to the position of all the points in the other set is meaningful and interpretable. The two sets of points 'correspond', rather than relate more precisely; hence 'correspondence analysis'.

Supplementary points

In the mapping procedure, using simple correspondence, the relationships between the categories of two variables, income and attitude, were explored. These can often be further explored by adding an additional row or column containing data for, for example, a 'contrast' group. Unlike the data in the original rows and columns, the profile of the new row or column is not used in the principal component analysis but it can be projected onto the map in the same way that the row profiles were positioned above. The supplementary points have zero mass and zero inertia but their positioning in the same space as the active categories is often illuminating.

Multiple correspondence analysis

This overview has described the main concepts and how maps are obtained in simple correspondence analysis. For the social science researcher, their usefulness might

Table 8.5   Overview row points[a]

'How satisfied with NHS Q8'		Score in dimension			Contribution				
					Of point to inertia of dimension		Of dimension to inertia of point		
	Mass	1	2	Inertia	1	2	1	2	Total
Very satisfied	.100	−.394	−.017	.016	.598	.040	.998	.002	1.000
Quite satisfied	.345	−.051	.019	.001	.034	.166	.882	.118	1.000
Neither	.176	.091	−.054	.002	.056	.710	.740	.260	1.000
Quite dissatisfied	.222	.191	.013	.008	.312	.049	.996	.004	1.000
Very dissatisfied	.157	−.010	.013	.000	.001	.035	.381	.619	1.000
Active total	1.000			.027	1.000	1.000			

[a]Row principal normalisation.

seem limited, especially if restricted to two variables plus supplementary points. A simultaneous consideration of several 'variables' is more typical of social science research. Hence, a generalisation of correspondence analysis is needed to analyse the relationships between categories of three or more variables.

From the technical viewpoint, the move from the framework of the bivariate case to the multivariate one is not simple and has led to the development of diverse approaches with the label 'multiple correspondence analysis'.[21]

One straightforward approach arranges the data in a two-way table that can then be explored using the same procedures as in simple correspondence analysis. Either an indicator matrix[22] with cases as rows and the 'response' categories as columns can be constructed, or a Burt matrix,[23] which has the response categories as both rows and columns can be used. The indicator coding does not necessarily have to be of the strict 1 or 0 form; it is possible to use 'fuzzy coding' in which values between 0 and 1 can be assigned.

One problem is that the resultant maps have a large number of points on them, making interpretation difficult. Restricting the plotting to a small number of dimensions can help, but this can hide configurations that would be clear if a higher number of dimensions were used.

This is necessarily a brief review, but some of the possibilities can be seen in the examples below. It should be clear that 'correspondence analysis' is now not one technique, but several. There is lively discussion about developments and direction in the literature. Given the complexity, it is worth emphasising that nothing that is happening to or with 'types' is in principle different to what is happening in the geometric example.

CORRESPONDENCE ANALYSIS

This section looks at two studies using correspondence analysis. It is of interest to reflect on their relations to both 'types' and the potential relations to case studies. In both cases, the treatment is highly selective.

1. Helene Fontaine: 'a typological analysis of pedestrian accidents'

Multiple correspondence analysis is a useful tool for the visualisation of types with several variables for consideration. Fontaine[24] selects 17 variables from secondary data on pedestrian accidents from a range of sources, including coding of detailed accident analyses over a period of 12 months (1275 pedestrians killed over 12months). The analysis '... reveals correlations between previously coded criteria'.

Nine of the variables related to the pedestrian (e.g. age, gender, reason for being out) and eight related to the environment (e.g. situation, day of the week, weather). To aid the visualisation, age and socioprofessional category were included as supplementary points. The aim was 'to identify some very distinct groups of pedestrian accident victims' to provide 'a typology (that) might serve as a basis for more in depth analyses' (Figure 8.5).

The horizontal axis distinguishes between fatal accidents occurring during the day in urban areas and, on the right-hand side, accidents in rural areas at night. The vertical axis relates to age, alcohol and activities, distinguishing between older people, with a high level of alcohol, walking or crossing the road, and younger victims playing or running. A consideration of the four quadrants suggests certain groupings/types of accident. There is the grouping in which the elderly predominate – generally crossing the road in a built-up area, on their own. There is a grouping in which victims tend to have a high alcohol rating to be walking alone at night in a rural area. A third grouping has a high proportion of child victims of daytime accidents in built-up areas, and a fourth group is dominated by young adults where the fatal accident is often subsequent to a previous incident of loss of control or initial non-fatal accident.

On the basis of the suggestions illuminated by the correspondence map, Fontaine went on

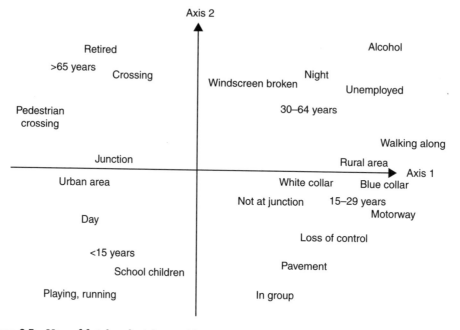

Figure 8.5   Map of fatal pedestrian accidents.
Source: (*Fatal accidents reports.*)

to conduct a hierarchical classification which supported the initial groupings. Figure 8.6 shows the final model.

Thus, analysis suggested some types that carried, from the beginning, an empirical warrant. Fontaine says that 'Rather than explain the causes of the accidents, the correlations reflect a "statistical proximity"'. She takes the emergence of a typology with what could be regarded as Weberian 'ideal types' (exaggeration, fiction …) as an obvious outcome, and remarks that 'The resulting typological breakdown should then serve as a basis for in-depth analysis to improve our understanding …'. It is hard not to see this as involving case studies.

2. Robert T. Green et al: 'societal development and family purchasing roles: a cross-national study'[25]

The research uses Rodman's[26] four-valued typology of societies, relevant to consumer decision-making, questioning existing

notions that power in a relationship derives from resources. The types are:

(1) Patriarchy: a traditional society with strong patriarchal family norms (e.g. India).
(2) Modified patriarchy: a patriarchal society rapidly modernising and accepting ideas such as equalitarianism in some classes (e.g. Greece).
(3) Transitional equalitarianism: equalitarian family norms replace patriarchal norms; power roles are achieved rather than ascribed (e.g. United States).
(4) Equalitarianism: equalitarian norms permeate the society (e.g. Sweden and Denmark).

Using data from the United States, France, Holland, Venezuela and Gabon, Green et al. explored whether Rodman's typology was an adequate framework for family purchasing decisions. These countries were chosen to represent a range of cultures from the relatively traditional to the relatively modern. Random samples of married middle-class and upper middle-class women were selected from four countries; a convenience sample was used for Gabon. Sample sizes ranged

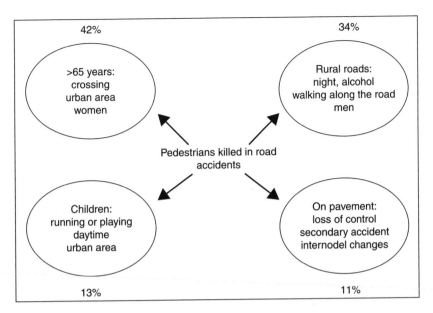

Figure 8.6   Final model: fatal pedestrian accidents.
Source: (*Fatal accidents reports*. The typology merely reveals the most distinctive characteristics, i.e. those overrepresented in each class compared with the pedestrian accident population as a whole.)

from 110 to 240 and the data were collected by questionnaires. The questionnaire asked the respondent to indicate who would make the decisions about the purchase of seven products and services, i.e. groceries, furniture, appliances, automobiles, savings, vacations and insurance. Possible answers were the husband, the wife or joint (Figure 8.7).

The vertical axis has wife-dominated decisions at one pole and husband-dominated decisions at the other; the horizontal axis has joint decisions at one pole and autonomous decisions at the other.

Three main clusters emerge clearly. Decision points about the purchases of groceries tend to lie close to the 'wife-dominated' pole for all five nations. At the bottom pole, the points suggest decisions about the purchase of automobiles and insurance tend to be dominated by the husband. Points towards the left-hand pole of joint decisions relate to the purchase of furniture vacations and appliances especially in the United States, France and Holland. However, at the right-hand side of the horizontal axis, the mapping suggests that decisions in Gabon about appliances, savings, furniture and vacation are more autonomous

and more husband-dominated than in the other countries. In Venezuela, too, decisions about appliances are more autonomous than in the other countries. Hence, the existence of a fourth cluster is suggested by the mapping.

Three of the countries in the study appear to fit three of Rodman's ideal types: Gabon is an example of a patriarchal society; Venezuela is modified patriarchal; France, Holland and the United States appear to fit the criteria for 'transitional equalitarianism'. So, this was a study with a powerful ideal-type input, where the main outcome was some warrant for the initial ideal types. The authors went on to run specific chi-square two-country tests. There remains an interesting potential fourth type, worthy of further investigation.

Correspondence analysis and case studies

Looking at in the context of case-study method, the outcome of these two studies is clear. Correspondence analysis is used at an early stage, on large-N data, and is seen as preliminary and exploratory. Although researchers using it expect that further work

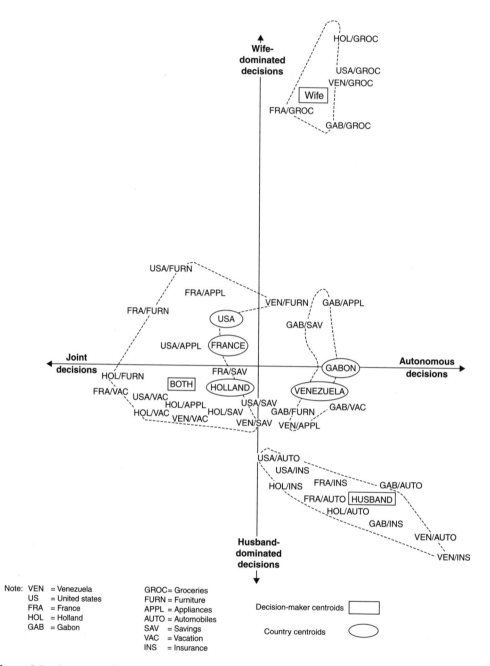

Figure 8.7 Correspondence map of family purchasing roles.

should follow, this is not explicit theory- and test-oriented work. Rather, case study, to explore and identify more detailed meanings in situations, is envisaged.

CORRESPONDENCE ANALYSIS AND METHODOLOGY

Methods, types and cases: three extremes

Correspondence analysis can be built into most leading methodological positions, each of which will generate versions both of 'type' and 'case study'. For simplicity, we take three extremes:

(i) A wholly inductive model

If your model of science is wholly inductive – a rare position since full positivism – then you have a major theorist in Benzécri, who has developed induction in new and productive ways, and opposes it to all versions of 'idealism'. Extreme (i) would claim that 'types' emerge from the data (observations), and that correspondence analysis demonstrates the machinery. An extreme inductivism has a nominalist understanding of theory, whereby its general terms are simply shorthand for all valid observations. Inductive science starts with the 'case study', but then analyses, simplifies and moves to observation of large numbers of simplified cases.

(ii) Attaching the highest value to testable theory

If your conception attaches the highest value to testable theory, specifying underlying variables or structures, and the relations between them, correspondence analysis is exploratory, and is a refinement of description. It is then a useful tool at a requisite (exploratory) stage in research. Additional (inferential) statistics will be marshalled for theory testing.

Extreme (ii) would subsume notions of type – eventually – into developed general theory. There is more to theory and its changes than operations on data. It is (usually) realist in its grasp of theory: for subsumption, 'types'

would have to have a status as real structures. Correspondence analysis provides candidates, usually in exploratory case study.[27]

Case studies are episodes in scientific development. Existing theory is applied to puzzles, and these can require theoretical reworkings. This may be preliminary to theory change. New exploration is therefore required – much of this will involve case study and descriptive techniques. In relation to both (i) and (ii), it is important that correspondence analysis works powerfully in the physical and biological sciences, for example in genetics.

(iii) Attaching the highest value to detailed understanding of cases

If your view attaches the highest value to detailed understanding of cases, as in histori- cal work or ethnography, and (some) cultural study, correspondence analysis can be, again, useful in an exploratory stage, or succession of stages. 'Case study' becomes the norm for social science, with no expectation of anything 'further'. A 'case study' involves, typically, embeddedness, history, temporality and defeasibility.

For (iii), all 'types' grow from everyday usage and practice, and all are embedded in multiple categorisations in reason and narrative. In the latter, we can include any social science theory and/or common sense narratives and standard or institutional processes of practical reason. 'Types' in social science are defeasible, and with temporal limitation. This limitation is like Weber's view that types can lose salience, over time. They can vanish from our interest (like 'criminal types', perhaps) or from the world, as with lost fashions. There is routine development and death of types of persons, as conditions of individuality, of recognition and of status.

Visualising types is not particularly a professional social scientific activity. It is a required competence in everyday life, and social scientific usage is a refinement, at best, for particular purposes. We can all imagine or visualise – and use – new and complex types, based on existing typifications. This constitutes the social world, rather than (merely) describing it.[28] What is unusual about (but not peculiar to) social science is spelling out the types employed, with an attempt at contrast and completeness; and claiming an empirical warrant, in the sense that the social scientist frequently wants to say that the types identified are those to be found in the segment of the social world under study, and that they are salient. Correspondence analysis certainly suggests new types, and how they may be visualised, to any competent person. However, it also suggests that the indicated types, and the space for them, already possesses some quantitative warrant, and this is its striking advantage. The cost of this warrant is its large-N character.

Mixes

If your preference is for a mix or moderation of these three – as in much work on 'case study' approaches – you will, in mixed ways, find value in correspondence analysis.

The argument is that whatever your position on social science method, correspondence analysis is of potential use to you.[29] In Benzécri's version, there are more resonances with position (iii) than would be expected for an approach that is inherently large-N, and 'inductivist'. The bias in favour of data and description fits (i) and (iii) better than (ii), but does not exclude it.

'Practical' social science

A fourth, perhaps unexpected, version of social science has marked resonance with correspondence analysis. This is practical social science. It has questions like: 'in which constituencies should I focus my heaviest campaigning?', 'how can I optimise the jury selection at the trial?' and market research issues. This is social science in immediate social, political, economic and administrative involvement. It is often heavily statistical. It is remarkably successful, and a prominent feature of contemporary social organisation. Perhaps it is superficial (in the sense of little relation to 'theory') and it needs to be rendered deeper for, e.g. academic

social science. Correspondence analysis is natural for it, in its closeness to the 'data', treated as unproblematic. Those concerned with practical questions find the speedy understandings and statements of quantity and distance immediately valuable.

Practical social science uses types, but these are heavily circumscribed, in salience, and time. Practical concerns provide many contexts within which 'inductivist' correspondence analysis can find a purchase. Hence, in France, the popularity of correspondence analysis outputs in the media, where the maps are read with little apparent difficulty. It is reasonable to say that, by comparison with much 'academic' social science, this is an influential success.

The 'model-free' character of correspondence analysis

In social science, the move is not from data to types but from initial types to transformed types, richer and often surprising. Like other empirical social research, correspondence analysis only simplifies in some respects. It might, and does, remove some of the surface accretions and complexities of the data, and reveal some underlying structure, but researchers typically finish with more questions than they started with.

Categories of contingency tables in social science already incorporate types and their relations. These may be no better than suspicions, but what we want is not to avoid them but to have them rejected, or heavily modified and extended. If this is 'idealism' (in Benzécri's sense), for sociologists it appears unavoidable. The suspicions built into contingency tables do not add up to statistical models, and in this sense the procedure is 'model free'. As with 'criminal types', the statistical procedure as such will produce results independent of the initial suspicions.

There is a necessary procedure of interpretation of the maps, which has to relate them to existing knowledge, formal or informal, and is not itself defined by the statistical procedures. Without ever intending it, where the procedure throws up correspondences that are readily interpretable in terms of initial suspicions, it can look confirmatory.

Correspondence analysis is a powerful contribution to inductive procedures. It imposes a genuine inductive contribution in appropriate research, and is itself a brilliant contribution to a valid account of induction. It is not surprising that what it does is to explore and suggest, rather than to compel particular interpretations. The notion of 'correspondence' introduced by Benzécri and his colleagues is philosophically, as well as statistically and methodologically, new and important. As much recent French philosophy would suggest,[30] the statistics here outruns and precedes the philosophy.

As part of this contribution, 'correspondence' links inductive procedure with description, and is a major contribution to the theory of description. It explains part of what it is for A and B to correspond, neither more nor less, rather than to be in other relations. It provides descriptive practices, including the simplification of complex data (data reduction).

If extended, thorough description is a valid part of science, it has perhaps not featured sufficiently in the standard philosophies of science. The balance between description, explanation and test varies within and between sciences, and at particular periods, and this is true of social science. However, case-study social science, and the elaboration of 'types' that goes with it, has a particular desire for effective and elaborated description, and wishes to be as inductive as possible. The bias in favour of description may persist, and not be outweighed by theoretical development. This is the resonance of case study and correspondence analysis. None of this encourages a view that induction is the whole of true science.

Correspondence analysis for visualising types

Correspondence analysis, as used in social science, provides a powerful constraint on the freedom to generate types, and forces direction on visualisation. It is not a tool for the visualisation itself – the correspondences require an interpretation that is not provided in the statistical treatment. Its largest virtue is that it comes with empirical warrant. In reflection, it will remain possible to reject the contingency table (with its suspicions), and look for a new one. This move might be triggered by the correspondence analysis maps.

For possible types, correspondence analysis provides swift overall appraisals, including quantity (counts of elements of potential types) and distance, how alike or unalike the possible types are. The ways in which 'types' feature in the analysis are multiple. Each category in the table is an ideal type, including, e.g. 'pedestrian' in Fontaine's study. We can take a cluster as a potential (empirical) ideal type. We can take the underlying dimensions as the simplest set of ideal types that the data suggest exist in this context.

Correspondence analysis is not a natural fit with case studies, despite the resonances. It is not (directly) a way of generating new understanding, nor a way of grasping underlying forces or factors (although it can contribute to this.) It helps to grasp, for a population, what are the choices/factors at work.

The 'preliminary' character of correspondence analysis

Limitations and criticism of the applicability of the technique for social science are largely related to its essentially exploratory and descriptive characteristics. It is natural that those working from a variable and generalising theory orientation would see it as only and essentially preparatory. Its productions would lead to further investigations and the formulation of testable models, preferably using interval metrics. Less obviously, those emphasising rich and qualitative conclusions, would want well researched and specified bases for the initial contingency tables, and would take the output as occasion for more precise and detailed studies, e.g. of 'small-N' or specific case studies. The limitations and criticisms tend to place correspondence analysis in wider contexts, rather than rule it out.

This argument resolves any issues between large and small N. Correspondence analysis usually belongs to exploratory work with fairly large-N samples or populations. But tested general theory is not necessarily the envisaged outcome. A survey can be, and often is, the preliminary work for a case study. The authors of each of our examples envisaged further, detailed case studies, which would draw on their analyses.

This further, perhaps less popular, Weberian emphasis is at least an important possibility. For Weber, fictive ideal types are an input to the detailed and particular studies of history.[31] This corresponds to the view that social surveys can be an input to detailed work like ethnographies or case studies, which generate the specific understandings we want, rather than serving the development of tested theory. Correspondence analysis has a place in indicating quantity, qualities, relations and distance, suggesting types for 'spiral', developing, understandings. And it is clear that its effective practice shatters the most pervasive of sociological method myths – that social statistics belongs *solely* to a 'natural science' method, characterised by hypothesis, theory and test.

NOTES

1. Greenacre, M. and Hastie, T. 1987 'The geometric interpretation of correspondence analysis' *Journal of the American Statistical Association* 82(398): 437–447
2. See, for example, Parsons, T. 1964 'Introduction' *Max Weber, The Theory of Social and Economic Organisation*. New York: Free Press, p. 14 *et seq*.
3. Schutz, A. 1967 *The Phenomenology of the Social World* (trans. Walsh, G. and Lehnert, F.). Northwestern University Press, chapter 1. In the present context, it is worth remembering that Schutz's work closely follows (in part) Husserl's 'Transcendental and Formal Logic'. Schutz's intersubjective grounding of the objectivity of social types reflects Husserl's intersubjective grounding of the objective concepts of mathematics. Husserl, E. 1969 *Formal and Transcendental Logic*. Martinus Nijhoff.
4. Ragin, C. 1987 *The Comparative Method: Moving Beyond Qualitative and Quantitative Strategies*. Berkeley, CA: University of California Press.

5. Bhaskar, R. 1979 *The Possibility of Naturalism*. Brighton, UK: Harvester
6. Maxwell, A.E. 1977 *Multivariate Analysis in Social Research*. London: Chapman and Hall.
7. Maxwell, A.E. 1977 *Multivariate Analysis in Social Research*. London: Chapman and Hall, p. 3.
8. Maxwell, A.E. 1977 *Multivariate Analysis in Social Research*. London: Chapman and Hall, p. 4.
9. Pearson, K. 1901 'On lines and planes of closest fit in systems of points in space' *Philosophical Magazine* 2: 559–572.
10. This includes exploratory factor analysis and optimal scaling. Procedures like correspondence analysis have been reinvented in different fields, with different names. Within social science it has been both discipline based (famously Bourdieu), and used in 'applied' social science such as market research. It has been used across a range of studies, from structural variables to event histories and textual analysis. Correspondence analysis is itself already a family of techniques, some more geometric than others: there will be some reference to this later. Dual scaling, principal components analysis of qualitative data, homogeneity analysis, optimal scaling are some of the alternative names. Nishisato gives a fuller list. Nishisato, S. 1980 *Analysis of Categorical Data: Dual Scaling and Its Applications*. Toronto: University of Toronto Press.
11. Benzécri, J-P. 1992 *Correspondence Analysis Handbook*. New York: Marcel Dekker.
12. Greenacre, M. 1993 *Correspondence Analysis in Practice*. London: Academic Press, p. 6. Benzécri is straightforwardly and robustly inductivist: he characterises alternatives as 'idealist'. A different context in which to look at 'induction' in the French school, is moves in French philosophy to change the force of science, from the domination of the world by interrogation based in existing theory and subjectivity, to an openness to surprise, new directions and attention to suppressed background understandings. These share with inductivism an absolute attention to the world: the other speaks through the researcher. These are much more general issues than data analysis and multivariate statistics.
There are related moves in mathematics, although the philosophy is very different to Benzécri's. See the excellent collection on the mathematical implications of Deleuze, S. Duffy (Ed.) 2006 *Virtual Mathematics: The Logic of Difference*. Manchester: Clinamen Press, Manchester. Among other things, there is opposition to set-theoretic formalisation of mathematics as logicism, an emphasis on problematics, on graphics and doodles, and the retention of historically abandoned possibilities – as well as fundamental primacy for mathematics over philosophy. None of this is intended to evade Benzécri's manifest espousal of induction.
13. E.g. fuzzy-set logic. Ragin, C. 2000 *Fuzzy Set Social Science*, Chicago: University of Chigago Press. This, by the way, is consistent with advanced forms of

correspondence analysis. See, for example, Verkuilen, J. 2001 *Measuring Fuzzy Set Membership Functions: A Dual Scaling Approach* APSA and Greenacre M. and Hastie, T. 1987 'The geometric interpretation of correspondence analysis' *Journal of the American Statistical Association* 82(398): 445. Chapter 7 in this volume presents the closely related case of cluster analysis as appropriate for case study. It is particularly interesting in that it takes its departure from the statistical sense of 'case', as opposed to 'variable' analysis, and does so within the framework of critical realism, rather than interpretivism. Cluster analysis is a case-based procedure in this full sense; correspondence analysis works with variables.

14. E.g. Benzécri, J-P. 1992 *Correspondence Analysis Handbook*. New York: Marcel Dekker.

15. Greenacre, M. 1993 *Correspondence Analysis in Practice*. London: Academic Press

16. This is a substantial simplification. Greenacre begins with a three-dimensional diagram, with vertical axes, and plots the points in this three-dimensional space. This is a three-dimensional scatter-plot (Greenacre, 1993, p. 12 *et seq.*) Then he shows that the points all fall within a triangle, which can be presented separately, without loss of information. For brevity, we have simply employed the triangle.

17. For the distance between 'very satisfied' and 'quite satisfied' in the row table: $S(\text{distance}) = \sqrt{(.149 - .250)^2 + (.278 - .342)^2 + (.573 - .408)^2}$

18. Reasons for the use of chi-square distance (as opposed to other distance measures) include correction for an overweighting by large numbers, the 'principle of distributional equivalence', whereby categories can be combined without affecting the rest of the geometry, and general utility in calculations for reduced dimensionality and contributions to inertia.

19. Here, the axes are close to the original variables: this is not usually the case, but derives from the simplicity of the present case. More complex data will lead to very different axes and labels, just as more unexpected possible types could very well also appear, forcing themselves on the researcher's attention. This is the surprising and worthwhile bonus.

20. Hence Benzécri's slogan: the model to follow the data.

21. See Blasius and Greenacre , especially Part 2. Blasius, J. and Greenacre, M. 1998 *Visualization of Categorical Data*. London: Academic Press.

22. One that indicates membership/non-membership using ones and zeros.

23. This is a symmetric matrix built up of a number of blocks in which each variable is tabulated against the categories of all the other variables and itself on the diagonal.

24. Fontaine, H. 1997 'A typological analysis of pedestrian accidents'. Paper presented at the 7th workshop of ICTCT, 26–27 October 1997, Paris.

25. Green, R.T., Leonardi, J-P., Chandon, J-L., Cunningham, I.C.M. Verhage, B. and Strazzieri A.

1983 'Societal development and family purchasing roles: a cross-national study' *Journal of Consumer Research* 9: 436–442.

26. Rodman, H. 1972 'Marital power and the theory of resources in cross-cultural context' *Journal of Comparative Family Studies* 1: 50–67.

27. Chapter 7 in the present volume is explicitly a critical realist treatment of a related statistical treatment. As opposed to our extreme (i) above, it does not presume identity of the data terms and the described world, with automatic 'validity'. As opposed to (iii) below, it is more concerned with relations between the 'real', and the statistical terms, including open issues of validity, than an interpretivist account would be. It shares with the present chapter a concern with new kinds of exploratory and descriptive statistics, appropriate for case study.

28. It is difficult to see how presuppositions of this sort could be reconciled with inductivism. It might be possible to separate a statistical inductivism, by which no statistically defined model precedes the encounter with the data, from an inductivism in social science. In the present chapter, the only implication is an attention to how, if at all, social types precede and organise the collection of data.

29. There could be exceptions. It is difficult to imagine two philosophies of social science more (apparently) opposed to each other, than Benzécri's inductivism and Bhaskar's transcendental realism. Benzécri shares the anti-Kantianism of much modern French philosophy, and it is on Kant that Bhaskar's analysis rests. A line of reconciliation does suggest itself: correspondence analysis as a way of stripping off superficial layers and accretions, and hence suggesting what the deep real structures might be. This would also begin from the everyday and ideological surfaces, and then allow the other (the data for Benzécri, the deep for Bhaskar) to speak. We shall not even imply the success of such a reconciliation. There is no mention of statistical social science in 'The Possibility of Naturalism'.

30. Duffy, S. (Ed.) 2006 *Virtual Mathematics: The Logic of Difference*. Manchester: Clinamen Press.

31. Weber, M. 1964 *Max Weber, The Theory of Social and Economic Organisation*. New York: Free Press, p.109. This presumes, which remains arguable, that what Weber refers to as 'history' is close to what we mean by 'case study'. The 'Social Psychology of World Religions', which makes plentiful use of ideal types in his sense, is one of the greatest of small-N case studies.

REFERENCES

Benzécri, J-P. 1992 *Correspondence Analysis Handbook*. New York: Marcel Dekker.

Bhaskar,R. 1979 *The Possibility of Naturalism*. Brighton, UK: Harvester.

Blasius, J. and Greenacre, M. 1998 *Visualization of Categorical Data*. London: Academic Press.

Duffy, S. (Ed.) 2006 *Virtual Mathematics: The Logic of Difference*. Manchester: Clinamen Press.

Green, R.T., Leonardi, J-P., Chandon, J-L., Cunningham, I.C.M., Verhage, B. and Strazzieri, A. 1983 'Societal development and family purchasing roles: a cross-national study' *Journal of Consumer Research* 9: 436–442.

Greenacre, M. 1993 *Correspondence Analysis in Practice*. London: Academic Press.

Greenacre, M. and Hastie, T. 1987 The geometric interpretation of correspondence analysis' *Journal of the American Statistical Association* 82(398): 437–447.

Husserl, E. 1969 *Formal and Transcendental Logic*. The Hague, the Netherlands: Martinus Nijhoff.

Maxwell, A.E. 1977 *Multivariate Analysis in Social Research*. London: Chapman and Hall.

Nishisato, S. 1980 *Analysis of Categorical Data: Dual Scaling and Its Applications*. Toronto: University of Toronto Press.

Parsons, T. 1964 'Introduction' in *Max Weber, The Theory of Social and Economic Organisation*. New York: Free Press.

Pearson, K. 1901 'On lines and planes of closest fit in systems of points in space' *Philosophical Magazine* 2: 559–572.

Ragin, C. 1987 *The Comparative Method: Moving Beyond Qualitative and Quantitative Strategies*. Berkeley, CA: University of California Press.

Ragin, C. 2000 *Fuzzy Set Social Science*. Chicago: University of Chicago Press.

Rodman, H. 1972 'Marital power and the theory of resources in cross-cultural context' *Journal of Comparative Family Studies* 1: 50–67.

Schutz, A. 1967 *The Phenomenology of the Social World* (trans. Walsh, G. and Lehnert, F.). Evanston, IL: Northwestern University Press.

Verkuilen, J. 2001 *Measuring Fuzzy Set Membership Functions: A Dual Scaling Approach*. Annual Meeting of the American Political Science Association (APSA).

9

How Classification Works, or Doesn't: The Case of Chronic Pain

Emma Whelan

The reality of pain is insistent and self-evident – but only to the one experiencing it. Others have access only to one's account, not to the pain itself. Because the experience of pain is private, it can only become a public object through representation; representation makes private pain tangible and workable by others. The implications of the elusive and intangible nature of pain, particularly for those in pain and their interactions with physicians, have been described compellingly by authors such as Scarry (1985), Kleinman (1988) and Jean Jackson (1992, 2000). However, the implications of pain's elusiveness for its assessment and standardization have been explored little in the social science literature on pain (for one exception, see Whelan 2003). This chapter presents a case study of one way of standardizing pain: the IASP *Classification of Chronic Pain* (Merskey and Bogduk 1994).

WHAT IS CLASSIFICATION AND WHY STUDY IT?

In their important work *Sorting Things Out*, Bowker and Star (1999, p. 10) define a classification system as 'a set of boxes (metaphorical or literal) into which things can be put to then do some kind of work – bureaucratic or knowledge production'. Of course, social scientists create and use such sets of boxes all the time, for example in close-ended survey questions. A census would be impossible without classifications of types of people, for example, although the specific typologies used to classify people in a census are up for debate. The choices we make about what to categorize and how to categorize may have far-reaching, varying, and unpredictable effects, especially upon those categorized. A couple of obvious examples make the case: one, the classification and, later, declassification of homosexuality as a category of psychiatric disorder by the American Psychiatric Association (Greenberg 1997); and two, the elaboration of classifications of the 'unfit' by the negative eugenics movement, by Nazi Germany, by sociologists, and arguably by modern-day geneticists (Carlson 2001). Bowker and Star (1999, pp. 6–7) confirm the social and moral significance of classification: 'Each standard and each category valorizes some point of view and silences another. This is not an inherently bad thing–indeed it is inescapable. But it *is* an ethical choice, and as such it is dangerous – not bad, but dangerous'. Thus, sociologists and science studies scholars studying fields other than pain have shown that standardization practices such as classification should not be seen as methods of reflecting reality transparently; instead, standardizations are ontological and political interventions that form the objects they seek to represent (Lynch 1990, 1991, Douglas and Hull 1992, Stemerding 1993, Ben-Ari 1994, Bowker and Star 1999, Clarke and Casper 1996, Curtis 1998). As Nelson Goodman put it, classifications are exercises in 'world-making' (cited in Downey 1992). Given their immense social, political, and ethical significance, studying classifications, and interrogating the classifications we ourselves use, is therefore crucial work for critical social scientists.

But '[i]n order to make a diagnosis or a decision about the absurdity, the danger, the amorality or the unrealism of an innovation, one must first describe the network' (Bruno Latour, cited in Singleton 1996, p. 459). So my task here is not to argue for or against the moral, social, or epistemic worth of any particular classificatory scheme, but instead to conduct a case study of the making of one professional classification system and the network of experts that created, resisted, and eventually accepted (partly, anyway) the system. After all, standardizations do not only affect those standardized; they can also affect those doing the standardizing, the subjects who use them. They direct their actions and goals – or, at least, they *try* to; as we will see, they do not always succeed.

Systems of pain standardization and classification try to define the object 'pain' for medical communities, and try to help constitute the members and membership of pain-studying communities in the process. Classification is especially important, because it puts pains in order, names their differences, sets them in relation to one another, and aims to make sense of their apparent variety and similarity. Classification creates a kind of 'pain cosmology', laying out the rules of pain's being, and hence the rules for engaging with pain. Although she does not discuss the issue in detail, Isabelle Baszanger's study of pain medicine notes that classification is essential to constitute pain as a workable object around which a professional community can organize: 'Working on pain implies knowing how to recognize it, how to interpret its diversity. It requires classification ... classification plays an essential role in creating a community of practice and can become a common basis for physicians to communicate among themselves and with others' (Baszanger 1995, p. 34; see also pp. 84–88).

However, attempts to develop tools for the classification of pain – indeed, for the classification of anything – raise several problems. While classifications are often thought to reflect the world transparently, indeed to be constituted by the world, Nelson Goodman and others have argued that we live in an always-already classified world, and that our world is preconstituted for us by the categories we use (see Douglas and Hull 1992). Thus, when developing any new classification, we must take account of pre-existing classifications, classificatory principles, and classifiers:

[S]peakers find themselves in a world already classified, in it they try to fulfill their projects, to do so they must organise, to organise they must adjust the classifications and adjust their habits ... the actors must secure each other's consent to the action they propose, ideas of justice [fit with reality] are invoked, the classifications are used to score accountability, to register degrees of success and failure. Where very exact fidelity is required, ambiguity has to be reduced, but how? The answer is partly technical, a matter of finding measures, and partly a matter of trust, a matter of agreeing measures. (Douglas and Hull 1992, p. 4)

Reducing ambiguity, and finding and agreeing upon measures, are not easy tasks. For example, comparability is the premise behind all standardization tools. Whereas pain classifications differentiate between classes of pains, and hence enforce boundaries between pains, they are also about grouping pains together, making pain cases comparable, which requires making pains, in some sense, the same. But not only can individuals and their accounts of their pains vary considerably; so can the accounts of those who document and assess. The variability in the documenters' and assessors' accounts – its acknowledgment, problematization, and solution – is the focus of this paper.

Although there are many systems for classifying pains, my focus will be on the chronic pain classification system developed by the International Association for the Study of Pain (IASP; Merskey and Bogduk 1994). The IASP is the primary international organization that has attempted to constitute pain, in and of itself rather than as a symptom of another medical condition, as a specialized but interdisciplinary field of research and clinical treatment. Its members include specialists in the highly diverse fields of anaesthesia, neurology, psychology, general practice, psychiatry, nursing, and social work, among others; thus, however influential its classification actually is or is not (and I shall discuss that), the IASP's intended theatre of operations is wide. The IASP *Classification of Chronic Pain* seems to be, first and foremost, an attempt to 'make pains the same' for diverse pain specialists – and also, thereby, to make pain specialists, in all their great disciplinary and international diversity, the same in some respects.

DEVELOPMENT OF THE IASP CLASSIFICATION

The IASP *Classification of Chronic Pain* was first published in its entirety in 1986 as a supplement to the IASP's journal *Pain*, the leading international journal in the field of pain medicine. The project was developed and organized by an IASP Subcommittee on Taxonomy (a subcommittee of the larger Committee on Standards) headed by Harold Merskey, a British-born psychiatrist at the University of Western Ontario, London, Canada. The *Classification*, now in its second edition (Merskey and Bogduk 1994), represents an impressive collaborative international effort, with official contributions from 103 specialists from 13 countries (and undoubtedly many unofficial contributors as well). The account of the *Classification*'s development provided here is based on the papers of this Subcommittee, including correspondence, minutes, reports, and publications, from the IASP Archives,[1] an oral history interview with Dr Merskey (Liebeskind 1994), and publications by advocates and critics of the IASP classification project.

The *Classification* defines key pain terms and provides descriptions of chronic pain syndromes developed by experts in those particular syndromes (Merskey and Bogduk 1994). The result is a 240-page book that describes hundreds of chronic pain conditions. It presents a system for the numerical coding of pain syndromes using five axes. The first axis, Regions, describes the primary anatomical site of the pain in the body (e.g. head, face, and mouth; abdominal region; lower limbs). The second, Systems, notes the system of the body 'whose abnormal functioning produces the pain' (Merskey and Bogduk 1994, p. 3) (e.g. the nervous system, the gastrointestinal system). The third, Temporal Characteristics of Pain, describes the occurrence of pain episodes (e.g. recurring regularly; continuous). The fourth, Patient's Statement of Intensity: Time Since Onset of Pain, records the pain as mild, medium, or severe and indicates its duration (1 month or less; 1 to 6 months; more than 6 months). The fifth, Etiology, relates to the cause or mechanism thought to produce the pain (e.g. genetic or congenital disorders; trauma; psychological origin). The classifier must code the pain on each of these five axes. The possible choices are delineated for each axis, with at least one 'other' category for each axis to cover cases that do not fit (e.g. Unknown, None of the above). Obviously, each of these components of the *Classification* depends on its own classification scheme, seemingly derived from already established, formal or tacit principles and classifications within pain medicine or biomedicine generally, such as a classification of systems of the body or time periods of illness. The *Classification* privileges location of pain because 'the majority of pains of which patients complain are commonly described first by the physician in terms of region and only later in terms of aetiology. An arrangement by site provides the best practical system for coding the majority of pains dealt with by experts in the field' (Merskey and Bogduk 1994, p. xii). The reader is thus directed to 'Give priority to the main site of the pain' (Merskey and Bogduk 1994, p. 3), a direction that has proved controversial, as we shall see.

Although he was not the President of the IASP at the time of its inauguration, the Taxonomy Subcommittee really got started on the initiative of Dr John Bonica, an American anaesthesiologist, probably the most prominent figure in the pain specialist community in his day, and the mastermind and founder of the IASP. Bonica was the first pain specialist to attempt a comprehensive classification of pain (Bonica 1953). Bonica's passion for developing a classification for chronic pain is evident in all his writings on the subject. His commitment to the manifest destiny of the IASP classification, that is, to its colonization of the world of chronic pain studies, is exemplified in a frequently cited editorial Bonica wrote in the journal *Pain* in 1979:

> The development and widespread adoption of universally accepted definitions of terms and a classification of pain syndromes are among the most important objectives and responsibilities of the IASP ... I hope ... that all IASP members will cooperate and use the classification of pain syndromes after this is adopted by IASP to improve our communications systems. This will require that they be incorporated in the spoken and written transfer of information, particularly scientific papers, books, etc., and in the development of research protocols, clinical records, and data banks for the storage and retrieval of research and clinical data. (Bonica 1979, p. 248)

Bonica's views about the purposes of classification emerge in his response to arguments about why classification won't work. Bonica writes:

> In the past, many people have considered the definition of pain and a uniform list of pain terms and classification of pain syndromes impossible because of so many differences of opinion among scientists and clinicians of different disciplines and also because of differences in national usage. Consequently, we have been markedly impaired in our communication pertaining to pain research and therapy. This became impressively clear to me during the time I wrote my book *Management of Pain* when I expended an immense amount of time and effort to analyse and synthesize the results reported by numerous writers who obviously were describing the same condition under a large variety of quite different names. (Bonica 1979, p. 247)

Here, Bonica advances two main aims for classification. First, we need to make *pains* the same – we need to group pains named and described differently into the same category as the same condition which, according to Bonica, they 'obviously' are. Second, and relatedly, we need to make *specialists* the same in some respects, in the name of scientific progress. That is, if research and treatment are to advance, we need to get everyone using the same language. We need to standardize terminology, and to overcome definitional differences – both national and disciplinary.

As Merskey puts it in his tellingly entitled paper 'Development of a Universal Language of Pain Syndromes', 'a workable system of classification is fundamental to both national and international comparison, to understand data from different clinics let alone different countries' (Merskey 1983, p. 44). Standardizing terminology is particularly important in pain medicine, a highly interdisciplinary field comprised of both scientist-researchers and clinicians, anaesthesiologists and psychologists, psychiatrists and neurologists, neurosurgeons and dental surgeons. Getting these diverse specialties to use the same language is not easy. This disciplinary diversity is, I think, a major reason for the insight and epistemological reflexivity of specialists within the pain field, but this reflexivity means that taxonomical work in the pain field is perhaps unusually difficult, because there is little consensus about the principles of classification. Add to this the fact that the IASP aims explicitly to be international, making translation between languages an essential, although not an easy, task, and a rather politicized one. These factors are reflected in Merskey's musings about why he, an Englishman who emigrated to Canada in the course of the Subcommittee's work, was chosen by Bonica to head the Taxonomy Subcommittee:

> I didn't really see why I was the guy that was selected. I know now, or at least I think I know now, because I think it needs about four things, which I happened to have combined. One was a fairly good knowledge of diagnosis in all the fields as a clinician. The second is a reasonable degree of tact. The third is the ability to express things in English well. And the fourth is not to be an American. [he laughs] And that's not my decision. That's the decision of several American presidents of the IASP ... who didn't want the United States to be thought to be hogging the appointments and to be unduly influential in the process ... I think they wanted it not to be American with taxonomy because maybe American interests would be too strong and at the same time they wanted somebody who would be strong in English. (quoted in Liebeskind 1994, pp. 97–99)

Combine the multidisciplinarity of the pain medicine field and the internationalism of the IASP and we have a rather motley crew of experts whose only bond is this shadowy object – pain. Solidifying the community then, in many respects, meant solidifying a common language to define that community.

In fact, this was the first major accomplishment of the IASP Taxonomy Subcommittee under Merskey's stewardship – the publication of a list of pain terms, including a number of new terms coined by the Subcommittee (Merskey et al. 1979). Merskey explains why this task was taken on first:

> When we got going, everybody was doubtful about whether we could classify chronic pain. People foresaw all sorts of troubles and I didn't even guess at what they would be, but nobody wanted to do it. But they did want to work on pain terms, and they did want definitions of pain terms. So I said, 'Let's do it' ... And after several revisions or circulations of the drafts, the terms were agreed. (quoted in Liebeskind 1994, pp. 100–101)

Merskey reports that the publication of these terms was well received:

> And those were a great success, at least in the sense that everybody liked them. Everybody felt pleased to have – or nearly everybody; nobody – it's never universal – everybody felt pleased to have terms they could use. (quoted in Liebeskind 1994, p. 102)

Indeed, *The Journal of the American Medical Association* published a commentary praising the Subcommittee's 'most useful list of pain terms'; the international membership of the Subcommittee which would ensure the uptake of the terms internationally; the simplicity of the definitions' wording; and the IASP's 'refreshing' emphasis on flexibility and room for growth. It even advocated the extension of this vocabulary to those not working in the field of pain medicine: 'Since the most common reason for patients seeing a doctor is pain, these 19 terms deserve use by all physicians regardless of specialty. It will make communication with our colleagues through conversation and publication that much easier and thereby provide that much better care for our patients' (de Jong 1980, p. 143).

Bonica, however, was 'greatly disappointed' to learn of the Subcommittee's decision not to pursue a classification immediately, although 'I suppose that the development of a glossary is a compromise which is better than nothing!' (Bonica, letter to Merskey, 15 July 1977).[2] In a letter to Merskey, he presents several suggestions as to how the Subcommittee might overcome the resistance of their colleagues to a classification, the anticipation of which contributed to the Subcommittee's reluctance to produce one. Bonica suggests, for example, that if the Subcommittee had got the classification ready in time for the Second World Congress on Pain, 'it could be presented to the General

Assembly for adoption and subsequently submitted to WHO [World Health Organization] for their consideration and probably official adoption [into their International Classification of Diseases]'. Bonica felt that, if this was achieved, 'this would make [the classification] acceptable by the majority if not most workers in the field throughout the world' (Bonica, letter to Merskey, 15 July 1977). He further suggests that, 'I believe that what "bugs" and misleads some of our colleagues is the misconception that once adopted, [the classification] is cast in steel for all time. Such a classification could be reappraised by a standing committee every three years and changes made whenever deemed necessary' (Bonica, letter to Merskey, 15 July 1977). Two strategies are suggested by Bonica, then: one, get the classification accepted by a higher power, the WHO, and the membership of the IASP will follow; and two, promise revisions as necessary – say that the standard is not such a standard after all – and the membership's discomfort with standardization will subside enough to permit the classification's adoption.

Bonica got his wish. Spurred on by the success of its pain term glossary, the newly confident Subcommittee decided to forge ahead with its original charge (Liebeskind 1994, p. 103). Merskey drafted a skeleton classification following the model of the National Institute of Dental Research in the US, whose classification 'started with etiology and then went through the characteristics of the pain' (Merskey, quoted in Liebeskind 1994, p. 104). This, however, was rejected by the other members of the Subcommittee:

And I think the reason ... probably was that we started with etiology ... the hardest thing on which to get agreement is how to classify any medical topic by etiology. You can say where it is; you can say what it sounds like. But to say what causes it, is the biggest topic for dispute. And ideas of etiology change ... So [Richard A.] Sternbach came up with the comment that 'What do doctors do? They classify by location first, at least with pain.' He says, 'When I see diagnoses from doctors, they refer to the low back or to the neck. Anatomy is where they start.' And I said 'Well, let's think of that.' (Merskey, quoted in Liebeskind 1994, p. 104)

Anatomy, as it happens, is where Bonica had started when he published his classification of chronic pain in 1953; pains were organized first according to the region of the body in which they appeared. Merskey consulted Bonica about basing the new classification on the same principle:

And he said to me, 'I'd be happy for that to be adopted, but I don't want to push it. In fact, the less you say about me the better' ... [he was sensitive to] having people feel that he was just sort of pushing people around to do it his way, which he wasn't. He wanted a classification. He was devoted to the idea of having a classification. He thought that was of extreme importance, but he didn't want to be the dictator ... he pushed for classification, but he didn't push for how to do it. So that's where we went next. With knowing that John was in sympathy with that, I circulated to the committee the way he'd done it. I circulated Sternbach's comments, or brought them up prominently, and said, 'Well, shall we try by region? By anatomy?' And the guys said, 'Okay, well, you could try by anatomy.' So then I prepared the scheme that we have, in broad outline. (Merskey, quoted in Liebeskind 1994, p. 104–105)

The Subcommittee, headed by Merskey, developed a long list of pain conditions which needed to be described in the classification, and sought experts internationally to draft the text, which was then edited and compiled by the Subcommittee. The *Classification* was a reality.

Not everyone shared Bonica's and Merskey's enthusiasm for standardization. Some actively resisted. Others, accepting the value of standardization in principle, have attempted to remake the *Classification* according to their own ideas and priorities. And not everyone has used the Subcommittee on Taxonomy's work in the ways originally intended: Merskey noted about the definition of pain published by the Subcommittee in 1979, 'There have been efforts, some inadvertent and some deliberate, to improve the definition, and it has not always been understood as I would have wished (what creator ever thought his work was fully appreciated?)' (Merskey 1994, p. S75). First, I will discuss a few particularly interesting objections to the IASP classification project during its development, which question the valorization of classification and the principle of standardization itself. Second, I will address some critical evaluations of the Subcommittee's *Classification* in the recent medical literature, that suggest the extent to which classification and standardization now have been accepted as virtues in principle, if not in practice.

TROUBLE IN THE SUBCOMMITTEE

A leading and particularly sharp-tongued opponent early on in the process was British neurologist Peter Nathan. Nathan, a long-standing acquaintance of Merskey, was an original member of the Subcommittee (Liebeskind 1994, p. 100). In response to Bonica's frustration about the lack of standardized descriptions of pain syndromes in textbooks, Nathan writes:

I agree with you that the descriptions in textbooks are not uniform. That is just as it should be; each clinician is impressed with certain aspects of the condition and he should be putting down his view of the condition. There is no one and only correct version. It is just this idea that is so wrong and that would appear if an I.A.S.P. committee were to pontificate on … every syndrome (Nathan, letter to Bonica, 1 January 1981).

Nathan's staunchly relativist position here is perhaps unusual, but Nathan makes other more specific and common critiques that call into question the purpose of standardization – through questions about usability, relevance, state of knowledge, disciplinary boundaries, and cultural and linguistic conventions. For example, reservations about whether the state of knowledge about pain is sufficient to produce a useful classification are expressed by other members of the Taxonomy Subcommittee. Nathan writes, in a letter to Merskey, 'This classification implies we have got all the answers, that we know it all already; and discourages further investigation. This is the history of medicine: giving a thing a name and then everyone thinks they know all about it' (Nathan, letter to Merskey, February 1977).

Related to this comment is the concern of Subcommittee members Bill Noordenbos and Howard Fields about the usefulness of the classification. Noordenbos writes, in an open letter to the Subcommittee, 'I must confess to feeling out of tune with the whole scheme as proposed by the committee at present. It is too complicated, depends on too many arbitrary decisions and eventually leads up to attempts to code complete case-histories. Such plans have a habit to end up in deep drawers or dusty attics' (Noordenbos, letter to the members of the Subcommittee on Taxonomy, March 1980). And Fields writes to Merskey:

I have decided that I am basically opposed to the comprehensive approach as unworkable and not useful. For example, I cannot see a cardiologist coding his patient's crushing substernal chest pain. It really isn't important to him or to those working with pain patients…We must constantly ask ourselves, who is going to use the classification scheme and for what purpose? To have classification is not a worthy enough goal in itself. (Fields, letter to Merskey, 5 January 1981)

So, how did the classification's champions – Bonica, the initiator, and Merskey, the man responsible for pulling the project together – effectively counter this resistance and get people on board with the project? Looking at what became of Peter Nathan is instructive. He ended up resigning from the Subcommittee in frustration, and despite making apparently major contributions in the early stages, received no formal credit in the publication, at least not in the second edition (and this is probably as he would have wanted it). Nathan's contributions, as well as his resistance, are effectively erased from the published record, although Merskey respectfully acknowledges Nathan's important contributions to the Subcommittee's work in an interview with John Liebeskind (Liebeskind 1994, p. 106). Others who became obstructive were dealt with in more blunt ways: One Subcommittee member who attended only one of two meetings had his $100 stipend cut to $50; another who attended neither got no stipend at all (Merskey, letter to Louisa Jones, 6 September 1978).

There are more subtle tactics, too. One of these is strategic reversal – the turning of an argument on its head. For example, both those critics wanting to abandon the classification project, and those advocates describing the day-to-day difficulties of the project, describe the linguistic, cultural, and disciplinary differences that make standardization difficult. Merskey, for instance, observes in a working paper early in the process that 'Linguistic descriptions in one language alone may have to be regarded as unacceptable for an international classification' (Merskey, 'First Working Paper on the Classification of Pain Syndromes', February 1977, appendix to letter to Taxonomy Subcommittee). In a letter to fellow sceptic Noordenbos, Howard Fields complains about the difficulties of the work the Subcommittee has asked him to do: 'I am supposed to find a description for "Fibrositis (indurative headache)". These are terms that are never used by neurologists. Fibrositis is a term used by rheumatologists' (Fields, letter to Bill Noordenbos, 5 January 1980).

But instead of using the point about linguistic incommensurability as evidence against the possibility of classification, Bonica, in a strategic reversal, uses it as a rationale for the necessity of a standard classification, thereby demonstrating the flexibility of scientific rhetorical strategies. In his editorial, Bonica argues that 'even if the adopted definitions and classification of pain syndromes are not perfect they are better than "the tower of Babel" conditions that currently exist (Bonica 1979, p. 247). Bonica knew that disciplinary and cultural differences in terminology had to be dismissed and disparaged if a standardized terminology and classification for pain were to be widely accepted. As science studies scholar Steven Ward points out, 'Those concepts which remain endemic to their academic and professional networks may serve to enforce boundary divisions between disciplines and sub-disciplines or between professional and lay knowledge to coordinate the internal activities of the group ... but they never succeed at becoming widespread truth' (Ward 1996, p. 12). For Bonica and Merskey, some disciplinary precision in vocabulary and focus had to be sacrificed for the good of a community consensus on pain – a

widespread truth about pain, if you like. And Bonica's often-stated goal to get the IASP classification included by the World Health Organization into the International Classification of Diseases aims to further solidify, standardize, and spread its truth.

Bonica draws on other strategies to quell the potential resistance of his colleagues in his introduction to the Merskey Subcommittee's work:

> The (following) report by the Subcommittee on Taxonomy of IASP is published with my strong endorsement and the approval of the Council. These terms represent the end result of many hours of discussion and much correspondence among the members of the committee, and their final consensus. The development and widespread adoption of universally accepted definitions of terms and a classification of pain syndromes are among the most important objectives and responsibilities of the IASP (pursuant to Section F of its by-laws). (Bonica 1979, p. 247)

Bonica's rhetoric here sells the Taxonomy Subcommittee's work in several ways. The first is an appeal to authority: the IASP's Executive is backing it, so IASP's membership should too. The second is an appeal to collegiality: the Subcommittee has worked very hard on the membership's behalf, and therefore should be rewarded with acceptance. The third is an appeal to duty: the IASP has a professional responsibility to come up with a classification – it's in the by-laws and hence must be done! In this way, the classification becomes an inevitability – the IASP as Borg, against which resistance is futile. But are pains and specialists so standardizable after all? Although forms like classifications embody attempts by their authors to direct action, they sometimes end up directing action in ways unintended by their authors – if they even end up directing action at all. The IASP *Classification* is no exception.

RESISTANCE POST-PUBLICATION

In what ways can and cannot the use of a classification be enforced or policed? While I was researching another medical classification, one physician told me that none of his colleagues paid any attention to the classification, preferring to rely on their own clinical experience as a guide to ordering patients' signs and symptoms in a meaningful way. This suggested to me that perhaps much of the systematization that goes on in medicine is more for appearance's sake than for practice's sake, and that practising medical experts might not always toe the line set out by their classification-promoting professional associations. So how influential is the IASP *Classification*, now almost 20 years old, in the field of pain studies?

This is a difficult question to answer based on a review of the medical literature alone, because the *Classification* is meant to be used in clinical practice, not just in research. Accessing representative and generalizable information about clinical practice is extremely difficult and well beyond the scope of this paper. It would be useful to see how often the *Classification* is cited in the literature, how often it is invoked to structure medical studies of chronic pain conditions; the most efficient way to do this would be through some database searches. But this is complicated by the fact that the *Classification*, although published as a supplement to a medical journal, is not classified as a medical journal article in the databases (some classification practices thereby complicate research on other classification practices!). Neither the 1986 nor the 1994 edition of the *Classification* is indexed in Medline; and the number of times the editions are cited is not provided in Web of Science (http://thomsonreuters.com/products_services/scientific/Web_of_Science).

However, while we may not be able readily to identify a fair sample of articles that merely *use* or *refer to* the *Classification*, we are able to conduct Medline searches for articles *about* the IASP *Classification*, that explicitly evaluate it or comment on it. And most of the few references to the IASP *Classification* that emerge from such a search are at least somewhat critical of it. This is probably as one would expect; those who have no problems whatsoever with the IASP

Classification would be unlikely to bother to write a journal article saying so. Still, this approach does give us some insights into the forms of resistance this classification project has to overcome in the field.

In general, what information is available suggests that the IASP *Classification* has enjoyed some success, but has not been adopted consistently by pain specialists. While Woolf (1999, p. 320) says of the *Classification* 'a measure of its importance is how widely it is used', Turk and Rudy point to the 'absence of an agreed upon classification of chronic pain syndromes and chronic pain patients that has been adopted on a systematic basis. The lack of availability of any universally accepted classification system has resulted in confusion and an inability of investigators as well as practitioners to compare observations and results of research' (Turk and Rudy 1990, p. 27). The 9-year gap between Turk and Rudy's evaluation and Woolf's later one suggests that there may be a growing acceptance and use of the *Classification*. However, some critics have argued that the *Classification* is 'too elaborate and difficult for the practitioner' (Procacci and Maresca 1991, p. 332) or take issue with its reliance on expert opinion and consensus-building rather than on systematic, evidence-based, empirical validation (Woda et al. 2005). Others critique the use of the construct of 'normal' pain throughout the *Classification*, arguing that it reflects and encourages a culture of clinical suspicion regarding the reality of patients' pain (Cronje and Williamson 2006).

Still others argue that the *Classification*'s privileging of anatomical site of pain as the primary principle of classification is clinically unhelpful and does not reflect current understandings of pain in the field. These critics tend to advocate a mechanism-based classification instead (Nicholson 2000, p. S1115, Woolf et al. 1998). Merskey has responded to this suggestion in print (he very often does to critics of the Subcommittee's work), arguing that 'During the preparation of the basis for the present IASP classification some 20 years ago, the Subcommittee on Taxonomy (as it then was) decided that it would be impossible to achieve a worthwhile classification using etiology as the first defining feature of syndromes. We have not made enough progress yet to change that position nor can I anticipate a date in the future for the ideal taxonomy' (Merskey 1999, p. 319). Turk and Rudy (1987) provide support for Merskey's position and for the *Classification*'s privileging of anatomical site as the most important axis in their evaluation of the *Classification*'s intercoder reliability. They found that although the reliability of the first axis, the anatomical Region of the pain, was good, the reliability of the fifth axis, Etiology (mechanism causing the pain), was low enough to produce 'reliabilities that are not clinically acceptable' for many pain conditions (Turk and Rudy 1987, p. 177). But despite their support for the *Classification*'s 'considerable potential and utility' and their argument that the 'IASP taxonomy system is on the right track and will eventually evolve into a scientifically sound diagnostic system', (Turk and Rudy 1987, p. 189), they nevertheless propose that the IASP system should be complemented by their own classification system, the Multiaxial Assessment of Pain, which addresses psychosocial and behavioural aspects of pain (Turk & Rudy 1990).

Perhaps the most damning published critique of the IASP *Classification* comes from Chaplan and Sorkin (1997, p. 82), who asked 'where do the rank-and-file members [of the American Pain Society (APS) and IASP] stand with respect to understanding and application of official vocabulary guidelines?' They recount an argument between a journal editor and another APS member regarding the definition of several of the IASP Subcommittee's pain terms: 'a few others joined in, several napkins were filled with stimulus response curves, and no consensus was reached' (Chaplan and Sorkin 1997, p. 82). Intrigued, Chaplan and Sorkin undertook an informal survey in which they sent a list of 10 of the Subcommittee's pain terms to 30 acquaintances in the APS, and to 135 randomly chosen APS members in 15 different specialties. Although the response rates they provide indicate a sample of only

28 to 42 respondents, 'the responses were frequently quite opinionated and somewhat surprising in that many did not define pain terms according to the IASP definitions' (Chaplan and Sorkin 1997, p. 82). Responses included blanks after some terms, complaints about the imprecise nature of the terminology, 'phrases indicating a lack of knowledge, and the statement 'I never use this term', as well as outright hostility toward some terms ('I HATE this word!' wrote one clinician/researcher)' (Chaplan and Sorkin 1997, p. 82). The authors conclude that 'Some clinical specialists in the field of pain management do not understand and do not like the approved terms, resulting in incorrect use of the words or avoidance of their use' and that 'many pain specialists are not in step with the officially mandated usage' (Chaplan and Sorkin 1997, p. 83).

Chaplan and Sorkin argue that the limited acceptance of the Subcommittee's terms is due in part to their lack of clinical usefulness, as they do not assist in the interpretation, diagnosis, or treatment of pains (they merely describe). Because the use of the terms is largely limited to pain specialists, Chaplan and Sorkin assert, they are not helpful in communicating with primary care physicians, the colleagues with whom pain specialists must communicate most often (Chaplan and Sorkin 1997, p. 83). Nor are they helpful in communicating with patients, they argue, as '[f]olk usage of the same terminology employed by the IASP is widespread, but the meanings may be entirely different' (Chaplan and Sorkin 1997, p. 83). Thus, while it may be possible to legislate the use of terms within pain medicine, extending this legislation to medicine as a whole or to the general public is a much more daunting task. But according to Chaplan and Sorkin (1997, p. 85), even articles published in *Pain*, the IASP's journal, do not apply the terms in the ways delineated by the Subcommittee. They ask some very pointed questions about the necessity of the IASP *Classification*, directly challenging the authority of the Subcommittee's work:

Part II of the 1986 Classification of Chronic Pain designated the 20 or so defined terms as the 'minimal standard vocabulary' for those who study and treat pain. Do we have to use the IASP terms to be understood and accepted? ... If the pain specialist, regardless of her or his area of specialization, is neither a researcher nor an academic, is it necessary that she or he use the IASP vetted terminology? Certainly, at present, many do not do so. Does use of specific pain terms in any way improve treatment or diagnosis? The answer would seem to be no. Could we not opt to forget about the semantic police and just enjoy good, well-described clinical and scientific observation? (Chaplan and Sorkin 1997, p. 85)

And yet, even Chaplan and Sorkin temper their criticism and, in the end, back the goal, if not the product, of Bonica, Merskey, and the Subcommittee on Taxonomy: 'Could we not opt to forget about the semantic police and just enjoy good, well-described clinical and scientific observation? We could, but this requires each observer to virtually reinvent the language, resulting in a Tower of Babel and a loss of cumulative learning experience in the field. We need a common language' (Chaplan and Sorkin 1997, p. 85). Chaplan and Sorkin go so far as to advocate the policing of correct usage and increased screening by journal editors and manuscript reviewers to improve correspondence with the officially mandated IASP terminology (Chaplan and Sorkin 1997, p. 86). Note their use of the phrase 'Tower of Babel', first used by Bonica in an editorial to describe the sorry state of linguistic chaos in the pain field, and to advocate the development of a classification back in 1979; his argument is cited approvingly in virtually every discussion of the taxonomy that I have read, and never contested.

Thus, despite the sometimes strenuous objections to the substance and taxonomic logic of the IASP Chronic Pain *Classification*, the victory of Bonica and Merskey is that few appear to challenge the *necessity* of a classification now. While the proper ordering principles of classification and representations of specific pains remain contested, all seem to agree that ordering principles and standardized representations of specific pains are indeed desirable goals. In seemingly achieving a consensus around the *need*

for a shared language, if not a consensus around the actual language to be used, the IASP *Classification* goes some way toward sharpening the boundaries of a shadowy object of study in a scientific community. In doing so, it helps to build and define the boundaries of the scientific community itself. In the end, the standardization of pain is more about making people the same, than making pains the same.

CONCLUSION

This chapter presents a case study of the processes involved in the development of one classification scheme in a specific field of medicine. What general lessons might social scientists take from this very particular case?

The case nicely illustrates and confirms Goodman's observation that classification is about 'world-making' – that rather than reflecting one reality transparently, classifications order reality for us. The making of this reality requires a long chain of material operations, papers, meetings, data manipulations, arguments, mediations, editing, financial and human resources. Classifications and categorizations, then, are not read off the nature (be it medical or social) they are meant to describe in any straightforward way; they are very human creations, and reflect the interests, goals, and perspectives of their creators.

We could also say that classifications are about world-*changing*, because new classifications must take account and potentially challenge or replace existing classifications that may order realities in very different ways. I use the plural 'realities' advisedly because there are multiple realities that the IASP classification had to try to take into account – the potentially conflicting realities defined by different medical specialties, and by clinicians versus researchers, as we've seen. It also has to try to mediate the potential conflicts between medical experts' and patients' realities. The IASP *Classification* organizes pain according to five axes, several of which, the reader will note, incorporate and in some ways privilege patient accounts of their experience. The first axis, which organizes the entire classification, is area of the body in which the patient reports experiencing pain; the third describes the patients' temporal experience of pain; the fourth describes patients' statement of pain intensity. But the second axis, system of the body that produces the pain, and the fifth, etiology, are entirely defined by physicians. Moreover, although pain is an entirely private and subjective experience, something roundly acknowledged within pain medicine, only the experts who treat and study pain patients were consulted in the development of the classification. The pain patients themselves, those experiencing this intrinsically subjective phenomenon, were not consulted (at least not officially or directly) in the development of the classification meant to organize that phenomenon.

We may choose to assume that including aspects of lay reports in our descriptions and classifications of laypeople's qualities or experiences means that we are describing them adequately. But that means we have to assume those of us designing the classification and applying it have chosen the right axes along which to classify, have privileged the most meaningful aspects of the layperson or their experience. However, aspects that define an identity or an experience and make it meaningful for our subjects may go entirely unrecognized by those of us doing the classifying. For example, an axis frequently used by those with chronic pain to measure describe their pain to others is functionality – what they are able to *do* during the pain (see, e.g. Whelan 2003) – and this is not reflected in the axes of the IASP *Classification*. When pain experts use the IASP *Classification*, they make a world that is not the same as the world of the people they are classifying, just as when social scientists use etic categories, the world they make is not the world of those they study.

All of this is fine, however, from the point of view of the pain experts doing the classifying. Those in the pain medicine community, or at least in the IASP's Subcommittee on Taxonomy, are quite epistemologically modest and reflexive. Their goal is not to capture patients' reality, but to impose an order that

they know fully well is artificial on a problem they acknowledge they do not yet really understand, in the hopes of creating order at some future point through coordination of activity toward common goals. Are we social scientists always so acutely aware of the artificiality of the categories we use, and the limits of their fit with the worlds, people, and experiences they attempt to represent?

Finally, an important lesson offered by this case is that standardizations do not always end up enforcing the standards they are meant to enforce. Even though the overall goals set out by Bonica and Merskey appear to have been agreed upon across pain medicine, the standardizations set forth by Merskey's committee continue to be debated, selectively taken up, challenged, revised, and ignored. As some science-studies scholars have noted, not everyone gets enrolled in the networks scientists attempt to build; some are partially enrolled, and others refuse to be enrolled altogether (see, e.g. Star 1991). As this case shows, it is not just laypeople who may resist scientific standardizations, but other scientists as well. In part, this is because standardizations are only so standardized after all. While the ideal classification is complete and exhaustive, its classificatory principles are consistently applied, and it provides mutually exclusive, clearly demarcated bins for every object to be classified, classifications in the real world do not fulfil these criteria (Bowker and Star 1999, pp. 10–11). Instead, 'people disagree about their nature; they ignore or misunderstand them; or they routinely mix together different and contradictory principles …. [and] mutual exclusivity may be impossible in practice, as when there is disagreement or ambivalence about the membership of an object in a category' (Bowker and Star 1999, pp. 11–12). Thus, when analyzing a classification, it is important to ask 'What happens to the cases that do not fit?' (Bowker and Star 1999, p. 9). There are always some that don't fit – both cases to be classified, and cases of classifiers.

Thus, while the critical study of documentary systems has tended to emphasize their (often oppressive) structuring of social life, the close study of classification and its consequences suggests that we need to pay equal attention to the agential side of the social equation. That is, we need to look at how the development of a classification is accomplished or thwarted by active subjects, and also at how classifications and other standardizations work, or don't, in the field – at the extent to which they are resisted, changed, or ignored, at how much they actually standardize social behaviour. As the spoiled ballot, the skipped survey question, and the medical classifications that 'end up in deep drawers or dusty attics' (Noordenbos, letter to the members of the Subcommittee on Taxonomy, March 1980) all attest, forms are not always forceful, and neither pains nor people can always be made the same.

NOTES

1. The IASP archives are housed in the John C. Liebeskind History of Pain Collection, History and Special Collections Division, Louise M. Darling Biomedical Library, UCLA. All documents cited in the text and not in the bibliography come from these archives (Ms. Coll. No. 124, Box 14). My thanks to Archivist Russell Johnson and Co-Director Marcia Meldrum for their assistance, to Dr Harold Merskey for copies of some of his many works on pain terminology and classification, and to the Faculty of Arts and Social Sciences at Dalhousie University for financial support of this research.

2. All the letters cited in the text are housed in the IASP archives (see note 1 for details about the Archives themselves). The letters, to my knowledge, are not published.

REFERENCES

Baszanger, I. 1995 *Inventing Pain Medicine: From the Laboratory to the Clinic.* New Brunswick, NJ: Rutgers University Press.

Ben-Ari, E. 1994 'Caretaking with a Pen? Documentation, Classification and "Normal" Development in a Japanese Day Care Center' *International Review of Modern Sociology* 24(2): 31–48.

Bonica, J.J. 1953 *The Management of Pain.* Philadelphia: Lea & Febinger.

Bonica, J.J. 1979 'The need of a taxonomy' *Pain* 6: 247–252.

Bowker, G.C. and Star, S.L. 1999 *Sorting Things Out: Classification and Its Consequences.* Cambridge, MA: MIT Press.

Carlson, E.A. 2001 *The Unfit: A History of a Bad Idea.* Woodbury, NY: Cold Spring Harbor Laboratory Press.

Chaplan, S.R. and. Sorkin, L.S. 1997 'Agonizing over pain terminology' *Pain Forum* 6(2): 81–87.

Clarke, A.E. and Casper, M.J. 1996 'From simple technology to complex arena: classification of Pap smears, 1917–90' *Medical Anthropology Quarterly* 10(4): 601–623.

Cronje, R.J. and Williamson, O.D. 2006 'Is pain ever "normal"?' *Clinical Journal of Pain* 22(8): 692–699.

Curtis, B. 1998 'From the moral thermometer to money: metrological reform in pre-confederation Canada' *Social Studies of Science* 28(4): 547–570.

de Jong, R.H. 1980 'Defining pain terms' *The Journal of the American Medical Association* 244(2): 143.

Douglas, M. and Hull, D. 1992 'Introduction' in M. Douglas and D. Hull (Eds) *How Classification Works: Nelson Goodman among the Social Sciences.* Edinburgh: Edinburgh University Press, pp. 1–12.

Downey, G.L. 1992 'Agency and structure in negotiating knowledge' in M. Douglas and D. Hull (Eds) *How Classification Works: Nelson Goodman among the Social Sciences.* Edinburgh: Edinburgh University Press, pp. 69–98.

Greenberg, D.F. 1997 'Transformations of homosexuality-based classifications' in R.N. Lancaster and M. di Leonardo (Eds) *The Gender/Sexuality Reader: Culture, History, Political Economy.* New York: Routledge, pp. 179–193.

Jackson, J.E. 1992 'After a while no one believes you: real and unreal pain' in M-J. Delvecchio Good, P.E. Brodwin, B.J. Good, and A. Kleinman (Eds) *Pain as Human Experience: An Anthropological Perspective.* Berkeley, CA: University of California Press, pp. 138–168.

Jackson, J.E. 2000 *Camp Pain: Talking with Chronic Pain Patients.* Philadelphia: University of Pennsylvania Press.

Kleinman, A. 1988 *The Illness Narratives: Suffering, Healing, and the Human Condition.* New York: Basic Books.

Liebeskind, J.C. 1994 *Oral history interview with Harold Merskey.* John C. Liebeskind History of Pain Collection, Ms. Coll. no. 127.26, History and Special Collections Division, Louise M. Darling Biomedical Library, UCLA, Los Angeles.

Lynch, M. 1990 'The externalized retina: selection and mathematization in the visual documentation of objects in the life sciences' in M. Lynch and

S. Woolgar (Eds) *Representation in Scientific Practice.* Cambridge, MA: MIT Press, pp. 153–186.

Lynch, M. 1991 'Method: measurement – ordinary and scientific measurement as ethnomethodological phenomena' in G. Button (Ed.) *Ethnomethodology and the Human Sciences.* Cambridge: Cambridge University Press, pp. 77–108.

Merskey, H. 1983 'Development of a universal language of pain syndromes' in J.J. Bonica, U. Lindblom and A. Iggo (Eds.) *Advances in Pain Research and Therapy* (Volume 5). New York: Raven Press, pp. 37–52.

Merskey, H. 1994 'Logic, truth and language in concepts of pain' *Quality of Life Research* 3(Supplement 1): S69–S76.

Merskey, H. 1999 'Comments on Woolf et al.' *Pain* 77 (1998): 227–229, *Pain* 82: 319–320.

Merskey, H. and Bogduk N. (Eds) 1994 *Classification of Chronic Pain: Descriptions of Chronic Pain Syndromes and Definitions of Pain Terms* (2nd edition). Seattle: IASP Press.

Merskey, H., Albe-Fessard, D.G., Bonica, J.J, Carmon, A., Dubner, R., Kerr, F.W.L, Lindblom, U., Mumford, J.M., Nathan, P.W., Noordenbos, W., Pagni, C.A., Renaer, M.J., Sternbach, R.A. and Sunderland, S. 1979 'Pain terms: a list with definitions and notes on usage. Recommended by the IASP Subcommittee on Taxonomy' *Pain* 6: 249–252.

Nicholson, B. 2000 'Taxonomy of pain' *The Clinical Journal of Pain* 16 Supplement 3): S114–S117.

Procacci, P. and Maresca, M. 1991 'Considerations on the taxonomy of pain' *Pain* 45:332–333.

Scarry, E. 1985 *The Body in Pain: The Making and Unmaking of the World.* New York: Oxford University Press.

Singleton, V. 1996 'Feminism, sociology of scientific knowledge and postmodernism: politics, theory and me' *Social Studies of Science* 26(2): 445–468.

Star, S.L. 1991 'Power, technology and the phenomenology of conventions: on being allergic to onions' in J. Law (Ed.) *A Sociology of Monsters: Essays on Power, Technology and Domination.* London: Routledge, pp. 26–56.

Stemerding, D. 1993 'How to make oneself nature's spokesman? A Latourian account of classification in eighteenth- and early nineteenth-century natural history' *Biology and Philosophy* 8: 193–223.

Subcommittee on Taxonomy, International Association for the Study of Pain (IASP) 1986 'Classification of chronic pain: descriptions of chronic pain syndromes and definitions' *Pain* (supplement 3).

Turk, D.C. and Rudy, T.E. 1987 'IASP taxonomy of chronic pain syndromes: preliminary assessment of reliability' *Pain* 30: 177–189.

Turk, D.C. and Rudy, T.E. 1990 'The robustness of an empirically derived taxonomy of chronic pain patients' *Pain* 43: 27–35.

Ward, S. 1996 'Filling the world with self-esteem: a social history of truth-making' *Canadian Journal of Sociology* 21(1): 1–23.

Whelan, E. 2003 'Putting pain to paper: endometriosis and the documentation of suffering' *Health* 7(4): 463–482.

Woda, A., Tubert-Jeannin, S., Bouhassira, D., Attal, N., Fleiter, B., Goulet, J-P., Gremeau-Richard, C., Navez, M.L., Picard, P., Pionchon, P. and Albuisson, E. 2005 'Towards a new taxonomy of idiopathic orofacial pain' *Pain* 116: 396–406.

Woolf, C. 1999 'Reply to Merskey et al.' *Pain* 82: 320.

Woolf, C.J., Bennett, G.J., Doherty, M., Dubner, R., Kidd, B., Koltzenburg, M., Lipton, R., Loeser, J.D., Payne, R. and Torebjork, E. 1998 'Towards a mechanism-based classification of pain?' *Pain* 77: 227–229.

Quantitative Approaches to Case-Based Method

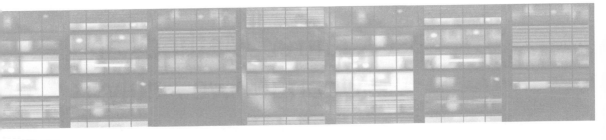

10

Case-Centred Methods and Quantitative Analysis

Ray Kent

INTRODUCTION

Case-centred methods are by no means limited to small-N research, but can also offer an alternative for large datasets in situations where the limitations and assumptions of mainstream frequentist quantitative methods restrict the conclusions that can be drawn from the analysis of quantitative data.

This chapter begins with a discussion of the assumptions made by and limitations of frequentist quantitative analysis in the social sciences. In particular, such methods are variable centred and tend to assume that the main patterns being sought between variables are ones of symmetrical covariation, that is, 'on the diagonal'. In practice, many patterns are triangular; frequentist methods cannot easily handle such patterns and, furthermore, are not particularly amenable to the analysis of asymmetrical relationships where causal sufficiency and causal necessity may be involved.

The chapter then turns to some of the alternatives to frequentist statistical methods. These include Bayesian methods,

configurational analysis, fuzzy-set analysis, neural network analysis and the theory of the tipping-point. Qualitative comparative analysis (QCA) and fuzzy-set qualitative comparative analysis (fsQCA), which are explained by Ragin in Chapter 31, can thus be seen as two of several options for the analysis of large-N data. The data that are entered into the software developed by Ragin and his associates (fsQCA) are in fact quantitative in the sense that they consist of variables that are either binary or they combine metric and non-metric measures together into fuzzy sets. Qualitative data, in the sense used by most qualitative researchers, by contrast, consist of words, phrases, narrative, text or images that would normally be analyzed textually, perhaps using different software such as that explained in Chapter 15.

THE FREQUENTIST TRADITION

What have become known as 'traditional', 'mainstream', 'classical' or 'frequentist' statistical approaches to the analysis of social science data were developed during the nineteenth century for use in astronomy, medicine, biology and to study the laws of heredity. Regression analysis, for example, was originally developed by Legendre and Gauss in the early years of the nineteenth century to fit data on the orbits of astronomical objects. According to Freedman (1999), the 'numerical method' in medicine goes back to Pierr's study of pneumonia in 1835, and John Snow's book on the epidemiology of cholera published in 1855. In the late nineteenth century, Francis Galton pioneered the use of frequency curves, particularly the 'normal' curve, while Karl Pearson refined the techniques of correlation to invent the correlation coefficient 'r' or 'Pearson's r' as it became known. Pearson also invented chi-square, one the most widely used statistics amongst social scientists today, and he pioneered the calculation of probable errors of statistics as well as the publication of statistical tables. George Udny Yule took Pearson's theory of correlation and laid the foundations of partial correlation and of linear regression for any number of variables. His interest in the practical application of statistics to social problems led him to consider the relationship between sets of categorical data, and he developed the analysis of contingency tables, inventing his famous statistic 'Q', still known as 'Yule's Q', for measuring association between attributes, which he published in 1900.

Galton was initially a mathematician who became an explorer and meteorologist. He was also cousin of Charles Darwin whose *On the Origin of Species,* published in 1859, had had a profound influence on him. His ambition became to apply statistics to the laws of heredity and, in 1875 he was conducting experiments with sweet-pea seeds to develop the laws of the inheritance of size. The idea of a regression line to measure correlation between sizes of seeds of mother and daughter sweet-pea plants emerged from this work. At the same time, he developed the use of frequency curves and had by 1889 even managed to invent a unit-free measure of association by using his ideas about the 'normal' curve and its properties. Galton became interested in the connection between heredity and human ability and he noted that able fathers tended to produce able children. He introduced the term 'eugenics' in 1883 in his book *Inquiries into Human Faculty* to describe the science that would utilize the principles of heredity to attempt to improve the ability of the human stock. In 1904 he founded a research fellowship in national eugenics at the University of London from which developed the Galton Laboratory of National Eugenics. At the same time Pearson was developing the parallel science of 'biometrics' – the application of statistical techniques to genetics. Like Galton, Pearson had studied mathematics at Cambridge and, in 1884, he became Professor of Mathematics and Mechanics at the University of London. By 1895, Pearson had established his Biometrics Laboratory, which in 1906 amalgamated with the Galton Laboratory to become the Eugenics Laboratory with Pearson himself as director.

Yule had been a student of Pearson', and when, in 1893, Yule returned from a period of study in Germany, where he had been working in the field of experimental physics, Pearson offered him a demonstratorship. While he was developing his ideas about correlation, Yule also became interested in the application of statistical techniques to social problems. He had come across Charles Booth's empirical studies of London poverty and in particular his book *The Aged Poor in England and Wales* (1894).

In 1895, Yule published an article in the *Economic Journal* entitled 'On the correlation of total pauperism with the proportion of out-relief'. At the time, paupers were supported either inside 'poor houses', or outside, depending on the policy of local authorities. Each local authority oversaw a number of small geographical areas called 'unions', rather like a parish. In the article, Yule drew attention to a statement made by Booth in his book to the effect that, 'The proportion of relief given out of doors bears no relation to the total percentage of pauperism'. This was one among many other conclusions 'to be drawn from the study and comparison of the official statistics' relating to all the poor law 'unions' in England and Wales. Yule, however, drew a scatterplot or 'correlation surface' as he called it for the years 1871 and 1891 showing the numbers of unions (of which there were about 600 at the time) combining a given percentage of population in receipt of relief (the rate of pauperism) with the number of out-paupers to one in-pauper (giving the ratio of out-relief to in-relief). Yule's correlation surface clearly showed a marked degree of correlation, but one that was distinctly skewed. Although he realized that, as a result, it was not strictly legitimate to compute Pearson's coefficient of correlation, Yule had no alternative statistics at his disposal. Although, apparently, no great weight could be attached to the value of the coefficient, 'its magnitude may at least be suggestive'. For 1871, Pearson's r turned out to be .26 and for 1891, it was .39. Yule concluded that the rate of total pauperism in the unions of England was positively correlated with the proportion of out-relief given, and that this correlation was distinctly greater in 1891 than it had been in 1871.

Yule's results could clearly be used by those who argued that giving more out-relief *caused* a higher level of pauperism; that to reduce the level of pauperism one needed to reduce the proportion of relief given outside the poor houses. In a later paper published in 1899 entitled 'An investigation into the causes of changes in pauperism in England, chiefly during the last two intercensal decades', Yule attempted to analyze what *were* the causes of changes in pauperism. However, far from concluding that the correlation between pauperism and level of out-relief could not legitimately be interpreted as one of direct causality, he found, using techniques of multiple regression and correlation, that five-eighths of the decrease in pauperism was 'accounted for' simultaneously by changes in out-relief ratio, the proportion of people over 65 and changes in population density. The latter two accounted for relatively small proportions of the changes in pauperism and were themselves being held

constant in the equation when the relationship between pauperism and out-relief was being investigated.

Yule concluded: '… in as much as changes in out-relief ratio helps to estimate changes in pauperism, change in pauperism would help to estimate change in out-relief ratio – it is difficult to imagine any causal relation between the two such that pauperism should influence out-relief ratio'. It did not, apparently, even cross Yule's mind that out-relief *should* respond to the level of pauperism! Yule appeared to be more interested in the elegance of his statistical methods than in the humanitarian consequences of his conclusions.

Yule's correlational techniques would clearly have been very useful in his attempts to establish the causes of poverty, yet there is no evidence that Booth even acknowledged Yule's articles of 1895 and 1899. It was unlikely that Yule, 'a courteous, even courtly man', did not at least inform Booth that he had used the latter's data in his 1895 paper, and the later paper appeared in the *Journal of the Royal Statistical Society,* a copy of which Booth would certainly have received as a member of the Society. Even more curious was that Booth's followers made no reference to the developments in statistical methods. Rowntree never made use of correlation in his highly statistical analysis of the causes of poverty even though he had consulted Pearson on several occasions. Bowley, who was a Professor of Statistics at the London School of Economics, wrote a book published in 1910 called *An Elementary Manual of Statistics*, but it contained no reference to Yule, Galton or Pearson. In fact the word 'correlation' did not appear in the index and the topic was not covered anywhere in the book (Kent 1981).

The origins of frequentist statistics thus at least in part reflect features of the culture and ideology of British society in this period, with its focus on heredity, racial improvement, class and intelligence. This is not to argue, suggests MacKenzie (1979), that their contemporary use continues to reflect the conditions of their origin, but rather that statistical techniques are not neutral, having been developed by individuals with clear social and political goals and, furthermore, that their development was never intended for the contemporary uses to which they are currently often put. They were designed for the analysis of large, homogeneous populations of cases that could be defined in advance and subjected to repeated tests and had only a small number of characteristics of interest. As soon as they are applied to social science data and in particular to the search for causal relationships, then, as Yule and Pearson found many years ago, problems in their application arise. The fundamentally altered context of their application has seldom been seriously analyzed.

THE LIMITATIONS OF FREQUENTIST STATISTICS

Frequentist statistics focus on frequency distributions of recorded values for a given set of cases and are based extensively on the use of regression analysis and related techniques including, for example, multiple regression, logistic regression, factor analysis and structural equation modelling. Regression-based techniques are by far the most frequently used in the social, behavioural, educational and health sciences (de Leeuw 2004). However, they make a number of assumptions that in practice may well not be justified. First, they assume that all variables are metric and that they are, furthermore, normally distributed. In practice, many variables used in the social sciences are derived from 7-point, 5-point or even 3-point rating scales and are *assumed* to be the equivalent of a metric scale with equal 'distances' between the points. Categorical variables may be introduced among the independent variables either in binary form or as dummy variables, but these, according to Schrodt (2006), quickly 'nibble the analysis to death'. Many variables like income that are genuinely metric may have distributions with very long tails (or there may well be outliers) that render the mean and variance as distribution descriptors potentially misleading.

Regression-based techniques, secondly, assume linearity – that data are best summarized with a straight line when in practice a non-linear function might be better. Third, it is being assumed that the independent variables are not themselves highly inter-correlated. In practice, there are often high levels of multicollinearity, which makes it difficult to evaluate the relative contribution of the independent variables. If these assumptions are unjustified or unexamined then, in the words of Berk (2004, p.38), the researcher has 'started down the slippery slope toward statistical ritual'. Coefficients that are relevant may turn out to be individually statistically insignificant, while the effects of outliers or anomalous sub-populations may be amplified. Linear regression results are, consequently, notoriously unstable: even the most minor changes in model specifications can result in estimates 'that bounce around like a box full of gerbils on methamphetamines' (Schrodt 2006).

Also included amongst frequentist techniques are other parametric techniques like analysis of variance plus a range of non-parametric procedures that are based on the use of chi-square, for example, phi and Cramer's V as measures of association, and loglinear analysis.

The key characteristics (many of which turn out to be limitations) that all frequentist approaches share include the following:

- they focus on the value distributions of variables rather than on cases as combinations of values;
- they focus on patterns of relationships between value distributions that are covariational, linear and, for the most part, additive;
- they are, contrary to common assumptions, not good at detecting, elaborating or demonstrating asymmetrical or causal relationships;
- they are limited in their ability to handle causal complexity in complex systems.

The focus on value distributions

Survey knowledge is typically produced by entering responses to questions, which may appear simply as ticks in boxes, as a row of values that profile a single respondent and then interpreting these entries in columns across respondents to produce *distributions* of values. These distributions, however, are no longer characteristics of individuals, objects or other kinds of case, but of a researcher-defined, closed set of cases. Characteristics of that distribution relate to the set, not to an individual case. A person does not have an 'average' age, but rather the average is a characteristic of the population from which the average was calculated; no single family has an 'average' of 2.4 children. Thus, although variables are treated as individual attributes during the data collection phase of survey research, analyses subsequently produced by the researcher loose both the identity of the individuals and the context in which the data were recorded. Furthermore, researchers are apt to assume not only that variables mirror aspects of the 'real' world, but that they can also act as concrete forces or agents with determining power. However, as Elliott (1999, pp. 101–102) points out, 'Although variables rather than individuals may become the subject of the statistician's narrative, it is individuals rather than variables who have the capacity to act and reflect on society'.

Variables are researcher constructions that emerge from whatever measurement process the researcher deems to be appropriate. Measurement might be direct (taking observations at face value), indirect (taking indicators) or derived by concocting a measure from some calculation on a number of scaled items; for example, Likert scales are based on the summation of a large number of items. Variables are thus whatever the researcher has defined them to be. Olsen and Morgan (2004) call them 'ficts' – statistical artefacts that are not necessarily concretely true and are potentially fictional. They have an existence more like a virtual reality. At best, variables are what Byrne (2002) calls 'variate traces' of some complex system or entity; they are not the entities or systems themselves. Any mathematical calculations performed on variables are purely abstract – treating them as 'real' amounts to reification. There may

well, furthermore, be errors arising from the measurement process, from survey design and execution or from any inadequacies arising from the sampling process (see Kent 2007).

The focus on covariation

Covariation implies that relationships between variables are seen to be symmetrical. In the case of binary variables, this means that any tendency for the presence of a characteristic on one variable to be combined with the presence of a characteristic on the other variable is also mirrored in their absence – cases are expected to 'lie on the main diagonal', as in Table 10.1. This gives a phi coefficient of 0.96. The implication of symmetry is that even the simple 'If X then Y' relationship cannot be tested *unless it also implies 'if not X then not Y'*. Table 10.2, however, shows a triangular pattern, such that if a case is a member of set X (a heavy television viewer), then he or she is also likely to be a member of set Y (has a large spend on convenience food); *but not being a member of set X implies nothing about membership of Y* (those whose television viewing is not heavy may or may not have a large spend on convenience food), resulting in a much lower value of phi (0.44), which is really only an index of diagonality, taking no account of set-membership relationships.

Table 10.1   A symmetrical pattern

Variable Y	Variable X		
	Set member	Non-member	Total
Set member	49	1	50
Non-member	1	49	50
Total	50	50	100

Table 10.2   A triangular pattern

Spend	Television viewing		
	Heavy	Not heavy	Total
Large	54	25	79
Not large	0	25	25
Total	54	50	104

In the case of metric variables, symmetry implies that if high values on one variable are associated with high values on the other, then low values are similarly associated. The simple statement 'If X is high then Y is high' cannot be tested *unless it also implies that 'low values on X are associated with low values on Y'*. Metric relationships are usually tested not only for symmetry, but also for linearity – that in fact the data-points on the scattergram will line up near the regression line. For every unit increase in one or more variables that are accorded the status of independent variable, there is a predictable increase (or decrease) in one or more variables accorded the status of dependent variable. This increase may be fixed over the range by which the independent variables vary, giving a straight line, or the increase may diminish or grow, giving a curved line.

Most multivariate techniques work on the basis of assessing the degree of linear covariation. Hair et al. (1998, p. 75) comment: 'An implicit assumption of all multivariate techniques based on correlational measures of association, including multiple regression, logistic regression, factor analysis, and structural equation modelling, is *linearity*. Because correlations represent only linear association between variables, non-linear effects will not be represented in the correlation value'. To most statisticians, 'non-linear' means any pattern other than a straight line, which may be curvilinear or one exhibiting heteroscedacity – unequal levels of variance across a range of predictor variables. The most direct remedy to both, according to Hair et al., is data transformation. 'If a non-linear relationship is detected, the most direct approach is to transform one or both variables to achieve linearity'; 'Heteroscedastic variables can be remedied through data transformations to those used to achieve normality'. In short, if the pattern is not a straight line, the solution is to transform the data to *make* it resemble a straight line.

In practice, patterns are commonly triangular (Ragin 2000), such that while high values of X are associated with high values of Y, low values of X may be found with a whole range of values for Y, as in Figure 10.1.

If variables are abstractions from real cases, then any bivariate or multivariate patterns that are discovered between variables

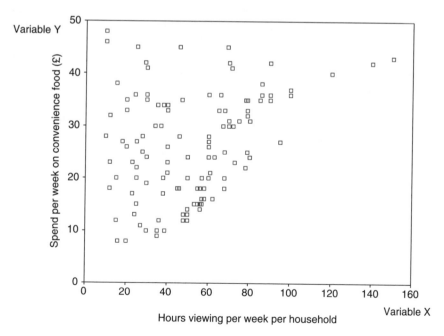

Figure 10.1   A triangular data pattern.

amount to a further abstraction – reification squared, according to Byrne (2002, p. 117). A correlation is a statistical artefact; a researcher construction that is twice removed from real cases. If patterns in the distributions of variables emerge, then this *may* throw some light on the way complex systems operate or are structured. The problem is that only one particular form of pattern is being sought; if none is discovered, then researchers are apt to conclude that there is 'no relationship' rather than seeing the result as a prompt to search for other kinds of pattern.

Causality and covariation

The objective of frequentist statistics is to 'account for' patterns of differences between variables. Different research objectives, however, give different meanings to the idea of 'accounting'. The research goal may be to predict differences, scores or categories in one or more dependent variables from one or more independent variables; it may be to 'explain' in a statistical sense the extent to which dependent and independent variables covary in some systematic fashion; it may be to reduce a set of differences or associations between a large set of variables to a smaller set; or it may be to generate evidence of causal influences. It is in respect of the last objective that frequentist statistics are, unfortunately, largely deficient.

It is common, even in books on multivariate analysis such as by Hair et al. (1998), to define the dependent variable as the 'presumed effect' and the independent variable as the 'presumed cause'. By contrast, Tabachnick and Fidell (2001) see independent variables as either the different conditions to which cases are exposed (shown an advertisement or not shown it), or characteristics that the cases themselves bring into the research situation (marital status or attitudes towards a retail outlet). Dependent variables are only 'outcome' variables in the sense that they are the ones in which the researcher is mainly interested. The distinction, the authors emphasize, is for the convenience of the researcher and to identify variables that

belong on one side of the equation or the other, *without causal implication*.

The paradigm for the provision of explanation of social phenomena is usually taken by both qualitative and quantitative researchers to be the process of causal analysis. Unfortunately, what this 'process' entails is variously interpreted; indeed, what we mean when we say that 'X causes Y' is open to an enormous range of possibilities. Historically, there has been fierce debate about what causality is and how it is established. There has even been controversy about what the key issues in the debate are about. The classical analyses are those of Aristotle and Hume. Aristotle recognized that people meant a variety of things by 'cause'. Causes could be material, formal, final or efficient. To Hume a cause is 'an object, followed by another, and where all the objects similar to the first are followed by objects similar to the second'. Causality is a matter of invariable sequence or constant conjunction. Since Hume, the literature on the philosophy of causality has been vast, controversial and inconclusive (Abbott 1998).

The modern philosophy of causality – and here it gets tied up with an equally complex literature on the nature of explanation – was set forth by Hempel's (1942) 'covering law'. This was already hinted at by Hume: where event A is followed by event B this is explained by a covering law of the form that B always follows from A, that is, A causes B. This formulation, however, has been criticized as being either 'trivial' or it fails to explain the covering law. Real explanation, so its critics argue, has to make sense of what social actors do. The alternative view of causal processes is based on narrative. Historians, for example, try to get the historical figure's own justification for action to understand what was 'reasonable' in the circumstances. Narrative itself is explanatory. The 'follow-ability' or plausibility of the story culminates by showing or making it understandable that the outcome was inevitable. Here, events, conditions and motivations are all combined. The thinking about causes is configurational and complex rather than linear and additive. Some will argue that this is a different kind of explanation; it is not causal at all, but interpretive.

Over the following years, however, despite these debates, the position adopted by most social scientists has come to embody a particular stance within these debates; cause involves a degree of 'forcing' or determination and it is sequential – the cause must come before the effect. Causality is, furthermore, typically seen by quantitative researchers in particular as both linear and additive, which implies that each independent variable makes a fixed contribution to the dependent variable and that these contributions can be added up. This justifies the common practice of apportioning causality in chunks, for example, that the decision to drop a product from the range is 35% determined by product diversity, 20% by company turnover and 15% by product line management policy. Such conclusions may be derived from multiple regression techniques.

Causality is now seen by most quantitative researchers as a property of mathematical and statistical propositions rather than a property of real social action (Abbott 1998). It is a mathematical framework to assist our understanding; it is not reality itself. Unfortunately, this caveat is frequently forgotten and researchers have come to believe that social and market activities look the way they do because forces and properties 'do' things to other forces and properties. More recent thinking about the concept of causality has rediscovered Aristotle's original idea that there are several different types of causal link. By the time he came to write the third edition of his book in 1965, Zetterberg included a lengthy analysis of varieties of linkage between determinants and results, distinguishing between reversible and irreversible relations, deterministic and probabilistic relations, sequential and co-extensive relations, sufficient and contingent relations, and necessary and substitutable relations.

In frequentist variable-centred statistical methods it is the variables that do the acting. Causality is established when one variable is seen to 'do' something to another variable.

Cases in effect do very little; they have lost their identity, their complexity and their narrative order that describes each as a story (Abbott 1992). Within a set of cases, there may, indeed, be patterns of various kinds; but while individuals can act as agents, 'causing' things to happen, variables are sets of values with distributions that might covary with other distributions or show some other kind of pattern. They are not and cannot, strictly speaking, act as causal agents. Social status cannot 'do' anything to repeat purchase; both are distributions of records accessed or constructed by the researcher. Variable centred analysis is, then, incompatible with any demonstration of causality, unless 'causality' is *defined* in terms of a demonstration of covariation, temporal sequence and lack of spuriousness, in which case causality is a convenient shorthand for describing certain kinds of pattern.

Frequentist statistics are blind to the dependent or independent status that researchers choose for their variables. Establishing covariation does not by itself demonstrate any degree or direction of any influence of one variable upon another. To some extent, temporal sequence can be studied using longitudinal data and spurious relationships may be detected using multivariate analysis, but establishing causal necessity and causal sufficiency is, on the whole, difficult with frequentist methods. It is possible, as explained above, to detect triangular patterns for two cross-tabulated binary variables or to examine the patterns in a scattergram with two metric variables.

Where patterns are triangular, as in Table 10.2 and Figure 10.1, then it may be possible to see that an interpretation of causal necessity or sufficiency is possible. Thus in Figure 10.1, high scores on the independent variable 'hours viewing per week per household' ensures a high score on 'spend per week on convenience foods'. In other words, a high score is *sufficient* to bring this about. However, a high score on hours viewing is not a *necessary* condition since high scores on spend per week can come about when viewing is low. In short, viewing is a sufficient, but not necessary condition for high spend on convenience food. Frequentist statisticians will try to apply a regression line through the data-points and will come up with an r^2 of 0.09 and are likely to report that there is 'no association' between the two variables. Table 10.1, similarly, can form the basis of an interpretation of a sufficient but not necessary condition.

Standard frequentist statistical measures normally look only at necessity and sufficiency jointly, not separately, although Clark et al. (2006) argue that standard linear regression models that include interaction terms can be used to test asymmetric hypotheses, measuring degrees of necessity and degrees of sufficiency. However, even if it is possible to modify frequentist methods to handle asymmetric relationships, they still cannot, as was pointed out by Smithson (1988) nearly 20 years ago, handle the simple conjunctions 'and' and 'or' in multivariate hypotheses. There is no adequate translation in frequentist terms, for example, for hypotheses of the form 'Y will be high if and only if X_1 and (or) X_2 is high'.

Complexity

In an everyday dictionary sense, complex systems have many varied interrelated parts; they are complicated, intricate and difficult to understand. Most social systems are characterized by causal complexity in which relationships are non-linear, non-additive, contingent, conjunctural or interdependent. Complex systems themselves may, furthermore, have emergent properties and open boundaries.

Non-linearity can take several forms. It may mean that systems change through phase shifts, which are radical transformations of kind (for which the term 'quality' is commonly used) rather than incremental development. It may mean the possibility of parallel universes or at least the possibility of alternative ways of outcomes or conditions happening. It may refer to the predominance of conjunctural and recursive relationships rather than ones of linear cause and effect.

Byrne (2007) points out that complex systems are evolutionary and unidirectional, that is, there is an arrow of time and that systems follow a path or trajectory in multidimensional space. The quality of openness means that systems are not independent, but tend to be nested (that is, systems within systems) or interpenetrating.

Frequentist statistics cannot handle any of these features with any degree of satisfaction. They cannot conceive that an outcome may happen in several different ways or that the effects of an event or a condition will vary considerably depending on a range of other events or conditions. Some commentators (e.g. Sayer 2000) have questioned the validity of applying frequentist methods in the social sciences at all. Such total dismissal is no doubt unwarranted; frequentist methods are, after all, transparent and parsimonious. Even though they are designed for closed systems, they may nevertheless offer insights and findings that further our understanding of systems with open boundaries. Even in open, dynamic and complex systems, there will often be regularities that can be detected using frequentist methods.

ALTERNATIVES TO FREQUENTIST APPROACHES

Frequentist statistics can be effective when conditions for their use are appropriate, but in practice they are commonly used without recognition of their limitations and minus the 'health warnings' that should, ideally, accompany the reports of findings from their use. Some critics, like Schrodt (2006), have gone further to suggest that the 'linear frequentist orthodoxy' seeks to impose as the sole legitimate form of social science a set of 'rather idiosyncratic and at times downright counterintuitive methodologies that come together to solve problems quite distinct from those encountered by most political scientists'.

If frequentist statistics are so circumscribed in their legitimate use, what should researchers do? There are, in fact, many other ways in which the analysis of (quantitative) data can be approached, most of which, while often used in the social sciences, seldom form part of the training of social scientists. An overview of some of these alternatives is presented below. Each of these approaches has its own limitations and not one of them can or should be seen as a total replacement for frequentist approaches. Rather, they are alternatives that should be considered when frequentist approaches are not appropriate or when they do not seem to be adequate to the task of finding patterns in a dataset.

Bayesian statistics

The goal of any science is to make predictions. These can be of various kinds. A forecast, which is usually short-term, is a prediction of events in a system that is not amenable to manipulation or intervention like a weather forecast. A prediction might be of the outcome, or likely outcome, of a deliberate act or intervention like the effect on sales of a manufacturer's decision to raise prices. The prediction might be hypothetical, for example, of the 'if X happens then Y will result' variety. In the frequentist tradition, prediction is of two kinds. One is to construct a model based on observed patterns of relationships between variables and then to use the model to make a statistical prediction of by how much one or more variables assigned the status of dependent variable will change as a result of changes in one or more variables assigned the status of independent variable. The other kind of prediction involves statistical inference. Frequentist inferential techniques assume that a random sample of observations has been taken and use probability in a distributional sense, for example, using a theoretical sampling distribution to calculate the probability of obtaining a result in a random sample from a population in which the null hypothesis is true. The null hypothesis is given, and it is the data that are evaluated by asking, 'How probable are these data, assuming that the null hypothesis is true?' While researchers talk about testing a hypothesis, the mathematics actually evaluate the probability of the data.

Bayesian statisticians turn the frequentist approach on its head and ask, 'What is the probability of a hypothesis, given the data?' The answer, based on a theorem developed by Thomas Bayes in 1763, is that the probability of the hypothesis, given the data (the 'posterior' in Bayesian terms) is equal to the probability of the data given the hypothesis (this is often called the 'likelihood function') multiplied by the probability of the hypothesis (which Bayesian call a 'prior') divided by the probability of the data. Bayes's theorem is usually written as:

$$P(H|D) = p(D|H) * p(H)/p(D) \qquad (1)$$

The 'hypothesis' can be a set of measures or 'parameters' of interest and might include measures like an expected mean, variance or regression coefficient.

According to Retzer (2006), the basic steps involved in Bayesian analysis are:

(1) Establish prior beliefs about the parameters before collecting the data.
(2) Collect the data and represent them in terms of what is referred to as a likelihood function.
(3) Update the prior beliefs from information in the newly acquired data using Bayes's rule.

For Bayes, the prior probability most likely came from previous observation, but researchers since have adopted the view that any educated guess could swerve as a prior or subjective probability estimate. Bayes's theorem thus mathematically incorporates prior probabilities into the current data or evidence to reassess the probability that a hypothesis is true. It is a formalization of what managers tend to do intuitively anyway: factoring in prior knowledge, hunch, and subjective probabilities into the assessment of the evidence or data before them. Instead of accepting or rejecting hypotheses, as in the frequentist approach, in Bayesian statistics, the probability of a hypothesis being true will be adjusted by any new observations. This approach allows for a range of hypotheses to be developed and provides a mechanism for deciding between them.

Bayesian analysis has not been greatly used in the social sciences until relatively recently largely because the mathematics can be very complicated. For all but the simplest problems, it requires calculus, in particular integration over the entire probability distribution. Two innovations, however, have helped the development of Bayesian statistical methods. One is Markov Chain Monte Carlo (MCMC) simulation which has enabled the estimation of complex models that would be nearly impossible with alternative methods (Bakkan 2005). The second innovation lies in writing models in hierarchical form. These are usually referred to as hierarchical Bayes (HB) models. These models have two levels: an upper level that provides average utility estimates across all individuals and a lower level that provides estimates of utility for each and every individual.

There is now a range of software available for undertaking various forms of Bayesian analysis. For an overview see Darren Wilkinson's Bayesian software links at http://www.mas.ncl.ac.uk or just put 'Bayesian software' into Google. A number of technical papers are available for free at http://www.sawtoothsoftware.com.

Although the logic behind the Bayesian approach is, say Rossi et al. (2005), 'compelling', it has not, in fact, been widely adopted. One problem is that the approach is highly statistical. The text offered by Rossi et al., for example, assumes 'a familiarity with matrix notation and basic matrix operations, including the Cholesky root'. Few textbooks on social research even mention Bayesian statistics and there are probably few social research courses that cover the topic. Smith and Fletcher (2004, p. 146) suggest a simplified 'domesticated' Bayesian approach which integrates an inverted p-value $(1 - p)$ from a standard test of significance with a prior to give a posterior probability. The Bayesian approach can also be used more as a metaphor than as an algorithm. Researchers in the social sciences often move back and forth between theory and data in an iterative process. A theory of probability that treats this activity as a process

involving the revision of prior beliefs is more consistent with actual practice than one that relies on a single pass through the data. In the Bayesian spirit, researcher preconceptions become priors rather than sources of bias.

One of the limitations of Bayesian approaches is that they require the determination of probabilities from previous data or from expert judgements. Lilford and Braunholtz (2003), however, argue that the results of qualitative research can be taken into account when making policy decisions by converting the data into a quantitative prior about the likely outcomes of an intervention. Bayes's theorem can then be used to combine this prior with quantitative data to produce a posterior.

Configurational analysis

Frequentist (and Bayesian) methods are variable centred. They look at the distribution of variable values across cases. In a case-by-variable data matrix, they focus on the columns, summarizing them and relating them together. Cases are treated as identical except for the variation in selected variables. As is explained earlier in various chapters in this Handbook, an alternative is to see each case as a particular combination of characteristics – as a configuration. Only cases with identical configurations can be seen as the 'same' type of case. In a case-by-variable matrix, the researcher now focuses on the rows, showing, for example, how outcomes are associated with particular combinations of features. A truth table (see pp. 528 for an explanation) shows the number of cases that possess each logically possible combination of measured characteristics that might, potentially, be seen as 'causal' variables and the outcome of interest to the researcher. From this perspective, variables are no longer isolated, analytically distinct aspects of cases, but rather components of configurations that allow the researcher to maintain the uniqueness of cases as complex entities.

If all variables are binary, manifesting the absence or presence of a characteristics or an outcome, it is possible to examine the *logical* relationships between the outcome being present, and the presence or absence of various combinations of factors. In particular it is possible to ask:

- What factors are found in all instances where the outcome is present?
- Is the outcome always present when particular factors or combinations of factors arise?

The first establishes that in all cases where the outcome occurs, these factors (which may be demographics, behaviours, system properties or events) are present – they are necessary conditions. The second establishes that in all cases where the factors occur, the outcome is present – they are sufficient conditions. A single factor may be necessary, but not sufficient – having a higher degree may be a necessary condition for being a university lecturer, but not all those with higher degrees are university lecturers. Alternatively, a factor may be sufficient, but not necessary. In all cases where a student studies hard, the exam performance is good. However, some students do well for other reasons.

A single factor may be neither necessary nor sufficient, but social phenomena are seldom the outcome of a single factor, so the researcher may look for combinations of factors that *jointly* are sufficient. Generating a truth table with a limited number of binary variables can be undertaken using multiway cross-tabulation (or 'layering') in SPSS. However, adding more variables exponentially complicates this process and considerable computing power is required. Ragin (1987) has suggested a technique that he calls qualitative comparative analysis (QCA) for which, with Drass and Ragin 1992), he developed a computer program that uses crisp-set binary data to generate a truth table. The program allows for probabilistic statements in the analysis so that the researcher could say, for example, that having a higher degree is 'almost always' or 'usually' necessary to be a lecturer or that studying hard is 'almost always' or 'usually' sufficient to ensure good examination performance.

Fuzzy-set analysis

Combinatorial logic depends on having crisp binary sets. Most categorizations used in the social sciences, however, are not well-defined; they are imprecise, vague, uncertain, ambiguous – in short, fuzzy – and cases tend to exhibit degrees of membership of categories like 'democratic country', 'loyal customer' or 'innovative organization'. Fuzzy sets extend crisp sets by permitting membership scores in the interval between 1 and 0. This means either taking binary categories and overlaying them with carefully calibrated measures of the extent to which cases are 'in' or 'out' of a set (e.g. a 'satisfied' customer) or, for continuous metric scales, overlaying the scale with conceptually appropriate criteria of what 'full membership', 'partial membership', and 'non-membership' of a set entails (e.g. how many units of alcohol per week classify a person as a 'heavy' drinker). The result is that they are binary and metric at the same time. They combine categorical and metric assessments in a single instrument. They distinguish between cases that are 'more in' a set than others with a cross-over point (of 0.5) for those who are neither in nor out – the point of maximum ambiguity.

The use of fuzzy sets enables the researcher to draw conclusions about logical relationships, as with QCA, but without having to reduce all the data to crisp binary sets. The analysis, as argued by Ragin (2000), now becomes sharper. If membership scores for each case concerning the causal factor are plotted against membership scores for the outcome, the result of a necessary, but not sufficient, condition would look like Figure 10.2.

High membership on Y (the outcome) presupposes high membership on X_1, but high membership on X_1 does not ensure high membership on Y and might be accompanied by high or low Y. Membership of X_1 is a necessary, but not sufficient, condition for membership of Y. Ragin (2000) argues that

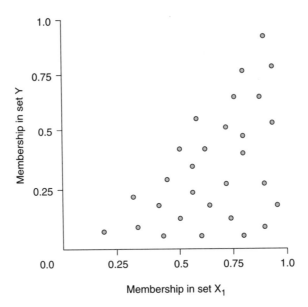

Figure 10.2   A fuzzy-set necessary but not sufficient condition.

we can be even more precise and say that the degree of membership of X_1 *sets a ceiling* on the degree of membership of Y. In this situation, membership of Y must always be *less than* or *equal to* membership on X_1 – scores, in short, are below the diagonal. The extent of membership of the category 'has a higher degree' (somebody might, e.g. have completed the degree but does not yet know the result of the dissertation component) sets a ceiling to the extent to which a person is a member of the category 'university lecturer' (he or she might be offered only casual employment or be put on probation).

The result of a sufficient but not necessary condition would look like Figure 10.3. High membership of the cause (X_1) ensures – *acts as a floor* for – high membership of the outcome (Y), but as it is not a necessary condition, then high membership of Y can come about in other ways, thus high membership of Y might be accompanied by a wide range of scores on X_1. In this situation, membership of Y must always be *greater than* or *equal to* membership on X_1. The degree of membership of the category 'studying hard' for an exam ensures a minimum membership of the category 'good exam performance', but high

grades may be achieved in other ways – being lucky in predicting the topics that come up, cheating or just being very bright.

Analysis of necessary and sufficient conditions using fuzzy categories can now be carried out using the principles of combinatorial logic. Each condition that might – for theoretical reasons – be necessary can be tested against the outcome. Each condition and each theoretically possible combination of all causal variables can now be tested for sufficiency. Combinatorial fuzzy scores are added using Boolean algebra. This means, for example, taking the *minimum* fuzzy score in each of the sets being combined. If a person is 0.8 in the category 'satisfied customer' and 0.6 in the category 'loyal customer', then he or she is 0.6 in the combined category 'satisfied and loyal customer'.

A number of software programs are available for performing fuzzy-set configurational analysis, the most advanced of which is that developed by Ragin called *fuzzy-set qualitative comparative analysis* (*fsQCA*). This can be downloaded for free at: http://www.u.arizona.edu/%7Ecragin/fsQCA/software.shtml along with a user guide and several articles that relate to how to

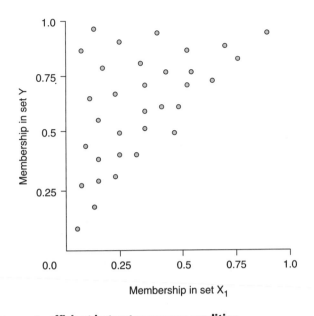

Figure 10.3 A fuzzy-set sufficient but not necessary condition.

interpret the output from the program. The program, which is explained by Ragin in Chapter 31 of this Handbook, covers both the crisp-set QCA and the fuzzy-set extension. The fuzzy-set extension can in fact handle a mixture of crisp and fuzzy variables.

A detailed example of a fuzzy-set analysis using *fsQCA* is shown in Box 10.1.

Fuzzy-set analysis thus represents a considerable advance on variable-centred analysis, focusing as it does on configurations of case characteristics that tend to produce the

BOX 10.1 A fuzzy-set analysis on the results of an e-mail survey in Norway

Kent (2005) reports the results of an e-mail survey in Norway into the effects on a range of e-mail response characteristics of e-mail use patterns, perceptions about technology, campaign elements and seeking different levels of permission from potential responders. The research sample was drawn from the customer database of a Norwegian company that issues loyalty cards that serve several different Norwegian retailers. Because of legislation that prohibits the use of unsolicited e-mail (or spam) in Norway, the company needed to ask every member registered in the e-mail database, through a medium other than e-mail, whether they would like to receive information via e-mail. By April 2002, approximately 40,000 members had accepted and given their 'basic' permission to receive information via e-mail. In a follow-up these members were e-mailed and asked if they would extend their permission by giving information on their personal interests and preferences; 65% of those who responded gave this 'extended' permission.

A random sample of 2100 of those who had given either basic or extended permission was selected and 1053 were returned, a response rate of 54%. In the survey, respondents were asked a series of questions about their use of e-mails. They were asked to indicate their strength of agreement or disagreement on a five-point scale with four items relating to their reaction to spam-based commercial e-mails, for example, 'Spam-based e-mail often has interesting content', 'I read all the spam-based e-mails I receive', 'I often click on links in spam-based e-mails' and 'I often make use of offers I receive in spam-based e-mails'. A similar set of items was used to get respondents' reactions to permission-based commercial e-mail. These were the 'outputs' (the dependent variables) being investigated. The causal factors included a number of e-mail use characteristics, for example the length of time using this medium, the number of e-mail addresses used, where read, how often read and so on.

In order to use fsQCA, the data first needed to be 'fuzzified'. This means all crisp-set variables need to be coded as either 0 or 1 and fuzzy variables given values between 0 and 1. This should be done in a way that 'makes sense'. For example, if the question was 'How long have you been using e-mail?' with the response categories 'Less than 1 year', '1–2 years', '3–4 years' and '5 or more years', it might 'make sense' to create a category called 'experienced user' with full membership of the set with a fuzzy score of 1 for those in the '5 or more years' category, a fuzzy score of 0.75 for those in the '3–4 years' category, being mostly in the category 'experienced user', a fuzzy score of 0.25 for those in the '1–2 years' category as being mostly out of the category 'experienced user' and a fuzzy score of 0 for those using e-mails for less than 1 year being totally out of that category. This recoding can be done in fsQCA, but is better achieved in SPSS first particularly if the user is familiar with SPSS and the features of the *Variable View* are required.

Figure 10.4 shows the 'fuzzified' data. Thus 'readspam' and 'readperm' are the five-value fuzzy scores ranging from 1 through 0.75, 0.5, 0.25 to 0.0. Thus a score of 0.75 means that this respondent is 'mostly in' the set 'reads spam'. The fuzzy variables 'respspam' and 'respperm' refer to the totals of the four-item Likert scales, which were created into fuzzy scores by taking the maximum score of 20 to be 'fully in' the set; the minimum score of 4 to be 'fully out'; the middle score of 12 was taken as the 'cross-over' point of 0.5 and the other scores were graded in intervals of 6.25%. A scattergram (XY plot) of the degree of membership of the set 'responds to spam' and the degree of membership of the set 'responds to permission e-mail' is also shown in Figure 10.4. A triangular pattern has clearly emerged – responding to permission e-mail is a necessary, *but not sufficient* condition for responding to spam. While this is in a sense an 'obvious' finding, it would not have emerged from a frequentist correlational analysis – it is also reassuring that the fuzzy analysis 'works'.

The degree of membership of the category 'responder to permission e-mails' was now taken as the output (dependent) variable with as causal factors whether or not extended permission had been given, whether or not e-mails were read mostly at home, the extent to which they are members of the set 'experienced user', the extent to

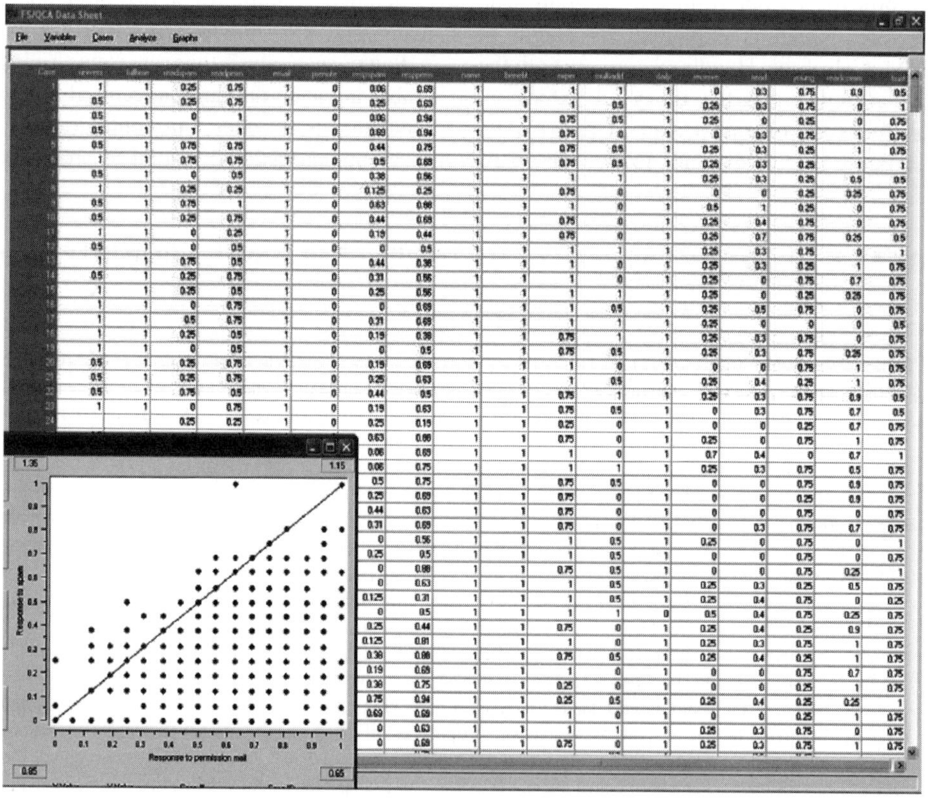

Figure 10.4   The fuzzified fsQCA dataset and XY plot.

which they are members of the set 'multiple-mail addresses' ('multiadd' in Figure 10.4) and the extent to which they are members of the set 'read commercial e-mails'.

For the analysis of causal sufficiency, fsQCA offers two algorithms: an inclusion algorithm and a truth table algorithm. The former lists every combination that meets the test criteria for sufficiency, then minimizes them by excluding those expressions that are contained or included in simpler expressions. The truth table algorithm constructs the equivalent of a truth table from fuzzy sets by imagining all combinations of causal factors as points in multidimensional space and assessing the nearness of each combination to a corner of vector space. This algorithm tends to be more parsimonious than the inclusion algorithm and gives measures of consistency (the extent to which the causal combination is a subset of the outcome) and coverage (the proportion of the total number of cases covered by the causal expression). Coverage is a proportional measure of the extent to which the solution 'explains' the outcome and, as explained by Cooper (2005), it plays a role analogous to variance explained in a regression analysis. The analysis of truth tables is more transparent than the inclusion mechanism, for example, it is possible to investigate the consequences of different simplifying assumptions and for situations where there is limited diversity. Ragin recommends the latter procedure, particularly for larger-N studies.

The truth table algorithm requires that the researcher selects a frequency threshold; this means that causal combinations below a certain frequency are excluded from the analysis (treated as 'remainders' in the terminology of the software). In a truth table, there are 2^k combinations, in this study 2^5 or 32 combinations. A frequency threshold of 10 was chosen, as there are over 1000 cases. This had the effect of excluding 14 combinations, leaving 18 with an empirical frequency of more than 10. The analysis gives a measure of consistency for each of the remaining combinations. A consistency of 0.8 would mean, for example, that the causal combinations are subsets of the outcome 80% of the time and can be interpreted as saying that the combination is 'nearly always' sufficient to bring about the outcome. This level was chosen for the analysis because there were 43 cases in one particular combination that just made this level. The 18 combinations are now reduced to a more parsimonious set using a particular algorithm, giving the four causal expressions below:

HOME*multiadd: consistency = 0.726

EXPER*readcomm: consistency = 0.723

EXPER*multiadd: consistency = 0.841

EXTPERM*EXPER: consistency = 0.699

Lower case indicates the negation, so the combination of being an experienced user and not having multiple e-mail addresses is sufficient in over 80% of cases to bring about a response to e-mails where permission has been given. The other causal combinations do not meet the chosen threshold. Overall, the analysis covers 90% of the cases included in the run. If consistency is raised to 0.9, using the same frequency threshold, the results become:

EXPER*multiadd*READCOM: consistency = 0.844

EXTPERM*EXPER*READCOM: consistency = 0.930

HOME*mulitadd*READCOM: consistency = 0.877

Consistency is now higher for each causal expression, but coverage has dropped to just over 0.5. There are now three causal expressions that meet the threshold, and reading commercial e-mails has emerged as an important factor. A separate analysis of necessary conditions suggests that only being an experienced user meets a consistency threshold of 0.8. The same model was run using the inclusion algorithm and a rather different result emerged. This showed that the combination of *not* being an experienced user, having several e-mail addresses and either having given extended permission or *not* reading e-mails mostly at home were jointly sufficient on 90% of the cases to give rise to a positive response to permission e-mails.

The analysis is thus far from conclusive and it is sensitive to changes in thresholds and algorithms used. It is also sensitive to the calibrations of fuzzy factors used or the manner in which more standard variables have been 'fuzzified'. The analysis above can be continued by inputting other potential causal factors and, by looking at those factors that may be necessary or sufficient for the negation (not responding to permission-based e-mails) and by looking at those factors involved in response and non-response to spam. Users need to live with the fact that there is no single solution as would be generated from a regression analysis. A standard regression analysis was carried out using the same model and it produced a multiple adjusted R^2 of just 0.13 and the only statistically significant standardized beta coefficient was the extent to which respondents read commercial e-mails.

outcome desired in all or nearly all instances. It straddles qualitative and quantitative procedures, and it sits midway between exploratory and hypothesis-testing research. It requires more cases than for qualitative research, but fewer than for quantitative. The analysis procedures used are the same for both metric and categorical variables – and for fuzzy-coded categories arising from qualitative data. It needs more understanding of potential causal factors than for exploratory research, as comparative analysts must specify the categories of phenomena that are of interest at the outset of the investigation, but hypotheses containing complex logical relationships can be difficult to formulate in advance to test. It focuses on cases as configurations of characteristics rather than on relationships between abstracted variables and it separates out necessary from sufficient conditions. It can be used in conjunction with frequentist analyses to locate patterns that the latter might miss. It is best used in situations where there are clear outcomes or dependent variables that are being analyzed and where the number of potential causal factors is fairly limited and fully understood. Although the results are not conclusive, it is possible, however, to see to what extent these results are sensitive to test criteria, giving some indication of robustness.

FsQCA has been used mainly with medium-sized datasets with Ns of 10 to 60 or so. This is perhaps unsurprising since frequentists would carefully avoid Ns of less than 60 or even less than 100. By the same token, qualitative researchers commonly have fewer than 10 or so cases. However, fsQCA has been applied to large-N studies, as in Box 10.1 and, for example, by Cooper (2005), who uses a dataset with over 5000 cases from the British National Child Development Study. Ragin (2003) discusses an application from the US National Longitudinal Survey of Youth that includes 758 black males. Ragin points out that with large-N studies it is important to establish a relevance threshold so that configurations with very few instances are excluded from the analysis. With large datasets, cases can be assigned to the wrong configuration through measurement error.

It is also true that when there are many cases, familiarity with individual cases is lost, which may limit possibilities for causal interpretations and the reasons for instances of limited diversity.

NEURAL NETWORK ANALYSIS

Neural networks mimic the human brain in its capacity to learn to solve problems. They are essentially pattern-recognition devices. The neural network is 'trained' on an appropriate set of data examples, but the modelling process is data-led. The model will progressively change to fit the data. Neural networks tend to be more robust and fault-tolerant than frequentist methods. They are better at handling noisy, incomplete or contradictory data. For example, the existence of outliers can severely handicap a traditional technique, but neural networks can handle them quite easily. Neural networks are not subject to the key assumptions of frequentist methods in terms of linearity, normality and completeness. Furthermore, they can capture the structured complexity of a dynamic process in the reality and can do so with imperfect datasets.

There are three basic types of neural network: the multilayer perceptron model, which is the most commonly used, the radial basis function, which is a more recent development and the Kohonen model, which is appropriate only for clustering problems.

The main element in a neural network multilayer perceptron model is a *node* (or neuron), which is analogous to the neuron of the human brain. This accepts a number of inputs from other nodes. Each connection with another node has an assigned weight, which is multiplied by each input value and summated in the same way that multivariate methods do in creating a composite variable. The summed value is then processed by an activation function to generate an output value, which is sent to the next node in the system.

The neural network is a sequential arrangement of three basic types of node: input,

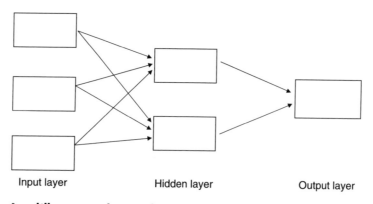

Input layer   Hidden layer   Output layer

Figure 10.5 A multilayer neural network.

output and intermediate or hidden nodes (Figure 10.5). An input node represents a single variable and receives initial data values from each case. Categorical variables need to be created into dummy variables. The hidden nodes are used by the neural network to represent more complex relationships. This, and the activation function, which is generally a non-linear S-shaped function, allows neural networks to represent non-linear relationships. Each node acts independently, but in parallel with all of the other nodes.

The key feature of a neural network that sets it apart from other multivariate techniques is its ability to learn or correct itself. The weights attached to the inputs act as a memory. Errors are distributed back through the system and the weights are changed proportionally, increasing or decreasing according to the direction of the error. Once all the weights have been recalibrated, the input for another case is entered and the process begins all over again. A large number of cases are passed through the network in this training phase so that it can make the best predictions across all the input data patterns.

The steps involved in doing a neural network analysis include: first, deciding on a training sample of cases used to estimate the weights and a separate validation sample to assess the predictive ability of the model. There need to be 10–30 cases in the training sample for every weight being estimated. The second step is to examine the data for skewness, non-normality and outliers.

The third step is to define the model structure. As the inputs and outputs are already selected, the decision is in effect to determine the number of nodes in the hidden layer. The consensus is that there should be only one layer of hidden nodes and the researcher should try to find the best fit with the minimum number of nodes. The fourth step is model estimation. This is an iterative procedure and the overall optimum solution might not be found. The goal is to achieve the best overall fit and yet not over-train the model with too many cases. The next step is to evaluate the model results against the predictions or classifications made. This uses the validation sample mentioned earlier. Finally, after the network has been trained and validated, the resulting model may be applied to data it has not seen previously for prediction, classification, time-series analysis or data segmentation.

One of the most common uses of neural networks in the social sciences is with classification problems – deciding to which group a classification belongs. This, according to Hair et al. (1998), corresponds to a discriminant or logistic regression problem. Using the same data, the authors compared a two-group discriminant analysis with four different levels of neural network sophistication (using more hidden layer nodes). The classification accuracy for the discriminant model was 97.5%. The simplest neural network model with four nodes achieved an 80% accuracy, with six nodes a 90% accuracy and 100%

for eight nodes and a model with two layers of hidden layers with four nodes each. The advantage of neural networks is therefore not dramatic.

More recently, neural network analysis has been combined with fuzzy-set analysis to produce what the authors call a 'neural network-based fuzzy modelling approach' (Stathacopoulou et al. 2007). The authors use fuzzy sets to provide a linguistic description of students' behaviour and learning characteristics that have been elicited from teachers. They use Zadeh's original concept of 'linguistic variables' (Zadeh 1975). Thus the amount of time a student has spent in a computer learning environment may be classified by teachers as 'very short', 'short', 'normal', 'long' or 'very long'. The actual observed time can then be used to identify degrees of membership of each of these categories, allowing for overlaps in classifications. This enables modellers to handle the inherent uncertainty associated with teachers' subjective assessments. If teachers' reasoning about how such factors may be related to outcomes is available and well defined, it can be encoded in the form of fuzzy rules, for example in a series of 'if–then' statements like 'If a student's total time at the computer is very long and the number of attempts to check answers is large and the number of random mouse moves and clicking buttons is small, then the student is very interested in the learning scenario'. Stathacopoulou et al. (2007) then use neural networks to add learning and generalization abilities to the fuzzy model by encoding teachers' experience through supervised neural-network learning.

THE TIPPING POINT

All the modes of data analysis mentioned so far operate within closed systems – systems with boundaries. The relationships between factors and variables may be complex, but they are at least seen to be stable. However, complex systems often overlap, they might be nested as systems within systems and they might be subjected to sudden phase shifts in which very small changes in one factor can, at critical points, produce huge consequences. These could take the form of a sudden take-off, a dramatic decline or the system becoming unstable.

In 2000, Gladwell, a writer for *The New Yorker*, published a book called *The Tipping Point*. He noted that major changes in society – ideas, behaviour, messages, product sales, fashions – often happen suddenly and unexpectedly, often spreading like outbreaks of infectious diseases. He used the phrase 'tipping point' to describe the moment when ideas, trends and behaviour cross a threshold, reach a critical mass or go on the boil to tip and spread like wild fire. It is the moment when little changes can make a big difference. Whether or not a tipping point happens is, according to Gladwell, affected by three factors: 'the law of the few', 'the stickiness factor' and 'the power of context'.

The law of the few states that the spread of any new idea is determined by the initial adoption patterns of a small group of socially infectious early-adopters that he calls 'connectors'. He draws on social network theory and research into the diffusion of innovation to explain how a combination of word of mouth advocacy and the copycat effect allows these connectors to drive diffusion of the idea or behaviour. Connectors are hubs in a peer network and a contagion effect quickly diffuses an idea.

The stickiness factor refers to the intrinsic contagiousness of the idea. This is a term borrowed from the media that is used to describe how 'sticky' a channel or a program is, that is, how 'glued' people are to it. A sticky idea is one that is easily understood, makes intuitive sense and is highly memorable.

The power of context points out that, like infectious diseases, ideas spread far and wide only when they fit the context into which they are launched.

Gladwell's book became a best seller, eagerly taken up by businessmen and marketing executives who were interested in how they could *create* a tipping point for new products, brands or services. Thus, companies should seek to develop special relationships with connectors, focusing innovation research on satisfying their needs rather than pandering to the fickle desires of the mass market. To create stickiness, companies need to tweak and test new products or services against a limited number of cross-category attributes that emerge as key drivers for product success. These have been recently articulated by Morris and Martin (2000), based on a meta-analysis of cult products and brands. To take advantage of the power of context, new products need to be adapted to fit the social, physical and mental context of their use. Marsden (2004) gives a number of examples of the use of tipping-point theory, including Post-It™ notes, Microsoft's launch of Windows 95® and Pfizer's launch of tetracycline.

The tipping point is a good example of case-oriented analysis, but one that focuses on successful cases to see what mix of conditions they have in common. The focus is more on what conditions may be necessary, but together might still not be sufficient to bring about the desired result. The tipping point is something that organization or governments might try to achieve, but dynamic, open, complex and adaptive systems commonly teeter on the edge of chaos; when they tip over they exhibit many of the features associated with chaos theory. In a chaotic system, minute changes in some initial conditions can, over a period of time – or even after a fairly limited number of iterations – bring about very large fluctuations in the outcome. This is the so-called 'butterfly effect' in which in principle a butterfly flapping its wings in one part of the world will in due course produce storms some months later in another part of the world. The effects are not random, but deterministic, but so complex that they are unpredictable. In this state, systems can spin towards various sorts of attractor states, which might be stable equilibria, recurrent cycles, out-of-control explosions or, somewhere between the two, strange attractors – trajectories through which systems move and gravitate towards.

Hibbert and Wilkinson (1994) explain a variety of mathematical techniques that could be used to identify systems that show chaotic tendencies and to distinguish them from random behaviour, but they require long data series of high quality. Attempts have been made to identify chaos in various economic and financial time series such as business cycles, stock process and employment rates, but have had limited success. In principle, if chaotic tendencies are detected, more detailed investigation of the underlying mechanism can be undertaken.

CONCLUSION

This chapter raises a number of issues about case-centred methods. First, what counts as 'case-centred' has become clouded. The study of individual cases and the methods for understanding them are clearly case based. The classification and comparison of several or many cases to determine similarities and differences and to explore complex and multiple causality is also case-centred, so will include methods like configurational analysis, cluster analysis and correspondence analysis. The idea of a tipping point can also be seen as emerging from a study of a number of cases. The extent to which neural network analysis and Bayesian statistics can be seen as case based, however, is less clear-cut. These are more variable centred than case centred, but not 'frequentist' in the sense of relying exclusively on analyzing the patterns of value distributions for variables. Perhaps it would be best to see these as alternatives to frequentist methods, but not 'case based' as used in this Handbook.

Second, this chapter raises the issue of the relationship between case-based methods and the number of cases being studied. Case-based methods have been implicitly related largely or even solely to small-N studies, although configurational analysis (which includes QCA, fsQCA and multivalue qualitative comparative analysis [MVQCA], as developed by Cronqvist and included in the TOSMANA software) has been positioned as being particularly appropriate for medium-sized datasets, but, as this chapter makes clear, can be and has been used also for large datasets. Cluster analysis and correspondence analysis have also been seen in this Handbook as case based and these are multivariate techniques that are used mainly on large-N studies.

Third, this chapter raises the issue of case-based methods and the distinction between qualitative and quantitative methods. Case-centred methods have often been seen as synonymous with qualitative research, but cluster analysis, correspondence analysis and configurational methods are quantitative multivariate techniques. Case-centred methods and quantitative analysis are not necessarily alternatives, but may overlap or be combined in various ways. Cluster analysis, qualitative comparative analysis and its fuzzy-set variation are all case centred, yet quantitative. The 'qualitative' in qualitative comparative analysis refers to the use of that word to mean 'quality', namely categorical or nominally scaled variables, not to textual or visual materials. This chapter has commented on the assumptions and limitations of 'frequentist' methods. These should not be equated with quantitative approaches generally, but rather they are a subset that focuses on value distributions and sampling distributions.

Fourth, this chapter raises the issue of what counts as a 'result' or 'solution' to the analysis of data. Some of the approaches, including frequentist methods, Bayesian statistics and neural networks give a single result or solution at the end of the analysis. Configurational analysis not only allows for multiple solutions or outcomes from a single analysis but shares with cluster analysis the characteristic that many different sets of solutions could be created, depending on which variables are included and what elements of the procedure are deployed. In short, there is no one best or correct answer, but many answers. Although this might be disconcerting to some researchers, this is probably a better reflection of the characteristics of complex systems. A related issue is that configurational

analysis and cluster analysis problematize what count as 'similar' and 'dissimilar' cases. In the former, only cases that share all the configurational characteristics can be regarded as similar. In cluster analysis, there are many different measures of similarity.

Fifth, Bayesian approaches and fuzzy-set analysis raise the issue of the extent to which it is appropriate to include subjective elements in quantitative analysis in a transparent fashion. A Bayesian 'prior' is often based on expert opinion or subjective experience. In fuzzy-set analysis the calibration of the degree of membership in sets is based on the researcher's substantive and theoretical knowledge. This is totally different from taking, in frequentist approaches, the mean and variance to determine the placing of a case on a scale of values.

Sixth, the idea of the tipping point and chaos theory are specifically concerned with system dynamics in a way that the other techniques are not. Frequentist techniques can use longitudinal data to measure system changes, whereas Ragin and Strand (2007) have suggested a way of using QCA and fsQCA to study causal order. However, neither approach is geared towards the study of the system dynamics involved in the sequencing of causal conditions.

Science is all about prediction, explanation and evaluation. Alternative explanations need to be evaluated before the best prediction can be had. A conclusion to be drawn from this chapter is that a multimethod approach to the analysis of datasets will considerably enhance the ability of researchers to make such evaluations. Collier et al. (2004) talk about 'sources of leverage' in causal inference. They argue that more important than the distinction between small-N and large-N studies or between qualitative and quantitative approaches is the distinction between experimental and observational data. Leamer (1983, p. 39) points out that with the latter, 'there is no formal way to know what inferential monsters lurk beyond our immediate field of vision'. The random *assignment* of cases to hypothesized causal conditions in experimental research eliminates many of the challenges to causal inference in a way that the random *selection* of cases in observational research does not. Here, researchers can only observe the values that independent variables acquire through the unfolding of social, political or economic processes. Frequentist methods were designed largely for and work best on experimental data. The analysis of observational data from open, complex and dynamic systems cannot normally be best achieved using techniques based on assuming symmetrical relationships, linearity and additivity. Bayesian statistics provide a better tool for evaluating uncertainty, whereas configurational approaches are a better way of examining situations in which there might be several different ways in which an outcome could come about.

Both Bayesian and configurational perspectives provide superior tools for evaluating arguments about necessary and sufficient causation. A major advance accomplished by the configurational approach and in particular the work of Ragin is that the study of necessary and sufficient causation is moved away from temporal implication (if X then Y) to one of set theoretic inclusion (all Xs are Ys, which, in set theoretic terms, can be seen as the Xs are a subset of the Ys). Only this approach can cope with situations where relationships between variables are asymmetrical. Both temporal implication and set theoretic inclusion, however, provide only evidence, not proof, of causal connections between identified factors or variables. Both require adequacy at the level of meaning before conclusions about causal relationships can be drawn, but only set theoretic inclusion can, for the most part, sort out causal necessity from causal sufficiency.

Although it would be unrealistic to expect researchers to be familiar with all the approaches outlined in this chapter, an awareness that they exist can only be an advantage. Researchers are apt to seek only one type of pattern, whether it is variable covariation, case configuration or evidence of tipping points. Failure to find

sought-for-patterns in one approach should not, ideally, lead to a 'no result' conclusion, but rather to a 'let's look for an alternative' approach. Each approach outlined in this chapter has its own strengths and weaknesses and none is a panacea for all situations. It is in some ways unfortunate that configurational analysis and fuzzy-set analysis have been seen as falling exclusively within the 'qualitative comparative analysis' framework. Although they are particularly suited to QCA, they are also very viable alternatives to frequentist statistical approaches. Data derived from social surveys will normally be analyzed using the frequentist statistics that are available on survey analysis software like SPSS. The results, however, are often slender. Differences between subgroups are often small and associations or correlations between variables are frequently tiny or non-existent. The same data can, however, be analyzed using software like *fsQCA* with very different results. Interestingly, in their recent book, Rihoux and Ragin (2007) have titled it 'configurational comparative analysis', dropping the 'qualitative' implication.

REFERENCES

Abbott, A. 1992 'What do cases do? Some notes on activity in sociological analysis' in C. Ragin and H. Becker (Eds) *What Is a Case? Exploring the Foundations of Social Inquiry.* Cambridge: Cambridge University Press.

Abbott, A. 1998 'The causal devolution' *Sociological Methods and Research* 27(2): 148–181.

Bakkan, D. 2005 'The Bayesian revolution in marketing research' ESOMAR Innovatel Conference, Paris.

Berk, R. 2004 *Regression Analysis. A Constructive Critique.* London: Sage.

Booth, C. 1894 *The Aged Poor in England and Wales.* London: Macmillan.

Bowley, A. 1910 *An Elementary Manual of Statistics.* London: Macdonald and Evans.

Byrne, D. 2002 *Interpreting Quantitative Data.* London: Sage Publications.

Byrne, D. 2007 'Complexity science and transformations in social policy' Online, available: http://www.whb.co.uk/socialissues/db.htm.

Clark, W., Gilligan, M. and Golder, M. 2006 'A simple multivariate test for asymmetric hypotheses' *Political Analysis* 14: 311–331.

Collier, D., Brady, H. and Seawright, J. 2004 'Sources of leverage in causal inference: toward an alternative view of methodology' in H. Brady and D. Collier (Eds) *Rethinking Social Inquiry. Diverse Tools, Shared Methods.* Lanham, MD: Rowman and Littlefield.

Cooper, B. 2005 'Applying Ragin's crisp and fuzzy-set QCA to large datasets: social class and educational achievement' *Sociological Research Online.*

de Leeuw, J. 2004 'Series editor's introduction' in R. Berk (Ed.) *Regression Analysis: A Constructive Critique.* London: Sage.

Drass, K. and Ragin, C.C. 1992 *QCA: Qualitative Comparative Analysis.* Evanston, IL: Institute for Policy Research, Northwestern University.

Elliott, J. 1999 'Models are stories are not real life' in D. Dorling and S. Simpson (Eds) *Statistics in Society.* London: Arnold.

Freedman, D. 1999 'From association to causation: some remarks on the history of statistics' *Statistical Science* 14(3): 243–258.

Galton, Sir F. 1883 *Inquiries into Human Faculty.* London: Dent.

Gladwell, M. 2000 *The Tipping Point. How Little Things Can Make a Big Difference.* New York: Little Brown and Company.

Hair, J., Anderson. R., Tatham, R. and Black, W. 1998 *Multivariate Data Analysis* (5th edition). Englewood Cliffs, NJ: Prentice Hall.

Hempel, C. 1942 'Studies in the logic of confirmation' *Mind* 54: 1(6): 97–121.

Hibbert, B. and Wilkinson, I.1994 'Chaos theory and the dynamics of marketing systems' *Journal of the Academy of Marketing Science* 22(3): 218–233.

Kent, R. 1981 *A History of British Empirical Sociology.* London: Gower Press.

Kent, R. 2005 'Cases as configurations: using combinatorial and fuzzy logic to analyze marketing data' *International Journal of Market Research* 47(2): 205–228.

Kent, R. 2007 *Marketing Research. Approaches, Methods and Applications in Europe.* London: Thomson Learning.

Leamer, E. 1983 'Let's take the con out of econometrics' *American Economic Review* 73(1): 31–43.

Lilford, R. and Braunholtz, D. 2003 'Reconciling the quantitative and qualitative traditions – the Bayesian approach' *Public Money and Management* July.

MacKenzie, D. 1979 'Eugenics and the rise of mathematical statistics in Britain' in J. Irvine, I. Miles and J. Evans (Eds) *Demysifying Social Statistics.* London: Pluto Press.

Marsden, P. 2004 'The tipping point: from dream to reality.' Market Research Society Annual Conference, Brighton. Online, available: http://www.WARC.com.

Morris, R. and Martin, C. 2000 'Beanie Babies: a case study in the engineering of a high involvement/relationship-prone brand' *Journal of Product and Brand Management* 9(2): 78–98.

Olsen, W. and Morgan, J. 2004 'A critical epistemology of analytical statistics: addressing the skeptical realist' Paper presented to the British Sociological Association, York, March.

Ragin, C. 1987 *The Comparative Method: Moving Beyond Qualitative and Quantitative Strategies.* Berkeley, CA: University of California Press.

Ragin, C. 2000 *Fuzzy-Set Social Science.* Chicago: University of Chicago Press.

Ragin, C. 2003 'Recent advances in fuzzy-set methods and their application to policy questions' Online, available: http://www.compasss.org/RaginDec_2004.pdf.

Ragin, C. and Strand, S. 2007 'Using QCA to study causal order: comment on Caren and Panofsky 2005' Online, available: http://www.compasss.org.

Retzer, J. 2006 'The century of Bayes' *International Journal of Market Research* 48(1): 49–59.

Rihoux, B. and Ragin, C. 2007 *Configurational Comparative Analysis.* London: Sage Publications.

Rossi, P., Allenby, G. and McCulloch, R. 2005 *Bayesian Statistics and Marketing.* Chichester, UK: John Wiley.

Sayer, A. 2000 *Realism and Social Science.* London: Sage Publications.

Schrodt, P. 2006 'Beyond the linear frequentist orthodoxy' *Political Analysis* 14: 335–339.

Smith, D and Fletcher, J. 2004 *The Art and Science of Interpreting Market Research Evidence.* Chichester, UK: John Wiley.

Smithson, M. 1988 'Fuzzy-set theory and the social sciences: the scope for applications' *Fuzzy Sets and Systems* 26: 1–21.

Stathacopoulou, R., Grigoriadou, M., Samarakou, M. and Mitropoulos, D. 2007 'Monitoring students' actions and using teachers' expertise in implementing and evaluating the neural network-based fuzzy diagnostic model' *Expert Systems with Applications* 32: 995–975.

Tabachnick, B and Fidell, L. 2001 *Using Multivariate Statistics* (4th edition). Boston MA: Allyn and Bacon.

Yule, G. 1895 'On the correlation of total pauperism with the proportion of out-relief' *Economic Journal* V: 603–611.

Yule, G. 1899 'An investigation into the causes of changes in pauperism in England, chiefly during the last two intercensal decades' *Journal of the Royal Statistical Society*, LXII.

Yule, G. 1900 'On the association of attributes in statistics: with illustrations from the material of the childhood society, etc' *Philosophical Transactions*, Series A, CLXXXIV: 257–319.

Zadeh, L. 1975 'The concept of a linguistic variable and its application to approximate reasoning' *Information Sciences* 8: 199–249.

Zetterberg, H. 1965 *On Theory and Verification in Sociology* (3rd edition). London: Bedminster Press.

11

The Logic and Assumptions of MDSO–MSDO Designs

Gisèle De Meur and Alain Gottcheiner

INTRODUCTION

Cases are meaningful

The MDSO–MSDO (**m**ost **d**ifferent cases, **s**imilar **o**utcome/**m**ost **s**imilar cases, **d**ifferent outcome) procedure is one of several techniques for comparative research in which the concept of cases, as defined by Charles C. Ragin and Howard S. Becker (1992), plays a central role.

Case studies in general, and MDSO–MSDO in particular, go beyond mere questioning about a limited number of variables and a large number of observations: they consider observations more in depth, using more parameters and data, expressed as 'variables'. When giving such detailed attention to observations, we will call them 'cases'. We will work in Ragin's (2002) way, considering each case as a separate and unique whole. In this view, a single decisive difference between two cases may signal a difference in kind, and not simply a difference in degree.

In order to give a well-established starting hypothesis, imagine a small number of cases (e.g. 10 to 20 countries, institutions, individuals) for which some given phenomenon (e.g. revolution, point of law, success) might or might not have happened. For each case, we are in possession of several dozens of variables.

The more variables, the more information about each case. However, checking whether each individual variable is relevant to the phenomenon under study, and treating every pair of cases, then every triplet, would take far too long; and, above all, it would lose links between variables, as set by cases.

Origins

The natural questions are: (1) how to reduce the system's complexity without losing relevant information? and (2) how to find cases that will transmit the most information through their comparisons, and the set of variables that are likely to have explanatory value?

In Book III, chapter VII, of his book *A System of Logic*, John Stuart Mill (1843/2002) holds as an explicative circumstance the one, and only one, that has the same value for all cases. In other words, among cases with the same outcome, if one variable has the same value, this is the one to use for explanation. Symmetrically, considering two cases with different outcomes, we would look for the one, and only one, variable with different values among those cases.

In practice, we shouldn't expect such a perfect configuration to happen very often. We therefore turn our attention to the notion of 'most similar system' or 'most different system', as put forward by Przeworski and Henry (1970), which allows for a small set of variables to vary concurrently with the outcome. This view of things also allows us to grasp relations between variables.

Methodological orientation

Going in this direction, De Meur, in her paper with Berg-Schlosser (1994), developed a method to accord due consideration to cases in which the same outcome appeared while being the least similar in their parameters (most different cases, similar outcome), in order to put forward variables having the same values for those cases. The same quest for homogeneous variables being tackled for cases with the fewest same-valued variables among those in which the outcome did not appear.

Conversely, when comparing cases 'with-outcome' with cases 'without-outcome', the pairs with the most same-valued variables (most similar cases, different outcome) will allow us to put forward the few different-valued variables, likely candidates as explanatory variables for the difference in result. The core idea is then to define three kinds of configuration, where comparisons will allow for detecting explanatory factors; that is, by reducing the initial data's complexity, putting forward a small number of variables and restricted configurations of cases. This is not about comparing cases, but rather about preparing the ground for efficient analyses.

Objectives for this procedure are twofold and deeply ingrained in the quest for genuine case comparisons.

As the gist of the cases does not reduce to one or two variables, especially not to *a priori* chosen variables, we need to keep track of the complexity produced by the variables, while at the same time endeavouring to reduce this complexity. The approach was therefore to focus our comparison-oriented attention on configurations that could contain a considerable amount of information. By locally reducing both the set of cases and the set of variables that group them the right way (groups of 'most similar' or 'most different' cases), we cut down unnecessary complexity (the 'background noise') and keep focused on tightly related elements. In this sense, our approach is radically prospective and we do not let ourselves reduce cases to one- or two-dimensional analysis. It is significant that, after conducing the reduction process, one given case might be included in several 'pertinent' configurations, under the light of different variables.

Warning

As MDSO–MSDO merely exhibits sets of cases, chosen for comparison efficiency, without conducting the comparison itself, it is a tool for steering the analysis and not for the actual analysis. It handles only dichotomized variables, which necessitate an educated choice of some dichotomization threshold. This is discussed later, in the section 'methodological discussion'.

It is therefore incumbent on researchers both to establish in advance the table of variables and to interpret the results of the reduction procedure, equipped with in-depth knowledge of their field of study and their own experience. This might also include adapting some parameters to help with the exhibition of meaningful variables. MDSO–MSDO never yields conclusions: the researchers remain solely responsible for their hypotheses, thesis, reasoning and conclusions. This being said, it is now time to tackle the technical aspects.

MEASURING SIMILARITY OR DISSIMILARITY BETWEEN CASES

The dissimilarity between two cases will be taken as the number of variables with different values in those cases. This is an integer, ranging between 0 (if both cases are identical in all variables) and the number of variables (if no variable takes the same value in both cases).[1] Hence, the first step of the procedure is computing a Hamming distance (the number of variables with differing values) for each pair of cases.

From here, we will describe technical aspects on the basis of the study by De Meur, Bursens and Gottcheiner (2006). The object of this study was the consideration of actor networks, classified as either tight (corporatist) or loose (pluralist) according to nine EU initiatives. 'tight' and 'loose' will be the two possible *outcomes*. Often, the outcomes will be in the yes/no format, i.e. 'did phenomenon X occur or not?' The method therefore uses the terminology of 'positive versus negative cases'. We shall, somewhat arbitrarily, consider 'tight' cases as positive ones.

We considered a set of 44 possible explanatory variables, labelled in five categories:

(1) Category A: formal aspects of the decision-making process (11 variables).
(2) Category B: characteristics of the interest groups (5 variables).

(3) Category C: characteristics of the decision-making institutions (11 variables).
(4) Category D: characteristics of the initiatives' contents (11 variables).
(5) Category E: formal aspect of the policy (4 variables).

The objects of the initiatives under study were as follows:

- Organization of the market in the rice sector (hereafter called case Rice or R).
- Organization of the market in the fodder sector (Fodder or Fo).
- Price setting in the sugar sector (Sugar or Sg).
- Price setting in the fruit sector (Fruit or F).
- European work councils (Council or C).
- Noise emissions (Noise or N).
- Gas emissions (Gas or G).
- Waste packaging (Waste or W).
- Safety and security in workplaces (Safety of Sf).

The complete set of variables can be seen in Annex 1 at the end of this chapter.

Consider the data matrix in Table 11.1, featuring our nine cases, of which five are positive (tight) and four negative (loose), and giving values for eleven Boolean variables meaning: presence of some characteristic ('1') or its absence ('0').

For example, we can see that cases R and Fo differ only by their value for variable A9: the two cases are quite similar, with a distance of 1.

Table 11.1   Data for nine cases, their outcome and eleven descriptive variables. 'Positive' cases, those for which the outcome phenomenon did occur, are conventionally written to the left of the table and their names are capitalized

Cases	Case1	Case2	Case3	Case4	Case5	case6	case7	case8	case9
Outcome:	Y	Y	Y	Y	Y	N	N	N	N
Variable A1	0	0	0	0	1	1	1	1	1
Variable A2	1	1	1	1	0	1	1	1	1
Variable A3	1	1	0	0	1	0	0	1	0
Variable A4	1	1	0	0	1	0	0	1	0
Variable A5	0	0	0	0	1	0	0	0	0
Variable A6	1	1	1	1	0	0	0	0	0
Variable A7	0	0	0	0	1	0	1	0	1
Variable A8	1	1	0	0	1	0	1	0	1
Variable A9	0	1	0	0	0	1	1	1	1
Variable A10	1	1	0	0	1	1	1	1	1
Variable A11	1	1	0	0	1	0	1	1	1

Table 11.2   Distances between cases

	Case1	Case2	Case3	Case4	Case5	case6	case7	case8
Case2	1		Zone 1					
Case3	5	6						
Case4	5	6	0					
Case5	5	6	10	10				
case6	7	6	4	4	8		Zone 2	
case7	6	5	7	7	5	3		
case8	4	3	7	7	5	3	4	
case9	6	5	7	7	5	3	0	4

Zone 3

We put the distance between pairs of cases into Table 11.2, computing the number of different-valued variables. By separating positive from negative cases, we get three distinct blocks: one for comparing positive cases between them, one for comparing negative cases between them, and one for cross-comparing positive and negative cases.

Most different, same outcome

The upper triangle (zone 1) gives distances between 'positive' (tight) cases. We can read a null distance between cases *Sugar* and *Fruit*, but a great distance between them and case *Council*: only variable A9 takes the same value. These are the kind of remarkable differences Mill was looking for: *Council* will be set against *Sugar* and *Fruit*, and variable A9 will be taken into account when looking for an explanation.

The right most triangle (zone 2) gives distances between 'negative' (loose) cases. We can read rather short distances, less than half the number of variables: every pair of cases has at least seven same-valued variables, which has limited interest, as we're looking for dissimilar cases.

Most similar, different outcome

The lower left part of Table 11.2 (zone 3) gives distances between the five positive-outcome cases and the four negative-outcome cases. Here, we're looking the other way round: as outcomes are different, we will attach price to

the paucity of different-valued variables, and hence will be looking for short distances.

We aren't lucky enough to have at our disposal some positive case and some negative cases with only one different-valued variable, but we will turn our attention to the pair with the shortest distance: *Fodder* and *noise* differ only in three variables. Pairs (*Sugar, noise*), (*Fruit, noise*) and (*Rice, waste*) differ only in four variables. There are five pairs with a distance of 5: (*Fodder, gas*), (*Fodder, safety*), (*Council, gas*), (*Council, waste*) and (*Council, safety*); we will not put these aside *a priori*.

Determining levels

To make interesting pairs more readable, we give 'level 0' to the most remarkable pairs: greatest distances within zones 1 and 2, shortest distances within zone 3. 'Level 1' is 1 away from level 0, whether there is a pair with this value of distance or not, and so on, up to some threshold level consistent with the idea of proximity or remoteness. As we are making comparisons on 11 variables, the threshold will be distance 6 (at least 6) for remoteness, distance 5 (at most 5) for proximity.

Within zone 1, the most remote pair is at distance 10; this is 'level 0'. Level 9 will be distance 9, and so on up to level 4 = distance 6, which is the only other existing value. Distances below 6 are not taken into account. Within zone 2, therefore, we will have to turn down each and every pair of cases (distances at most 4). Turning down some pair will be marked by a dash.

Table 11.3 Distance levels

	Case1	Case2	Case3	Case4	Case5	case6	case7	case8
Case2	–		Zone 1					
Case3	–	4						
Case4	–	4	–					
Case5	–	4	0	0				
case6	–	–	1	1	–	Zone 2		
case7	–	2	–	–	2	–		
case8	1	0	–	–	2	–	–	
case9	–	2	–	–	2	–	–	–

Zone 3

Within zone 3, we have to consider similarities. The shortest distance (3) is given 'level 0'; levels 1 and 2 will correspond to distances 4 and 5; greater distances are turned down. This gives us a simplified table (Table 11.3), in which remarkable pairs – those that were given level 0 – are instantly visible; other levels, if they make sense, are also written in this table.

GENERALIZING BY USING CATEGORIES

So far, we have kept off a further level of complexity. A well-documented qualitative study might yield several score variables, and the risk of losing sight of interesting variables among the mass. However, variables can be rather different in nature: for example, if we endeavour studying failures at, say, 15 schools in one city, an important dimension characterizing educational establishments might be 'political': organizing authorities, help from the city council, the presence of an active board of governors/parents, partnership with other infrastructures; demography is another dimension: proximity from the town centre, density of population; and the social dimension: well-off or low-income part of the town, level of unemployment, proportion of unskilled workers.

Hence, we will need to split the bunch of variables into several categories, making them as homogeneous as possible (geographical variables, or social, or political). Heuristics tell us categories shouldn't be too small: four

variables in a category are a minimum. However, getting homogeneous categories is more important than grouping the same number of variables in each category.

For each category, we will perform the same piece of work as above. In each category, level 0 will be given to most different pairs (within zones 1 and 2) and to most similar pairs (within zone 3), then level 1 and so on, as long as the distance remains higher (within zones 1 and 2) or lower (within zone 3) than half the number of variables in that category. We then aggregate the tables produced for each category in such a way as to produce a string of results for every pair of cases (Table 11.4).

Now, we look – for each zone – for the pairs with the most maximal distances across categories (zones 1 and 2) or the most minimal distances (zone 3), i.e. the pairs with the most 0s in Table 11.4 (this number may vary from zone to zone). Within zone 1, this will be (*Fruit, Council*), with its three 0s. Note, too, the pair (*Sugar, Council*), whose score isn't far away: two 0s and a 1. Within zone 2, the pair (*gas, waste*) comes first, with its three 0s. The pair (*waste, safety*) yields '0' twice and '1' once. Within zone 3, pairs with the most 0s, i.e. the most minimal across categories, are (*Fruit, safety*) and (*Council, safety*). The pairs (*Sugar, safety*) isn't far behind; while (*Fruit, safety*) and (*Council, safety*) yield '0' twice and '1' twice, (*Sugar, safety*) has '0' once and '1' twice.

For the sake of synthetic vision, we write the results as a string of integers: the first number will be the number of 0s for the pair;

THE LOGIC AND ASSUMPTIONS OF MDSO–MSDO DESIGNS

Table 11.4 Level for each pair of cases across five categories

	Case1	Case2	Case3	Case4	Case5	case6	case7	case8
Case2	–		Zone 1					
Case3	–	4–2–						
Case4	–	4–	–					
Case5	–0	4–0	0–10	0–00				
case6	–333–	–3–3–	13–1–	13–0–	–1		Zone 2	
case7	–113–	211–	–131–	–132–	22–1	–		
case8	1–2–	0–2–	–	–	2–11	–2–0–	–000–	
case9	–013–	2033–	–011–	–010–	210–0	–1–	–	–100–

Zone 3

Table 11.5 Aggregated levels for each pair. Pair (Case4,Case5), with only three '0s', gets 3 as its first aggregated level, after which its score remains at 3. Pair (Case5,case9), with '0' twice, '1' once and '2' once, shows successive aggregated levels of 2, 3 and 4

	Case1	Case2	Case3	Case4	Case5	case6	case7	case8
Case2	–		Zone 1					
Case3	–	–112						
Case4	–	–1	–					
Case5	11111	11112	23333	33333				
case6	–33	–22	–2233	12233	–1111		Zone 2	
case7	–2233	–2333	–2233	–1233	–1333	–		
case8	–1222	11222	–	–	–2333	11222	33333	
case9	12233	11244	13333	23333	23444	–1111	–	23333

Zone 3

the second will be the total of 0s and 1s, and so on. This string of aggregated results allows for easier visualization of pairs with the largest number of first places (first integer), and also of second places, etc. (Table 11.5).

Within each zone, we consider the highest first integer, the highest second integer, etc., yielding a string of highest levels:

- 33333 within zone 1
- 33333 within zone 2
- 23444 within zone 3.

Note that, in the present case, each string of highest levels corresponds to some given pair of cases, but that this isn't necessarily the rule: one '22344' string and one '11245' string will yield a string of highest levels of '22345'.

Mentioning aggregate level numbers allows for the determination of a new set of remarkable pairs to add, in a second stage, to those coming from considering only 0s; and

so on. This expands the set of 'remarkable pairs': considering the second integer in each string, within zone 1, pair (*Sugar, Council*) is added to pre-existing pair (*Fruit, Council*), as it has the same aggregated number of 0s and 1s. Similarly, within zone 2 (*waste, safety*) is added to (*gas, waste*), and within zone 3, pair (*Sugar, safety*) is added to pairs (*Fruit, safety*) and (*Council, safety*) (Figure 11.1).

CASE PATTERNS AND VARIABLES

Fetching relevant variables

The MDSO–MSDO procedure determines the cases with the smallest number of same-valued variables and identical outcome (zones 1 and 2: MDSO pairs) and the cases with the smallest number of different-valued variables and different outcome (zone 3: MSDO pairs).

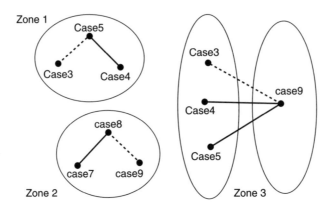

Figure 11.1   Most relevant pairs.

Those variables that are indeed same-valued for MDSO pairs, or different-valued for MSDO pairs (italicized in Table 11.6) are deemed relevant. Within zone 1, considering the number of 0s tells us we should check Case 4 (*Fruit*) against Case 5 (*Council*). Considering only actual case patterns in Table 11.6 gives us a listing of same-valued variables for Case 4 and Case 5, across the five categories.

Within Category A, we have already seen that variable A9 was the only same-valued variable. Categories B and C are not helpful to us because too many variables (at least half of them) are same-valued; categories D and E yield variables D1, D5, D7 and E3.

Extending the check to 0s and 1s, the case pattern for zone 1 also includes Case 3 (*Sugar*), but this does not change anything to the selection of relevant variables.

Table 11.6   Data sorted by case configurations

Cases	Zone 1			Zone 2			Zone 3			
	Case4	Case5	Case3	case7	case8	case9	case9	Case4	Case5	Case3
Outcome	Y	Y	Y	N	N	N	N	Y	Y	Y
Category A										
A1	0	1	0	1	1	1	1	0	1	0
A2	1	0	1	1	1	1	1	1	0	1
A3	0	1	0	0	1	0	0	0	1	0
A4	0	1	0	0	1	0	0	0	1	0
A5	0	1	0	0	0	0	0	0	1	0
A6	1	0	1	0	0	0	0	1	0	1
A7	0	1	0	1	0	1	1	0	1	0
A8	0	1	0	1	0	1	1	0	1	0
A9	0	0	0	1	1	1	1	0	0	0
A10	0	1	0	1	1	1	1	0	1	0
A11	0	1	0	1	1	1	1	0	1	0
Category B										
B1	0	0	0	1	0	0	0	0	0	0
B2	1	0	1	1	1	1	1	1	0	1
B3	0	0	0	0	1	0	0	0	0	0
B4	0	0	0	0	1	0	0	0	0	0
B5	0	0	0	0	1	0	0	0	0	0
B6	0	0	0	0	1	0	0	0	0	0
B7	0	0	0	0	1	0	0	0	0	0

Within zone 2, checking case 7 against case 8 yields variables B2, C1, C2, C5, C11, D4, D6, D8 and D11. Other categories would yield too many variables. Adding case 9 to the case pattern, as suggested by taking into account the aggregate numbers of 0s and 1s reduces relevant variables to: B2, C1, C11, D4, D8 and D11.

Within zone 3, the case pattern contains three cases from scratch: *Fruit* and *Council* are in opposition with *safety*. To be considered as relevant, variables shall be same-valued for *Fruit* and *Council*, and different-valued between those two and *safety*. The only such variable is A9. It remains relevant if we add Case 3 by considering pairs with the same aggregate number of 0s and 1s.

Back to brass-tacks

The MSDO–MDSO procedure is now complete and we can tackle comparative analysis. MSDO–MDSO is not, in itself, a method for understanding cases; it is a method for identifying variables and cases that could be used with most success in explaining the phenomenon under study. Variables that are relevant in several pairs, be they MDSO or MSDO, are of special value. When a small set of relevant variables and relevant cases has been identified, they can be used in classical case analysis, in which the social science researcher's knowledge about the meaning of each variable, and interpretations of the link between variables and outcomes, is essential.

The MSDO–MDSO procedure can also be used as input for a qualitative comparative analysis (QCA)-type analysis. This needs a small set of possible explanatory variables (usually between three and six); when there are so many possible explanatory factors, MSDO–MDSO helps us select the 'right' ones without any preconceived idea.

If two variables seem to explain one MSDO pair, one might wonder whether they're strongly dependent. If they aren't, the difference in outcome needs using both variables for explanation. However, if some value of one variable has as corollary some

value of the other, then the explanation might need only one variable. Looking at the values for those variables in other cases might give us an answer.

The process of 'dialogue between theory and data' is therefore essential. Singling out a small number of variables and looking at what they do in the model can lead to new ideas about its functioning and new variables; these, in turn, could be put into one more round of MSDO–MDSO calculations, to see whether they induce some change ; and so on. This could also create the need for rethinking the partition into categories (see p. 217).

ANOTHER STUDY

In their 1994 paper, Gisèle De Meur and Dirk Berg-Schlosser discuss how political systems in European countries evolved as they were submitted, after WWI, to pressure tending to make them evolve into fascist or authoritarian systems. A 'positive' result would be maintaining a democratic form of government all the way through the interwar period; a 'negative result' would be the advent of some type of dictatorial form of government.

Przeworski and Henry (1970) had found that there were no ideal Mill pairs (see the section 'Most different, same outcome', above and this consideration was seminal in the creation of MSDO–MDSO. They studied a set of eighteen European countries, eight of which had experienced a 'positive' outcome (Sweden, Finland, Belgium, the Netherlands, France, Great Britain, Czechoslovakia and Ireland), while ten had fallen into some form of authoritarianism (Austria, Germany, Italy, Hungary, Romania, Estonia, Portugal, Spain, Greece and Poland).

A set of 61 variables were labelled into seven fairly natural categories: historical facts; socioeconomic indexes; social composition (e.g. ethnical and language minorities); elements of political culture; influence of specific actors (e.g. syndicates, employers' associations, militia); bases of the political systems; foreign elements (e.g. economic dependency, colonial system). Some variables were naturally dichotomic (was the country among the winners or losers of WWI?), whereas others needed a choice of threshold, as is the case for quantitative welfare indexes or the size of the country's population.

Results

MDSO pairs included, for positive cases, Czechoslovakia as opposed to Sweden or Great Britain; and Finland as opposed to any of Great Britain, Ireland, Belgium and the Netherlands. For negative cases, Germany was opposed to Greece, Portugal and Romania, whereas Spain was opposed to Estonia and Greece.

MSDO pairs were: Finland/Germany; Finland/Estonia; Sweden/Estonia; Sweden/Hungary; Ireland/Estonia; Ireland/Hungary; France/Spain; France/Greece; Great Britain/Greece; Czechoslovakia/Austria and Czechoslovakia/Hungary.

If we look, for example, at MDSO 'positive' pairs Czechoslovakia/Sweden and Czechoslovakia/Great Britain, we see that common characteristics include a strong separation of state and church, high gross national product (GNP) and political tolerance. These variables are nominees to the title of relevant variable.

It is now necessary to look back at the cases, to try and understand what these parameters did for preservation of democracy. This is, of course, the Political Science researcher's job. Of special interest are pairs that include Finland. This country is very different, in many aspects, from other 'positive' outcome cases. It is geographically, culturally and historically close to Estonia; yet we have to explain Finland's narrow escape versus Estonia's failure. Variables that distinguish between those countries, while they group together Finland and north-western European countries, will be twice essential. The same holds true of oppositions between Czechoslovakia on one side, and Hungary and Austria on the other.

One important political fact that plays a role in both Finland's and Czechoslovakia's cases is the strong involvement of the state's head in favour of democracy, while Estonia, Hungary and Austria gave free rein to military interventionism. This distinction is present in nearly all MSDO pairs, and should be considered of special importance in the way events unfolded in those countries.

METHODOLOGICAL DISCUSSION AND CONCLUSION

In explaining arguments and methods, we used dichotomized variables, without questioning this choice. This gives an impression of some Manichean world, made of rich and poor, executives and workers, etc.

Dichotomization

Studies with an orientation towards variables usually make use of three kinds of variable: nominal, ordinal and cardinal (numerical). Although the latter are very important in the realm of natural science, they usually distort things when tackling human science. For example, age isn't a linear, explanatory variable: in considering exposure to illnesses, a distribution might be bimodal or even U-shaped; sometimes it isn't even ordinal, e.g. when considering coming of age, retirement. In the same way, nominal variables are sometimes taken as ordinal. When considering age as related to professional activity, it can't be an ordinal variable, given that the top level of activity lies *between* youth and retirement. Using nominal variables therefore allows us to avoid several pitfalls. However, forced dichotomization of all variables might seem excessive. This is especially true of normal (Gaussian) distribution of a continuous variable: where should we place the threshold when most of the weight of the distribution is around the centre?

The generic answer to that problem is to decide, not by looking at the variable's distribution (normal, U-shaped, bimodal) but at its hypothesized relation with the outcome. The real problem is not to split a set of values in two subsets at every cost, but rather to think about the most sense-containing threshold. Choosing as threshold the average, the median, a local minimum, … as such would therefore be a crass error. Taking the case of variable 'age', 'young' and 'old' people would be split quite differently when considering retirement, studies, marriage, motherhood.

MDSO–MSDO isn't able to tackle three-valued variables, like 'yes/no/no opinion' or 'left-wing/ centre/right-wing'. Data will always need reduction, according to the outcome to be explained. For example, 'if we need to look at the influence of a positive statement by some person on the final decision, 'no opinion' will be grouped with the noes.

A fortiori, a ten-valued nominal variable, like socioprofessional category, should be expressed in another way: white collar/blue collar, self-standing/wage earner, once again according to the study's features and necessities.

On the other hand, an ordinal four-valued answer like 'positively/rather /rather not/absolutely not' could be made into two variables, one stating the positive/negative opinion aspect, the second the degree of conviction: 'clear-cut/qualified'. This will hit on the head the 'radicality' nail, which would have been less apparent, possibly even brushed aside, in an ordinal vision.

Categories

Does making categories out of a set of variables contain a large part of arbitrary decision? Our feeling is that grouping variables according to their affinity is best, in order to compare comparable things.

Some variables might be 'in-betweens': is women's preference for liqueur (and men's for dry spirits) inborn, or has it a social component? If it is inborn, variable 'gender' should be put into category 'physiological', else into 'educational'. If doubt remains, one should conduct the study twice, with both configurations.

A website takes charge of the most off-putting part of calculations. It can be reached at: http://www.jchr.be/01.

What if there is a paucity or plethora of remarkable pairs?

The technique above usually cuts down a fair amount of complexity. However, it may happen that too many pairs appear in one configuration. In this case, in lieu of using the second-rank digits from Table 11.5 (giving the number of 0s and 1s), one should only use pairs with the best first-rank digit, that is, taking only 0s in consideration.

Conversely, if one needs a larger number of cases present in the configurations, one could create more pairs by loosening constraints. In lieu of demanding, for each pair, one digit at the best level, one accepts two digits at suboptimal level (of some other number of such digits). Here, we don't create another pair for zone 1, but within zone 2, pair (*noise, waste*), with string 11222; has three submaximal digits compared to the referent string 33333. Adding pair (*noise, waste*) to already given pairs (*gas, waste*) and (*waste, safety*) yields the following configuration (Figure 11.2):

> Within zone 3, with two subminimal digits, we get pairs (*Rice, noise*), (*Sugar, noise*), (*Rice, gas*), (*Fodder, gas*), (*Sugar, gas*), (*Fruit, gas*), (*Council, gas*), (*Council, waste*), (*Rice, safety*). With three, only pairs (*Sugar, noise*), (*Fruit, noise*), (*Rice, gas*), (*Fodder, gas*), (*Sugar, gas*), (*Council, gas*), (*Council, waste*), (*Rice, safety*) would remain. With four, only (*Fruit, noise*), (*Fodder, gas*), (*Council, waste*), (*Rice, safety*).

We see, therefore, new pairs appear on the graph for zone 3 (dotted strokes). Pair (*Rice, safety*) does not help the configuration, as one and only one variable was selected by this configuration. Pair (*Fodder, gas*) is independent of any other and will be dealt with separately. Two new configurations are interesting: *Fruit* versus *noise* and *safety*, and *Council* versus *waste* and *safety*. See Annex 2, which is made up on the basis of those new configurations.

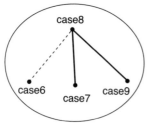

Zone 2

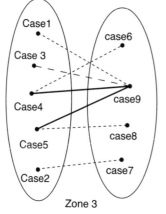

Zone 3

Figure 11.2   Most relevant pairs after loosening constraints

The following question should also be asked: When getting new configurations, do we need to use each and every one of them in the final analysis? For example, one might decide to take new pairs into account only when they graft onto already existing configurations. In that case, pair (*Fodder, gas*) wouldn't be kept.

Note that those techniques may be used independently on the three zones, as they ask three totally different questions, namely comparisons between cases with positive outcomes, between cases with negative outcomes and between cases with different outcome.

As a conclusion, we would like to insist on the flexible features of the procedure: it makes use of several parameters, which aren't predetermined. On the contrary, these should be set during research, possibly even modified thereafter: this is not about manipulating

data but rather adapting tools to data, as if focusing a microscope according to the size of the object under view. Dichotomization thresholds, number of levels to be considered, creation of new pairs from loosening constraints: all those are the researcher's decision.

We purposely declined to give 'automatic decision modes', which would have allowed the user to avoid thinking about the logic of one's choices. We're thoroughly convinced that the discomfort arising from this will be more than compensated by the gain from decisions: more legitimate and more adapted to each application's features.

However, we found it a good idea to make the researcher's job easier by sparing them mechanical calculations as much as possible: a piece of software, both quick and easy to use, which operates selections based on the choices put in by the researcher is available online at: http://www.ulb.ac.be/soco/matsch/

NOTE

1. This so-called 'Hamming distance' is commonly used by computer scientists and gene theorists.

REFERENCES

De Meur, G. and Berg-Schlosser, D. 1994 'Comparing political systems – establishing similarities and dissimilarities' *European Journal for Political Research* 26: 193–219.

De Meur, G., Bursens, P. and Gottcheiner, A. 2006 'MSDO–MDSO revisited for public policy analysis' in *Innovative Comparative Methods for Policy Analysis.* New York: Springer, pp. 67–94.

Mill, J.S. 1843/2002 *A System of Logic.* Honolulu: University Press of the Pacific (1st edition published 1843).

Przeworski, A. and Henry, T. 1970 *The Logic in Comparative Social Inquiry.* New York: Wiley.

Ragin, C.C. 2002 'Préface' in G. De Meur and B. Rihoux (Eds) *L'analyse quali-quantitative comparée (AQQC–QCA), approche, techniques et applications en sciences humaines.* Louvain-la-Neuve: Bruylant Academia.

Ragin, C.C. and Becker, H.S. (Eds) 1992 *What Is a Case? Exploring the Foundations of Social Inquiry.* Cambridge: Cambridge University Press.

ANNEX 1: THE FULL SET OF THE EXAMPLE'S DATA

Our example comes from a study on drawing up modes for nine European directives, with forty-four variables grouped in five categories. It was discussed in De Meur et al. (2006).

1	2	3	4	5	6	7	8	9	Cases: European Directives
T	T	T	T	T	L	L	L	L	Type of configuration: (T = Tight and L = Loose)
									Category A: Formal aspects of the decision-making process
0	0	0	0	1	1	1	1	1	A1 consultation procedure (0) – cooperation/co-decision procedure (1)
1	1	1	1	0	1	1	1	1	A2 protocol based (0) – treaty based (1)
1	1	0	0	1	0	0	1	0	A3 Commission's own initiative (0) – Council based initiative (1)
1	1	0	0	1	0	0	1	0	A4 short preparation (0) – long preparation (1)
0	0	0	0	1	0	0	0	0	A5 consultation of an advisory Committee 0) – no consultation of an advisory Committee (1)
1	1	1	1	0	0	0	0	0	A6 COREPER (0) – Special Committee Agriculture (1)
0	0	0	0	1	0	1	0	1	A7 implementation Committee (0) – no implementation Committee (1)
1	1	0	0	1	0	1	0	1	A8 Qualified Majority Voting (0) – unanimity (1)
0	1	0	0	0	1	1	1	1	A9 short procedure (0) – long procedure (1)
1	1	0	0	1	1	1	1	1	A10 package deal (0) – no package deal (1)
1	1	0	0	1	0	1	1	1	A11 time limit (0) – no time limit (1)
									Category B: Characteristics of the interest groups
0	0	0	0	0	1	1	0	0	B1 large content-related interest (0) – small content-related interest (1)
1	1	1	1	0	1	1	1	1	B2 large institutional interest (0) – small institutional interest (1)
0	0	0	0	0	0	0	1	0	B3 representative groups (0) – also non-representative groups (1)
0	0	0	0	0	0	0	1	0	B4 European umbrella organizations (0) – also non-European umbrella organizations (1)
0	0	0	0	0	0	0	1	0	B5 social-economic groups (0) – also other groups (1)
0	0	0	0	0	1	0	1	0	B6 strong groups (0) – weak groups (1)
0	0	0	0	0	1	0	1	0	B7 organizations (0) – also individual actors (1)
									Category C: Characteristics of the decision-making institutions
1	1	0	0	1	1	1	1	1	C1 closed Commission (0) – open Commission (1)
0	0	0	0	0	1	1	1	0	C2 much expertise inside Commission (0) – little expertise (1)
0	0	0	0	1	1	1	0	1	C3 large content-related interest Commission (0) – small content-related interest Commission (1)
1	1	1	1	0	0	1	0	1	C4 large institutional interest Commission (0) – small institutional interest Commission (1)
1	1	1	1	0	1	1	1	0	C5 much expertise inside European Parliament (0) – little expertise EP (1)
1	1	0	0	0	1	1	0	0	C6 much left–right opposition EP (0) – little left–right opposition EP (1)
1	1	1	1	1	0	1	0	1	C7 much materialism–non materialism opposition EP (0) – little materialism–non materialism opposition (1)
1	1	1	1	1	1	1	0	1	C8 much left–right opposition Council (0) – little left–right opposition Council (1)
1	1	1	1	1	0	1	0	1	C9 large institutional interest Council (0) – small institutional interest Council (1)
0	1	0	0	0	0	1	0	0	C10 much national interest opposition Council(0) – little national interest opposition Council (1)
0	1	0	0	1	0	0	0	0	C11 imminent presidency change Council (0) – no imminent presidency change Council (1)
									Category D: Characteristics concerning the content of the legislative initiative
1	0	1	1	1	1	1	0	1	D1 polarization (0) – no polarization (1)
0	0	1	1	0	1	1	0	1	D2 radical changes (0) – marginal changes (1)
0	0	1	1	0	1	1	0	1	D3 broad scope (0) – small scope (1)
0	0	0	0	1	0	0	0	0	D4 technically difficult (0) – technically easy (1)
1	1	1	1	1	1	1	0	1	D5 spill-over (0) – no spill-over (1)

(Continued)

(*Continued*)

0	1	0	1	0	1	0	0	1	D6 exceptions for member states (0) – no exceptions for member states (1)
0	0	0	0	0	0	1	0	0	D7 social-economic basis (0) – other basis (1)
0	0	1	1	0	0	0	0	0	D8 heavy efforts required (0) – none or light efforts required (1)
0	0	1	1	0	1	1	0	1	D9 basic proposal (0) – complementary proposal (1)
0	0	0	0	1	0	0	1	0	D10 changing proposal (0) – new proposal (1)
1	1	1	1	0	0	0	0	0	D11 directive (0) – regulation (1)
									Category E: Formal aspects of the policy concerned
0	0	0	0	1	1	1	1	1	E1 strong integration (0) – weak integration (1)
1	1	1	1	0	0	0	0	0	E2 young policy sector (0) – old policy sector (1)
0	0	0	0	0	1	1	1	0	E3 social-economic policy sector (0) – other sector (1)
0	0	0	0	1	1	1	1	1	E4 (re)distributive (0) – regulative (1)

ANNEX 2: ENRICHED CASE CONFIGURATIONS

	Zone 2				Zone 3							
Cases:	case7	case8	case9	case6	Case2	case7	Case4	case9	case6	Case5	case9	case8
Outcome	N	N	N	N	Y	N	Y	N	N	Y	N	N
Category A:												
A1	1	1	1	1	0	1	0	1	1	1	1	1
A2	1	1	1	1	1	1	1	1	1	0	1	1
A3	0	1	0	0	1	0	0	0	0	1	0	1
A4	0	1	0	0	1	0	0	0	0	1	0	1
A5	0	0	0	0	0	0	0	0	0	1	0	0
A6	0	0	0	0	1	0	1	0	0	0	0	0
A7	1	0	1	0	0	1	0	1	0	1	1	0
A8	1	0	1	0	1	1	0	1	0	1	1	0
A9	1	1	1	1	1	1	0	1	1	0	1	1
A10	1	1	1	1	1	1	0	1	1	1	1	1
A11	1	1	1	0	1	1	0	1	0	1	1	1
Category B:												
B	1	0	0	1	0	1	0	0	1	0	0	0
B2	1	1	1	1	1	1	1	1	1	0	1	1
B3	0	1	0	0	0	0	0	0	0	0	0	1
B4	0	1	0	0	0	0	0	0	0	0	0	1
B5	0	1	0	0	0	0	0	0	0	0	0	1
B6	0	1	0	1	0	0	0	0	1	0	0	1
B7	0	1	0	1	0	0	0	0	1	0	0	1
Category C:												
C1	1	1	1	1	1	1	0	1	1	1	1	1
C2	1	1	0	1	0	1	0	0	1	0	0	1
C3	1	0	1	1	0	1	0	1	1	1	1	0
C4	1	0	1	0	1	1	1	1	0	0	1	0
C5	1	1	0	1	1	1	1	0	1	0	0	1
C6	1	0	0	1	1	1	0	0	1	0	0	0
C7	1	0	1	0	1	1	1	1	0	1	1	0
C8	1	0	1	1	1	1	1	1	1	1	1	0
C9	1	0	1	0	1	1	1	1	0	1	1	0
C10	1	0	0	0	1	1	0	0	0	0	0	0
C11	0	0	0	0	1	0	0	0	0	1	0	0

(*Continued*)

(*Continued*)

Cases:	Zone 2				Zone 3							
	case7	case8	case9	case6	Case2	case7	Case4	case9	case6	Case5	case9	case8
Outcome	N	N	N	N	Y	N	Y	N	N	Y	N	N
Category D:												
D1	1	0	1	1	0	1	1	1	1	1	1	0
D2	1	0	1	1	0	1	1	1	1	0	1	0
D3	1	0	1	1	0	1	1	1	1	0	1	0
D7	0	0	0	0	0	0	0	0	0	1	0	0
D5	1	0	1	1	1	1	1	1	1	1	1	0
D6	0	0	1	1	1	0	1	1	1	0	1	0
D7	1	0	0	0	0	1	0	0	0	0	0	0
D8	0	0	0	0	0	0	1	0	0	0	0	0
D9	1	0	1	1	0	1	1	1	1	0	1	0
D10	0	1	0	0	0	0	0	0	0	1	0	1
D11	0	0	0	0	1	0	1	0	0	0	0	0
Category E:												
E1	1	1	1	1	0	1	0	1	1	1	1	1
E2	0	0	0	0	1	0	1	0	0	0	0	0
E3	1	1	0	1	0	1	0	0	1	0	0	1
E4	1	1	1	1	0	1	0	1	1	1	1	1

12

The Case for Qualitative Comparative Analysis (QCA): Adding Leverage for Thick Cross-Case Comparison

Benoît Rihoux and Bojana Lobe

INTRODUCTION

When Charles Ragin launched Qualitative Comparative Analysis (QCA) both as an approach and as a technique, it was clear that case-based knowledge was a crucial companion to QCA. Indeed, QCA was conceived as an 'aid to [the] interpretive analysis' of cases (Ragin 1987, p. 120). Thus, before engaging in QCA proper – the formal, computer-run part of it – 'it is necessary to gain familiarity with the relevant theories, the relevant research literature and, *most important of all*, the relevant cases' (Ragin 1987, p. 121; emphasis is ours).

This chapter thus concentrates on the connection between QCA and cases. In particular, we aim at addressing two core questions that are subject to regular debates. On the one hand, does QCA relate to a specific conception of 'what is a case?' (Ragin and Becker 1992) or, alternatively, can researchers with different conceptions of what a case is fruitfully exploit QCA? On the other hand, in concrete terms, how does (or should) the 'dialogue with the cases' be conducted during the successive stages of a QCA procedure? These two questions can be subdivided in several subquestions. Before tackling these, we briefly present QCA as an approach with its specific goals, assumptions and qualities, then as a set of techniques that can be used for different purposes.

A main, over-arching argument in this chapter is that QCA should fundamentally be considered as case oriented, rather than as some middle way between case-oriented and variable-oriented analysis – even though it resorts to variables in its analytic phase.

QCA: A BIRD'S EYE VIEW[1]

QCA[2] designates both an approach (or research strategy) and a set of specific techniques. On the technical side, it is an umbrella term for three specific techniques (see section below). The whole approach, as well as the first technique (crisp-set QCA; csQCA[3]) was launched by Charles Ragin's seminal volume, published in 1987. The purpose of this first section is to offer a short presentation of QCA before addressing the two core questions outlined above.

QCA as an approach

As a research strategy, or as a way to envisage the 'dialogue between ideas and evidence' (Ragin 1987), QCA is first and foremost of *comparative* nature. More precisely: it is (or at least was intended to be, when it was launched; see below) geared towards multiple-case studies, in a small- or intermediate-N research design. As all rigorous empirical comparative approaches, it strives to meet two apparently contradicting goals: gathering in-depth insight in the different cases and capturing the complexity of the cases (gaining 'intimacy' with the cases), and also producing some level of generalization (Ragin 1987).

As discussed throughout in this volume, there is now a renewed interest in case-oriented research (see also Mahoney and Rueschemeyer 2003, George and Bennett 2005, Gerring 2006). There is naturally a quite tight connection between case-oriented research and the number of 'cases' (or units of observation). In social science research, many relevant and interesting objects are naturally limited in number (e.g. collective actors, firms, nation states, regions, policy sectors). In such situations, we face naturally limited or small-N (or intermediate-N) populations. In some other circumstances, when the population of cases is larger, there are still some good reasons for a researcher to pick out a more limited set of cases. Indeed, in comparative research, small- or intermediate-N situations may either be the result of limited

number of cases, or of a deliberate choice of the researcher to select a limited number of cases (De Meur and Rihoux 2002, Tilly 1984).

The problem is that, when it comes to comparing more than, say, two or three cases, in many instances the comparison of the case study material is rather loose or not formalized – hence the scientificity of case studies is often questioned (Gerring 2006). This particularly occurs when such comparisons are conducted *ex post*, and when the collection of the case study material has not been designed to be used for subsequent comparative analysis.

Ragin's intention was to develop an original 'synthetic strategy' as a middle way between the case-oriented or qualitative, and the variable-oriented or quantitative approaches (Ragin 1987, 1997). The goal of this strategy was to 'integrate the best features of the case-oriented approach with the best features of the variable-oriented approach' (Ragin 1987, p. 84). Despite criticism of this statement (e.g. Berg-Schlosser 2004, Swyngedouw 2004), we can take Ragin's initial statement as a starting point, provided some qualifications and nuances are added.

On the one hand, indeed, QCA embodies some key strengths of the qualitative, case-oriented approach (Ragin 1987, Berg-Schlosser et al. 2008). To start with, it is a holistic approach, in the sense that each individual case is considered as a complex entity, as a whole that needs to be comprehended and which should not be forgotten in the course of the analysis. Thus, QCA is in essence a case-sensitive approach. From a mainstream statistical viewpoint, this might be considered as a weakness; quite the contrary, from a qualitativist, case-based perspective; this is a strength of QCA.

Furthermore, QCA develops a conception of causality that leaves room for complexity (Ragin 1987, Berg-Schlosser et al. 2008). In most hard sciences, complexity is neutralized by experimental design – something that is not usually available to us in the social sciences. QCA's strategic response to this is the concept of *multiple conjunctural causation*.

This implies that: (1) most often, it is a combination of conditions (independent or 'explanatory' variables) that eventually produces a phenomenon – the outcome (dependent variable, or phenomenon to be explained); (2) several different combinations of conditions may produce the same outcome; and (3) depending on the context, a given condition may very well have a different impact on the outcome. Thus, different causal paths – each path being relevant, in a distinct way – may lead to the same outcome. Like J.S. Mill, Ragin rejects any form of permanent causality because causality is context- and conjuncture-sensitive. The bottom line is that by using QCA, the researcher is urged not to specify a single causal model that fits the data best, as one usually does with standard statistical techniques, but instead to 'determine the number and character of the different causal models that exist among comparable cases' (Ragin 1987).

On the other hand, QCA indeed embodies some key strengths of the quantitative, or analytic-formalized approach. First, it allows one to analyze more than just a handful of cases, which is seldom done in case-oriented studies. This is a key asset, as it opens up the possibility to produce generalizations. Moreover, its key operations rely on Boolean algebra which requires that each case be reduced to a series of variables (conditions and an outcome). Hence, it is an analytic approach which allows replication (Berg-Schlosser et al. 2008). This replicability enables other researchers to eventually corroborate or falsify the results of the analysis, a key condition for progress in scientific knowledge (Popper 1963). This being said, QCA is not radically analytic, as it leaves some room for the holistic dimension of phenomena. Finally, the Boolean algorithms allow one to identify (causal) regularities that are parsimonious, i.e. that can be expressed with the fewest possible conditions within the whole set of conditions that are considered in the analysis – although a maximum level of parsimony should not be pursued at all costs.

QCA as a set of techniques

In terms of techniques, the label QCA is used as an umbrella term that captures the whole group of them. QCA using conventional Boolean sets (i.e. variables can be coded only '0' or '1', and thus have to be dichotomized) was developed first, which is why the label 'QCA' has been often used to name this first technique. However, the standard practice (following Schneider and Wagemann [2007] and Rihoux and Ragin [2008]) is now to distinguish between four labels: (1) when referring explicitly to the original Boolean version of QCA, we use csQCA (where 'cs' stands for 'crisp set'); (2) when referring explicitly to the version that allows multiple-category conditions, we use mvQCA (where 'mv' stands for 'multi-value'); (3) when referring explicitly to the fuzzy-set version, which also links fuzzy sets to truth-table analysis, we use fsQCA (where 'fs' stands for 'fuzzy set'); and (4) we use fuzzy sets to designate the original fuzzy-set analysis as developed by Ragin (2000, 2008b), the latter technique is the only one which does not implement truth-table analysis.

Below, we present, in short, the main operations of csQCA: basically, this sequence is similar for the three other techniques, with some specificities and enrichments that are too long to present here (see Cronqvist and Berg-Schlosser 2008, Rihoux and De Meur 2008, Ragin 2008a, 2008b). The more formalized steps, based on the formal logic of Boolean or set-theoretic algebra[4] and implemented by a set of computer programs[5], aim at identifying so-called 'prime implicants' in a truth table. The key philosophy of csQCA is to '[start] by assuming causal complexity and then [mount] an assault on that complexity' (Ragin 1987, p. x).

The researcher must first produce a data table, in which each case displays a specific combination of conditions (with 0 or 1 values) and an outcome (with 0 or 1 values). The software then produces a truth table which displays the data as a list of configurations. A configuration is a given combination of some conditions and an outcome. A specific configuration may correspond to several observed cases.

The key following step of the analysis is Boolean minimization; that is, reducing the long Boolean expression, which consists in the long description of the truth table, to the shortest possible expression (the minimal formula, which is the list of the prime implicants) that unveils the regularities in the data. It is then up to the researcher to interpret this minimal formula, possibly in terms of causality.

As a technique, csQCA can be used for at least five different purposes (De Meur and Rihoux 2002, p. 78–80, Berg-Schlosser et al. 2008). First, the most basic use is simply to summarize data, i.e. to describe cases in a synthetic way by producing a truth table, as a tool for data exploration and typology building. This use is basic in the sense that it does not rely on a more elaborate, stepwise design of typology building, such as recently developed by George and Bennett (2005). Second, it can also be used to check coherence within the data: the detection of contradictions allows one to learn more about the individual cases. The third use is to test existing theories or assumptions to corroborate or refute these theories or assumptions – csQCA is hence a particularly powerful tool for theory testing (e.g. Sager 2004, Mahoney and Goertz 2004). Fourth, it can be used to test some new ideas or assumptions formulated by the researcher, and not embodied in an existing theory; this can also be useful for data exploration. Fifth, and finally, csQCA allow one to elaborate new assumptions or theories: the minimal formula ultimately obtained can be interpreted – i.e. confronted with the cases examined – and lead the researcher to formulate new segments of theory. This is probably why csQCA is sometimes referred to as a kind of analytic induction – it is indeed inductive to the extent that it allows the researcher to discover more through a dialogue with the data. However, there is also a significant input of theory in csQCA. For instance, the selection of variables that will be used in the analysis, and the way each variable is operationalized, must be theoretically informed (Berg-Schlosser and De Meur 2008). Arguably, though, a more inductive use of csQCA raises more methodological difficulties than a simple, deductive theory-testing (Ebbinghaus 2005).

csQCA is also a particularly transparent technique insofar as it forces the researcher not only to make choices on his or her own (i.e. the researcher decides, not the computer), but also to justify these choices from a theoretical and/or empirical perspective. At several stages during the course of the procedure, the researcher is confronted with choices. For instance, he or she must decide whether or not to obtain the shortest solution possible, to achieve a maximal level of parsimony. If this choice is made, some cases that exist logically but have not been observed in the data, will be included in the Boolean minimization. In practice, the software will attribute a 0 or 1 outcome value to these logical cases, thus making 'simplifying assumptions' about these cases. However, the researcher might reject this option, privileging complexity over parsimony. One also has to make clear choices as to the way each variable is dichotomized, and as far as the choice of variables is concerned.

Finally, let us note that csQCA allows one to consider phenomena that vary both qualitatively and quantitatively. Both of these phenomena can be operationalized in the conditions and outcome variables used for software treatment (Berg-Schlosser et al. 2008).

REFLECTIONS ON CONCEPTION(S) AND TYPE(S) OF 'CASES' IN QCA

Ragin opted for the label 'qualitative' to indicate that csQCA enables the researcher to analyze phenomena that vary in nature, that are present or absent, and not only in degree (Ragin 2002), that csQCA allows examination of constellations, configurations and conjunctures (Ragin 1987) and, last but not least, that each case is considered as a complex and specific combination of features. Beyond this quite self-evident statement, which conception(s) of cases are best compatible with QCA, if any? Further, which types of cases can be processed with QCA?

Revisiting two dimensions of debate of 'what is a case?'

Ragin (1992, pp. 8–11) suggested two key distinctions to differentiate answers to the question of 'what is a case?'. The first distinction is: are cases primarily conceived as empirical units (a *realist* perspective) or as theoretical constructs (a *nominalist* perspective)? In other words: '*a realist sees cases as either given or empirically discoverable, [whereas] a nominalist sees cases as the consequences of theories or of conventions*' (Ragin 1992, p. 8).

The second distinction is: are cases primarily conceived as specific or as general? In other words: are cases developed in the course of one's research (this is the specific view) and are they thus designations specific, or are they general and '*relatively external to the conduct of research*'? Following the second, *general* perspective, cases basically exist prior to the research and are largely 'given' and recognized as such by the researcher. Conversely, following the first, *specific* perspective, cases have to be 'produced' in the course of the research, and '*what the research subject is "a case of" may not be known until after most of the empirical part of the [research] project is completed*'. Ragin also argues that this distinction partly overlaps with the quantitative–qualitative divide – the quantitative template being more 'general' and the qualitative template being more 'specific' with regards to the conception of cases.

On the first distinction, we would argue that the most straightforward approach of cases from a QCA perspective is the *realist* one. Indeed, for the cases to be selected in a small- or intermediate-N design – even before engaging into the technical part of QCA proper – they need to be identified as distinct empirical 'wholes'. For instance, a comparison of political parties across Europe will, by definition, connect to a 'real

world', whereby the different parties can be differentiated according to their country of origin. Of course, these practical steps of case selection are not a theoretical, as the selection of a specific type of parties (say, Green parties) will have to dwell upon the theoretical literature to define what a 'Green' party is. By forcing the researcher to carefully define the selected cases by a series of attributes – which will allow him or her to differentiate 'cases' (of a given population) versus 'non-cases' (i.e. cases of another type of population) – QCA indeed calls for quite a lot of theoretical qualification.

In engaging in this *realist* perspective for the purpose of QCA, researchers voluntarily choose to simplify the 'real world', for instance by considering that the cases are bounded objects (whereas it is clear that real-life social scientific objects have unclear or disputable boundaries), or by reducing the cases to a set of core condition and outcome variables (for the purpose of formalized comparison through QCA proper), or by considering that 'all cases are equal' (whereas some cases might be substantively more important than others from the researcher's viewpoint; see Platt 1992). One has to accept these (temporary) simplifications because they are needed to perform the technical (analytical) part of QCA – in a way, one is being 'positivist' to some extent, but always being conscious that the actual 'real world' is much more complex.

On the second distinction, probably different positions can be held. For one thing, it depends on the empirical nature of the cases one has to consider. In quite a lot of research situations, the cases are formalized macro-level entities (e.g. countries, institutional systems), or well-identified meso-level entities (e.g. a political organization, a business firm). In such a situation, cases are mostly 'given' and can largely be taken for granted for the next steps. However, if the cases refer more to processes or a rather 'open' system of actors, e.g. a policy process with a given outcome, the cases still have to be constructed, at least to some extent, in the course of the research. This also depends on whether the outcome of interest is unambiguously defined from the outset – if it not so, then cases will be gradually 'discovered' by fine-tuning the outcome, as well as the articulation between the outcome and the conditions. For instance, by iteratively discovering that the key outcome to be explained in Green parties (the initial 'cases') is the occurrence (or non-occurrence) of 'major formal organizational adaptations', Rihoux (2001) is led to define his 'cases' rather as *units of observation*: a given party organization observed during a time period of 2 years before the outcome occurs (or not). This is consistent with the notion that cases are gradually identified in the course of the analysis (Platt 1992, p. 41).

Thus, to conclude with regard to this second dimension: QCA is quite compatible both with the general and the specific perspectives – and with a mix of both, as there is naturally a continuum between these two ideal types.

Which types of case for QCA?

A first way to distinguish types of cases is quite straightforward: following the micro–meso–macro distinction. So far, because QCA has been initially mostly applied in some fields such as historical sociology, comparative politics, policy analysis or management studies, most QCA applications have been geared towards macro- or meso-level phenomena. Even in such applications, this does not mean that more micro-level phenomena are neglected. For instance, as a key determinant of formal organizational adaptation in political parties (a meso-level outcome), Rihoux (2001) identifies factional change or leadership change which has much more to do with small groups dynamics within parties. Similarly, Scouvart et al. (2007) also consider micro-level conditions that impact on the macro-level outcome of deforestation in regions of the Amazon basin.

In the majority of such meso- or macro-level applications, with a few exceptions (e.g. Chanson 2006), the knowledge about cases mostly derives from secondary sources, such as documents, newspapers articles and monograph accounts of other people or reports.

Therefore, this knowledge is limited by contextual restrictions (i.e. a cultural setting, language), especially as quite a few QCA applications are cross-national or cross-cultural. Researchers thus do not possess intimate knowledge about the cases deriving from close interaction with their cases, and fail to acquire an in-depth understanding of the cases and the context surrounding them. Many interpretations of QCA results (of the minimal formulae) are therefore limited.

Some first micro-level applications of QCA have recently been conducted (Lobe 2006, Scherrer 2006), with individuals as the units of analysis. Micro-level cases, namely individuals who possess a certain set of characteristics relevant for a given research, provide an extensive amount of primary information, gathered through multiple sources, qualitative and quantitative. For example, one can conduct a long-term ethnographic observation of a certain community and decide to study the key informants who would be those opinion leaders who impact on the community as a whole. The study would be even more complex if we study key informants across various communities, not taking communities as cases, but rather their most representative and outspoken members. The data about such micro-level cases (i.e. individuals) can be gathered through direct ethnographic interaction with each specific case. Further, in-depth interviews about, say, their personal history, can be conducted. A quantitative survey on their demographic characteristics can also be run, followed by a focus group with a group of such cases, in order to study their interaction and dynamics. Throughout this direct and intensive day-by-day interaction with individual cases, a researcher is able to acquire in-depth knowledge about each one of them. This 'intimate' case knowledge (in Ragin's original sense; see above) about each case enables one to make the interpretations from a relatively privileged position in comparison to most macro- and meso-level QCA applications.

Researchers with a qualitative background who focus on individuals as cases might doubt of the usefulness of QCA, as there is already a broad range of qualitative methods to analyze individuals. The point is that qualitative (e.g. ethnographic) approaches, which are often most appropriate to study individuals, can be supplemented by (or substituted with) QCA for two main reasons. On the one hand, QCA can be used to achieve a systematic comparison across a smaller number of individual cases (e.g. a sample of between 10 and 30 cases) in order to preserve complexity, and yet being as parsimonious as possible and illuminating otherwise often hidden causal paths on a micro level. On the other hand, QCA can complement qualitative interpretive analysis, by offering a certain degree of 'reduction' of rich qualitative data. With QCA, cases can be systematically compared only through a small number of variables (conditions and outcome; see above). The final interpretation can then be a combination of long, narrative-like interpretive accounts, supplemented by a few causal models that were discovered (via QCA) among comparable individual cases.

Whatever the level of the cases, it is useful to clarify the core assumptions made by QCA, as an approach, with regards to the properties of the cases. Two core assumptions probably need to be singled out: complexity and diversity.

The assumption of case complexity was clearly laid out by Ragin in his seminal work (1987): indeed the starting point of the whole QCA enterprise was, first, to recognize the need to gather in-depth insight into different cases and to capture their complexity and, second, to find (through QCA) some 'connections' across cases. In other words: QCA allows one to perform systematic cross-case comparisons, while at the same time giving justice to within-case complexity (Rihoux and Ragin 2008). In short, within-case complexity means that each case is characterized by a large number of components (each case is a bounded system with many constituent parts and a given purpose), that a potentially huge number of factors (or conditions) – both endogenous and

exogenous – could influence the outcome of interest, and that the direction of the influence of individual conditions on the outcome is not so straightforward.

Thus, transforming cases into *config-urations* (a set of conditions leading to a given outcome) is already a vast simplifi-cation of the reality of the cases. And yet complexity remains, because with QCA the conditions are envisaged in a combinatorial way – hence enabling one to model quite a high level of complexity even with only a few conditions (see 'multiple conjunctural causation', above). In other words, QCA techniques strive to achieve some form of 'short' (parsimonious) explanation of a certain phenomenon of interest, while still providing some allowance for causal complexity.

Because of this specific conception of com-plexity and causality, QCA is naturally also geared towards *cross-case diversity* (Ragin 2006); actually, diversity is a companion of complexity. In practical terms, this implies that each 'causal path', no matter how many cases it covers, is potentially meaningful – thus with QCA there is, a priori, no 'deviant' or 'outlier' case, also because QCA has a different, more specific (vs. general) look at causal connections (Ragin and Rihoux 2004, Ragin and Sonnett 2004, Rihoux 2008b).

These assumptions of complexity and diversity are also valid – even more so, possibly – for micro-level cases. Individuals are indeed inherently complex, as every case displays its own physical, psychological, social, economical and political character-istics, each of which intertwines with the others. Further, distinct attitudes, beliefs, behaviour of individual cases add to the initial complexity in macro- and meso-level cases. In other words, what is specific about micro-level cases is that they are not only bounded systems (as meso- or macro-level cases; see above), but they are bounded systems with a self.

Unless one makes very strong assumptions about human behaviour (e.g. assumption of rationality), each individual is, in essence, a system of its own. Because one must, for the purpose of systematic comparison, select individuals who are comparable – while at the same time being unique in his or her way – one should also take on board the assumption of cross-case diversity. For instance, we could consider individual cases of twelve leaders of specific political parties across Europe to examine their impact on the popularity of the party. Are they charismatic persons? Do they possess special leadership and communication skills? Are they very sociable and down-to-earth individuals? Are they very stable and psychologically powerful? Do they interact with their peers more than others? How do they behave in everyday life? Do they have a family? Do they belong to a younger or older generation? What are their values and beliefs? Do they practice what they preach? It is probable that each leader will possess a specific, unique profile.

To sum up these reflections, we may conclude that QCA does not call for one given conception of cases. Different types and conceptions of cases can be taken on board, provided one also takes on two core assumptions: complexity and diversity.

QCA AND CASES: FIFTEEN DIALOGUES ALONG THE WAY

It should by now be quite clear that QCA, as an approach, is largely case oriented. As will be demonstrated below, at virtually every step of the QCA procedure, as a set of techniques, there is a dialogue with the individual cases, whether they are macro-, meso- or micro. The whole process emerges from the cases to which the researcher returns at every successive step of the inquiry.

How does this translate in concrete terms with regards to the QCA techniques and their usage? As cases are inherently complex and as the key enterprise of QCA techniques is to reduce this complexity and reach some level of parsimony, we may take this complexity/parsimony continuum as a guiding rail for our reflection. If we look at the whole process of QCA, as a first approximation, we can represent this process as a 'funnel of complexity' (Figure 12.1).

Indeed, there are three main phases in a QCA procedure, and each one of these corresponds to some evolution along the

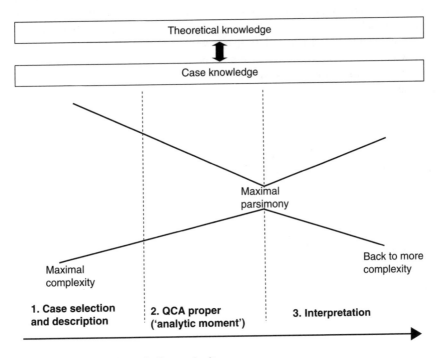

Figure 12.1   QCA and the funnel of complexity.

complexity/parsimony continuum. In the first phase (case selection and case description), the complexity is maximal as the user must, for each case considered, produce a case description (or case report). By definition, this case description contains (or should contain) at least some amount of 'thick', historical information on the case, also relating to some of its specificities (cultural, etc.). However, by producing standardized case descriptions, and thus by entering a comparative template, one already diminishes the level of complexity – one begins to synthetize the 'thick' case information. In the second phase, through the various technical steps of QCA proper – the 'analytic moment' – one further diminishes the level of complexity. Selecting conditions (variables), summarizing the information in numerical scores, then performing all the steps to finally obtain the minimal formulae: at each one of these steps, one gains further parsimony. The maximal level of parsimony is therefore obtained at the end of the analytic, computer-aided part of QCA. Finally, in the third phase, the different 'causal paths' obtained through the minimal formulae are interpreted, which necessitates a 'return to the cases' and to their narratives, and thus a move back to more complexity.

Relative merits of this 'back and forth' dynamic within a research design were already recognized more than a decade ago (Fielding and Fielding 1986, Eckert 1987, Phelan 1987, Greene et al. 1989, Greene and Caracelli 1997). This was further refined with the formalization of a 'feedback loop' logic by Lobe (2006, 2008), in a mixed methods research design which is easily applied in connection with QCA (see below). Considering QCA beyond simple analysis and looking at its multi-cycled dialogue with each case, we can clearly see that the whole process is actually a thorough combination of qualitative and quantitative sources about the case.

The summary in Figure 12.1 is correct, but the picture is not fine-grained enough to illustrate this multi-cycled interaction with each case, as these three phases can be divided in many more concrete operations, and also as

it does not make justice to the fundamentally iterative nature of QCA. Further, it does not make explicit *how* and *at what stages precisely* a 'dialogue' with the cases is requested. This will be the purpose of the next sections.

Four practical notes must be made here. First, for reasons of space, we shall mainly focus the argument on csQCA – but naturally all the csQCA steps also apply to other QCA techniques. Second, the emphasis will be laid on the more frequent research design for QCA, namely small- or intermediate-N research, with a relatively low number of cases. This is not to say that larger-N applications cannot be conducted (see, e.g. Ishida et al. 2006). Third, many of the points discussed below are in line with and are usefully complemented by the QCA 'good practices' which have been recently laid out (Wagemann and Schneider 2007, Rihoux and Ragin 2008). Fourth, for the purpose of illustration, we shall use two particular 'real-life' applications: an analysis of the determinants of major organizational reforms in West European Green parties (Rihoux 2001) and an analysis of the conditions of community conflict escalation and de-escalation in post-WWII Europe (Rihoux et al. 2008[6]). A few other published applications will also be referred to for some particular points.

In all, we have listed a sequence of fifteen well-identified practical operations – five operations in each one of the three main phases outlined above (and in Figure 12.1).

Before the 'analytic moment'

1. Comparative research design and case selection

Naturally, case selection in QCA does not equate with a statistics-style 'sampling' procedure, as every case must be selected purposefully (Ragin 2004, Ragin and Rihoux 2004, Berg-Schlosser and De Meur 2008). In most QCA designs, one selects cases that display some common background features (thereby controlling for those features in a quasi-experimental way; see, e.g. Lijphart

[1971, 1975], Collier [1993]), and that display some variation on some aspects – those that will be the variables (conditions and outcome) in the model. This already necessitates at least *some* 'thick' within-case knowledge. Note that this first operation is also tightly connected to operation nr.3 (defining the outcome), because the choice of 'meaningful' features (constants or variables) will depend on the research question – and therefore on the outcome of interest – and because the cases also have to be selected in order to ensure some variation in the outcome.

In a small- or intermediate-N design, the delineation of the 'population' of comparable cases is often not so straightforward. A crucial problem to tackle is that of 'borderline cases' – for each one of these, the user will have to make an informed decision on whether the case is 'in' or 'out' of the population. For instance, the French environmentalist party of the 1990s *Génération Ecologie* is not a 'Green' party proper, and the Roma issue in Hungary, Slovakia and the Czech Republic displays some profound specificities (e.g. it is a non-territorial conflict; the contours of the 'community' are not clear, etc.), which make comparison impossible with other 'community conflicts' broadly defined within Europe. To make those two qualifications, one needs some level of within-case knowledge.

Finally, it should be noted that the list of cases for the QCA remains open – it could still be modified and fine-tuned at further stages.

2. Gaining case knowledge

This phase is naturally intertwined with the previous one. There are many different data-collection strategies and methodologies, which cannot be discussed at length here. It is certainly a challenge to gain enough 'intimacy' with each case if one works on, say, twenty or thirty cases. Actually, in QCA, there is always a certain trade-off between the number of cases considered (breadth) and the degree of intimacy gained with each individual case (depth). This operation is even more difficult if one studies cases in different cultural contexts (e.g. cross-national

comparison), with sources in different languages and of different quality. One option is then to rely on case experts (a different expert for each case), but even in such a strategy, the person(s) who will perform QCA properly should become really well acquainted with each individual case.

In short, we can say that different methods apply for different levels of cases. At the macro and meso levels, multiple sources of data and evidence must usually be 'crossed': existing case studies, official statistical data, textual data (e.g. from various documents, publications, newspapers), archival records, surveys, etc. Expert interviews can also be conducted in some cases to gain further knowledge from an actor perspective. In his analysis of strategic changes in business firms, Chanson (2006) went further: he not only conducted interviews of key players (other example: Rihoux et al. 2008), but he also resorted to on-site, direct observation to get a first-hand grip of the 'field' of each firm. At the micro level, with individuals as cases, one quite naturally shifts to more qualitative methods. Participant observation, in-depth interviews, direct observation, testimonials, narratives and focus groups can be conducted. At this level, it is important to establish a direct connection with each case (each individual): observing their practices, spending time with them, interviewing them, studying their online appearance if applicable (through blogs, forums, personal web pages, etc.).

3. Defining the outcome of interest

At first sight, defining the outcome of interest would seem to stem more from theory and the research question and less from the cases. However, the cases also play a key role here – outcome definition should be case informed as well as theory informed. For instance, Scouvart et al. (2007) build upon Scouvart's on-site observation of the cases, subregions with settlers in the Amazon basin, to define and operationalize the speed of deforestation (her outcome of interest), moving away from a simple, quantitative measure. In another application, Rihoux (2001) uses theory to define what a 'major' (as opposed to minor) organizational reform is for a political party (using Panebianco's [1988] theory). However, the fine-tuning of the definition of the outcome, and its connection with some potential conditions, could only be achieved by mobilizing a deeper case knowledge, e.g. observing that, in Green parties, formal rules play a more important role for the party activists, as compared to other parties, and thus deciding to focus specifically on *formal* organizational reforms.

As explained above, this step is tightly linked with case selection. In some events, the user might discover that the outcome does not vary for some cases. For instance, in their study of community conflict escalation in Europe (outcome [1], vs. de-escalation as outcome [0]), Rihoux et al. (2008) found out that, in some countries, the outcome seems to be non-relevant, as there is neither escalation nor de-escalation (the conflicts never escalate, e.g. Belgium and Estonia). However, these cases were kept for further analyses, with an alternative definition of the outcome, conflict 'non-escalation' becoming the outcome [1].

4. Model specification: selection of conditions

The way this phase is conducted depends on the use of QCA. If it is mostly used for theory testing, naturally, theories provide the key 'ingredients'. However, so as to decide whether the theory to be tested is applicable to the cases under scrutiny, one must also rely on case knowledge. For instance, for the explanation of organizational reforms in Green parties, some segments of Harmel and Janda's theory (1994) are not really applicable because they specifically apply to larger parties or to parties with a particular orientation of primary goals. This example shows that, even in a deductive use of QCA, there can be some dose of induction and case input. Incidentally, if one develops a more complex model – such as the 'two-step' model advocated by Schneider and Wagemann (2006), in which one differentiates 'remote' and 'proximate' conditions – some key qualifications could also be made relying on case expertise.

Conversely, if QCA is mostly used for exploratory purposes, or for simple synthesis, or for theory building (or conjecture building), then cases play a central role. Chanson (2006) has pursued a fully 'case-driven' strategy for model specification in his study of nine major business firms. First, he gathers some in-depth historical information on each case through in-depth interviews of key firm managers. Second, for each case, he elaborates a 'reputational' list of all the factors (potential conditions for QCA) that were said (by the interviewees) to have had an impact on the 'story' leading to the outcome (occurrence/ non-occurrence). Third, and last, he constructs an inclusive model: if a condition is mentioned in at least one case, it is added to the model that results in quite a long model with eighteen conditions.

Note that, whatever the use of QCA, if there are too many conditions for few cases, if one wants to reduce the number of conditions by aggregating them, one can proceed in a theory- and/or case-driven way. For instance, Rihoux (2001) was able to aggregate different conditions pertaining to variation of organizational size (budget, staff, dues-paying members) into one single condition, because he could demonstrate – in a case-informed way – that those conditions basically follow the same trends. There is also a specific technique to diminish the number of conditions, called MSDO/MDSO, which can also be used in a case-informed way (De Meur and Berg-Schlosser 1994, 1996, Berg-Schlosser and De Meur 2008).

5. Visualizing/synthetizing cases and the models

One useful step, intermediate even before engaging in QCA proper (the computer-run part) is to synthetize the cases so as to get a better, global view of each one of them. One way to do this is to elaborate graph-like 'synthetic case descriptions' (SCDs; Rihoux et al. 2008; see also Rihoux 2001, Yamasaki 2007). In their basic form, SCDs consist of a time line with a graphical display, along this time line, of the key trends and changes on the outcome *and* on all the individual conditions for the whole period considered (one line for each variable). This proves to be a really useful 'semi-simplification', as a form of visual summary that still portrays complexity but in which only the key elements, changes and trends are made visible. Compiling and observing the SCDs, the user can already, intuitively, grasp some cross-case commonalities, some core differences, as well as some puzzling case profiles.

The key point here is that SCDs allow one to grasp more intuitively, on one single graph, the unfolding of each case as a whole. They also help the user, following a more inductive and case-informed logic, to make some choices on how to tackle the temporal articulation between the conditions and the outcome. For instance, Rihoux (2001), observing the temporal articulation between some 'stimuli' (conditions) and the outcome of interest, was able to choose a time span of 2 years as an informed rule of thumb, also because this could be justified from a more qualitative observation of the actual processes of organizational reforms in Green parties.

During this first main phase, we have thus demonstrated that it is possible and useful to engage the dialogue between each step and case knowledge. Following the logic of feedback loops and cycling (Lobe 2008), these dialogues can be defined as 'analytic cycling', moving back and forth to improve the analytic model before entering the analytic, computer-aided part. In this first phase, the combination between qualitative and quantitative data that can be collected with various qualitative, quantitative and mixed methods and contributes to case knowledge, has to be given special attention. Of course, using multiple data sources tends to improve the validity of the QCA model.

The 'analytic moment': synthesis and minimization

This second main phase corresponds to the computer-aided part, with TOSMANA and/or FSQCA. Note that, most often, this is not the most labour-intensive phase – it is rather the previous phase, 'upstream', that is most

time-consuming. However, the analytic phase of synthesis and minimization also has a lot to gain from case knowledge – precisely that case knowledge and 'intimacy' which has been patiently gathered during the previous phase.

6. Dichotomization: threshold-setting

Concrete guidelines on how to dichotomize conditions and the outcome cannot be discussed here (for details, see Rihoux and De Meur 2008). Let us rather focus on one key 'good practice': threshold-setting should not be performed mechanically and should rather rely on informed judgement, theory-and/or case-driven. Therefore (within-)case knowledge also plays a crucial role here, especially because, in the social sciences at least, purely theory-informed cut-off points are seldom undisputed. For instance: in the study of community conflicts in Europe, Rihoux et al. (2008) decide that a community conflict dimension (e.g. religious, territorial, demographic) is coded as 'salient' (score of [1] on that condition) only if this dimension is highly salient in the policy discourse *and* in the actual political initiatives. This operationalization was drawn from historical, 'thick' case knowledge, observing the processes of conflict escalation and de-escalation in the specific cases.

7. Truth-table exploration and contradiction solving

Before performing the core QCA operation (minimization; see below), it is often useful to examine the truth table, at least in two ways. First, in a more descriptive fashion, the way the cases are clustered in configurations (with a [1] or a [0] outcome) can be instructive, as the cases in the same configuration (provided it is non-contradictory; see right below) are 'logically equivalent' from the perspective of the QCA software. The user can then 'discover' that two or more cases which were apparently different (e.g. in different countries and in a different period) are actually quite similar in their core features. The narratives of these cases can then be examined in a comparative way, in a more descriptive use of QCA (see different uses of QCA, above).

Second, and probably more crucially, one must solve the so-called 'contradictory configurations' before proceeding further. These are configurations whose outcome is, in some cases, equal to [1] and in some cases equal to [0], while displaying the same values on the conditions. Among several possible strategies (Rihoux and De Meur 2008), two key strategies are fundamentally case driven. On the one hand, one can re-examine in a 'thick', historical way the cases are involved, and check whether the cases are really so proximate on each and every variable (the conditions as well as the outcome), which in turn might lead the user to reconsider the way some conditions (and/or the outcome) have been dichotomized.

On the other hand, in this process of systematically reconsidering clusters of cases, one may 'discover' some factor that had not been taken into account. This might lead one to add one more condition, thereby further enriching the model. One might also discover that a given case really lies 'at the margin' of the considered population of cases – it could eventually be dropped for the further steps. For instance, Rihoux (2001) found out that one reason why the Swiss Green Party was always involved in contradictory configurations was that Swiss party organizations are fundamentally confederal in nature, and therefore that most crucial evolutions take place at the cantonal level (the federal party being more of an 'empty box'). Given the fact that the outcome of interest was examined at the national/federal level in the comparative analysis, it was decided to drop the Swiss case. Thus, contradiction solving is actually a very useful heuristic device in the dialogue between QCA and 'thick' case knowledge; in this example, it also helps the user to loop back to the phase of case selection.

8. Minimization and logical remainders

For the core step of Boolean minimization, one key decision is to take into account or not the 'logical remainders' that enable one to obtain a more parsimonious minimal formula.

If one chooses for the radical strategy of allowing the software to exploit *all* useful logical remainders (so as to obtain the most parsimonious minimal formula possible), no particular 'return to the cases' is requested. However, if one opts for the 'intermediate solution', i.e. a minimal formula derived with the aid of only those logical remainders that are consistent with the researcher's theoretical and substantive knowledge (see Ragin and Sonnett 2004, Ragin 2008a), one must go back to the cases and, on that basis, decide which logical remainders will be used by the software. Quite often, as most social science theories are relatively 'soft' (see above), one must also rely on one's case expertise to make statements on non-observed cases – in the form : 'considering the cases I have observed so far, if I were to observe a case with such and such values on the conditions, I would *rather* expect the outcome value to be [1] (or [0])'.

9. Solving 'contradictory simplifying assumptions'

When one performs, separately and with the inclusion of logical remainders, the minimization for the [1] outcome configurations and the minimization for the [0] outcome configurations, the danger is that one could make 'contradictory simplifying assumptions' (CSAs). In short, a CSA occurs when the same logical remainder is used both in the minimization of the [1] outcome configurations and in the minimization of the [0] outcome configurations, thereby making two contradictory assumptions regarding the outcome value of that logical remainder.

In such a situation, the strategy to be advocated is exactly the one outlined above with regards to the solving of contradictory configurations (see above, step 7), as one must also 'orientate' (in terms of outcome value) those problematic logical remainders (see Rihoux 2001, Vanderborght and Yamasaki 2004). In their analysis of the factors explaining why the policy of 'basic income' reaches (or not) the political decision-making agenda, Vanderborght and Yamasaki bump into this difficulty. By orientating a few key CSAs (using their case knowledge), they are actually able to obtain a more elegant *and* meaningful minimal formula. This shows how fruitful a 'return to the cases' can be at that stage. Eventually, one must run again the minimization procedure, once again checking for CSAs, and so on until no CSAs remain – thus it is an iterative process.

10. Minimization: arbitrating between (terms of) minimal formulae

Quite often, there is more than one minimal formula; or rather, at some stage of the minimization procedure, the software cannot arbitrate between some alternative terms (combinations of conditions) because they are equally 'short' (parsimonious). Once again, the user must intervene and select those terms that 'make more sense'. This can be a theory-driven process, but most often one must crucially rely on 'thick'-case expertise – especially as those terms to be arbitrated between usually concern a particular subgroup of cases. For instance, in the final QCA tests on community conflict escalation (outcome [1]), the researchers had to arbitrate between equally 'short' combinations of conditions for the case of Cyprus in the 1950s to the 1970s (strong escalation). Consulting case experts, Rihoux et al. (2008) decided to concentrate on those combinations that included decolonization processes, because considering the Cyprus case such 'external' factors (the end of the British rule, and its consequences) played a quite crucial role in the escalation.

Thus, during the successive steps of this second main phase, one can cycle back and forth either all the way back to the previous main phase (e.g. gaining case knowledge, or reconsidering some of the conditions and the QCA model) or cycle within this phase (e.g. when solving contradictory simplifying assumptions, one can cycle back and forth to the truth table, excluding or fine-tuning some problematic conditions).

Downstream: interpretation

It should be stressed that the analytic (computer-aided) part of QCA is only one step in the QCA process; a series of crucial operations must still be performed, otherwise the whole point of QCA is missed and, once again, 'returning to the cases' plays a central role.

11. Factoring out conditions in the minimal formulae

Quite often, it is possible to further 'summarize' (*note*: not to make more parsimonious, because no element is taken out) the minimal formula given by the computer. In substance, one can consider the minimal formula as a standard linear algebraic equation and factor out some conditions to make them more visible. There are at least two types of criteria to decide on which condition(s) to single out this way: more technical criteria (e.g. which condition is present in the largest number of terms of the minimal formula? Which condition, if singled out, 'covers' the largest number of cases?) and more theory- or case-informed criteria.

As an example of a case-informed strategy to factor out conditions, Rihoux (2001) has factored out the 'factional change' condition because, according to the 'real-life' cases and processes he had observed (Green parties in Europe), it is so that factional change often acts as a catalyst, which is thus more 'proximate' to the occurrence of the outcome, namely major organizational reform.

12. Case-by-case interpretation

Beyond the minimal formulae, one must still provide interpretations – by 'interpretation', in the broad sense, we mean asking more focused 'causal' questions about ingredients and mechanisms producing (or not) an outcome of interest. By definition, interpretation is case oriented, because QCA is precisely conceived as a lever to better understand purposefully selected cases (Curchod et al. 2004). Actually, there are not one but three distinct ways to interpret the minimal formulae, from the narrowest to the broadest in scope: case-by-case interpretation, cross-case interpretation and 'limited historical' generalization.

The first, case-by-case type of interpretation is quite straightforward: we re-examine some 'thick', individual case narratives, using the core conditions indicated by the QCA minimal formula. To use an metaphor: each case is a 'black box', and the QCA minimal formula acts like a flashlight which indicates some precise spots to be looked at to better understand the outcome. One way to do this, among many others, is to translate the various conditions in the minimal formula (and leading to a given outcome of interest) into a 'causal' narrative. Note that if the same term of a given minimal formula applies to different cases, it could very well be that the same combination of conditions should be translated into *different* narratives (e.g. different sequences of these conditions) for the different cases.

13. Interpreting cross-case patterns

The logic of this step is basically the same as in the previous one, but in an extended way. The researcher strives to identify similarities (or contrasts) across the 'thick' case narratives, building on the terms of the QCA minimal formula; typically, those cases that are clustered in connection with a given parsimonious term are examined in parallel. Thus, with QCA (the technical part of it) as a heuristic help, we are able to make sense out of 'multiple-case narratives', i.e. to identify common (bits of) narratives across several cases. This is a rejoinder to Abbott's views on the comparison of case narratives (1992, p. 72). This way of proceeding is also actually quite similar to 'thick' binary comparison, with one key difference: QCA helps us make *several* such 'local' (e.g. binary), 'thick' comparisons across small groups of cases.

By engaging in these cross-case, focused comparative interpretations, we not only discover common (bits of) narratives across cases, but also some other, unsuspected elements that were not comprised in the QCA model. For instance, Rihoux (2001) discovered that the German, Belgian and Austrian Greens shared some core elements in their respective narratives leading to a major organizational reform. This led him to ponder

on whether some other factors were at play, e.g. in terms of cross-national diffusion – the influence of the German Greens' experience of reforms on two also quite institutionalized and geographically and/or culturally proximate parties. In the Rihoux et al. QCA of community conflicts, the same combination of escalating factors often comes up in former Yugoslavia (e.g. Kosovo), at different historical stages of escalation – leading the researchers to reflect on the possible role of collective memory of previous violent periods (this memory being instrumentalized by 'community entrepreneurs') as a key catalyst for renewed escalation.

14. 'Limited historical' generalization

This further step goes beyond the observed cases – it is also some form of interpretation of moving beyond what is immediately perceived. In more concrete terms, a well-executed QCA should go beyond plain description, and QCA results could be used in support of 'limited historical generalization' (Ragin 1987, p. 31). More specifically, from a systematic comparison of comparable cases, it is possible to formulate propositions that we can then apply, with appropriate caution, to other similar cases – that is, cases that share a reasonable number of features with the cases that were the subject of the QCA – which are sufficiently close to the initial 'homogeneity space' of the observed cases. Note that this view on generalization is much more modest than statistical inference which allows very broad generalizations (from a sample of, say, a few hundred respondents of a survey to a population of millions of individuals).

The question to be asked is: which other cases could be a case for the same 'demonstration' as the cases included in the QCA? For instance, Rihoux (2001) suggested that his core findings could be expanded, beyond the case of Green parties strictly defined, to other Left-Libertarian and New Left parties (e.g. 'Red–Green' parties in Scandinavia), because the latter are also smaller, 'amateur–activist' parties, with a particular sociodemographic profile of activists, even though their ideological proximity with the

Greens is not always so obvious. However, he argued that his results could not be generalized further to smaller, growing activist parties in previous historical periods (e.g. the Socialists in the early twentieth century), because the whole political context and the internal features of those parties were too distant from the Greens. Note that such a process of modest generalization is mainly supported by historical case knowledge.

15. Cumulation

QCA techniques are particularly transparent. They demand that the researcher, at virtually all stages of the analysis, acts with transparency in his or her choices – selecting variables, processing them, choosing tools for the analysis, intervening during the analysis and so on. During this process, as has been amply demonstrated above, the researcher regularly refers back to the cases, with all their richness and specificity. This back-and-forth dialogue with the cases, combined with the transparency of choices, is unquestionably a virtue of QCA techniques. What also makes this transparency possible is that the formal language used by the software takes its inspiration from principles used in everyday life and, for this reason, can be more easily understood by non-specialists.

Because of those features, QCA is very well suited for cumulation. Namely: it is possible for other researchers, taking a given QCA analysis as a starting point, to 're-visit' this analysis, for instance taking a few cases out or bringing a few cases in, adding one or two conditions, changing the way some conditions have been dichotomized, etc. In doing so, those other researchers might dwell upon their own knowledge of some specific cases. Because QCA is a case-sensitive technique (De Meur et al. 2008), the result of these other analyses will most probably yield some different minimal formulae – at least partly different, which in turn will further enrich cross-case interpretation (see step 13).

To sum up: towards the end of this third and last phase, we can cycle between the steps within that phase, looping between case-to-case interpretation and interpretation

of cross-case patterns. More importantly, we once again loop back to the initial case knowledge in order to make meaningful and case-based interpretations of the minimal formulae.

CONCLUSION

We hope to have demonstrated that QCA, both as an approach and as a set of techniques, is centrally concerned with cases, and that 'thick' a case-based knowledge plays a key role in the practical procedures. Even more so: the 'dialogue' between QCA and cases is (or should be) continuous, at each and every step of the whole process, both before ('upstream'), during and after ('downstream') the analytic, computer-aided part of the analyses.

More precisely, many 'returns to the cases' are needed, each time for a clear purpose. This is also what makes QCA techniques fundamentally iterative, and also often labour-intensive, which, from a case-oriented perspective, should rather be seen as a strength. Those returns to the cases often lead the researcher to 'loop back' to previous steps in the analysis, because the look back at the cases reveals that some prior choice (e.g. the selection of a given case or the operationalization of a given condition) needs to be modified. Hence we are now able to revise and complete Figure 12.1, displaying the fifteen core operations, as well as the main 'feedback loops' back to previous steps, most often by means of a return to the cases (Figure 12.2).

Observation of Figure 12.2, as well as a careful consideration of the text above, indicates that a serious return to the cases must at least be conducted at three or four crucial steps of the analysis, and even, ideally, at each one of the fifteen steps. Naturally, a return to the cases is time-consuming and work-intensive, so the researcher should consider the 'cost' and potential 'benefits' of each return to the cases. If a problem can be solved without re-examining some cases (e.g. by relying mostly on theory), it is perfectly

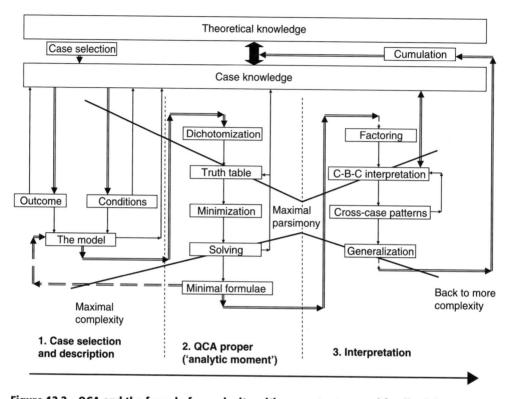

Figure 12.2   QCA and the funnel of complexity with concrete steps and feedback loops.

acceptable as long as the argumentation is correct and clearly laid out.

Figure 12.2 also reminds us vividly that, far from being a push-button-type technique, the use of QCA is (or should be) a fundamentally iterative and creative process. This is in line with current methodological preoccupations, at least in the field of comparative analysis: there is a concern that some techniques (typically: mainstream statistical techniques) are being too frequently used in a mechanical, push-button type. By contrast, the philosophy of QCA is that the researcher should play a more active role, that he or she should interact more actively with the cases and also with the software tools.

The logic of iterations and feedback loops we have repeatedly discussed here also means that QCA can naturally be combined/ sequenced with several other techniques, be they more 'qualitative' or 'quantitative'. In this chapter, we have mostly laid the emphasis on qualitative aspects (e.g. returning

to the cases and considering their historical narratives), but quantitative tools can also be useful (e.g. using a clustering technique to modify the dichotomization of a given condition, etc.). The bottom line is that, by design, and also in practical terms, QCA fits quite well into a 'mixed methods' design (Lobe 2006, 2008, Rihoux and Ragin 2008).

This chapter has also tried to demonstrate that the potential of QCA is quite broad, beyond mainstream QCA applications so far, i.e. examining a small- or intermediate-N of macro- or meso-level cases. Some micro-level cases are now beginning to be fruitfully analyzed with QCA. This raises particular challenges, but we see no reason why more micro-level applications should not develop in the future, especially since – as we have demonstrated – it is possible for a researcher to gain a very good knowledge of each particular micro-level case. In this sense, a bridge could possibly be built between QCA and 'ethnographic case studies' that *'begin and end with the individual and his or her small group'* (e.g. Harper 1992, p. 147).

As for larger-N applications, at whatever level (macro-, meso- or micro-level cases), our view is more critical. The practical difficulty is that it is simply not feasible to gain in-depth case knowledge with each individual case in a large-N research design. Indeed, large-N design is more focused on *categories* of cases (typically: groups of respondents in a survey), not *individual* cases. We can, indeed, gain more insight into some quantitative, larger-N datasets by using QCA or linked techniques such as fuzzy sets (e.g. Ragin 2006), but then the goal of the QCA is displaced. If 'thick', individual cases are the core starting point – this was indeed a chief preoccupation of Ragin when he launched QCA in his seminal volume – then the template discussed in this chapter is only applicable if one engages in small- or intermediate-N research.

In conclusion: much can still be done to improve the 'dialogue with the cases' in QCA, in real-life applications. There are many avenues for further improvements. One such improvement could come from the side of research practices. In this chapter, we have only considered the usual practice, i.e. an *individual* researcher engaging into QCA to gain leverage in his or her within- and cross-case knowledge. Perhaps a qualitative leap could be achieved if we could, in real-life projects, create cohesive networks of case-specific experts, who could then engage in more collective QCA applications. These case experts would follow exactly the same template and would be consulted by the coordinator (who would perform the technical QCA steps) at many stages, to make some arbitrations and perform some 'feedback loops' together, in a coherent way. Some recent QCA applications have attempted to make some steps in that direction.[7] Such collective efforts are assuredly difficult research enterprises, but they could pave the way, with the leverage of QCA, for *collective* cross-case knowledge.

NOTES

1. For overviews of QCA, see Rihoux (2006; 2008a; 2008b). For more detailed information, see the textbook edited by Rihoux and Ragin (2008), as well as Schneider and Wagemann (2007).

2. QCA first existed as a single technique, using dichotomous data. It is now referred to as 'csQCA' (crisp-set QCA), one among different techniques (Rihoux and Ragin 2008). See the next section.

3. Previously known as QCA; see footnote 2.

4. For an accessible presentation of key elements of Boolean logic and operations, see Ragin (1987). For details on using the software for analysis, see Rihoux and De Meur (2008), Schneider and Wagemann (2007), as well as the COMPASSS resource site: http://www.compasss.org.

5. Two main free-access software programs are being developed. FSQCA is available at http://www.compasss.org and at http://www.u.arizona.edu/~cragin/QCA.htm, and performs csQCA as well as fsQCA. TOSMANA performs csQCA and mvQCA, with some additional features. It is available at http://www.compasss.org and at http://www.tosmana.net/. Some other efforts are under way, such as the development of a QCA module in the 'R' and stata package.

6. For this example (in the PEACE-COM project, EU FP6 funding), in the course of the QCA the core substantive (case) expertise was provided by Elise Féron, whom we thank for this.

7. For example, the 'inter-war project' (Berg-Schlosser and Mitchell 2003), the data from which is being re-analyzed in the Rihoux and Ragin textbook (2008), or the PEACE-COM project (Rihoux et al. 2008).

REFERENCES

Abbott, A. 1992 'What do cases do? Some notes on activity in sociological analysis' in C. Ragin and H. Becker (Eds) *What Is a case? Exploring the Foundations of Social Inquiry.* Cambridge: Cambridge University Press, pp. 53–82.

Berg-Schlosser, D. 2004 'Review of: L'analyse quali-quantitative comparée (AQQC-QCA), by G. De Meur and B. Rihoux 2002 Louvain-la-Neuve: Academia Bruylant' *European Sociological Review* 20(2): 162–165.

Berg-Schlosser, D. and De Meur, G. 2008 'Comparative research design: case and variable selection' in B. Rihoux and C. Ragin (Eds) *Configurational Comparative Methods. Qualitative Comparative Analysis (QCA) and Related Techniques.* Thousand Oaks, CA: Sage.

Berg-Schlosser, D. and Mitchell, J. 2003 *Authoritarianism and Democracy in Europe, 1919–39. Comparative Analyses.* Hampshire, UK: Palgrave Macmillan.

Berg-Schlosser, D., De Meur, G., Rihoux, B. and Ragin, C.C. 2008 'Qualitative comparative analysis (QCA) as an approach' in B. Rihoux and C. Ragin (Eds) *Configurational Comparative Methods. Qualitative Comparative Analysis (QCA) and Related Techniques.* Thousand Oaks, CA: Sage.

Chanson, G. 2006 *Contributions a l'étude des déterminants de la décision d'externalisation. Une analyse dans le secteur de l'édition scolaire.* Unpublished doctoral dissertation, IAE, Lille.

Collier, D. 1993 'The comparative method' in A.W. Finifter (Ed.) *Political Science: The State of the Discipline (II).* Washington: American Political Science Association, pp. 105–119.

Cronqvist, L. and Berg-Schlosser, D. 2008 'Multi-value QCA (MVQCA)' in B. Rihoux and C. Ragin (Eds) *Configurational Comparative Methods. Qualitative Comparative Analysis (QCA) and Related Techniques.* Thousand Oaks, CA: Sage.

Curchod, C., Dumez, H. and Jeunemaître, A. 2004 'Une étude de l'organisation du transport aérien en Europe: les vertus de l'AQQC pour l'exploration de la complexité' *Revue Internationale de Politique Comparée* 11(1): 85–100.

De Meur, G. and Berg-Schlosser, D. 1994 'Comparing political systems: establishing similarities and dissimilarities' *European Journal of Political Research* 26(2): 193–219.

De Meur, G. and Berg-Schlosser, D. 1996 'Conditions of authoritarianism, fascism and democracy in inter-war Europe: systematic matching and contrasting of cases for "small N" analysis' *Comparative Political Studies* 29(4): 423–468.

De Meur, G. and Rihoux, B. 2002 *L'analyse quali-quantitative comparée (AQQC-QCA): approche, techniques et applications en sciences humaines.* Louvain-la-Neuve: Academia-Bruylant.

De Meur, G., Rihoux, B. and Yamasaki, S. 2008 'Addressing the critiques of QCA' in B. Rihoux and C. Ragin (Eds) *Configurational Comparative Methods. Qualitative Comparative Analysis (QCA) and Related Techniques.* Thousand Oaks, CA: Sage.

Ebbinghaus, B. 2005 'When less is more: selection problems in large-N and small-N cross-national comparisons' *International Sociology* 20(2): 133–152.

Eckert, J.K. 1987 'Ethnographic research on aging' in S. Reinharz and G.D. Rowles (Eds) *Qualitative Gerontology.* New York: Springer, pp. 241–255.

Fielding, N.G. and Fielding, J.L. 1986 *Linking Data.* Beverly Hills, CA: Sage.

George, A.L. and Bennett, A. 2005 *Case Studies and Theory Development in the Social Sciences.* Cambridge, MA: MIT Press.

Gerring, J. 2006 *Case Study Research: Principles and Practices.* Cambridge: Cambridge University Press.

Greene, J.C. and Caracelli, V.J. (Eds) 1997 *Advances in Mixed-Method Evaluation: The Challenges and Benefits of Integrating Diverse Paradigms (New Directions in Evaluation, 74).* San Francisco: Jossey-Bass.

Greene, J.C., Caracelli, V.J. and Graham, W.F. 1989 'Toward a conceptual framework for mixed-method evaluation designs' *Educational Evaluation and Policy Analysis* 11(3): 255–274.

Harmel, R. and Janda, K. 1994 'An integrated theory of party goals and party change' *Journal of Theoretical Politics* 6(3): 259–287.

Harper, D. 1992 'Small N's and community case studies' in C. Ragin and H. Becker (Eds) *What Is a Case? Exploring the Foundations of Social Inquiry.* Cambridge: Cambridge University Press, pp. 139–158.

Hicks, A.M. 1994 'Qualitative comparative analysis and analytical induction: the case of the emergence of the social security state' *Sociological Methods and Research* 23(1).

Ishida, A., Yonetani, M. and Kosaka, K. 2006 'Determinants of linguistic human rights movements: an analysis of multiple causation of LHRs movements using a Boolean approach' *Social Forces* 84(4): 1937–1955.

Lijphart, A. 1971 'Comparative politics and the comparative method' *American Political Science Review* 65(3): 682–693.

Lijphart, A. 1975 'The comparable-cases strategy in comparative research' *Comparative Political Studies* 8(2): 158–177.

Lobe, B. 2006 *Mixing qualitative and quantitative methods in the environment of new information-communication technologies.* Unpublished doctoral dissertation, University of Ljubljana, Faculty of Social Sciences.

Mahoney, J. and Goertz, G. 2004 'The possibility principle: choosing negative cases in comparative research' *American Political Science Review* 98(4): 653-669.

Mahoney, J. and Rueschemeyer, D. 2003 *Comparative Historical Analysis in the Social Sciences.* Cambridge: Cambridge University Press.

Panebianco, A. 1988 *Political Parties: Organisation and Power.* Cambridge: Cambridge University Press.

Phelan, P. 1987 'Compatibility of qualitative and quantitative methods: studying child sexual abuse in America' *Education and Urban Society* 20(1): 35–41.

Platt, J. 1992 'Cases of cases… of cases' in C. Ragin and H. Becker (Eds) *What Is a Case? Exploring the Foundations of Social Inquiry.* Cambridge: Cambridge University Press, pp. 21–52.

Popper, K.R. 1963 *Conjectures and Refutations: The Growth of Scientific Knowledge.* London: Routledge and Kegan Paul.

Ragin, C.C. 1987 *The Comparative Method. Moving beyond Qualitative and Quantitative Strategies.* Berkeley, CA: University of California Press.

Ragin, C.C. 1992 'Introduction: cases of what is a case?' in C. Ragin and H. Becker (Eds) *What Is a Case? Exploring the Foundations of Social Inquiry.* Cambridge: Cambridge University Press, pp. 1–18.

Ragin, C.C. 1997 'Turning the tables : how case-oriented methods challenge variable-oriented methods' *Comparative Social Research* 16: 27–42.

Ragin, C.C. 2000 *Fuzzy-Set Social Science.* Chicago: Chicago University Press.

Ragin, C.C. 2002 'Préface' in G. De Meur and B. Rihoux (Eds) *L'analyse quali-quantitative comparée (AQQC-QCA): approche, techniques et applications en sciences humaines.* Louvain-la-Neuve: Academia-Bruylant, pp. 11–14.

Ragin, C.C. 2004 'La place de la comparaison: jalons pour la recherche comparative configurationnelle' *Revue Internationale de Politique Comparée* 11(1): 118–129.

Ragin, C.C. 2006 'The limitations of net-effects thinking' in B. Rihoux and H. Grimm (Eds) *Innovative Comparative Methods for Policy Analysis.* New-York: Springer, pp. 13–41.

Ragin, C.C. 2008a 'Qualitative comparative analysis using fuzzy sets (fsQCA)' in B. Rihoux and C. Ragin (Eds) *Configurational Comparative Methods. Qualitative Comparative Analysis (QCA) and Related Techniques.* Thousand Oaks, CA: Sage.

Ragin, C.C. 2008b *Redesigning Social Inquiry: Fuzzy Sets and Beyond* Chicago: Chicago University Press.

Ragin, C.C. and Becker, H.S. 1992 *What Is a Case? Exploring the Foundations of Social Inquiry.* Cambridge: Cambridge University Press.

Ragin, C.C. and Rihoux, B. 2004 'Qualitative comparative analysis (QCA): state of the art and prospects' *Qualitative Methods: Newsletter of the American Political Science Association Organized Section on Qualitative Methods* 2(2): 3–13.

Ragin C.C. and Sonnett, J. 2004 'Between complexity and parsimony: limited diversity, counterfactual cases, and comparative analysis' in S. Kropp and M. Minkenberg (Eds) *Vergleichen in der Politikwissenschaft.* Wiesbaden: VS Verlag für Sozialwissenschaften.

Ragin, C.C., Berg-Schlosser, D. and De Meur, G. '1996 Political methodology: qualitative methods' in R.E. Goodin and H.D. Klingemann (Eds) *A New Handbook of Political Science.* Oxford: Oxford University Press.

Rihoux, B. 2001 *Les partis politiques: organisations en changement. Le test des écologistes.* Coll. Logiques Politiques Paris: L'Harmattan..

Rihoux, B. 2006 'Qualitative comparative analysis (QCA) and related systematic comparative methods: recent advances and remaining challenges for social science research' *International Sociology* 21(5): 679–706.

Rihoux, B. 2008a 'Qualitative comparative analysis (QCA) and related techniques: recent advances and challenges' in S. Pickel, G. Pickel, H.J. Lauth and D. Jahn (Eds) *Neuere Entwicklungen und Anwendungen auf dem Gebiet der Methoden der vergleichenden Politikwissenschaft – Band II.* Wiesbaden: Westdeutscher Verlag.

Rihoux, B. 2008b 'Case-oriented configurational research using QCA (qualitative comparative analysis)' in J. Box-Steffensmeier, H. Brady and D. Collier (Eds), *Oxford Handbook of Political Science: Methodology.* Oxford: Oxford University Press.

Rihoux, B. and De Meur, G. 2008 'Crisp-set qualitative comparative analysis (csQCA)' in B. Rihoux and C. Ragin (Eds) *Configurational Comparative Methods. Qualitative Comparative Analysis (QCA) and Related Techniques.* Thousand Oaks, CA: Sage.

Rihoux, B. and Ragin, C. (Eds) 2008 *Configurational Comparative Methods. Qualitative Comparative Analysis (QCA) and Related Techniques.* Thousand Oaks, CA: Sage.

Rihoux, B., Joly, J. and Dandoy, R. 2008 *Deliverable 8. The Key Determinants of Community Conflict Escalation and De-escalation in Europe: A Systematic Comparative Analysis (QCA).* Brussels: European Commission.

Sager, F. 2004 'Metropolitan institutions and policy coordination: the integration of land use and transport policies in Swiss urban areas' *Governance: An International Journal of Policy, Administration, and Institutions* 18(2), 227–256.

Scherrer, V. 2006 *Citoyens sous tensions. Analyse qualitative des rapports à la politique et des configurations d'appartenances à partir d'entretiens projectifs sur les proches.* Unpublished doctoral dissertation, Paris: Institut d'Etudes Politiques de Paris.

Schneider, C.Q. and Wagemann, C. 2006 'Reducing complexity in qualitative comparative analysis (QCA): remote and proximate factors and the consolidation of democracy' *European Journal of Political Research* 45(5): 751–786.

Schneider, C.Q. and Wagemann, C. 2007 *Qualitative Comparative Analysis (QCA) und Fuzzy Sets. Ein Lehrbuch für Anwender und jene, die es werden wollen.* Opladen & Farmington Hills: Verlag Barbara Budrich.

Schneider, C.Q. and Wagemann, C. *Qualitative Comparative Analysis (QCA) and Fuzzy Sets. A User's Guide.*

Scouvart, M., Adams, R.T., Caldas, M., Dale, V., Mertens, B., Nédélec, V., Pacheco, P., Rihoux, B. and Lambin, E.F. 2007 'Causes of deforestation in the Brazilian Amazon: a Qualitative Comparative Analysis' *Journal of Land Use Science* 2(4): 257–282.

Swyngedouw, M. 2004 'Review of: L'analyse quali-quantitative comparée (AQQC-QCA) by De Meur, G, and Rihoux, B. Louvain-la-Neuve: Academia

Bruylant, 2002' *European Sociological Review* 20(2): 161–162.

Tilly, C. 1984 *Big Structures, Large Processes, Huge Comparisons.* New York: Russell Sage Foundation.

Vanderborght, Y. and Yamasaki, S. 2004 'Des cas logiques... contradictoires? Un piège de l'AQQC déjoué à travers l'étude de la faisabilité politique de l'allocation universelle' *Revue Internationale de Politique Comparée* 11(1): 51–66.

Wagemann, C. and Schneider, C.Q. 2007 'Standards of good practice in qualitative comparative analysis (QCA) and fuzzy-sets' *COMPASSS Working Paper* (51): 35.

Yamasaki, S. 2007 *Policy change in nuclear energy. A comparative analysis of West European countries.* Unpublished doctoral dissertation, Université catholique de Louvain (UCL): Louvain-la-Neuve.

13

On the Duality of Cases and Variables: Correspondence Analysis (CA) and Qualitative Comparative Analysis (QCA)

Ronald L. Breiger

One of the most innovative, most highly developed, and most widely influential strategies for moving beyond the well-worn dichotomy of 'qualitative' versus 'quantitative' approaches to comparative social research is the Qualitative Comparative Analysis (QCA) approach of Charles Ragin (e.g., Ragin, 1987, 2000, in press). In this chapter, I build on one of the foundations of QCA: the duality of cases and variables. By 'duality' I mean co-constitution, as in Breiger (1974, 2000) and Breiger and Mohr (2004). Within QCA, cases are productively understood as configurations of variables, that is, 'as combinations of aspects and conditions' (Ragin 2000, p. 13). At the same time, variables may be seen as configurations of cases. This idea, I believe, is fundamental to QCA, although it is not as prominently articulated as the

other side of the duality. In this chapter I will illustrate some of the insight that results from thinking in this way, both for crisp sets and for fuzzy-set analysis of the sort that has been pioneered by Ragin in a way that allows powerful new modeling of qualitative case variation (Ragin 2000, in press).

Rather than beginning with a section on formal methods, I will organize this chapter around the analysis of two examples: a crisp-set and a fuzzy-set example. To aid comparison, I will re-analyze examples that have been already studied by means of QCA. My purpose is not at all to propose a 'better' approach, but rather to propose a complementary approach, one that asks somewhat different questions and that leads to some new but highly complementary and useful insights.

EXAMPLE 1: ETHNIC POLITICAL MOBILIZATION

Ragin (1987, pp. 137–149; 2000, pp. 123–141) takes the example of ethnic political mobilization as a central one for demonstrating the benefits of crisp-set QCA analysis. As is typical of Charles Ragin's work, the 'example' dataset is both the result of serious scholarship and an occasion for his furthering of substantive research (Ragin bases the central table on his synthesis of data from three different studies; 1987, pp. 137–138). What have been the configurations of conditions relevant to political mobilization of territorially based linguistic minorities in Western Europe? Four variables are identified, for each of 36 ethnic minorities (some of which are: Magyars in Austria, Basques in France, and Catalans in Spain). The variables are whether the size of the subnational group is large (SIZE), whether its linguistic base is strong (LING), whether the minority region is relatively wealthy (WEALTH) in comparison to the core region of the host nation, and whether the minority region is growing economically (GROWTH) or declining. The dependent variable is the presence of a high degree of political mobilization within the minority region. The data, in the form of a binary table (thirty-six minority groups by five variables), are given in Ragin (1987, p. 141; 2000, p. 124).

Analysis of necessity

An analysis of necessary conditions (Ragin 2000, pp. 91–102, 131–133) involves selecting only those cases manifesting the dependent variable, which in this case takes us directly to the 19 cases (ethnic groups) that were coded as having mobilized. This subset of the data is shown in Table 13.1.

Boolean intersections are fundamental to QCA analysis (and their generalization as the 'minimum' of two vectors are at the core of fuzzy-set QCA). One of the main concerns of QCA is the search for minimal combinations of variables (the smallest number of 'configurations') that maximally 'cover'

Table 13.1 Causal conditions for the nineteen ethnic groups that have mobilized

Ethnic group	Variable			
	SIZE	LING	WEALTH	GROWTH
AalandersFinland	0	1	1	0
SlovenesItaly	0	1	1	1
ValdotiansItaly	0	1	1	1
WestFrisiansNeth	1	0	0	1
CatalansFrance	1	0	0	1
OccitansFrance	1	0	0	1
WelshGreatBritain	1	0	0	1
BretonsFrance	1	0	0	1
CorsicansFrance	1	0	0	1
FriuliansItaly	1	0	1	1
OccitansItaly	1	0	1	1
BasquesSpain	1	0	1	1
CatalansSpain	1	0	1	1
WalloonsBelgium	1	1	0	1
SwedesFinland	1	1	1	0
SouthTyroleansItaly	1	1	1	0
AlsatiansFrance	1	1	1	1
GermansBelgium	1	1	1	1
FlemingsBelgium	1	1	1	1

Source: Ragin 1987 (p. 141); Ragin 2000 (p. 124).

(account for) the cases (see also the discussion of coverage in Ragin 2006). Because of the set-theoretic nature of QCA analysis, we may consider a variety of techniques for accomplishing goals that are somewhat similar: Boolean factor analysis (Mickey et al. 1983, De Boeck and Rosenberg 1988), Galois or 'dual' lattice analysis (Kim 1982, Mohr and Duquenne 1997, Mische and Pattison 2000, Mische 2007), and correspondence analysis, for example (Breiger [2000] relates correspondence analysis to the concept of duality that is applied here). Notable relations among these techniques are being developed (Pattison and Breiger 2002). In this chapter, I work with a variety of correspondence analysis (CA).

Barycentric correspondence analysis is a form CA that is particularly well suited for analyses performed on Boolean strings and Galois lattices (on the latter point, see Wolf and Gabler 1998, p. 88). Greenacre (1984) and Le Roux and Rouanet (2004) are standard references on barycentric analysis, based on the work in France of Jean-Paul Benzécri and his colleagues. The technique is not widely

Table 13.2   Barycentric CA scores: ethnic mobilization, groups that have been mobilized

(A) Scores for causal conditions

	Dimension		
	[1]	[2]	[3]
SIZE	0.7942	−0.1596	−1.287
LING	−1.5717	−1.5552	0
WEALTH	−0.9391	1.5921	0
GROWTH	0.7942	−0.1596	1.287

(B) Scores for ethnic groups

	Dimension		
	[1]	[2]	[3]
AalandersFinland	−1.2554	0.0185	0
SlovenesItaly	−0.5722	−0.0409	0.429
ValdotiansItaly	−0.5722	−0.0409	0.429
WestFrisiansNeth	0.7942	−0.1596	0
CatalansFrance	0.7942	−0.1596	0
OccitansFrance	0.7942	−0.1596	0
WelshGreatBritain	0.7942	−0.1596	0
BretonsFrance	0.7942	−0.1596	0
CorsicansFrance	0.7942	−0.1596	0
FriuliansItaly	0.2164	0.4243	0
OccitansItaly	0.2164	0.4243	0
BasquesSpain	0.2164	0.4243	0
CatalansSpain	0.2164	0.4243	0
WalloonsBelgium	0.0056	−0.6248	0
SwedesFinland	−0.5722	−0.0409	−0.429
SouthTyroleansItaly	−0.5722	−0.0409	−0.429
AlsatiansFrance	−0.2306	−0.0706	0
GermansBelgium	−0.2306	−0.0706	0
FlemingsBelgium	−0.2306	−0.0706	0

known to or used by American researchers; an exception is Faust (2005), who provides an exposition and applications to the study of social networks. A brief technical introduction is provided in the Appendix to this chapter.

Barycentric CA scores for the Table 13.1 data are given in Table 13.2. Here is what is distinctive and very helpful about the 'barycentric' analysis. Consider, for example, the Slovene minority group in Italy. From the second row of Table 13.2(B), we see that their barycentric 'scores' on the three dimensions are:

	[1]	[2]	[3]
SlovenesItaly	−0.5722	−0.0409	0.429

The second row of Table 13.1 shows that this group stands at the intersection of LING, WEALTH, and GROWTH. (Note the three '1's in the second row of Table 13.1.) The barycentric scores for these three variables are (from Table 13.2(A)):

	[1]	[2]	[3]
LING	−1.5717	−1.5552	0.0000
WEALTH	−0.9391	1.5921	0.0000
GROWTH	0.7942	−0.1596	1.2870

Now, if we take the means of these three variables on each dimension respectively, we obtain – once again – precisely the scores shown above for this ethnic group! For example, on dimension 1, the mean of −1.5717, −0.9391, and 0.7942 is −0.5722, which is the score on dimension 1 given above for the Italian Slovenes; the same is true for the two other dimensions. This definitional property is what makes the barycentric analysis so appealing for working with set-theoretic intersections. The quantitative score for each ethnic group is (given a somewhat unconventional, but quite appropriate, interpretation of the mean) at the 'intersection' of the causal conditions that, so to speak, comprise the case. In this sense, using a dictionary definition of the term *barycentric*, each case is placed at 'the center of gravity' of the causal conditions that constitute it (for further discussion, see the Appendix at the end of the chapter).

As Table 13.1 has nineteen rows but only four columns, a correspondence analysis using three dimensions is sufficient to reproduce the data table completely. This quality renders our example particularly easy to interpret using barycentric CA. In more general situations, where there are more than four causal conditions, the analysis becomes more complex but still leads to portrayals of the space of cases and causal conditions that can be quite helpful to an analyst. One technique that helps in these more complex situations is to use what CA analysts call 'disjunctive coding', that is, to code each case not only on each condition it manifests, but (doubling the number of conditions) also on each condition it does not manifest. I will use disjunctive coding in a 'sufficiency' analysis of the ethnic mobilization data, but for the 'necessity' analysis disjunctive coding is not necessary.

Figure 13.1 portrays the nineteen ethnic minority groups and the four causal conditions in a two-dimensional space. This represents a reduction of the data (albeit not much of one, as the first dimension accounts for 73% of the 'inertia' or association in the table, and the second dimension accounts for an additional 17%). Quite a few of the ethnic groups are plotted at exactly the same coordinates. These four sets of 'equivalent' cases are labeled A, B, C, and D in Figure 13.1, and the memberships of these sets are defined in Table 13.3. (Astute readers of Table 13.3 will note that the sets of ethnic minorities grouped together in sets B, C, and D are internally homogeneous across all four variables, whereas those grouped together in set A are all fluent, wealthy, and *one* of either large or growing. The special features of set A will be further discussed below.)

The first dimension of Figure 13.1 contrasts LING and WEALTH, on the left of the diagram, with GROWTH and SIZE, on the right. The diagram helps the analyst to see the cases as intersections of the causal conditions. For example, ethnic groups in set D (defined in Table 13.3) manifest both GROWTH and SIZE, and none of the other conditions. That is why set D is located precisely at the coordinates of GROWTH and SIZE in Figure 13.1. Minority groups in set C manifest GROWTH and SIZE, and also WEALTH; hence these groups are located precisely on the line that connects GROWTH and SIZE to WEALTH in Figure 13.1 (and these cases in set C are precisely twice as close to GROWTH = SIZE as they are to WEALTH). Similarly,

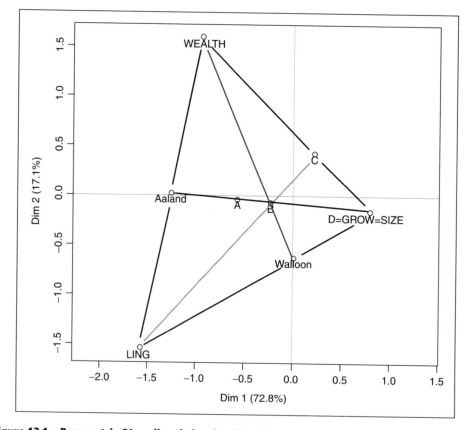

Figure 13.1   Barycentric CA on linguistic minorities data, necessity analysis, first two dimensions (see Table 13.3 for definitions of 'A', 'B', 'C', 'D').

Table 13.3   Sets of ethnic groups that are equated in Figures 13.1 and 13.2

Set A:	Dimension			Variable			
	[1]	[2]	[3]	SIZE	LING	WEALTH	GROWTH
A1: SlovenesItaly	−0.57	−0.04	0.43	0	1	1	1
A1: ValdotiansItaly	−0.57	−0.04	0.43	0	1	1	1
A2: SwedesFinland	−0.57	−0.04	−0.43	1	1	1	0
A2: SouthTyroleansItaly	−0.57	−0.04	−0.43	1	1	1	0

Set B:	Dimension			Variable			
	[1]	[2]	[3]	SIZE	LING	WEALTH	GROWTH
AlsatiansFrance	−0.23	−0.07	0	1	1	1	1
GermansBelgium	−0.23	−0.07	0	1	1	1	1
FlemingsBelgium	−0.23	−0.07	0	1	1	1	1

Set C:	Dimension			Variable			
	[1]	[2]	[3]	SIZE	LING	WEALTH	GROWTH
FriuliansItaly	0.22	0.42	0	1	0	1	1
OccitansItaly	0.22	0.42	0	1	0	1	1
BasquesSpain	0.22	0.42	0	1	0	1	1
CatalansSpain	0.22	0.42	0	1	0	1	1

Set D:	Dimension			Variable			
	[1]	[2]	[3]	SIZE	LING	WEALTH	GROWTH
WestFrisiansNeth	0.79	−0.16	0	1	0	0	1
CatalansFrance	0.79	−0.16	0	1	0	0	1
OccitansFrance	0.79	−0.16	0	1	0	0	1
WelshGreatBritain	0.79	−0.16	0	1	0	0	1
BretonsFrance	0.79	−0.16	0	1	0	0	1
CorsicansFrance	0.79	−0.16	0	1	0	0	1

the Belgian Walloons exhibit GROWTH and SIZE, and also LING; therefore, this group lies precisely on the line connecting LING to GROWTH and SIZE.

The Finnish Aalanders exhibit WEALTH and LING; therefore, they are located in Figure 13.1 on the line connecting these two causal conditions, at a point precisely half-way between WEALTH and LING. The ethnic groups in set B exhibit all four conditions. Therefore, the barycentric correspondence analysis has placed set B on the line connecting GROWTH and SIZE to the Aalanders (who are positioned at the intersection of LING and WEALTH), precisely half-way between these points. Set B is also at the intersection of the line connecting WEALTH to the Walloons (= GROWTH, SIZE, LING) and the line connecting LING to set C (= GROWTH, SIZE, WEALTH).

As I have already mentioned, the two-dimensional barycentric CA portrayal of Table 13.1 provides a reduction of the mobilization data. I would like to think of this 'reduction' as very loosely analogous to the kinds of 'probabilistic criteria' that Ragin develops and brings to bear in crisp-set QCA analysis. Given that Figure 13.1 is a reduction of the data, what has been lost from the picture of Figure 13.1? We can find out by examining the third dimension. Figure 13.2 plots the third dimension against the first. Only four of the ethnic groups, along with two causal factors, have non-zero scores on the third dimension. This new dimension separates GROWTH and SIZE, which are in fact not identical with respect to the groups that manifest them. (Compare the respective columns for GROWTH and SIZE in Table 13.1.) They are 'close'

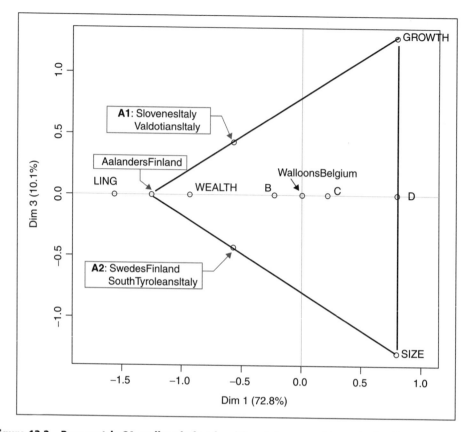

Figure 13.2   Barycentric CA on linguistic minorities data, necessity analysis, dimensions 1 and 3.

to identical, however, which is why their coordinates are identical across the first two dimensions of the reduced diagram of Figure 13.1. Figure 13.2 shows the difference: the Italian Slovenes and Valdotians (set A1 of Table 13.3) manifest LING and WEALTH *and* GROWTH, whereas the Finnish Swedes and Italian South Tyroleans (set A2) manifest LING and WEALTH *and* SIZE. The four groups just mentioned are the ones that comprise set A of Figure 13.1. Moreover, the Italian Slovenes and Valdotians lie precisely on the line (in Figure 13.2) connecting GROWTH to the Aalanders. Why? Because the Aalanders are constituted precisely by LING and WEALTH. (Furthermore, these two Italian groups are precisely one-third of the distance between the Aalanders and GROWTH. Why? Because the Aalanders have *two* causal conditions shared by the

Italian groups, whereas GROWTH is the third condition.)

In his discussion of the necessity criterion as it pertains to the political mobilization data, Ragin (2000, pp. 131–132) points out that there is no single cause (and therefore no combination of causes) that is uniformly present in the outcome, and hence no necessary conditions can be identified. GROWTH and SIZE come the closest; each is present in 16 of the 19 cases. As Ragin points out at some length, one might well consider probabilistic criteria in the investigation of necessity. But even if the cases were independent of one another (an assumption to which I will return) and the underlying probability of a case manifesting GROWTH (let's say) were as low as 0.65, the binomial probability of observing sixteen 'successes' in nineteen cases would be above 0.05 (Ragin 2000, p. 132).

I see little reason, however, to assume that the nineteen cases of ethnic political mobilization are statistically 'independent' of one another, which is the key assumption involved in Ragin's extensive reliance on binomial reasoning and its generalizations. We see from Figure 13.2 that there are four cases that exhibit one of GROWTH and SIZE, but not both. (Each of the remaining fifteen cases manifest either *both* of these causes or *neither* of them.) An important point that is revealed in Figure 13.1 is that *all four* of these exceptions (Slovenes, Valdotians, and South Tyroleans in Italy, and Swedes in Finland; set A in Figure 13.1) manifest both LING and WEALTH. It is this commonality among the four exceptional cases that (so to speak) motivates the barycentric analysis to identify GROWTH and SIZE in the diagram (Figure 13.1) that accounts for 90% of the inertia (or 'association') in Table 13.1.

In brief: nothing I have said changes the truth of Ragin's conclusion (2000, p. 132) that no causal combination is necessary for the outcome, according to the veristic criterion. Moreover, I am not proposing a new probabilistic criterion. I am pointing out that, descriptively, the analyst's identification of GROWTH and SIZE accounts for 90% of the inertia in the outcomes dataset, and that the four cases that have only one of GROWTH or SIZE also have both of LING and WEALTH, and in this sense are not best thought of as independent cases. If the analyst were willing to construct a new variable, defined as {GROWTH or SIZE}, then this new variable would be present in eighteen of the nineteen cases that manifest the outcome of political mobilization. Applying the binomial calculation that Ragin (2000, p. 132) discusses, but to the set-theoretic union of GROWTH and SIZE, then if the underlying probability of a case manifesting one of these variables were as low as 0.65, the binomial probability of observing eighteen 'successes' in nineteen cases would be 0.003, which is considerably below 0.05

To summarize: in no sense has the barycentric analysis 'supplanted' the crisp-set QCA analysis of necessity. However,

the barycentric analysis has provided a very useful aid toward visualizing the cases as intersections and/or unions of the causal conditions. Moreover, it has constructed a common 'space' that allows the researcher to visualize the cases and the causes within the same diagram. Finally, the barycentric analysis has made it clear that, in this dataset, GROWTH and SIZE are causal conditions that treat the cases in very much the same way.

Analysis of sufficiency

The analysis of sufficiency (Ragin 2000, pp. 92–102, 132–141) is the study of whether a postulated set of configurations of variables always (or 'almost' always, in the case of approximate solutions) leads to the outcome in question (the mobilization of ethnic groups, in our example). Table 13.4 shows all thirty-six cases, with disjunctive coding applied (the final column of Table 13.4 will be discussed later). For example, the South Tyroleans in Italy (fourth up from the bottom in Table 13.4) are large, fluent, wealthy, not growing, and mobilized – hence the '1' entries in the columns labeled SIZE, LING, WEALTH, MOBZ, and 'growth' in Table 13.4, where lower-case labels (like 'growth') represent the absence of a given condition. Thus, each row of Table 13.4 has five entries of '1', with the corresponding case being accounted for (with respect to presence or absence) on each variable, including the dependent variable.

Figure 13.3 displays the two-dimensional barycentric CA solution for the Table 13.4 data. Variables, which are circled in the figure, are shown in single upper-case letters (such as 'M' for mobilization), and their complements are shown in lower-case and with the complement symbol (such as '~m' for the absence of mobilization). Notice that the barycentric solution, given the disjunctive coding of cases (Table 13.4), imposes that each variable and its complement are connected by a straight line through the origin of the plot, indicating that they have a cosine (correlation) of –1.00. It is notable that the first dimension of the plot is, in this example, essentially synonymous with mobilization

Table 13.4 Disjunctive coding for all thirty-six ethnic groups (dependent variable = MOBZ), sufficiency analysis. Note that the variable names in lower-case (such as 'size') are the complements of those in upper-case (e.g., 'SIZE')

Ethnic group	Variable					Complement of variable					
	SIZE	LING	WEALTH	GROWTH	MOBZ	size	ling	wealth	growth	mobz	MOBZ and
LappsFinland	0	0	0	0	0	1	1	1	1	1	
LappsSweden	0	0	0	0	0	1	1	1	1	1	
LappsNorway	0	0	0	0	0	1	1	1	1	1	
FinnsSweden	0	0	0	0	0	1	1	1	1	1	
AlbanianItaly	0	0	0	0	0	1	1	1	1	1	
GreeksItaly	0	0	0	0	0	1	1	1	1	1	
NorthFrisiansGermany	0	0	0	1	0	1	1	1	0	1	
DanesGermany	0	0	0	1	0	1	1	1	0	1	
BasquesFrance	0	0	0	1	0	1	1	1	0	1	
LadinsItaly	0	0	1	0	0	1	1	0	1	1	
MagyarsAustria	0	1	0	0	0	1	0	1	1	1	
CroatsAustria	0	1	0	0	0	1	0	1	1	1	
SlovenesAustria	0	1	0	0	0	1	0	1	1	1	
GreelandersDenmark	0	1	0	0	0	1	0	1	1	1	
AalandersFinland	0	1	1	0	1	1	0	0	1	0	LW
SlovenesItaly	0	1	1	1	1	1	0	0	0	0	LWG
ValdotiansItaly	0	1	1	1	1	1	0	0	0	0	LWG
SardsItaly	1	0	0	0	0	0	1	1	1	1	
GaliciansSpain	1	0	0	0	0	0	1	1	1	1	
WestFrisiansNeth	1	0	0	1	1	0	1	1	0	0	SG
CatalansFrance	1	0	0	1	1	0	1	1	0	0	SG
OccitansFrance	1	0	0	1	1	0	1	1	0	0	SG
WelshGreatBritain	1	0	0	1	1	0	1	1	0	0	SG
BretonsFrance	1	0	0	1	1	0	1	1	0	0	SG
CorsicansFrance	1	0	0	1	1	0	1	1	0	0	SG
FriuliansItaly	1	0	1	1	1	0	1	0	0	0	SGW
OccitansItaly	1	0	1	1	1	0	1	0	0	0	SGW
BasquesSpain	1	0	1	1	1	0	1	0	0	0	SGW
CatalansSpain	1	0	1	1	1	0	1	0	0	0	SGW
FlemingsFrance	1	1	0	0	0	0	0	1	1	1	
WalloonsBelgium	1	1	0	1	1	0	0	1	0	0	SGL
SwedesFinland	1	1	1	0	1	0	0	0	1	0	SLW
SouthTyroleansItaly	1	1	1	0	1	0	0	0	1	0	SLW
AlsatiansFrance	1	1	1	1	1	0	0	0	0	0	LWSG
GermansBelgium	1	1	1	1	1	0	0	0	0	0	LWSG
FlemingsBelgium	1	1	1	1	1	0	0	0	0	0	LWSG

Source: Ragin (1987, p. 141; 2000, p. 124)

(see the straight line connecting M with ~m). All the cases manifesting mobilization have scores greater than 0 on dimension 1 of Figure 13.3, and all cases with no mobilization have scores less than 0. Cases evidencing mobilization are indicated as intersections of variables. For example, 'LWG' stands for those ethnic groups which have mobilized and which also manifest fluency (L) and wealth (W) and growth (G), as well as the absence

of large size (~s). A complete enumeration of these groups is provided in the final column of Table 13.4: for example, 'LWG' stands for the Slovenes and the Valdotians, both of Italy. To avoid clutter, cases that do not manifest mobilization are indicated by unlabeled points in Figure 13.3.

Ragin's (2000, p. 138) finding for sufficiency is, in my notation, $S\,G + L\,W \rightarrow M$. Note that in this regard all four of these

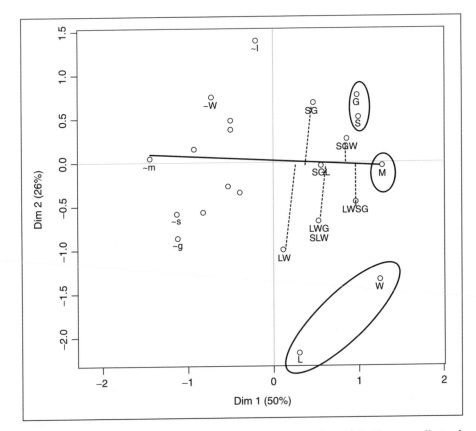

Figure 13.3   Barycentric CA on the Table 13.4 data, sufficiency analysis, first two dimensions. Note that variables are shown in single upper-case letters (such as 'G' for 'Growth'), and their negations are shown in lower-case, with complement signs (such as '~g'). Cases that manifest mobilization are shown as intersections of variables (compare Table A-1).

independent variables are on the same side of the Figure 13.3 plot as is the dependent variable; all have dimension 1 scores greater than 0, as do all the cases manifesting the dependent variable. S and G clearly cluster together. To see this, draw a line from each of these variables to the origin, and note that the angle so formed is small (which means that the cosine, or correlation among these variables, is large and positive). A similar, not quite so strong, result obtains for L and W: the angle formed by connecting both of these points to the origin is acute, indicating a positive association among these variables across the thirty-six cases.

From Figure 13.3 it can be seen that all cases manifesting mobilization are at the intersection of variables SG and/or LW. This is the key result of the QCA sufficiency analysis. In this example (other examples are not guaranteed to produce such felicitous analytical outcomes) this QCA result is in accord with the barycentric CA analysis, although the latter was not designed to produce it. At the same time, a somewhat different, though compatible, interpretation is suggested by Figure 13.3. Following interpretive procedures suggested by Goodman (1996), let us project each of the cases onto the line connecting the variables Mobilization (M) and its complement (~m). These projections are shown in Figure 13.3 as lines intersecting line M.~m at right angles. From the plot, we see that cases manifesting all four independent variables (LWSG) have what Goodman's (1996) interpretive procedures would identify as the strongest positive association with mobilization (because the projection of LWSG onto the line M.~m is closest to M). Next, any combination of three of these variables (SWG, SGL, LWG, SLW) has the next-highest association with M. Finally, two intersections each entailing two variables (SG and LW, the QCA sufficiency configurations) also are seen to have positive association with mobilization, although this is association of a magnitude less than that of the three- and four-variable configurations. All other configurations, those with scores less than 0 on dimension 1, have negative association with mobilization ('negative' in the sense brought out in Goodman's 1996 discussion of procedures for interpreting plots such as this one). The line of reasoning undertaken in this paragraph provides further support for the QCA finding that SG and LW are the minimal configurations needed to demarcate the set of cases exhibiting mobilization from those in which mobilization is absent.

A more general point is illustrated by the projections discussed in the preceding paragraph. We have just seen that the CA allows us to speak of configurations that are *more* or *less* associated with the outcome variable, mobilization, even in a crisp-set analysis such as this one. Cases (such as Flemings in Belgium) manifesting all four independent variables are seen in this example to have a *higher* positive association with mobilization than do cases that have only three variables, and these cases have a *higher* association with mobilization than do cases manifesting only SG or LW. These and similar points are developed further in the Appendix to this chapter, which shows why the association scores on Mobilization, which are given for all cases in Table A-1, are consistent with the geometric interpretation of the projections in Figure 13.3. The main finding of interest here is that we may use correspondence analysis to discover 'strong' versus 'weak' association of both cases and causal combinations with the outcome variable in a crisp-set analysis.

EXAMPLE 2: DEMOCRACY IN INTERWAR EUROPE

Ragin (in press) provides fundamental new conceptualization and development of QCA using fuzzy sets (or fsQCA). I believe that the ideas of the previous example can be extended to aid in thinking about this new work. I will illustrate using the same dataset that Ragin (in press) takes as his example. The outcome variable is breakdown of democracy in eighteen European countries in the inter war period. The potentially causal conditions are fuzzy-coded membership in being developed (D), urban (U), literate (L), industrial (I), and unstable (N).

These five variables suggest $2^5 = 32$ combinations at the 'corners' of the vector space formed by the causal conditions. In brief, these 'corners' so to speak stake out the limits of the fuzzy-space of variables (but see Section 2.1 of Ragin [in press] for a more complete discussion and for the relation of this space to the pillars of Ragin's analysis, including the concept of calibration and correspondence between vector space corners and truth table rows). However, some of these thirty-two combinations manifest no observed instances among the eighteen nations in the study. Only ten of the thirty-two combinations are associated with greater than 0.5 membership of at least one nation, as shown in Ragin's Table 5.8. The first row of that table, for example, is the (crisp-set) combination D = 0, U = 0, L = 0, I = 0, N = 1, or in notation I will employ, 'duliN'. Three cases (Greece, Portugal, and Spain) appear at this 'corner'.

To obtain values on 'duliN' (and on the other nine configurations) for each of the eighteen countries, I use the fuzzy-set codings for each of the variables (D, U, L, I, N) that Ragin obtains from his calibration procedure and displays in his Table 5.2. For the negations (such as 'd') I use 1 minus the given values (for example, d = 1 – D, from the fuzzy codings in his Table 5.2).

The result is an 18 × 10 table, showing countries as rows and the ten causal combinations (from Ragin's Table 5.8) as

Table 13.5 Fuzzy-set membership of each nation in each causal combination. Shown in parentheses after the country's name is the fuzzy 'democratic breakdown' score for those nations whose score is greater than 0.5 (Finland's score, at 0.36, is the highest breakdown score below 0.5)

Nation (break-down score)	Causal combination									
	duliN	dulin	DULIN	DuLIN	duLiN	duLin	dULIn	DuLin	DuLIn	DULIn
Austria (0.99)	0.02	0.02	0.14	0.65	0.24	0.24	0.14	0.24	0.35	0.14
Belgium	0.01	0.01	0.04	0.04	0.01	0.01	0.01	0.02	0.11	0.89
Czechoslovakia	0.03	0.03	0.13	0.04	0.04	0.04	0.58	0.04	0.04	0.42
Estonia (0.88)	0.04	0.04	0.02	0.02	0.13	0.85	0.02	0.15	0.02	0.02
Finland	0.02	0.02	0.03	0.09	0.49	0.51	0.03	0.43	0.09	0.03
France	0.03	0.03	0.02	0.07	0.03	0.03	0.02	0.17	0.83	0.02
Germany (0.99)	0.02	0.02	0.77	0.17	0.04	0.04	0.15	0.04	0.17	0.23
Greece (0.97)	0.62	0.35	0.05	0.05	0.11	0.11	0.1	0.05	0.05	0.05
Hungary (0.59)	0.19	0.09	0.08	0.08	0.8	0.09	0.08	0.08	0.08	0.08
Ireland	0.04	0.04	0.02	0.02	0.07	0.38	0.02	0.62	0.02	0.02
Italy (0.99)	0.49	0.51	0.11	0.25	0.38	0.38	0.11	0.25	0.25	0.11
Netherlands	0.01	0.01	0.01	0.01	0.01	0.01	0.03	0.01	0.01	0.94
Poland (0.88)	0.45	0.02	0.02	0.02	0.55	0.02	0.02	0.02	0.02	0.02
Portugal (0.99)	0.88	0.02	0.01	0.02	0.02	0.02	0.01	0.02	0.02	0.01
Romania (0.75)	0.22	0.78	0.02	0.02	0.15	0.15	0.02	0.02	0.02	0.02
Spain (0.97)	0.59	0.14	0.04	0.04	0.08	0.08	0.08	0.04	0.04	0.04
Sweden	0.01	0.01	0.13	0.13	0.07	0.07	0.07	0.3	0.7	0.15
United Kingdom	0.01	0.01	0.04	0.02	0.02	0.02	0.02	0.02	0.02	0.96

Source: Table 5.8 from Ragin (in press).

the columns. This 18×10 array is shown as Table 13.5 of this chapter. The same table also indicates which ten nations are coded high on 'democratic breakdown' (which I operationalize as fuzzy scores above 0.5).

To study dual intersections of cases (nations) and causal conditions, I perform a barycentric correspondence analysis on the table just described. The resulting two-dimensional plot is shown in Figure 13.4. Purely as an aid to interpretation subsequent to obtaining Figure 13.4, I have circled most of the memberships greater than 0.5 (as these memberships appear in Table 13.5).[1] Furthermore, Figure 13.4 distinguishes causal combinations (shown as dark circles) from nations with low scores on democratic breakdown (shown as open circles) and from nations with high scores (greater than 0.50) on the breakdown variable (shown as open triangles in Figure 13.4).

Perhaps the first point to note about Figure 13.4 is that, along its most salient dimension, a set of highly developed, highly urban, highly literate, highly industrial, and highly stable countries – by name: the Netherlands, the UK, and Belgium – are separated from all the others. Moreover, we know (from Ragin's Table 5.2) that these countries had exceptionally low scores on democratic 'breakdown'.

Figure 13.4 shows that the nations (indicated by open triangles) that did experience breakdown are to a considerable extent arrayed along the line (shown in the figure) that connects DULIN to duliN. Ragin's interpretation (in press, section 2.5) locates two paths to breakdown: DLIN and dui. Figure 13.4 shows that the countries that experienced breakdown are (with the exception of Estonia) divided into opposite quadrants: Germany and Austria (sharing DLIN) are toward the lower left, in contrast to Portugal, Spain, Greece, Romania, Poland, Italy, and Hungary, all of which are in the upper-right quadrant. The latter quadrant is also the location for causal configurations duliN, dulin, duLiN, which share as a common denominator dui. Thus, the 'two

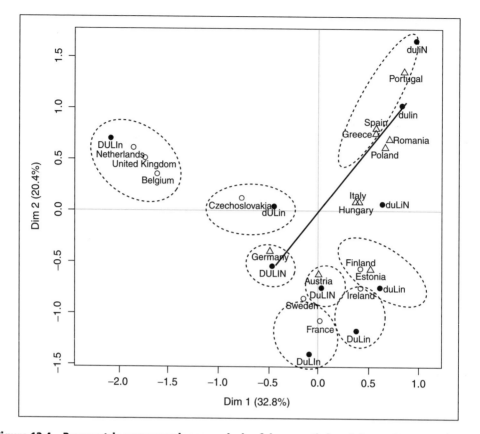

Figure 13.4 Barycentric correspondence analysis of democratic breakdown: Causes and cases.

paths to breakdown' identified by Ragin have a natural representation as oppositions in Figure 13.4.

Estonia is an exception. It has a high breakdown score (of 0.88) but is orthogonal to the line shown in Figure 13.3 and appears in the lower-right quadrant. Like the countries at the upper right, Estonia is a strong member of causal configuration dui. However, like Germany and Austria, it has high literacy. Finland is very close to Estonia. If I had binarized 'breakdown' to include one additional country, Finland (with a breakdown score of 0.36) would have been the one added.

Figure 13.4 contains no insight that is not already present in Ragin's analysis (in press). It does, however, embed some of that insight within a somewhat wider tableau of cases and configurations; for example, clearly distinguishing the Netherlands, the UK, and Belgium (all DULIn) from the countries that did exhibit high breakdown. Figure 13.4 does not provide a means for 'discovering' sufficiency – indeed, the dependent variable was not even included in the data (Table 13.5) on which CA was performed – but it does add insight to a visualization of sufficiency, within a reduced-form map of the dual relation of causes and cases.[2]

DISCUSSION: EXPLOITING THE DUALITY OF CASES AND VARIABLES

Ragin's work, and that of a broader community of researchers (see, for example, the work collected in Ragin and Becker, 1992), develops a case-oriented approach to causal reasoning, one that requires 'a constant iterative engagement with social reality in a programme founded on integrative method'

(Byrne 2002, p. 156). I have sought to build on and extend the idea that variables are constituted by the cases that comprise them, as well as vice versa. The principal machinery for such building has been barycentric correspondence analysis, a form of analysis that is especially well suited for set-theoretic work and its extensions.

This chapter has not been simply an example of how correspondence analysis (CA), even in its barycentric guise, can be imported to aid in QCA. Rather, in the spirit of the iterative engagement to which David Byrne refers in the quotation in the preceding paragraph, QCA has been used to tailor correspondence analysis. For example, I have introduced to CA the concept of 'dependent variable' from the configurational world of QCA; such a concept most often has no place within CA.[3] Much more fundamentally, Ragin's (in press) reworking of fuzzy-set analysis provides a highly innovative sort of 'input' to CA (see Table 13.5), one that has not heretofore been used with the CA approach.

One issue that is sometimes raised about QCA is that a relatively large number of causal combinations in the solution may all be presented as equally relevant.[4] For example, a QCA study of how courts interpret the law in their rulings in AIDS cases resulted in six simplified configurations for the thirty-six cases considered (Musheno et al. 1991, pp. 766–767). New work on the concept of 'coverage' (Ragin 2006) speaks to this criticism to a considerable extent (see also De Meur et al. in press). My discussion of Figure 13.3 (as well as this chapter's Appendix) suggests that combinations can be ordered with respect to their association with the outcome variable. In addition, and in the spirit of duality that guides this chapter, barycentric CA provides ways to talk about importance of variable combinations by reference to the arrangement of cases in a dual case-variable space. Figures 13.3 and 13.4 provide examples relevant to crisp-set and to fuzzy-set analysis respectively.

Another benefit of the linking of CA and QCA is that the joint approach provides a visual representation of key comparisons.

Thus, the CA representation could be used as a guide for case selection in the iterative process that leads from QCA analysis to the in-depth study of cases found to be interesting in the previous analysis. Comparative case-study research is always preoccupied with finding the 'best' cases to study in an in-depth manner. To take an example: Figure 13.4 shows that the analyst needs to look at only one case in the DULIn cluster (where Belgium, the UK, and the Netherlands are situated similarly), and only one case in the duliN cluster of Spain, Greece, and Portugal. Figure 13.4 also shows that the analyst needs to pay attention to Estonia versus Finland (as mentioned in my discussion of Example 2), and also to Sweden versus Austria, and perhaps to Germany versus Czechoslovakia. In short, assuming the right causal conditions have been selected, the dimensional portraits of barycentric CA set up a way of seeing one's way to the selection of cases for further in-depth study. This is another benefit of combining features of QCA and CA.

Finally, I would like to call attention to the way that the CA analysis treated highly correlated conditions (SIZE and GROWTH) in Table 13.1. It equated these conditions by (in effect) taking the set-theoretic union of them, equating the two conditions in Figure 13.1. The tendency of QCA is to complicate; as Charles Ragin pointed out in a personal communication, each new causal condition doubles the size of the analytic space formed by these conditions. Ultimately, there must be some redundancy among the selected causal conditions, and CA, as a data reduction technique, exploits that redundancy in a way that the more principled QCA cannot (by design).

At the broadest level, in this chapter I have tried to link the duality that has always been fundamental to Ragin's QCA with similar concepts of co-constitution among levels that have been used in social network analysis, in sociology more generally, and in somewhat-related procedures (such as CA and the analysis of dual lattices). There is much more work to do along these productive lines of research.

NOTES

1. To avoid clutter in Figure 13.4, I have suppressed two clusters of memberships greater than 0.5 that appear in Table 13.5. One cluster is {Italy, Romania, dulin}. The other is {Hungary, Poland, duLiN}.

2. Also including the dependent variable, in a fuzzy-set analogue to the sufficiency analysis of Example 1 in this chapter, is a subject for further work.

3. For one exception, showing how a variable may be treated as dependent within CA, see Bartholomew et al. (2002, p. 106). The QCA context explored in this chapter is, however, different from the typical one studied by researchers using correspondence analysis.

4. I am grateful to Charles Ragin for his generous contribution of a good deal of the insight in this paragraph and in the two following paragraphs.

REFERENCES

Bartholomew, D.J., Steele, F., Moustaki, I. and Galbraith, J.L. 2002. *The Analysis and Interpretation of Multivariate Data for Social Scientists.* London: Chapman and Hall.

Blasius, J. and Greenacre, M. 2006 'Correspondence analysis and related methods in practice' in M. Greenacre and J. Blasius (Eds) *Multiple Correspondence Analysis and Related Methods.* Boca Raton, FL: Chapman & Hall/CRC, pp. 3–40.

Breiger, R.L. 1974 'The duality of persons and groups' *Social Forces* 53: 181–190.

Breiger, R.L. 2000 'A tool kit for practice theory' *Poetics* 27: 91–115.

Breiger, R.L. and Mohr, J.W. 2004 'Institutional logics from the aggregation of organizational networks: operational procedures for the analysis of counted data' *Computational and Mathematical Organization Theory* 10: 17–43.

Byrne, D. 2002 *Interpreting Quantitative Data.* London: Sage Publications.

De Boeck, P. and Rosenberg, S. 1988 'Hierarchical classes: model and data analysis' *Psychometrika* 53: 361–381.

De Meur, G., Rihoux, B. and Yamasaki, S. 'Addressing the critiques of QCA' in B. Rihoux and C. Ragin (Eds) *Configurational Comparative Methods: Qualitative Comparative Analysis (QCA) and Related Techniques.* Newbury Park, CA: Sage Publications (in press).

Faust, K. 2005 'Using correspondence analysis for joint displays of affiliation networks' in P.J. Carrington, J. Scott and S. Wasserman (Eds) *Models and Methods in Social Network Analysis.* Cambridge: Cambridge University Press, pp. 117–147.

Goodman, L.A. 1996 'A single general method for the analysis of cross-classified data: reconciliation and synthesis of some methods of Pearson, Yule, and Fisher, and also some methods of correspondence analysis and association analysis' *Journal of the American Statistical Association* 91: 408–428.

Greenacre, M.J. 1984 *Theory and Applications of Correspondence Analysis.* London: Academic Press.

Kim, K.H. 1982 *Boolean Matrix Theory and Applications.* New York: Marcel Dekker.

Le Roux, B. and Rouanet, H. 2004 *Geometric Data Analysis: From Correspondence Analysis to Structured Data Analysis.* Dordrecht, the Netherlands: Kluwer.

Mickey, M.R., Mundle, P. and Engelman, L. 1983 'Boolean factor analysis' in W.J. Dixon (Ed.) *BMDP Statistical Software.* Berkeley, CA: University of California Press, pp. 538–545.

Mische, A. 2007 *Partisan Publics: Communication and Contention across Brazilian Youth Activist Networks.* Princeton, NJ: Princeton University Press.

Mische, A. and Pattison, P.E. 2000 'Composing a civic arena: publics, projects, and social settings' *Poetics* 27: 163–194.

Mohr, J.W. and Duquenne, V. 1997 'The duality of culture and practice: poverty relief in New York City, 1888–1917' *Theory and Society* 26: 305–356.

Musheno, M.C., Gregware, P.R. and Dass. K.A. 1991 'Court management of AIDS disputes: a sociolegal analysis' *Law & Social Inquiry* 16: 737–774.

Pattison, P.E. and Breiger, R.L. 2002 'Lattices and dimensional representations: matrix decompositions and ordering structures' *Social Networks* 24: 423–444.

Ragin, C.C. 1987 *The Comparative Method: Moving beyond Qualitative and Quantitative Strategies.* Berkeley, CA: University of California Press.

Ragin, C.C. 2000 *Fuzzy-Set Social Science.* Chicago: University of Chicago Press.

Ragin, C.C. 2006 'Set relations in social research: evaluating their consistency and coverage' *Political Analysis* 14: 291–310.

Ragin, C.C. 'Qualitative comparative analysis using fuzzy sets (fsQCA)' in B. Rihoux and C. Ragin (Eds) *Configurational Comparative Methods: Qualitative Comparative Analysis (QCA) and Related Techniques.* Newbury Park, CA: Sage Publications (in press).

Ragin, C.C., and Becker, H.S. (Eds) 1992 *What Is a Case? Exploring the Foundations of Social Inquiry.* Cambridge: Cambridge University Press.

Weller, S.C. and Romney, A.K. 1990 *Metric Scaling: Correspondence Analysis.* Newbury Park, CA: Sage Publications.

Wolf, K.E. and Gabler, S. 1998 'Comparison of visualizations in formal concept analysis and correspondence analysis' in Blasius, J. and Greenacre, M. (Eds) *Visualization of Categorical Data.* San Diego: Academic Press, pp. 85–97.

APPENDIX: NORMING OF SCORES IN CORRESPONDENCE ANALYSIS

A correspondence analysis of a rectangular matrix provides sets of scores on dimensions for the row categories and sets of scores for the column categories. There are numerous different ways to norm the scores. Any two legitimate normings for rows (or any two for columns) will be linear transformations of each other, and hence correlated perfectly. Nonetheless, the choice of norming is consequential. A lucid discussion of this point (and many others) is Goodman (1996); (see also Faust, 2005) and Blasius and Greenacre (2006) for barycentric correspondence analysis).

Correspondence analysis

The fitted cell values (F_{ij}) of the correspondence analysis (CA) of a rectangular table may be expressed as follows, with respect to the sum (N) of cases in the table and the proportion of all the cases that fall in each row (p_{i+}) and the proportion of all cases that fall in each column (p_{+j}):

$$F_{ij} = Np_{i+}p_{+j}(1 + \lambda_{ij}) \qquad (1)$$

The λ_{ij} are the interaction terms. If all $\lambda_{ij} = 0$, then the correspondence analysis model devolves to the simple model of statistical independence. Above and beyond the independence model, the CA model posits that all interactions may be represented as a multidimensional structure:

$$\lambda_{ij} = \sum_{m=1}^{M} r_{im}c_{jm} \qquad (2)$$

where the analyst postulates M dimensions for rows (the r scores) and for columns (the c scores). We will call the r_{im} scores and the c_{jm} scores 'weighted scores' (following

the terminology of Weller and Romney 1990, p. 62). These scores are normed as follows:

$$\sum_i r_{im}p_{i+} = 0; \qquad \sum_i r_{im}^2 p_{i+} = \sqrt{L_m} \quad (3a)$$

$$\sum_j c_{jm}p_{+j} = 0; \qquad \sum_j c_{jm}^2 p_{+j} = \sqrt{L_m} \quad (3b)$$

where L_m is the principal inertia (Blasius and Greenacre 2006; speaking somewhat loosely, L_m is a descriptive measure of the association in the table that is accounted for by dimension m of the CA).

Barycentric correspondence analysis

Because we find it useful to do so, we may define transformations of the row and column scores (and, hence, alternative normings for them). For example, we may define transformations of the row scores as

$$u_{im} = \sqrt[4]{L_m}r_{im} \qquad (4)$$

(i.e., multiplying the row scores r_{im} of eq. 2 by the fourth root of the principal inertia, L_m). Following terminology common in the literature, the row scores u_{im} of eq. 4 are referred to as 'principal coordinates'.

We may choose to apply a different transformation to the column scores of eq. 2:

$$v_{jm} = \left(1 / \sqrt[4]{L_m}\right) c_{jm} \qquad (5)$$

(i.e., dividing the column scores c_{jm} of eq. 2 by the fourth root of L_m). The literature refers to the column scores v_{jm} of eq. 5 as 'standard coordinates' (or sometimes as 'optimal' or 'canonical' scores).

The squares of the standard coordinates for the column scores of eq. 5 are normed, not to $\sqrt{L_m}$ (as in eq. 3b), but to 1. The squares of the principal coordinates for the row scores of eq. 4 are normed, not to $\sqrt{L_m}$ (as in eq. 3a), but to L_m.

The asymmetric normalizations of row scores and column scores, as defined above, produces a barycentric correspondence analysis. The definitive feature of barycentric CA is as follows (Blasius and Greenacre 2006, p. 32). With respect to data tables, x, such as those often presented in QCA publications, tables showing cases as rows and variables as columns, the score u_{im} for any case (row point, in principal coordinates) is the weighted mean of the scores for variables (column points, v_{jm}, in standard coordinates). The weights are given by the ith row of table x (showing the proportion of that row's counts that appear in each cell). An example is given, for the Slovenes of Italy, in the first section of this chapter.

Many common statistical packages perform correspondence analysis and identify scores normed to 'principal coordinates' and to 'standard coordinates'. Any of these CA programs can be used to construct a barycentric CA. For purposes of this chapter, the author used programs he wrote in the R language.

Degree of association of cases and causal combinations with the outcome variable

If the row scores and the column scores are the 'weighted scores' shown in eq. 2 and normed as in eq. 3, then Goodman (1996) shows that the interaction structure of the model may be written equivalently to eq. 2 as:

$$\lambda_{ij} = dist(i)\, dist(j) \cos(i, j) \qquad (6)$$

which 'says' that the association between row category i and column category j as postulated by the M-dimensional CA model is equal to the (Pythagorean) distance of row category i from the origin, times the distance of column category j from the origin, times the cosine of the angle formed by connecting the points representing both categories to the origin. This equation provides the basis for the geometric interpretation of 'degree of association' with the outcome variable in crisp-set analysis that I have illustrated in discussing Figure 13.3 (in discussion of sufficiency analysis for the ethnic mobilization example). Substitution of eqs. (4) and (5) into eq. (2) shows that eq. (6) also holds if row scores (for

Table A-1 Interaction scores λ_{ij}, where j = Mobilization and i indexes the thirty-six ethnic groups

Ethnic group	Interaction score	Comment (compare Table 13.4)
FlemingsBelgium	1.25	
GermansBelgium	1.25	LWSG and
AlsatiansFrance	1.25	Mobilization
CatalansSpain	1.10	
BasquesSpain	1.10	SWG and Mobilization
OccitansItaly	1.10	
FriuliansItaly	1.10	
WalloonsBelgium	0.73	SGL and Mobilization
SouthTyroleansItaly	0.73	SLW and Mobilization
SwedesFinland	0.73	
ValdotiansItaly	0.72	LWG and Mobilization
SlovenesItaly	0.72	
CorsicansFrance	0.58	
BretonsFrance	0.58	
WelshGreatBritain	0.58	SG and Mobilization
OccitansFrance	0.58	
CatalansFrance	0.58	
WestFrisiansNeth	0.58	
AalandersFinland	0.20	LW and Mobilization
FlemingsFrance	−0.48	SL and Not mobilization
GaliciansSpain	−0.64	S and Not mobilization
SardsItaly	−0.64	
BasquesFrance	−0.65	
DanesGermany	−0.65	G and Not mobilization
NorthFrisiansGermany	−0.65	
LadinsItaly	−0.65	W and Not mobilization
GreelandersDenmark	−1.01	
SlovenesAustria	−1.01	L and Not mobilization
CroatsAustria	−1.01	
MagyarsAustria	−1.01	
LappsNorway	−1.17	
GreeksItaly	−1.17	
AlbanianItaly	−1.17	Ø and Not mobilization
LappsSweden	−1.17	
FinnsSweden	−1.17	
LappsFinland	−1.17	

points i) are normed to principal coordinates and column scores (for points j) are normed asymmetrically to standard coordinates, as is the case with barycentric CA.

Table A-1 shows the interaction scores, λ_{ij}, where j = Mobilization (the dependent variable in the crisp-set analysis) and i ranges across all ethnic groups. Notice that the interaction scores in Table A-1 are proportionate to distances formed by the projections in Figure 13.3. This result (on which see Goodman 1996) provides the foundation for thinking of 'degree of association' in Mobilization, the dependent variable of the crisp-set analysis, with respect both to cases and to configurations of independent variables (see Example 1, above, Analysis of sufficiency).

14

Using Cluster Analysis, Qualitative Comparative Analysis and NVivo in Relation to the Establishment of Causal Configurations with Pre-existing Large-N Datasets: Machining Hermeneutics

David Byrne

In the social sciences, with the availability of online datasets we often have large-N – up to several thousand – datasets that contain large amounts of quantitative information about sets of cases. With all the appropriate and necessary provisos about casing (see Ragin 1992) taken into account, the cases in these datasets are typically rather tightly bounded institutions or administrative units, which can be taken as cases for the purpose of exploration and causal analysis. Typically, these datasets are available as spreadsheets, usually in some format that can be read into Excel and hence into statistical packages such as SPSS (Statistical Package for the Social Sciences) and into qualitative comparative analysis (QCA) software. A range of such sets is typically the product of the administrative collections of statistical information. Here, we can illustrate how we can type data using cluster analysis in SPSS and then use QCA as a preliminary quantitative exploratory tool in relation to outcomes for institutions and then move on to further qualitative investigation – if you like a tool-based version of the hermeneutic circle. The essential basis of such exploratory use revolves around identifying contradictory configurations in a first pass with QCA and the moving from these contradictory configurations into qualitative further investigation. This is often surprisingly easy, as, for a range of public institutions, not only do we have online datasets but also online qualitative reports based on inspections. These reports represent 'found' field studies and can be interpreted in order to establish further distinctive aspects among the cases within a contradictory configuration. In effect, we can use the packages and the methods contained within them in a machine shop fashion. SPSS allows us to create types, which is particularly useful in relation to outcome variables. As Rihoux and Ragin (2004, p. 18) have remarked:

> ... policy researchers, especially those concerned with social as opposed to economic policy, are often more interested in different kinds of cases and their different fates than they are in the extent of the net causal effect of a variable across a large encompassing population of observations. After all, a common goal of social policy is to make decisive interventions, not to move average levels or rates up or down by some minuscule fraction.

Studies of this kind are particularly valuable when we are trying to assess achievement of clearly defined objectives for case entities in the form of public institutions that have such objectives specified for them by governments. However, we can extend the idea beyond this to consider outcomes as state conditions for any set of entities for which we have this kind of mix of quantitative and qualitative information. An example of the first kind that will be used to illustrate the procedure here is the set of English state secondary schools. For this set, we have a range of statistical descriptors and inspection reports available online. We can define outcomes in terms of the clear and specific goals associated with maximizing performance by cohorts of pupils in public examinations. An example of the second kind would be 'post-industrial' cities in the European Union that we can classify using

a clustering technique and contemporary data, and then use historical data and qualitative materials to try to establish multiple causal paths towards different post-industrial city-system states in the present.

The first thing to appreciate is that we are here concerned with understanding that is to do with the establishment of cause. Our methods do involve interpretation, but in a rather different mode from that which Vulliamy (2004, pp. 276–277) has described:

> ... ethnographers, influenced by traditions such as poststructuralism, postmodernism, feminism and postcolonialism, that stress multi-perspectivism and the complex interrelationships between language, knowledge and power, have been critical of code and retrieval software packages and the grounded theory approach underpinning them. ... Instead they have experimented with the textual presentation of data through hypertext and hypermedia programmes, where the reader can choose different pathways through both selections of qualitative data – such as field notes, documents or interview transcripts – and the author's discourse analysis of them. They argue that hypertext software helps preserve the complexity and multi-meanings of social life by enabling a presentation of text that is non-sequential, unlike code and retrieval packages which privilege the sole linear account of the researcher.

The second thing to appreciate is that we should always regard any quantitative measure describing a case as an attribute of that case. It is really rather important to stress that attributes should be distinguished from variables as that term is normally understood. In traditional variable-centred causal analyses the variables can work outside the cases and can and do have causal power assigned to them as abstract 'de-caseified' entities in their own right. Following Byrne (2002), variate measures describing cases are here understood as traces of the cases represented by the systems which are the cases. The use of the term 'attribute' reinforces this integral character of the measures. They are part of the cases and not extractable from them as reified active variables. As we shall see the term attribute can be carried over into our qualitative work in a useful and meaningful way.

STATE SECONDARY SCHOOLS IN THE NORTH EAST OF ENGLAND

It is convenient to work with a dataset describing all 126 state secondary schools in the North East Government Office Region of England, although we could equally well do this with all of the some 3000 secondary schools in England as whole. The data came from administrative returns for 2006. Here, we have information on all of the cases so no issues of sampling arise. From the large set of descriptive attributes available for these schools, we have selected and constructed the following subsets:

School identifier

Local Education Authority identifier

% pupils getting 5 or more A to C grades GCSE

% pupils getting 5 or more A to G grades GCSE

% pupils getting at least one pass any grade GCSE

Average point score of pupils at GCSE

% of days lost to authorized absences

% of days lost to unauthorized absences

% of pupils with any special need

Comp, VA or VC (i.e. non-selective school)

Religious school

Binarized high AC5 – constructed variable

Binarized high average point score – constructed variable

Binarized state high special needs – constructed variable

Low-binarized state AC5 – constructed variable

Low-binarized average points score – constructed variable

Mixed

6th form

% of pupils eligible for free school meals – deprivation measure

Binarized % of pupils eligible for free school meals – deprivation measure, constructed variable

Binarized two-step cluster 2 – constructed variable

A notable absence from the dataset are data on the ethnic composition of school pupil cohorts. This would matter a great deal in an all-UK study, but the North East of England has a very small ethnic-minority population and no secondary school has more than about 7% of its pupils from ethnic minorities.

All of the binarized attributes were constructed using the Visual Bander in SPSS to partition the corresponding continuous aggregate measure. The binarized cluster membership variable was constructed using two-step cluster with each of the following attainment measures used to construct the clusters: % 5 A–C GCSE, % any pass GCSE, average point score GCSE. The result was a split into an 'adequately performing' and 'inadequate' set, as in Table 14.1.

We can see that the clusters are relatively distinctive by comparing box-plots of the distribution of the average GCSE points score (Figure 14.1).

Using the conventional difference-of-means test to examine cluster differences, all the variables used to construct the clusters can be seen to be highly significantly different in relation to mean scores. This is not a process of inferring from samples; we have a population here. Rather, it is a convenient way of using existing statistical tools to establish that the two clusters really do seem to contain different

Table 14.1   Two-cluster solution for school cohort pupil performance

		Good achievement in public exams		Average uncapped GCSE and equivalent point score per pupil – adjusted		% of pupils achieving any qualifications	
		Mean	Standard deviation	Mean	Standard deviation	Mean	Standard deviation
Cluster 1	171 cases	52.8	11.0	412.0	43.75	99	1
Cluster 2	284 cases	28.7	8.0	321.4	44.2	96	3

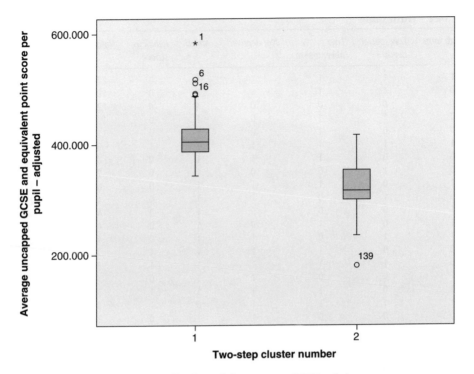

Figure 14.1   Box-plots of the distribution of the average GCSE point score.

sorts of cases in relation to overall pupil cohort attainment profiles.

We next carried out a crisp-set QCA using the cluster membership as effect and the following variables as input:

Comp, VA or VC (i.e. non-selective school)

Religious school

Mixed

6th form

Binarized state high special needs – constructed variable

Binarized % of pupils eligible for free school meals – deprivation measure, constructed variable

Binarized % of days lost to unauthorized absences – order measure, constructed

This generated the following truth table (Table 14.2):

Let us explore this table. We can see that six positive configurations were fully resolved, containing nine cases. Eight negative configurations were resolved containing

20 cases. However, for the purpose of exploratory use of QCA beginning with quantitative attribute sets, it is precisely the contradictory configurations that are interesting. Many of these configurations are almost resolved, with a minority being in the non-dominant category for the configuration. We can look more closely to see what is different about the case(s) in the configuration that has the minority outcome. This is a way of deploying the logic of what De Meur and Gottcheiner (Chapter 11) refer to as a 'most similar different outcome' design as a basis for a move from quantitative to qualitative comparison. An example is row 3 in Table 14.2 (bold text), above which there is just one school that is in the configuration:

No sixth form – not low special needs – not low deprived – not low absenteeism – not religious – mixed– is in the adequate achievement cluster

What is different about this school? We can identify schools in this configuration by using Select If in SPSS to extract the configuration

Table 14.2 Truth table

Has sixth form	Low special needs	Low absenteeism	Not deprived	Mixed	Religious school	Number	% in adequate attainment cluster
1	1	1	1	1	0	27	82
0	1	1	1	1	0	18	61
0	*0*	*0*	*0*	*1*	*0*	*12*	*8*
0	1	1	0	1	0	12	17
0	0	1	0	1	0	11	27
1	1	1	1	1	1	9	78
0	0	1	1	1	0	8	63
0	1	0	0	1	0	7	0
1	0	1	1	1	0	6	33
0	1	0	1	1	0	4	25
1	0	0	0	1	0	4	0
1	0	1	0	1	0	4	0
1	1	0	1	1	0	4	25
0	0	1	1	1	1	3	67
0	1	1	1	1	1	3	100
1	0	0	1	1	0	3	33
1	0	1	1	1	1	3	100
1	1	1	1	0	1	3	67
0	0	0	1	1	0	2	0
0	1	0	1	1	1	2	50
1	0	0	0	1	1	2	0
1	1	0	0	1	0	2	50
0	0	1	0	1	1	1	0
0	1	0	0	1	1	1	0
0	1	1	0	1	1	1	0
1	1	0	1	0	1	1	100
1	1	0	1	1	1	1	100
1	1	1	0	1	0	1	100

Table 14.3 School achievements

School	Number of pupils	% special needs	% achieving level 2	% functional English and Maths	Average GCSE points score	Average no. qualifications	% score absenteeism	% free school meals
C	910	11	28	85	311.6	9.6	2.9	40
D	839	13	38	93	326.1	9.5	1.9	23
E	726	15	16	73	266.0	11.1	1.7	28
F	941	16	9	77	274.6	8.9	1.9	24
G	335	28	21	94	309.8	10.0	1.9	21
H	880	18	31	90	315.1	9.5	1.7	31
A	**543**	**16**	**34**	**95**	**427.0**	**12.7**	**2.9**	**35**
B	810	15	20	82	388.3	11.7	2.8	31
I	520	19	19	83	243.6	8.4	3.5	40
J	805	15	21	77	240.6	8.2	2.1	32
K	743	15	18	79	180.0	7.7	7.6	27
L	898	18	27	86	341.3	10.5	2.8	21

as a separate dataset and can examine their quantitative profiles below. The adequate achievement school here is School A. We can see from Table 14.3 that this school is doing much better on GCSE scores than most of the others in the set, although, School B is only 10% behind it and its performance is above the mean for the adequate performance cluster.

There is clearly a threshold effect in cluster allocation here but that reflects reality itself. School A is not significantly better on any of the measures of deprivation, special needs or order – indeed, it does not do best of the set on any of these single criteria being third highest or worst on all three criteria. Neither is size an issue. It is one of the smaller schools but by no means the smallest. So what it makes it different? This is where we go qualitative.

Before going into how we use NVivo (a qualitative data analysis software package) to explore further in search of causality, a methodological mark is in order. We are pursuing path dependency in relation to causation when we work forward from a single configuration. In other words, we are not attempting to add something to our causal account for all cases but rather to add something to account for difference in this particular set of cases – a set of non-religious, mixed-sex, 11–16 schools with high proportions of special needs and poor children and with relatively high absentee rates. One of them is different. What makes it different from others like it? This might not make a difference for other sorts of schools but it will for these sorts of schools. We can, of course, add any newly discovered factors or set of factors to the truth table analysis and apply the factor to all cases. For many it will be irrelevant. Sorting that out is the job of the Boolean reduction part of QCA. But for these schools with this character it will matter.

This has practice implications. In policy, it is perfectly appropriate to recognize the inherent truth of the apocryphal Irish directional instruction – I wouldn't start from here if you want to get there. Schools in this set cannot hope to emulate the City Technology College, Emmanuel College, which combines creationist teaching with active overt selection and that, whereas it has a high proportion of special needs children, has only 6% of children on free school meals, one-third the regional average. Such schools also cannot realistically hope to emulate the more straightforward excellent local comprehensive, Lord Lawson of Beamish (named after an ex-miner-turned Labour MP and then peer), which is the

second best performer at GCSE and has 10% special needs and 10% children on free school meals. However, they can imitate School A, because this is the same sort of entity that they are.

For English secondary schools, we have available qualitative documents in the form of regular inspection reports prepared by Ofsted teams. We can look at these quite comprehensive documents, which include some quantitative information (and in particular ranking statements in relation to management and aspects of teaching) alongside a good deal of straight text-based qualitative commentary. That for School A is available online – as all Ofsted reports are – at: http://www.ofsted.gov.uk/oxedu_providers/full/(urn)/111733/(type)/8192/(typename)/Secondary%20education.

What most people do with NVivo is work through the texts they have and code blocks of text to one or more 'nodes' or subnodes representing themes. The purpose is largely to retrieve illustrative material for a textually based argument. Occasionally, but not that often, the model-building facility is used to construct a visualization of the relationship among themes. However, a case-based approach is different; it begins with attributes. The NVivo package works on the basis of the construction of nodes. Generally, these are thematic nodes, that is, they represent a particular theme, which emerges from the interpretative reading of texts generated by qualitative research. For example, Byrne and Doyle (2005) found that a set of focus groups that were discussing the cultural implications of the end of coal mining in a town in the North East of England spent a lot of time talking about 'dirt', but with very different interpretations of the meaning of dirt. This was an '*in vivo*' theme, to use the grounded theory approach. However, we can also identify case nodes in NVivo so each focus group, and also each individual within each focus group, is also represented as a case node. NVivo allows for the creation of a special form of node – the case node – to which we can attach all information not about themes but about each case with which we are working.

Creating case nodes is literal casing. In the mining study cases were people with attributes such as age, sex, work experience and so on identified and coded. We also had case nodes for each group with attributes defining type of group, location, numbers of people and so on. NVivo has a facility that allows for the importation and export of attributes as .dat files. In our schools example, we are working with predetermined cases in the form of the schools, so we would create a case node for each school and import our existing SPSS .dat file to create our preliminary attribute set.

We then read carefully through all our qualitative information – in this case in the first instance the Ofsted inspection reports, which we can conveniently and easily download from the web as text documents.

Note that attributes are understood in a different way here from variables – when we measure variables we go to the world with an operationalized mechanism for constructing data. It is perfectly true that with 'open-ended' questions we do actually see what the world is telling us before we construct the coding frame through which we constrain text – information held in the natural language of everyday life as Bateson (1984) called it – into data expressed as numbers. However, we do not generally recognize what a revolutionary process this is. We actually let people tell us about the world before we construct our measurements and we do so on the basis of what they have said. Thinking and working in this fashion we generate attributes as measures, which emerge from our engagement with textual and other representations of the world. Note what NVivo says below:

Attributes are information about the people, sites or other items represented by the documents or nodes in your project.

In other words, attributes can be constructed as information about cases, but this information can be developed through a grounded and continuing interpretive engagement with actual information about the world expressed as text and images.

Another aspect of NVivo, which can be useful to us, is 'sets'. This is simply a way of organizing things into categories. In general, in the creation of attributes we should have a unique set of attributes for each case node, although we might want to organize documents associated with a particular case into sets.

Working in the first instance with Ofsted reports, which are already in existence and can be turned into files that can be read straight into NVivo as documents for thematic coding, we can explore what is different between the adequately performing school in this set and those that are not doing well. This will allow us to explore thresholds and how cases approach them. We are not, of course, confined to the Ofsted reports; we can go down the whole qualitative route if we can get access: we can interview significant actors in the schools, we could observe ourselves (if permitted) to reinforce or contradict the 'secondary observation' in the form of Ofsted reports that we have mined in order to work from thematic coding through to the construction of new attributes, and with the new attributes constructed we can refine our QCA analyses to see what difference they make to our account of causality. One qualification is that Ofsted reports come out at different dates, but all those reviewed were written since 2003.

In many ways, this looks like a twenty-first-century version of the hermeneutic circle in its traditional form. As Crotty (1998, p. 92) puts it:

> … in order to understand something one needs to begin with ideas, and to use terms, that presuppose a rudimentary understanding of what one is trying to understand. Understanding turns out to be a development of what is already understood, with the more developed understanding returning to illuminate and enlarge one's starting point.

In a very preliminary run through of some of the Ofsted reports for the set of schools addressed here, I have identified differences in relation to staff turnover, exclusion policies, presence of disruptive minorities and teaching styles as significant. A comparison between School A and School C was particularly informative. School C's Ofsted report was generally very positive and management/leadership was just as strongly endorsed as was the case for School A – the school has made very considerable improvement over recent years – but there were comments on continuity of staff and on the negative impact of a minority of pupils, not so much in behavioural terms as in relation to non-attendance, very poor performance and lack of parental interest. This group was identified as exceptional in relation to general good engagement with the school by pupils and parents, but no such group was identified in School A. Specific mention was made in relation to School A of a very effective targeted mentoring programme. School C was praised for its initial mentoring but it is plain that mentoring is a much more targeted and extensive process at School A. So even on a preliminary scan something has emerged that could explain a difference and could be transferred as good practice from one locale to the other.

Table 14.4 was constructed after reading through Ofsted reports for the schools in this set that still exist; one school has been closed and another school has been transformed into a Church of England Academy and no Ofsted reports are available in consequence. It is readily evident that using Mills' original method of difference we can establish that staff-led intensive mentoring is the single distinguishing feature of the successful school in the set. So, immediately, we have a policy recommendation that is achievable.

To employ a very useful expression suggested by Charles Ragin, this study has taken the form of a possibility analysis. In other words it has enabled us to establish something that makes a difference and about which something can be done. The children in these schools would certainly do better if they were less deprived, and as the current author is a life-long social democrat from a family with a four- (becoming five-) generational commitment to that political position, he regards greater social equality as achievable. That said, it is, in the current political climate, a medium-term objective. Introducing mentoring schemes based on School A's style can be done very quickly.

Let me conclude with a comment on generalization here equivalent to scope as discussed in several chapters in this Handbook. This study can make no claims for generalization of its causal account beyond the limits of a particular set of schools in the North East of England in the first decade of the twenty-first century – and that does not matter at all. The point has not been to make generalizable claims but rather to demonstrate the effectiveness of the method as a way of managing available quantitative and qualitative data in order to establish what works. We have found something that works here and now – what is transferable is the method of approach, both generally as a way of working which combines the quantitative and qualitative, and specifically in policy analyses where we have this kind of data available. The causal claims here are local and

Table 14.4 School data

School	General overall view inspectors took of the school	Management assessment	Presence of disruptive minority	High staff turnover	Specific mention of staffed mentoring scheme
C	+ve	+ve	Yes	No	No
D	+ve	+ve	Yes	No	No
E	−ve	−ve	Yes	Yes	No
F	−ve	+ve	Yes	No	No
H	+ve	+ve	No	No	No
A	**+ve**	**+ve**	**No**	**No**	**Yes**
B	+ve	+ve	No	No	No
I	+ve	+ve	No	No	No
J	−ve	+ve	No	No	No
L	+ve	+ve	Yes	No	No

real for a certain kind of secondary school in a particular region in a particular time period. The generalizable claim is for the approach as a technique.

As a final demonstrative point, it is worth contrasting the configurational approach to these issues with the most obvious frequentist statistical method – binary logistic regression. This was done with the same variable set but using the continuous (i.e. not binarized) data for percentage free schools meals (deprivation), percentage of pupils with special needs and percentage of unauthorized absences. The categorical variables input were gender of intake, whether or not religious, and whether or not the school had a sixth form. The model worked well. It had a Nagelkerke R square of 0.628 and the Hosmer and Lemeshow test showed a significance of 0.000 in terms of difference between observed values on performance cluster and those predicted by the model. This can be illustrated best by the prediction table generated by fitting the model (Table 14.5). When all cases were assigned to the most common outcome category, 56% were correctly assigned. However, when the model was fitted assignation improved to 86%.

Exploring for high residuals identified the deviant cases listed in Table 14.6.

School A is case 49 and is picked out by this method as 'misclassified' but logistic

Table 14.6 Deviant cases, revealed after exploring for high residuals

Case	Observed Two-step cluster number	Predicted group
16	1**	2
49	2**	1
52	2**	1
89	1**	2
145	2**	1

regression gives us none of the details of this, unlike QCA, which shows us which set of schools it belongs to and enables us to move to qualitative exploration. This is a good illustration of Kent's point (see Chapter 10) to the effect that configurational methods enable a much more detailed exploration of complex causation than is possible with conventional frequentist statistical methods.

REFERENCES

Bateson, N. 1984 *Data Construction in Social Surveys*. London: Allen and Unwin.

Byrne, D.S. 2002 *Interpreting Quantitative Data*. London: Sage.

Byrne, D.S. and Doyle, A. 2005 'The visual and the verbal – the interaction of images and discussion' in C. Knowles and P. Sweetman (Eds) *Exploring Cultural Change Using Visual Methods*. London: Routledge.

Crotty, M. 1998 *The Foundations of Social Research*. London: Sage.

Ragin, C. 1992 'Introduction' in C. Ragin and H. Becker (Eds) *What Is a Case? Exploring the Foundations of Social Inquiry*. Cambridge: Cambridge University Press, pp. 1–19.

Rihoux, B. and Ragin, C. 2004 'Qualitative comparative analysis: state of the art and prospects'. Presented at American Political Science Association Convention, Chicago, IL.

Vulliamy, G. 2004 'The impact of globalisation on qualitative research in comparative and international education' *Compare* 34(3): 261–284.

Table 14.5 Classification table[a]

Observed		Predicted		
		Two-step cluster number		Percentage correct
		1	2	
Step 1	Two-step cluster 1	55	11	83.3
	number 2	10	74	88.1
	Overall			86.0
	percentage			

[a]The cut value is 0.500.

Qualitative Approaches to Case-Based Research

15

Computer-Based Qualitative Methods in Case Study Research

Nigel Fielding and Richard Warnes

INTRODUCTION

In recent years the practice of qualitative data analysis has been substantially influenced by the emergence of CAQDAS – computer-assisted qualitative data analysis. Qualitative software has enabled more formal and systematic approaches to qualitative data analysis, facilitated closer integration of findings from qualitative and quantitative research and stimulated engagement with multimedia data sources. However, both the methodological literature and developers of qualitative software have largely confined their attention to code-based rather than case-based approaches to qualitative data analysis, and software developed to support the analysis of case study data in the pursuit of causal analysis has been neglected outside that field. The case study field may benefit from a closer engagement with qualitative software,

and users of qualitative software may benefit from widening their horizons to include software developed with case study analysis in mind.

This chapter profiles the affordances of qualitative software in order to draw out how features to enable code-and-retrieve analytic work can be used by the case study researcher. In addition to code-and-retrieve functionality, relevant features include the ability to construct Boolean searches, facilities for analytic memo-ing and data annotation, features supporting data visualization and conceptualization, and procedures enabling interrelation of quantitative, qualitative and sociodemographic data. Following an extended empirical example of synthesis between code-based and case-based analysis, the chapter outlines other computational applications that can extend the range, depth and dimensionality of case study research.

QUALITATIVE ANALYSIS, QUALITATIVE SOFTWARE AND CASE STUDY RESEARCH

The contemporary field of case study research takes the 'turn to the case' as a deep, fundamental departure from the conventional form of scientific explanation whereby the engine of explanation is causality and causality is explained by examining the operation of variables on cases. Cases are the subordinate element in this logical framework, being the determined result of the play of variables on empirical instantiations of the phenomenon of interest. Colloquially, the position is that, to achieve causal explanation, science has to get its head up from the particularities of individual cases and instead focus on the cross-case commonalities that remain once tests of necessity and sufficiency have stripped out mere association. Being the dominant element, the successful identification of operative variables carries the kudos, and a concern with the particularities of cases suggests the kind of character defect associated with being more interested in the trees than the wood.

Contributors to the debate over the 'turn to the case' note, however, that this picture of scientific explanation is overdrawn and that, in reality, science closely studies individual cases, notably where they appear anomalous. This important observation does not alter the dominance of attention to variables relative to cases. Any scientist would concede that cases are useful, as they are the test-bed against which models expressed as variables are elaborated, then to be refined against anomalous cases. But case study method would not stand as a distinct and rising field of interest not only in social science but in natural sciences like biology, biomedicine and physics, if individual cases merited attention only when apparently anomalous. Those interested in the 'turn to the case' see further value in considering individual cases beyond a concern with the anomaly. To consider a case in and of itself can suggest alternative variables, alternative mechanisms and processes that help us understand phenomena but that are not best-captured under the rubric of 'causality', and can also help us do causal explanation without recourse to variable-centred method.

The conventional juxtaposition in social science by which the tension is captured between variable-centred methods and alternative analytic agendas is the juxtaposition between quantitative and qualitative methodology. In fact, there is no logical reason that quantitative methods cannot be employed in pursuit of explanations other than those based on the analysis of variables and factors, nor any logical reason that qualitative methods cannot be used in pursuit of causal explanation. There are, however, rather compelling practical obstacles to such endeavours. It is necessary to point this out because by simply resting with the bipolar quantitative/qualitative distinction one might assume that all qualitative methods offer a more conducive framework for case study research and that, therefore, computational support for qualitative research will necessarily offer effective tools for case study research. In fact, the position is rather different.

Whereas it is certainly true that most qualitative researchers would endorse an understanding of cases as specific and unique instances to be understood in their own terms (tagged by the editors as 'the ideographic project'), the sway of the variable-centred method extends deep into much qualitative research. A form of reasoning that thinks in terms of small samples is still a form of reasoning that pursues the logic of sampling, and the instinctive approach to qualitative research is to look for similarities and differences across cases. Samples may not permit confident generalization to a population, but, in purely logical terms, the instinctive posture is indistinguishable from variable-centred method. In the dominant approach to qualitative analysis, which was also the dominant inspiration for the large majority of developers of qualitative software, the interest in cross-case comparison is entirely explicit. That approach is, of course, grounded theory, and in their seminal statement, Glaser and Strauss (1967) subtitled grounded theory as 'the constant comparative method'.

Thus, for many qualitative researchers, the essential computational support for their analytic work is that which enables substantive, generic 'codes' to be applied across a set of cases as well as within each individual case, with a view to the 'retrieval' for analytic purposes of all similarly coded data. As we will see, there are some important variations in features supporting different analytic strategies, but it is not coincidental that qualitative software is sometimes referred to as 'code-and-retrieve software'. It needs to be noted, though, that there is nothing inherent in such a procedure that prevents its use in case study work. This part of the chapter aims to show how computational procedures for the analysis of qualitative data that were largely modelled on code-based analytic strategies can be applied in case study research.

Other features of qualitative software (or CAQDAS; Fielding and Lee 1991) also show their origin in the tenets and procedures of grounded theory but are equally adaptable. A prominent element of grounded theory procedure is the expectation that the analyst will regularly break off from the work of coding in order to write an 'analytic memo'. Such memoranda might be about some quality of the code, with a view to informing the eventual drawing up of a doctrinal 'code definition' that will ensure consistent application of the code, but they could also be about other features of the data. Grounded theorists take the position that the conditions in which a given analytic insight emerged might lend further understanding of the insight, so some memoranda are about the analyst's current or general circumstances, or are only weakly connected with the data segment that has in some way prompted the writing of a memo.

A third principal feature of CAQDAS is the provision of tools and features to support the visualization and conceptualization of relationships within the data. While features like graphic idea maps – which use directed graphs, arrows, mathematical symbol sets and other visual means to represent relationships between data, analytic categories and conceptual schema – might seem to have little necessary tie to the dominant data reduction mechanism of the 'code', the reality is that the fundamental unit and nodal point in features like 'tree structures' or 'network views' is the code label. Thus, if one invokes the 'tree structure' in one of the variants of the *NUD*IST* package (currently *N*7), the representation is of a hierarchical coding scheme, downward progress through which takes one to N degrees of specificity beneath the top level codes. If one operates the 'network view' in *ATLAS.ti*, the nodal points are code labels, between which one can assign directed lines, and to whose lines one can assign either free text labels or an array of logical relationship types (such as 'is a kind of' or 'leads to' or 'causes'). If the graphical representation features of CAQDAS provide users with the most free play for their analytic imagination, then it is still an imagination organized around codes.

The fourth principal feature of CAQDAS that will be remarked here is the provision of features to enable quantification of the dataset held in the software, or its export to a statistical package, or for statistical information to be imported into the software. The key tools here are the data matrix (Miles and Huberman 1994) comprising row-and-column tables, and a set of features derived from content analysis methodology (Berelson 1952) and software, such as simple word counts, Key Word In Context features and wild card (word root) searches. In the mainstream practice of qualitative research using CAQDAS, the data matrix rows are often populated with codes and its columns with cases (i.e. 'data with this code can be found in this case') or with data segments (i.e. 'data with this code can be found between these line numbers'). Once again, a key feature of qualitative software is organized around codes.

Thus, the field of qualitative software is very much modelled on code-based rather than case-based approaches to qualitative analysis. Happily, the obstacles to case-based use posed by the dominant paradigm in qualitative software are not intrinsic to the features themselves and the operations they support. Rather, they are largely a question of nomenclature, leaving the case study researcher with a requirement to translate, but not, at least, to invent anew. It is a premise of the new seriousness with which case-based analysis is being addressed that the in-depth investigation of single cases can contribute to the intellectual project of generalization by revealing relationships and processes that compensate for the vulnerability of causal explanation to spurious explanation in terms of simple association. The centrality of the coding paradigm to qualitative software is an obstacle but not a bar, because the procedures and features we have mentioned are generally amenable to use within single cases. While some case study work results in a holistic account at the level of the case, it is here assumed that getting to grips with the case will involve a good deal of work examining its elements and the components of the data (of various sorts) available to the researcher. We need now to specify these procedures and to note how some of the twenty or so qualitative software packages in common use support them, remarking in the course of the discussion how given features might be used by the case study researcher primarily concerned with exploring a single case.

COMPUTATIONAL SUPPORT FOR QUALITATIVE RESEARCH

A key publication, Weitzman and Miles (1995), the sourcebook for many when negotiating the process of evaluating, selecting and using qualitative software (but now obsolete in the specific programs reviewed), demonstrated that computers are now routinely used at each stage of qualitative research, from the design and data collection stages to analysis and presentation. While early development work sought to refine basic procedures of data management, code assignment, annotation of extracts or codes and the search-and-retrieval process, another contribution of CAQDAS is that it makes our analytic work more transparent and self-documenting, creating an

'audit trail' allowing users to trace how given findings and conditions have been derived. This helps rebut a principal criticism of qualitative research, that analysis takes place 'in the researcher's head' and is thus non-reviewable and unsystematic.

Managing qualitative data is often repetitive and tedious, conditions ripe for error. CAQDAS's support for formatting, segmenting and marshalling data into meaningful units ready for analysis helps address this. Qualitative software can help with other major bottlenecks, such as transcription, and can support work with multimedia data. For example, the *HyperResearch* package's *HyperTranscribe* tool supports transcription of digital audio and video, and podcasts. Several CAQDAS packages can handle video data, sometimes with all the same functionality offered for managing and analyzing text. Qualitative software's data management capacities are often the principal attraction to users, but most will also exploit the code-and-retrieve data analysis routines and Boolean retrieval features. Leading packages all include graphical tools for idea mapping, procedures and tools to handle quantitative data, and even facilities to operate other software directly within the qualitative program. As not every feature is available in every package, and users will want tools specific to their approach, informed choice is crucial.

In the seminal typology of qualitative software, Tesch (1990) contributed the important idea that, to answer the question 'what is the best package', one had to be clear about what kind of analytic work was intended, both in current and future projects. Tesch thus organized her typology around different kinds of analytic work. Choice begins by learning what is available. The best-known classification is that of Weitzman and Miles (1995): the three types are named for the analytic work characterizing them: text retrievers, code-and-retrieve packages and theory-building software. Kelle (1997) argues that this typology represents successive generations of software, and Mangabeira (1995) argues that the distinctive feature of third generation software is that it supports model building.

While the threefold typology remains broadly valid, it is important to note the increasing convergence of features as developers learn from each other and from users.

Weitzman and Miles's 'text retrievers', such as *Metamorph, WordCruncher, ZyIN-DEX* and *Sonar Professional* are akin to content analysis programs. They focus on recovering data using keywords selected by the user. Entering 'case study' thus retrieves every occurrence of the phrase in the chosen text. Strings of characters that are not words can also be retrieved, searches can be confined to a sub-set or performed across all files, and searches can be performed for things that sound similar or have similar meanings. Being able to search for strings mixing characters and numbers is useful when searching within bureaucratic documents including alphanumeric unique identifiers, such as social security card or health service records. Analytic memos can be linked to the data segments, to code terms, or to the beginning of each case (e.g. to interview transcript headers). Like other qualitative software, text retrievers readily provide various counts, such as the number of data segments or cases with a given code, how many segments have been coded and how many are 'noise', and so on.

Text retrievers retrieve data very quickly and can handle very large documents, but have limited features. Nevertheless, counting occurrences of a theme or category can be highly informative, and sophisticated analyses can be based on simple counts. Anderson et al. (2001) counted the number of lines of text in field observation notes between occurrences of codes representing children's reasoning strategies; the decreasing number of lines verified an increasing convergence of argumentation strategies between the children as they worked in problem-solving groups. An exception to the 'limited features' point is the *QDA Miner* package, which offers both strong content analysis features modelled on contemporary text mining principles, and functionality similar to that of highly specified qualitative software. For case study researchers the principal utility

of text retrievers probably lies in being able to do a first sift of the data quickly, to get an initial sense of recurrent themes and patterns, and of the distribution of 'hits' between different key terms.

'Code-and-retrieve' packages occupy the core ground of qualitative software. As developers aimed especially to support grounded theory, which generates a thematic analysis based on codes expressing aspects of the themes derived from the data, these packages particularly support dividing texts into segments, attaching codes to segments and retrieving segments by code. In case study work, the researcher taking Yin's (1994) approach might design main codes relating to pattern-matching, explanation-building and time-series analysis. Retrievals can be done that combine more than one code or are based on how codes relate to each other, for example, where data coded 'case study methods' coincides with data coded 'code-based methods'. Retrievals can be selective of only particular respondents or other divisions in the data. Code sets can include information that has been collected for all respondents, such as sociodemographic variables like age, sex and marital status or organizational information like a condition that varies between case study sites, such as whether a hospital does or does not have an Accident and Emergency (A & E) department. Retrievals can thus combine conceptually-based codes and sociodemographic or organizational features, such as length of hospital stay by patient age by presence of an A & E department by expressed attitude towards hospitalization. Searches can use the basic Boolean operators AND, OR, NOT and XOR, such as retrieval of data only where two characteristics apply but not a third, for example, data from TEENAGE respondents and who were ADMITTED UNDER THE INFLUENCE OF ALCOHOL and who were NOT released within 24 hours. Proximity operators like NEAR and CO-OCCUR are usually available.

While providing full code-and-retrieve capacities, 'theory-building' software, the third main type of qualitative software, also helps users create higher-order, more abstract classification schemes, semantically oriented typologies and representations of data other than those derived from codes, such as tools to formulate and test propositions using hypothesis-testing features. Theory-builders provide graphical features to visually represent relationships in the data. Code names, analytic memos, header file information or any other object within the worked project are displayed as nodes that can be linked to other nodes. Values can be assigned to links between nodes, as can relationship types (such as 'leads to', 'is a kind of', 'causes' and so on). In some packages, like *MAXqda*, the link is purely a visual representation whose function is confined to symbolizing relationships, but in packages like *Qualrus*, *N-Vivo7* and *ATLAS.ti*, the links are functional, so data can be retrieved based on the links between codes. Thus in *ATLAS.ti*, the data associated with an expressed relationship can instantly be inspected to check how well the relationship applies (Figure 15.1).

N-Vivo7's relationship nodes provide another way to link categories: the relationship itself acts as a code. This means that the relationship automatically enters the code set, a form of 'system closure' enabling automation of retrievals in subsequent iterations of the coding scheme (Figure 15.2). With system closure, the results of every analytic query are 'banked' and added to the dataset, and the composition of a complex retrieval is retained so it can be repeated as new data are added. Automated coding based on the previous retrieval can then be performed each time the dataset is changed.

Some theory-builders offer artificial intelligence system features. *Qualrus* users can define criteria that must be satisfied for a code to apply to a given extract and if these are not satisfied the program will prompt the user that they have violated the rule. *Qualrus* will suggest codes based on several computational strategies, including grounded theory constant comparison. When selecting a segment to

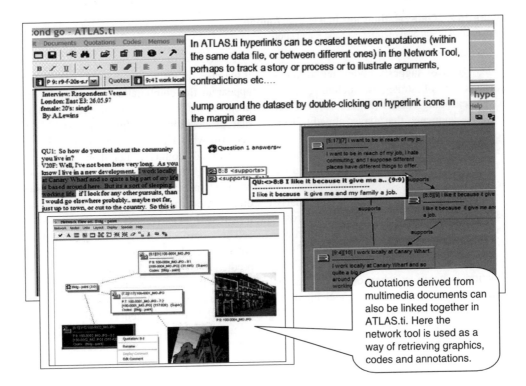

Figure 15.1   Hyperlinking in ATLAS.ti (version 5).
Source: Lewins and Silver (2007). © Sage Publications.

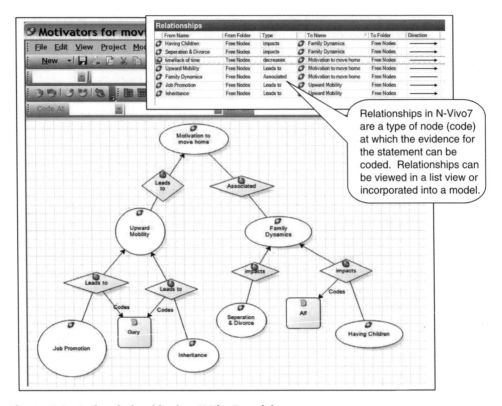

Figure 15.2   Code relationships in a N-Vivo7 model.
Source: Lewins and Silver (2007). © Sage Publications.

code, *Qualrus* suggests codes based on a combination of strategies, including case-based reasoning (CBR) (Figure 15.3). CBR reviews segments that have already been coded, identifies those most similar to the current segment and suggests codes applicable to it based on those applied to the similar segments.

Hypothesis test features can be particularly useful in case study research involving cross-case comparison. This tests hypothetical relationships between the occurrence of one entity in the data and that of another. The function is iterative: when co-occurrence is found, this can be used as an element of a further hypothetical relationship. IF/THEN rules can take the form 'For a given case, IF code A is present AND code B is present AND code C is present THEN ADD code D'. To construct meaningful hypotheses several IF/THEN rules may be needed. The *Hyper-Research* program majors on this feature.

It searches for instances where the code words appear in the combinations required by the proposition. When they do, the case supports that proposition. A helpful approach is to perform what Hesse-Biber et al. (1991) call 'directional' coding rather than 'coding for content'. Codes like 'self image' do not help when it comes to hypothesis testing. To signal direction one needs two codes: 'positive self image' and 'negative self image'.

This approach clearly relates to analyses where causal explanation, modelling and prediction are pursued, but relies on an epistemological perspective that regards qualitative data as reliable, valid and a secure base for generalization. Consistent code application is essential to it. Analytic memo writing can help ensure consistency of coding, as can the criteria prompts provided by artificial intelligence (AI) software like *Qualrus*.

Related to coding consistency, and as important to the premises of case-based

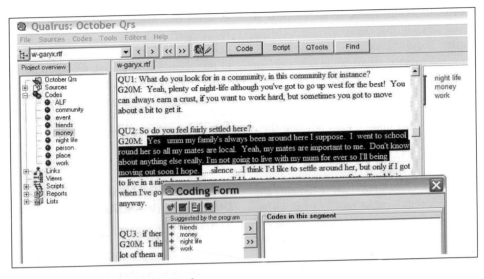

Figure 15.3   Code prompting in Qualrus.
Source: Lewins and Silver (2007). © Sage Publications.

reasoning, is clarity about data segmentation. Determining criteria for defining the content, and extent, of segments is critical because the data segments effectively function as *de facto* cases against which researchers test their emergent understanding. Segmentation runs the gamut from whole research sites or interviews through to the linguistic components of individual utterances. In many cases, the completed analysis will draw on segments all along such a range, as in our extended example below. Particularly where a holistic case study is intended, the questions arise of the most suitable level of segment granularity, and whether there are generic segment types that are likely to be present in any case study of field sites of a given kind. Such questions oblige us to be explicit about the ways in which cases are understood, and in particular, how they are understood both as a whole and by way of their parts.

A system theory and social constructionist's take on this would involve an additive explanation of the phenomenon and also provide for contingency, whereby a different 'whole' would result if the same 'parts' behaved differently than in the observed instantiation. Thus, in a political protest outside an animal research facility, one might identify as key parts the actors and activities

comprising the event *in toto*: activists, onlookers, facility staff, police, journalists. Speech acts and physical behaviour are driven by contingencies of personality, networks of social relationships, specifics of the issue, the formal and informal regulatory framework, the physical circumstances (e.g. climate, site layout) and so on, and could eventuate in different outcomes through variation in any of the parts. It might develop into a 'riot', result in a 'negotiation' or 'fizzle out'. But the event would remain an instance of the general class of 'political protest' rather than 'war' or 'carnival' because of the parts from which it came into being and their purposes in calling it into being.

Ultimately, the researcher's sense of what should be the necessary 'parts' depends on analytic perspective and theoretical approach, although Lofland and Lofland's (1994) distinction between acts, actors and activities offers an accessible heuristic adaptable to any theoretical position. What is important to say in the context of software is that the computational support can and should be used to reflect the researcher's conception of key parts and overarching whole. For example, memo writing and annotation tools can be organized in a hierarchy if the researcher takes an 'organization chart' perspective on the case, including blank levels or cells if data are missing that the researcher's theory indicates should logically be present. The latter circumstance might be an occasion, in software with expert systems functionality, to build in code prompts reminding the researcher to look for signs of what was not found in the first coding pass but that their theory suggests should be there.

While CAQDAS packages provide tools to organize, manage, explore, inter-relate and interpret qualitative data, it remains the user who decides what tools to use, what constitutes a segment (and, indeed, whether to analyze at case level or use codes), what codes to apply and with what level of granularity (utterance by utterance, paragraphs, whole case), what retrievals to perform, and whether the results are analytically significant. While Figure 15.4 shows that qualitative software offers a lot, it also indicates that users face many choices. Lewins and Silver (2007) provide comparative reviews of a wide range of CAQDAS packages at a feature-by-feature level of detail that might be particularly useful in making such choices.

We have emphasized that coding is the dominant paradigm in computer-based qualitative data analysis, as it is in offline qualitative data analysis. However, there is an important strand of thinking that does not employ coding but uses instead the hyperlinking capacities of some qualitative software packages to simply link, without labelling, sections of text (or other data) that are in some way associated. Some testify that this approach better reflects the thought processes involved in making connections as one reads qualitative data (Stanley and Temple 1995). Also an advantage for such users is that the links can reflect the fact that not all researchers read transcripts and other case study material in strict chronological order. In elaborating a theme, researchers might well have a prior idea of where they need to look, and this might especially be so in case study work of the sort expounded by Yin (1994), in which the final case study is the result of a highly systematic series of procedures designed to render the case

in terms that make it immediately available for comparison with other cases. Weaver and Atkinson (1995) provide a detailed exposition of this approach. Although the software with which they illustrate the argument is now obsolete, a number of contemporary packages enable segments to be linked without the application of a code label.

COMPUTATIONAL SUPPORT FOR QUANTITATIVE ANALYTIC STRATEGIES

While this chapter's prime focus is qualitative software, there is other computational support for case study research involving statistical and other quantitative techniques. Several of these relate to mainstream statistical techniques and any standard statistics software package such as *Stata*, *R* or *SPSS* will support them. It is not, therefore, proposed to profile the operation of such software, but it is worth briefly noting some of the analytic strategies themselves.

Qualitative data that have been quantified, such as by recording separately for each case the presence/absence of a given code, enable the calculation of the frequency of the code's occurrence and the production of a case-by-variable matrix. Statistical techniques like cluster analysis, correspondence analysis and multi-dimensional scaling are then in frame. To illustrate, types of adaptation to labour force position that have been documented in non-standardized interviews can be made the basis of a probabilistic cluster analysis, in order to relate perceived social class to income measures. The proximity and probability of classification of each respondent towards the centre of the relevant cluster (i.e. type) can thus be visualized and categories reduced to a smaller number of dimensions by multiple correspondence analysis. Kuiken and Miall (2001) used this technique to specify experiential categories they had identified from interview responses in social psychological research comparing different readers' impressions of the same short story, where

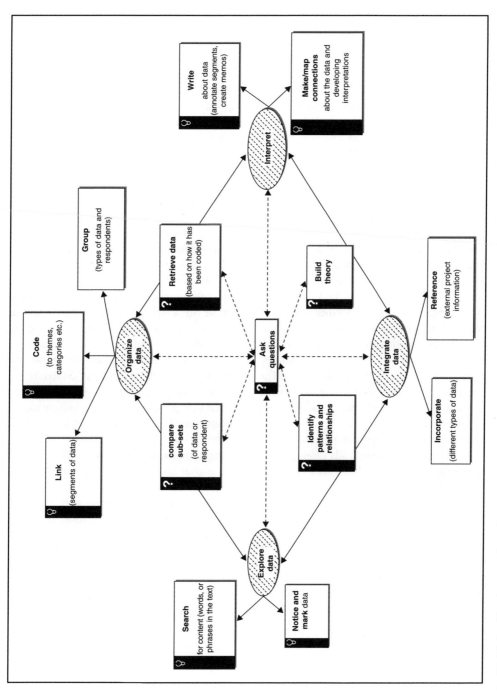

Figure 15.4   Multiple affordances of qualitative software.

each reader was an individual case. After identifying attributes qualitatively, categories were specified by a quantitative cluster analysis that systematically varied the presence of individual attributes. There was then a further qualitative inspection of the clusters in order to further differentiate the types. For a review and a detailed worked example of the use of correspondence analysis in case study research, see Phillips and Phillips (Chapter 8).

In research into the design of mixed methods projects, Niglas (2004) used scales to measure variation on several design characteristics. Cluster analysis produced eight distinctive groups and indicated the characteristics discriminating between them. Niglas then compared the characteristics to commentaries written during her initial reading of each project, producing summary descriptions of each group. These were used as elaborated definitions to assign studies into categories representing variables for further statistical analysis. For a critical assessment of the logic of similarity and dissimilarity underpinning cluster analysis as an exploratory statistical technique, see Uprichard (Chapter 7), and for an extended example of the application of the technique, see Downward and Riordan (Chapter 23).

Having noted the ways that qualitative software might be used in case study research, and some principal numerically based techniques with affinities for case study method, we now briefly consider Ragin's rendering of case study analysis in terms of 'qualitative comparative analysis'.

QUALITATIVE COMPARATIVE ANALYSIS

Ragin (2000) argues that the governing analytic interest of the social sciences should be in set-theoretic relationships rather than causal models based on relationships between variables. This naturally directs analytic attention to case-based reasoning. Code-based analysis predominates in contemporary qualitative research, but qualitative software readily supports case study research and case-based reasoning. There is specialist software to support one principal form of case-based analysis, Ragin's (1987) 'qualitative comparative analysis' (QCA). QCA is based on the Boolean algebra of sets and logic. It seeks patterns of causation in small to moderate numbers of cases by analyzing the configuration of possible causal elements associated with the presence or absence of the outcome whose causes are in question. The focus on configurations accommodates the possibility that different combinations of conditions can produce the same outcome, and allows for contradictory patterns of causation, where a positive outcome may result when a given condition is combined with one set of variables but a negative outcome results when it is combined with others.

In a process of 'Boolean minimization', the researcher prepares a 'truth table', which lists various combinations of variables that appear in a dataset. Each case, listed as the rows of a truth table, might be an interview respondent and each variable an attribute or an attitude that was or was not associated with the respondent. Software like Ragin's own *QCA* and *fsQCA* programs, or the CAQDAS package *AQUAD*, systematically compare each configuration in the truth table with all the others, removing ineffective configurations. Where two rows differ on only one causal condition but result in the same outcome, the condition that differs between the rows is 'ineffective' and can be removed, creating a simpler combination of causal conditions (Table 15.1).

Imagine you have two cases relating to a court's use of prison sentences. Upper case letters below show the presence of a condition, lower case its absence. The dash between terms signifies an AND relation:

Case 1: CRIMINAL RECORD – NO RELATIONSHIP – SUBSTANCE ABUSE – unemployed = PRISON

Case 2: CRIMINAL RECORD – no relationship – SUBSTANCE ABUSE – unemployed = PRISON

In case 1, imprisonment occurs where there is a previous criminal record, no steady

Table 15.1   Example of a truth table

Case	Criminal record	No relationship	Substance abuse	Unemployment	Prison sentence
A	0	0	1	1	1
B	1	0	1	0	0
C	0	1	1	1	0
...					
N	1	0	0	1	1

relationship, substance abuse, but the defendant is employed. In case 2, imprisonment occurs with a defendant who has a previous criminal record, abuses substances, is employed, but is not in a steady relationship. Imprisonment happens in one case where there is a steady relationship but not in the other. One can then infer that a steady relationship does not influence sentencing to imprisonment. The two configurations can then be combined excluding relationship issues, yielding,

CRIMINAL RECORD – SUBSTANCE ABUSE –
unemployment = PRISON

Imprisonment, on these two cases, occurs where there is a long criminal record and substance abuse despite defendants being in work. Resulting from such simplifications of conditions is a Boolean expression containing only the logically essential 'prime implicants'. To systematically achieve a formal analysis of case study data, QCA has real strength. It can be used with smaller datasets than those needed for multivariate statistical analysis, and it makes no assumptions about the nature of the variables (Fielding and Lee 1998). The *QCA* software manages the manipulation of the textual data and the production and iteration of relevant truth tables. A variant on this software package, *fsQCA*, provides support for the fuzzy set approach to qualitative comparative analysis (see below). The fuzzy set option enables work with sets whose membership is not 'crisp', that is, showing degrees of fit rather than full membership or full non-membership. These conditions are more often applicable to the kinds of relationships with which

social scientists work. The *fsQCA* package enables calibration of fuzzy sets using interval scale variables and provides an algorithm that renders a similar outcome to the truth table procedure but that accommodates the fact that conventional truth table analysis cannot be reliably performed in work with fuzzy sets because there is no simple way to sort cases according to the combination of causal conditions they display, since each case's array of membership scores may be unique.

As a procedure, QCA forces researchers to select cases and variables systematically, reducing the temptation to ignore 'inconvenient' cases. It acknowledges the context-specific character of causation. Although data analysis is always a matter of data reduction, QCA's data reduction is radical. But it is not unproblematic. One issue is in determining what should be the input conditions (Amenta and Poulsen 1994). Combinations of dichotomous variables grow exponentially from a base of two and, if there are many independent conditions, QCA becomes unwieldy. Size also decreases the chance that every logically possible combination will have an empirical referent. Combinations that are logically possible might be unlikely to occur in practice or be hard to detect or measure. Also, deriving conditions directly from empirical data, it can be hard to know what to select. Using theory might replicate orthodoxy or miss important conditions that existing theory does not address. How input conditions are to be defined and measured can be unclear. QCA uses dichotomous variables, so if we are working from qualitative case data some prior means of data reduction is needed. While software helps manipulate key elements of the data, it is a relatively limited part of QCA work, with most key decisions occurring offline.

A DETAILED EXAMPLE

To highlight the application and use of these methods in a practical context, an extended empirical example is drawn from ongoing research on counter-terrorist policing and security measures. This research draws on a series of interviews of senior police, security officials, military specialists and academic advisors in seven case study countries. Once transcribed, the interviews are being subjected to the comparative textual analysis of 'Grounded Theory' and the computer-assisted causal analysis of QCA as a means of developing explanatory knowledge in this field. Consequently, this is a multi-case, multi-method and multi-analytical research model. Ultimately, it is hoped that any explanatory knowledge generated can be utilized to develop computer-assisted causal modelling with the aim of identifying 'best practice'; those measures introduced by the case study countries that have effectively minimized, prevented and controlled terrorist threats, and any lessons to be drawn from them.

Research questions

A generic, semi-structured interview plan was utilized for all interviewees in the seven countries chosen as case studies: the UK, Ireland, France, Spain, Israel, Turkey and the USA. Given that there are considered to be three levels of research – exploratory, descriptive and explanatory/causal (Silke 2004) – and that this research hopes to develop explanatory knowledge in the field of counter-terrorism, the predominant level of questioning utilized in the research was based around 'how' and 'why' questions, which are more likely to generate explanatory data. Such focused how and why questions are 'likely to lead to the use of case studies, histories and experiments as the preferred research strategies. This is because such

questions deal with operational links needing to be traced over time, rather than mere frequencies or incidence' (Yin 2003, p. 6). In the counter-terrorism research the normal sequence was inverted, becoming 'why' and 'how'. Thus, 'why' has a particular Western nation had to respond to specific types of terrorist threat, whether religious, nationalist-secessionist, extreme right, extreme left or single issue, and 'how' has that particular nation responded with counter-terrorist measures, such as diplomatic–political, legal, security, policing, intelligence, military, economic and technical interventions, and what are their concomitant impact on civil liberties?

The questions were also designed and grouped in such a way as to make the resulting interview transcripts more amenable to the use of comparative code-based thematic analysis as part of the grounded theory research method. Whereas this research method stresses the importance of avoiding the forcing of the research material to 'fit' a particular hypothesis, and of allowing such a hypothesis to 'emerge' from the data, it was felt essential to provide some basic framework in the interviews to ensure that the particular terrorist threats and various counter-terrorist responses of the different nations were effectively covered. This was based around the 'threat' and 'response' categories previously mentioned. Although the interviewees in the different nations were asked the same general questions, they were free to respond and expand as they wished. Indeed, as a semi-structured interview plan, when an interviewee began to develop an interesting line of information or comment this was encouraged by the researcher's use of additional questions and if necessary, clarification was sought.

Case study design and unit of analysis

The level of questioning previously highlighted tends to lend itself to the development and use of case studies as a research strategy. As Yin (2003, p. 1) points out, 'in general, case studies are the preferred strategy when "how" or "why" questions are being posed, when the investigator has little control over events, and when the focus is on a contemporary phenomenon within some real-life context'. Yin further notes that a case study approach is particularly useful 'when the boundaries between phenomenon and context are not clearly evident' (Yin 2003, p. 13). Ragin (1987, p. 51–52) argues that such methods have a number of benefits:

> First they are designed to uncover patterns of invariance and constant association ... the second distinguishing feature follows from the first: the method is relatively insensitive to the frequency distribution of types of cases ... third, case-orientated methods force investigators to consider their cases as whole entities ... fourth, case-oriented methods stimulate a rich dialogue between ideas and evidence.

As part of the research design there is a need to define the nature of the 'case', which effectively forms the 'unit of analysis' being utilized in the research. For the purposes of this research design, the initial proposed 'case' unit of analysis was at a nation-state level, by 'country', thus examining each country's counter-terrorist responses as an individual case. As the research design was based on a comparative analysis, and as 'multiple cases offer the researcher an even deeper understanding of processes and outcomes of cases, the chance to test (not just develop) hypothesis, and a good picture of locally grounded causality' (Miles and Huberman 1994, p. 26), the research required a multiple 'case' study, with comparative analysis between the seven individual cases. While it can be argued that all the 'case study' nations should be considered 'Western' in terms of their orientation, political systems, international agendas and foreign policies, each nation was selected to represent a variety of different historical, political, legal, policing and cultural/religious backgrounds. In addition, each had both historically and more currently, suffered from significant levels of various types of terrorism, resulting in the introduction of widely differing forms of counter-terrorist response.

SYNTHESIS OF RESEARCH METHODS

Having obtained field data in the form of around 100 interviews from counter-terrorist 'practitioners' in the various case study countries and built up a large collection of primary and secondary documentary material, the material in the interview transcripts is being subjected to a synthesis of two main research methodologies: grounded theory originally outlined by Glaser and Strauss (1967), further developed by Strauss and Corbin (1998), and QCA, as developed by Ragin (1989). Whereas the former research method subjects the research data to 'constant comparative analysis', the later allows the identification of elements of 'causal analysis' from the material. A synthesis of these two research methodologies, and the use of multiple 'case studies', is more likely to develop generalizable explanatory knowledge.

Grounded theory

The first research method, grounded theory, is a form of 'constant comparative textual analysis' (see Bottoms 2000 for overview). According to Glaser and Strauss (1967, p. 102), 'the purpose of the constant comparative method of joint coding and analysis is to generate theory more systematically ... by using explicit coding and analytic procedures'. Such thematic analysis and coding allows the systematic 'comparative analysis' of the qualitative data obtained in the semi-structured interviews, leading to the 'emergence' of a more formal theoretical hypothesis.

Three main processes embody grounded theory. First, the interview transcript is subjected to 'textual analysis' through 'open coding', which fragments the material and identifies concepts within the data. 'The analyst starts by coding each incident in his data into as many categories of analysis as possible, as categories emerge or as data emerge that fit an existing category' (Glaser and Strauss 1967, p. 105). This process has been defined as 'breaking down, examining, comparing, conceptualizing and categorizing data' (Strauss and Corbin 1990, p. 61). As the coding of the interview transcripts progresses, sub-categories, links and other analytically developed thoughts are often identified and should be recorded in the form of memos, which can be examined later to aid in the development of a hypothesis. At first, the transcript material can be 'manually' coded to develop the researcher's skill in the process, but as this continues, computer software such as *N-Vivo7* may be used to assist with both coding and systematic retrieval, including the use of Boolean operators.

The second process to which the interview transcripts will be subjected is 'axial coding', which seeks to 'begin the process of reassembling data that were fractured during open coding. In axial coding, categories are related to their sub-categories to form more precise and complete explanations about phenomena' (Strauss and Corbin 1998, p. 124). Whereas Strauss and Corbin later developed a specific 'coding paradigm' for this part of the coding process, based around the four categories of conditions, interaction among the actors, strategies and tactics and consequences, this was explicitly rejected by Glaser, who argued that it went against the original concepts of grounded theory, namely 'emergence' and 'discovery', by attempting to fit the data into preconstructed paradigms (see Dey 1999, pp. 106–107). Rather, Glaser developed a much wider range of coding families to allow greater flexibility, while at the same time acknowledging that they were preconceived and insisting they be used only if they emerged from the data. Given the complex and varied nature of the data arising from multiple national 'case studies', it is more appropriate to follow Glaser's model.

Having linked and integrated categories and sub-categories in the data, in effect re-assembling the raw data, the interview material will be subjected to 'selective coding' where integration will occur around a central category which 'emerges' from the data. 'A central category has analytic power. What gives it that power is its ability to pull the other categories together to form an explanatory whole. Also, a central category should be able to account for considerable variation within categories' (Strauss and Corbin 1998, p. 146). Both Glaser and Strauss provide separate guides to the criteria necessary for such a central category (see Dey 1999, p. 111, Strauss and Corbin 1998, p. 147). In their original formulation, Glaser and Strauss (1967) emphasize the virtue of parsimony in variables, from which the number of categories will be reduced and theoretical saturation will be achieved. In summary, 'selective coding is the process of integrating and refining the theory. In integration, categories are organized around a central explanatory concept ... once a commitment is made to a central idea, major categories are related to it through explanatory statements of relationships' (Strauss and Corbin 1998, p. 161).

Such a procedure allows a great deal of flexibility in the initial stages of gathering and processing of the research material, and given the complex nature of the subject field this initial flexibility is essential, allowing the necessary range for objective analysis. Nevertheless, the incorporation of a formal, systematic procedure in the form of QCA offers greater depth and validity.

QCA allows the construction of 'truth tables' utilizing a binary system and a list of independent variables to assess the various causal factors of an event. Ultimately, the method minimizes down the various factors to define the key 'prime implicants', those factors which are logically necessary or sufficient causes. While there are various rules associated with the use of Boolean algebra (see Ragin 1989, pp. 85–102), the use of *QCA* or *fsQCA* software replicates the manual processing of data by such rules, managing and simplifying the use of the textual data. Effectively, through retrodiction, this will help identify causal factors from the data. Consequently, one of the most important factors in this analytic approach is the construction of the independent variables that form the input conditions.

A true synthesis between grounded theory and QCA would be to base the independent variables utilized for the 'truth tables'/input conditions in the QCA on factors that emerge as a result of subjecting the interview transcripts to grounded theory. Hence, along with a hypothesis, it is proposed to allow the pertinent independent variables to 'emerge' from the data through the process of grounded theory. The transcribed interviews will firstly be subjected to comparative analysis through grounded theory before the independent variables that 'emerge' from the material are utilized to subject some of the data to causal analysis through QCA. This synthesis between the two analytic approaches is an appropriate design for the research as both methods favour the use of case studies and comparative analysis. Whereas grounded theory allows the flexibility and range necessary to study such a complex subject without trying to fit the results to conform to a preconceived hypothesis, QCA helps identify elements of causality which will help develop explanatory research.

Quality of research design

Having outlined the extended empirical example with its case-based research design, attention can be focused on the quality of the design. Yin (2003, pp. 33–39) highlights four key tests that can be applied to an empirical case-based design to assess its quality. These are construct validity, internal validity, external validity and reliability.

In terms of construct validity (triangulation), a major concern of any research is that its methodology fails to be effective or operationally valid, leading to a significant element of subjectivity entering into the field research and the assessment of the resultant data. Two measures introduced to overcome such a problem in the research design are the use of multiple sources of evidence and the establishment of a logical chain of evidence. Consequently, the extended example utilizes a number of different research methods, both to 'triangulate' the results of the research from different sources and to ensure a logical 'evidential chain'.

The concern with internal validity in relation to any explanatory/causal research measure is that the researcher might make incorrect inferences if all aspects of the research subject are not considered and rival explanations are not addressed. Consequently, rival explanations contained in opposing propositions and their associated literature will be considered and addressed; for example, that the risk from terrorism has not significantly increased, and that Western nations have deliberately heightened public 'risk perceptions' for their own political agendas. A third concern is external validity, whether the results of the research can be applied beyond the immediate case research itself. This is particularly problematic if the research is based on a single case study, and consequently, the openness of the research to replication will be increased by its utilization of comparative analysis in a holistic multiple case design.

The final concern is whether the research is reliable; could the same logical steps be followed and replicated at a later stage and do the methods effectively measure what they are meant to measure? Consequently, each research step has been recorded and all data is retained in a logical manner to maintain a form of database, comprising copies of questions, interview transcripts, computer data and back-up CD-ROMs. Whereas the example highlights the examination of Western societies' counter-terrorist measures, and their effectiveness in response to the threat of terrorism, the approach outlined here is equally applicable to many research fields and topics.

New computational technologies and case study research

This chapter closes by outlining some emergent applications of grid and high performance computing that can extend the range, depth and dimensionality of case study research. In recent years, the data archiving community has promoted common standards for the formatting and annotation of data to facilitate secondary analysis. The idea is that such standards enable cognate data derived from different projects to be compared or combined. The role of the computer mark-up language XML is central to these developments. Using XML and software to read/edit XML documents also enables qualitative data analysis facilities to be incorporated into groupware applications like document bases and collaborative workspaces and to be used across networks (Carmichael 2002). Such developments address the increasing requirement for tools enabling dispersed research teams to collaboratively work on a dataset of shared interest. Combining XML with a scripting language like Perl facilitates collaborative analytic work on a qualitative dataset by offering CAQDAS-type functionality (retrieval by text and codes, annotation of text segments by memos, generation of tables, matrices and other data summaries) simply using a standard web browser. For case study researchers a particular benefit might be that this also makes it easier for research participants to collaborate more directly in the interpretation of data from research projects. Rather than a passive form of participation, simply providing data, participants can make their own input, offer their own views on the researcher's interpretations, and so on. Grid computing resources facilitate the Internet-based coexistence of raw datasets, proprietary CAQDAS software with XML integration, and other project-specific applications.

We earlier noted the basic procedures of QCA; QCA procedures systematically elaborate outcomes against conditions, enabling causally significant conditions to be identified. However, we also noted difficulties in defining input conditions and handling the exponential growth in combinations of conditions from a base of two. QCA is essentially a qualitative method, as field data are used to capture the conditions in each case studied, but the richness of field data poses a multitude of choices when it comes to defining input conditions. The resources made available by high performance and parallel computing can help resolve this problem. Such resources could enable QCA software to analyze definitive volumes of cases and conditions, and handle the many combinations generated by the exponential proliferation of logically possible input conditions. As one of the principal affordances of grid computing resources is the facility to radically speed up any numerical calculation, the computations required by the statistical procedures associated with other kinds of case study analysis, such as cluster analysis and multiple correspondence analysis, also stand to gain from exploiting new computing power (Crouchley and Fligelstone 2003; Crouchley and Allan, 2008).

With an orientation to the ways that humans use approximate information in conditions of uncertainty to generate decisions, fuzzy set theory resembles human reasoning in being specifically designed to mathematically represent uncertainty and vagueness (Zadeh 1965). It provides formalized tools for dealing with imprecision. It replaces the Boolean logic we considered earlier by a multi-valued logic allowing a gradual transition between members of binary states, and is thus suitable to many social science fields (Smithson 1988; note, however, that the analogy has limits; strictly, whereas fuzzy sets are often multi-valued, fuzzy logic and multi-valued logic are distinct). In the terms of Ragin's rendering of QCA, the application of fuzzy set principles permits membership in the interval between 0 and 1 while retaining the two states of full membership and full non-membership. Applications are as diverse as the control of traffic signals (Niittymaki 2001) and judicial decision-making (Cook 2001). Each of the five system types identified by McNeill and Thro (1994) as appropriate applications for fuzzy logic apply to social science problems: (i) complex systems that are hard to model and lack a mathematical basis; (ii) systems controlled by humans which a computer model is supposed to emulate; (iii) systems with complex and continuous inputs and outputs that behave in a non-linear way; (iv) systems whose rules are derived from human skills or that use common sense and intuition as the basis for a model; (v) systems that are naturally vague because their underlying mechanism is both unknown and dynamic. Zadeh (2001) suggests that, while more certain branches of mathematics and statistics have yielded large scientific advances, the ability to understand the behaviour of systems containing human interactions requires fuzzy logic techniques. High performance computing offers resources of speed and performance to those using the intensely computational techniques associated with the application of fuzzy logic to modelling case studies of human behaviour and its results.

ACKNOWLEDGEMENTS

The authors thank RAND Europe, Bramshill National Police Staff College, the Airey Neave Trust and institutions and individuals in the policing, intelligence, military and academic fields, whose support and insight enabled and facilitated the research discussed in the principal empirical example.

REFERENCES

Amenta, E. and Poulsen, J. 1994 'Where to begin: a survey of five approaches to selecting independent variables for QCA' *Sociological Methods and Research* 23: 22–53.

Anderson, R., Nguyen-Jahiel, K., McNurlen, B., Archodidou, A., Kim, S., Reznitskaya, A., Tillmens, M. and Gilbert, L. 2001 'The snowball phenomenon: spread of ways of talking and ways of thinking across groups of children' *Cognition and Instruction* 19(1): 1–46.

Berelson, B.R. 1952 *Content Analysis in Commmunication Research.* Glencoe, IL: Free Press.

Bottoms, A. 2000 'The relationship between theory and research in criminology' in R. King and E. Wincup (Eds) *Doing Research on Crime and Justice.* Oxford: Oxford University Press.

Carmichael, P. 2002 'Extensible markup language and qualitative data analysis' *Forum Qualitative Sozialforschung/Forum: Qualitative Social Research* 3(2).

Cook, B.B. 2001 'Fuzzy logic and judicial decision making' *Judicature* 85(2): 70–100.

Crouchley, R. and Allan, R. 2008 'Longitudinal statistical modelling on the grid' in N. Fielding, R.M. Lee and G. Blank (Eds) *The Handbook of Online Research Methods.* London: Sage.

Crouchley, R. and Fligelstone, R. 2003 *The Potential for High-end Computing in the Social Sciences.* Lancaster: University of Lancaster Centre for Applied Statistics.

Dey, I. 1999 *Grounding Grounded Theory: Guidelines for Qualitative Inquiry.* San Diego CA: Academic Press.

Fielding, N. and Lee, R.M. (Eds) 1991 *Using Computers in Qualitative Research.* London: Sage.

Fielding, N. and Lee, R.M. 1998 *Computer Analysis and Qualitative Research.* London: Sage.

Glaser, B. and Strauss, A. 1967 *The Discovery of Grounded Theory.* Chicago: Aldine.

Hesse-Biber, S., Dupuis, P. and Scott Kinder, T. 1991 'HyperResearch: a computer program for the analysis of qualitative data with an emphasis on hypothesis testing and multimedia analysis' *Qualitative Sociology* 14: 289–306.

Kelle, U. 1997 'Theory building in qualitative research and computer programs for the management of textual data' *Sociological Research Online* 2.

Kuiken, D. and Miall, D. 2001 'Numerically-aided phenomenology: procedures for investigating categories of experience' *Forum Qualitative Sozialforschung/Forum: Qualitative Social Research* 2(1).

Lewins, A. and Silver, C. 2007 *Using Qualitative Software: A Step-by-step Guide.* London: Sage Publications.

Lofland, J. and Lofland, L. 1994 *Analyzing Social Settings.* Belmont, CA: Wadworth.

Mangabeira, W. 1995 'Computer assistance, qualitative analysis and model building' in R.M. Lee (Ed.) *Information Technology for the Social Scientist.* London: UCL Press.

McNeill, F.M. and Thro, E. 1994 *Fuzzy Logic: A Practical Approach.* Boston: AP Professional.

Miles, M. and Huberman, A.M. 1994 *Qualitative Data Analysis: An Expanded Sourcebook.* Thousand Oaks, CA: Sage.

Niglas, K. 2004 *The Combined Use of Qualitative and Quantitative Methods in Educational Research.* Tallinn, Estonia: Tallinn Pedagogical University.

Niittymaki, J. 2001 'General fuzzy rule base for isolated traffic signal control-rule formulation' *Transportation Planning and Technology* 24(3): 227–247.

Ragin, C. 1987 *The Comparative Method: Moving beyond Qualitative and Quantitative Strategies.* Berkeley, CA: University of California Press.

Ragin, C. 2000 *Fuzzy Set Social Science.* Chicago: University of Chicago Press.

Silke, A. (Ed.) 2004 *Research on Terrorism: Trends, Achievements and Failures.* London: Frank Cass.

Smithson, M. 1988 'Fuzzy set theory and the social sciences: the scope for application' *Fuzzy Sets and Systems* 26: 1–21.

Stanley, L. and Temple, B. 1995 'Doing the business? Evaluating software packages to aid the analysis of qualitative data sets' in R.G. Burgess (Ed.) *Studies in Qualitative Computing. Volume 3, Computing and Qualitative Research.* Greenwich, CT: JAI Press.

Strauss, A. and Corbin, J. 1990 *Basics of Qualitative Research: Techniques and Procedures for Developing Grounded Theory.* Thousand Oaks, CA: Sage.

Strauss, A. and Corbin, J. 1998 *Basics of Qualitative Research: Techniques and Procedures for Developing Grounded Theory (2nd edition).* Thousand Oaks, CA: Sage.

Tesch, R. 1990 *Qualitative Research: Analysis Types and Software Tools.* New York: Falmer Press.

Weaver, A. and Atkinson, P. 1995 'From coding to hypertext: strategies for microcomputing and qualitative data analysis' in R.G. Burgess (Ed.) *Studies in Qualitative Computing. Volume 3, Computing and Qualitative Research.* Greenwich, CT: JAI Press.

Weitzman, E. and Miles, M. 1995 *Computer Programs for Qualitative Data Analysis.* Beverley Hills, CA: Sage.

Yin, R. 1994 *Case Study Research (2nd edition).* Thousand Oaks, CA: Sage.

Yin, R. 2003 *Case Study Research: Design and Methods (3rd edition).* Thousand Oaks, CA: Sage.

Zadeh, L.A. 1965 'Fuzzy sets' *Information and Control* 8: 338–53.

Zadeh, L.A. 2001 'From computing with numbers to computing with words: from manipulation of measurements to manipulation of perceptions' *Cajal and Consciousness: Annals of the New York Academy of Sciences* 929: 221–252.

16

Extending the Ethnographic Case Study

Seán Ó Riain

A CASE OF ETHNOGRAPHY

In 1997, I spent three months working at the Irish office of USTech, a Silicon Valley software company. Immersed in the work of the software team, I became a moderately competent technical writer and lived through the challenges of deadlines, arguments with managers and the tensions of workplace relationships. My time within the small partitioned space that enclosed the team's six members allowed me to unpick some of the key elements of the social world of the software team and their 'local' context (Ó Riain 2000).

I entered USTech searching for what remained of local relationships of production within a global corporate network and 'virtual' model of corporate organization. My hopes of using ethnography to reveal the crucial local foundations of global production were not disappointed – information sharing, cooperative relationships, tacit skills and the use of local relationships to resist global managerial control were all obvious within the team. The ethnographic case study had revealed the importance of place and after a month I was convinced that my study was a case study of the persistence of solidaristic local social worlds within virtual organizational forms.

This was, therefore, a classic example of the intimate tie between the ethnographic method and the case study, of an ethnographer burrowing into the social relationships of a specific local social world and revealing at least some of its internal dynamics and layers of meaning. However, the process was in fact much more complex – even for this modest ethnographic study.

The team reached the high point of this collective identity and solidarity the week that we submitted our latest version of the software program to our US managers – 'we' had done it! However, within days I found myself surprised and even dismayed to notice that our solidarity had dissipated. My co-workers were now in tense and sometimes open competition with each other for improved roles in the next project and access to interesting technical work. Suddenly the case I was studying was no longer my local world of solidarity but a local social world that shifted and changed with the pressures and opportunities of global markets, brought into the workplace through the rhythm of project deadlines. If software work was highly socialized, it turned out that software careers were highly individualized (Benner 2002). The theoretical debates to which I extended the case proved to be multiple and varied across the lifecycle of the ethnography itself.

As my theoretical questions shifted, so too did my search for empirical evidence. I began to follow these individualized careers, first through interviews with workers at USTech and subsequently with software developers in other firms. I followed workers through their networks and out into the technical communities of the Dublin region that turned out to be so critical to sustaining their work lives with technical tips in times of crisis, information on new jobs and sources of recommendations and warnings about industry developments. 'Networking', it turned out, was a crucial part of the software workplace and following those networks brought me far from the six men in a cubicle where I had started.

More surprising than these extensions in space were extensions in time. As I started writing the first analyses of the research, I realized that the world of software development in 1990s Ireland had been familiar to me – despite my complete lack of experience in the information technology industry. How was it that I had managed to begin to make sense of this world, even in the very short three months spent in the software team? As I read through the life histories of my co-workers, the similarities between their lives and my own became evident. Despite the differences between education and software, it turned out that our shared experiences in those months was embedded within a shared history of the Irish professional classes. I had spent some years on the opposite side of a university campus from one of my colleagues, many of us had emigrated for more challenging work and rewarding careers and then later returned, and I worked the same long, irregular hours that I criticized in the software workplace.

Therefore, this ethnographic case study had been significantly extended from that first month. It had been extended in space as I followed the networks of my co-workers and interviewed other workers like them. It extended in time as the dynamics of the project unfolded and as I realized that the starting point of this ethnography lay somewhere in my own personal history, entwined with the social history of the middle classes. It extended theoretically as the research became a case of quite different phenomena – of the foundations of global production in local relationships, of the global pressures of the deadline and how it formed and dissipated local solidarities, of the new deal being constructed between the Irish middle classes and their high-tech employers. With each extension came new questions, new interviewees and new situations to be explored. The extensions of the ethnographic case depended on the extension of the personal journey of the ethnographer – from the team into the industry, forward into the exploration of careers and backwards through the recognition of shared personal histories. These extensions made the boundaries of the case porous, the unit of analysis complex and the object of study a moving target. Yet, despite these various extensions, at the heart of what I learned about changing global workplaces was the time I spent embedded in the local context of the software team as participant and observer. The ethnographic context remained crucial but that context had been extended theoretically, empirically and personally. The character of the ethnographic case been made more inclusive but also more problematic.

ETHNOGRAPHY, CASES AND CONTEXT

What does this complication of the ethnographic case mean for ethnography? Ethnographic research has long been synonymous with case studies, typically conceived of as grounded in the local and situated in specific, well-defined and self-contained social contexts. Furthermore, these contexts were typically to be seen as cases of some larger phenomenon. Even when not theorized explicitly by ethnographers, the best ethnographies built arguments regarding more general processes of cultural formation, inequality generation, community formation, labelling of deviance and other significant sociological processes. However, even as case study research has increasingly emphasized the constructed, contingent character of cases (Ragin and Becker 1992), ethnographic research has itself begun to grapple with challenges to existing conceptions of ethnographic sites (Marcus 1998, Burawoy et al. 2000, Gille 2001, Gille and Ó Riain 2002). Ethnographers have sought to move beyond the concept of the fixed context, linked unproblematically to a case, and have sought to carry out ethnographies that are linked across sites, embedded in history, that incorporate their own personal histories and that link micro processes to macro structures and dynamics. How is ethnographic research transformed if it moves away from its moorings in the context-specific case study towards extended case methods (Gluckman 1961)?

This section of the chapter outlines the roots of ethnography in a 'contextualist' paradigm of social science (Abbott 1997, Burawoy 1998) and then goes on to explore some of the reasons why ethnographers might be particularly likely to challenge notions of cases as fixed context-specific entities (Ragin and Becker 1992).

Ethnography has been in many ways the paradigm of case study research, but has also been accused of the worst sins of case study research. Indeed, whereas some of the criticisms levelled at ethnographic research are specific to ethnographic data collection (e.g. personalized methodological decisions, unreliable data collection, inability to replicate studies) there are others that are aimed at the case study character of ethnography. These criticisms are typically levelled at the apparently unrepresentative character of ethnography and what Goldthorpe (2000) refers to as the problems of sampling within and across locations. We will discuss these criticisms in more detail later in the chapter but it is clear that ethnography and the case study

are intimately related – for both practitioners and critics.

Indeed, Abbott (1997, p. 1149) sees the classic Chicago school ethnographies of urban life in Chicago as the roots of a 'contextual paradigm' of social research that provides the best viable alternative to the variable-based approach to social scientific study. For Abbott, this paradigm is rooted in the study of social contexts: 'In a single sentence, the Chicago school thought – and thinks – that one cannot understand social life without understanding the arrangements of particular social actors in particular social times and places' (Abbott 1997, p. 1152). This is in essence the definition of ethnography – research that is based upon sharing the time and space of those who one is studying.

Understanding local contexts is crucial, moreover, to understanding broader cultural and social structures because contexts are the sites where these structures are produced, maintained and transformed. The link to ethnographic methodology is again clear: 'practical rationality and judgment evolve and operate primarily by virtue of deep-going case experiences. Practical rationality, therefore, is best understood through cases – experienced or narrated – just as judgment is best cultivated and communicated via the exposition of cases' (Flyvberg, 2001, pp. 135–136, Eliasoph 2005).

Ethnographic case study research sits, therefore, at the heart of the contribution that sociology can make: 'our discipline has the strongest theoretical tradition in social science founded on the idea of interaction and contextual determination' (Abbott 1997, p. 1177). Nonetheless, many of the 'first-wave' sociological and anthropological ethnographies did follow methodological conventions that restricted ethnographic cases to their immediate context and placed the ethnographer in the often uncomfortable but relatively clear position of 'alien' in a 'foreign' social world. Such an approach broadly shared certain assumptions, even if in practice the studies violated them – making the understanding of a specific social world the object of study, conceiving of those social worlds as self-constitutive and imagining the social group as a dense cluster of networks in a relatively bounded location (Glaeser 2006, p. 31).

These assumptions have been largely abandoned today, creating new challenges of defining, locating and studying 'the case'. To achieve a link between context-specific data and meso- or macro-level generalizations, ethnographers have adopted a number of strategies – and become more reflexive about those strategies. We can think of those strategies as falling under three interlocking extensions of ethnographic case research:

(1) *Personal extensions*: given the reflexive turn in social research, there has been a corresponding concern with how ethnographers themselves shape the cases that they study – no longer are ethnographers simply aliens uncovering unknown worlds. The embodied experience of the ethnographer is a crucial resource but also poses challenges in defining, and generalizing from, cases. The fluidity of ethnographic cases, the shaping of the boundaries of the case by the ethnographer's location within the field and the question of how ethnographers can convey their personalized experiences and tacit learning to readers become central questions.

(2) *Theoretical extensions*: as ethnographers became increasingly dissatisfied with treating the social worlds they studied as semi-autonomous and self-constitutive, they sought to understand those worlds in terms of the larger structures and processes that produced and shaped them. The bridge to these structures were the macro-sociological theories that ethnographers brought with them to the field and which they sought to prove, disprove and reconstruct (Burawoy et al. 1991).

(3) *Empirical extensions*: these theoretical extensions were often complemented – and at times problematized – by creative efforts to experiment with the empirical boundaries of the ethnographic case. Historical ethnographies, global ethnographies, embedding cases within studies of social networks and other methods were employed as ethnographers became increasingly explicit in their dissatisfaction with the notion of the social world as a dense, relatively bounded, cluster of networks.

The next section reviews the complexities of the personal journeys undertaken by ethnographers in a world of cases with uncertain boundaries. It suggests that whereas the fluid and multi-faceted aspects of the ethnographic case pose dilemmas for ethnographers, they can also become resources for ethnographers in exploring theoretical and empirical questions. The following section then goes on to explore three strategies employed by ethnographers in making these theoretical and empirical explorations – theoretical discovery, theoretical extension and theoretical reconstruction (Snow et al. 2003).

PERSONAL EXTENSIONS: EMBODIED LEARNING AND THE FLUIDITY OF CASES

At the heart of ethnography is the body of the ethnographer – a thinking, feeling, sensuous person constantly collecting 'data' from around them. The cool judgements formed of others within team meetings, the feelings of surprise at the change in the character of the software team after the deadline, the sudden sweat on my brow when under pressure to meet a deadline – all were valuable ways of learning about life inside USTech that could not have been achieved without ethnographic participation. Ethnography is irreducibly personal and the definition of the ethnographic case is in part traced by the ethnographer's personal journey through particular situations, roles, identities, networks, institutions and spaces and their embodied and interactive experiences with that journey (Wacquant 2004, Eliasoph 2005). Some ethnographers have fully embraced the personal dimension of ethnographic work, as indicated in the turn towards auto-ethnography, where the personal journey of the ethnographer is placed at the centre of the ethnographic research and writing process (Reed-Danahay 1997).

It is perhaps useful to think of ethnography as somewhat akin to an apprenticeship where the apprentice learns not only the skills necessary to practice a particular craft, but also learns what it means to be a member of that particular 'community of practice' – including the often tacit and apparently instinctive skills of posture, accent, tone and so on (Lave and Wenger 1990, Wacquant 2004). Learning these skills is a critical part of ethnography, one that can only be attained by 'being there': 'We, like the people we study, must learn the practices – be they boxing or fiddling or perhaps even shuffling papers in a cubicle – till they become second nature' (Eliasoph 2005, p. 160).

But this has also led ethnographers into a dilemma – the tension between the need to immerse oneself in the social world to learn its secrets and the analytical orientation that turns these runs of experience into elements of a case that can be examined sociologically. The concern with getting inside the social world and the interpersonal loyalties forged in that process has led to a strong emphasis on authenticity. However, the ethnographer's inevitable departure to write about his or her 'objects of study' raises issues of the moral and ethical commitments that stretch across and beyond the definition of 'the case' in space and time. This uncomfortable situation of the ethnographer is perhaps the underlying reason for the 'morality wars' that break out now and then with one group of ethnographers disparaging the political-moral credentials of others (e.g. Wacquant 2002, Katz 2004).

However, as Zussman (2005) points out, what ethnographers need to ply their trade and to provide useful understandings of social worlds and their formation is not authenticity but situatedness. It might in fact be the case that contemporary ethnography, with its many extensions beyond the immediate context, will render the ethnographer more of an 'alien' across multiple settings. Ethnographers of transnational connections, for example, do not face a journey into the heart of a community, with the associated search for acceptance, but instead a networked search for networked community across a range of people who may themselves have many and often partial memberships of the social worlds through which the ethnographer travels.

What these personal extensions do suggest is that there are new challenges to ethnography once the assumption of self-constitutive, relatively bounded social worlds is dropped. The processual character of ethnographic research is emphasized in this new context. All research methods involve a certain degree of evolution of theoretical focus and methodological strategy over the course of the research. However, ethnography is the most fluid of all the methods. The survey instrument that underpins statistical analysis 'fixes' the kind of substantive data that can be generated through the study – this becomes a crucial moment of definition of the research agenda. However, although there are certainly decisive turning points and decisions within ethnography, the ethnographer has significant flexibility in shifting theoretical focus, location within the field, the kinds of data being sought, and so on. The ethnographic case is therefore fluid and always open to re-definition on the ground. This is more so in the case of historical research, where the question may shift but the underlying sources cannot be generated anew (see e.g. Walton 1992). The personal journey of the ethnographer is not simply a question of moving through the case, but is part of the process of definition of the case.

Does this then simply dissolve the ethnographic case, or leave it floundering in the morass of personal predilections and the specificity of the ethnographer's location? As Eliasoph (2005) argues, we learn through embodied experience but this knowledge is very difficult to communicate to others. Some argue that a literary, evocative language might be necessary instead of sociology's dominant realist language. Others also turn to rhetoric and the ethnographic imagination as a solution (Willis 2000). Van Maanen (1988) argues that there are two moments of ethnography, the collection of data (which has received a great attention) and the process of writing the text (which has received much less). Can the rhetoric of ethnographic writing – once we recognize it for the sets of conventions that it consists of – bridge the gap between experience and understanding or explanation?

There is undoubtedly a strong evocative dimension to most, if not all, great ethnographic studies. Many ethnographies not only report on 'being there' inside the case but bring us as readers inside the case. However, this cannot be all that ethnographic cases are based upon if they are to aspire to some degree of the 'systematic generalization' that is the basis of a broad conception of science (Burawoy 1998). The embodiment of ethnographic experience and the evocation of that experience by bringing the reader inside the case are crucial and irreducible parts of ethnographic research. However, they do not solve the question of how we might formulate the ethnographic case but only pose the question all the more urgently given the fluidity of the case and its dependence on personal experience and location. It is essential, therefore, that we have additional sets of conceptual and practical tools if ethnographers are to locate their cases within broader social processes and not solely within their own personal trajectories.

Snow et al. (2003, p. 184) see a further moment between data collection and writing: 'the practices that ethnographers employ in order to transform their field data into narratives'. It is to these (often glossed over) practices and strategies that we can look for guidance as to how ethnographers can formulate case studies that are both contextual and extended. In fact, if such strategies are deployed creatively and thoughtfully, then the multi-faceted and shifting character of the ethnographic case can become a resource where different elements of theoretical interest can be explored as the research develops, where emerging theoretical questions or empirical trends can be explored rather than controlled for, and where the 'fit' between theory and data can be strengthened rather than weakened. The following section explores three such sets of strategies for extending the case, bridging theory and data.

VARIETIES OF EXTENSIONS OF CASE STUDIES

David Sudnow's ethnographic examinations of the criminal justice system are perfect examples of the enlightening potential of the bounded case study. Through a close examination of the work of the public defender's office in the US, Sudnow (1965) finds a system where routinized organizational practices structure legal outcomes (and particularly plea bargaining) more than the 'facts of the case' (which are often treated as largely irrelevant). Sudnow brilliantly explicates the internal dynamics of the situation in this particular institutional context and documents the processes at work.

However, he has little to say about the broader institutional and political conditions that sustain these processes, how these processes themselves shape patterns of power and inequality beyond the defendant processing system itself, about resistances to the process, or indeed about how other institutional regimes might create different kinds of 'normal crimes' – all topics that many ethnographers today would be concerned to explicate through similar kinds of case studies. In many cases, in these classic studies, the kinds of theory that were generated operated more as orienting frameworks that would allow researchers to identify particular patterns within the social world rather than to confront specific causal explanations (see e.g. Fine 1979).

The dilemma many contemporary ethnographers face is how to reach from the observable processes that are the bedrock of Sudnow's work out to these broader structures and processes that cannot be directly observed from within the case study itself. It is perhaps no surprise then that ethnographers themselves have sought to explicate the ways in which ethnography allows them to make causal arguments that link micro- and meso- or macro-level processes. These efforts range from 'weak' programmes that seek to identify points of potential causal explanation (e.g. Katz 2001, 2002, 2004) to 'strong' programmes that seek to establish ethnographic case-based research as a second approach to scientific generalization (Burawoy 1998).

Snow et al. (2003) seek to identify more systematic ways through which an 'analytic ethnography' can 'develop systematic and generic understandings and propositions

Table 16.1   Theoretical development and ethnographic case studies

	Theoretical discovery	*Theoretical extension*	*Theoretical reconstruction*
Dominant mode of empirical extension of case	Limited extension	Empirical extension to related cases	Selection of theoretically significant (and often 'negative') cases
Dominant mode of theoretical development	Domain-specific findings	Comparison of cases	Theoretical reconstruction in light of negative cases
'Carrier' of accumulated knowledge	Knowledge of findings in specific domains of study (e.g. the workings of the criminal justice system)	Middle-range theories and sets of findings regarding classes of cases (e.g. welfare state types and their dynamics)	Large-scale theories (e.g. theories of the general process shaping the organization of work under capitalism)

about social processes' (Snow et al. 2003, p. 181). The primary approaches that they suggest all relate to ways in which evidence might be extended to connect to theoretical debates – theoretical discovery, theoretical extension and theoretical refinement (or, to use Burawoy's phrase, theoretical reconstruction). In Table 16.1, I identify some of the main dimensions along which these approaches differ in significant ways. For each of the three approaches, I identify the dominant approach the ethnographer uses in exploring the boundaries of the empirical case – strategies that range from circumscribing the boundaries of cases, to comparing cases, to linking cases to existing theoretical and historical accounts of macro-structures. The table then outlines how each of these strategies relates to a mode of theoretical development and how that leads to an accumulation of knowledge. Again, the approaches vary in their ambitions and level of analysis – ranging from domain specific knowledge, through comparative analysis of cases at the middle range, to more general theories of macro-structural processes.

Snow et al. (2003) first identify the familiar approach within ethnography of *theoretical discovery*, the inductive uncovering of new concepts and conceptual tools in a manner similar to that of grounded theory (Glaser and Strauss 1967). Katz (2001, 2002) seeks to move ethnography from descriptive and interpretive goals to causal explanation without becoming hamstrung by weighty epistemological constraints or over-formalization of

these methodological strategies. He suggests a series of 'luminous' moments or forms within ethnographic descriptions that might serve to alert ethnographers to possibilities for intervention within the narrative description of 'how' the field works to offer causal explanations of 'why' it works as it does. These 'luminous descriptions' include, for example, data that shows subjects in poignant moments, that describe how conduct is socially situated, or that is a strategic resource for ruling out competing explanations (Katz 2002, p. 64). Elsewhere, Katz (2004) argues that the central method available to ethnographers for 'extending' ethnographic description is through the linking of the 'here and now' to the 'there and then' – a goal to be achieved through the strategic points of intervention in the ethnographic narrative identified in the earlier article. This programme seeks to extend the craft of ethnography to a set of tools and tricks of the trade that enable the creation of specific, localized causal explanations (see also Becker 1998). However, while Katz (2001, 2002) does seek to use illuminating moments within ethnographic cases to shed light on broader contextual effects, he does not offer a strong theory of how this knowledge accumulates across ethnographies or how existing theories and findings are incorporated into ongoing ethnographic cases.

However, Snow et al. go on to suggest that a more fruitful – and indeed more common – ethnographic approach to theoretical elaboration is that of *theoretical extension*: 'in this process, one does not discover or develop new theory per se, but extends existing theoretical or conceptual formulations to other groups or aggregations, to other bounded contexts or places, or to other sociological domains' (Snow et al. 2003, p. 187). What distinguishes theoretical extension is the re-use of concepts in new and often surprising situations – they offer Morrill's study of 'vengeance' rituals (familiar from anthropological studies) among corporate executives as a case where an existing concept yields new insights through its application in a surprising setting. Generally speaking, they argue that 'the likelihood of theoretical development is greatest under conditions of either pronounced contextual similarity or dissimilarity' (Snow et al. 2003, p. 194). The model of theoretical development in this approach is essentially the comparative use of concepts across varieties of cases.

Others see case studies accumulating into knowledge of broader structures through use of other cases as data. This process of generalization is aimed at the construction of middle range theory, through the extension of theories to other cases through theoretical sampling and comparative analysis (Snow et al. 2003, Mjøset 2005).

Finally, Snow et al. (2003) suggest Burawoy's (1998) 'extended case method' as a third approach – one which they call 'theoretical refinement' or as Burawoy might have it, '*theoretical reconstruction*'. In Burawoy's 'strong' programme of theoretical development through ethnographic research, theories themselves serve as vital 'carriers' of the accumulation of case-based knowledge. Furthermore, he sees these theories as themselves much more coherent and systematic attempts at synthetic explanation than the accumulation of concepts and micro-explanations in the programmes of either Katz or Snow et al. Finally, the connection between theory and evidence is quite different. Where the other approaches used concepts strategically to generate explanations as needed, the explicit goal of Burawoy's extended case method is the reconstruction of theory. In order to achieve this, the ethnographic case is used as a negative case of the preferred

theory, with the ethnographer seeking, on the one hand, to critique the theory he or she considers most plausible and, on the other, to reconstruct the theory so that it can accommodate these same critiques. In this way, ethnographic cases – no matter how deep and localized the ethnography itself – can carry unusual theoretical weight in advancing a programme of research (Burawoy et al. 1991, Burawoy 1998).[1] Theories can be refined or reconstructed in a process that is theoretically led as cases are selected in terms of their ability to allow the ethnographer to strategically intervene in the process of developing the theory. The case study is used to challenge and reconstruct the preferred theory and it is the theory itself that carries the accumulated knowledge of previous studies.

MODES OF THEORETICAL DEVELOPMENT IN ETHNOGRAPHIC CASE STUDIES

Burawoy's claims for the scientific status of ethnography and for the range of its theoretical ambition constitute a 'strong programme' for the location of ethnography within the leading methods of sociological science, understood as 'systematic generalization' (1998). Others have pursued and developed this programme (see e.g. Eliasoph and Lichterman [1999] on developing the 'extended case method' to take account of culture as well as structure). However, it is clear that other ethnographers are uncomfortable with the approach. Some disparage it as 'aristocratic', arguing that the case serves the master narrative of the theory (Katz 2004) – although in this view the alternative conception of knowledge accumulation is not made explicit. In particular, Burawoy's extended case method appears to be built on a notion of all-encompassing structures, within which cases can be located – allowing them to become strategic negative cases rather than simply aberrations on the margins of a distribution of particular cases. How do we know that the socialist and capitalist factories that Burawoy himself analyses (Burawoy 1985, 1992) are strategic cases for assessing the dynamics of those macro-social structures, rather than statistical aberrations that are atypical of factories within each system (Fitzgerald 2006)?

Glaeser notes that if efforts at theoretical reconstruction are to avoid a kind of structuralist determinism, implying totalizing social structures, then those ethnographies need to conceive of structures as ' that incredibly dense thicket of partially independent and partially interacting social processes' (Glaeser 2006, p. 24). But can we extend our cases to tell us stories about the dynamics of social structures if those cases are structured by a variety of interlocking and loosely coupled structures, which are themselves contingent outcomes of other social processes, further removed in time and space?

Although a programme of theoretical extension aimed at developing middle range concepts is less ambitious, for its proponents it is also more flexible and allows for multiple levels of analysis. Mjøset (2005) argues for precisely such a model of case study research. Mjøset argues – much like Snow et al. (2003) – that grounded theory approaches in practice tend to engage quite strongly with theoretical and conceptual concerns but that they do so in a systematically different way than in Burawoy's extended case method. He argues that in grounded theory, explanations of specific cases can be turned to contextual generalizations, not through the challenging of favoured theories, but through theoretical sampling of additional cases. Grounded theory generalizes through research questions to representative concepts, a quite different theoretical goal than in Burawoy's model of reconstruction of what is a more 'grand' conception of theory. However, Mjøset argues that when Burawoy talks about reconstructing quite specific sets of theories this comes close to what grounded theory does in practice, as grounded theory often is engaged in the project of reconstructing middle range theories (as in Snow et al.'s agenda for theoretical extension). Where Burawoy boldly argues the differences

between socialist and capitalist workplaces based on two of his ethnographies (e.g. Burawoy 1985), Mjøset argues that where ethnographic cases seek to reconstruct large-scale theories (e.g. globalization, modernity) the link between reconstruction and specific cases typically becomes quite tenuous.

These issues are also central to the recent heated debate over urban ethnographies in the US. Wacquant's (2002) critique of some of the most prominent ethnographies of urban poverty accused the authors of many sins, but a failure to place local contexts of interaction within their structural contexts and to explain their dynamics in terms of those structures was a central element of the critique. Duneier (2002) defends his chosen strategy of extending his case empirically rather than theoretically (see below), framing this as a choice that different analysts will make in varying ways and for different reasons. Newman (2002) explicitly critiques Wacquant's strategy for understanding local cases in terms of theories of structural dynamics:

> Unlike Wacquant, none of us believe that the diverse behaviors of ghetto dwellers can be explained solely by a unitary logic of oppression or exclusion. That is why our books move beyond a listing of macrosociological forces impinging on the ghetto. Political-economic forces create the structure within which the ghetto exists, as we duly note, but ghetto dwellers are not simply bearers of social relations or victims of social structure. Understanding life in the ghetto requires granting its residents far more agency than Wacquant allows and being prepared to accept an understanding of causation more varied and less deterministic than a single uniform logic of racial exclusion that sweeps all in its path. (Newman 2002, p. 1595)

Thus, the concept of 'the case' among these urban ethnographers depends heavily upon their concept of the primary causal factors at work.

Gowan (forthcoming) seeks a way through the morass with a careful exploration of the moralities of homeless recyclers, linked to their own biographical and historical stories. Most crucially for this discussion, she identifies three critical aspects of the intertwining of biography and history, of agency and structure within 'ethnographies of the street'. The first is a sensitivity to political, social and cultural context and the forms of life that different conjunctures make possible, even within particularly powerful structural forces. Second, she undertakes a comparative analysis of different cities, which allows her to empirically explore the question of contextual mediation of structure and agency fairly directly. Third, while this contextual, comparative approach is helpful, Gowan herself points to the difficulty of 'extending' from the local to the macro level in contexts of abandonment and displacement (as in most ethnographies of urban poverty), rather than of incorporation and exploitation (as explored in ethnographies of the workplace). For her, it is telling that the ethnography of urban poverty that has been most successful in making this extension has been Lyon-Callo's (2004) study of homeless shelters – which crucially relied on the institution of the shelter itself as a link between the micro and macro. Where such institutions have been weakened in the social world, the task of the ethnographer becomes all the more challenging. When successful, however, this approach allows Gowan to seek out a space between the exploration of individual motives and actions, and the overwhelming power of structural forces – instead she argues that the aim of her study 'should not be a celebration of "decency" in unlikely places, but an illumination of the process whereby a specific configuration of urban space, political culture and recycling policy enabled a bearable way of life to flourish' (Gowan [forthcoming]).

It seems that the boundaries between grounded theory and the extended case method, or between theoretical extension and theoretical reconstruction, are more blurred than has apparently been the case. For those undertaking theoretical extension, once cases accumulate sufficiently to allow for new theoretical assumptions, in practice, theory will be reconstructed. Similarly, in a strategy of theoretical reconstruction, the theoretical accounts of the macro-structures that cases confront have often been built up out of comparative ethnographic, historical

and statistical analysis of cases – so that (again, in practice) theoretical extension is a component of theoretical reconstruction. In the end, then, it may be that the debate is less about empiricism versus theoreticism and more about the level and type of theory being constructed. In either case the ability of ethnography to systematically generalize from cases to theories – the definition of science (Burawoy 1998) – is not in question.

EMPIRICAL EXTENSIONS: EXTENDED PLACE METHODS

Gowan's dilemma of studying a world of 'disconnection' leads us, then, to a different type of extension of the ethnographic case method – the search for conceptual mechanisms for empirically extending cases in time and space. These mechanisms are crucial to both extensions to the meso-range (as in theoretical extension) and to the macro-range (as in theoretical reconstruction). This has become an increasing concern for Burawoy's own work – whereas the first compilation of students' ethnographies (Burawoy et al. 1991) posed a straightforward dualism between structural power and agentic resistance, the second (Burawoy et al. 2000) sought to make sense of a much more complex set of cases in which the boundaries were often unclear and the structures about which theories were offered were more varied and interacting. How, for example, do we understand the social organization of work when it is shaped by the interaction of global forces of neo-liberalism, global connections of high-tech professionals and the global imaginations of corporate elites and local and global trade unionists (Burawoy et al. 2000)?

And yet, ethnography is well situated to tackle this problematization of the boundaries of cases. Among social scientific methods, ethnography relies least on a rigid or static notion of the case itself and is best placed to explore the empirical extensions of the case.

Glaeser (2006) notes that when we investigate contextualized action processes, we are investigating the very processes that bring history and distance into the local, making non-simultaneous space and time simultaneous (see also Abbott 1997). Within the social action of the localized social world, therefore, are the clues to uncovering the time and space extensions of social action – and of the ethnographic case, if we can uncover them.

Abbott notes that the Chicago school of sociology distinguished degrees of contextuality (1997, p. 1152). Temporally, this involved 'natural histories' of social processes (e.g. revolutions) with internal logics, careers with medium levels of contextuality and interactional fields with massive contextuality. Spatially, it involved natural areas, area-careers and once again the highly contextual interactional field. The interactional field is highly contextual and becomes the point at which temporal and spatial processes and degrees of contextuality intersect (Abbott 1997, p. 1157). This indeed is why Burawoy's extended case method works – because the time-space ties to the larger structures are present within the local context and because in practice contextuality decreases as we move to the macro-level.

Extensions across space

Ethnography is an especially suitable methodology with which to investigate social structures that are constituted across multiple scales and sites (Burawoy et al. 2000). Even the most sophisticated statistical methods tend to rely on a nested hierarchy of scales and units of analysis whereas ethnography can strategically locate itself at critical points of intersection of scales and units of analysis and directly examine the negotiation of interconnected social actors across multiple scales. At the same time, globalization also poses problems for ethnography. The potential and uneven de-linking of the spatial and the social under conditions of globalization upsets ethnography's claim to understand social relations by 'being there' and thus demands that we rethink the character of 'global ethnography' (Gille and Ó Riain 2002).

Marcus (1998) argues that the study of an increasingly globalized world requires multi-sited ethnography involving fieldwork across multiple sites, extending the research site in space. The extension of ethnography to multiple sites is a seemingly excellent way to meet the challenges posed by globalization to place-based studies. However, while finding connections is certainly not difficult, deciding which of them are worth pursuing seems somewhat arbitrary, a feature of multi-sited ethnography that Marcus acknowledges when he calls it a kind of constructivism (1998, p. 90). Marcus identifies the methods of such construction: connecting sites by following people; following objects, metaphors, plots, stories, allegories; following conflicts and biography. What ties together fieldwork locations is the ethnographer's discovery of traces and clues, her 'logic of association' (Gille and Ó Riain 2002).

Ethnographies of transnationalism provide useful examples of the multi-sited approach and show where it works well – when there are clearly defined patterns of connection between relatively highly concentrated sites, e.g. of migration process (Schiller 1997, Smith and Guarnizo 1998, Portes et al. 1999, Kyle 2000, Fitzgerald 2006). Similarly, Donham's (1999) study of Marxist modernization in Ethiopia involves two sites. However, these are sites that can be understood as clearly located within a well-established hierarchy of scales – the national capital, which is the centre of mobilization of modernization projects, and a village, where they are implemented and contested. Eade and his collaborators (1997) take a different approach – fixing their ethnographic site in London but using a variety of studies carried out by a large research team to explore the multiple connections of their research site to many parts of the world (see also Fitzgerald [2006] for proposals regarding teams of researchers). Such extensions can also enrich areas of study that have largely passed over the external networks of the field. Stoller's (2002) study of African traders in New York mirrors Duneier's study of (primarily) African American traders in the same city. However, his focus on immigrants leads him to an exploration of the wider trading networks of which they are a part – suggesting different and more complex patterns of structural influence and strategic social action.

Other studies explore more complex and 'multi-scalar' ethnographic sites (for an extended discussion of issues relating to the politics of scale and place in the construction of ethnographic sites, see Gille and Ó Riain [2002]). Tsing (2005) provides an 'ethnography of global connections' where she explores various dimensions of the social shaping and constitution of the Indonesian rainforest. The case of the rain forest, where Tsing spent significant amounts of time, provides a window into global connections but Tsing uses interview, historical and other methods to extend the case empirically into the various networks of social relations around the rainforest. Furthermore, she argues for a view of globalization that emphasizes the points of 'friction' within global processes, where global processes are grounded, if only for tense moments (see also Burawoy et al. 2000). The ethnographic moment is crucial to the exploration of such crucial moments of 'friction' in social relations.

Extensions across time

Ethnography has also increasingly come to recognize that history is critical to the ethnographic enterprise and even to what can be seen as a site (Gille 2001). In sociology, historical analysis has too often implied unilinear development, as spatial variation is translated into temporal variation, into 'stages' in social change or simply an 'effect' of the global on the local (see Miller 1995). By contrast the Comaroff (1992) practice of historical ethnography defies the imposition of the microsociology/macrosociology dichotomy on the local/global one. 'Even macrohistorical processes – the building of states, the making of revolutions, the extension of global capitalism – have their feet on the ground. Being rooted in the meaningful practices of people, great and small, they are in short, suitable cases for anthropological treatment' (Comaroff 1992, p. 33).

The Comaroffs re-define the role of archival research in their historical ethnography, treating it as a source of textual traces of an ethnographic site (and case), which the ethnographer can reconstruct without having to accept archives as objective documentary record. While much of comparative-historical sociology has relied on historical documents, letters, diaries, official record, etc., this approach requires that sociologists re-evaluate archival research. Ethnographic research can be a powerful entrance into such re-interpretation of archival materials, often aided by analyses of 'social memory'. Contemporary stories regarding historical events can be measured against the archival record to reveal how historical events are reconstructed and contested as part of contemporary culture. Whereas ethnographic interpretation can be aided by historical materials, the detailed knowledge of the contemporary site can cast new light on archival materials and the intended and unintended consequences of historical actions (Gille and Ó Riain 2002). Although sympathetic, Mary Des Chene finds that this historical ethnography is still too bound to a particular locality. As she argues, 'spatial contiguity is not essential to every kind of historical anthropological research' and 'the field may not be a place at all, but a period of time or a series of events, the study of which will take a researcher to many places' (Des Chene 1997, p. 71). Des Chene seeks to combine the extensions of space and time in the ethnographic case.

Of course, history can be incorporated more directly into ethnographic research, albeit over a more limited time span. Donham's (1999) study of Marxism in Ethiopia provides a fascinating example of a historical ethnography – only in this case incorporating 're-visits' to sites of earlier fieldwork. Such re-visits to the site of an earlier ethnography are very demanding of individual ethnographers, and one way to introduce a historical component to ethnographic research is to 're-visit' the sites (or similar sites) studied by other ethnographers. Burawoy (2003) argues that whereas 're-visits' typically seek to debunk the original study, they may be better deployed to analyze historical change – using the earlier ethnography as historical data.

Institutional and cultural extensions

There are other ethnographers who also extend beyond the immediate context of the case but do not deal explicitly with issues of time and space. Nonetheless, when ethnographers study organizations, social movements or other institutions, they are studying fields where time and space are being integrated through forms of social organization. Duneier (1999, 2002), for example, argues that he extended his study of 'public characters' in New York through an 'extended place method', following the empirical clues regarding the broader structural forces at work that were provided through his fieldwork on the street. In practice, this meant carrying out interviews with people working in those institutions (largely public or civic) that dealt with people living and/or working on the streets. The mode of extension of the street was not the transnational networks of the people themselves (as in Stoller 2002) but the institutions which integrated the social world of the street into the broader welfarist and punitive structures of the state and civil society – echoing Gowan's (forthcoming) point about the difficulties of studying milieux where institutions have been systematically weakened.

In a similar vein, Glaeser (2006) argues that formal institutions can be particularly valuable sites for studying ethnographically how local contexts shape, and are shaped by, broader structural forces – precisely because they integrate actors and actions across time and space. An interesting example of this kind of ethnography is Steve Lopez's (2007) study of the local context of care work in a Michigan nursing home – where through this local context he explores the character of the 'mock bureaucracy' first analysed by Alvin Gouldner (1954) and sheds light upon organizational processes from within the local context. The extensions here are theoretical – Lopez tackles Gouldner's concept directly – as well as empirical as state regulation of

nursing homes looms large within the nursing home and the ethnographic study.

Another interesting case is that of the burgeoning field of studies of cultural production. As Becker's (1982) classic study shifted the terrain of the sociology of culture from the textual reading of cultural forms to the ethnographic study of the process of cultural production, this has been a fertile field for ethnographers. In many cases, these have been 'classic' localized ethnographic studies – where the ethnographer gets inside the process of production of cultural forms such as the news, the talk show, the software programme, the video game, and so on. Hidden within this, however, is a quite different organizing principle of these case studies than in the classic Chicago school ethnographies. The focus of study in studies of cultural production is the cultural form that is being produced and this becomes the focus of the case – rather than a 'complete description' of the social world being studied.

Grindstaff (2002) studied the making of two US talk shows, from her position as an intern. On the face of it a classic insider account of the social world of the talk show, the theoretical concern and the organizing principle of the empirical investigation was in fact the construction of particular kinds of moral narratives and class and other social identities through these talk shows. Similarly, King-O'Riain's (2006) comparative study of Japanese American community beauty pageants was not a classic study of the social world of different Japanese American communities, but an explication of the process through which racial categories were produced in different ways in each of the different communities.

A somewhat different example is that of Best's (2006) exploration of car culture among Californian youth. The focus of the study is a particular cultural icon – the car – and how it is woven through young peoples' lives. There are certain sites that present themselves for study, including the main street where Best observes and participates, to a limited degree, in cruising. But Best's study must draw on other methods to follow this icon off the street and out into the lives of young people – interviews with youth regarding car culture and documentary research on the cultural construction of the car in US history extending the ethnographic site in space and in time.

The 'classic' model of extended stays in a site extends to multi-sited ethnography quite poorly. Becoming part of a site remains a critical part of ethnography – the issue of gaining entry – but the very nature of that membership changes for the ethnographer as it changes for those around her or him. Place becomes a launching pad outwards into networks, backwards into history and ultimately into the politics of place itself (Gille and Ó Riain 2002). The need to pursue actors through space, time, institutions and contexts of cultural production and use in order to explore social relations across different sites seems likely to increase our use of interviews, history, tracing networks and so on and decrease our time simply spent 'being on site'. So we see a variety of methods being used to supplement site-based ethnographic studies – life history interviews with former community pageant contestants (King-O'Riain 2006), observation of harassment in public places through systematic sampling of public settings (Gardner 1995), 'going along' with people and asking them to interpret their lives as they go (Kusenbach 2003), mapping of social and trading networks (Stoller 2002), the reading of musical 'texts' (DeNora 2000), and so on. Nonetheless, it is crucial to note that immersion in a particular context does inform these alternative methods in crucial ways, enriching them even as they extend ethnography. The ethnographic skill of getting inside social contexts and social processes remains a crucial contribution and the reduction of ethnography to these supplementary methods would be a dangerous development indeed.

ETHNOGRAPHY AND THE ACCUMULATION OF KNOWLEDGE

Many of the questions we have discussed relate to how ethnographers can make sense

of cases by locating them within a wider structural context. We will now turn to a brief discussion of how ethnographic knowledge accumulates, or might do so.

Ethnography has long been vulnerable to critique for not being 'adequately scientific'. For some scholars, ethnography was hopelessly mired in subjectivism – and even some of the most prominent ethnographers, including Herbert Blumer, were inclined to accept this argument.[2] In our discussion of personal extensions of the case we have touched on these issues in emphasizing the crucial importance of the personal learning of the ethnographer through their embodied experience. Knowledge of the empirical world becomes transformed into 'experience' that, in auto-ethnography, is communicated to the reader through a writing process where the experience of the ethnographer self is the dominant mode of learning and of communication. But the ethnographer's personalized learning is only part of the process of ethnographic study and this embodied experience is a vehicle for collective learning, not the collective learning itself.

It is also worth noting that the distinction made here between contextualized and decontextualizing research is fundamentally different to the distinction often made between quantitative 'objective' methods and the ethnographic study of the 'subjective' (Abbott 1997). The scientific contribution of ethnography is to systematically study social action in context, while variable analyses seek to make universalizing claims that extend across contexts but at the same time erase context. While this contextual paradigm is not limited to ethnography – there has been a related revival in the use of comparative historical methods, network analyses, contextualized use of statistical analyses and other methods that take context seriously – there appears to be an irreducible ethnographic moment implied in the recognition of the contextuality of social action.

This then shifts the ground from the alleged subjectivism of ethnography to its lack of generalizability. Goldthorpe's (2000) recent statements *On Sociology* have argued strongly for the variable-based probabilistic model of sociological research. For Goldthorpe, ethnographic work is bedeviled by a lack of attention to issues of sampling, and particularly probabilistic sampling. Ethnography should engage in a much more systematic process of sampling, both within and across contexts being studied; for example, through locating cases using survey data. Locating cases and ruling out idiosyncrasies are sensible strategies in the field but Goldthorpe pushes his case much further, arguing for a fundamental disjuncture between the contextuality of ethnographic case methods and the search for a universal (albeit probabilistic) social science.

However, the critique runs into trouble on this point. In practical terms, it is not at all clear that probabilistic locating of case materials will solve sampling problems. Scheper-Hughes (2000), for example, provides a comprehensive catalogue of what she left out of her account of Clochan, a small village in Ireland, some decades before. But the issues and patterns she missed were missed due to her theoretical blinders rather to a lack of exposure to the necessary empirical materials. Without re-visiting her data, or the field, she was able to list a series of processes that could have been incorporated in her initial study – but a modified probabilistic strategy, while it might have been of other uses, would not have solved this problem.

More abstractly, Goldthorpe's notion of theory is one that applies across all contexts. Studies that are deeply shaped by the contextuality of their cases cannot hope to rise to this level of theory. However, ethnographic studies show that the models of action which can apply across all cases (for Goldthorpe, this is 'rational action theory') are profoundly impoverished when explaining actual processes of action and interaction in specific social contexts (see also Abbott 1988). Being able to account for this contextuality of social action is also a crucial element of any social science – and one where ethnographic case methods have a distinct advantage over variable-based approaches (Mjøset 2005).

Is it possible then to generalize at all from ethnographic cases or has ethnography found a new morass of contextuality to fill the place of subjectivism? Hodson (2001) provides an interesting approach that re-codes ethnographies of work to provide more valid data for variable analysis of social processes within various kinds of workplaces. The study has much to recommend it, but loses precisely that sense of process and context that is so rich and informative in ethnographic case studies. So there is no easy answer here.

Nonetheless, Burawoy (1998) argues that the contextualist approach to research can make equal claim to scientific status as the variable-based, decontextualized approach to social science research. He argues that ethnography can systematically generalize precisely by taking context seriously and locating those contexts that are being studied within broader social-historical processes. As we have seen, there is debate among ethnographers exactly how this is regarding achieved – whether to be through theoretical discovery, extension or reconstruction. Our discussion implies that it proceeds in practice through an interaction of theoretical extension and reconstruction, made possible by a variety of new developments in conceptualizing how cases extend in time and space. Ultimately, the grounding of ethnographic case studies in specific contexts creates certain problems with generalization but avoids others facing decontextualized social science.

CONCLUSION

The ethnographic case study remains firmly grounded in the ethnographer 'being there' within the time and space of those he or she is studying, learning through mutual experience and his or her situatedness within the social world. However, we see an increasing range of ways in which ethnographers are extending their cases – personally, theoretically and empirically.

Without empirical extension, theoretical extension is often limited to the locating of the case within a unitary structure and requires some heroic assumptions about the degree to which local processes are determined or shaped by these kinds of structures. However, without theoretical extension, empirical extension is often aimless-wandering through strings of linked social interactions with little rationale for why particular empirical extensions are being followed, whereas others are forsaken. Taken together, however, theoretical and empirical extensions of classic ethnographic cases are creating exciting new ethnographic approaches. They are also creating new methodological challenges, including a new emphasis on the ongoing process of theoretical sampling within the process of the ethnographic study, with close attention to be paid to the paths chosen and rejected, and the reasons for these decisions.

Furthermore, this all suggests an uncomfortable set of personal extensions, where the ethnographer may move across settings, perhaps 'accepted' in the main site but moving uneasily across interviews with the officers of institutions that shape that site, or out into family or business networks that individuals hide from others in the site but reveal to the ethnographer, or uncovering historical facts that have become carefully constructed secrets within the site. Even in an era of reflexive ethnography, the moral and ethical questions may be more difficult rather than less. However, there are equally important benefits to be obtained from ethnographies where the ethnographer is multiply, if perhaps a bit uncomfortably, situated.

We have reviewed the three main approaches that ethnographers have used to try to generalize their cases, even in such an uncertain setting. While theoretical discovery seeks to bound cases in pursuit of domain-specific findings, theoretical extension and theoretical reconstruction seek a broader set of generalizations through the strategic use of comparative cases and negative cases, respectively. We found that theoretical extension and reconstruction might be more closely intertwined than ethnographers have suggested and that ethnographers from both approaches have sought new and creative

ways to extend their cases across space, time and institutional structures and practices.

Each of these kinds of ethnography has provided outstanding studies but at different levels of generality and generating different kinds of theory. The challenge to ethnographic case studies is less that the theoretical and methodological approach will generate biased findings but that definitions of the case will rule in and out certain social processes. This is a problem that is shared with variable oriented studies and in fact ethnography is better placed to deal with it as it can question the boundaries of the case as the study proceeds. The processual character of ethnography that renders it complicated is also a resource in the research process. The de- and re-construction of the case that so many have seen as the death knell of ethnography instead places ethnography at the centre of a resurgent contextualist paradigm of social inquiry, a paradigm that is increasingly self-consciously exploring its own theoretical and methodological foundations.

NOTES

1. Snow et al.'s concept of theoretical refinement is less ambitious than Burawoy's strong programme. They end with a series of rules of thumb that enhance refinement – approach the field with a repertoire of concepts rather than have theory drive the ethnography, pursue heavy immersion in the field but with an eye to the generality of what is being observed, allow data and theories to speak to each other as much as possible, and revisit notes as refinement of theories proceeds (Snow et al. 2003, p. 193)

2. It is interesting in this respect to see Herbert Gans' retraction of his original defensiveness regarding the weak scientific status of his classic study *The Urban Villagers*. Although the original methodological appendix yielded science to positivism, by the second edition, in 1981, Gans has not changed his view of the strengths and weaknesses of participant observation but is now equally critical of other methods – which he argues are just as much combinations of art and science as ethnography is (Gans 1981, p. 415).

REFERENCES

Abbot, A. 1988 'Transcending general linear reality' *Sociological Theory* 6: 169–186.

Abbott, A. 1997 'Of time and space: the contemporary relevance of the Chicago School' *Social Forces* 75(4): 1149–1182.

Becker, H. 1982 *Art Worlds*. Berkeley, CA: University of California Press.

Becker, H. 1998 *Tricks of the Trade*. Chicago: University of Chicago Press.

Benner, C. 2002 *Work in the New Economy*. Oxford: Blackwell.

Best, A. 2006 *Fast Cars, Cool Rides*. New York: New York University Press.

Burawoy, M. 1985 *The Politics of Production*. London: Verso.

Burawoy, M. 1992 *The Radiant Past*. Chicago: University of Chicago Press.

Burawoy, M. 1998 'The extended case method' *Sociological Theory* 16(1): 4–33.

Burawoy, M. 2003 'Revisits: an outline of a theory of reflexive ethnography' *American Sociological Review* 68: 645–679.

Burawoy, M., Burton, A. and Ferguson, A.A. 1991 *Ethnography Unbound*. Berkeley, CA: University of California Press.

Burawoy, M., Blum, J.A. and George, S. 2000 *Global Ethnography: Forces, Connections and Imaginations in a Postmodern World*. Berkeley, CA: University of California Press.

Comaroff, J. 1992 *Ethnography and the Historical Imagination*. Boulder, CO: Westview Press.

DeNora, T. 2000 *Music in Everyday Life*. Cambridge: Cambridge University Press.

Des Chene, M. 1997 'Locating the past' in A. Gupta and J. Ferguson (Eds) *Anthropological Locations*. Berkeley, CA: University of California Press, pp. 66–85.

Donham, D. 1999 *Marxist Modern*. Berkeley, CA: University of California Press.

Duneier, M. 1999 *Sidewalk*. New York: Farrar, Straus and Giroux.

Duneier, M. 2002 'What kind of combat sport is sociology?' *American Journal of Sociology* 107(6): 1551–1576.

Eade, J. (Ed.) 1997 *Living the Global City: Globalization as Local Process*. New York: Routledge.

Eliasoph, N. 2005 'Theorising from the neck down' *Qualitative Sociology* 28(2): 159–160.

Eliasoph, N. and Lichterman, P. 1999 'We begin with our favorite theory … reconstructing the extended case method' *Sociological Theory* 17(2): 228–234.

Fine, G.A. 1979 'Small groups and cultural creation: the idioculture of Little League baseball teams' *American Sociological Review* 44: 733–745.

Fitzgerald, D. 2006 'Towards a theoretical ethnography of migration' *Qualitative Sociology* 29(1): 1–24.

Flyvberg, B. 2001 *Making Social Science Matter*. Cambridge: Cambridge University Press.

Gans, H. 1981 *The Urban Villagers*. New York: Free Press.

Gardner, C. 1995 *Passing By: Gender and Public Harassment*. Berkeley, CA: University of California Press.

Gille, Z. 2001 'Critical ethnography in the time of globalization: toward a new concept of site' *Cultural Studies-Critical Methodologies* 1(3): 319–334.

Gille, Z. and Ó Riain, S. 2002 'Global ethnographies' *Annual Review of Sociology* 28: 271–295.

Glaeser, A. 2006 'An ontology for the ethnographic analysis of social processes: extending the extended case method' *Social Analysis* 49(3): 18–47.

Glaser, B. and Strauss, A. 1967 *The Discovery of Grounded Theory*. Chicago: Aldine.

Gluckman, M. 1961 'Ethnographic data in British social anthropology' *Sociological Review* 9(1): 5–17.

Goldthorpe, J.H. 2000 *On Sociology*. Oxford: Oxford University Press.

Gouldner, A. 1954 *Patterns of Industrial Bureaucracy*. New York: Free Press.

Gowan, T. 'New hobos or neoromantic fantasy? Work and ethics among homeless recyclers in San Francisco' *Qualitative Sociology* (forthcoming).

Grindstaff, L. 2002 *The Money Shot*. Chicago: University of Chicago Press.

Hodson, R. 2001 *Dignity at Work*. Cambridge: Cambridge University Press.

Katz, J. 2001 'From how to why: on luminous description and causal inference in ethnography (part I)' *Ethnography* 2(4): 443–473.

Katz, J. 2002 'From how to why: on luminous description and causal inference in ethnography (part II)' *Ethnography* 3(1): 63–90.

Katz, J. 2004 'On the rhetoric and politics of ethnographic methodology' *Annals of the American Academy of Political and Social Science* 595: 280–308.

King-O'Riain, R. 2006 *Pure Beauty*. Minneapolis, MN: University of Minnesota Press.

Kusenbach, M. 2003 'Street phenomenology: the go-along as ethnographic research tool' *Ethnography* 4(3): 455–485.

Kyle D. 2000 *Transnational Peasants*. Baltimore, MD: Johns Hopkins Press.

Lave, J. and Wenger, E. 1990 *Situated Learning: Legitimate Periperal Participation*. Cambridge: Cambridge University Press.

Lopez, S. 2007 'Efficiency and the fix revisited: informal relations and mock routinisation in a nonprofit nursing home' *Qualitative Sociology* 30(3): 225–247.

Lyon-Callo, V. 2004 *Inequality, Poverty, and Neoliberal Governance: Activist Ethnography in the Homeless Sheltering Industry*. Broadview Ethnographies and Case Studies. Peterborough, Ontario: Broadview Press.

Marcus, G.E. 1998 *Ethnography Through Thick and Thin*. Princeton, NJ: Princeton University Press.

Miller, D. 1995 *Worlds Apart: Modernity Through the Prism of the Local*. London: Routledge.

Mjøset, L. 2005 'Can grounded theory solve the problems of its critics?' *Sosiologisk Tidsskrift/Journal of Sociology* 13(4): 379–408.

Newman, K. 2002 'No shame: the view from the left bank' *American Journal of Sociology* 107(6): 1577–1599.

Ó Riain, S. 2000 'Net-working for a living' in M. Burawoy, J.A. Blum and S. George (Eds) *Global Ethnography: Forces, Connections and Imaginations in a Postmodern World*. Berkeley, CA: University of California Press.

Portes, A., Guarnizo, L.E. and Landolt, P. 1999 'Introduction: pitfalls and promise of an emergent research field' *Ethnic and Racial Studies*. 22(2): 217–237.

Ragin, C. and Becker, H. (Eds) 1992 *What is a Case?* Cambridge: Cambridge University Press.

Reed-Danahay, D. (Ed.) 1997 *Auto/Ethnography: Rewriting the Self and the Social*. Oxford: Berg.

Scheper-Hughes, N. 2000 'Ire in Ireland' *Ethnography* 1(1): 117–140.

Schiller, N.G. 1997 'The situation of transnational studies' *Identities* 4(2): 155–166.

Smith, M.P. and Guarnizo, L. (Eds) 1998 *Transnationalism from Below*. New Brunswick, NJ: Transaction Publishers.

Snow, D., Morrill, C. and Anderson, L. 2003 'Elaborating analytic ethnography: linking fieldwork and theory' *Ethnography* 4(2): 181–200.

Stoller, P. 2002. *Money Has No Smell*. Chicago: University of Chicago Press.

Sudnow, D. 1965 'Normal crimes: sociological features of the penal code in a public defender's office' *Social Problems* 123(3): 255–275.

Tsing, A. 2005 *Friction: An Ethnography of Global Connection*. Princeton, NJ: Princeton University Press.

Van Maanen, J. 1988 *Tales of the Field*. Chicago: University of Chicago Press.

Wacquant, L. 2002 'Scrutinising the street: poverty, morality and the pitfalls of urban ethnography' *American Journal of Sociology* 107(6): 1468–1532.

Wacquant, L. 2004 *Body and Soul*. Oxford: Oxford University Press.

Walton, J. 1992 'Making the theoretical case' in C. Ragin and H. Becker (Eds) *What is a Case?* Cambridge: Cambridge University Press, pp. 121–138.

Willis, P. 2000 *The Ethnographic Imagination*. Cambridge: Polity Press.

Zussman, R. 2005 'The black Frenchman' *Qualitative Sociology* 28(2): 201–207.

17

Scope in Case Study Research

Gary Goertz and James Mahoney

INTRODUCTION

One might ask what a chapter on scope is doing in a volume on case study methodology. If one's concern is with understanding particular cases, then aren't scope considerations irrelevant? In fact, however, we suggest that scope concerns are at least as crucial in case studies as in large-N statistical analyses. Because they study many cases, large-N researchers can assert that their findings are general even if it is unknown whether they can be extended to cases beyond the sampled population. By contrast, researchers who study one or few cases are much more vulnerable to the charge that their findings are not generalizable. And when they do generalize, they are much more likely to be taken to task for bias in case selection, e.g., choosing idiosyncratic cases. Thus, case study researchers often must go to great lengths to justify their choice of cases and the scope of their arguments.

The idea of 'scope' is of course commonplace, but the concept rarely receives sustained analysis and discussion. For example, a JSTOR search in social science journals for 'scope' in the title or abstract turns up virtually

nothing except the widely-cited article by Walker and Cohen (1985). A nonsystematic survey of leading research methods textbooks also reveals little or no discussion of the issue of scope (e.g., Nachmias and Nachmias 1976, Hoover 1984, Isaak 1985, Coffey and Atkinson 1996, Alford 1998, Singleton and Straits 1999, Babbie 2001). In this chapter, we try to make explicit some of the often implicit ways in which analysts – and especially case study analysts – understand scope and make choices about the scope of their theories.

Scope is intimately related to generalization. A scope statement sets empirical and theoretical limits on the extent to which an inference can be generalized. In one sense, case studies are clearly useful for establishing these limits. For example, in his classic discussion of kinds of case study, Eckstein (1975) shows that many case studies are explicitly used to test or define the scope of more general theories. Eckstein also shows that case studies are used to develop new theories, and these kinds of case studies almost inevitability raise issues about the extent of generalization. 'How generally do your findings apply?' is indeed a typical question that case study researchers must answer.

How should case study researchers address this question?

Quite frequently, these researchers respond by arguing that the scope of their theory is limited and cannot be extended to many cases. Scope limitations are often the refuge of presenters during Q&A periods. When confronted with a good counterexample, the presenter says that the example is outside the theoretical or empirical scope of her theory. This response often has a bit of an *ad hoc* feel. The scope limitations were not set out at the beginning but used as an escape clause. A good case study should be upfront about scope conditions.

In this chapter, we provide some methodological observations that are intended to be of use to case study researchers – and also large-N researchers – when formulating scope statements. We argue that researchers need to set limits on the scope of their arguments in light of concerns about both conceptual homogeneity and causal homogeneity. In terms of conceptual homogeneity, researchers need to make sure that measurement stability holds across all units and variables of a theory. We suggest reasons why case study researchers might be especially concerned about this kind of homogeneity. In terms of causal homogeneity, researchers need to make sure that posited causal relations are stable across all observations. In case study research, this often means making sure that causal relations at different levels of conceptual aggregation are stable. If either conceptual or causal homogeneity cannot be maintained, it is appropriate for analysts to limit the scope of their arguments. Generalization is restricted at the point where homogeneity of one kind or another breaks down.

HOW SCOPE IS DISCUSSED IN CONTEMPORARY SOCIAL SCIENCE

Social scientists discuss and debate scope when they try to identify the appropriate domain for testing a theory. In large-N research, the concern is often whether the observations selected for analysis are sufficiently homogeneous to sustain valid findings. Thus, much of the debate is whether scope restrictions need to be introduced to distinguish heterogeneous subgroups present within the large-N population. Some theories propose not restricting the scope, but this move is often criticized on the grounds of introducing heterogeneity. For example, rational choice theory in a purist sense might not apply scope conditions:

> Most rational choice theorists (including structural realists) do not claim that their theories should be limited in time or space, and so would expect the same relationships found in politically relevant dyads, or other subsets, to hold among all dyads. In fact, among formal rational choice theorists, Bueno de Mesquita (1981) explicitly argues that the expected utility theory of war should apply to all regions and periods. Kenneth Waltz, writing in a less mathematical formulation, similarly argues that the constraints and inducements of system structure (as opposed to internal domestic factors) affect all states equally through time. (Bennett and Stam 2000, p. 555)

However, a number of other scholars suggest that the scope of rational choice theory is limited to 'highly structured settings' in which the rules of the game are transparent and the consequences of different actions are clear (Bates 1997; see also Elster 1979, Tsebelis 1990, Geddes 2003). Outside of this domain, the theory is not expected to apply. Likewise, there is debate among neorealists in the field of international relations over whether its central claims apply more widely than the modern Westphalian international system (for example, see the debate between Fischer [1992, 1993] and Hall and Kratochwil [1993]).

With small-N studies, the concerns are often different. Here, the issue is less whether the cases analyzed are homogeneous (although some case experts might also raise this concern). Rather, the bigger issue is whether the findings for the initial set of cases can be generalized to other cases. For example, Skocpol (1979) developed a causal theory of social revolutions in France, Russia, and China. The big question for many after her was the extent to which one could extend the scope of her theory to contemporary developing countries. Skocpol herself argued that the causes of social revolution in other settings were different and required a separate theory, one which she later helped formulate (Goodwin and Skocpol 1989). There are various reasons why Skocpol felt that separate theories were needed and that they could not be combined into one single and overarching theory of social revolution. For example, the combination of the two theories would have come at a considerable expense of parsimony and elegance; moreover, it is possible that the two theories could not be combined because all of the relevant changes in the interrelations among variables were not known. Alternatively, the combination of the two theories might have introduced serious concept and measurement validity problems. These are the typical kinds of concern that arise when qualitative researchers consider extending their arguments beyond an initial case or set of cases.[1]

In short, in contemporary social science, scope concerns arise in large-N research when scholars question whether the population under analysis actually exhibits unrecognized heterogeneity. These concerns push large-N research in a case study direction. By contrast, scope concerns arise in small-N research when scholars ask whether the findings for the initial cases can be extended more generally. These concerns push case study research in a large-N direction.

CONCEPTUAL SCOPE

Conceptual scope refers to restrictions on generalization that arise from the need to maintain stability in the definition and measurement of the core conceptual entities of a theory. Most fundamentally, conceptual homogeneity requires that the analyst: (1) consistently define and measure the specific kind of observations (or units) to which the theory applies; and (2) consistently define and measure independent and dependent variables. Case study researchers may restrict the scope of their theory because they believe that

the introduction of new cases will produce instability in the measurement of their key concepts (Zelditch 1971).

Homogeneity of observations

In almost all causal research, the observations under examination are assumed to be of a specific kind. The assumption is that causal hypotheses will apply to only a certain kind of observation; the introduction of other kinds of observations to test hypotheses will introduce heterogeneity into the design and produce instability in causal inference. For example, it would be relatively senseless to perform an experiment to test the effect of hammer blows on the universe of objects in a house. Whereas we can perhaps assume homogeneity of the treatment (i.e., force of hammer blow) and dependent variable (break or no break), the variety of observations in the study makes it of little value. More directly relevant to political scientists, studies of economic development usually define the unit of analysis as a 'state' (Kuznets 1951); they at least implicitly assume that the introduction of other kinds of observations such as subnational regions or nonstate organizations would introduce heterogeneity and produce unstable estimates of causal effects. Accordingly, the scope of theories of economic development is normally limited to a certain class of observations.

We use the expression *observation homogeneity* for these kinds of assumptions because the analyst believes that the observations are fundamentally similar with respect to some concept. For example, if the observations of a study are 'states,' the researcher assumes that each observation is homogeneous with regard to its 'stateness.' To empirically substantiate this assumption, of course, one would need a definition and set of measures for the concept of state, and then one would need to show that all observations in fact are good instances of this concept.

In controlled experimental work, researchers also assume that observations are homogeneous with regard to concepts under study, and they frequently expend considerable effort in making sure that units are of the same kind.

For example, researchers might be interested in the strength of iron under hammer blows. To explore this issue, they would normally make sure that the iron rods (for example) are really made of iron with as few impurities as possible. The scope of their causal inference would be limited to the kinds of units that are tested in the experiment.

In much of social science, by contrast, the assumption of the homogeneity of observations is often not directly explored and deeply problematic in various ways. First, the concept with which the observations are assumed to be similar may have a contested or inconsistent meaning. For example, with respect to the concept of state, Gleditsch and Ward (1999) have proposed a different set of criteria than the standard Correlates of War (COW) definition. Second, there might be a significant gray zone in which we are not certain if an observation represents an instance of a concept. For many concepts, there is an underlying continuum (e.g., Hug 2003) and there is no obvious or correct place to draw the line. For example, do political entities such as the Vatican, Monte Carlo, and so on count as states? Third, some subsets of a given kind of observation may be systematically removed from the analysis. For instance, microstates (e.g., tiny island countries) are often eliminated from data sets, yet these entities fit the criteria for a state.[2]

The introduction of heterogeneous observations or the systematic exclusion of certain kinds of homogeneous observations can create unstable causal inference. Indeed, what looks like heterogeneity in the causal sense might in fact be a result of heterogeneity in the observations. In other words, a theory could have a correctly specified causal model but still produce unstable estimates of causal effects because the observations are not of the same kind.

Case study researchers might impose scope conditions to avoid these kinds of problems. For example, if one wants to explore the phenomenon of corporatism, case study researchers usually focus on good cases of corporatist states and contrast them with states that are clearly not corporatist. A theory of corporatism based on odd or marginal corporatist states is suspect (Hicks 1988). States like Switzerland and Japan are not very clearly either corporatist or pluralist states. Although they can be used, they are chosen exactly because of their marginal status.

Case study researchers often also try to get the *ideal* case of some phenomenon. Here one is explicitly not getting a typical empirical case but an ideal theoretical one, one that best exemplifies the 'pure' concept. With some concepts, however, this approach might not be appropriate. As an illustration, Figure 17.1 shows the empirical distribution for the polity

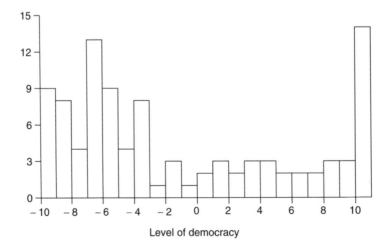

Figure 17.1   Ideal cases: polity democracy measure.

concept of democracy. The huge spike at the right-hand end means that this concept and measure are not useful for studying ideal democracies. For example, according to the polity measure, the United States has a maximum level of democracy starting in 1870 and continuing until the present.

One must go to the literature on the 'quality' of democracy to get a concept that extends further to the right (e.g., Diamond and Morlino 2004). Here, one typically adds more dimensions and requirements onto minimalist definitions of democracy. Dahl's work is notable in this regard because he explicitly conceptualizes democracy such that it never appears in practice: 'polyarchy [democracy in practice] is one of the most extraordinary of all human artifacts. Yet it unquestionably falls well short of achieving the democratic process' (Dahl 1989, p. 223).

An upshot of this discussion is that case study researchers who define their units with ideal type concepts might be especially reluctant to extend the scope of their arguments. Insofar as most real cases do not approximate the ideal type, then most real cases will introduce heterogeneity into the analysis.

Homogeneity of independent and dependent variables

Just as homogeneity of the unit matters, so does homogeneity of the independent and

dependent variables. If one does not achieve consistency and stability in the measurement of these variables, it obviously follows that problems can arise when making causal inferences using these variables.

To explore these issues in case study research, consider a study focused on explaining 'revolution.' Table 17.1 lists six underlying components (violence, popular involvement, etc.) and shows how different authors use them to define three kinds of revolution: social revolutions, political revolutions, and rebellions. These three categories are defined using the classical approach to concepts built around the logic of taxonomical hierarchy (Sartori 1970). Thus, social revolution has the largest number of defining components (all six must be present) and the fewest number of empirical examples. Rebellion, by contrast, has only two necessary conditions and many more empirical instances.[3]

This example illustrates how, in case study research, conceptual homogeneity on the dependent variable is often linked to questions of the appropriate level on a hierarchy at which one should work. Suppose that we have a theory designed to explain the occurrence of political revolution. As social revolution is a subset of political revolution (i.e., all social revolutions have the defining components of political revolutions), one might think that social revolutions could be included as positive cases of political revolution when

Table 17.1   Variation in the dependent variable: 'revolution'

Scholar	Violence	Popular involvement	Change in governing body	Minor political structural change	Major political structural change	Stratification changes
Social Revolution						
Skocpol	Y	Y	Y	Y	Y	Y
Moore	Y	Y	Y	Y	Y	Y
Political Revolution						
Huntington	Y	Y	Y	Y	N	N
Johnson	Y	Y	Y	Y	N	N
Davies	Y	Y	Y	Y	N	N
Rebellion						
Gurr	Y	Y	N	N	N	N

Source: Adapted from Kotowski (1984, 422).

testing the theory. But social revolutions are not the same thing as political revolutions (i.e., social revolutions involve major political structural and stratification changes, whereas political revolutions do not), and scholars often argue that one needs different theories to explain social revolutions and political revolutions. As a result, it is possible that the inclusion of cases of social revolution as instances of political revolution would introduce conceptual heterogeneity into the analysis.[4]

As another example, consider again the concept of 'democracy.' In the Polity IV data set, this concept is measured along a -10 to $+10$ scale. Conceptual homogeneity requires that all countries with a given score, say 5, on this scale in fact have the same level of democracy. The same score must mean the same thing across all cases.

Case study researchers will often express real concern for this aspect of homogeneity. A scholar with expertise in a particular region may look at various instances of 5 and worry whether they are really the same. Case expertise may lead the analyst to see concept heterogeneity where a large-N dataset assumes homogeneity.

For example, Bowman et al. (2005) argue that the use of inappropriate data sources causes the leading quantitative datasets on democracy (i.e., Gasiorowski 1996, Marshall and Jaggers 2004, Vanhanen 2004) to seriously miscode the Central American countries. Because of poor underlying data, two cases might have the same score for democracy across measures but actually have quite different levels of democracy. Indeed, these authors' own assessment of the level of democracy in Central America (the BLM index) produces results that are only weakly correlated with existing indices (and for certain periods there is no correlation at all). From this perspective, then, the scores in the other measures often suffer from conceptual heterogeneity.

Conceptual homogeneity concerns also arise through what we call 'substitutability' (Goertz and Mahoney 2005) or what might be called functional equivalence (Przeworski and Tuene 1970, van Deth 1998). The Polity IV concept of democracy is an aggregation of five component parts. Hence, there are a variety of ways to score a 5 on the polity scale. Concept homogeneity assumes that in terms of causal effect all these configurations are homogeneous. The key assumption is that some differences *within* democracies have no causal effect and hence can be treated as equivalent. Przeworski et al. (2000) provide an illustration of this homogeneity assumption. Their concept of democracy has four component parts. Their coding rules state that if a country has a zero value (dichotomously) on any one of the four components, then the country is coded as a nondemocracy. Democracy can be achieved in only one way (i.e., a one on all four components), whereas nondemocracy can occur in fifteen different ways (i.e., $2^4 - 1 = 15$).

The question is whether these fifteen different ways of becoming a nondemocracy have the same causal consequences when introduced into analysis (or, alternatively, are produced by the same causal factors). For example, when assessing the consequences of nondemocracy on fertility rates, as Przeworski et al. (2000) do, can we assume that a country that has zero value on only one of the components performs in the same way as a country that has a zero value on all four components?

This kind of homogeneity issue is especially important when scholars are working with dichotomous categories, which is common in case study research. Quite frequently, the author will be centrally concerned with the homogeneity of the positive value for the dichotomous category (e.g., democracy, war, revolution) but give less attention to the homogeneity of negative values (e.g., nondemocracy, nonwar, and nonrevolution). However, in causal analysis, it is essential that the negative value mean the same thing across all observations, otherwise unstable inferences may result.

CAUSAL SCOPE

Causal scope refers to restrictions on generalization resulting from the need to maintain stability in the hypothesized causal linkage between independent and dependent variables. This is often discussed under the rubric of 'causal homogeneity.' Although the concept of causal homogeneity is used in somewhat different ways by different authors, it fundamentally refers to the assumption that independent variables work in analogous or identical ways across a given population of observations. In statistical research, for example, a typical definition of causal homogeneity is 'the assumption that, other things being equal, a given set of values for the explanatory variables always produces the same expected value for the dependent variable within a given set of cases' (Seawright and Collier 2004, p. 276). In case study research causal homogeneity is understood roughly as the assumption that particular outcomes can be explained in light of independent variables that exert the same effects across all observations.

Given these definitions, causal heterogeneity is an extension of a model specification problem. Unstable causal inference is generated by the failure of a theoretical model to identify key independent variables and/or correctly specify their interrelationships. When one says causal relationships are not stable, even though conceptual heterogeneity is not a problem, one typically means that there are unknown variables or relationships that cannot be adequately modeled when moving from one population to the next.

In this section we discuss some of the issues that arise in restricting or expanding the scope for three kinds of causal arguments in case study research.

Simple causal explanations

A common explanatory claim in case study research concerns necessary condition counterfactuals: if not-X then not-Y. X is a cause of Y because without X, Y would not have occurred. As various methodologists point out, this understanding of causation is common in historical explanation:

> I wish to show that one kind of causal argument is peculiarly characteristic of historical explanation. Historians, I shall argue, sometimes explain events in a perfectly good sense of 'explain,' by referring us to one or a number of their temporally prior *necessary* conditions; they tell us how a particular event happened by pointing out hitherto unnoticed, or at least undervalued, antecedent events, *but for which*, they claim on broadly inductive grounds, the event in question would not or could hardly have happened. (Gallie 1956, p. 161; see also Nagel 1961, pp. 581–582; Fearon 1996, p. 40)

How do scope issues relate to arguments by case study researchers about necessary causes? First, as Eckstein's (1975) work suggests, the necessary cause might be associated with a more general theoretical framework. The case study might be intended to illustrate that the scope of the existing framework extends to the case under analysis. While the full scope of the framework might not be known precisely, the case study itself provides information about this scope. Theory-confirming case studies are confirming precisely because they fall within the scope of a larger theory. For example, one might argue using process tracing that labor repression in the rural sector was a necessary cause of sustained high growth in Chile. This finding is interesting because it confirms a broader theory that suggests that labor repression was necessary for high growth in East Asia.

Second, it is also possible that the necessary cause contradicts a more general theory. These necessary causes suggest limitations in the scope of the more general theory. Insofar as the theory was previously expected to apply to this kind of case, this is valuable information. An example would be the debate over the role of ideational factors in producing the end of the Cold War. Scholars who believe ideational factors (e.g., Soviet New Thinking) were necessary causes may set up their argument as a challenge to realist theories that deny the importance of these causes.

A variant that combines the first two types might be path-dependent arguments. These arguments may identify an idiosyncratic necessary cause that contradicts a general theory. In that sense, they put limits on the scope of the more general theory. However, these examples also suggest the generality of the framework of path dependence. In that sense, they are confirming instances *vis-à-vis* the framework of path dependence.

Finally, what about instances in which the necessary cause is not associated with any pre-existing more general theory? In these instances, usually the analyst is working in a theory-developing mode. If the analyst believes that the new theory only works to explain the particular case under study, then the general lessons from the case study might involve understanding why the case requires an idiosyncratic theory. However, we believe that it is common for case study researchers to argue not only for the necessity of Z in the present case, but also to make suggestions that one is likely to see the same in other cases. With just the one case analyzed, these suggestions might well have a speculative feel to them, leaving it to other scholars to undertake theory-testing case studies. Ideally, however, the analyst will try to make reference to features in the case that were necessary for the necessary cause to exert its effect. These pre-condition contextual factors (themselves necessary causes) then become the scope of the argument.

In short, necessary condition hypotheses often lie at the core of case study explanations. Case studies can be used in the theory confirming, generating, or falsifying mode. However, they all deal with evaluating the empirical and theoretical homogeneity of claims about a key variable.

Equifinality: multiple causal path explanations

A second use of case studies involves the study of equifinality, or separate causal paths to the same outcome. Case studies often postulate a particular causal path to an outcome. Subsequent case studies then may examine if there are other potential paths to the same outcome. If there are, then case study research leads to the discovery of equifinality, i.e., multiple causal paths to the same outcome. A theory-generating case study can thus incite researchers to explore the scope of their argument, leading to the discovery of equifinality.

One sees this quite clearly in the literature on the welfare state. For various reason's much of the early work focused on what might be called the social-democratic or the Scandinavian route to a welfare state. However, some researchers began to explore in more detail other countries, particularly Catholic ones, and proposed that there was a conservative route to a welfare state. The end result was Esping-Andersen's extremely influential three worlds (i.e., paths) of the welfare state. Another example would be Gerschenkron's (1962) work on modernization in Germany, which helped stimulate Moore (1966) to identify three separate paths to the modern world.

The idea of multiple paths presents a nice contrast with the necessary condition counterfactual. Whereas the necessary condition counterfactual stresses that certain factors are essential and must be present, equifinality stresses that there are alternatives. In addition, whereas necessary condition counterfactuals target individual causes, equifinality normally calls attention to combinations of variables. To identify domains of causal homogeneity with equifinality, one needs to make sure that multiple combinations of variables have stable effects. That is, the question is not whether X_1 and whether X_2 have a stable effect, but whether $X_1 * X_2 * X_3 * \ldots$ and $X_1 * X_4 * X_5 * \ldots$ have stable effects.

One might be tempted to believe that the discovery of different causal paths to a given outcome amounts to the study of causal heterogeneity. For example, Ragin's (1987, 2000) methods, which explicitly are intended to study equifinality, are sometimes understood to apply to heterogeneous populations. This belief grows out of the fact that these methods assume that any particular independent variable may have quite different – even opposite – effects, depending on the other variables with which it is combined in an interaction. For example, one might explain some outcome Y in terms of the following model (the '+' stands for the logical OR):

$$Y = ABC + aBD \qquad (1)$$

In the first configuration – ABC of eq. (1) – variable A must be present for Y, whereas in the second configuration variable A must be absent (i.e., a) for Y. Hence, both the presence of A and absence of A may be crucial to the occurrence of Y, depending on the values of the other variables with which they interact. Given that the effects of A are not constant and that the 'average' effect of A is not meaningful, qualitative researchers sometimes conclude that they study causal heterogeneity.

In fact, however, this model of causation still requires the analyst to make assumptions about causal homogeneity. The difference with much quantitative research is that these assumptions of homogeneity are linked to combinations of variables rather than singular variables. The approach assumes that a given combination of causal factors will produce the same effect on an outcome within the population under study. For example, in eq. (1) the assumption is that ABC and aBD are sufficient for Y across all cases analyzed. The difference is that when equifinality is studied, case study researchers are more concerned with making sure that combinations of interacting variables have stable effects than with ensuring that the individual effect of each variable is constant.

This discussion has two different implications for case studies that are worth emphasizing. On the one hand, the discussion suggests that it is very difficult to identify the scope of a qualitative argument, because one must not only be concerned with the stability of individual causes, but also of interacting combinations of causes. Insofar as one believes that these interactions are not likely to be stable across large populations, one will be pushed in the direction of a restrictive scope. On the other hand, the discussion also underscores how case studies can be used to develop theory by identifying new combinations of causes that lead to a particular outcome. These new combinations might then be combined with already existing ones into a single overarching theory. In that sense, the discovery of additional causal paths can encourage one to broaden the scope of their argument through theoretical modifications that take into consideration multiple paths.

CONCLUSION

Scope is really a series of homogeneity claims – arguments about the homogeneity of not only causal relations, but also core conceptual entities. We think that including concept homogeneity as part of scope is essential, since instability in causal relationships is not necessarily a result of poor model specification but may in fact be a problem with the measurement of key concepts. A few inappropriate cases or measures of independent or dependent variables can wreck havoc with the causal claims involving theory-limiting or causal variables. Cleaning up the concepts may be more effective than trying to rework the theory.

At the same time, when one does focus on more traditional issues of causal homogeneity, it is important that one pays close attention to the specific causal claims that are invoked. The scope issues that arise for the kinds of causal arguments developed in case study research are different from those that arise in large-N research. In addition, within the case study tradition itself, different kinds of causal arguments raise distinct considerations for specifying theory scope.

When scholars choose a case, typically it is in part because it is a case of *something*. We propose that one is implicitly thinking about generalizations to other instances of that something. There is a belief that either the concepts or the causal patterns (or both) under investigation are relevant for understanding phenomena elsewhere (including by way of contrast). It is worth recalling that almost all of Eckstein's types of case studies involve some relationship to general theories or larger descriptive patterns. We suggest research could be improved by making the scope claims inherent in most case studies more explicit.

NOTES

1. These scope issues also occasionally arise in large-N, quantitative research. For example, consider the debate over Przeworski et al.'s (2000) 'exogenous theory' of democracy, which holds that development does not generally increase the likelihood that authoritarian countries will become democratic (instead, development makes democracies, once established, less likely to become authoritarian). In their critique of Przeworski et al.'s empirical work, Boix and Stokes (2003) find that this conclusion is, significantly, a product of a focus on recent cases. 'By restricting their analysis to post-1950 cases, Przeworski, Limongi, and their associates underestimate the endogenous effect of development on transitions to democracy' (Boix and Stokes 2003, p. 519). Boix and Stokes argue that pre-1950 and post-1950 cases exhibit heterogeneous causal patterns, and they suggest that explaining the source of this heterogeneity should be a major topic of future research.

2. The rationale for excluding very small states can vary. For example, Kuznets (1951) excludes them because they are highly economically dependent on surrounding countries, whereas many conflict scholars would exclude microstates because of their small likelihood of experiencing military conflict.

3. Kotowski (1984) argues that the defining characteristics in the columns are necessary conditions. Thus, as one adds more necessary conditions, the inclusiveness of the concept must remain the same or go down.

4. This example suggests that the best contrast or 'negative' cases in qualitative research are often those from the category just below the dependent variable of interest (see Mahoney and Goertz 2004). For example, in her work on social revolution, Skocpol's (1979) negative cases are often instances of political revolution. Analogously, useful negative cases for a theory of political revolution are instances of rebellion.

REFERENCES

Alford, R. 1998 *The Craft of Inquiry: Theories, Methods, Evidence.* Oxford: Oxford University Press.

Babbie, E. 2001 *The Practice of Social Research* (9th edition). Belmont, CA: Wadsworth.

Bates, R. 1997 'Comparative politics and rational choice: a review essay' *American Political Science Review* 91: 699–704.

Bennett, D. and Stam, A. 2000 'A cross-validation of Bueno de Mesquita and Lalman's international interaction game' *British Journal of Political Science* 30: 541–560.

Boix, C. and Stokes, S. 2003 'Endogenous democratization' *World Politics* 55: 517–549.

Bowman, K., Lehoucq, F. and Mahoney, J. 2005 'Measuring political democracy: case expertise, data adequacy, and Central America' *Comparative Political Studies* 38: 939–970.

Bueno de Mesquita, B. 1981 *The War Trap.* New Haven, CT: Yale University Press.

Coffey, A. and Atkinson, P. 1996 *Making Sense of Qualitative Data.* Newbury Park, CA: Sage Publications.

Dahl, R. 1989 *Democracy and its Critics.* New Haven, CT: Yale University Press.

Diamond, L., and Morlino, L. 2004 'The quality of democracy: an overview' *Journal of Democracy* 15: 20–31.

Eckstein, H. 1975 'Case study and theory in political science' in F. Greenstein and N. Polsby (Eds) *Handbook of Political Science. Volume 7 Strategies of Inquiry.* Reading, MA: Addison-Wesley.

Elster, J. 1979 *Ulysses and the Sirens* (revised edition). Cambridge: Cambridge University Press.

Fearon, J. 1996 'Causes and counterfactuals in social science: exploring an analogy between cellular automata and historical processes' in P. Tetlock and A. Belkin (Eds) *Counterfactual Thought Experiments in World Politics.* Princeton, NJ: Princeton University Press.

Fischer, M. 1992 'Feudal Europe, 800–1300: communal discourse and conflictual practices' *International Organization* 46: 467–491.

Fischer, M. 1993 'On context, facts, and norms: response to Hall and Kratochwil' *International Organization* 47: 493–500.

Gallie, B. 1956 'Essentially contested concepts' *Proceedings of the Aristotelian Society* 56: 167–198.

Gasiorowski, M. 1996 'An overview of the political regime change dataset' *Comparative Political Studies* 29: 469–483.

Geddes, B. 2003 *Paradigms and Sand Castles: Theory Building and Research Design in Comparative Politics.* Ann Arbor, MI: University of Michigan Press.

Gerschenkron, A. 1962 *Economic Backwardness in Historical Perspective.* Cambridge: Cambridge University Press.

Gleditsch, K. and Ward, M. 1999 'A revised list of independent states since the Congress of Vienna' *International Interactions* 25: 393–413.

Goertz, G. and Mahoney, J. 2005 'Two-level theories and fuzzy-set analysis' *Sociological Methods and Research* 33: 497–538.

Goodwin, J. and Skocpol, T. 1989 'Explaining revolutions in the contemporary Third World' *Politics and Society* 17: 489–509.

Hall, R. and Kratochwil, F. 1993 'Medieval tales: neorealist "science" and the abuse of history' *International Organization* 47: 475–491.

Hicks, A. 1988 'National collective action and economic performance: a review article' *International Studies Quarterly* 32: 131–153.

Hoover, K. 1984 *The Elements of Social Scientific Thinking* (3rd edition). New York: Saint Martin's Press.

Hug, S. 2003 'Selection bias in comparative research: the case of incomplete data sets' *Political Analysis* 11: 255–274.

Isaak, A. 1985 *Scope and Methods of Political Science*. Homewood, IL: Dorsey Press.

Kotowski, C. 1984 'Revolution' in G. Sartori (Ed.) *Social Science Concepts: A Systematic Analysis*. Beverly Hills, CA: Sage Publications.

Kuznets, S. 1951 'The state as a unit in study in economic growth' *Journal of Economic History* 11: 25–41.

Mahoney, J. and Goertz, G. 2004 'The Possibility Principle: choosing negative cases in comparative research' *American Political Science Review* 98: 653–669.

Marshall, M. and Jaggers, K. 2004 'Polity IV project: political regime characteristics and transitions, 1800–1999' Manuscript. Online, available: http://www.cidcm.umd.edu/inscr/polity/2004.

Moore, B. 1966 *Social Origins of Dictatorship and Democracy: Lord and Peasant in the Making of the Modern World*. Boston: Beacon Press.

Nachmias, D. and Nachmias, C. 1976 *Research Methods in the Social Sciences*. New York: Saint Martin's Press.

Nagel, E. 1961 *The Structure of Science: Problems in the Logic of Scientific Explanation*. New York: Harcourt, Brace and World.

Przeworski, A. and Teune, H. 1970 *The Logic of Comparative Social Inquiry*. New York: John Wiley.

Przeworski, A., Alvarez, M.E., Cheibub, J.A. and Limongi, F. 2000 *Democracy and Development: Political Institutions and Well-being in the World, 1950–1990*. Cambridge: Cambridge University Press.

Ragin, C. 1987 *The Comparative Method: Moving Beyond Qualitative and Quantitative Strategies*. Berkeley, CA: University of California Press.

Ragin, C. 2000 *Fuzzy-set Social Science*. Chicago: University of Chicago Press.

Sartori, G. 1970 'Concept misformation in comparative politics' *American Political Science Review* 64: 1033–1053.

Seawright, J. and Collier, D. 2004 'Glossary' in H. Brady and D. Collier (Eds) *Rethinking Social Inquiry: Diverse Tools, Shared Standards*. New York: Rowman and Littlefield.

Singleton, R. and Straits, B. 1999 *Approaches to Social Research* (3rd edition). Oxford: Oxford University Press.

Skocpol, T. 1979 *States and Social Revolutions: A Comparative Analysis of France, Russia, and China*. Cambridge: Cambridge University Press.

Tsebelis, G. 1990 *Nested Games*. Berkeley, CA: University of California Press.

van Deth, J. (Ed.) 1998 *Comparative Politics: The Problem of Equivalence*. London: Routledge.

Vanhanen, T. 2004 'Polyarchy dataset: measures of democracy 1810–2002' Manuscript. Helsinki: University of Helsinki.

Walker, H. and Cohen, B. 1985 'Scope statements: imperatives for evaluating theories' *American Sociological Review* 50: 288–301.

Zelditch, M. 1971 'Intelligible comparisons' in I. Vallier (Ed.) *Comparative Methods in Sociology: Essays on Trends and Applications*. Berkeley, CA: University of California Press.

18

Small-N Access Cases to Refine Theories of Social Exclusion and Access to Socially Excluded Individuals and Groups

Nick Emmel and Kahryn Hughes

INTRODUCTION

Steinmetz (2004) concludes his critical realist interrogation of sociological method with the observation that case studies, small-N comparisons, and the semi-autonomous development of social theory are the three core activities of any social science. In this chapter, we will describe the lessons we have learnt about these three core activities in research to develop methodological strategies to recruit and research socially excluded people.[1] In particular, our attention will focus on what we characterise as access cases in this methodological research. Access cases provide the organisational structure for the large dataset we produced during a study aiming to develop and refine access methodologies and our understanding of

experiences of social exclusion. In addition to organisational structure, however, these cases provide bounded units in a potentially limitless open social system, enabling us to theorise the contingent development (Abbott 1992) of both methodologies of access and the experience of social exclusion. These cases allow for interrogation of relational, transactional, and dynamic networks (Emirbayer and Goodwin 1994, Emirbayer 1997) amongst social actors and allow us to describe potential trajectories through and out of social exclusion. The use of access cases in this research therefore provides a methodological strategy through which we are able to refine anti-categorical theory and address substantive questions about social action and experiences of social exclusion.

FROM A GEOGRAPHICAL CASE STUDY TO ACCESS CASES

An earlier study[2] to the one we will describe in detail in this chapter, in the same geographical area, made us aware that it is difficult to recruit socially excluded people to research. The geographical area, a low-income estate already selected by our funders, was our case in this earlier research. As a case study, there were challenges in working at this putative scale. Administrative boundaries did not correspond with the estate's geography. A municipal ward boundary ran through the centre of the estate, aggregating demographic and census data in two much larger administrative areas; health, social service, and police data were all collected at different scales. We were obliged to make inferences from the available data, our local knowledge, and the local knowledge of service providers, to produce a rough-and-ready picture of demographic, health, and other social statistics. We sought to enhance our understanding of the demography and social make-up of the estate through the lay-knowledge of the participants we could readily access through schools, church groups, and community organisations. In doing so, we were able to theorise that there were groups within the estate we had not been able to access. This theorisation became the basis for the research described in more detail here, a study with the aim of combining method development and identification of the dimensions of social exclusion to produce methodological advances in the access to and recruitment of socially excluded individuals.

In this qualitative methodological research we sought to move, in an iterative and reflexive way, between 'finding'(asking questions such as 'who are socially excluded people?' and 'what are the methods of access to socially excluded people?') and 'defining'(asking questions such as 'how do socially excluded people interpret their exclusion?' and 'are the recruitment strategies appropriate and effective?'). These questions sought to address the four objectives of our study: (1) identification of socially excluded people; (2) development of methods of access; (3) commentary on the success or failure of these methods of access; and (4) theorisation of the methodological implications of the methods used in accessing socially excluded people.

We initially tried to gain access to socially excluded people and groups by talking with those we could access most easily: service providers such as health visitors, drug workers, social workers, workers for government agencies such as the Anti-Social Behaviour Unit (ASBU) and Youth Offending Team (YOT), voluntary organisations, and those living and working on the low-income estate whom we had accessed in our earlier research. We understand that, as researchers, we have a common linguistic and cultural capital with the health- and social-care workers, in particular (Bourdieu 1999). The residents we accessed were those who were better educated, more articulate, and involved in community organisation. We identified and interviewed 39 of these workers and residents. In the first round of interviews we sought to capture what they understood by social exclusion; the nature of the contact they had with those they considered socially excluded and whom we were trying to access; and what they considered their ability to provide us with access to the people they had identified.

Based on these 39 interviews, we purposefully sampled five service providers and one resident. Our sample captured a continuum from formal service providers, whose role is to address the pathology of social exclusion through implementing specific measures to control, supervise, and rehabilitate socially excluded individuals, to informal service providers whose relationship is one of befriending, supporting, and protecting those who they consider to be vulnerable and misunderstood in the community. Each of these service providers agreed to act as a gatekeeper to socially excluded people they identified, and whom we were trying to access.

In the research, we produced 30 access cases. An access case includes all data on every interaction involved in an attempt to access a socially excluded individual or group. These data include telephone conversations, informal conversations where permission was granted, and near-verbatim notes in cases where participants and gatekeepers declined to be taped but agreed to the field notes. Access cases additionally include ethnographic field notes and taped conversations between the research team theorising the cases of access. In 12 of the 30 cases, access was successful. Where we were successful in accessing a socially excluded individual or group, our access case includes transcripts of a taped life-history interview that sought to understand both the experience of social exclusion through production of a life-history narrative and interrogation of the appropriateness of the way we had accessed the participant. Six of these interviews were with more than one person, ranging from two to seven people; in total, 27 socially excluded participants were interviewed.

These 30 successful and unsuccessful access cases are the focus of this chapter. These access cases are developed within the geographical case of the low-income estate. The geographically bounded estate is characterised by low income: over 65% of households claim council-administered benefits, compared with the city average of 26.8%, for instance. In-depth interviews with service providers and others from outside the estate frequently describe the area as socially excluded, reflecting high levels of drug abuse, teenage pregnancy, crime and criminal behaviour, and unemployment. These categorisations, generated from statistics and interview data with service providers to those who live on the estate, however, are disrupted in the interviews. Service providers relate particular relational practices identified as characteristic of this area. Different sorts of boundaries and boundedness are discussed. Through these interpretations, the geographical case facilitated an understanding of place and space as relational. This single-N geographical case has within it heterogeneous explanations of the embodied relational practices we are concerned to investigate in this research. To understand these, a method is needed that facilitates comparison within particular cases and between cases

that is not facilitated through the single case. Before investigating this potential strength of multiple cases further, however, we consider how the use of access cases allowed us to manage the data in the research.

ACCESS CASES AS AN ORGANISATIONAL STRUCTURE

The access cases allow us to manage three main activities in the research. First, the management and organisation of extremely large datasets, particularly qualitative data. Second, the management, tracking, and analyses of relational flows between ourselves and gatekeepers, gatekeepers and participants, and participants and other participants. Third, analyses of relational flows between different parts of the data in order to facilitate the contingent processes of methodological and theoretical development.

Organisation

One of the significant challenges facing qualitative researchers is to manage and organise large datasets. At a practical level, these access cases provided a filing system to organise our data. A typical access case in our dataset where access was successful included the initial interview with the gatekeeper, follow-up interview with the gatekeeper, telephone conversations and other interactions with the gatekeeper, ethnographic field notes edited from the field-worker's diary, team meeting notes edited from team meetings, initial interviews with some of the participants, and a life-history interview in successful cases of access.

Relational flows

Length and size are not the only complexities to be dealt with in managing qualitative datasets. Access cases became the organising principle for tracking relational flows, research processes, and gatekeeper and participant negotiations in the 30 access cases, making audit of our activities and planning of field-work possible. Through analysis of the relational flows between researcher/ gatekeeper and gatekeeper/participant, the access cases enabled us to understand the nature of the participants' lives that made them difficult to access; the features of particular relationships participants have with different types of gatekeeper, in the context of emerging understandings of experiences of social exclusion, which allowed or impeded access; and so manage the fundamentally contingent process of methodological and theoretical engagement and development.

Relationship between different parts of the data: the interplay between the empirical and the theoretical

The relationships between different parts of the data also have to be managed. A research project with field-work carried out over 2 years includes reflection on an emergent process of data collection that is iteratively refined as the research progresses. In our study, the products of such iteration are the empirically and theoretically generated access cases. The process of theorisation was made tangible in the evolving series of access strategies we used over the course of the field-work. The access case therefore becomes a temporal record of data generation, the theorisation from these data, and the insights that lead to empirical activities that emerge from that theorisation.

An example of this interplay between empirical research and theorisation and the generation of strategies of access is shown in a case where we failed to access a participant. In access case K, we gained access to a participant through the referral of a particular gatekeeper, but were refused access by the participant when she was asked to sign a consent form. The access case provided the organisational structure for the material needed to interrogate data to theorise why access had been refused. These data included the gatekeeper's detailed historical and contextual description of the

participant and her household; ethnographic field notes from the interaction between researcher and participant; and a telephone interview with the gatekeeper who had spoken with the participant after she had turned the researcher away from her door. With these data, we were able to sharpen and refine our understanding of processes of access and strategies used to ensure ethical access. This particular case allowed us to theorise that the consent form acted as a generative mechanism that impeded access. This theorisation was facilitated not only by data collected within this case of access, but also through interrogation of other cases where it became clear that the consent form is associated with officialdom for our prospective participants and, given our contextual understanding of K's informal economic activities and childcare arrangements, signing a form is considered risky and constitutes a potential threat. This theorisation enabled us to further consider our participants' perceptions of risk. Specifically, K's case highlighted how often the relationship between formal gatekeepers and our participants were often described as punitive, or leading to punitive action (e.g., with ASBU and YOT). Our analysis of K's case access also provided a theory, albeit a fairly blunt instrument at this stage, to be applied and tested in other access cases, about the 'punitive' character of officialdom, and form filling in particular. We stopped using informed consent forms after this event and instead gained recorded verbal consent.

The insights gained from this experience in the research enriched our understanding of those who are socially excluded and their approach to risk and trust. This, alongside the other Ns in our research, allowed us to develop more penetrative questions about why and how particular gatekeeper relationships facilitate or impede access, informed by the ongoing production of more robust theories about the nature of social exclusion.

Before considering what we have learnt about the value of comparison between access cases to develop more substantial tested theory, however, we consider the limitations of theorisation within single cases in more detail.

FROM SINGLE-N CASE STUDY TO SMALL-N 'CASING' FOR SOCIAL THEORY

The case study is ubiquitous in qualitative research (Walton 1992, Patton 2002, Steinmetz 2004). One area where case studies are particularly prevalent is in the rich descriptions of methods to access hard-to-reach groups. Case studies are used to illuminate methods of access including snowballing; incentives; peer interviewers using matched researchers by age, gender, and background and privileged access; support and endorsement from leaders (Berg 1999); advertising and innovative service delivery approaches (Urwin 2003); and techniques for building trustful relationships (Sixsmith et al. 2003).

Each of these examples provides a rich case description of a particular method of access applied. Typical of these case studies is the description of access to a close-knit urban community developed by Sixsmith et al. (2003). This case study describes how researchers spent considerable amounts of time in the community involving themselves in community activities, walking the site, and chatting with groups of residents in a strategy of being there and being seen. In Sixsmith's and colleagues' study, two researchers were employed who had similar experiences to those who live in the low-income community, each was from a working-class background and had experience of working in socially deprived communities. Sixsmith et al. (2003) draw out from their case study features of their access that they considered important in gaining access to otherwise invisible members of communities. Credibility, rapport, and generating trustful relationships with groups in the community are all identified as important features of gaining access and maintaining that access throughout the research process. Similarly, the case studies developed by Elliott et al.

(2002) and Kuebler and Hausser (1997), who each use a strategy of peer interviewers to access drug users, highlight how these peer interviewers are able to introduce and vouch for outside researchers and build relationships of empathy and mutual trust with groups that are difficult to access.

These single-N case studies are invaluable in providing insights into how access might be achieved. However, as we have observed above, the single case study is a blunt instrument in the process of theorisation. As Elliott et al. (2002, p. 178) note, their interrogation of the use of peer interviewers 'makes some attempt to explore the essence of (peer interviewers) skills within the context of other debates about the nature of lay expertise in qualitative research'. This understandable caution arises out of the methodological strategy used. As in the geographical case of the low-income community we described at the beginning of the chapter, the single-N case study can only ever have limited, but possibly useful explanatory potential.

In considering the limitations of the single-N case we have identified two reasons for this limitation in this research. First, the case must involve the necessary bounding of a potentially infinite open system social world that might be incorporated into the researcher's gaze (Bhaskar 1979). The case study is, therefore, for the inevitable and practical purposes of social research, an ecological unit, and our ability to make sense of the case rests in understanding where the boundaries of the case are set. In knowing, or, at the least, having a partial understanding and acceptance of these limits we avoid the risk of ecological fallacy and making claims for generalisability and transferability of findings that cannot empirically be supported.

Alongside the problems of defining the boundary of a single case study, the single case highlights the categorical at the expense of illuminating relational practices. Thus, the description of the single geographical case outlined in the introduction is beset by categories, indicators of low income and normative descriptions of the low-income estate as a whole. Reification is an ever present danger in analysis. Drawing on network analysis, Wellman (1983, p. 165), rejects explanations of 'social behaviour as the result of individuals' common possession of attributes and norms rather than as a result of their involvement in structured social relations'. This anti-categorical imperative, informed our research too. We sought to illuminate dynamic processes of access and social exclusion over time. Single cases provide only limited opportunities to capture the ways in which actors may respond to and interact with structures in very different ways despite the apparent similarity of the context in which they act. These intentional acts (Bhaskar 1979) may lead to an elaboration of structures by social actors or their reproduction (Archer 1998). The focus of our access cases, in recording the process of access to one individual or group, facilitates analyses of how relational practices are constitutive of particular relational networks that are themselves productive of, and located within, broader social processes.

The example below demonstrates how multiple access cases inform each other in theory building about the dynamic elaboration or reproduction of social processes we are concerned to investigate. Here two individuals, P and C, have apparently similar backgrounds. They live on the same low-income estate, are both heroin addicts, and have families living on the estate. Yet, when they describe their relational networks and how they use these networks, their accounts are markedly different.

First, P's network, which – like all the networks described – first considers home and family and his relationship with important others:

> Yeah, the opportunities in G, ... em, were limited, ... em, a very rough area. Certain families ... er run working class areas, there's no getting away from that. You go into any, most working class areas and you'll have two or three families that actually control that area (AS: right). They'll control crime there, they'll control drug dealing there, ... errmmm, and they'll control whether you can walk down that street or not, and ... that was the life I was ... er, brought up in as a child.

> Fortunately, ... em, my family home was quite an open home. In my family home there was five of us, I've got two brothers and two sisters and we all had a lot of friends each and we made connections with the most important people on these communities, you know, crime families, and fortunately ... em, you know, we didn't get no pressure or no hassle from these families because we made friends with them. (pp. 26–27)

The importance of these networks is explored further by P. In particular, the networks that exist within the estate that are important to his economic activity. P, a recovering heroin addict, describes in some detail his 'graft', which, he explains 'is for a heroin addict going out and doing crime' (p. 39). P goes on to explain how individuals specialise in particular activities. P specialises in stealing building equipment. Further, he explains why he can pursue this particular graft and draws attention to the networks within the estate that are important in this economic activity:

> I'd only nick fucking ... er work tools, now that's my bit of a speciality because in 10 year I've always nicked work tools, you get good fucking pay for 'em, they're small, you can conceal 'em, it's a pretty quick graft, and anybody buys work tools. There's enough builders or roofers or joiners in fucking working class areas to be able to sell this stuff to. And it wor very very good money, I mean you go, you know, many many times I've nicked generators and for generators you're looking at two, three hundred quid. (pp. 36–37)

P focuses on the networks through which he is able to conduct this informal economic activity. His narrative also describes his successful efforts to put heroin and graft behind him. One of the main impetuses to address these issues in his life is defined through his relationship with his family, friends, and neighbours. In particular, P emphasises the impact on his family of their neighbours' negative attitude towards him as a drug addict. P talks about 'family breakdowns, '... errr while I were on heroin, not because I'd ever done anything bad to 'em or anything immoral or anything like that, just because I embarrassed them, I embarrassed 'em in the community' (p. 53). But these relationships with family alone were not the key to P's success in addressing heroin addiction. P needed further networks to address this addiction, in particular P describes his relationship with his probation officer and key-worker, and the importance of these professionals in supporting him:

> But, your Probation Officer is there to help you, you know, they are fucking there to help you, and they do, ... I've had my Probation Officer 10 year, and she were fantastic and ... err supported housing after the ... er after the bail hostel – fantastic – SH, ... er, KL (names of hostels about five miles from G) it is, ... er, you get your own key-worker, ... em, you don't have to see her if you don't want to, although you've gotta have two monthly sessions, ... em, half-an-hour sessions, just to let her know how you're going on, how its developing, etcetera, etcetera, how you're progressing. I think they supported me a lot. (p. 70)

P notes these workers' importance in finding him housing outside G and establishing contact with health workers.

P's network is an exemplar of a 'big' network comprising family, friends, neighbours, economic collaborators, and health- and social-care professionals. Not only is a wide-ranging network described, so too are the activities of the network that impact on P's life decisions. Importantly, much of P's narrative is embedded and defined within the constraints of a place, but it also includes references to other places outside G: the hostels, his girlfriend's address, his new flat, which are outside this socially excluded place. In the interviews, P talks of the opportunities he has had to return to the local library to study, to start training, to involve himself in a community programme that requires him to be clean of drugs, and the implications of both this big network and the richness of activities on the network that lead him to aspire to be a journalist. Through moving out of G, moving out of his drug-using networks, towards further education and employment, through the utilisation of these significant relationships and resources beyond G, we consider the trajectory of P's life is one out of social exclusion.

C's network, by contrast, is a 'small' network. His narrative is characterised by his awareness of a lack of networks and the lack of support and value he perceives from the networks he does have. C, like P, is a heroin addict. Early in his narrative C emphasises the smallness of his social space:

> It's like, I'm round at my house all the time and that, and very rarely go out so, so that's it. I've no, I just like to keep myself to myself, do you know what I mean. So I don't really bother with going to people's houses or ... like, you know, stuff like that (AS: right). I just like stay in the house. And then it's just, I go round to t'house and that's it then, in the house all the time. I don't know, I've nowhere else, I don't go anywhere else at all. Except just like, I get up and go out, I just go to score. And then I come back and then I'm in the house all the time (AS: right). I don't like go anywhere else so really the only important thing is my house. That's all. (pp. 19–20)

The limits of C's networks are constantly reinforced throughout the interview. C has a wife and two children, but claims to play no part in supporting them or engaging with them. In fact, he observes that heroin addiction makes it impossible for him to play with his children as he might wish. His talk of family is restricted to describing from whom within the family he borrows money to support his heroin addiction. In his account, there is no discussion of friends and neighbours.

Despite the pervasive limits to networks in C's narrative, the relational nature of C's networks are emphasised. C describes two very different experiences of trying to address his addiction to heroin. First, he talks of a positive experience, a doctor who prescribed medication to support him in getting off heroin. 'When I had a break off it [heroin] before, I had a doctor from AV Medical Centre, and that's how I got off it before. I did it through him' (p. 31). But C moved house and, as he explains:

> It were a good doctor that I had. But with us like moving up this end, we wasn't in his catchments area so he had to take us off his register ... and then we went down to the doctor down there and he said no, can't help you. If he'd have just carried on giving me what my doctor would have given me, I wouldn't be on it now. It's like, in a way, I blame the doctors in a way for me going back to it because if he had carried on giving me the help I was getting

off the other doctor, I wouldn't have gone back to it because I was, like, not bothering. (p. 32)

C describes a relationship with the first doctor who is willing to treat his drug addiction. He does not receive this mediation to services he needs from the second doctor. Indeed, throughout the narrative C talks about being rebuffed by professional drug and health workers, the inappropriateness of referral mechanisms, and his inability to build bonds of trust with those who deliver services. C's small and isolated network contrasts sharply with P's big networks of family, friends, neighbours, economic opportunities, and health- and social-care providers. It has none of the richness of reciprocity and perceived benefit gained through the relationships that P draws on to live his day-to-day life. C is constrained in a place of social exclusion. Our analyses led us to conclude the trajectory of C's social exclusion is one of perpetuation of his condition.

These two cases demonstrate that while, as observed, a place might be labelled as socially excluded, a much finer grain of investigation is needed to understand the trajectories of social exclusion of those who live within that place and the sociocultural and psychosocial interactions that lead to different trajectories through social exclusion. If P's or C's case were to stand alone it is quite easy to see how very different theory could emerge. These cases are dissonant; P's account describes big networks, C's describes small networks. Yet, when analysed alongside each other they enable us to consider more than the individual narratives about the size of networks that emerge from single access cases. Rather, they emphasise that social exclusion is differentially experienced and mediated depending on particular relationships of which they are part. This has important implications for developing understandings of how particular relational networks are productive of, and located within, broader social processes and, in the context of our research, of processes of social exclusion and researchers' access to socially excluded individuals and groups.

COMPARISON OF SMALL-N CASES

In this chapter, our argument is that comparison of small-N ($= 30$) case studies aids more robust theory development through insights into the relational and transactional character of the participants' lives. Our research seeks to identify how embedded actors' relationships and stories shift over time and space, rather than seeking out categorical stability in action (Somers and Gibson 1996). Comparison between N cases facilitates development of new conceptual characteristics. As Walton (1992 p. 127) observes, 'new cases become strategic when they challenge or respecify received causal processes'. Through comparison we propose that we are able to refine theory. This is not to dismiss the importance of within-case analysis (Ragin 2006), but to observe that the single case remains a blunt instrument in theory development. Casing of small-N case studies is a methodological step in research to facilitate sharpening of the theoretical insights from research. As we have shown in the example of P and C above, by presupposing an open social system and examining the relational context of the participants, comparison of small-N cases implies that the relationships investigated between cases may be neither recurrent nor contingent. Similarly, generative causal mechanisms may be congruous across cases or, as importantly, be particular to one case. Conjunction across small-N cases is the methodological tactic through which mechanisms and phenomena triangulate a particular theoretical position, or expose dissonance.

To develop this assertion further with an example: the life-history narratives elicited from socially excluded individuals and groups in our research provide accounts of intentional practices aimed at transforming their material and social world. The life history narratives are not seamless autobiographical accounts of a life lived on a low-income council estate, rather they are accounts that express moments in the life course that are important to the teller – for Denzin these are epiphanies: 'those interactional moments and experiences that leave a mark on peoples' lives' (Denzin 1989, p. 70). Typical of these accounts is C's earlier description of his relationship with two different medical practices, one doctor that supported his attempts to address heroin addiction and a second doctor that would not. These are moments C describes when he felt he has some control over his life and also, in juxtaposition, the moments when he felt he could not address the issues in his life that concerned him. C's life history, like all the life histories we collected from socially excluded individuals, express moments that we theorised as epiphanies of powerlessness. Importantly, power is seen here as 'the relations of force that obtain between the social positions which guarantee their occupants a quantum of social force' (Bourdieu and Wacquant 1992, p. 220). Powerlessness is a description of constrained or enabled relationships between social actors (Emirbayer and Goodwin 1994) to address issues in the teller's life.

In our investigation of other accounts across the cases we identified further experiences of relationships of powerlessness. An exemplar of this expression of powerlessness is offered in an insight made by a manager of a voluntary organisation that works with families on the estate. This manager, who acted as a gatekeeper, describes a conversation with a retired man about a storage container deposited by the council in the grounds of the community centre next door to the man's house. This was used by local children as a place to play, climbing and jumping on the metal box through the night making a noise and disturbing nearby residents.

> ... 'Oh it's terrible you know, and on a night it's so noisy you can't do anything.' And I [the manager] said 'Oh we'll get it shifted.' He said 'Oh no can't.' I said 'Why not?' He said 'Well they [local councillors] won't listen to us will they?' (AM p. 281)

However, further interrogation and theorisation of our cases allowed us to refine our theory of powerlessness as an important part of any description of experiences of social exclusion, for while powerlessness is ever

present in the life-history narratives and talk about life on the estate, the extent of such powerlessness is emphasised by glimpses of constrained powerfulness. In a narrative rich in these stories of powerlessness, S talks of the constraints on her ability to have control over life events. Here, S describes her attempts to have a water heater repaired. Importantly, she introduces another theme – that of mediating her demands through a professional, a doctor – to address this particular problem:

> They [the Public Health Department] used to do tests, because of the old lead piping (AS: right) ..., so they [the children] kept having tests for that done, and, ... err, I eventually got all the lead piping in the house replaced with this plastic stuff, but still get doctors coming. A head doctor or somebody came out to talk to us, and I thought 'Oh bugger it, I'll tell him'. So I'd had no hot water for 2 to 3 months, no hot water, and I'd already reported it, and I said 'Well could you have a word with the council'. And he's gone 'Why?' 'Well' I said 'I've had no hot water'. He said 'How long for?' '[I] said "Don't know, about 12 weeks, sommat like that".' He's gone 'Well how do you bath your kids?' Well I had an old twin tub then with a heater on it so you take the bloody agitator out and, I showed it, I filled it up with cold water and I put the heater on and I warmed the water up and that's how. I strip washed my kids, in me washing machine, I said they don't have to turn it on, but that's how I washed me kids for nearly 3 months ... But within 24 hours of him contacting the rent office I had a new gas water heater and I thought that was not very nice. Why did they have to wait for somebody else to do it when I needed it myself, when I'd already been up and complained about it umpteen times? (S p. 22)

A common theme in these life-history narratives is how health- and social-care providers – doctors, nurses, social workers, voluntary workers – are used to mediate problems falling without their ostensible professional remit that need resolution in the teller's life. These stories talk to the constrained agency of socially excluded people and the coping mechanisms developed to address particular problems. Again, drawing on network analysis, these coping mechanisms are attempts to fill 'structural holes' or gaps in the tellers' social network. These are attempts to address disparities in access to information and benefits (Burt 1992). It is notable in S's account that in describing her strategy of trying to get the doctor to lever change she does not know the doctor, nor is she sure he will help. In colloquial northern English 'Oh bugger it' means something along the lines of 'I'll give it a try'.

However, and emphasising the relationality of the networks under investigation in the small-N cases, a great many of the accounts of attempts to mediate change through service professionals describe heightened powerlessness, rather than success is addressing a particular problem. The professional frequently does not deliver on something that has an impact of these socially excluded people's lives, and might sometimes additionally burden the asker with punitive measures. This, too, is a theme in S's description of her attempts to get her water heater mended and in C's discussion about the second doctor's refusal to address his heroin addiction.

Furthermore, through theorisation of social action in social exclusion, refined by comparison between and across our access cases, we were able to theorise why access was possible through some gatekeepers but not through others. Reflecting the increasingly sophisticated, nuanced, and real-life experience of social exclusion back on the successful and failed access cases, the role of gatekeepers in mediating constrained powerfulness and the possibility of access became clear. As we have described elsewhere, the role of the gatekeeper in the lives of socially excluded people, the relationships of trust that are possible and the perception of risk of being associated with a gatekeeper or the researchers are important in understanding access to socially excluded people (Emmel et al. 2007). These insights into social action in social exclusion were made possible through developing access cases throughout the research. Theorisation of the mechanisms and relationships within cases were made more robust through triangulation between cases and in doing so, this methodological strategy facilitates a refining of a relational rather than categorical social theory.

THE RESEARCHER AS SOCIOLOGIST AND CASING

In addition to building more robust relational theory, a further consequence of a case methodology is to make the role of the sociologist in the construction of theory an explicit and practical enterprise. Steinmetz (2004) in his translation of Bourdieu suggests that sociologists neither takes the position of the *other*, the participant in the research, nor are they detached *quasi-divine observer* of the events they have chosen to make problematic and investigate. Methods are needed that facilitate an integration of 'the vision of the observer and the truth of the practical vision of the agent' (Steinmetz 2004, p. 391).

In our research, this was made possible through the use of cases. As we have noted above, we treated the deliberations of the researchers as data that were incorporated into each case. These deliberations included our team-meeting notes, individual researcher's mimeographs from their analysis of interview data, and, often, personal reflections on the emerging findings in the research. These, inevitably, included our thoughts about how we felt about particular incidents and experiences gained from being involved in the research – given that we were researching with vulnerable and excluded groups making sense of these lives included emotional responses as well as cool headed sociological theorisation.

In the production of access cases as described above, we simultaneously produced two field sites: (1) the research field, namely the social world we sought to clarify and understand through interviews with key informants, gatekeepers, socially excluded participants, and field notes; and (2) the research team, understanding how we as researchers engaged in this production through team meetings, the processes of theorisation discussed above, and personal reflections. It is not our intention to imply here that the field therefore becomes more a conceptual production by the research team; indeed, it was our theoretical endeavour to ascertain the material practices inscribing and constituting this social world through the accounts of those we interviewed.

In addition to critically engaging with, and understanding, the boundaries of the bounded social world defined through the case, we also attempt to recognise the explicit contributions of our own sociological backgrounds, intentions, and understandings in forming, say, interview schedules, interview formats, ethical procedures, etc. In doing so, we sought theoretically to engage with what we describe as the space within and between cases.

Indeed, we suggest the production of these two fields provide the conditions for the analysis in the research, in which theoretical development is a hermeneutic process where, as Habermas (1988, p. 166) observes, 'it is meaningless to classify hermeneutic understanding as either theory (what happens in the research-team-field) and experience (what happens in the field). It is both, and yet not completely either'. Our purposeful distinction between two research sites provides the space within cases and between cases where theorisation is facilitated. We further understand this space as involving a series of extended relationships between researchers, gatekeepers, and participants where proximity, of understanding, engagement, and participation is sought through ongoing case analysis and access in the field.

Furthermore, the types of data included in our access cases can be understood as representative of relational context often seen as difficult for qualitative research. The access cases include gatekeepers definitions of social exclusion, operating to clarify the definition of who was being recruited to the study and why their lives, as experienced by the gatekeeper, reflected what we as researchers had spoken about in discussing our research with them. In doing so, these gatekeepers provided definitions of social exclusion that they mobilised in their working lives which, as described by the participants we accessed through them, often involved mediating wants and needs that fell without their professional remit. Also, we interviewed different gatekeepers who sometimes mentioned the same person. In gaining access to that person, we were able to reflect on the relational flows and the characteristics of these relationships,

which facilitated or impeded access, therefore allowing us to refine methodological strategies in gaining access based on sharper theorisation of these relationships. Further, the participants themselves described how they considered these relationships mediated in their day-to-day access of things they needed in order to live their lives. Finally, participants' accounts described the relational networks in which they were embedded and how and which relationships (kin, friendships, acquaintances, professionals) comprised their everyday lives. In moving beyond individual accounts, and encapsulating researcher, gatekeeper, and participant observations, the access cases facilitated an understanding of both professional and intimate relational practices, and therefore context, of the socially excluded participants' lives. Through interrogating relational practices within access cases and between access cases we are able to demonstrate that successful access to 12 of our 30 access cases is not because these are the most networked individuals and groups, as we had hypothesised at the outset of our study. Instead, particular relational practices are at play that allow us, as researchers, to access these socially excluded people through the mediation of gatekeepers, which in turn are engaged in particular relational practices with those whom we wish to access.

CONCLUDING OBSERVATIONS

With a few notable exceptions (Williams and Windebank 2002, Cattell 2004), the empirical literature on social exclusion is bereft of understandings and insights from those who are socially excluded. Social exclusion is most commonly defined through a lens of categorical multiple deprivations, which are considered to conspire together to increase the likelihood of an individual being socially excluded (Social Exclusion Unit, 2004). Invariably, social exclusion is framed as the deviance of an individual in the context of his or her responsibilities to society. Researchers' understandings of social exclusion are often through measurement of deprivations and deviances (Gordon et al. 2000). Typical of this Durkheimian approach is the working definition developed by Burchardt et al. (2001, p. 30) in which an individual is socially excluded if 'he or she does not participate in key activities of the society in which he or she lives' (see also Burchardt et al. 1999). These authors identify four key activities as: (1) consumption – the capacity to purchase goods and services and production; (2) participation in economically and socially valuable activities; (3) political engagement – involvement in local and national decision making; and (4) social interaction – integration with family, friends, and community. This definition is problematic for sociologists for two reasons. First, the key activities are beset by problems of definition; and second, each term can be problematised in sociological research. These problems are ignored through asserting that each key activity is empirical, measurable, tangible, and uncomplicated. Furthermore, it is assumed that each key activity will cause an effect of social exclusion. This approach reifies the relational nature of social exclusion, conflating structure and agency and denying a role for social action.

Through our investigation of the use of access cases in research to understand social exclusion and access to socially excluded individuals and groups we have shown how these cases facilitate the refinement of theory. The case study is ubiquitous in the social sciences, yet single-N cases are a blunt instrument in processes of theorisation. Small-N comparison provides an opportunity for more robust development of theory. Access cases provide the opportunity to explore multiple and varying relationships that happen in an open social system and to triangulate these in sharpening theoretical development. Access cases facilitate a critical engagement with sociological constitution of boundaries of the social world under investigation. Through this critical engagement we produce a dialogue between empirical enquiry and theoretical development in which analyses of the relationality of social practices constitutive of context leads to refined and sharpened theoretical insights.

NOTES

1. This chapter arises from research funded by the Economic and Social Research Council to develop methodological strategies to recruit and research socially excluded groups ESRC Research Methods Programme Grant H333250001.
2. This earlier research was carried out for a Primary Care Trust, the most local body in the management of health care delivery in the UK National Health Service. The reference to this study is omitted to ensure anonymity of the research site.

REFERENCES

Abbott, A. 1992 'What do cases do? Some notes on activity in sociological analysis,' in C. Ragin and H. Becker (Eds) *What is a Case? Exploring the Foundations of Social Inquiry*. Cambridge: Cambridge University Press, pp. 53–82.

Archer, M. 1998 'Realism and morphogenesis' in M. Archer, R. Bhaskar, A. Collier, T. Lawson and A. Norrie (Eds) *Critical Realism: Essential Readings*. London: Routledge, pp. 356–382.

Berg, J.A. 1999 'Gaining access to under researched populations in women's health research' *Health Care for Women International* 20: 237–243.

Bhaskar, R, 1979 *The Possibility of Naturalism: A Philosophical Critique of the Contemporary Human Sciences*. London: Routledge.

Bourdieu, P. 1999 'Understanding' in P. Bourdieu (Ed.) *The Weight of the World: Social Suffering in Contemporary Society*. Cambridge: Polity Press, pp. 607–626.

Bourdieu, P. and Wacquant, L.J.D. 1992 *An invitation to reflexive sociology*. Cambridge: Polity Press.

Burchardt, T., Le Grand, J. and Piachaud, D. 1999 'Social exclusion in Britain 1991–1995' *Social Policy and Administration* 33(3): 227–244.

Burchardt, T., Le Grand, J. and Piachaud, D. 2001 *Degrees of Exclusion: Developing a Dynamic Multidimensional Measure*. Oxford: Oxford University Press.

Burt, R.S. 1992 *Structural Holes: The Social Structure of Competition*. Cambridge, MA: Harvard University Press.

Cattell, V. 2004 'Social networks as mediators between the harsh circumstances of people's lives, and the lived experience of health and wellbeing' in B. Phillipson, G. Allan and D. Morgan (Eds) *Social Networks and Social Exclusion: Sociological and Policy Perspectives*. Aldershot: Ashgate, pp. 142–161.

Denzin, N.K. 1989 *Interpretive Biography*. Newbury Park, CA: Sage.

Elliott, E., Watson, A.J. and Harries, U. 2002 'Harnessing expertise: involving peer interviewers in qualitative research with hard-to-reach populations' *Health Expectations* 5: 172–178.

Emirbayer, M. 1997 'Manifesto for a relational sociology' *The American Journal of Sociology* 103(2): 281–317.

Emirbayer, M. and Goodwin, J. 1994 'Network analysis, culture, and the problem of agency' *The American Journal of Sociology* 99(6): 1411–1454.

Emmel, N.D., Hughes, K., Greenhalgh, J. and Sales, A. 2007 'Accessing socially excluded people-trust and the gatekeeper in the researcher-participant relationship' *Sociological Research Online* 12(2), available: http://www.socresonline.org.uk/12/2/emmel.html.

Gordon, D., Adelman, L., Ashworth, K., Bradshaw, J., Levitas, R., Middleton, S., Pantazis, C., Patsios, D., Payne, S., Townsend, S. and Williams, J. 2000 *Poverty and Social Exclusion in Britain*. York: Joseph Rowntree Foundation.

Habermas, J. 1988 *On the Logic of the Social Sciences*. Oxford: Basil Blackwell.

Kuebler, D. and Hausser, D. 1997 'The Swiss hidden population study: practical and methodological aspects of data collection by privileged access interviewers' *Addiction* 92(3): 325–334.

Patton, M.Q. 2002 *Qualitative Evaluation and Research Methods*. London: Sage.

Ragin, C. 2006 'Systematic cross-case analysis with small-Ns' in Research Methods Festival, Oxford, 19 July 2006.

Social Exclusion Unit (SEU) 2004 *Breaking the Cycle: Taking Stock of Progress and Priorities for the Future*. London: Social Exclusion Unit.

Sixsmith, J., Boneham, M. and Goldring, J.E. 2003 'Accessing the community: gaining insider perspectives from the outside' *Qualitative Health Research* 13(4): 578–589.

Somers, M.R. and Gibson, G.D. 1996 'Reclaiming the epistemological "other": narratives and social constitution of identity' in C. Calhoun (Ed.) *Social Theory and the Politics of Identity*. Oxford: Blackwell, pp. 37–99.

Steinmetz, G. 2004 'Odious comparisons: incommensurability, the case study, and "small Ns" in sociology' *Sociological Theory* 22(3): 371–400.

Urwin, C. 2003 'Breaking ground, hitting ground: a Sure Start rapid response service for parents and their under fours' *Journal of Child Psychotherapy* 29(3): 375–392.

Walton, J. 1992 'Making a theoretical case' in C. Ragin and H. Becker (Eds) *What is a Case? Exploring the Foundations of Social Inquiry*. Cambridge: Cambridge University Press, pp. 121–138.

Wellman, B. 1983 'Network analysis: some basic principles' in R. Collins (Ed.) *Sociological Theory*. San Francisco: Jossey-Bass, pp. 155–200.

Williams, C.C. and Windebank, J. 2002 'The "excluded consumer": a neglected aspect of social exclusion' *Policy and Politics* 30(4): 501–513.

19

Using Comparative Data: A Systems Approach to a Multiple Case Study[1]

Fred Carden[2]

INTRODUCTION

> Another contribution of the study is the methodological strides it is making. Not many cross-case studies have been conducted with the same attention to comparability of theory, method, and data. This work will surely have much to tell researchers about methods to adopt, adapt, and avoid.
>
> (Weiss 2003, p. 7)

This chapter presents the methodology used to carry out a study of the influence of research on public policy. The study under discussion was initiated by the International Development Research Centre (Canada) (IDRC) to get a better understanding of how the research we support has an influence on public policy. The intent was to inform both the agency and the researchers it supports on the factors that affect/influence so that they could take these into account. A multiple case method was used; 25 case studies were initiated. Of these, 22 cases were completed within a 12-month period and one additional case was completed the following year and included in the analysis. These studies covered a wide range of fields of research in countries as varied as Ukraine, Tanzania, Vietnam and Guatemala. This complexity called for a careful design to ensure some learning from this cross section of cases. At the same time, the diversity of cases strengthened our confidence in any common findings.

The study has had a significant effect on the work of the Centre. The concepts it introduced and the findings from the cases have affected both how research projects are designed and how they are evaluated. In the words of IDRC's President, it 'has changed the way we fund projects'.[3] The active engagement of Centre staff and partners at all stages of the study were significant in achieving this influence. That story forms the centre-piece of this chapter.

The study began in January 2001 (Carden et al. 2001). A series of staff interviews and preliminary searches of the literature were carried out in the first months of the year. This was followed by the development of several background research activities. These included consultations with Centre staff and experts in the field, an in-depth literature review, use of external expertise and research into the Centre's data.

Because of the varied nature of the Centre's work and the range of regions in which its programs work, the study was made up of a number of sub-studies brought together to build a corporate picture of our work. A range of methodologies was necessarily used. These are outlined following a discussion of the evaluation questions and the state of the art in this field as it relates to the Centre. The data was collected, discussed and analysed as far as possible in collaboration with the users; a number of methods were used to ensure participation. As soon as sub-studies were completed they were posted for full and open access. This chapter goes into some depth on the implementation of the evaluation because of the focus here on use. The process of the study is considered central to the use of the findings.

Before presenting the methodology, some important considerations are reviewed as to definitions, limitations and methodological issues. A glossary at the end of the chapter provides definitions of evaluation terms used.

DEFINITIONS

Kingdon (1984, p. 3) considers public policy-making as a:

> ... set of processes, including at least (1) the setting of an agenda, (2) the specification of alternatives from which a choice is to be made, (3) an authoritative choice among those specified alternatives ... and (4) the implementation of a decision.

Succinctly stated, this definition includes the idea of policy as a set of processes, activities or actions resulting in a decision. IDRC recognizes that:

> ,... decision making occurs at various levels and is carried out by a broad range of decision makers, from heads of families to program directors in other donor agencies, to government policymakers. (IDRC 2001, p. 1)

While both 'policy' and 'policy-makers/decision-makers' can be defined quite broadly, for the purpose of this study policy is defined as *public policy*. As such, the central focus of the study was on issues surrounding policy processes as they relate to municipal, regional and national levels of government. Community and household level decision-makers were not the central focus of this work.

It should be noted that not all Centre projects or programs have or are expected to have an influence on policy. However, it is an area of increasing importance to a wide range of activities across the Centre.

LIMITATIONS

The study was limited in three respects. First, it is a study conducted only once thus far; therefore any learning and change over time will not be captured unless some effort is made to repeat the exercise at a later date. Second, because the study was not planned prior to the implementation of the projects, it had to rely to a certain extent on memory and the tracking down of individuals and project documents, not all of which were easily available. As far as possible, data was triangulated through more than one source but, inevitably, some selective memory creeps into a study of this type. Third, the study did not intend to provide an overview of IDRC project 'success' in influencing public policy. Rather, it used a positive sample to better understand where and how the Centre's support has led to policy influence. In this regard it responds to Flyvberg's (2001) argument that social science is primarily reflective rather than explanatory or predictive.

METHODOLOGICAL ISSUES IN UNDERSTANDING INFLUENCE

Evaluation of research in support of development faces several key challenges. These challenges have to do with how development support is evaluated. In many cases, evaluation attempts to look at the final impact of a project. It looks not so much at how the project succeeded but at whether or not it succeeded. Evaluation normally also tries to determine the direct effects of a project, that is, it tries to establish cause and effect links between the project and the final impact. A third problem is that of time. Contribution to development by donors and national governments is often carried out in a series of short projects, 3–5 years in duration. However, development, and especially the policy influence process, is usually a much longer-term process. As a result, the issue of when to evaluate is problematic. Projects can distort organizational processes, so if we look at influence during, or too soon after, completion of a project, we may be looking at project effects, not sustained influence, something also referred to as the 'project trap' (Lusthaus et al. 2002). Finally, the social sciences struggle with the issue of whether or not there is a generalizable social science, with findings that can be applied through a general model, or whether social science is more case and context specific. The social sciences struggle with gaps in research and evaluation methods suitable to the specificities of the social sciences.

IMPACT OR INFLUENCE?

While it is generally understood that development happens because of a range of factors coming together to create change, there is considerable pressure on both development (and development research) projects and the agencies that fund them, to demonstrate a significant positive impact on development. It is also understood that development results occur when a local partner takes ownership of the actions and makes the project their own. Nevertheless, there is increasing pressure on projects and on agencies (including multilaterals, bilaterals and non-governmental organizations [NGOs]) to demonstrate 'good performance'. As a result, the project and the donor tend to elevate their own position in identifying any change that occurs. There is a tendency to focus on the final results, and ignore the important information on *how* the project achieved anything. It is then almost impossible to identify the critical success factors and the development of new relationships and patterns because these have not been tracked. It is therefore extremely difficult to apply the experience to other settings. Outcome mapping (Earl et al. 2001) makes the case that development (research) contributes to outcomes, which then work with other outcomes and events to create impacts in local contexts. The intent here is to identify the real level at which a project or program provides assistance and to assess those contributions, not the final impacts, which remain the responsibility of the local partners.

ATTRIBUTION

Closely related to the concept of impact is that of attribution. There is a call to attribute changes in a setting (a country, an organization, etc.) to projects that were supported. Donors (whether national governments, foundations, external aid agencies, the private sector or NGOs) want to know how their resources are spent and, through evaluation, seek to know what changes have been caused by their support, what impacts are the result of programs and projects they have supported. Iverson notes that, 'Insofar as multiple and often unknown confounding variables are the norm, complex systems present a serious obstacle for attribution' (Iverson 2003, p. 36). In most development and development research, the project and program support is to one or several dimensions of a development issue. It is highly unusual that a development impact can be clearly linked to a single program or intervention, unless all the other conditions have already been met and factors are already aligned. In this situation, the supporters of the final project claim full credit for the change or impact, even though it was only possible because of a whole series of preceding events and activities that created the right conditions for change. Within this frame of reference, the challenge in development (research) evaluation is that we can only claim credit for change by effectively discrediting others and raising our contribution's importance above the contributions of others.

As Flyvberg notes, 'proof is hard to come by in social science because of the absence of 'hard' theory, whereas learning is certainly possible' (Flyvberg 2001, p. 73). The focus here is on learning about and from the contributions made through IDRC-supported research, in order to contribute more effectively to change on an ongoing basis.

TIME

A persistent issue in evaluation is that of timing: when is the evaluation 'final'? When can you give a judgement that is permanent? What happens over time when good things turn bad and bad things turn good? How do you modify the findings of the evaluation and take this into account? This problem is further exacerbated in the study of influence on public policy, a notoriously long-term affair. If we consider a successful development effort as one in which the local partner has taken ownership of the ideas or knowledge and is using them directly for development purposes, the external agent is further and further removed from the impact. Thus over time, if the program is successful, the external agent plays a smaller and smaller role – precisely at the time impact occurs. Paradoxically, if all goes well, projects and funding agencies are being asked to assess their contribution at

the point when they are least involved with the change.

SOCIAL SCIENCE RESEARCH

The final evaluation challenge that informed the design of this study is the debate on research approaches in the social sciences. The debate here is not about qualitative versus quantitative research methods; both are used and useful. Rather, the debate is around whether, in the social sciences, general knowledge is more valuable than concrete, practical knowledge. As Flyvberg notes, 'context counts' (Flyvberg 2001, p. 38) in the social sciences. He goes on to clarify that the issue for the social sciences in understanding how people and societies function is that this means there is a context dependent relationship between the context, how people act and how they interpret what has happened. The rules are not the game just as the map is not the territory. Both are far more complex and subtle than can be captured through an understanding of the governing rules and systems. Understanding values and interests – and how they differ among parties – plays a key role. Here, we are trying to find out why things happened, and how they happened so that we can use this knowledge in support of future activities.

Flyvberg and others before him (Yin 1994) make the case that the approach best suited to understanding context and the relationships which are part of development is the case study method. Case studies are widely criticized in the social sciences, to the point that Yin refers to this problem on page 1 of his book outlining case-study design and methods. Case studies are often seen as explanatory and are used in teaching. In these contexts they may contain evident bias to generate discussion around a particular interpretation of events. However, case study as a research method must be concerned with the rigorous and fair presentation of data. Case studies are particularly useful in answering 'how' and 'why' (reflexive) questions, whereas one might use a survey or other method to answer 'what' questions. Here our preoccupation is with the how and the why.

THE MULTIPLE CASE APPROACH

Based on a utilization focused approach to evaluation, the design and implementation of this evaluation study started with an extensive exploration to identify who would use the findings and how they would be used. These preliminary discussions informed both the design and the process of analysis. Past experience in evaluation at IDRC (and I would argue more generally) has demonstrated that in many cases, the users have not worked this through on their own and generally have a very vague idea of how they will use the results. Potential for use is greatly enhanced when the users go through the process of specifying the nature of their needs and interests in conducting the study. Active engagement with researchers, program staff and Centre management throughout the study was a hallmark of its implementation.

Early in the design stage, the Centre approached Dr Carol Weiss for her input to the study because of her expertise in this field. External expertise was matched with an internal implementation team ensuring both methodological rigour and internal relevance.

Because of the varied nature of the Centre's work (support of research on information and communication technologies, environment and natural resources management, social and economic policy and science and technology policy for innovation) and the range of regions in which we work (Africa, Asia, Latin America, Middle East and North Africa), the study was made up of a number of sub-studies brought together to build a corporate picture of our work. A range of methodologies was used. Data were collected, discussed and analysed as far as possible in collaboration with the users; a number of methods were used to ensure participation. Products of the study started to appear late in 2001 and continued through to the presentation of the final report in 2007.

USERS

The first user identified was IDRC program staff. They have a mandate to develop research activities (projects or programs) with a view to supporting 'the production, dissemination and application of research results leading to policies and technologies that enhance the lives of people in developing countries'. The study is intended to provide them with a rich review of Centre experience from which staff can draw out the most useful and relevant lessons for their purposes.

The second primary user was the corporation as a whole, through its program managers. The evaluation addressed two corporate needs: (1) it provided a picture of how we are doing now; (2) it provided input to the development of the next strategic program framework (2005–2010). Ongoing user involvement in design and in analysis was crucial and the methodology reflected that priority throughout. Members of both user groups (program staff who support projects, and Centre managers who set directions) were involved in the identification of issues as well as preliminary identification of cases. Members of both groups maintained involvement in the study until it was completed. The range and level of interest to date demonstrate the clear relevance of the issues within the Centre.

KEY QUESTIONS

The strategic evaluation was discussed with all levels of staff involved in project and program delivery including in the Centre's Regional Offices. These initial discussions with Centre staff and preliminary reviews of the literature as well as of Centre documents, pointed to three straightforward questions that the evaluation could fruitfully address:

(1) What constitutes public policy influence in IDRC's experience?
(2) To what degrees and in what ways has IDRC supported research-influenced public policy?

(3)   What factors and conditions have facilitated or inhibited the public policy influence potential of IDRC-supported research projects?

ELEMENTS OF THE STUDY

In order to deal with the diversity of interests and needs, as well as the complexities of the research-policy linkages, this strategic evaluation was conducted using a range of methods. Exploratory case-study research is combined with deductive theory building, continually adjusted to accommodate one another (Burns 1981). It is a hypothesis-generating approach rather than a hypothesis-testing approach, given the limited range of work that has been carried out in this field. Collaboration with the users extended beyond the strict confines of each study to engage users in the synthesis and hypothesis generation across elements around both the implications to programs and to the corporation as a whole. In addition, it is anticipated that partners of the Centre may be brought into the discussions in various ways. This reflects the core focus in systems thinking on relationships (Maruyama 1976) and on equifinality, or the achievement of the same ends through multiple different pathways (Katz and Kahn 1969).

Three critical mechanisms were put in place to support user involvement. First, a small IDRC advisory group worked with the evaluation team throughout the study. They represented key users in different parts of the Centre and advised on design, research and on use issues. Second, consultations with regional offices were carried out. Key outputs of these consultations are reported in workshop reports (IDRC 2003b, 2003c, 2003d). Third, the evaluation design team established a space within the Evaluation Unit's intranet site for the posting of documents and other information. The creation of the site was posted in Echonet, our internal newsletter. As materials became available they were posted to the site. Most materials are also posted to the Evaluation Unit's public internet. While the study is clearly focused on learning for the Centre, the implementation of research,

and any subsequent policy influence, are carried out by our partners, not by the Centre itself. The study therefore sought to integrate the perspectives and views of partners in the study. This was achieved both through interview processes in the study, and through partner engagement in regional and Ottawa-based consultations on findings.

The study was divided into three main parts: background research, case studies and analytical outputs. They are addressed here, each in turn.

Background research

Six studies were undertaken to ensure we had a good history of the Centre's approaches and prior experience in this domain:

(1)   Literature review (Neilson, 2001).
(2)   Framework paper (Lindquist, 2001): Lindquist prepared a background paper on frameworks for examining policy influence providing a preliminary framework that was tested and modified through the document reviews, case studies and consultations.
(3)   Project completion report review (Edwards, 2001): project completion reports (PCRs) are completed by program officers on IDRC projects with a value of over $150,000. These provide insights into the results and management of the projects.
(4)   Program review (Gillespie, 2003): in order to develop a clear picture of the priority given to policy influence, a review was conducted of the programming documents, including program objectives and a survey of project objectives, for all centre programs to identify the nature of policy-related objectives in each case.
(5)   Evaluations review (Adamo, 2002): a review was carried out of the 80 evaluations submitted to IDRC from July 1999 to March 2001, to identify those that had a mandate to address policy influence.
(6)   Policy influence and IDRC: a history of intent (Gonsalves and Baranyi 2003): this study explored and documented the evolution of thinking on the relevance of policy influence in the evolution of the Centre's programming.

These background studies were widely shared and discussed with Centre staff and management to inform the development of the study and relate the documents to the tacit understandings of how the Centre carries out its work.

Case studies: the research

The case studies are the heart of this evaluation. Three key issues are treated here:

(1) Selection of a suitable set of cases.
(2) Conduct of the studies by reviewers from the countries where the research took place.
(3) Collective analysis involving program staff and partners. This last element is critical to the success of the study given the study's strong use orientation.

Twenty-two case studies were completed within 12 months of initiation; one was completed about 12 months later and integrated into the analysis. Two case studies were not completed.

Case selection

The cases were identified through a consultative process with Centre staff and interviews with former senior officers of the Centre. Criteria for selection were considered in the context of developing a good cross section of IDRC-supported projects. These included: range, uniqueness, comparability, type of influence, type of organization doing the research, type of organization being influenced, duration of IDRC involvement with the partners, intentional vs. unintentional influence, and to cover the range of IDRC programming mechanisms. In recognition of the finding from the literature that policy influence often takes a very long time, the study deliberately sought out some projects of long duration and some that had been initiated more than ten years prior to the start of the study.

In all cases, the projects selected were ones where there was a claim of influence that could be clearly identified and articulated by the staff member(s) proposing the case. The purpose of the study was not to determine the extent of influence overall in IDRC-supported research but rather to better understand how influence happens. Therefore, a purposive sample was seen as appropriate. It is worth noting that not all the case studies were selected prior to commencement of the casework. A sub-set of 16 cases was identified at the beginning of the study. As the research became well known throughout the Centre, staff came forward with further examples of projects they felt should be included. Nine additions were made based on a combination of merit, geographic spread and subject area coverage. This process permitted us to bring in some excellent cases that would have been left out had we made the full selection from the initial sample. Further, these additions provided the opportunity to balance coverage.

Consultant selection

Consultants were identified in each region to carry out the case studies. Criteria for selection of consultants included: (1) experience with qualitative methods; (2) capacity for social/gender analysis; (3) participatory learning approaches to evaluation; (4) experience in the policy domain; (5) ability to work across sectors; (6) strong knowledge of region of work; and (7) availability. Our preference was for consultants from the countries where the studies took place. In all, 21 consultants were engaged to carry out the 25 studies. Of these, 12 (6 female, 6 male) were from the South and 9 (5 male, 4 female) from the North; of the 9 from the North, 6 were IDRC staff and 3 were external consultants.

Pre-testing and case-study preparation

Before full implementation, two test-case studies were carried out. Based on experience in these two cases, consultants for the first group of case studies were convened for an orientation session. The consultants met as a group with Centre staff, including program staff, Centre management and the evaluation team working under the direction of the Evaluation Unit. Although not all consultants were able to participate in this workshop, the workshop was seen as invaluable to the successful completion of the studies. The common frame of reference and shared language that developed among the evaluators resulted in a commonality across the case studies. This greatly enhanced comparability among the cases.

Case content

It was important that the cases present detailed stories of the policy influence process. The case studies were developed based on a common semi-structured interview guide that provided significant comparative data. Based on our background research and the test-case studies, the following common elements guided the interviews and case development:

Perspectives of decision-makers Interviews with decision-makers were an important element of the investigation, although this has to be tempered in some contexts with the willingness of decision-makers to give credit to others in the decisions that are taken. Further, as Weiss notes:

> Individuals in policy-making positions do not act alone or in isolation from everything going on around them. They are bound by the availability of resources, the constellation of interests affected, the line-up of supporters and opponents.[4]

The ability of any individual decision-maker to extract the influence of a piece of research on any decision or line of thinking is weak in most cases.

What is often more interesting is the extent of their knowledge on who to ask if they do want to know something, their level of confidence in the research they do receive and their abilities to use data and knowledge in the decision process.

Pertinence to issues of the day – context While research is frequently anticipatory and precedes policy demand, context matters greatly in the use of the findings for policy processes. An understanding of the history of the investigation, from its entry to the research agenda to timing on policy influence, is an important factor in understanding policy influence. Issues become pertinent through a variety of routes: leadership, crisis, and

advocacy being three of the most common. Understanding how issues have become pertinent is important to understanding where and how research plays a role – whether in influencing the decision-makers, the advocates, or being available in a timely way to respond to crisis.

The relationships of researchers to relevant communities The study investigated the capacities of the researchers to introduce their findings to decision-makers and to other relevant communities – groups representing those affected, public interest groups, advocacy coalitions and NGOs, and so on. This was reflected *inter alia* in communication skills, trust in the quality of research by the other groups, ability to relate the findings to issues with currency.

Research quality In the IDRC case studies, we investigated whether and how there had been any influence on public policy from a set of research activities that were deemed to be of reasonably high quality by the IDRC Officers who knew these projects well. We did not independently investigate the quality of the research, nor did we encounter in the (high number of) interviews for the case studies any reference that would cause us to question the quality of the research. In any case, research quality is an essential element.

The nature of influence The study started from the perspective that there were three different types of influence possible:

(1) Change in policy itself (or the decision not to change).
(2) Strengthening policy capacities (of researchers and/or policy-makers).
(3) Broadening policy horizons (opening up understanding of the range of factors coming into play in a policy decision outside the sometimes narrow scope of research or decision).

One could conceive of 'regime change' as a further category here; it is not the one that emerged in our case studies.

The evolution of the policy community

There is no clear divide between the research and policy communities. Rather, these two overlap significantly (and differentially in different countries); so to understand policy influence it is important to understand the evolution of the policy community in a given context. For example, in the development of the policies around the economics of fisheries in Southeast Asia, it was important to follow the careers of the first trained fisheries economists, many of whom became directors of influential research institutions and some of whom became decision-makers in their countries; and all of whom maintained a close contact with each other through a network to exchange findings, results, outcomes of policy decisions and so on.

Use of case material

The approach used in this study put considerable responsibility on the user of the findings to delve into the products of the study and engage in their analysis in some depth. The second dimension of this approach is that it also put more responsibility on the implementation team to ensure appropriate dissemination of the various products. The core findings around context have been used to interrogate research proposals for projects intended to influence policy; the methodology and framework have formed the foundation of project level evaluations in all program areas in which the Centre is active since they were presented. The core concepts have been central in IDRC program team discussions in their reflection and work planning meetings in 2005–2006.

Analytical outputs

In order to analyse the case material, a three-stage process was undertaken. First, a series of regional workshops was held to review the case studies and obtain input and perspectives from Centre staff and research partners (IDRC Evaluation Unit 2003a, 2003b, 2003c, 2003d, 2003e). Detailed reports of these workshops were analysed to identify key issues identified across the regions. The cases were then analysed around the core issues identified.

Regional analysis workshops

Using a variety of methods, the workshops were structured around:

- Review of the cases themselves.
- Review of the IDRC role and position in the research and policy influence process.
- Discussion of the policy influence typology developed for the study and position of the cases within this typology.
- Discussion of performance based on an analysis of the cases around context, motivation and capacities.
- Small group discussions on the contributors and inhibitors to influence.[5]

These workshops resulted in a rich preliminary analysis of the findings and provided insights for the review team on key foci for the full cross-case analysis. Upon completion of the case studies, and the development of a regional analysis, a cross-case analysis was undertaken.

Cross-case analysis

In order to identify categories for cross-case analysis, the evaluation team analysed detailed workshop reports from the preliminary analysis and found the key common issues cutting across the discussions. These issues formed the basis for the final analysis (Weiss et al. 2004). On an ongoing basis, findings were presented and discussed at a series of workshops with some of the Centre's regional offices, with partners and with other organizations engaged in similar work, such as the Overseas Development Institute. This iterative approach to the analysis strengthened its relevance to the Centre and strengthened the use of the data.

SOME COMMENTS ON IMPLEMENTATION

Implementing a study with 25 distinct cases posed significant challenges. These challenges were compounded by the focus on use of the study results. This meant the active engagement[6] of the key users in all phases of the study. Six core issues emerged from experience as central to the experience.

Selection of cases

In order to make the study meaningful to the wide range of actors within the Centre, it was essential that the cases represent their core interests in some way. Achieving that meant ensuring staff involvement in the selection of cases, ensuring coverage across the range of development problems around which we support research and the regions in which we operate. This required several iterations and a flexible design that permitted the initiation of some casework while case selection was still going on. As indicated earlier in the chapter, a first set of sixteen cases was identified. The Centre-wide discussions of the study raised the level of interest in it and raised additional cases from those staff who had not made suggestions in the first round of consultations. In addition to choosing cases that appeared to demonstrate some sort of policy influence (based on a set of questions asked of the proponents), we also had to ensure coverage. This balancing act meant that some potentially good cases were left out. Given that the case studies would investigate policy influence, we had to make choices based on the assertions of our informants with limited real data about how events transpired in the case. The process of case selection benefited from this conduct while the major consultations and workshops were going in within the Centre, deciding the design of the study, development of a framework and literature review. The engagement of staff in these other exercises enhanced the level of understanding of what we were trying to achieve – and enhanced our understanding as the study team, of what Centre staff needed to know more about tin their support of research for policy influence.

Identification of evaluators

We sought evaluators from the region of the case. We had a hunch that context

played a key role and therefore felt it important that the evaluators, as far as possible, were steeped in the context and could interrogate it more deeply as a result. We were successful in identifying just over half of the evaluators from the South. In addition to location, we were looking for a specific skill set: experience in qualitative methods, experience in evaluation, strong knowledge of the region, ability to work across sectors, strong interview skills.

Timing

Because of the importance of comparability across cases, it was important that the studies be conducted more or less simultaneously. Therefore, availability of the consultants was a key factor. With sufficient lead time, we were able to secure the services of our first choices.

A second aspect of timing related to this study is that as an emergent design, there was considerable overlap between the main elements of the study. As the timeline in Figure 19.1 indicates, the design of the study continued until the case studies were virtually complete and well into the analysis phase of the study. Use of the findings started well before the analysis was complete; and dissemination activities started during the design phase and continued well past completion of the analysis. This attention to timing and overlap in stages of the study were inevitable in a use-oriented study. This approach certainly contributed to the success of the study. The effort necessary to sustain the balance between responsiveness and focus on the study itself should not be underestimated.

Consistency

Cases in such varied sectors and regions posed a particular problem in terms of comparability. In order to ensure some comparability we:

- Developed a common, semi-structured interview guide that was used in all cases.

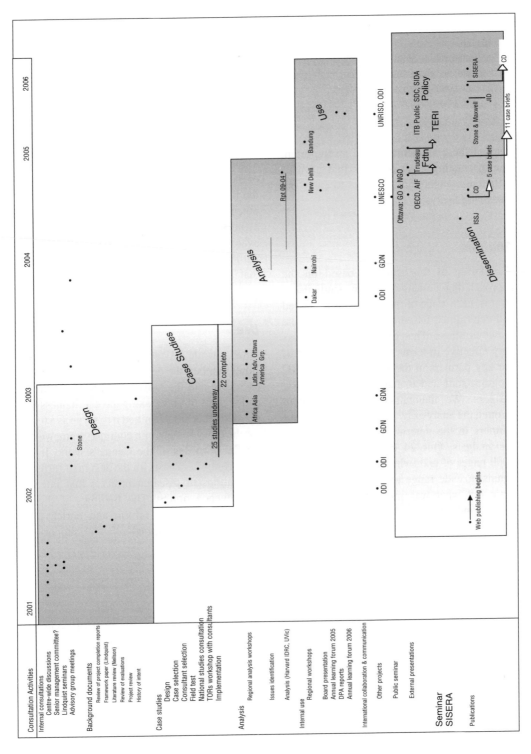

Figure 19.1

- Brought the consultants together to review the guide and its purpose.
- Created opportunities for the consultants to discuss their cases while they were conducting the research.
- Requested copies of all data so we could review it should we encounter significant problems of comparison in the cross-case analysis.
- Engaged in ongoing dialogue with the case study authors.

Each of these elements played an important role in creating a set of cases that gave us sufficient comparability of data to carry out cross-case analysis.

Analysis

The design of this study is based on the approach that it emerges over the study itself. That is, each stage of the study was reviewed and determined based on the findings of the previous stage. This emergent design was very effective in terms of the engagement of our key partners in the study, notably IDRC program staff and managers but also IDRC partners. We maintained this engagement through the analysis by actively involving our partners in the determination of key issues for analysis. Our 24 cases totalled almost 3000 pages of text, which could be analysed against a wide range of factors. In order to tease out what was most important to the Centre and its researchers we conducted a series of four workshops with sub-sets of the cases. Workshops in three regions (sub-Saharan Africa, Asia and Latin America) each brought together program staff, managers and researchers from that region to consider the findings of the cases from that region. A fourth workshop in Ottawa worked with a cross section of cases from all regions. In all cases, we brought the evaluators to the workshops as well to highlight key findings from the cases. Each workshop was thoroughly documented, including a final workshop of the advisory committee (IDRC Evaluation Unit 2003a, 2003b, 2003c, 2003d, 2003e). The reports of this preliminary analysis were themselves then analysed to

identify key cross-cutting issues. This resulted in a remarkably consistent set of issues emerging from the regional workshops. These core issues guided the final analysis by the research team.

Engagement

As noted earlier in this chapter, engagement of our key partners was critical to the success of the study. Engagement was sustained through a constant focus on the issues and interests of the partners and through attempting to link the findings to their issues. As Patton (1997) noted in his description of utilization-focused evaluation, 'evaluators should facilitate the evaluation process and design any evaluation with careful consideration of how everything that is done, *from beginning to end,* will affect use' (emphasis in the original).[7]

Use

Finally, while 23 case studies is a relatively small number, the depth of data collection in each case and the range of fields of research and regions of undertaking gave a richness to the study that has permitted it to serve as a tool for the development of a common framework for the purposes of the Centre's work. It is serving now as a basis for the design of further evaluations of research projects that intend to influence policy. The findings of these studies should help inform and enrich the framework as it is applied to Centre-supported research.

CONCLUSIONS

As Carol Weiss notes, 'Instead of concentrating solely on the effect of research on individuals in policy-making positions, they have begun to take the policy-making *system* as their canvas' (Weiss 2003, p. 5). This has significant implications for the evaluation of the influence of research on policy. It is no longer a matter of looking at how individuals are influenced but at how systems evolve, how they are influenced.

Context matters. This brings us back to the points raised at the beginning of this chapter: the effect on evaluation of attribution, impact and time. Bringing context to bear increases the difficulty in claiming impact, increases the difficult in identifying attribution and brings into play changes over time in what the (positive or negative) effects might have been. Bringing into play a use-oriented evaluation approach that calls on the users throughout the study reduces the risk of irrelevance of an evaluation and increases the opportunities to ensure users define the areas of evaluation and modes of analysis. Involving users complicates life for the evaluation team, not only in terms of the time involved but also in insuring methodological integrity. Evaluation should never be done for its own sake, though, and the trade-off is that user involvement dramatically increases the potential for influence and relevance, two of the most important goals in evaluation.

Glossary[8]

Emergent design: An implementation plan in which the specification of every step depends on the results of previous steps, sometimes also known as a cascading or rolling design.[9]

Evaluation: A process by which a strategy, issue or relationship is studied and assessed in-depth.

Impact: Significant and lasting changes in the well-being of large numbers of intended beneficiaries.

Inputs: Resources that are invested into a program in order to encourage results through the relevant activities.

Outcome: Changes in the behaviour, relationships, activities and/or actions of a boundary partner that can be logically linked to a program (although they are not necessarily directly caused by it).

Output: Directly achievable and observable, though not necessarily short-term, products of a program.

Partners, Boundary: Those individuals, groups or organizations with whom the program interacts directly and with whom the program can anticipate some opportunities for influence.

Triangulation: The use of multiple sources and methods to gather similar information.[10]

Utilization-focused evaluation: utilization-focused evaluation (U-FE) begins with the premise that evaluations should be judged by their utility and

actual use; therefore, evaluators should facilitate the evaluation process and design any evaluation with careful consideration of how everything that is done, *from beginning to end*, will affect use.[11]

Utility: The extent to which an evaluation produces and disseminates reports that inform relevant audiences and have beneficial impact on their work.[12]

NOTES

1. The copyright of this chapter belongs to the International Development Research Centre.

2. Director of Evaluation, International Development Research Centre, Canada; and Research Fellow in Sustainability Science, Harvard University Center for International Development. The views expressed are those of the author and do not necessarily reflect the views of the centres.

3. Interview with the author, March 2006.

4. Carol Weiss, speech at IDRC, March, 2003.

5. See Lusthaus et al., Organizational Assessment, for an outline of this performance frame-work.

6. I use 'engagement' here rather than 'participation'. Participation has become overused and is often abused, tending to mean anything in which someone outside the core team has been consulted for their opinion. Engagement implies a commitment and an active involvement with the data and its analysis.

7. Utilization-Focused Evaluation Checklist, Michael Q. Patton, January 2002. Online, available: http://www.wmich.edu/evalctr/checklists/ufe.pdf_.

8. Other than those indicated, definitions are taken from Earl et al., Outcome Mapping Glossary. Online, available: http://www.idrc.ca/evaluation/ev-28407-201-1-DO_TOPIC.html.

9. Western Michigan University, Evaluation Center, Glossary of terms. Online, available: http://ec.wmich.edu/glossary/prog-glossary.htf#S-U.

10. Western Michigan University, Evaluation Center, Glossary of terms.

11. Utilization-Focused Evaluation Checklist, Michael Q. Patton, January 2002. Online, available: http://www.wmich.edu/evalctr/checklists/ufe.pdf.

12. Western Michigan University, Evaluation Center, Glossary of terms.

13. IDRC-published references cited here are available at http://www.idrc.ca/evaluation-policy. Or they can be obtained in hard copy from the Evaluation Unit by email request to: evaluation@idrc.ca.

REFERENCES[13]

Adamo, A. 2002 *Strategic Evaluation of Policy Influence: What Evaluation Reports Tell us about Public Policy*

Influence by IDRC-Supported Research. Ottawa: IDRC Evaluation Unit.

Burns, T.F. 1981 *Planning networks and network agents: an approach to adaptive community governance.* Unpublished doctoral dissertation. University of Pennsylvania.

Carden, F. and Neilson, S. with Smutylo, T., Deby, D., Earl, S., den Heyer, M. 2001 *IDRC-Supported Research in the Public Policy Process: A Strategic Evaluation of the Influence of Research on Public Policy.* Ottawa: IDRC Evaluation Unit.

Earl, S., Carden, F. and Smutylo, T. 2001 *Outcome Mapping: Building Learning and Reflection into Development Programs.* Ottawa: IDRC.

Edwards, K. 2001 *PCRs and Policy Influence: What Project Completion Reports Have to Say about Public Policy Influence by Centre-Supported Research.* Ottawa: IDRC Evaluation Unit.

Evaluation Center, Western Michigan University, Glossary of terms http://www.wmich.edu/evalctr/checklists/ufe.pdf.

Flyvberg, B. 2001 *Making Social Science Matter: Why Social Inquiry Fails and How it Can Succeed Again.* Cambridge: Cambridge University Press.

Gillespie, B. 2003 *Intent to Influence Policy in IDRC Programs and Projects: What Program and Project Level Goals and Say about IDRC's Approach to Influencing Policy.* Ottawa: IDRC Evaluation Unit.

Gonsalves, T. and Baranyi, S. 2003 *Research for Policy Influence: A History of IDRC Intent.* Ottawa: IDRC Evaluation Unit.

International Development Research Centre (IDRC) 2001 *Closing the Loop, Communication for Change at IDRC,* Ottawa: IDRC, p. 1.

International Development Research Centre, Evaluation Unit 2003a 'Cases, concepts and connections'. Report of a workshop, Ottawa, March 2003. Ottawa: IDRC Evaluation Unit.

International Development Research Centre, Evaluation Unit 2003b 'The influence of research on public policy'. Report of a workshop, Johannesburg, November, 2002. Ottawa: IDRC Evaluation Unit.

International Development Research Centre, Evaluation Unit 2003c 'The influence of research on public policy'. Report of a workshop, Montevideo. December, 2002. Ottawa: IDRC Evaluation Unit.

International Development Research Centre, Evaluation Unit 2003d 'The influence of research on public policy'. Report of a workshop, Bangkok, January, 2003. Ottawa: IDRC Evaluation Unit.

International Development Research Centre, Evaluation Unit 2003e 'The influence of research on policy'. Advisory committee retreat, February 20–21.

Iverson, A. 2003 *Attribution and Aid Evaluation in International Development: A Literature Review.* Ottawa: IDRC Evaluation Unit.

Katz, D. and Kahn, R.L. 1969 'Common characteristics of open systems' in F.E. Emery (Ed.) *Systems Thinking.* Harmondsworth, UK: Penguin Mondern Management Readings, pp. 86–104.

Kingdon, J. 1984 *Agendas, Alternatives and Public Policies.* Boston: Little Brown.

Lindquist, E. 2001 *Discerning Policy Influence: Framework for a Strategic Evaluation of IDRC-Supported Research.* Ottawa: IDRC Evaluation Unit.

Lusthaus, C.A., Adrien, M-H., Anderson, G., Carden, F. and Montalvan, G.P. 2002 *Organizational Assessment.* Washington and Ottawa: IDB & IDRC.

Maruyama, M. 1976 'Toward cultural symbiosis' in E. Jantsch and C. Waddington (Eds) *Evolution and Consciousness: Human Systems in Transition.* Reading, MA: Addison Wesley, pp. 198–213.

Neilson, S. 2001 *Knowledge Utilization and Public Policy Processes: A Literature Review.* Ottawa: IDRC Evaluation Unit.

Patton, M.Q. 1997 *Utilization-Focused Evaluation.* Thousand Oaks, CA: Sage.

Patton, M.Q. 2002 Utilization-Focused Evaluation Checklist. Online, available: http://www.wmich.edu/evalctr/checklists/ufe.pdf.

Weiss, C.H. 2003 'Studying research utilization'. A speech at IDRC, 24 March. Ottawa: IDRC Evaluation Unit.

Weiss, C.H., Karuskina-Drivdale, S. and Paksima, S. 2004 *IDRC-Supported Research and its Influence on Public Policy: Results from a Cross-Case Analysis.* Ottawa: IDRC Evaluation Unit.

Yin, R.K. 1994 *Case Study Research: Design and Methods* (2nd edition). Applied Social Science Methods Series, Volume 5. Thousand Oaks, CA: Sage.

PART THREE

Case-Based Methods in Disciplines and Fields

The ten chapters that comprise this last part of this Handbook have in common a deployment of a case focused orientation in a discipline and/or field. Again, there is a fuzziness and overlap with Parts 1 and 2. All of the authors address methodological debates and describe the actual methods they employ, sometimes in considerable detail, but they do so in relation to the issues, which emerge from a specific focus of interest. The first two chapters, by Walton and Amenta, are examples of single-case studies, which employ historical materials in the construction of narratives of change. Amenta's materials take the form of the conventional primary documentary sources of the historian whereas Walton uses literary sources in relation to more conventional historical materials. Much of Walton's methodological argument is devoted to making a wholly persuasive case for the value of literary materials as sources at the interface of history and ethnography – as he says:

> … literature may provide insight into how social relations actually function, a kind of latent sociology. … evidentiary literature typically explores the normative world, the rules that govern conduct to a greater or lesser degree, and the reaction to rule breaking. When these standards are met we may learn a good deal about history from literature and literature may be treated as valid evidence provided we know what the evidence is about. (see p. 381)

Walton recognizes the ideographic character of his story of Big Sur but he also contends, in our view correctly, that ideographic accounts of this kind can be the basis of a more general account when reviewed in careful comparison with other, often literature based, narratives of places that are, to use Ragin's phrase, here 'sufficiently similar'.

Amenta presents a study in historical sociology (or sociological history – the ordering of disciplines does not matter here) dealing with the US Old Age Pension movement. He uses this detailed case to carry three methodological arguments. The first is for the significance of path dependence in unravelling chains of complex causation: '… when something happens is often key to its influence in processes of major change' (see p. 352). The second is about practice and amounts to a demand for a deep engagement with materials relating to cases. He argues for a historian's care and attention to primary sources, and given that he is dealing with change the historical emphasis is appropriate, although the requirement of deep engagement is equally characteristic of anthropological work. His final point represents a departure from traditional historiography – the requirement to generalize or perhaps it is better to say as he does devise: '... scope conditions around one's theoretical claims' (see p. 352). Amenta's discussion of scoping is particularly interesting and he organizes his chapter by presenting an extensive review of the issues relating to generalization before working through them in relation to a demonstration based on a specific case study. This tension between the desire to have generalizable theory and the limitations of the nature of case-based evidence runs through many of the chapters in this book, although in most there is either an explicit or implicit rejection to greater or lesser degrees of the claims for superiority of nomothetic, universalist models of explanation that characterize positivist conceptions of scientific practice.

Bergeson takes up the cultural theme in relation to artistic cases studies. Generally, these are informed by an insertion of the social into German idealist philosophy's aesthetic theory. Walton regards approaches that focus only on meaning as incomplete in that they do not take account of the social component in the actual production of the art object itself. His argument resonates strongly with critical realist ontological positions as delineate by Harvey, Carter and Sealey, and Byrne in Part 1 of this Handbook and he generalizes it to case study practice as a whole:

> ... there is something inherent in the various forms of art that determine which kinds of meanings they will signify. There are two implications of this for case study analysis. The relation between the specific case and the thing it purportedly represents is not an independent relationship, and second, variation in meaning derives not from applied interpretative grids, but from the internal structure and the other properties of the case study itself. This is strongest for art case studies, but I suspect the point is general. (see p. 385)

The argument is developed through an engagement with art theory in relation to the objects which constitute the field of fine art and in particular with the frames of reference which inform the interpretation of painting. Walton shows how the shift of recognition from the materiality of art objects towards

attention being directed primarily, and indeed often only, to the 'idea' or concept, informs not only art theory but also the practice of art in the turn first to abstraction and then to the purely conceptual. This chapter is perhaps the most assertive statement of the agentic capacity of reality itself in this whole collection.

Downward and Riordan's chapter uses a cluster-analysis-based approach to 'social interactions and the demand for sport' to take on the general line of reasoning in that most positivist of social sciences – economics. Their arguments are set in the framework of a developing school of 'Heterodox Economy', which challenges the fundamental assumptions of conventional neoclassical economic theory by recognizing that: '... economic choice reflects the interaction of human agency with a pre-existing social structure, that nonetheless will evolve following human agency' (see p. 394). This chapter demonstrates how the use of particular methods as techniques has implications for basic understanding of social processes. Cluster analysis as a typological method enables researchers to see patterns of social relationships across sets of human actors, rather than understanding choice solely in relation to the isolated individual. Downward and Riordan undertake a large-scale cluster analysis of UK General Household Survey data to explore these issues. They employ the term 'lifestyle' but relate lifestyles to economic and demographic statuses. In other words, evidence demonstrates that categories of choice displayed in relation to sporting and leisure activities are generatively related to wider social relations and thus sustains the criticisms that heterodox economists mount against conventional economic orthodoxy.

Mahoney and Larkin Terrie return to issues that have been addressed in relation to the specific case by Amenta. However, they extend them beyond the specific case to consideration of the whole process of generalization in contemporary political science. Much of their discussion is devoted to comparing and contrasting case based comparative methods with methods based on the statistical testing of hypotheses. They take a rather respectful view of the latter set but their comparison of the approaches is particularly methodical and clear. Three core traits of difference are identified: explanatory goal, conception of causation, and method of theory testing.

We characterize comparative-historical analysis in the following way: (a) it asks questions about the causes of effects (i.e., why particular dependent variable values occurred in specific cases); (b) it relies on a conception of causation built around necessary and sufficient causes and their derivatives (e.g., INUS causes); and (c) it tests theories with a combination of comparative set-theoretic methods and process tracing. By contrast, we characterize statistical analysis as follows: (a) it asks questions about the effects of causes (i.e., the causal influence of particular independent variables); (b) it uses an average effects conception of causation; and (c) it tests theories with regression techniques. (see p. 412)

To demonstrate 'how these methodological traits fit together in practice' Mahoney and Larkin Terrie examine how they are deployed in two classic texts: Orloff and Skocpol (1984), which employs conventional statistical approaches, and Huber et al. (1993), which works in set theoretic mode. Key issues addressed here are those of conceptual and causal heterogeneity, reviewing again crucial themes raised by Goertz and Mahoney in Part 2 of this Handbook. The chapter concludes with a statement that could be summed up as 'horses for courses' – in other words, statistical methods based on variable analysis and comparative case methods are doing different things and both are valid methods of dealing with understanding in this area. This view is well and persuasively articulated but it is not held by all of the other contributors to this Handbook nor by one of the editors.

Fiss's chapter deals with case studies and organizational phenomena. There is something of a contrast here with the methodological arguments in political science outlined by Mahoney and Larkin Terrie. Case studies have a long history in the study of organizations and have indeed been the dominant method of description and to a considerable extent of theory development. However, the approach also has a long history of criticism directed

at its capacity to develop generalization. The issues are exactly the same as with political science but they are, as it were, come at from opposite directions. In political science, the case study has had to establish its position. In organizational studies it has had to defend it. Fiss argues strongly for the configurational nature of the case study and suggests that since cases are to be understood in configurational terms, then the appropriate methods for understanding them are configurational techniques and in particular QCA. He takes a stronger line here than do Mahoney and Larkin Terrie. For him, traditional quantitative methods are not appropriate because their causal logic does not reflect the set theoretic nature of organizational causality. The chapter takes us through the issues associated with case study research in organizational contexts with a developed discussion of casing followed by a careful consideration of the nature of organizational configurations. Fiss makes use of the interesting idea of limited diversity, which resonates with complexity theory's notion of restricted attractor spaces discussed in chapters in Part 1 of this Handbook. He extends his discussion to include consideration of organizational levels and develops a detailed consideration of the issues that arise for understanding complex causation on the basis of qualitative analysis alone. The chapter considers whether regression based multilevel modelling can resolve issues of understanding of cross level causation in organizations but considers that they are limited since they can only handle complex causation through a treatment of inter-action effects. Fiss's note that interaction effects beyond two-way interactions are almost never addressed in regression based studies has general force. The chapter concludes with an argument for combining qualitative procedures with systematic QCA illustrated by relevant examples. This has much in common with Byrne's position in his chapter in Part 2 of this Handbook.

Griffiths draws on her double repertoire as both a sociomedical researcher and as a clinical practitioner in considering the nature of the case in medicine. Interestingly, this is one chapter in the Handbook where the use of the case as a teaching tool has considerable significance. This reflects the history, including the 'pre-scientific' history of medical education, where the demonstration of the case has been a crucial method of exposition to trainee practitioners. Griffiths draws on the methodological debates, and in particular Ragin's discussion of casing, to consider how cases are understood in medical science and medical practice. All the issues encountered thus far in earlier chapters re-emerge here. What is a case? Is it a person? General (family medicine) practitioners like Griffiths have never confined the case simply to the body but have always included relations of people with others in their social world – the 'family' in the first instance but with no 'stop-line' necessarily imposed. Changing medical science changes the ways in which cases are defined. In an almost actor–network style, new modes of measurement and new instruments change conceptions of what represent pathological deviations from normal function, and hence what is a case of, for example of breast cancer or diabetes. Moreover, those who define a case are not just physicians. People themselves, and those around them, both define a case 'to present' – for someone to be ill – and define the nature of the case in terms of social extent and duration in time. So Griffiths presents us with three cases from her routine of work as a GP – she takes us through them as she would an apprentice physician – explaining how she and her patient and in some instances members of the patient's family, interact in constructing cases and in deciding how to proceed with them. To be identified as a 'case of a disease' is to be classified – diagnosed, as a basis for treatment – prescription. This can be beneficial but it is only part of the process. It is necessarily a process of abstraction but the actual management of a health problem may require questioning of the boundaries of that abstraction by both physician and patient. At the same time, developments in medical science redefine the nature of conditions. There is a considerable resonance between Griffith's

discussion and many other chapters here, but particularly with Whelan's discussion of pain classification. The social scientist examining the construction of medical knowledge and the practitioner (who is also a social scientist) engaging with real people use similar accounts of what the issues of casing are in health contexts, although Griffiths is more explicitly realist in her treatment of these issues.

Dopson and her colleagues present an account of 'the team-based aggregation of qualitative case study data in healthcare contexts'. This chapter has much in common with Carden's discussion in his chapter, in Part 2 of this Handbook and either chapter could have been included in either part since both give us an account of the processes of doing research in relation to substantive issues. Both, moreover, are concerned with how to integrate material deriving from a range of separate case studies so as to generate 'increased external validity' as a basis for generalization. The chapter begins with a review of methodologically derived arguments about the possibility and/or desirability of developing generalizable knowledge from case studies. It then proceeds to an example of aggregation in which the aggregation is not a meta-analysis of research done by others but rather was based on a re-review of primary materials by the two groups of researchers who had generated these materials. The process is described in some detail and has much in common with the methods employed by Carden and his colleagues, although it deals with a different field – health instead of development – and the studies were less methodologically diverse although they did differ in important respects. Dopson et al. give us a full account of their procedures in detail and then consider what methodological issues arise in work of this kind. Issues of conceptualization and definition emerge here again as they have so often in the contributions to this book. Context matters. The processes under review are complex and are constructed in considerable part by communities of practice. The knowledge generated is itself complex and fluid. And in work of this kind, everything revolves around mutual trust amongst those engaged in the process.

Bevan addresses the issues arising from what Ragin has called 'the dialogue between ideas and evidence' in relation to the history of development studies as a field of understanding and practice. She identifies development studies as an 'outlier' in the social sciences given *inter alia* the diversity of its objects of interest, the degree of change in the entities it studies in less developed countries, and the historical dominance of the field by neoclassical economics and its quantitative models, which, Bevan argues, have not produced accounts of much practical use to either donors of less developed countries themselves. Her exposition is framed around the example of a case based research programme in Ethiopia conducted between 2002 and 2007. Her chapter reviews the history of development studies and identifies, following Kanbur, two types of poverty research framework – neoclassical approaches with a quantitative style and 'broad social sciences' approaches, which are typically qualitative and involve community based participatory research. The project described was concerned with producing new conceptual frameworks in relation to integrated multimethod research. Bevan takes us through the ways in which a consideration of a synthesis of critical realism, complexity theory, and case-based understanding enabled her and her co-workers to develop a 'complex dynamic system Q-integrated approach' that moves beyond the Q-squared programme for integrating qualitative and quantitative approaches in development studies and development practice. Important aspects of this approach include a shift from measured variables as outcomes to a focus on the whole relational structure of the nested social systems within which development practice is located. Policy thus moves from a process of technical resolution to something embedded in politics and culture.

Olsen also addresses development issues but her focus is at a micro-level of individuals and households. The study deployed a set of tools – EXCEL, NVivo and fuzzy-set QCA – in the collection, management, and interpretation of data. It provides a worked-through example of the way in which quantitative data construction through conventional survey techniques can be combined with the construction of attributes on the basis of interpretation of qualitative research products – in this case interview transcripts – in order to develop a dataset that can be used in fuzzy-set QCA. The fuzzy outcome set described a range of degrees of resistance to landlord or employer. Clustering was used to construct this outcome measure with membership of different clusters being the basis for assigning the degree of membership of the outcome set. This chapter provides a worked-through example of the deployment of a whole range of techniques towards the delineation of complex and multiple configurations related to 'resistance' as action by households. In particular, Olsen includes an extensive discussion of how she interprets the products of fuzzy-set QCA, which demonstrates exactly how she reasons and interprets rather than simply 'decides' in classic hypothesis testing mode.

The concluding chapter in Part 3, and in the book as a whole, is a report by Byrne et al. based on a project funded by the UK Economic and Social Research Council's Methods Initiative, which combined a programme of teaching researchers how to think about and use case-based methods with a focus-group-style participatory research exercise directed at exploring those researchers understanding of the role of case-based methods in relation to their practice, and in particular their practice as applied social researchers. It illustrates how there is a cross-cutting relationship between methodological arguments based around the distinctions between quantitative accounts of causal processes and qualitative interpretation on the one hand and the force of evidence of different kinds in the policy process on the other. This has particular significance in an era in which politics has, at least on the surface and especially in the UK, become less a matter of ideological contestation and more a matter of demonstration of competency in the delivery of services and general economic satisfaction. We have moved towards an evidence-based process of political administration and the question asked of researchers, and indeed asked by them, was what is the place of case-based methods in the formulation and utilization of such evidence? This theme has underpinned several of the preceding chapters in this Handbook, e.g. Carden, Dopson, and Bevan. Here it is elaborated in relation to qualitative research on researchers themselves. Researchers were generally attracted to case approaches, recognizing how they offered the possibility of instantiated thick description of causal mechanisms. At the same time, they worked in an environment in which ideas of hierarchies of evidence, associated with the Cochrane and Campbell collaborations, privilege quantitative and indeed even experimental bases for evidence. And yet, the researchers note how in policy discussion even quantitative evidence becomes transformed into instantiated narratives and that it is instantiated narratives that have the most influence on policy makers and on practitioners. Methods and methodology are political at every level, but it is clear from this study that case-based methods do offer a mode of synthesis that can take us beyond sterile opposition between the quantitative and the qualitative.

REFERENCES

Huber, Evelyne, Charles, Ragin, and John D. Stephens, 1993. "Social Democracy, Constitutional Structure, and the Welfare State". *The American Journal of Sociology*, 99: 711–49.

Orloff, Ann Shola and Theda, Skocpol, 1984. "Why Not Equal Protection? Explaining the Politics of Public Social Spending in Britain, 1900–1911, and the United Sates, 1880s–1920". *American Sociological Review*, 49: 726–50.

20

Making the Most of an Historical Case Study: Configuration, Sequence, Casing, and the US Old-age Pension Movement

Edwin Amenta

Methodological and metatheoretical break-throughs in historical sociology over the last two decades seem to have put historical sociologists in a bind. This bounty of thinking and applications has provided new insights, such as a focus on path dependence and time order in explanations, and new tools, such as formal qualitative techniques for historical sociologists and historical institutionalists in political science (Hall and Taylor 1996, Pierson and Skocpol 2002). Historical sociology has become unbound from the primitive small-N comparative methods present at its founding. At the same time, historical social scientists are expected to act more like historians in their use of archival materials and understanding of time (Sewell 2006). Social scientists are to take a prospective

outlook, rather than the retrospective views of old-style comparative and historical research. These injunctions tend to turn historical social scientists toward case studies. Yet the expectations for greater sophistication in causal argumentation, methods of analysis, and in historical thinking and practices have made historical sociological investigations more difficult to undertake and to make the claims in them stick.

Historical sociology has become more historical in two key ways. The first is analytical and associated with social scientists. Historical sociologists have become increasingly sensitive to time order in explanations and to the possibilities of path dependence (Abbott 1992a, Griffin 1992, Pierson 2000). In narrative causal accounts, as opposed to standard variable-based discussions, when something happens is often key to its influence in processes of major change (Griffin 1992, Sewell 2006). Similarly, the possibility of path dependence, or the process of increasing returns for institutions once they are formed, means that causes of the rise of these institutions will have a different influence, possibly none at all, once the institutions are set in place (Mahoney 2000, Pierson 2000).

The second historical turn is a matter of practice. Historical social scientists are expected to act more like historians (Sewell 2006). Instead of relying on secondary sources, historical social scientists nowadays develop a deep knowledge of their case or cases. Following this lead typically this means an engagement in the kind of archival research that will ward off misunderstandings and reveal how key actors thought about what they were doing. It is no longer considered sufficient simply to maintain a broadly comparative perspective, and the comparative method of Mill as well as the far more sophisticated comparative methodologies that have arisen since can be handled appropriately only when the investigator has a sufficiently deep knowledge of the empirical material. Historical social scientists are also warned against biases and gaps in historiography (Lustick 1996). In addition, the narrative causal accounts of historians are viewed as based more on rhetorical form and convention than systematic attempts at developing time-ordered causal arguments that combine structures, mechanisms, and events (Griffin 1992). Being historical in this second sense is both time-consuming and demands skills, such as interpreting documents, in which social scientists are usually untrained.

At the same time, however, historical sociologists and historical institutionalists in political science are expected to retain social science's concern with the general. There are few academic rewards for social scientists knowing a case well. This means theorizing in a causal way about conditions beyond the observed instances and devising scope conditions around one's theoretical claims. These claims are expected in turn to be more sophisticated, combining events and structures and considerations of time order and the possibility of path dependence. Social scientists are also expected to provide plausible empirical demonstrations of their claims. Although formal qualitative methods have been developed to address some of these concerns, these methods typically involve creating, manipulating, and analyzing datasets in newly sophisticated ways, and thus raise their own questions.

Given these competing demands, what are historical social scientists – aside from engaging in further metatheoretical critique – to do? I argue that these developments provide more opportunities than constraints by way of research on the impact of social movements on policymaking (Amenta et al. 2005, Amenta 2006). Specifically, I trace the influence of the Townsend Plan and the old-age pension movement on the rise of US old-age policy and what is commonly known here as Social Security. In this research, I have sought to take history seriously in both senses of the word. First, I think explicitly about timing and sequence and pay attention to multiple and conjunctural causation. I try to indicate the combinations and sequences of events, actions, and structures that led to a major institutional shift in policy, based on competing visions about the role of and reasons for public social provision. I attend to the historical understandings of all the key actors, with all the archival legwork that implies, while seeking to address general theoretical arguments about the consequences of social movements and the development of welfare states. In doing so, I am aided by a search to understand and make sense of what the episode in history is a case of (Ragin 1992). This exercise can help a scholar devise and propose scope conditions, conceptually based delimitations around the theorizing, advancing theoretical speculation about other situations in which the claims might also hold good. I suggest that scholars go deeper into their cases, but not so far native as to neglect more general theorizing, and that recent developments in historical sociology can help.

HISTORICAL SOCIOLOGY TODAY

Historical sociology has always taken as its subject the explanation of major institutional changes and shifts – revolutions, the rise of states, the appearance of democratic institutions, the initiation of welfare states, and the like (see Mahoney and Rieschemeyer 2003). Before the breakthroughs in metatheoretical and methodological thinking, scholars would use standard comparative or quantitative analyses to delineate and isolate key factors or sometimes merely one key factor posited to produce the shift or phenomenon. But it is no longer generally considered to be the best practice to develop or appraise causal accounts deploying standard comparative methods on a reading of secondary literature on the subject in the manner of Moore's (1966) or Skocpol's (1979) early work and isolating general structural factors leading to institutional changes. Moore notably attempted to say something very general based entirely on limited secondary sources. Today, scholarship tends to seek less general claims rooted in more in-depth knowledge.

Configurational and sequential causation

Analytical, metahistorical, and methodological developments in historical sociology have yielded several insights that have achieved something like consensus among today's historical social scientists. Some of these insights have come from the upgrading of the standard comparative methods that were initially viewed as the keystone of historical sociology (and, indeed, the main organization in sociology promoting historical sociology is a section called Comparative and Historical Sociology). First, any causal account must take into consideration the likelihood that the outcome is the result of more than one cause – a configuration or conjuncture of causes – and also that there is more than one causal configuration possible to produce the outcome (Ragin 1987). Scholars are expected to seek out multiple, conjunctural causes for major social and political changes

(Katznelson 1997), or what is sometimes referred to as 'equifinality' (George and Bennett 2005).

On top of the understanding that causation is likely to be multiple and conjunctural, causes of institutional shifts are considered to be in the social science sense of word historical. The timing and sequence of causes matter. Not only will a causal factor be expected to have an effect only in conjunction with others, but a potential causal condition will work differently depending on where it appears in a sequence of causes and events (Griffin 1992), and events can alter structures in different ways (Sewell 2006). These causes might include structures, actors, and events and in ways that do justice to time order and possible path dependencies. In short, causal recipes, like recipes in cookbooks, need to list more than the combinations of causal ingredients deemed necessary and sufficient to cause the change. Scholars are expected to address issues of order, timing, and pace in making conjunctural causal arguments.

Yet the causes in any configurational sequence may also be contingent or accidental (Sewell 2006). Some conditions, events, or actions may be necessary for major institutional change to happen, but may be idiosyncratic to the case (Isaac et al. 2004). Indeed, in Stinchcombe's (1968) account of 'historicist' causation, factors in which the accidental may be central provoke institutional change that is impervious to change. As Pierson (2000) has shown, institutional change often provides self-reinforcing mechanisms that help to prevent further change (see also Mahoney 2000, Mahoney and Schensul 2006). From this understanding of path dependence, a set of conditions provokes institutional change, but afterward the reappearance of these conditions would not have the same effect. For instance, control of the US government by a right-wing regime in the late 1930s would have been sufficient to abolish Social Security as social insurance, but a Republican regime holding all branches of government after 2004 could not do so given how far the program had developed and the size of the constituency backing it.

Every historical social scientist an historian

Aside from needing to take into account issues of timing and pace in the manner of historians, historical sociologists have been enjoined to act like historians in more mundane ways that go beyond simply employing data that they do not initially collect (Miriampolski and Hughes 1978). Social scientists need to engage debates in historiography and often assess historical materials independently. That is because there are likely to be selection problems and biases in the extant historiography on many subjects (Lustick 1996), and thus even a comprehensive knowledge of the secondary sources on a given subject may be insufficient. Even if historiography were somehow comprehensive, other issues would arise. Although historians often produce narrative accounts in the sense of making time-order causal claims, these claims are frequently done unsystematically and are considered by historical, in the first sense, social scientists to be suspect (Griffin 1992). These warnings suggest that historical social scientists need to read historiography critically, but also engage in some independent inspection and interpretation of the materials from which historians have drawn inferences.

Other demands on historical social scientists firmly suggest a strong engagement with case materials. Theoretical processes need to be understood and appraised, and the best way to do so is by a way of deep historical knowledge. Specifically, arguments in historical social science often concern the thinking of key actors behind their actions, and historiography may give only a partial or biased account of this thinking. When general social scientific arguments are unpacked for their mechanisms, the bits of theory connecting major claims, they are also best appraised by detailed examinations of case materials. Process tracing (George and Bennett 2005, Hall 2003) of this sort tends to require deep knowledge of cases.

But acting more like historians makes historical sociology more time-consuming and difficult. There are no shortcuts to mastering historiography or engaging in archival work. More significantly, these strictures tend to force historical social scientists deeper into their cases and tend toward the case study. That is to say, social scientists seeking deep historical knowledge will be pushed toward studies of developments in fewer countries or places within a country over briefer periods of time. For some subjects, notably studying social movement organizations and challengers, the push is even stronger; demands on time due to the need for historical reconstruction are typically great (Tilly 2006), because their traces of activity are more difficult to locate.

The ever-present concern for the general

Yet even sociologists willing to shed the general linear reality of standard quantitative methods, as Abbott (1992a) has called it, usually seek to develop or appraise theoretical arguments that are in some ways or in some parts transportable to other cases, however defined. A case study that provides a complete theoretical informed explanation of some large institutional shift is typically not sufficient for sociological analyses. An understanding of what is accidental is often important in these explanations, but accidental events cannot be the focus of historical sociology. A key part of the social science project is to isolate theoretical argumentation of some form or another that would be expected in well-defined circumstances or contexts to produce similar phenomena. Typically, these contexts, or scope conditions, are defined conceptually (George and Bennett 2005). One may expect certain structures, short-term causes and events to lead to similar outcomes in rich democratic societies during the period of the rise of welfare states. Sometimes, however, scholars set contexts not conceptually, but by way a specific place and a historical period, such as in the US between the wars. Scholars employing the latter 'proper name' strategy (Przeworski and Teune 1970) may do so because they are not adept at theorizing or because they doubt the validity and usefulness of extensive theorizing (Collier and Mazzuca 2006). For those theorizing scope conditions a deeper historical knowledge of cases may make the conditions more plausible.

The extensiveness of the transportable parts of social science theorizing in any case study varies according to the preferences and inclinations of scholars. Theoretical causal claims range from the expansive and heroic generalizations of rational choice theorists (Kiser and Hechter 1991) to complete explanations of individual institutional shifts or developments across one case or very similar cases (Steinmetz 2004). The causal claims may also involve among other things drawing deep analogies (Stinchcombe 1978), isolating 'mechanisms' that are general but with different influences in different temporal and institutional contexts (McAdam et al. 2001), or developing claims meant to explain developments across a defined population over a period of time (Ertman 1997). Regardless of whether one seeks the invariant generalizations once common among comparative social scientists (Skocpol and Somers 1980) or adequate causal explanations of specific cases, the problem of empirical demonstration remains. Historical social scientists are expected to provide evidentiary demonstrations that support their more sophisticated theoretical claims and cast doubt on plausible alternatives. One question is whether case studies can do more than simply suggest hypotheses and build theory, which would require appraisal on other cases, disconfirm very general theoretical claims, or stand as a single instance of support for some theoretical claim (Lijphart 1971, cf Rueschemeyer 2003, George and Bennett 2005).

Do formal qualitative methods solve the problem?

Quantitative and formal qualitative methods have been developed to address some of the issues surrounding multiple, conjunctural, and time-order causation. The formal qualitative methods include among others fuzzy-set qualitative comparative analysis (fsQCA) and event structure analysis (Griffin 1993, Isaac et al. 2004). Fuzzy-set qualitative comparative analyses notably make it possible to isolate conditions necessary and sufficient for highly unusual results, such as major institutional change, although the measures themselves may need to be converted into ones that are sensitive to time order to make arguments historical in the social science sense (Caren and Panofsky 2005). Each of these approaches is in some ways limited for scholars of case studies. The crisp and fuzzy forms of qualitative comparative analysis typically imply comparative analyses, not case studies, though it is possible to use them to make sense of individual cases (but more on that below). And event-structure analyses tend either to provide specific interpretations and causal accounts of events or provide aid in the development of theory in the social science sense of historical.

Yet analyzing any dataset with time-sensitive quantitative or formal qualitative methods, no matter how sophisticated, does not address being historical in the second sense – for historical social scientists to think and act as historians do. Only a deep knowledge of the case materials can aid in understanding where timing might and might not matter and in addressing the many counterfactual questions inherent in historical research. Scholars can be widely comparative from this way of thinking only with an encyclopedic knowledge of cases. What is more, deeply historical methods like process tracing (George and Bennett 2005) that seek to appraise mechanisms or the smaller bits and connections in wider theoretical arguments are far more labor-intensive than the manipulation of pre-packaged datasets across many cases. The stricture to gain a deeper understanding tends to focus scholars studying relatively recent phenomena in what are typically considered 'case studies' (cf Ragin 1992) – analyzing developments in one country across a given period of time.

The availability of new time- and configuration-sensitive formal qualitative and quantitative techniques does not solve the problems flowing from the need for deep knowledge. These qualitative methods necessarily rely on the manipulation of datasets, which in turn are produced or assembled by someone. If that someone does not have a deep knowledge of the cases at hand and the historical circumstances surrounding them, the connection between concepts and measures may become tenuous and the results of analyses worthless. Even event structure analysis, a formal qualitative tool that forces scholars to be explicit about their counterfactual reasoning, requires valid basic accounts before it can be employed. To use event structure analysis to explain a particular event and generate more general hypotheses, for instance, about specific lynchings (Griffin 1993), scholars need first to have valid and reasonably complete factual accounts of them or the means to reconstruct them.

Similarly, in standard crisp qualitative comparative analyses, designing the truth table is a task with steep knowledge requirements (Ragin 1987). Decisions about break points and degree of membership in categories of fuzzy sets also depend on such knowledge (Ragin 2000). That said, as I argue below, gaining deep knowledge of cases can help to exploit the full benefits of methods like fsQCA, rather than using them as a kind of alternative to quantitative techniques for the testing of more sophisticated configurational and multicausal hypotheses.

Casing and historical sociology

More generally, historical social scientists like other qualitative researchers share deeper concerns about the sort of theoretical case that is uncovered, discovered, or created in the process of research. What is the case a case of? (Becker 1992, Ragin 1992) is a question that scholars are enjoined to ask themselves as they complete their investigations. Scholars paying attention to this issue can make theoretical connections that help to draw new conceptual lines around phenomena previously seen as disparate and not obviously comparable. The study may thus prompt the investigator to identify a new class of phenomena that

might have similar causes and consequences or add new instances to existing classes of phenomena. Scholars engaged in what are typically known as case studies, in that they focus one country, movement, or policy, are typically enjoined to develop extra observations to make their claims compelling (King et al. 1994). But these case studies also provide an opportunity to think more deeply and conceptually about the phenomena revealed during the analysis and scope conditions on arguments (George and Bennett 2005). Thus disadvantages in empirical demonstrations can be turned into analytical advantages.

One of the advantages of casing over other candidates for addressing general is that it retains the entire case as an analytical unit, subject to understanding and explanation. By comparison, if one is addressing theories based on mechanisms, the mechanism itself becomes the analytical unit, and in the search for similar mechanisms in different circumstances the advantages of understanding the case as an entire configuration or something with a beginning middle and end may be lost. A focus on mechanisms may come at the expense of explaining and understanding, say, a social movement that acts in a time and place with a beginning and an end or a period of policy reform that starts from almost nothing and ends with the building of durable institutions.

There is also the advantage in generalization in casing. Typically, social scientists choose cases on the basis of their being a part of some larger theoretical population; cases can be claimed to be typical of a larger group or they may be seen as atypical and thus extra worthy of explanation (Walton 1992). In the process of engaging in research, scholars can refine the understanding of this more general population and situate the case more precisely with respect to others deemed as otherwise similar. However, one can also think of a case study as containing empirical instances of more than one conceptual or theoretical construct (Platt 1992, Ragin 1992). Thus, scholars can influence several theoretical debates in the context of one case study, rather than being limited to one, as is the case for most large-N research.

In short, historical social science expects more sophisticated theorizing, a kind of explanatory richness that takes into account the possibility of historical and multiple conjunctural causation and path dependence. Scholars may need to employ more sophisticated methods that can address combinations of time-ordered causes. Historical social scientists also must remain alert to issues surrounding cases. In the minimal sense this sensitivity includes seeking out other information and analytical opportunities that might help to make causal claims more convincing (King et al. 1994); these demonstrations can range from gathering related large-N datasets to comparisons of similar cases with secondary sources to imaginary experiments. In addition, claims rely on a deep knowledge of the case or cases. Yet for all these new strictures, historical sociology is presented many opportunities and some of the insights provide opportunities to overcome the problems provoked by others. The concern with thinking about types of case can help when scholars seek to abstract out what is general in their explanations. A deep knowledge of cases increases the chances that any datasets derived from them will be valid. They will also provide scholars the opportunity to explore and appraise arguments about the determinants of institutional shifts and other unusual outcomes, as well as to help make better sense of their cases.

THE HISTORICAL CASE: THE TOWNSEND PLAN AND SOCIAL SECURITY

In my study of the Townsend Plan, old-age pension movements, and the rise of Social Security, I wanted to know whether the Townsend Plan had an impact on old-age policy. In particular, did the pension movement produce social security as we know it today, or fundamentally turn US social policy toward the old-age welfare state that it has become? After all, Social Security and Medicare are now the two biggest-budget items and much of Medicare is also slanted toward old age (see Amenta et al. 2005 and Amenta 2006 for most of the support for the following). I was asking both specific questions about whether a movement had an impact on a major institutional shift in public policy and if so which combinations of structures and circumstances caused that result. I was seeking to be historical in both main senses of the word. I was also seeking explanations with applicability beyond the instance I was examining – which made it pressing to understand what my case was a case of, with possibly more than one answer. In dealing with the strictures to become historical in both senses I went native for a while as an historian, but tried to emerge from the archives with social science theoretical insights and demonstrations of argument.

The Townsend Plan was a crusade named after Dr Francis E. Townsend, a California physician who was 73 in 1933 when he began a career in activism. The Townsend Plan, the name of both organization and program, called for a national, generous old-age pension for any citizen of age 60 or older who agreed to be retired and to spend the money quickly. It was designed to end poverty in old age and the Great Depression. In 1936, two million older Americans were members of approximately 8000 Townsend clubs. The Townsend Plan was one of the 57 voluntary associations ever to win membership from 1 per cent or more of the US adult population (Skocpol 2003). Although no version of Townsend's program ever became law, contemporaries, historians, and social scientists disagree about whether and how much the organization advanced US old-age policy. The Townsend Plan was later joined by a series of pension organizations that worked mainly at the State level. After 1950, however, the Townsend Plan was no longer a serious challenger and in 1980 became one of the few of the 57 to fall out of existence, suffering the fate of the International Workers of the World and the second Ku Klux Klan.

Questions and answers

The question was, at bottom, about the impact of the Townsend Plan and the pension movement on the vision animating old-age policy. The model pressed by the Townsendites and the pension movement was to provide stipends to citizens in a generous, equal, and universal fashion. The main alternatives included a compulsory, government-administered annuity for individuals, paying out according to what individuals paid in; social insurance for the risk of growing old without an income or a family breadwinner; means-tested and minimal stipends with supervision and loss of citizenship rights; and the existing non-system of wholly inadequate and idiosyncratic State and local public aid. The Social Security Act provided a combination of the means-tested model, applied immediately in States with some national standards and individual State decisions, and a national annuity model, designed for the future. The Townsend Plan and the pension movement sought to implode the means-tested model, engaging State by State in action to increase the stipends and their liberality, while removing restrictions on beneficiaries' rights, such as allowing them to bequeath rather than forfeit their property. For the long run, the Townsend Plan and pension movement sought to replace the annuity model at the national level with its own universal and generous pension.

I also theorized about the conditions under which political impacts by movements were likely. My political mediation model claims that collective action is political mediated in its political influence (see Amenta et al. 2005, Amenta 2006 Chapter 2). The essential idea was that the favorable political contexts, generally based on the partisanship of regimes in power, would increase the productivity of collective action. I also argued that assertive, rather than noninstitutional, action would be the most productive, though there were also political contexts, such as underdemocratized polities, where collective action over policy would be fruitless without prior structural political reform, and highly favorable political conditions that would amplify the impact

of action. I developed specific claims about matches of different strategies in different political contexts and fine-grained arguments about small and medium amounts of influence. The alternative arguments in the social science literature about the impact of social movements were largely one-factor claims about strategies, form of organization, or political contexts that were expected to work regardless of other circumstances.

I theorized as well the special case in which radical and far-reaching outcomes, such as creating a shift in public policy along the lines demanded by the Townsend Plan, would occur. As controlling the government through a new party is rarely an option in a political setting like the US, and initiatives and referendums are available only in some States, I argued that a challenger with far-reaching goals will need to have several things, many of them outside the challenger's control, happen at the same time to have a major influence: a favorable political context, its issue on the political agenda, high and widespread challenger organization and mobilization, credible claims-making directed at elites and the general public, and plausible assertive action. Although I was studying and theorizing major shifts in public policy, I was thinking that the same was likely to be true for bids to transform politically the structural position of groups, such as through voting or civil rights.

One of the important parts of political contexts included the institutionalization of old-age policy. Working from the standard historical institutionalist idea that new policy – key events that change structures – transforms politics, I understood the institutionalization of policy as a target that might pick up speed and move to different places. At the earliest stages, I expected that a movement would have the greatest opening for influence but, as time went on, the train would be moving further and faster away from the station, picking up reinforcements along the way. Any new program develops an interested clientele and provides the political problems associated with its retrenchment (Pierson 1994) or alteration. This constituency's growth and extension into the middle-class decreases the chances of fundamental change (cf. Mahoney and Schensul 2006). By voting for a program, legislators become more committed supporters, even those who have agreed to it as a compromise become politically invested. Executive bureaus running a program also typically gain resources and power over time. The Social Security Board has been regarded an especially powerful domestic bureaucracy in the US setting, and legislation establishing the old-age programs was enacted in 1935 and upgraded in 1939. Part of the idea behind the upgrade was to gain greater support for the national part of the program by increasing the number of current beneficiaries. All the same, although the policy was changing and the target moving, it remained easily within reach at least until 1950, when amendments buttressed the social insurance component.

Deep knowledge and interpretation as data

Addressing the impact of the Townsend Plan centered on answering counterfactual questions. The challenge was to demonstrate that specific consequences in social policy would not have happened in the absence of the challenger and its collective action. Scholars sometimes simply assume that challengers cause outcomes they seek, but often other actors and conditions may also influence outcomes beneficial to the constituencies of challengers. For instance, US programs benefiting the aged may have come as a result of the Depression or the rise to power of the Democratic Party rather than the Townsend Plan. To assess the historical impact of a challenger, scholars can survey the views of participants, contemporary observers, and historians. My key primary sources included congressional debates over the Social Security Act and its amendments; congressional committee minutes on the investigation of the Townsend Plan; contemporaneous reports of key actors; their published recollections; governmental statistics; archived traces of Townsend Plan activity; the Townsend Plan newspapers; and the national press. Following these paper trails

helped to address the counterfactual questions in several ways. Policy-makers often indicated what they were planning before the Townsend Plan existed and before it had engaged in various actions. I could ascertain whether the Townsend Plan induced changes in proposals and in which directions. I could also trace whether such strategies as efforts to endorse congressional candidates influenced members of Congress to act differently from what partisan or regional affiliations would imply.

I had to start almost from scratch, however, as the historiography had many gaps, a chronic problem in studying social movements (Tilly 2006). There was only one extensive extant account of the Townsend Plan (Holtzman 1963), which was limited by being a political science treatment in an era in which social movements were not expected to be influential. Neither was historical chronology one of the goals. I had to ascertain many basic facts about the organization, its strategies, and changes over time by way of inspecting its newsletter and the other archival material available, some of which had not previously been inspected. By the end, I was reasonably certain that no living being knew any more about the Townsend Plan, the pension movement, and their campaigns than I did, and a handful knew as much about the development of Social Security and US old-age policy in its formative years. This in itself was not enough to appraise my theoretical claims in ways that social scientists would find plausible or develop theory.

I focused on the main campaigns of the Townsend Plan and the pension movement, and the many episodes of old-age policy-making. I systematically analyzed whether the movement was influential and, if it was, what it was about its actions made it so, in each of the campaigns and episodes. Analyses of the political process in the development of legislation helped in establishing the challenger's impact. I traced whether a challenger altered the plans and agendas of political leaders, influenced the content of the proposals as devised by executives, legislators, or administrators, influenced the votes of representatives on key legislation, or influenced the implementation of laws. These interpretive decisions were informed by selected 'most similar' comparisons, such as between the pension movement and other social spending challengers, including Huey Long's Share Our Wealth, veterans' and unemployed workers' organizations. I also compared Old-age Assistance with Aid to Dependent Children, a similarly structured program. The answers to the counterfactual questions about the campaigns and episodes of policy making became the dependent variable of my study – a series of results that were largely interpretations of historical episodes.

Making the case

I wanted to make sense of the pattern of influence of the Townsend Plan and the pension movement at these moments and places. I had some variation here. The Townsend Plan contended for an extended period of time and employed almost every strategy short of armed revolt – from letter-writing and educational campaigns to initiative drives and the launching of a new political party – at different levels of mobilization in many different political contexts. I traced these changing efforts to turn policy into senior citizens' pensions over multiple rounds of the policy process, as old-age policy was altered over time and thus changed the possibilities for further influence. These episodes helped to appraise my larger model about matching strategies and political contexts. It also gave me an opportunity for process tracing and congruence appraisals (George and Bennett 2005 Chapters 9 and 10), as I was able to examine one by one changes in resource mobilization, political contexts, and framing and political strategies. The evidence suggested that these single-factor explanations were incongruent with the pattern of influence and instead provided some support for my arguments about matching strategies and contexts (Amenta 2006, conclusion). I also collected Old-age Assistance data across states and voting data on old-age policy in Congress and engaged with coauthors in some

quantitative analyses (Amenta et al. 2005) that helped to confirm my claims. These efforts were pretty much out of the King et al. (1994) playbook (see also Amenta 1991), but did not much help in explaining the transformations that I was most interested in.

I also sought out key, transformative episodes for explanation and the conditions under which unusual outcomes were possible. I was looking both at the national and at the State level – where radical attempts were more likely. I sought to ascertain the conditions under which States were willing to dump the means-tested model in favor of generous and widespread pensions. I also asked about what would make national political leaders support pensions. I became especially interested in one episode of national policy making. In 1941, the Townsend Plan and the pension movement almost converted US old-age policy into one based on universal pensions for senior citizens. President Roosevelt and the Democrats in Congress had agreed to allow the passage of a universal pension of $30 per month as part of a revamped Social Security program. All signs suggested passage of this legislation in early 1942; it was going through similar steps and was receiving contemporary political commentary in the press in ways analogous to the amendments to the Social Security of 1939. But the US was bombed into the Second World War, upgrades in social policy left the political agenda (Amenta 2006 Chapter 6), and configurations in Congress quickly turned conservative after 1942.

Still, this near miss was of considerable theoretical interest. The movement reached the brink of transforming old-age policy; the reasons for it not happening were largely accidental. A series of conditions suggested by the political mediation model seemed necessary to reach this point. The framing of the Townsend Plan and the pension movement was fairly consistent and remained plausible – perhaps even more so given that the administration was adopting a 'spending solution' to the Depression (Brinkley 1996) in consonance with the Townsend Plan's call for stimulating the economy. Its resource mobilization remained reasonably high with revenues and membership reaching a secondary peak after dropping back in 1937. More important, the Townsend Plan was able to organize more extensively in the East and Midwest, where it was previously lacking in Townsend clubs, buttressed by State-level pension organizations in the West, and thus the movement was finally organized nationwide. The political alignment was also fairly favorable, with a left-center Democrat remaining President with large, if no longer overwhelming, majorities in Congress. The Townsend Plan was plausibly engaged in its most assertive brand of action, working for the election of a large contingent in Congress in the 1940 elections, including both Republicans and Democrats. However, many of these favorable conditions were also there in 1939, when it was possible for the movement to have influence, but not to transform old-age policy.

Two new aspects were based on previous events and processes of learning within the organization and depended on prior political developments. The Townsend Plan had ended its tilt toward the Republicans. In a legislative maneuver designed to do that in 1939, the Democratic House leadership allowed a vote on a Townsend-sponsored bill. In the bill's overwhelming defeat it transpired that many Republicans supported Townsend pensions because they believed they would never come to a vote; in the 1940 campaign the Townsend Plan sought to force such Republican 'traitors' from office and supported more Democratic challengers. Its electoral activity, while seemingly similar, became far more forcible. More important, the Townsend Plan achieved a rapproachement with the Roosevelt administration. The new organizational leader of the Townsend Plan, Sherman Bainbridge, was a longstanding ally of the Townsend-supported Sheridan Downey, a Californian who was one of the Senate's most reliable New Dealers, and similar alliances were effected with others, notably Florida's Claude Pepper. Townsend quit criticizing Roosevelt, who reciprocated, no longer disparaging the pension movement's ideas as 'fantastic,' and was willing to override the resistance of his own Social Security Board to pensions. The Townsend Plan's congressional delegation was also granted autonomy from the organization to cut deals. For the first time, an alliance based on political strength was forged between the pension organization, the President, and the ruling Democratic leadership. The regime was pro-social policy, but now also favorably disposed to the organization.

Using formal qualitative methods

With coauthors (Amenta et al. 2005), I also engaged in both quantitative and formal qualitative analyses. Despite similar federal incentives for all states to create old-age assistance programs, they did not converge in their generosity and coverage. Thus old-age assistance programs varied widely, and the pension movement sought to convert them into pension-like programs in which benefits would be generous and coverage would be widespread. Political contexts in States also varied widely – some polities had structural hindrances, but those that did not often varied greatly in more recent developments. These analyses pooled all observations at the State level from the inception of the program in 1936 until 1950, when the Social Security Act was amended to make the insurance model supreme. We examined a large number of cases and controlled for other variables that might also have influenced old-age policy, such as left party regimes, powerful domestic bureaucracies, favorable public opinion, and economic and demographic developments. We also examined key old-age votes, focusing on 1939, the year that the Social Security Act was amended and which universal and more generous pensions also came up for votes in Congress. These analyses were deeply informed by the history of the case and the rhythms of social movement campaigns and policy making.

Although the quantitative techniques found the influence of the pension movement on both outcomes in expected ways (Amenta et al. 2005), the analyses were limited to single factors or minor interactions. These analyses also placed the usual limitations on cases noted by Abbott (1992b), as they converted 48 stories into about 400 'cases,' or observations, with the usual unrealistic simplifications of the explanation. I was most interested in the extreme cases of states where benefits were highly generous and relatively unrestricted. I also wanted to understand and explain why 17 senators voted for the Lee amendment, which would have replaced the current old-age policy with pensions of the type supported by the movement. My best guess was that several structural, medium-term, and short-term conditions would have to converge. The methods of fsQCA seemed ideal to address these sorts of questions and appraise this multifaceted argument. Although accounting for these unusual outcomes was not the same thing as explaining a major policy shift at the national level, the analyses were consonant with understanding the conditions under which major shifts in policy were possible.

My political mediation model included both long-term and more short-term political developments. Two large-scale political structural situations were important. One was the disfranchisement of much of the less well off South near the turn of the century. A second process was the establishment of patronage-based traditional political parties largely in the Northeast and Midwest, also mainly after the Civil War. I expected that challengers like the Townsend Plan would have grave difficulty organizing in under-democratized polities and high hurdles in the patronage-based polities, and difficulties in gaining support from political leaders in these polities even where they managed to organize. These presumptions were supported. In the shorter run, the simultaneous processes of organizing the aged and swinging state and local Democratic Party organizations behind the national New Deal and gaining power would promote old-age breakthroughs. But also necessary was extensive and recent assertive action through electoral processes by the pension movement, either in congressional elections or through initiative processes. The movement was expected to be less influential where it endorsed a successful candidate if the movement was unable to back that candidate with extensive organization.

The initial results on both Senate voting and where states stood on benefits supported the political mediation arguments. Perhaps most interesting were the Senate results, which were analyzed by way of crisp sets, given the ordinal nature of most of the measures, and focused on the combinations where positive votes were simply possible. Senators in democratized polities and not dominated by patronage-oriented parties that had a Democratic or radical third party affiliation in a state that was well organized by the pension movement and that received the Townsend Plan endorsement provided the greatest support for the radical amendment (see Amenta et al. 2005). There were two other combinations for which support was possible, but these did not cover many cases. But applying QCA to medium-N datasets has additional value for those focused on cases – an unusual situation given the standard division of labor between social scientists who analyze datasets and those who do not.

We reflected theoretically on cases that did not quite fit, addressed additional potential determinants, and better situated cases. The initial analyses made us rethink what 'democratized' meant, as Florida, a case counted first as underdemocratized given its lower voting participation and status as a former member of the Confederacy – the usual means of categorization – seemed inappropriate. The State combined a well-democratized south with an underdemocratized north and had recently repealed its poll tax. Both of its senators were pension supporters as was a significant fraction of its House delegation – the only place in the South for which this was true – leading us to use the poll tax as the main measure of democratization. We also added measures from other perspectives on the development of social policy, such as high public opinion for a national pension; at the same time, we combined into one measure theoretically similar factors, such as the movement being well organized and offering an endorsement. The public opinion measure joined in the major combination and added to the explanation, but was not enough to cover the outcome. It would take more influences than previously theorized to secure such votes in circumstances where the administration was opposed to such a bill. Examining more closely the states where pensions were generous revealed different pathways to that point. Colorado organized, campaigned, and won high pensions very quickly through a referendum, which merely had to be defended later; in California the process was drawn out, involving referendums, but mainly failed ones.

What it was a case of?

As I was nearing the end of the study, I thought more about what sort of case this case was, an analytical advantage of case studies often left unexploited. The social movement literature is based on case studies, but scholars tend to view their cases as typical – to paraphrase the Townsend Plan slogan, every movement a Middletown – and expect that broad explanatory claims should apply all movements, possibly following McAdam's (1982) influential analysis of the US Civil Rights movement. Its theoretical model was posited to apply to all movements regardless of how unusual that one might have been. Although there has been much subsequent debate over what constitutes a social movement, the casing issue has mainly been neglected. The consequences of social movement literature, following Gamson (1990/1975), has taken a slightly different approach, placing cases into one of four categories, based on whether they gained new advantages and whether they were accepted by opponents.

I realized that the Townsend Plan did not readily fit anywhere into this two-by-two scheme. One off-diagonal case, 'co-optation' fit somewhat in that the Townsend Plan was not nearly 'successful' in gaining what it demanded and achieved some acceptance, with its many political allies. In States where pension organizations won, such as in Colorado and California, they ultimately lost because the insurance model won out at the national level. But the Townsend Plan and the main pension organizations were not co-opted in the standard sense; they never gave up principles to have their leaders incorporated into national positions. The movement died off, but not mainly because it was 'preempted,' with political officials winning over a movement's supporters by conceding just enough to win their allegiance. The movement largely imploded on its own. Nor was it just another failed displacement organization, seeking to replace its opponents or the economic or political system, which tend to doom any challenger in a democracy. The Townsend Plan sought to displace only a policy. Also, this was a wide movement with a dominant national organization, rather than just simply a challenging organization. The exercise suggested that the relevant characteristics of movement consequences went beyond success and failure along these dimensions; it was better to think of movements seeking substantial change by ways of their degrees of influence and continued leverage.

From this way of thinking, the US pension movement was a political movement with far-reaching aims that was highly influential, if not successful, and that took another form later with new organizations. In this way, the pension movement had much in common with some other US political movements in the middle of the twentieth century, notably the first feminist movement, the anti-alcohol movement, the nativist movement, and anti-war movements. It was somewhat less similar to movements that gained influence but with more long-term leverage and continuous organizational presence, such as the labor movement, the civil rights movement, the second feminist movement, and the environmental movement. It seems quite possible that any generalizations from my study might apply best to the far-reaching, influential, died-off sort of movement and to require modification to apply to influential movements with more consistent leverage.

Any analysis of the impact of a social movement on policy is also an analysis of policymaking, and this leads to the second advantage of casing. Cases can be cases of more than one thing. Thus I found it worthwhile to reflect back on the case of policymaking here. The establishment of Social Security, which in many accounts was inherent in the 1935 legislation, was instead a kind of compromise that no one envisioned or wanted. The initial policy as designed hastily by the Committee on Economic Security was at best muddled and at worst contradictory, securing only the principle that poverty in old-age need to be addressed by the national government. Major administrative players fought over the ideas and goals behind old-age policy, notably whether it should be social insurance or a guaranteed income for the poor. Although the more conservative and less powerful Social Security Board was losing initially, it was the main domestic administrative body left standing after the dismantling of the Work Projects Administration and the National Resources Planning Board during the conservative rise to power after the 1942 elections. The Board saw old-age insurance as the entering wedge of a complete social insurance system, but that did not come close to passing Congress. The political organizations of business fought unsuccessfully for a kind of minimalist/non-national model on the order of health policy. The pension movement had its own vision that was realized only in part, only in a few places, only briefly, but formed the main political impetus driving the process.

CONCLUSION

To gain a deep knowledge of a subject matter and making theoretical sense of issues surrounding timing, sequence, and configuration, historical social scientists have turned more and more to case studies and the well-known problems of how to make arguments convincing. Historical social scientists nowadays seek something less general than Barrington Moore, heroic in the broadness of claims and shallowness of source material, based on in-depth knowledge. Indeed, scholars may become so focused on developing an adequate

explanation that they may not theorize outside the parameters of the case.

But historical case studies of transformative periods also open the way for new theorizing that employs configuration and time-order claims in ways that combine structures and events. From adequate explanations of individual episodes of major social change addressing issues of structure, action, and contingency, it is possible and worthwhile to distill arguments suitable for application to other cases. There seems to be no disadvantage to doing so. Although misunderstanding or being ignorant about basic information surrounding a case may ruin a study, being wrong is no major problem for a theory, which serves mainly a guide and a challenge to other scholars.

There are other advantages to the new approach. Historical social scientists may also be able to develop datasets that aid in answering more important questions than simply explaining variance. They can deploy their deep knowledge not simply to provide the sorts of extra observations often deemed lacking in case studies. Social scientists can also strategically analyze in detail the circumstances surrounding structural transformations and allied extraordinary occurrences. I examined national votes to transform old-age policy and campaigns in states that sought to convert means-tested benefits into universal pensions. Formal qualitative methods have developed to the point that social scientists can both test extant arguments and suggest compelling alternatives. When applied in an iterative way, these methods can also help scholars make better sense of their cases. Historical sociologists like other qualitative researchers can also innovate in their casing strategies and advance their more sophisticated forms of theorizing. Once one's case is understood, it takes only a cursory knowledge of other cases to address the question of what the case is a case of. The answers can help to set scope conditions around sophisticated theoretical arguments and guide research on similar cases.

It remains true that the academic returns to social scientists for the labor expended into knowing a case well are relatively minor. I was able very quickly to publish a couple of articles in the two top sociology journals about the causes and consequences of the Townsend Plan. Empirically, the studies were based on multivariate analyses of data gleaned from secondary sources, government documents, and hasty searches through primary documents on the organization. I otherwise leaned on the main secondary source for my information, without knowing, as I learned later, such basic things as that back in the day almost everyone called the organization and phenomenon the 'Townsend Plan' and not the 'Townsend Movement.' In one paper, I relied on the one-size-fits-all propositions from the movement literature and thus neither developed a deep knowledge of the case nor thought outside the general linear box. I wanted to get to know the subject thoroughly some day, but in the meantime was well on my way to a successful tenure review. By contrast, writing the book and engaging in quantitative analyses with greater validity, more interesting outcomes, and more sophisticated ideas about causality took a long time, and the book came out more than a decade after the original articles. Its generation cost countless hours at the New York Public Library and archives around the country, as well as microfiche-related eye strain. I amassed a lot of information, mainly notes from said archives and microfiche, that I could not publish.

All the same, the academic rewards for publishing monographs that combine deep understanding of cases with sophisticated theoretical thinking remain high. And, despite the decline in the market for books, top academic presses remain eager for such work. Young social scientists can still earn tenure and established ones can earn promotions by publishing these books. Much knowledge about cases can be imparted between theory-heavy introductory and concluding chapters. No doubt fewer Barrington Moore Jrs will walk among us, but if more scholars young and old take history seriously in both senses social science will be the empirically and theoretically richer for it.

REFERENCES

Abbott, A. 1992a 'What do cases do: some notes on activity in sociological analyses,' in C. Ragin and H. Becker (Eds) *What is a Case?* New York: Cambridge University Press, Chapter 2.

Abbott, A. 1992b 'From causes to events: notes on narrative positivism' *Sociological Methods and Research* 20: 428–455.

Amenta, E. 1991 'Making the most of a case study: theories of the welfare state and the American experience' *International Journal of Comparative Sociology* 32 (1991): 172–194.

Amenta, E. 2006 *When Movements Matter: The Townsend Plan and the Rise of Social Security.* Princeton, NJ: Princeton University Press.

Amenta, E., Caren, N. and Olasky, S.J. 2005 'Age for leisure? Political mediation and the impact of the pension movement on old-age policy' *American Sociological Review* 70: 516–538.

Becker, H. 1992 'Cases, causes, conjunctures, stories, and imagery' in C. Ragin and H. Becker (Eds) *What is a Case?* New York: Cambridge University Press, Chapter 9.

Brinkley, A. 1996 *The End of Reform: New Deal Liberalism in Recession and War.* New York: Vintage.

Caren, N. and Panofsky, A. 2005 'TQCA: a technique for adding temporality to qualitative comparative analysis' *Sociological Methods and Research* 34: 147–172.

Collier, R.B. and Mazzuca, S. 2006 'Does history repeat?' in R.E. Goodin and C. Tilly (Eds) *The Oxford Handbook of Contextual Political Analysis.* New York: Oxford University Press, Chapter 25.

Ertman, T. 1997 *Birth of the Leviathan: Building States and Regimes in Medieval and Early Modern Europe.* Cambridge: Cambridge University Press.

Gamson, W.A. 1990/1975 *The Strategy of Social Protest.* Homewood, IL.: Dorsey Press.

George, A.L. and Bennett, A. 2005 *Case Studies and Theory Development in the Social Sciences.* Cambridge, MA: MIT Press.

Griffin, L.J. 1992 'Temporality, events, and explanation in historical sociology: an introduction' *Sociological Methods and Research* 20: 403–427.

Griffin, L.J. 1993 'Narrative, event-structure analysis, and causal interpretation in historical sociology' *American Journal of Sociology* 98: 1094–1133.

Hall, P.A. 2003 'Aligning ontology and methodology in comparative research' in J. Mahoney and D. Rueschemeyer (Eds) *Comparative Historical Analysis in the Social Sciences.* Cambridge: Cambridge University Press, pp. 373–404.

Hall, P.A. and Taylor, R.C.R. 1996 'Political science and the three new institutionalisms' *Political Studies* 44: 936–957.

Holtzman, A. 1963 *The Townsend Movement, a Political Study*. Madison, WI: Bookman Associates.

Isaac, L.W., Street, D.A. and Knapp, S.J. 2004 'Analyzing historical contingency with formal methods: the case of the "Relief Explosion" and 1968' *Sociological Methods and Research* 23: 114–141.

Katznelson, I. 1997 'Structure and configuration in comparative politics' in M.I. Lichbach and A.S. Zuckerman (Eds) *Comparative Politics: Rationality, Culture, and Structure*. New York: Cambridge University Press, pp. 81–112.

King, G., Keohane, R.O. and Verba, S. 1994 *Designing Social Inquiry: Scientific Inference in Qualitative Research*. Princeton, NJ: Princeton University.

Kiser, E. and Hechter, M. 1991 'The role of general theory in comparative-historical sociology' *American Journal of Sociology* 97: 1–30.

Lijphart, A. 1971 'Comparative politics and the comparative method' *American Political Science Review* 65: 691–693.

Lustick, I. 1996 'History, historiography, and political science: historical records and selection bias' *American Political Science Review* 90: 605–618.

McAdam, D. 1982. *Political Process and the Development of Black Insurgency, 1930–1970*. Chicago: University of Chicago Press.

McAdam, D, Tarrow, S. and Tilly, C. 2001 *Dynamics of Contention*. New York: Cambridge University Press.

Mahoney, J. 2000 'Path dependence in historical sociology' *Theory and Society* 29: 507–548.

Mahoney, J. and Rieschemeyer, D. 2003 *Comparative and Historical Analysis*. New York: Cambridge University Press.

Mahoney, J. and Schensul, D. 2006 'Historical context and path dependence' in R.E. Goodin and C. Tilly (Eds) *The Oxford Handbook of Contextual Political Analysis*. New York: Oxford University Press, Chapter 24.

Miriampolski, H. and Hughes, D.C. 1978 'The uses of personal documents in historical sociology' *The American Sociologist* 13: 104–113.

Moore, B. Jr 1966 *The Social Origins of Dictatorship and Democracy*. Boston: Beacon Press.

Pierson, P. 1994 *Dismantling the Welfare State? Reagan, Thatcher, and the Politics of Retrenchment*. New York: Cambridge University Press.

Pierson, P. 2000 'Path dependence, increasing returns, and the study of politics' *American Political Science Review* 94(2): 251–267.

Pierson, P. and Skocpol, T. 2002 'Historical institutionalism in contemporary political science' in I. Katznelson and H.V. Milner (Eds) *Political Science: State of the Discipline*. New York: W.W. Norton, pp. 693–721.

Platt, J. 1992 'Cases of cases …. of cases' in C. Ragin and H. Becker (Eds) *What is a Case?* New York: Cambridge University Press, Chapter 1.

Przeworski, A. and Teune, H. 1970 *Logic of Comparative Social Inquiry*. New York: Wiley.

Ragin, C.C. 1987 *The Comparative Method*. Berkeley, CA: University of California Press.

Ragin, C.C. 1992 'Introduction: cases of "What is a case?"' in C. Ragin and H. Becker (Eds) *What is a Case?* New York: Cambridge University Press, pp. 1–17.

Ragin, C.C. 2000 *Fuzzy-Set Social Science*. Chicago: University of Chicago Press.

Rueschemeyer, D. 2003 'Can one or a few cases yield theoretical gains?' in J. Mahoney and D. Rueschemeyer (Eds) *Comparative Historical Analysis in the Social Sciences*. Cambridge: Cambridge University Press, pp. 305–336.

Sewell, W. Jr 2006 *Logics of History*. Chicago: University of Chicago Press.

Skocpol, T. 1979 *States and Social Revolutions: A Comparative Analysis of France, Russia, and China*. Cambridge: Cambridge University Press.

Skocpol, T. 2003 *Diminished Democracy: From Membership to Management in American Civic Life*. Norman, OK: University of Oklahoma Press.

Skocpol, T. and Somers, M. 1980 'The uses of comparative history in macrosocial inquiry' *Comparative Studies in Society and History* 22: 174–197.

Steinmetz, G. 2004 'Odious comparisons: incommensurability, the case study, and "small N's" in sociology' *Sociological Theory* 22: 371–400.

Stinchcombe, A.L. 1968 *Constructing Social Theories*. New York: Harcourt, Brace, and World.

Stinchcombe, A.L. 1978 *Theoretical Methods in Social History*. New York: Academic Press.

Tilly, C. 2006 'Why and how history matters' in R.E. Goodin and C. Tilly (Eds) *The Oxford Handbook of Contextual Political Analysis*. New York: Oxford University Press, Chapter 22.

Walton, J. 1992 'Making the theoretical case' C. Ragin and H. Becker (Eds) *What is a Case?* Cambridge: Cambridge University Press, Chapter 5.

21

Poetry and History: The Case for Literary Evidence[1]

John Walton

A horseman high alone as an eagle on the spur
of the mountain … draws rein, looks down

At the bridge-builders, men, trucks, the power-
shovels, the teeming end of the new coast-road
at the mountain's base.

He sees the loops of the road go northward,
headland beyond headland, into gray mist …

He shakes his fist and makes a gesture of
wringing a chicken's neck, scowls and rides
higher.

I too

Believe that the life of men who ride horses,
herders of cattle on the mountain pasture,
plowers of remote

Rock-narrowed farms in poverty and freedom, is
a good life. At the far end of those loops of road

Is what will come and destroy it, a rich and vulgar
and bewildered civilization dying at the core …

from *The Coast-Road*
The Selected Poetry of Robinson Jeffers (1927a)

Robinson Jeffers (1887–1962) settled on the
thinly populated coast of central California
in the early twentieth century and began
writing stories of pioneering families and their
majestic surroundings that would define the
poet and the place called Big Sur. In the 1920s
and 1930s Jeffers became one of the nation's
most celebrated (if least enduring) poets. His
art was the narrative poem, major works
running one or two hundred pages based on
the land and legends of the California coast.
Jeffers wrote about real people and places,
sometimes by name, often in recognizable fictional characters and settings, always rooted in
social context, and plotted in perennial human
dramas. Jeffers's poetry is suffused with a
sense of the place and people of Big Sur.
Here, by his own testimony, Jeffers found his
poetic mission. As Henry Miller (1957, p. 45)
observed, '[t]he rugged pioneers who settled
here needed only a voice to make known their
secret drama. And Jeffers is that voice.'

In the opening lines of *The Coast-Road*,
Jeffers describes the construction of a two-
lane highway that would open Big Sur to
through traffic in the late 1930s and mark deci-
sively a movement already in progress from a
homesteading pioneer community to a scenic
redoubt of wealthy ranchers, tourists, artists,
and service workers. Jeffers portrayed this

transition in moralistic terms, from poor-but-free frontier to rich-and-vulgar civilization. Although the road builders and their allies saw the transition in different terms, all were aware of it. Jeffers illuminates varied individual reactions to the sea change as well as the broader advance of modernity affecting local society and its moral order.

A CASE STUDY OF LITERATURE AS EVIDENCE

The purpose of this chapter is to explore the methodological issues involved in using literature as evidence in social history. I employ a particular research method to explore the problem: a case study of a small world in space and time, a local place where one may know the actors as individuals, the terrain on which they operate, and the quotidian events shaping their world. The eclectic and intimate detail of a case study is essential for comparing literary descriptions of people and places with other types of evidence in the process of establishing validity or triangulating on empirical claims.

A perennial issue in historical research, particularly studies of little known events and places, is the matter of sources. Classical studies of microhistory depend upon the rare diary, transcript, ledger, or eye-witness account (e.g. Ginzburg 1982, Davis 1983). In other cases, however, the historical record is sparse. Sometimes the only detailed accounts of a time and place come in the form of 'fiction.' One of the early and enduring contributions of post-modernist scholarship has been a reconsideration of the nature of fact and fiction, the 'facticity of fact' in a turgid but revealing phrase. Apparent facts are sometimes fiction (erroneous, made up), and seeming fictions are sometimes true. More fundamentally, facts in the form of empirical observations are typically lodged in broader narratives that assume temporal and causal connections not inherent in the evidence. Narrative form itself conveys a certain 'emplotment' (White 1987). Most 'facts' and socially and culturally mediated; the evidence we rely upon for

understanding society and history derives from human processes of observation, collection, categorization, interpretation, and representation. Literature is no different from official statistics or journalism in the sense that their value as evidence requires examination of the manner in which they are socially constructed (Trouillot 1995, Arnold 2000, Walton 2001). The implication of these insights is that so-called fictions judiciously interpreted can have evidentiary value.

Social scientists have long recognized the uses of literature in social and cultural research. Literature is employed sociologically in at least three different ways. First is the illustrative approach: Dickens tells us much about the life and institutions of nineteenth-century London, and Willa Cather about the American plains and pioneers. Novel accounts may not constitute facts but they do provide a feel for the times, one author's impressions, contemporary perspective, or empirical content (e.g. Dickens's description of the chancery court or Cather's portrait of frontier women). Second, the sociology of literature directly studies artistic production: for example, the historical conditions that gave rise to the realist novel as a new literary form (Watt 1957) or the social history of the crime story (Mandel 1984). Third, social research deals with the *interplay* of literature and society, how for example, John Steinbeck's *Grapes of Wrath* grew out of the great Dust Bowl migration to California and how Steinbeck's novel affected the political climate of the state (Gregory 1989). In each of these approaches literature is employed as evidence, albeit evidence of a qualified sort.

In this case study I pursue a fourth and somewhat stronger use of literature as historical evidence. I shall argue and endeavor to demonstrate that, under some circumstances and with certain precautions, literature can be used reliably as historical evidence. The argument, though rare, is not unprecedented. Oxford historian Keith Hopkins (1993, p. 3) has written about 'novel evidence for Roman slavery' using the text of *The Life of Aesop* 'to sketch the slave's experience of slavery, and the fears and anxieties which slavery evoked in Roman masters.' Hopkins argues that Roman stories about slavery are perhaps a better (or no less valid) indicator than surviving records of the Roman Senate, for example, because stories reveal the boundaries of morality, the fears of slave owners, and thus the normative order within which all Romans operated. So-called 'real history' based on diaries, autobiographical accounts, tax records, or criminal statistics should be no more privileged when it comes to interpreting culture than stories, especially stories passed down through generations.

French historian Louis Chevalier (1973) offers a related argument in his study of the laboring classes and the dangerous classes in nineteenth-century Paris. Living conditions of the urban poor are described in a wealth of French demographic data and also, equally, in evidence of the 'opinions' about those conditions held by contemporaries. 'This city emerges from the muted roar that rises from the great bulk of qualitative documents, and especially from the popular novels of every kind and at every level, whose testimony acquires its full value when checked by quantitative research' (Chevalier 1973, p. 19). Evidence of opinion, best expressed by the popular novels of Hugo and Balzac, as well as demographic facts about crime and public health are necessary and complementary sources of social knowledge.

This chapter explores a California case of literary evidence as a source for studying local society. The case study simultaneously expands and limits analysis. It expands the variety of research tools and evidence employed (from demography to diary). It also narrows and focuses the scope of inquiry to specific places, individuals, roles, and events in literary descriptions and it compares these with complementary historical evidence (e.g. newspapers, memoirs, censuses). Insofar as that comparison validates the reliability of the evidence, I shall argue further that literary evidence illuminates social relations in additional ways that are seldom found in conventional sources. It provides an account of life *as experienced* that may be interpreted (triangulated) in light of other more conventional

sources ('facts'). The issues posed by the case study include: What constitutes evidence in social research? What kind of evidence is found in literature? What leads us to believe in some forms of evidence more than others? What role does the method of data collection play in its credibility? How does literary method (if we grant such to novelists and poets) compare with the methods of ethnographers or diarists?

THE SETTING

El Sur, the south, was the name Spanish colonists gave to the great expanse of rugged land lying along the central California coast below the missionary capital established in 1770 in Monterey. The Esselen Indians who occupied what is now Big Sur numbered perhaps 1200 and were among the smallest of California Indian groups. These hunter-gatherers lived in small bands, left curious rock paintings in backcountry caves, and struggled to maintain their independence even as colonial forces surrounded them (Breschini and Haversot 2004). Under Mexican rule (1821–1846) large tracts of land were granted to ex-soldiers and associates of provincial governors. The 8,814-acre San José y Sur Chiquita grant stretched ten miles south from Carmel Mission. The 8,949-acre *El Sur* grant, awarded initially to Governor Alvarado and soon passed on to Captain John Rogers Cooper, was the only working ranch in Big Sur when homesteaders began moving in after the US acquired California in 1846 and following the Homestead Act of 1862 and Timber Culture Act of 1873.

As the Native American population virtually disappeared owing to disease and absorption into the agricultural labor force, a new tribe of Anglo homesteaders slowly settled the Sur. Michael and Barbara Pfeiffer, who were of Alsatian origin, arrived in 1869 with four children. Former *vaqueros* on the Cooper Ranch, Manuel Innocenti, an Indian, and David Castro bought small farms. Many of the settlers were Yankees, like William Brainard Post, who married

Anselma Onesimo, a Rumsen Indian (Norman 2004). Because Big Sur was isolated and its rugged terrain generally inhospitable to the Mexican hacienda, a good deal of coastal land was still available for distribution under US public land laws in the late nineteenth century. Through preemption, homesteading, timber claims, re-sales, and squatting, a growing number of settlers in the 1870s and 1880s acquired farms, typically beginning with the 160-acre allotments for homestead and timber claims. Land moved from public ownership to small private holdings with successfully patented homesteads, and some of these were subsequently consolidated in larger farms and ranches.

In 1879, the voter registration roll for Sur Precinct listed twenty-six men, all identified as farmers save two stock raisers, two laborers, one lumberman, and one miner. By 1896 there were sixty-two voters (all male until 1919), agrarians to a man except the lighthouse keeper and an engineer. The US Census of Agricultural Production for Monterey County in 1880 lists only a handful of farmers on the coast suggesting the others were subsistence farmers with no measurable production for the market. Michael Pfeiffer's farm included over 500 acres, 12 of which were tilled, 200 cows and pigs, and a yearly income of $1,100, mostly from butter production, but no paid labor, owing perhaps to a family that grew to eight children. Kentuckian Thomas Ingram produced $1,500 worth of cattle and butter on his 400-acre ranch and paid $300 for hired labor. Charles Bixby, whose principal business was timber, owned a profitable ranch on Mill (later Bixby) Creek valued at over $4,000 and paid $800 in wages. Bixby built a ship's landing for export from his sawmill and employed ranch and mill workers in the construction of the first wagon road linked to Monterey. By 1900, the US manuscript census lists 331 persons living in 95 households in the section of Monterey Township from the Carmel River to the San Luis Obispo County line.

Big Sur began to change at the turn of the century. Agricultural production on family farms remained the staple of the economy

specializing in dairy (butter, cheese), livestock, and honey. Gold and coal mining had short-lived successes. Limestone mines and kilns for processing quick lime prospered for two decades. Elaborate tramways were built to carry the processed lime from kilns on the hills to ship landings along the rocky and treacherous coast.

The more sustained industry was timber, principally redwood and oak bark used in leather tanning. Forest products were exported from a series of landings (e.g. Notley's, Bixby's, Partington) or 'dog hole' ports along the coast and carried to Monterey and San Francisco by a regular steamship service in the years surrounding 1900. Like mining, however, timber and tanbark faltered as economically accessible supplies were exhausted. By 1900, the industry of the future began to emerge as campers and sports enthusiasts appeared in growing numbers at outdoor resorts (Idlewild, Pfeiffer's). Wealthy city people began purchasing cattle ranches for their scenic and recreational value. Finally, Big Sur's legendary bohemian community of poets, artists, writers, spiritual seekers, and sundry eccentrics came for the inspiration imparted by the natural beauty and one another's company. The coast road was steadily improved allowing automobile traffic as far as Sur precinct twenty-six miles south of Carmel in the 1920s. With a final assist from the Works Progress Administration (WPA), the seventy-mile connection to San Simeon was completed in 1938. The highway marked the area's final passage to modernity as a series of local place names (Palo Colorado, Mill Creek, Idlewild, Sur) were absorbed into the aggregate place name Big Sur (Clark, 1991).

LOCAL KNOWLEDGE

Robinson Jeffers settled in Carmel in 1914 with wife and poetic muse, Una. He had been educated in European schools by an austere father – a professor of theology who supervised his study of Greek, Latin, and the classics. Although Jeffers had already published a volume of poetry, his work was obscure and tentative. But now, Jeffers says, 'certain accidents changed and directed my life,' the first was Una who:

> ... by her presence and conversation has co-authored every one of [the poems]. A second piece of pure accident brought us to the Monterey coast mountains, where for the first time in my life I could see people living amid magnificent unspoiled scenery ... Here was contemporary life that was also permanent life ... [Jeffers goes on to describe the people and events that informed his stories, for example] the Indian woman and her white husband, real persons whom I had often seen driving through our village in a ramshackle buggy. The episode (in *Roan Stallion*) of the woman swimming her horse through a storm-swollen ford at night ... was part of her actual history. (Jeffers 1927a, pp. xv–xvii)

Una, who was more sociable than the brooding poet, provided much of the local knowledge that Jeffers wove into his work. Reflecting on their early days in Carmel, Una wrote:

> [T]he big adventure of our first winter was a trip down the coast on the horse stage with [legendary local teamster] Corbett Grimes, who carried the mail and occasional passengers three times a week ... This was the first of a thousand pilgrimages, that we, and later our twin sons with us, have made down the coast and into the back country, where with books and maps and local gossip we have tried to piece together a fairly complete picture of this region: its treasures of natural beauty and vivid human life have been inexhaustible (quoted in Bennett 1966, p. 71)

Jeffers's stories are infused with the people and places of Big Sur. Place settings in the poems often bear their true name (Point Lobos, Soberanes Canyon, Mill Creek, Cooper's Ranch) but frequently, and according to no apparent pattern, appear also as pseudonyms (Manvil's Landing for Notley's, Thurso's Landing for Bixby's). Real people usually have pseudonyms, often sound-alikes, such as Fraser for the pioneer Pfeiffer family, Hanlon for resort owner Charles Howland, or Alera for the Cooper-Molera family (cf Hughey and Hughey 1996). Sometimes real names are employed (e.g. Vasquez), although not necessarily in reference to the particular person: 'Onorio Vasquez who comes into

several of the stories was drawn at the first from a man down the coast we knew slightly' (Una Jeffers to Lawrence Clark Powell, 1932). Close reading of Jeffers's work demonstrates his long experience and detailed knowledge of local society. Carmel poet George Sterling said of Jeffers, 'Probably there was never anyone since the Indians to whom this coast was so presently familiar' (quoted in Powell 1940, p. 83).

Obviously, Jeffers did not write history or ethnography as such. His stories blend local events and places with plot ideas from a rich variety of sources. '*Tamar* grew up from the biblical story ... and from the strange, introverted, and storm-twisted beauty of Point Lobos' (Jeffers 1927a, p. xvi). *Cawdor* deals with a farm family whose generational and sexual conflicts recall the Greek legend of Phaedra and play out in a twisted version of the Oedipus myth. *The Loving Shepherdess*, who wanders along the Big Sur coast with her sheep, 'was suggested by a footnote in one of the novels of Walter Scott' (Jeffers 1927a, p. xvii).

The poems themselves address universal and often tragic themes of power, death, insanity, perverted love, jealousy, hate, suicide, nature, and the cosmic insignificance of humans. But the people, places, and events through which the drama is enacted come from the real history of Big Sur. Novelist Henry Miller, a long-term resident of Big Sur in a later period, notes that:

> Robinson Jeffers is unerring ... His figures and their manner of behavior are not falsely exaggerated as some believe. If his narratives smack of Greek tragedy, it is because Jeffers rediscovered here the atmosphere of the gods and fates which obsessed the ancient Greeks (Miller 1957, p. 145)

THE STORIES

Although Jeffers's oeuvre spanned nearly fifty years beginning with his first published volume in 1912, his major and defining work came in the 1920s and 1930s, the years of his great narrative poems that also defined Big Sur. Jeffers was not the first to write about the region. California author Gertrude Atherton published *Patience Sparhawk and Her Times* in 1897, about a girl raised in poverty and backwardness at Point Lobos. Jack London's 1913 novel *Valley of the Moon* described the bohemian set of Carmel and their frolics along the Big Sur coast. Others, including John Steinbeck, Lillian Bos Ross, and Henry Miller, would follow Jeffers. But more than any other, Jeffers portrayed the scenic and human drama of Big Sur in a manner that influenced subsequent artists whether poets, novelists, painters, or photographers such as Ansel Adams and Edward Weston.

In 1916, Jeffers published *Californians*, a minor work yet one that introduced many of the settings and characters that would animate later plots. The poem 'Ruth Allison' tells the story of a beautiful farm girl who falls in love with Paul, heir to the vast Alera ranch, who betrays her by an affair with the bored adulterous wife of mill owner Manvil. The abandoned limekilns and tramway leading to Manvil's landing are vivid images from Jeffers's first trip down the coast that recur in later works. Ruth dies of a broken heart: 'Had he been faithful she would have been most happy, being of her nature beautiful, and bound to the great nature of that lonely place'. Meanwhile, a rapacious timber industry has stripped the hills. Nature and economy ruined, settlers displaced, and homes deserted:

> [Y]ou will see on the bleak ocean-cliff, under bare windy hills, a settlement of cottages about one building, broad, three-storied, capable of many beds, and thereby an old mill. These vacant stand ... and there is hardly a tree for miles around. (Jeffers 1916, p. 69)

The scene depicted in these last lines is Palo Colorado, site of Notley's landing and the remarkable three-storied Swetnam family farmhouse, which, in fact, has been occupied to this day.

Tamar, written in the early 1920s, is the first of the long narrative poems (Hunt 2001). Unlike the innocent Ruth Allison, Tamar is the daughter of a Point Lobos farm family who is simultaneously having an incestuous affair with her brother, pregnant as a result,

and an incest rape victim of her despised father who is now ruined with age and religious obsession. Two demented aunts and various spirits of the dead, including her mother, also occupy their lonely, storm-battered house. Tamar starts an affair with a neighbor lad to conceal the origin of her pregnancy and incites her brother's jealousy ending in a fight and killing. Violence, otherworldly interventions, and destruction visit the family all of whom finally die in a house fire. Jeffers's biographer James Karman (1987, p. 87) describes *Tamar* as 'extremely dense. On one level it is a tale of gothic horror. On another it is a study of what the strange landscape around Carmel can do to people.' Indeed, Jeffers believed that the awesome natural landscape of Big Sur somehow corrupted the sanity of people who lived there.

The Women at Point Sur (Jeffers 1927b) continues with themes of fire, incest, family conflict, fanaticism, mysticism, and the ultimate force of nature. It also helped advance Jeffers's reputation as a poet of great power whose work, nevertheless, was tragic, morbid, and too 'dirty' for the polite reading public (Bennett 1966). The prelude to this book-length poem sets the scene with a great oil-tank fire in Monterey that lights up the whole region, an actual and long-remembered event of 1924 (Conway 2003, p. 115). The Reverend Dr Barclay abandons his church and family, comes to the coast, and is taken in to the 'gaunt' house of a poor farm family near the great rock promontory of Point Sur. Barclay, who is seeking a power beyond God, believes 'I have something fiery here that will burn the world down to significance.' He gathers a small band of followers who share his mission. Barclay's own family joins him, including his daughter, who he rapes, and his wife whom he torments. Among the other women of Point Sur is the lighthouse keeper's daughter (once pregnant by the farm-family head and despised for having had an abortion) and other relatives who have in common rape, incest, extra-marital affairs, homosexuality, or pregnancy. In the end, Barclay dies attempting to lead his disciples into a brush fire that he believes is the route to power beyond human insignificance.

Jeffers was surprised that his early efforts, although regarded as critical achievements, were also considered less spiritually transcendental than morbidly decadent (Bennett 1966). The works that followed grew richer in local color, plot, human drama, and clarity. *Cawdor* (1928) is the story of another farm family living on the steep Big Sur headlands who take in a blind father and his daughter (Fera) whose home has been destroyed by fire (again) (Hunt 2001). Living on Cawdor's farm are his grown sons (George and Hood) and two Mexican servants, farmhand Jesus Acanna and housekeeper Concha Rosas, the 'dark fat woman' who has moved into Cawdor's bed replacing his deceased wife. Cawdor lusts for the beautiful Fera, offering to care for her blind father if she will marry him. Fera agrees for the sake of her father's security. Soon, however, Hood returns from a hunting trip and the two young people develop a chaste attraction. Cawdor, however, believes that Fera and Hood are having an affair and shoots his son in a jealous rage. Believing that Hood is dead, Cawdor discovers that there was no affair and in his shame and misery puts out his own eyes.

Infidelity also figures prominently in *Thurso's Landing* (1932) (Hunt 2001) . The county road builders are working their way toward Thurso's Landing where the limekilns have been shut down, leaving Reeve Thurso and his wife Helen in precarious straits on their farm. Helen is forlorn, exasperated by Reeve's dogged attachment to the family's shrinking holding. 'Look how I'm stuck in a rut: do I have to live there? I'll not let the days of my life hang like a string of naughts between two nothings.' Then on the trail she encounters Rick Armstrong who works on the road-building crew. Rick is a vision who would swim in the ocean and emerge 'naked and very beautiful, all his blond body gleaming from the sea.' Helen and Rick make love and decide to run away together to the desert. Reeve pursues the couple, intends to kill Rick but spares him, and returns with the unresisting Helen in tow. Helen's chance for happiness is doomed, like the life of the coast itself. Reeve is paralyzed in a cable accident that robs him of his last asset of physical strength. In his weakened condition, Helen forgives him for his obstinacy. In a final act of compassion to relieve his pain she kills him by cutting his throat and herself with rat poison.

Give Your Heart to the Hawks (1933) comes near the end of the Big Sur cycle of poems and plays on familiar themes of sex and family violence but without the metaphysical power of earlier works (Hunt 2001). Lance Fraser accidentally kills his brother Michael by pushing him off a sea cliff during a drunken party. Michael had been having an affair with a neighbor girl, who is pregnant. She goes to San Francisco for an abortion and later in despair drowns herself. Lance is guilt ridden and haunted by Michael's ghost. Lance's wife Fayne, who is also pregnant, urges they leave the coast to escape the torments of their dysfunctional family. Father Fraser is an abusive parent and religious fanatic who prays for everyone's punishment. In the end, Lance leaps from the cliffs to his own death leaving Fayne and his unborn child to 'change the world.' Although the plot parallels the biblical story of Cain and Abel, Jeffers gives it a more decisive ending. As in all his work, Jeffers employs actors in real places and obvious references to local people. The scene is Sycamore Canyon, Pfeiffer ('Fraser') Point, and the eponymous Wreck Beach where a series of ships ran aground. Bootleg liquor that fuels the ill-fated party comes from Drunken Charlie's, a thinly disguised local moonshiner during prohibition. Similar to the fates of Lance and Michael Fraser, a number of lives were lost in accidents on the sea cliffs.

POETRY AND FACT

Are Jeffers's stories true? That is, though obviously fictional, are the poems based on real events? Do they accurately represent the time, place, and social circumstance? Do they provide historical information, evidence perhaps, not available in conventional primary sources? Let us take these questions in order moving from the issue of verisimilitude to interpretation.

In the first place, Jeffers drew freely from actual events in plotting his stories. In *The Loving Shepherdess* (1929) he writes of the following incident:

Three men came in the door without knocking, wherever they moved, water and black oil ran down. There'd been a shipwreck. I gave them the house, then one of them found the ax and began chopping firewood, another went back across wild rain to the fall of the hill … and saw the great, black, masted thing almost on shore, lying on its side … All that morning the people came up like ants, poor souls they were all so tired and cold, some hurt and some crying (Hunt 2001, pp. 343–344)

In December 1909, the schooner Majestic ran aground in a storm at Pfeiffer Point. The Majestic was part of the lumber fleet that worked the coast. Twenty-one members of the crew made it to shore and climbed a bluff:

It was wet and slippery, and it took the half drowned men nearly an hour to reach the top … A few miles away lay the house of John Pfeiffer, and they made for the place where they received breakfast, dry clothes, and transportation to Monterey … The sailors speak in the highest praise of the treatment they received at the Pfeiffer Ranch' (*Monterey Daily Cypress* 7 and 10 December 1909)

Devastating fires occur with regularity in Jeffer's stories. Monterey's great oil tank fire set the scene for *The Women at Point Sur.* On 12 April 1905, a range fire destroyed the Vasquez ranch in the same way Fera's homestead was ravaged in *Cawdor*. Like the Point Lobos family home in *Tamar*, Notley's Landing burned in November 1905 and Pfeiffer's Resort in April 1910. Jeffers's seeming preoccupation with destructive fires reflect the risks that people lived with.

Suicide was a personal risk that people confronted in a world of physical isolation, economic uncertainty, and family instability. It is difficult to determine whether the suicide *rate* was higher in Big Sur than elsewhere, but there is no doubt that the act was common. One of Jeffers's predecessors, the poet Nora May French, killed herself in Carmel to escape a love triangle (*Monterey Cypress* 15 November 1907). Jose Soberanes, son of a prominent ranching family, shot himself

after a marital quarrel (*Monterey Cypress* 10 September 1910). Lee Fook, an unemployed Chinese laborer who lived in a shack on the Cooper Ranch, was distraught over financial failure and attempted to save face by hanging himself before friends intervened (*Monterey Cypress* 18 January 1913).

Jeffers used similar circumstances in his stories and in several places inserted an actual suicide. In the poem 'Ruth Allison,' Manvil is the owner of a lumber mill and ship landing whose wife leaves him as his business is failing:

[W]hen she left the stars were dead to him. Yet he would not have died; but government, that justly indignant God, waxed hot against him for tan-oaks on the public lands despoiled … Therefore – he would have slept in prison else, with shame and loss beyond his power to bear – he ended, a revolver in his mouth. (*Californians*; Jeffers 1916, pp. 68–69)

The owner of Thurso's Landing in the poem of the same name chose 'to pop himself off because he went broke … Because the lime kilns failed and the lumber mill ran out of redwood' (Jeffers 1927a, p. 280). In fact, Godfrey Notley, owner with his brother William of Notley's Landing and mill, shot himself in a Santa Cruz saloon 'in a fit of temporary insanity, induced by overwork and nervous prostration.' (*Monterey New Era* 29 March 1905) There is no record of marital dissolution or government trouble preceding Notley's demise, but the economically available supply of tanbark was declining. Cutting trees on accessible public lands would have attracted the ire of government foresters. The business was in trouble and Notley's Landing was sold to a tanning company within a few years.

Events in *Thurso's Landing* turned on the disabling injury Reeve suffered while attempting to cut down a cable from the abandoned tramway. In fact, on 10 October 1900 (*Monterey New Era*) five years before his suicide, Notley himself was badly injured when repairing a ship mooring at the mill. On 16 May 1906 (*Monterey New Era*) Joseph Pomber, one of Notley's employees, was killed by a falling tree. Like suicides, industrial accidents are common and Jeffers wove them into his stories providing a grounded sense of the risks looming over frontier life.

Jeffers explains the source of these story ideas in his recollection of a 1914 trip down the coast:

> At Notley's Landing we saw the ruinous old lumber-mill (which blew down this present year, after having stood for so many) and heard a story about it. In the gorge of Mill Creek we passed under a rusted cable sagging to a stuck skip, and we were told about the lime-kilns up canyon, cold and forgotten with the forest growing over them... On a magnificent hillside opposite a mountain peak stood a comparatively prosperous farmhouse, apple trees behind it, and the man who lived there had killed his father with rat-poison and married his step-mother. (Lyon 1971, p. 10)

In *Thurso's Landing*, after the mercy killing of Reeve, Helen takes her own life with a dose of rat poison.

The factual bases of Jeffers's work goes well beyond incorporation of specific incidents. Dating from 1900, the pioneer community of Big Sur begins a fundamental shift in economy and culture. Although the timber and mining industries are failing, agriculture persists on the larger ranches, themselves expanding at the expense of small holders and former homesteaders. Even at this early date, the tourist economy is appearing with several resorts and campgrounds. Wealthy outsiders are purchasing ranches for their scenic appeal. The extensive Cooper Ranch prospered with a dairy, creamery, cattle, and even experimental oil drilling. The ranch defended its expanding borders with trespass warnings and lawsuits.

Jeffers is concerned with losers in the modernization process, with corrupt civilization and its powerless victims. Dispossession is at the root of family hardship (in *Californians*, *Thursos's Landing*, *Cawdor*, *The Women at Point Sur*). In 1906, the newspaper reported that Notley Company:

> [Has] taken the bark from nearly all the ranches in that neighborhood, and residents there estimate that there will be no more tan bark there for the next ten years [while at the same time] the coast section is becoming more popular yearly with summer visitors and many of the ranchers are building additions to their houses to accommodate summer visitors. (*Monterey New Era*, 27 September 1906)

The Monterey Lime Company closed its works at Mill Creek in June 1911.

Doubtless, one of the most controversial features of Jeffers's work is the frequent, even obsessive, use of rape and incest. Psychoanalytical interpretations of the work explain these preoccupations by Jeffers's childhood in the company of a distant father and nourishing mother or by his education in Greek and biblical classics (Everson, in Jeffers 1916). Obviously, too, Jeffers exploited sensational symbols of human self-indulgence against the background of all-powerful nature. Yet, according to biographer James Karman (1987, p. 41), 'Jeffers defended himself by saying that he drew his stories from events that occurred around him.'

In September 1922, George Leist was charged with felonious relations with his thirteen-year-old daughter, Victoria, who was pregnant at the time of the trial. Although Victoria's brother corroborated her claim of rape, their accounts differed and a jury voted for acquittal. A second trial charging a similar offense several months later resulted in a hung jury despite the presence in the courtroom of a delegation of forty women, in support of the child and prosecutor (*Monterey Cypress*, 22 and 23 October 1920).

In 1914, Esteban Apesteguia, a farmhand on the Cooper-Molera ranch was arrested and charged with the rape of sixteen-year-old Edna Ramos, the feeble-minded daughter of ranch foreman Angel Ramos. The affair had progressed for some time until Esteban began to worry about its consequences and regretfully confessed to his sister, who told the parents. Esteban pleaded guilty and offered to marry Edna, which her mother opposed but the judge considered reason for a probationary sentence (*Monterey Cypress*, 9 January, 14 March, and 5 April 1914).

Jeffers used incidents of this sort, and their public condemnation, to portray the gravity of sexual abuse. Pregnancies lead to suicides, rapes to homicides, and dysfunctional families to mutual destruction, often by fire. In *Tamar*, we hear the story of:

> Sylvia Vierra and her man [who] lived in the little white-washed farm-hut ... two years ago they had had much wine in the house, their friend Verdugo came avisiting, he being drunk on the raw plenty of wine they thought abused nine-year-old Mary, Sylvia's daughter, they struck him from behind and when he was down unmanned him with the kitchen knife, then plotted drunkenly – for he seemed to be dead – where to dispose of the body. [Riding by the hut later that evening, Tamar noticed a great bonfire and] saw by the firelight a man's feet hang out of the fire. (Hunt 2001, pp. 87–88)

The story is attributed to an eyewitness account of two girls from Point Lobos who passed it on to Una Jeffers (Bennett 1966, p. 109).

Among the most memorable stories of Big Sur is the tragic life of Mary Ellen Pfeiffer Dani. Mary Ellen (born 1866) was one of eight children of Big Sur pioneers Michael and Barbara Pfeiffer. She was raped at the age of twenty-two while at home alone and subsequently bore a child. Perhaps as a consequence of the rape, she suffered a mental breakdown:

> Miss Ellen Pfeiffer, daughter of Michael Pfeiffer who resides over on the coast below Monterey, was examined by Drs Tuttle and Trimmer last Monday, adjudged insane and committed to the asylum at Stockton. The unfortunate girl was the victim of a mysterious brutal outrage alone at the home of her parents about 3 months ago. (*Salinas Weekly Index*, 6 December 1888)

Following her confinement Mary Ellen returned home. She kept the child, suggesting perhaps that the father was not unknown (several men including two older brothers and her future husband lived in the area). Seven years later, she married Alvin Dani of another pioneer family and together they had a second child in 1897. But her life never righted itself. Suffering 'fits of despondency' she killed herself three years later – with strychnine poison (*Monterey New Era* 26 September 1900).

Jeffers's stories are steeped in actual events and although one may question the frequency with which suicide, incest, or insanity occurred, the effects of such traumatic events would have endured in experience and memory. They were psychologically salient in people's lived experience.

POETRY AND SOCIAL RELATIONS

So far, we have addressed the credibility of narratives, their consistency with the empirical world they purports to describe. The next question concerns their sociological coherence, how they square with the ways in which groups and societies characteristically function. Jeffers's work, I would submit, displays verisimilitude of people and place. But what does it say about less directly observable social processes? Does it describe an intelligible world?

The society Jeffers portrays, of course, is the rural American frontier at the turn of the twentieth century, a geographically distinct, isolated, sparsely populated coastal community in the throes of social and economic transition. For Jeffers, this is fundamentally a family-centered society. Other institutions existed: rural schools, markets, community gathering places, a Grange Hall – although, interestingly, no permanent churches. Households were too far from one another to provide the nucleus of a residential community. Schools within walking or wagon distance served only a handful of children. Dances at a ranch or mill brought people by horse and wagon who camped overnight before the long return trip. Most people spent most of their lives in the company of a nuclear family. This is borne out in the manuscript census that lists large-family households with occasional farm hands or relatives attached, but only a few single-male households or worker dormitories (one exception was the dozen or so Japanese laborers on the Cooper ranch). Everyone of Jeffers's stories centers on a nuclear (or surrogate) family and much of his drama involves family relations of love, jealousy, power, hate, sex, sacrifice, loss, and death. Indeed, the moral conflicts central to so many of the stories – incest, infidelity, and abandonment – represent the most basic threats to family survival. They are poems about family morality.

The family-centered character of the Big Sur community is corroborated in a rare diary kept by Ellen Jane Swetnam who lived with her family at Palo Colorado near Notley's Landing from 1897 to 1905 (Swetnam 1897–1904). Isaac Newton Swetnam, Ellen's husband, built their landmark three-storied house that Jeffers mentions in several poems. The Swetnams had eight children ranging in age from school age to adults when they were living at Palo Colorado. Ellen's diary is devoted to daily affairs: farm work, children's activities, making clothes, sickness, household accounts, and the comings and goings of local people. The death of one son killed in Cuba during the Spanish–American War is described in the diary. Another older daughter lives in San Francisco, makes good money, and sends some of it home. Family members visit between one another's homes frequently. Ellen keeps in touch with relatives in Kentucky and England but is absorbed on a daily basis with work and the children at home, two of which marry in these years. One daughter is epileptic and requires close attention, although she marries later. The daughters marry, divorce, and remarry with surprising regularity for the time, all the while maintaining a close loyalty to the family. Together Ellen, Isaac, the older children, and one or two hired men maintain the farm that supplies Notley's Mill and produces butter and honey for the market in Monterey, where Isaac takes their produce every two weeks. Ellen provides accommodation and meals for travelers, which adds to the comfortable family income. As the diary entries show, Ellen's life revolves around the family. Her only regular involvement outside the family is with the local school, where she plays a key role in hiring and firing teachers. Ellen is a proud and proper woman who would never mention sex or scandal in her diary, although she does chastise farm hands for drunkenness and suitors who she thinks are no

good for her girls. Robinson Jeffers and Ellen Swetnam each describe a world that exists in and through the family, albeit a family that is plagued by intrigue in one case and consumed by work in the other.

Jeffers also sketches a broader context of the stories, a world beyond the family that limits and influences the actors. Although isolated and struggling economically, the families have links to the wider society. The coast road is penetrating their community in *Thurso's Landing*, bringing new threats and opportunities. World War I, which Jeffers opposed, is taking the young men in several stories: Tamar's brother–lover, Lee, wants to join the army; Reeve Thurso served in France with his brother Mark who limps from a permanent war injury. Wild youngsters escape to San Francisco and Monterey, the girls for abortions and the boys for boredom-relieving lust, 'He'd put away the boyish jets of wickedness, loves with dark eyes in Monterey back-streets, liquor and all its fellowship, what was left to live for but the farm-work?' (*Tamar* 2001, p. 29, (Hunt 2001))

The facts support this picture. Monterey newspapers report regularly on the state of the coast road describing accidents due to poor conditions, surveys and contracts let for improvements, the thrice-weekly twenty-six mile stagecoach trip from Monterey to the Sur post office and its gradual replacement by the automobile road. Telephone service arrives in 1912. Local boys go off to war and the conflict in Europe competes with local news. Ellen Swetnam's diary shows an impressive interest in international affairs from Cuba to the Philippines and South Africa. Yet it is in the family that these influences come together.

Closer to home, Big Sur families lived among neighboring farmers and a working class of Hispanic laborers. Jeffers's stories accurately reflect these social facts, which can also be inferred from the manuscript census. Itemized households often contain a wife and husband, three to six minor children, as well as the Hispanic 'hired man' or female 'servant.' Several Hispanic ranch owners boasted ancestry and social status dating from the colonial era. Jeffers's eye sweeps the social landscape. In *Cawdor*, Concha Rosas, the 'dark, fat … Indian-blooded woman' is housekeeper and mistress, but always inferior to the young white Fera, who replaces her in Cawdor's harsh affections. When Fera first notices Concha she asks, 'Who's that wide-lapped dark o' the moon.' Thurso's farm employed 'the dark Spanish woman Olvidia' and the mestizo Johnny Luna. The 'Indian house-girl, Maruca' appears in *The Women at Point Sur*. In that story, and in several others, Onorio Vasquez has a farm in the hills and appears often as a mystic or good Samaritan.

Jeffers captures the nuances of race relations in California scarcely fifty years after its acquisition from Mexico. Hispanics had been the governors and landowners until immigrant whites steadily supplanted them. Indians were absorbed through intermarriage, mostly with Hispanics, although in a few cases with Europeans. Over time, Hispanics and mestizo offspring formed the working class whose racial and occupational status placed them at the bottom of the social ladder. Yet there were qualifications. Some Hispanic or intermarrying families like the Cooper-Molera clan were among the landed upper class. Others lived along side or within white households. Race and class interact in the allocation of social honor.

California of the late nineteenth century had a race problem centering less on Hispanics than on the Chinese and Japanese who entered the country as laborers and stayed to become successful agriculturalists and merchants despite various legislative exclusion acts. Jeffers seldom touches on Asians, perhaps because they hardly affected Big Sur. Yet the Asian question loomed large in the surrounding society. Newspapers used unabashed racial slurs, reporting 'chinks get in bad' for gambling (*Monterey Cypress* 15 September 1913), 'Japs want school of their own' (*Monterey Cypress* 2 May 1913), or 'Nigger Sue arrested' for selling liquor (*Monterey New Era* 30 July 1907). It is another measure of Big Sur's insularity that racial distinctions were played out in the ambivalent Hispanic relations rather than

exhibiting common vitriolic attitudes toward Asians and Blacks.

This was a family-centered and relatively egalitarian society; a network of similarly endowed farm families who knew one another sent their children to small local schools, and gathered occasionally for dances and the Fourth of July barbeque. Jeffers correctly stresses the relative autonomy of families, but he also situates their actions in a distinct social context:

[E]very week-end night was dancing and the wail of violins at Hanlon's place. From Manvil's lumber camp, and from the lime-kiln on the Mill Creek hills, men came; and many ranches roundabout, or ranchers' sons, with joy forgathered there to celebrate the term of week's toil. (*Californians*; Jeffers 1916, p. 58)

A celebratory dance begins the ill-fated affair in *Thurso's Landing*. Inter-family romances and infidelities have tragic effects in *Tamar* and *Cawdor*. But families also helped one another in shipwrecks and accidents. The homeless are taken in, albeit with unfortunate results.

Interfamilial conflict is a more characteristic Jeffers theme. Claire, *The Loving Shepherdess*, explains to Onorio Vasquez:

[T]he neighbors were never our friends. Oh, they feared my father; sometimes they threatened our shepherd, a Spanish man who looked like you … we live lonely. (Hunt 2001, p. 338)

Reeve Thurso quarrels with the road crew that has broken his fence. In fact, Ellen Swetnam's diary records persistent conflicts with neighbors (Swetnam, 1847–1904). Cows belonging to the neighboring Smith family break fences and get into their pasture. Ellen suspects poisoning when several of their hogs die mysteriously; her suspicions were grounded. Isaac Swetnam and his son-in-law Horatio Parmelee advertised a $500 reward for information leading to the arrest of anyone poisoning livestock (*Monterey New Era* 22 December 1900). Farm animals were maimed and poisoned in disputes among ranchers (*Monterey Cypress* 1 April 1909).

For her part, Ellen is angry over troubles at Palo Colorado school. Smith and Swetnam children quarreled often and Ellen blamed the teacher, with whom she had differences. School politics, the hiring and firing of teachers, was a persistent source of friction and Ellen's uncharacteristic anger. Although Jeffers makes no mention of schools, his overriding emphasis on conflict is accurate.

Finally, family and local society are ruled by Jeffers's all-powerful force of nature. Storms and fires put an end to the feeble schemes of men and women. Rock and ocean are the only permanent elements of the world. In *The Coast Road*, Jeffers compares the growing penetration of the outside world to:

> ... an old drunken whore, pathetically eager to impose the seduction of her fled charms [he then asks], Where is our consolation? [and his answer is] beauty beyond belief, the heights glimmer in the sliding cloud, the great bronze gorge-cut sides of the mountains tower up invincibly, not the least hurt by this ribbon of road carved at the sea-foot. (Jeffers 1927a, p. 581)

Big Sur, in fact, is an awesome landscape that has captured the admiration and fear of residents from the early homesteaders to inspired artists. The weather is always problematic: fog, gloom, wind, and storms alternating with brilliant panoramic vistas. People were at the mercy of nature. 'Demented man lost in mountains succumbs to cold and starvation' (*Monterey New Era* 20 May 1903) could be the fate of a Jeffers character. Nature ruled. The steep canyons that once provided bark, timber, and limestone stopped providing. Fires swept the hills and landslides cutoff road access. Wagons and automobiles went over unstable cliffs and bridges collapsed:

> Big flood at Sur, houses are washed away and others wrecked – roads almost impassable ... the Sur post office was washed up against the hillside ... piles of driftwood are wedged up against the Palo Colorado school. (*Monterey Daily Cypress* 26 March 1907)

Although Jeffers turned nature into a metaphysical premise, he did not exaggerate the risks and uncertainties it posed in people's daily lives.

CONCLUSION

The case study provides a frame and context within which a variety of evidence may be fitted together, compared, evaluated, and interpreted. Conventional sources and poetry validate one another; census data describing large, isolated extended families fit literary accounts of family morality. Newspaper reports of natural disasters provide a foundation for poetry about a threatening world. Combined and compared the evidence generates an understanding of the lived experience that surpasses any singular standpoint, no matter how factual.

This case study supports two propositions. First, Jeffers's poetry recounts the experience of real people and actual events affecting their lives. This literature is true, if not necessarily representative of local life. Second, the poetry captures the social relations that pattern local life the role of families, neighbors, race, and the environment. The poems are about a known world, they reflect that world in believable ways, and they are consistent with the facts. Yet they are neither themselves facts nor necessarily the best source for discovering facts. What, then, is the point?

Chevalier distinguishes between facts, meaning demographic evidence, and opinion embodied in literature. Opinion is the perception by contemporary nineteenth-century Parisians of the crime, disease, and poverty that official statistics documented. For historical purposes, fact and opinion are equally important and complementary. Evidence of opinion is 'obtained from the comparison which we cannot fail to establish between the social facts a demographic assessment identifies as having been important and the description of them given deliberately, or, far more often, involuntarily in what they [the writers] cannot help saying' (Chevalier 1973, p. 57). Demographic facts enter social history when they are experienced and transmitted as opinion. Novelists do exactly this, sometimes involuntarily (e.g. unavoidably including accounts of hazardous Parisian sewers or Big Sur sea cliffs), which makes their novels meaningful to contemporaries and therefore a unique source on the opinion of an era.

How does this work in the case of Big Sur? First, although Jeffers was the region's most prolific writer, he was not the only one and he was not alone in focusing on the perils of life on the coast. In Gertrude Atherton's (1897) novel set at Point Lobos, Patience Sparhawk's once-beautiful mother is widowed, becomes a drunk, and accidentally sets fire to her house where she dies while passed out. John Steinbeck's *To a God Unknown* (1935) tells how farmers in the Salinas Valley are saved from drought when the gods of nature (known to Indians) in the Big Sur mountains are propitiated by human sacrifice. The classic novel of the region, *The Stranger in Big Sur* by Lillian Bos Ross (1942), ends happily only after Hanna, the mail-order bride, is raped by her backwoods husband who then has an affair with hot-blooded Maria (whose Spanish–Indian ancestry excluded her as a potential wife), and the couple reconcile when Hanna has a child. Literary opinion about life in Big Sur consistently stressed hardship, threats to families, race, sex, and violent death.

Returning to the general question that initiated this inquiry, what is the value of poetry as historical evidence? And specifically, what does Jeffers tell us that we would not have known from a study of conventional sources alone? Historian Keith Hopkins analyzed ancient fables as a method for deriving evidence about Roman slavery. The significance of these stories is found in the emphasis they placed on:

> ... the boundaries of morality, or what one can call the penumbra of moral ambiguity. [The stories] help us map out Roman attitudes to morality, just as they helped Romans themselves to sort out what was allowable, legitimate, and praiseworthy. Individual stories do not tell us directly what was normal, but they do indicate which abnormalities met with overt disapproval, and for these purposes... it does not matter so much whether these stories were true. It matters more that they were told and retold. (Hopkins 1993, p. 5)

Jeffers poetry is consistent with the facts of time and place – he was there and knew what he was writing about. Yet, beyond that, Jeffers also tells us about the normative order that prevailed in this rural community, the morality illuminated by the fears and sanctions the defined deviant conduct. Jeffers may overdo, say, the frequency of incest, but we know that it was a fact and we know that it was feared in an isolated, family-centered society. Similarly, sexual anxieties, jealousies, and infidelities were especially threatening and proscribed acts. We learn of them through literature rather than from memoirs in which such taboo events are detectable but also suppressed. Jeffers talked about them in a way that conveyed their potent effect.

Other discoveries flow from this interpretation. The nuclear family was the center and principal arena of people's lives. Neighbors shared in communal activities but also experienced frequent conflict. Racial considerations suffused local society, albeit in nuanced ways. The physical environment dominated daily life to an extent difficult to imagine today. Morality loomed large in the regulation of a family-centered world and its characteristic forms of deviance. Incest and infidelity were the major crimes people worried about rather than the robbery or assault that might preoccupy city residents. The dark side for Jeffers is a special kind of darkness. This climate of opinion is not evident in conventional historical sources or even in personal memoirs that tend to silence any scandal that might affect families or come back to harm the writer.

Certain principles of case-study methodology emerge from this inquiry. Literature is valuable as historical evidence when authors do 'research' – collect data, observe people and places, talk to informants, or otherwise engage in fieldwork. Robinson and Una Jeffers were diligent in this regard. Literary work is credible when consistent with other fictional accounts of the time and place. Jeffers is believable in part because he echoes Atherton, Steinbeck, Ross, and Miller. Literary evidence can be validated when it allows comparison of fact and opinion, when the literary work elaborates on events gleaned from conventional sources such as census, newspaper, or economic data. Finally, evidentiary literature typically explores the normative world, the rules that govern conduct and the reaction to rule breaking. These are some of the tests that may be applied to literature as valid historical evidence.

The case-study method can incorporate analyses of literature because cases and stories both deal with characters, places, events, and narratives. Poetry of the sort Jeffers wrote is also ethnography with many of the empirical properties one finds in, say, Malinowski's account of society among Pacific islanders. The case study provides a coherent picture of a small world, a story limited in time and space. Yet the part reveals things about the whole in which it is contained.

The story of Big Sur, a hundred-mile strip along California's coast in the early twentieth century, goes some distance toward explaining the nature and hazards of frontier settlement, the conflicts pervading our heroic pioneer myth, the trials homesteaders suffered, the rapid disappearance of their hard-won autonomy, their bitter experience of war and insanity. Laurel Thatcher Ulrich's great book *A Midwife's Tale* shows how the diary of a pioneer woman in eighteenth-century Maine 'connects to several prominent themes in the social history of the early Republic.' But, she says, it does more than that. 'By restoring a lost substructure of eighteenth-century life, it transforms the nature of the evidence upon which much of the history of the period has been written' (Ulrich 1991, p. 27). The same can be said of Jeffers's ethnography. It charts the substructure of life among pioneer homesteaders, the experience from which Western history is built. It demonstrates the physical and moral hazards of frontier life, the meanness of rural society, and the rapid economic transition that absorbed 'the West' within a few decades of its invention. The grand narratives of Western America are transformed when set against the texture of daily life that is perhaps best captured by the poet.

NOTES

1. For critical comments on earlier drafts, I am grateful to Howard Becker.

REFERENCES

Arnold, J.H. 2000 *History: A Very Short Introduction.* Oxford: Oxford University Press.

Atherton, G. 1897 *Patience Sparhawk and Her Times.* New York: John Lane.

Bennett, M.B. 1966 *The Stone Mason of Tor House: The Life and Work of Robinson Jeffers.* Los Angeles, CA: The Ward Ritchie Press.

Breschini, G.S. and Haversat, T. 2004 *The Esselen Indians of the Big Sur Country: The Land and the People.* Salinas, CA: Coyote Press.

Chevalier, L. 1973 *Laboring Classes and Dangerous Classes in Paris During the First Half of the Nineteenth Century.* Princeton, NJ: Princeton University Press.

Clark, D.T. 1991 *Monterey County Place Names: A Geographical Dictionary.* Carmel Valley, CA: Kestrel Press.

Conway, J.D. 2003 *Monterey: Presidio, Pueblo, and Port.* Monterey, CA: City of Monterey.

Davis, N.Z. 1983 *The Return of Martin Guerre.* Cambridge, MA: Harvard University Press.

Ginzburg, C. 1982 *The Cheese and the Worms: The Cosmos of a Sixteenth-Century Miller.* New York: Penguin.

Gregory, J.N. 1989 *American Exodus: The Dust Bowl Migration and Okie Culture in California.* New York: Oxford University Press.

Hopkins, K. 1993 'Novel evidence for Roman slavery' *Past and Present* 138 (February): 1–13.

Hughey, R.K. and Hughey, B. 1996 'Jeffers Country revisited: beauty without price' *Robinson Jeffers Newsletter* 98/99 (Spring and Summer): 9–81.

Hunt, T. 2001 *The Selected Poetry of Robinson Jeffers.* Stanford, CA: Stanford University Press.

Jeffers, R. 1916 *Californians.* Introduction by W. Everson. New York: Macmillian (reprinted 1971, Cayucos Books).

Jeffers, R. 1927a *The Selected Poetry of Robinson Jeffers.* New York: Random House.

Jeffers, R. 1927b *The Women at Point Sur and Other Poems.* New York: Liveright.

Jeffers, U. 1932 'Letter to Lawrence Clark Powell'. Reprinted in A.N. Ridgeway 1962 *The Selected Letters of Robinson Jeffers, 1897–1962.* Baltimore, MD: The Johns Hopkins Press.

Karman, J. 1987 *Robinson Jeffers: Poet of California.* San Francisco: Chronicle Books.

Lyon, H. 1971 *Jeffers Country: The Seed Plots of Robinson Jeffers' Poetry.* San Francisco: Scrimshaw Press.

Mandel, E. 1984 *Delightful Murder: A Social History of the Crime Story.* Minneapolis, MN: University of Minnesota Press.

Miller, H. 1957 *Big Sur and the Oranges of Hieronymus Bosch.* New York: New Directions Paperbook.

Norman, J. 2004 *Images of America: Big Sur.* Charleston, SC: Arcadia.

Powell, L.C. 1940 *Robinson Jeffers: The Man and His Work.* Pasadena, CA: San Pasqual Press.

Ross, L.B. 1942 *The Stranger in Big Sur.* New York: Morrow (republished 1985, Santa Barbara, CA: Capra Press).

Steinbeck, J. 1935 *To a God Unknown.* New York: Bantam Books.

Swetnam, E.J. 1897–1904 Unpublished diary. Big Sur, CA: Big Sur Historical Society.

Trouillot, M-R. 1995 *Silencing the Past: Power and the Production of History.* Boston: Beacon Press.

Ulrich, L.T. 1991 *A Midwife's Tale: The Life of Martha Ballard Based on Her Diary, 1785–1812.* New York: Vintage Books.

Walton, J. 2001 *Storied Land: Community and Memory in Monterey.* Berkeley, CA: University of California Press.

Watt, I. 1957 *The Rise of the Novel.* Berkeley: University of California Press.

White, H. 1987 *The Content and the Form: Narrative Discourse and Historical Representation.* Baltimore, MD: Johns Hopkins University Press.

22

Cultural Case Studies

Albert J. Bergesen

INTRODUCTION

With case studies of cultural objects, like painting and sculpture, the object's meaning is usually thought to be the product of some interpretative grid, world view, set of assumptions, received categories, and so forth, brought by the person who views or studies the case.

This opinion is rooted in German idealist philosophy with the central argument being that art objects are comprised of material things – paint, marble, wood, chalk, and so forth – and these non-human entities are incapable of emitting human meanings in and of themselves. Everyone recognizes, though, that art has a human meaning, and so the default solution has been to locate that meaning in the apprehending, or interpretative eye, of the beholder. Since that person is part and parcel of some society, class, gender, or race, meaning is pushed ever further from the art object itself, for what a painting means now becomes a matter of one's class position, national origin, religious affiliation, and so forth.

The first assumption of what an artistic case study means, then, is that art object

meaning resides within the interpretative grid of the observer; not the object's internal structure. The second assumption is that variation in such meaning, since all paintings don't mean the same thing, resides in variation in the interpretative grid the audience brings to apprehending the art object. There are a number of dimensions to such variation, from civilizational differences at the most macro level down to national, class, regional, city, family, and personal biographical factors at the more micro level. There is also a hierarchical dimension, particularly tied to economic class, as seen in Bourdieu's (1984) concept of the habitus, or an internalized class-based interpretative grid that yields different meanings, or distinctions, about art objects.

While seeming reasonable on the surface, this position is, in fact, a mistaken notion. Art objects, as case studies, are not neutered objects incapable of emitting any meaning on their own. They don't just lie there awaiting interpretation from a socially constructed grid designed to meet the needs of some class, nation, gender, race, or other social category. They emit meaning on their own, independent of the interpretative grids that are laid upon them. This does not mean there is no social factor in art objects, it is just that the social enters into the art object in its very construction, not in the secondary act of its apprehension. The eye sees what it must see, which means nature is harnessed by social forces in the form, or structural configuration, of the art object itself. Art, or for that matter any cultural object, isn't just physical material; a painting isn't just paint; sculpture isn't just marble; dance isn't just a human body in motion; a building isn't just glass, steel, and cement; and music isn't just sounds. They are those, of course, and on that account Mannheim (1952) and Panofsky's (1955) labeling theories are correct. But what they failed to grasp is that these basic vocubularic elements are structured by style grammars into larger wholes and it is that that the eye apprehends. Their eye doesn't see just paint or marble, but a structured painting or piece of sculpture; we don't experience just steel and cement in a building, but architecturally carved space; and we don't just watch a body move, but we watch a choreographically structured set of movements.

We know from linguistics that syntactic structure affects sentence meaning independent of the meaning of specific words. For example, the words *bites*, *dog*, *man* are the same in sentences 1–3, yet their meanings are entirely different, as seen below:

(1) Dog bites man.
(2) Man bites dog.
(3) Bites man dog.

On analogy with an art object, like a painting, a sentence is a structured complex of elements, like the above words and phrases. Structural complexes (1) and (2) emit different meanings, and (3) has no meaning at all, yet all three are comprised of the same basic elements, the three words; *bites, man, dog*. Variation in emitted meaning (dog bites man vs. man bites dog) therefore, does not arise from the different meanings of the constituent elements (the words); but from their order, structure, syntax, or to put it in artistic terms, their style. That is, we often speak of the language of art, or of art grammar,

or style syntax, but it is just as reasonable to speak of sentence style as it is of a painting's pictorial syntax.

Now, let's try a thought experiment. Suppose there is cultural grid, or interpretative framework brought to these sentences whose content states: 'dogs biting men'. When applied to (1) we can say that the resultant interpretation is reasonably derived from that cultural grid. But when that grid is applied to (2), it fails to explain the meaning emitted by that structural complex, for here what is said is that 'men bite dogs'. Nor does it help for (3) which doesn't say anything at all. Therefore, it appears to be variation in form, style, composition (art terms), or in syntax and grammar (linguistic terms), that constrains the kinds of meanings these entities can emit, and bringing a cultural grid does not override the internal structure of the cultural entity like these sentences.

Now, consider another case. Let's apply the general principles from our sentence examples to a couple of paintings. We again begin with identical sets of constituent elements; not the words *man*, *bites*, *dog*, but the subject matter, *Jesus*, *disciples*, *a table*, and *a supper*. Like the sentence case, let us now assemble these identical constituent elements into two paintings: (4) Leonardo da Vinci's *The Last Supper* (1495–98) and (5) Tintoretto's *The Last Supper* (1594). Structural complexes (4) and (5) have the same basic elements whose meaning is unchanged (Jesus, table, etc.), just like the three words in the dog bites man example. But when they are arranged differently they emit two different style meanings that everyone recognizes. The da Vinci last supper emits the style meaning High Renaissance, while the Tintoretto emits the meaning of Mannerist style. Here we have the same subject matter, that is, the same vocubularic elements, yet one is considered an instance of the Mannerist style and the other of the High Renaissance style. Importantly, neither style is understood to be the result of cultural grids brought to bear upon these structured objects to make them yield the meaning High Renaissance or Mannerism. The different style meanings arise instead from the internal structure of the paintings, like the internal structure of sentences (1–3). In linguistics we know rules for arranging basic elements affect the meaning emitted by sentence objects, but in art we mistakenly think meaning is brought to the art object. But in fact it is emitted from the object, and further varies with variation in the internal structure of the object, whether that is called the grammar, or style, of art. But, from Mannheim (1952) through Panofsky (1955), Danto (1964), Dickie (1974), Becker (1982), and Bourdieu (1984), a consensus has emerged that the meaning of art is almost wholly dependent upon what global views, iconologies, cultural grids, or artworld interpretations brought to the assumed neutral form of the art object.

In the face of this consensus I argue the opposite: there is something inherent in the various forms of art that determine which kinds of meanings they will signify. There are two implications of this for case-study analysis. First, the relation between the specific case and the thing it purportedly represents is not an independent relationship, and second, variation in meaning derives not from applied interpretative grids, but from the internal structure and other properties of the case study itself. This is strongest for art case studies, but I suspect the point is general. Sociology, and other disciplines as well, have traditionally assumed that the frame, the external imposed interpretation, is what gives the case-study art object its meaning. In some cases this is no doubt true. But such a social construction perspective, while initially formulated to overcome what appeared as fixed essentialist assumptions about types of persons, groups, and art objects, has now become a fetter to scientific analysis. Advances in linguistics provide a challenge to the purported cultural turn in art theory. Internal structure, here in the case of something like an art grammar or style syntax, constrains the range of possible meanings.

The key point is that in art, form and meaning co-vary, and by possible extension, other case-study structures, and what they represent, may also systematically co-vary. While the focus here is upon form and meaning in painting, the point about a case and its larger meaning co-variation is general. Given different art syntactical forms, then, yes, some art will have its meaning arise outside the art object, whether that larger cultural context of interpretation is called a *weltanschauung*, iconology, the grid of Bourdieuian distinction, or a Becker (1982), Danto (1964), Dickie (1974) *Art-worlds*. The key point is that these are interchangeable ways of saying the same thing: some art forms are context-dependent for their meaning, but in other art forms contextual interpretation is less necessary, for such forms speak their own interpretation.

This is accomplished through the pictorial language of an elaborated code, where the extensiveness of art vocabulary and art rule flexibility is such that the form can express its own meaning without relying upon the larger artworld, institutional or societal, context. The forms that require such context are more abstract, minimal and austere ones. They function as restricted codes of visual expression, unable to signify any particular signification and thereby rely upon their social context to fill in the explicitness of which they are morphologically incapable of signifying.

This necessary role of contextual interpretation for particular kinds of forms can be represented a general model of form/meaning relationships. Aesthetic communication is composed of two elements: the medium of communication, the explicit vocabulary and syntax of the art object, and the message, the semantics, the meaning the form emits. Medium or message reminds of McLuhan, but the distinction is general and also appears as Saussure's signifier/signified, along with the form or meaning distinction in art history. Semiotically, this means a signifier is variable; it is not a fixed symbol pointing to, or embodying, a fixed meaning. This is because signifiers have a grammar or syntax that allows for a variety of combinatorial possibilities, and like syntactic shifts within sentences, they yield variable meanings (Bergesen, 2005). We have tended to think of signifier with its signification as a one-to-one relationship, but variation in the form of the signifier results in variation in the types of significations produced.

From this point of view the semiotic process is deeply sociological, for signifiers in their extremely abstract form are context-dependent and require a large web of societal understandings to produce their meaning or signification. To visualize the balance between form and added interpretation, imagine a playground teeter-totter that balances on a fulcrum point in the middle. On the right hand side is the form, the explicit component (pictorial vocabulary or syntax), the Wölfflin (1994, 1966, 1932) side, and on the other is the meaning side, the interpretive component of art, the more subjective Panfosky and Mannheim side. Both sides are continuous variables. The left hand interpretation side varies from interpretations that are more literal, specific, objective, and factual, to being more concerned with more generalized universal ideas. It is the difference between what the subject matter is in itself (objective meaning), and what it symbolically represents in more philosophical and theoretical terms (iconological meaning). The right hand Wölfflinian side also varies from being composed of a narrower pool of pictorial vocabulary and more rigid, strict, formal syntactic rules of art to a wider pool of pictorial vocabulary and more flexible, loose, and supple rules of art composition (Bernstein 1975).

The pool of vocabulary for art is the range of colors, shapes, textures, and materials that comprise the basic building blocks to be structured by the rules of art, the pictorial syntax, which yield the visual configurations known as styles of art (Bergesen 2000, 1991a, 1991b, 1979). Formalism in art theory is not just a question of identifying static eternal shapes, but specifying the changing syntactic rules of art codes, which clearly shift over time in response to different historical circumstances. Wölfflin's distinctions between Linear or painterly, planar or recessional, clear or unclear, open or closed, and multiplicity or unity style rules can be considered something like art's grammar employed in the act of producing meaningful artist outputs (paintings, sculptures, etc).

These rules of art, as procedures and moral constraints, are also exercises of power and control, and as such have direct implication for the symbolic reproduction of social hierarchy and domination.

POWER OF FORM

Social power is essential for understanding the operation of Wölfflin's various aspects of form, which are not neutral but embody the exercise of power over our visual imagination. To understand this we need to realize there is a hierarchy of principles involved in the production of art objects that begins with the basic act of separation and division. Establishing visual boundaries that define shapes and separate colors is the most basic act of manufacturing pictorial representations, and the theoretical concept of line (where the boundary of one stops and another begins) is principally utilized for this end. In art grammatical terms, line, as a syntactic device, represents a rule, or procedure that structures and orders visual composition. That is, line is a visual portal through which social power is manifest in visual form. To bound some figures and start others, or to separate forms from each other, are all the visual responsibilities of line. At the most basic level if one figure isn't separable from another then that form doesn't exist, as it cannot be differentiated and thereby brought into visual existence. Also, when the eye gravitates to line as the most important reality for defining a subject's pictorial existence, this is an exercise of symbolic power, and line becomes an act of control. Often legitimated as the experience of beauty, symmetry, and balance, as in classic art, line visually orders consciousness in a pleasing and calm way, and just as raw power is stabilized in human relations by being translated into authority relations, so too in the realm of visual relations is power translated into the visually stable and enduring peace and tranquility that are the clear firm lines of classic art.

Conversely, a weakening of line is a weakening of the power to order and control vision. When line wavers, wobbles, or is established in a more impressionistic way through a looser gestural application of pigment, the power to control and order content's definition is weakened and relaxed. Subject matter, released from the grip of line, now asserts its own interests, as figures and shapes seem more animated from within rather than defined from their outer borders by the grid of line. With a weakening of line, principles of order recede, composition loosens, and subjects are less well-held in place, a condition Wolfflin called the *painterly style of representation*. But these are not so much separate modes of expression as opposite ends of a single variable of the power to bound and define, and thereby bring into visual existence content and subject matter. Wolfflin's style distinction between the linear and the painterly, then, is sociologically the strong presence of, or absence of, an ability to bound form in a clear and orderly fashion. Linear or painterly represents opposite ends of a form-bounding variable, which reflects the presence and absence, of power to control visual representation. The stronger and more powerful the syntactic rule, the more clearly delimited the figures within the overall form; the weaker the rule, the more vague, unclear, and impressionistic the form's visual definition.

A second syntactic rule is plane, the ordered placement of shapes and figures parallel to the picture plane. This is also an exercise of power and control. To order forms on a single plane means they have to be willfully moved, placed, and arranged in pictorial space in a very formal way. When this rule is in operation shapes and figures are not allowed to recede into the picture space, but are arranged next to each other on a singular plane, or for foreground-background effects, placed before and behind each other on a series of planes. Painterly forms could, in principle, be aligned along such a plane, but planetric ordering is greatly facilitated by line which creates more discrete figures that can serve as pictorial building blocks that are then ordered side by side. Things more clearly defined and separate from each other are more easily separable

entities to be visually grasped and laterally aligned. When the plane principle weakens or loosens, shapes are now free to slip and slide within the picture space. They can move behind each other, be partially hidden, and recede back into the picture. The weakening of the power of planetric ordering is Wolfflin's recessional motion, but plane and recession like linear and painterly are but opposite ends of a single power variable.

In general, then, form is most fundamentally defined by establishing a boundary. When the power of art rules are strong, the separating and defining boundary is a clear and precise line. When the rule weakens, the line wavers, shivers, and looses its form-creating ability, appearing as a more impressionistic sense of the beginning and ending of subject matter, rather than a more firmly established edge. The same is true with spatial location. When the rule is strong forms are placed side by side along a single dimension or plane. When the rule is weak, forms are free to move, recede, and advance, forward and backward, in the picture space. The visual mooring of shape along the planetric row is now gone, and shapes float, mix, recombine, and interconnect, receding and advancing at will, without the power of a planetric grid to order their position and assign their place. From these two basic rules – to bound (line) and assign place (plane) – the other rules of Wolfflin are largely derivative, but still part of the overall set of syntax that makes up the basic rules of art.

Here is the key point. Variation along the line and plane axes is associated with variation along the meaning axes from literal or objective to general or theoretical (Bergesen 1984). A larger pool of artistic vocabulary is required to visually sculpt meaning specificity because the artistic ability to articulate explicit, literal, and factual meaning requires flexibility in both line and plane. Rule relaxation manifests as painterly recessional forms, drawing from a larger pool of pictorial vocabulary is the pre-condition for more specific realistic representations. In this case the artwork's form is carrying more of the semantic burden for the overall meaning of the composition and so the necessity of added interpretation or theory is less. A seventeenth century Dutch painting of domestic life is just that an objective primary meaning. Jackson Pollock's drips of paint, though, are interpreted as the essence of the human condition. With the Dutch art we see great visual elaboration and little larger meaning; with Abstract Expressionism we see little visual elaboration yet greater meaning.

This syntactic capacity to depict lifelike representations not only makes additional interpretation less necessary, but actually cordons off the possibility of larger generalized interpretation. Realism reduces its interpretative capacity to the boundary of its innate forms. Theoretically, realism in art overrides, or blocks out, any larger general iconological interpretation. As is well known, realistic art has long been noted as being devoid of larger theoretical implication. The northern realism of seventeenth-century Flemish, Dutch, and German art is more devoid of principles of art theory and larger ideas of cosmic harmony, symmetry, and balance than the more classic styling of Renaissance Italian art. Michelangelo disapproved of Flemish art for its straightforward reproduction of nature saying, 'the green grass of the fields, the shadow of trees, and rivers and bridges, which they call landscape … all this … is done without reason or art, without symmetry or proportion, without skillful selection or boldness, and finally, without substance or vigor … for good painting is nothing but a copy of the perfections of God and a recollection of his painting' (quoted in Nochlin 1985).

Michelangelo is not alone in faulting realism for its lack of principles of selectivity, its ordinary subject matter, and its failure to follow more classic rules and principles of painting. From the Neoclassical revival in the eighteenth century to the sparse abstraction of twentieth-century Abstract Expressionism and Minimalism, clear, clean, simple, austere, minimalistic, and abstract expression in art has been praised above the particularistic, literal, factual, and realistic representations of everyday reality (Greenberg 1939, 1940, 1969).

There is an interesting irony here. The weight of form results in lighter interpretations, and the lighter the form, the heavier serious, more theoretical, and more absolute the interpretation. Elaborately detailed Dutch realism can be dismissed as just a representation or copy of real life, whereas Jackson Pollock's drips of paint off a stick has been interpreted as the existential angst of the nuclear age, the equal of the Old Masters, and a revolutionary challenge to the very direction of art itself. This is a very profound set of ideas and interpretations to be taken from such a few drips of paint, and, on the other side, not much implication is drawn from all the intricacy, composition, coloring, perspective, and drawing that goes into a Dutch realist painting. But this is the way it has to be: minimal form cannot specify any particular interpretation, and the more abstract that form becomes, the deeper into the culture are the interpretations that are read into it. There is, then, a systematic relation between degree of abstraction and social distance of the added on interpretation. To see this start with an explicit realism in form. In this compositional situation, meaning is virtually co-terminus with form, which is why Mannheim called it *objective meaning*. Meaning and material art object are one. Next, reduce, restrict, minimalize, and abstract the form, and the meaning now begins to inch away from the form, and begins to be added on by the social institutions at an every greater social distance from the artist or art object in direct proportion to the abstractedness of the form. At a close distance meaning is added by the world of artists, galleries, dealers, agents, and museums (the Becker/Danto *Art-Worlds*), which is a broader social web than the form (the art object) *per se*. At another point of distance comes class or region as a source of meaning imputation (Bourdieu's class-bound grids) that are invoked to supply interpretation. Finally, there is the most basic, general, and universal religious-philosophical assumptions of the trans-societal, global, or the civilizational sort, like Mannheim's *weltanschauung* or Panofsky's iconology

(Bergesen 2007). In general ever more abstraction in form yields ever larger scale of social structure as the foundation for the ever more general interpretation.

The point for case-study analysis to remember is that such widened interpretative frames are elicited, or demanded, by the ever more abstract and minimal shape of the art object. That is, the generalization of meaning in classic and abstract art comes from reducing the flexibility of said forms to articulate anything specific. As line and plane increase their ordering ability, and as the pool of pictorial vocabulary narrows, the ability of form to signify anything specific accordingly declines. The art object's form now has no choice but to articulate the general and universal. If a particular nose, face, or torso cannot be represented because of the growing restriction in the vocabulary and rigidity of line and plane then what is represented is the nose, face, and torso, in general. With this shift in form there is a direct shift in the generality of meaning, as meaning increases in generality in direct proportion to restrictedness of form. The figure is less that specific person, but humanity in general; less that person's plight, but the plight of mankind; less that person's suffering, but the suffering of all of us. The change in the code of form will not allow otherwise. An artist cannot articulate a specific, realistic, objective meaning if the representation is general and abstract. The same is true in the other direction. More objective realism is associated with a lack of larger ideas and themes, for what is visually articulated is a particular person, place, tree, or shrub, which is not the essence of people, places, or nature.

In principle, there is a one-to-one relationship between these changes in form and types of meaning they emit. As the painting becomes more and more abstract, the meaning emitted becomes more universal, or philosophical, and at the same time, it has to be more and more imputed from outside the art object properly. In effect, with more classic or abstract art solely the form itself cannot establish the intended signification, and therefore the necessity of additional interpretative theory increases. If, though, the form/meaning equation tilts far enough to the imputed meaning side, the meaning of the art will reside entirely on the supplemental theory side, as the material form will have virtually disappeared. Art is now all interpretation or theory, that is, all concept and idea. This would be the purest example of the Becker/ Bourdieu/Danto/Dickie Institutional Theory of Art, where the art is not only what the artworld says it is, but is nothing but that interpretation. What was called *Conceptual Art*, or *Idea Art*, of the 1970s is an example of a form-meaning equation where form is so minimalized that it virtually disappears leaving only supplemental theory to constitute the experience of art. In this situation what is lost in the physicality of the form must now be made up for in the amount of, and conceptual generality of, supplemental, non-form emitting, theory. The less the art object is a physical sense of something painted or sculpted, the more the add-on interpretation or theory increases until the art object becomes nothing but theory. It is an art where the object is not the form in the traditional sense of a painting or a piece of sculpture, but is now an idea, a thought, a theory, or a concept. This condition does not occur very often in the history of art, but it is possible, and as the highly condensed minimalism of the 1970s demonstrated, it occasionally occurs.

Actually, such a turn toward abstraction in the 1940s–1950s was probably the basis for the social constructionist, or Art World, or Institutional Theory of Art that swept the academic disciplines of sociology, philosophy, art history, and cultural studies. Theorized as the natural state of art–audience relations, it actually only represents a very specific condition of a high degree of abstraction, where a signifier of form is incapable of signifying a specific meaning and hence of necessity, must rely upon extra form interpretative meaning. A painting is only what you think it is when its abstract nature leaves it open to audience intrusion on artistic intention. When an artist disarms himself by leaving his artistic form at such a general level that no specific signification can be made, then that painting, as a communicative object, is vulnerable to redefinition by an apprehending audience armed with interpretative cultural grids. But this is a rare event and the Art World or Institutional Theory of Art based on such a rare event has led a generation of art scholars astray with the false claim that art objects must attain their signification from the outside. In fact, for most art, over most art history, the internal form of the object frames the type of meanings it will emit.

Wolfflin's types of form and Panofsky's types of meaning, then, are not independent of each other. They are not only correlated in art's historical fact – classic and abstract art has more theory and manifestoes, realistic art less – but they have a necessary causal connection. The syntax of line and plane limits the specificity that form is capable of emitting and as such, limits the range of meanings such forms can emit or produce. Line and plane in full force produce more classic art, Wolfflin's basic point, and classic art is one of more generalized Panofskyian iconological interpretations. A loosening of these rules allows more suppleness of line and a more precise crafting of specific images, places, and subject matter. A loosening of the rule of planetric ordering also allows forms to twist, turn, bend, slip, and slide around each other to realize more lifelike postures, making rule loosening a prerequisite for more natural realism, which in turn is associated with more specific, literal, objective, primary Panofskyian meanings. As the essential, universal, and general features of subjects disappear, interpretation and meaning also drop down to the level of more historically contingent and naturally specific representations. Form and meaning, then, are neither separate nor independent.

SUMMARY AND CONCLUSION

This might have seemed like a digression into some fine and arcane points about art theory.

But it is important to how we approach the case study within culture generally and art specifically. I have argued the following:

(1) Part or whole relations are implicit in the very conception of a case study. The case is a portal to knowledge of the whole.

(2) But in the sociology, philosophy, and cultural studies of art, the part or whole tables are turned. The art object is theorized as devoid of sense-making capabilities, hence the viewer must bring them to the object, or they are overridden by the apprehender's suffocating cultural grid comprised of extra-art meanings that are imposed upon the object's form. Either way, art is thought today to mean what sources of meaning emission other than the object's own internal structure and form want it to say.

(3) But we now know that pure vocabularic elements, in and on their own, do not constrain the meaning they emit when combined into a structural whole. 'Man bites dog' and 'Dog bites man' have identical meanings only at the level of their constituent vocabularies, not at the level of their structural combination. Art objects, from paintings to sculpture, architecture, music and dance, and the decorative arts of fashion and design, are apprehended as such structural combinations. Therefore, the meanings emitted at the structural level are different, if the vocabularic combinations are structurally different. Jesus, a table, disciples, and a meal signify the same thing only at the vocabularic level. Combined with rule, combinations of plane vs. recession, or linear vs. painterly or multiplicity create da Vinci's and Tintoretto's paintings of the last supper. While vocabularicly identical, they are structurally different, and as such yield different style interpretations or meanings: High Renaissance vs. Mannerism.

(4) The top down assumption of neutered cultural objects is only a rare event of highly minimalized and abstracted expression. Otherwise, hence for most art, form syntax, shaping art vocabularic constituents, yield, or put forward, meanings on their own.

(5) When performing a case study of a cultural object, look to the internal structure of the, object (Bergesen 2007, 2005, 2000), for it will provide itself hints of the larger phenomena it represents. It is the structure of Tintoretto's *The Last Supper* painting as a case study that points to Mannerism as the larger phenomena,

as da Vinci's syntactical combination of the same constituent subject matter points to the High Renaissance style.

(6) Case studies of fine art and popular cultural objects have too long rested on the false assumption that the meaning they illicit is brought to them, that they are labeled, or socially defined, or socially constructed, to mean this or that. In fact, cultural objects, as case studies, are quite competent to express their meaning. Look, see, hear, feel the syntax, grammar, and ordered vocabulary. Occasionally they will be so minimal as to invite outside meaning providers to fill in what they cannot speak. But remember: that is the exception, not the rule.

REFERENCES

Becker, H. 1982 *Art Worlds*. Berkeley: University of California Press.

Bergesen, A.J. 1979 'Spirituals, jazz, blues, and soul music: the role of elaborated and restricted codes in the maintenance of social solidarity' in R. Wuthnow (Ed.) *New Directions in the Empirical Study of Religion*. New York: Academic Press, pp. 333–350.

Bergesen, A.J. 1984 'The semantic equation: a theory of the social origin of art styles' in R. Collins (Ed.) *Sociological Theory 1984*. San Francisco: Jossey-Bass, pp. 187–221.

Bergesen, A.J. 1991a 'A theory of pictorial discourse' in R. Wuthnow (Ed.) *Vocabularies of Public Life*. New York: Routledge, pp. 158–168.

Bergesen, A.J. 1991b 'Decoding modern dance: With A. Jones' in R. Wuthnow (Ed.) *Vocabularies of Public Life*. New York: Routledge, pp. 169–181.

Bergesen, A.J. 2000 'A linguistic model of art history' *Poetics* 28: 73–90.

Bergesen, A.J. 2005 'Culture and cognition' in M. Jacobs and N. Hanrahan (Eds) *The Blackwell Companion to the Sociology of Culture*. New York: Basil Blackwell, pp. 35–47.

Bergesen, A.J. 2007 *The Depth of Shallow Culture: The High Art of Shoes, Movies, Novels, Monsters and Toys*. Boulder: Paradigm Publishers.

Bernstein, B. 1975 *Class, Codes and Control*. New York: Schocken Books.

Bourdieu, P. 1984 *Distinction: A Social Critique of the Judgment of Taste*. Cambridge: Harvard University Press.

Danto, A. 1964 'The artworld' *The Journal of Philosophy* 61: 571–84.

Dickie, G. 1974 *Art and the Aesthetic: An Institutional Analysis*. Ithaca: Cornell University Press.

Greenberg, C. 1939 'Avant-Garde and Kitsch' *Partisan Review* Fall: 34–49.

Greenberg, C. 1940 'Toward a newer laocoon' *Partisan Review* July-August: 296–310.

Greenberg, C. 1969 'After abstract expressionism' in H. Geldzahler (Ed.) *New York Painting and Sculpture: 1940–1970*, New York: E.P. Dutton, pp. 360–371.

Mannheim, K. 1952 'On the interpretation of *Weltanschauung*' in K. Mannheim (Ed.) *Essays in the Sociology of Knowledge*. New York: Oxford University Press, pp. 33–83.

Nochlin, L. 1985 'The realist criminal and the abstract law' in R. Hertz (Ed.) *Theories of Contemporary Art*, Englewood Cliffs: Prentice Hall.

Panofsky, E. 1955 *Meaning and the Visual Arts*. Chicago: University of Chicago Press.

Wolfflin, H. [1888] 1966 *Renaissance and Baroque*. Ithaca: Cornell University Press.

Wolfflin, H. [1898] 1966 *Classic Art*. London: Phaidon Press.

Wolfflin, H. [1915] 1932 *Principles of Art History*. New York: Dover Publications.

Wolfflin, H. 1994 *Prolegomen zu einer Psychologie der Architekur*. Munich: Dr. C. Wolf and Sohn. His doctoral dissertation, reprinted in English as 'Prolegomena to a Psychology of Architecture' in *Empathy, Form, and Apace: Problems in German Aesthetics, 1873–1893*. Santa Monica: The Getty Center for the History of Art and the Humanities.

23

Social Interactions and the Demand for Sport: Cluster Analysis in Economics

Paul Downward and Joseph Riordan

INTRODUCTION

This chapter explores the use of cluster analysis within economics by applying it to the General Household Survey (GHS) of 2002 to examine sports participation. It argues that cluster analysis can be used to interpret the behaviour of individuals as interacting with a social and economic context as would be suggested by various theoretical arguments in economics. These are explored in the next section ('Economic choice theory'). This is not to suggest, however, that cluster analysis will provide decisive tests that discriminate between the theoretical arguments. However, it can provide a very useful tool for exploring data and, in particular, how it may be classified so as to add a further level of detail to theoretical and empirical discussions.

The section ('Cluster analysis: techniques and previous applications in sport') briefly investigates the application of these choice

theories to participation in sport. This is important because each of the theoretical traditions in economics suggest the need to examine social interactions in choice, although this is not typically explored empirically. In contrast, in the context of sport, cluster analysis has been used to classify the activities and socioeconomic profiles of participants. It is argued that these applications of cluster analysis have typically been presented in an 'a-theoretical' way. Consequently, the next section ('Cluster analysis of the General Household Survey (GHS) 2002') presents an application of cluster analysis that explicitly links theoretical discussion to the choice of clustering method and the interpretation of results. Conclusions then follow, suggesting that the cluster analysis helps to reveal elements of different individual lifestyles, as the individual (case) is associated with an array of socioeconomic characteristics that are shared by others, however, the specific interpretation of the clusters will hinge upon the methodological presuppositions of various economic theories. Suggestions for future research are discussed by way of a summary.

ECONOMIC CHOICE THEORY

Economics can be distinguished as comprising an orthodox, dominant school of thought, neoclassical economics, and a looser set of heterodox economic ideas (Downward 2007). There are differences in both the central theoretical conceptions in each school, as well as their philosophical underpinnings. These two schools of thought are now discussed.

Neoclassical economics

The neoclassical approach to economics focuses upon the allocation of scarce resources, as originally postulated by Lionel Robbins (Lawson 2003). The approach is built on six key elements (Gravelle and Rees 2004):

(1) Goods and services are the central objects of economic activity, which involves the production and exchange of these commodities.
(2) Prices are allotted to each commodity as a unit of account, or rate of commodity exchange.
(3) Markets are where commodities are bought and sold.
(4) The individual is at the heart of the decision-making process.
(5) Rationality is central to consumption and production decisions, as defined by fully informed optimisation.
(6) The method of analysis can be described as a static equilibrium methodology.

The application of these elements for consumer choice is made more specific by assuming that the individual has insatiable preferences, that is, a desire to increase utility by consuming more goods and services; and, it is argued that the consumer is only constrained by incomes and prices. Perfectly informed optimising decision making by the individual thus requires balancing the ratio of the marginal utilities of the alternative goods and services against their relative costs.

Although its philosophical description can be debated, neoclassical economics can be described as having a positivist philosophical orientation (Friedman 1953, Putnam 2002), which is also described as empirical realist (Lawson 1997). This is because it examines real objects that are purported to exist independently of the research, but knowledge of the objects is produced by examining, through the above theoretical account of individual choice, the constant conjunctions of events. Consequently, the realism of these assumptions is unimportant, and the role of theory is to offer predictions about these events, which can then be tested. For example, if prices change, the model can be used to predict how the consumer will reallocate their consumption activities to a new position of equilibrium.

As Downward and Riordan (2007) argue, a natural focus of neoclassical economics is to model the demand for sport as representing an individual agent maximising subjective utility subject to constraints. The income–leisure trade-off model treats leisure, i.e. sport demand, as a residual from the demand for work (for example, see Gratton and Taylor 2000). Significantly, the approach predicts that rising incomes may increase or decrease sports participation because either work is substituted for leisure because of, say, an increase in the wage rate, or that the same consumption of other goods is possible with an income rise whilst allowing for more time to be spent on sport. A more comprehensive foundation is, however, provided by Becker (1965) in which the consumption decisions of individuals are based on the allocation of time and 'market goods' to support consumption activities in the context of a household. An implication of this approach, as detailed by Becker (1974), is that individuals can invest in personal capital, skills and capabilities, or social capital and reputation which provides the greatest return for the household. This suggests that individuals are more likely to participate in a sport having already done so and, naturally, these consumption skills are more likely to promote participation in other sports. This approach predicts that demand for sport will reflect lifestyle factors.

Heterodox economics

Heterodox economics is more problematic to define because it comprises a wide variety of theoretical approaches (Lawson 2003, 2006). However, Lawson (2003) and Lewis (2004) argue that a common approach can be established based on shared characteristics. The first is that economic choice reflects the interaction of human agency within a pre-existing social structure that, nonetheless, will evolve following human agency. Naturally, the interaction of structure and agency might lead to the emergence of a lifestyle for different agents. The second is a methodological commitment to exploring the processes that really underpin events, and the problematic nature of prediction in economic analysis. In the context of consumer choice, Lavoie (1994) identifies post-Keynesian, institutionalist, Schumpeterian evolutionists, social economists, behaviouralists, marketing specialists and other non-orthodox economists as the proponents of heterodox economics. What these groups have in common is that they all criticise the neoclassical theory of consumer choice and, in particular, the central role of marginal utility theory and optimising behaviour. Synthesising their contributions, Lavoie (1994) argues that the following six guiding principles, or axioms, are relevant to consumer choice:

(1) procedural rationality
(2) satiable needs
(3) separability of needs
(4) subordination of needs
(5) growth of needs
(6) non-independence.

In this regard, Earl (1986) and Shackle (1966) emphasise the importance of rule, habits and social convention as an expression of rationality when cognitive limitations are present. Agents satisfice rather than optimise. This requires reaching acceptable levels of satisfaction with elements of consumption activity.

Consequently, needs can be satiable, which is contrary to a presumption of optimising behaviour requiring a constraint to limit consumption. Needs can also be separable, and hierarchically organised as argued by Robinson (1956) and Nell (1992). Thus, income bounds might constrain active participation in sport as opposed to the substitution of leisure time and the opportunity to purchase goods and services. Further, Veblen (1899) and Galbraith (1958) emphasise that individual preferences are not independent but actually shaped explicitly according to the social context in which a person operates. Social class and values influence demands for different bundles of activities. Not surprisingly, there are overlaps of the heterodox approach with sociological theory. For example, Bourdieu postulates that 'distinction' is achieved via exclusive lifestyles, dispositions, world views and cultural interventions (Stempel 2005). The individual can thus accumulate economic, social and cultural capital to facilitate distinction. Sport could be an element of this. Accumulation of such capital proceeds through habitus, as:

> A system of principles which generate and organise practices and representations that can be objectively adapted to their outcomes without presupposing a conscious aiming at ends or an express mastery of the operations necessary in order to attain them. (Bourdieu 1990, p. 53)

These principles are not rules as such. Social structure does not necessarily determine behaviour, and individuals are not necessarily conscious of the cultural forces that can guide their actions. These forces can be unconscious signals, which can be learned through dispositions or habitus. This implies that these principles are adaptable over time, subject to constraints.

This is clearly at odds with the neoclassical economics assumption of rational agents and fixed utility. The implication of habitus is, however, that different attributes of economic and cultural capital are associated with different types of lifestyle, which can be viewed in the context of social hierarchy. The agency of individuals is thus placed in the context of a structural process, so social class both determines and is determined by the behaviour of individuals. Social approaches therefore, also imply the importance of lifestyles, which emerge from these interactions.

Social theory also emphasises that activities can be gendered. This naturally applies to sport too. It can be argued that masculinity is constructed out of competitive activities and femininity through less participation in sport or an emphasis on particular activities, such as keep fit, concerned with body type. In this respect Kay (2004) sees demographic and social factors as 'drivers' of changes in participation. Roberts (1999), further, emphasises that sociological analysis needs to focus on clusters of activities that are not easy to disentangle, rather than carry out separate studies in sport, leisure and physical education. The implication is that this is true of heterodox economics, which seeks to draw upon such factors.

In short, the use of cluster analysis would enable the researcher to investigate the presence of social interaction and lifestyles in sport. Both traditions of economic theorising would suggest that this is an appropriate focus for investigation. The aim would be to explore the possibility and characteristics of particular 'lifestyles'. The interpretation, however, will be determined from the philosophical underpinnings of the research.

CLUSTER ANALYSIS: TECHNIQUES AND PREVIOUS APPLICATIONS IN SPORT

Cluster analysis is a numerical taxonomy method that explores particular multivariate relations in the data (Byrne 2003). In particular, it identifies and classifies objects into similar types. Cluster analysis can be used to group variables according to their distributions or group the cases or individuals according to similarities in the values of the variables that are used to describe the behaviour of cases.

As Downward and Riordan (2007) note, there are a wide variety of methods of cluster analysis, but they are typically of two broad

types. Hierarchical analysis forms individual cases into successively larger groups of cases – clusters – sequentially until one single cluster is constructed. The researcher can then explore alternative classifications. In relocational methods, cases are allocated to best fit a predetermined number of clusters. In either case a distance measure is required to calibrate the similarity or dissimilarity of cases. Similarity and dissimilarity of cases is calibrated using a variety of forms of distance function for ratio, interval and ordinal data and 'matching' coefficients for nominal data (Romesburg 2004).

There have been two previous cluster analyses of large-scale data in the UK examining sport participation. They were data descriptive and not grounded in explicit theoretical discussion. Burton (1971) attempted to identify 'recreational types' by employing cluster and factor analysis, to establish the demand for recreational facilities. Burton argues that:

> The particular reason for employing groups of pursuits rather than individual pursuits is the hypothesis that correlations between the former and socio-economic variables – the presumed causal factors – will be more accurate and more stable over time than correlations for the latter. (Burton 1971, p. 22)

Burton (1971) drew samples from 500 households in Billesley and a further 500 in the All Saints areas of Birmingham in the UK. These data represent a random sample taking one in every eight houses from an electoral register of 4,000 households. A household questionnaire asked the head of the family nine questions regarding its composition. An activities questionnaire and a time budget were also left for family members to complete. The latter required the respondents to log their activities over a 24-hour period. The purpose of this was to gain insight into the relationship between recreation and other activities.

Sixty activities were cited in the questionnaire, and respondents were given further opportunity to add to the list any activities not covered therein. Each activity was treated as a separate variable, and respondents' observations were recorded as 0 for non-participation, and 1 for participation. Correlation coefficients were then calculated between pairs of variables for the whole sample of observations. These could take three critical values: 1 if all respondents take part in both activities; 0 if none did either activity; −1 if none took part in activity 1, but all took part in activity 2.

Activities were then grouped together according to their correlation coefficient, such that there was a large correlation within grouped activities, but a low one between groups. This was achieved by applying McQuitty's elementary linkage method. This approach implies first, taking the highest pairwise correlation (in Burton's case, cricket and football). These variables are then compared to other variables, to see if any other variables have their highest correlation with the identified variables (Burton found tennis and table tennis to be linked to soccer). The process is continued until no members have links to activities outside their group.

The next group is then started by finding the next highest correlation after ignoring any correlations with the original group. A major potential criticism with this approach is that it only takes account of the highest correlations. So we could have a situation in which football and cricket have a correlation of 0.536, whereas football and athletics have a correlation of 0.535 and athletics ends up in

a different group. Furthermore, the dominant variable that starts off a group might end up having little in common with other variables in the group. A possible solution would be to look at the second-best correlations as well, which was undertaken by Burton, and the results found to be generally similar to the highest correlation groupings.

Burton identified fourteen different groups amongst seventy-one activities (sixty were precoded activities, and a further eleven were later coded as a result of respondents including extra activities). These are summarised in Table 23.1, below.

Tests of homogeneity were carried out between groups, and eight major characteristics were identified as associated with participation: skills; group activities; active participation; risk and danger; urban or rural; cost; water based; and speed and dexterity requirements. Burton (1971) recognised however, that this left a need to study how recreation types are correlated with different socioeconomic groups.

A more recent analysis by Sturgis and Jackson (2003), commissioned by the Department of Culture, Media and Sport (DCMS), identifies clusters of sports activities in the UK Time Use Survey (2000). Data were obtained from combined household and individual questionnaires presented to 10,648 UK residents aged eighteen years old and over,

Table 23.1 The fourteen cluster groups identified by Burton (1971, p. 191)

Group	Activities
1	Rugby, athletics, basketball, badminton, keep fit, cycling, amateur dramatics/music
2	Archery, go-karting, winter sports, fencing, surfing, water skiing, aqualung diving, canoeing, hunting
3	Hill walking, rambling, camping/youth hostelling/caravanning, walking, visit to museum/art gallery
4	Soccer, cricket, tennis, golf, table tennis, fishing
5	Hobbies/do-it-yourself, outdoor bowls, motor racing, motor-cycle racing, scrambles, rallies, flying/gliding/sky diving, squash, boxing, wrestling, judo/karate, other activities
6	Picnicking, driving in countryside, gardening, dining out, visit to a pub or club, bingo, dancing
7	Visit to community or church centre, old time dancing, photography
8	Ice skating, roller skating, bird watching, horse riding, youth club
9	Sailing, rowing, motor-boat cruising, messing about in boats, evening classes
10	Visit to a cinema, visit to a theatre/concert, visit to a library
11	Hockey, netball, gymnastics
12	Mountaineering, pot-holing
13	Painting/drawing/sketching, going to a party
14	Tenpin bowling, swimming

and also from time-use diaries. Data were weighted to allow for unequal selection probabilities, seasonality and non-response. Due to the requirements for large numbers for statistical purposes, and the lack of variation over the two-day period of diary data collection for sports activities, four weekly participation data were used, rather than the diary data.[1]

The purpose of the study was to look for distinct clusters of activities with different social and individual characteristics associated with participation in each cluster. Clusters were identified on the basis of the similarity of activities to one another, where such similarity is 'defined as the probability of their co-occurrence within individuals over a defined reference period' (Sturgis and Jackson 2003, p. 5). The within-group activities are therefore relatively homogeneous in terms of their covariance, whereas between-group variation is maximised.

Similarity between activities was established using the Pearson correlation coefficient. Variables were grouped together iteratively into homogeneous clusters via 'centroid clustering'. The results of the cluster analysis are presented in Table 23.2, below.

Sturgis and Jackson (2003) then treated these clusters as the dependent variable in a logistic regression to identify the factors associated with participation in any activities within the group. The greatest impact on cluster membership identified from the study was the predominance of people doing no activities at all. Other key predictors were age, sex, income, social class, education level, household access to a car, region of residence.

The main problem with these studies, however, is that they group activities together.

Table 23.2 DCMS sport and cultural clusters (adapted from Sturgis and Jackson 2003, p. 3)

Cultural clusters	Sports clusters
Cultural consumer activities	Active aerobic
Arts and related activities	Non-active competitive
Heritage activities	Outdoor competitive
Family outdoors	Outdoor non-competitive

It is, perhaps, more useful to group people, that is cases, together with similar lifestyles. This is more in keeping with the view that sports participation mutually emerges from, and is therefore an *integral part of*, a lifestyle, as indicated by an array of characteristics being used to describe cases. In some ways, this suggests how neoclassical and heterodox uses of cluster analysis might vary. As discussed in the previous section, the emphasis of neoclassical economics is on prediction, i.e. the values of variables. By contrast, heterodox economics, which emphasises examining structure and agency, will be concerned with the case descriptions. These descriptions are conceptualised as emergent from structure and agency interaction. This broad methodological difference should, however, recognise that in as much that neoclassical economics has a theory of social interactions, rooted in the work of Becker (1974), then this distinction is not necessarily true. The ultimate difference will lie in the interpretation of the results. This issue is discussed further in the penultimate section of the chapter.

CLUSTER ANALYSIS OF THE GENERAL HOUSEHOLD SURVEY (2002)

The focus of the current study is to identify how the decision to participate in different activities, can be thought of as arising from a complex array of interdependent individual and socioeconomic factors as is suggested in economic theories of choice. This study employs the use of cluster analysis, therefore, but in a different way to that used in the previous studies in the UK. Instead of clustering activities *per se*, cases are clustered to identify the nature of lifestyles, part of which is reflected in the decision to participate in an activity and subsequently its frequency. Only clearly assigned cases are profiled, so this enables us to focus on lifestyles.

As well as the economic theories referred to above, which suggest that lifestyles described by arrays of individual and socioeconomic characteristics may be identified in the data, it is also expected, *a priori*, that the cases are clustered according to different types of activity. The Council of Europe (1980) and Rodgers (1978) developed essentially separate classifications of leisure, recreation and sport which have become accepted categories, and were implied in the 1993 Council of Europe, European Sports Charter. According to this classification, leisure is characterised as activities involving physical activity, carried out for recreational purposes. Recreation has the same basic characteristics as leisure, yet often is competitive in nature. Sport contains the same elements but is also characterised by an institutional framework for the activities. Thus, we might expect to find, for example, that a higher proportion of sportspeople are young males.

Data

This study analyses data from the GHS (2002). Although the GHS is an annual study of thousands of UK households, the questions relating to activities classified as 'sport and leisure' appear only periodically (1993 and 1996 prior to the 2002 study).[2] The survey

asks respondents to provide information on their participation or otherwise in each of forty activities (see Table 23.6, p. 401) over a four-week period immediately prior to the interview. Furthermore, respondents are requested to provide information on the frequency of participation of those activities undertaken during that period of time. Data are also available on individual, social and economic characteristics of the cases taking part. Data used in this investigation are confined to those aged 16 years and above, and only those who completed a full interview. This implies a sample size of 14,827.

Tables 23.3, 23.4 and 23.5 identify the individual and social characteristics of responses, their economic characteristics and their sports and leisure participation. Their measurement and definition are also provided.

Having defined the variables, the next section explains the analysis techniques employed in this study to identify clusters.

Cluster analysis techniques

The method employed in this work is two-step cluster analysis from SPSS, to extend the

Table 23.3 Individual and social characteristics

Variable name	Type of variable	Definition
Age	Continuous	Reports mean age ± 1 standard deviation
Sex	Categorical	Male or female
Marital status	Categorical	Single never married, married, married and separated, divorced, widowed
Nadfems	Continuous	Number of adult females in household
Nadmales	Continuous	Number of adult males in household
N0–4	Continuous	Number of pre school children in household
N5–15	Continuous	Number of school age children in household
Highest education	Categorical	Highest level of educational attainment: Higher degree, first degree, teaching qualification, other higher qualification, nursing qualification, A level (2+), A levels (1), GCSEO (5+), GCSEO (<5), SUBC1GCSE/CSE, apprenticeship, other qualification, no qualification
Ethnicity	Categorical	White/non-white
Health	Categorical	Describes the state of health of the respondent: not good/fairly good/poor
Longstanding illness	Categorical	Does the respondent have a longstanding illness?: Yes/No
Illness limits activity	Categorical	Does the respondent suffer from an illness which limits participation in a particular activity?: Yes/No
Smoking*	Categorical	Does the respondent smoke?: Yes/No
Smoke cigar	Categorical	Does the respondent smoke a cigar?: Yes/No
Smoke pipe	Categorical	Does the respondent smoke a pipe?: Yes/No
Drink nowadays	Categorical	Does the respondent drink alcohol?: Yes/No

* Categories are based on an aggregation of the original categories.

Table 23.4 Economic characteristics

Variable type	Variable name	Definition
Employment status		
	Empman	Employer or manager
	Prof	Professional
	Nonman	Non-manual
	Personal	Personal services
	Skillman	Skilled manual
	Semiskill	Partially skilled manual/technical worker
	Unskill	Unskilled worker
	Working	In work
	Retired	Retired from work
	Keephouse*	Keeping house
Region		
	North	Northern England and Yorkshire
	Mids	East and West Midlands and East Anglia
	South	South West and South East England
	Wales	Wales
	Scotland	Scotland
Access to motor vehicle	Usevcl1	Own or use a motor vehicle
Income	Weekinc	Gross household income (£000s)
Hours worked	Tothrs	Total usual hours of work per week
Unpaid hours	Unpaidhr	Total weekly unpaid hours work
New class	NewCl	New social class I to V

* Categories are based on an aggregation of the original categories.

Table 23.5 Sport and leisure characteristics

Variable name	Type of variable	Definition
Sp4walk, sp401–sp440	Categorical	For each of 40 sports, and walking participation or not in last 4 weeks
Sp401sc–sp440sc	Categorical	For each of 40 sports, participation or not in last 4 weeks in a sports club
Sp401oc–sp440oc	Categorical	For each of 40 sports, participation or not in last 4 weeks in a club that is not primarily a sports club
Sptime1–40	Continuous	For each of 40 sports, number of times participated in last 4 weeks
Numsportw	Continuous	Number of sports participated in during last 4 weeks
Voltime	Continuous	Hours spent volunteering in sport
TV	Categorical	Watched TV or not in last 4 weeks
Radio	Categorical	Listened to radio or not in last 4 weeks
Records	Categorical	Listened to records or not in last 4 weeks
Books	Categorical	Read book or not in last 4 weeks
Music	Categorical	Played music or not in last 4 weeks
Acting	Categorical	Acted or not in last 4 weeks
Paint	Categorical	Painted or not in last 4 weeks
Dance	Categorical	Danced or not in last 4 weeks
Enroll	Categorical	Watched TV or not in last 4 weeks
Educpres	Categorical	Attending leisure recreation class
Writing	Categorical	Attending non-leisure classes
Volcult	Categorical	Volunteer or not in other leisure
Voltime2	Rank/ordinal	Hours volunteered on other leisure
Numcultw	Continuous	Number of other leisure activities participated in over the last 4 weeks

work of Downward and Kay (2007). This is because this method allows for the analysis of both categorical and other data scales. The method first aggregates cases into a smaller number of cases. The aggregated cases are then further aggregated into an even smaller number of cases. This method is chosen over traditional hierarchical clustering, as it is more efficient and can handle larger datasets. As explained above, the latter starts off with a cluster for every case, and then reduces these down subsequently to one cluster. The two-step cluster analysis can be used to identify a prespecified number of clusters or also allows the number of clusters to be assigned automatically, using maximum likelihood measures. In each case, continuous variables are assumed to follow a normal distribution and categorical variables a multinomial distribution. Results are thus presented in terms of means and standard deviations for the former variables for each cluster, and frequencies for the latter variables for each cluster. Based on an initial specification of clusters, changes in the log-likelihood of cases belonging to specific clusters are identified, and then these initial clusters are compared to a new set of clusters.

It is important to note that there is no reason to presuppose that one method is superior to others. Methodological and theoretical motivation clearly matters. However, as the emphasis of this research is to explore possible alternative explanations of sports participation, the maximum likelihood method of automatically identifying clusters is employed.

Results

The analysis produced three distinct clusters for 9,738 (66%) of all of the cases. The first cluster contained only 281 cases (3%), the second cluster contained 2,012 cases (20.5%) and the final largest cluster contained 7,445 cases (76.5%). This suggests that of the total sample of 14,827 cases, 9,738 cases had relatively distinct profiles. A further 5,089 cases produced an indistinct pattern of behaviour and as such can be treated as outliers to the structures that have been uncovered.

Table 23.6 presents the basic characteristics of each cluster according to their participation in sports and leisure activities; these are listed in the first column. They are grouped according to which cluster contains the most cases, as indicated by the column 'mode'.

Thus, the first batch of activities are examples of primarily Cluster 3 behaviour, the second Cluster 2 behaviour and the third Cluster 1 behaviour. Tied and close distinctions are noted in the tie/close column. It is argued that these clusters can be associated with leisure, recreational activities, and team and more competitive sports respectively. Of course, other classifications could be used according to different sets of variables. After all, cluster analysis captures a multidimensional characterisation of cases. It should be recognised, then, that the interpretation is epistemologically relative to the focus of attention. It is in this context that an emphasis is placed upon an examination of the 'sports and leisure' variables.[3]

The second, third and fourth columns in the table indicate how many participants engage in the specified activity according to each cluster. The total number of participants is given by the column headed 'N'. Columns 8, 9 and 10 then reproduce these frequencies of participation as percentages of the total number of participants for that activity. For example, the table shows that 3,770 cases undertook a walk of 2+ miles in the last four weeks. Of these, 142 cases can be identified for Cluster 1, 1,042 for Cluster 2 and 2,568 for Cluster 3. These frequencies represent 3.77%, 27.64% and 68.59% of the total number of cases undertaking a walk.

Table 23.7 explores the profile of the clusters in more detail, by exploring each cluster in respect of key household characteristics; the sex of individuals, their age, the number of preschool and school-age children in the household, as well as the number of adult females and males in the household, the marital status of households, household income and the number of sports and other leisure activities undertaken, ethnicity, health and education.

In Table 23.7, with the categorical variables the frequency of cases associated with each cluster are presented in columns 3 to 5. Columns 7 to 9 then also report these frequencies as percentages of the total set of cases identified in the clusters; that is 9,738 cases. In this respect each block of percentages for each

Table 23.6 **The basic characteristics of each cluster according to their participation in sports and leisure activities**

Four-week activity	Cluster 1	Cluster 2	Cluster 3	N	Mode	Tie/ close	Cluster 1 (%)	Cluster 2 (%)	Cluster 3 (%)	N
Walk of 2+ miles	142	1042	2586	3770	3		3.77	27.64	68.59	3770
Snooker past	68	343	454	865	3		7.86	39.65	52.49	865
Watched TV	279	1992	7372	9643	3		2.89	20.66	76.45	9643
Listened to radio	265	1918	6629	8812	3		3.01	21.77	75.23	8812
Listened to records/tapes	263	1873	6321	8475	3		3.10	22.10	74.58	8475
Read books	190	1505	4647	6342	3		3.00	23.73	73.27	6342
Sung/played instrument	43	323	680	1046	3		4.11	30.88	65.01	1046
Performed in play	9	62	97	168	3		5.36	36.90	57.74	168
Painting	31	253	590	874	3		3.55	28.95	67.51	874
Dancing	41	322	705	1068	3		3.84	30.15	66.01	1068
Enrolled on course	29	205	499	733	3		3.96	27.97	68.08	733
Attending leisure class	37	285	335	657	3		5.63	43.38	50.99	657
Written stories/poetry	17	109	200	326	3		5.21	33.44	61.35	326
Running of Arts events	269	1794	7415	9478	3		2.84	18.93	78.23	9478
Swimming/diving	73	652	624	1349	2	3	5.41	48.33	46.26	1349
Swimming/diving outdoors	30	202	75	307	2		9.77	65.80	24.43	307
Cycling	69	459	437	965	2	3	7.15	47.56	45.28	965
Indoor bowls	0	53	22	75	2		0.00	70.67	29.33	75
Outdoor bowls	4	27	9	40	2		10.00	67.50	22.50	40
Tenpin bowling	27	163	158	348	2		7.76	46.84	45.40	348
Keepfit/aerobics	57	688	558	1303	2		4.37	52.80	42.82	1303
Martial arts	39	39	14	92	2	1	42.39	42.39	15.22	92
Weight training	76	454	84	614	2		12.38	73.94	13.68	614
Weight lifting sport	18	97	15	130	2		13.85	74.62	11.54	130
Gymnastics	0	19	2	21	2		0.00	90.48	9.52	21
Football indoors	43	123	22	188	2		22.87	65.43	11.70	188
Football outdoors	63	187	96	346	2		18.21	54.05	27.75	346
Cricket	2	48	8	58	2		3.45	82.76	13.79	58
Tennis	19	133	21	173	2		10.98	76.88	12.14	173
Badminton	19	145	20	184	2		10.33	78.80	10.87	184
Squash	28	95	16	139	2		20.14	68.35	11.51	139
Table tennis	18	74	18	110	2		16.36	67.27	16.36	110
Jogging/running	72	359	92	523	2		13.77	68.64	17.59	523
Angling	20	101	68	189	2		10.58	53.44	35.98	189
Ice skating	2	39	0	41	2		4.88	95.12	0.00	41
Golf past	29	309	202	540	2		5.37	57.22	37.41	540
Skiing past	8	33	3	44	2		18.18	75.00	6.82	44
Horse riding	8	71	26	105	2		7.62	67.62	24.76	105
Climbing	23	45	3	71	2		32.39	63.38	4.23	71
Motor sports	11	25	25	61	2	3	18.03	40.98	40.98	61
Shooting	29	47	29	105	2		27.62	44.76	27.62	105
Rugby	28	4	3	35	1		80.00	11.43	8.57	35
American football	3	0	0	3	1		100.00	0.00	0.00	3
Gaelic sports	2	0	0	2	1		100.00	0.00	0.00	2
Hockey	17	0	2	19	1		89.47	0.00	10.53	19
Netball	13	2	2	17	1		76.47	11.76	11.76	17
Basketball	21	14	4	39	1		53.85	35.90	10.26	39
Athletics	12	3	2	17	1		70.59	17.65	11.76	17
Sailing	35	20	12	67	1		52.24	29.85	17.91	67
Canoeing	20	7	0	27	1		74.07	25.93	0.00	27
Windsurfing	14	3	0	17	1		82.35	17.65	0.00	17
Curling	3	0	0	3	1		100.00	0.00	0.00	3
Volleyball	19	2	0	21	1		90.48	9.52	0.00	21

Table 23.7 Key household characteristics of clusters

Variable	Cluster profiles	1	2	3		1 (%)	2 (%)	3 (%)
Sex	Male	219	1174	3334	Male	2	12	34
	Female	62	838	4111	Female	1	9	42
Age	Mean	36	41	45				
	+1 standard deviation	48	54	59				
	−1 standard deviation	24	28	32				
Numbers of preschool children aged 0 to 4 (N0 to 4)	0	240	1741	6420	0	2	18	66
	1	26	214	815	1	0	2	8
	2	14	53	195	2	0	1	2
	3	1	4	15	3	0	0	0
Number of school-age children aged 5 to 15 (N5 to 15)	0	206	1425	5457	0	2	15	56
	1	40	287	1105	1	0	3	11
	2	25	239	675	2	0	2	7
	3	9	52	166	3	0	1	2
	4	1	6	28	4	0	0	0
	5	0	2	9	5	0	0	0
	6	0	1	3	6	0	0	0
	7	0	0	2	7	0	0	0
Number of adult females in the household (Nadfems)	0	40	224	563	0	0	2	6
	1	211	1547	5874	1	2	16	60
	2	27	193	866	2	0	2	9
	3	3	43	127	3	0	0	1
	4	0	5	10	4	0	0	0
	5	0	0	5	5	0	0	0
Number of adult males in the household (Nadmales)	0	10	227	1047	0	0	2	11
	1	199	1472	5305	1	2	15	54
	2	57	247	918	2	1	3	9
	3	11	57	158	3	0	1	2
	4	4	9	16	4	0	0	0
	5	0	0	1	5	0	0	0
Marital status (Marstat)	Single never married	118	634	1661	Single never married	1	7	17
	Married	138	1142	4538	Married	1	12	47
	Married and separated	6	56	213	Married and separated	0	1	2
	Divorced	18	150	784	Divorced	0	2	8
	Widowed	1	30	249	Widowed	0	0	3
Household income (£ week)	Mean	1690	888	612				
	+1 standard deviation	5155	1768	1150				
	−1 standard deviation	−1775	8	73				
Number of sports (Numsportw)	Mean	5	3	1				
	+1 standard deviation	7	5	2				
	−1 standard deviation	2	2	0				
Number of leisure activities (Numcultw)	Mean	4	4	4				
	+1 standard deviation	5	5	5				
	−1 standard deviation	3	3	3				

variable sums to 100% allowing for rounding. In the case of continuous variables, such as age, the mean and values up to one standard deviation around the mean are presented to give an idea of the range of data.

Table 23.7 reveals that Clusters 1 and 2, that is, sport and recreation activities, are more likely to be undertaken by males, whereas the opposite is true for Cluster 3, that is, leisure activities. Males are, in fact, up to 3.5 times more likely to participate in sports than females, but less so with recreational activities. As far as the age profiles of participants is concerned, the data reveal that sports activities are more likely for those typically aged between 24 and 48, recreational activities for those aged between 28 and 54 and leisure activities for those aged between 32 and 59.

The data reveal that whereas the majority of cases in each cluster have no preschool children, or no school-age children, Cluster 3 cases are much more likely to include those with more children of any of these ages. It would appear that the presence of children does hinder participation in sport and recreation. Likewise, in each cluster there is evidence to suggest that it is most likely to be the case that households comprise a single male and female and that these will be married.

In terms of household weekly income, the results indicate that both the average and dispersion of income is greater for households in Cluster 1, than in 2 and 3 respectively. This is consistent with the age profiles as Cluster 3 is more likely to include those on lower more fixed incomes, given that they are likely to be older, and separated. This suggests that Cluster 1 households reflect those who are either on high or very low incomes as, typically, younger either married or never married single males.

The remaining social and individual characteristics are represented in Table 23.8.

Again, data are presented in a similar manner to those in Table 23.7. Columns 3 to 5 represent the frequency of cases assigned to Clusters 1, 2 and 3. Columns 6 to 9, represent these frequencies as a percentage of total assigned cases for each category.

For higher education, for example, there are 634 cases in total with a higher degree. Of these, 34 are assigned to Cluster 1, 232 to Cluster 2 and 368 to Cluster 3. Thus columns 7, 8 and 9 read 0.35%, 2.38% and 3.77%, respectively. This enables us to investigate the cluster assignment of cases with different education, health, drinking and smoking levels. In general, the results suggest that Cluster 1 frequencies tend to rise in relative terms compared to Cluster 3 as educational level increases, the same is the case with cases reporting good health, and drinking. Interestingly, however, the data does not suggest any ethnic effects.

Having investigated the individual and social characteristics of the clusters, the next section looks at the economic variables. Table 23.9 disaggregates the results for each cluster in terms of the economic variables and is set out in a similar manner to Tables 23.7 and 23.8. The first column contains the variable description explaining the economic status of the individual. The second and sixth columns explain the cluster profiles. Columns 3 to 5 provide the number of cases assigned to each of Clusters 1, 2 and 3 respectively. Columns 7 to 9 express these numbers in percentage terms of the total number of participating cases in each variable category. For example, if we take the variable 'Own/use motors', there are 8,384 cases who own/use motor vehicles and 1,354, who do not. Of these, 255 are assigned to Cluster 1, 1,882 to Cluster 2 and 6,247 to Cluster 3. These represent 2.6%, 19.3% and 64.2% respectively of total responses in this category. The exception to this is the variable 'Weekly unpaid work'. The mean for each cluster is presented in columns 3 to 5, and the standard deviations of the means are given below the cluster means in the two following rows.

The results for social class and economic status, perhaps not surprisingly, reinforce the findings in Table 23.7. Whereas Cluster 3 is always the largest constituency, the results imply that greater social and economic advantage will be associated with higher chances of belonging to Cluster 1 and thus more specialised sports participation. There are

Table 23.8   Other social and individual variables

Variable	Cluster Profiles	1	2	3	Descriptors	1(%)	2(%)	3(%)
New social class	I	29	174	298	I	0.3	1.8	3.1
	II	104	876	1977	II	1.1	9.0	20.3
	IIIN	54	427	1722	IIIN	0.6	4.4	17.7
	IIIM	52	341	1739	IIIM	0.5	3.5	17.9
	IV	28	160	1267	IV	0.3	1.6	13.0
	V	14	34	442	V	0.1	0.3	4.5
Economic Status	Working	258	1721	5254	Working	2.6	17.7	54.0
	Unemployed (ILO)	4	29	118	Unemployed (ILO)	0.0	0.3	1.2
	Permanent unable to work	2	23	439	Permanent unable to work	0.0	0.2	4.5
	Retired	8	150	930	Retired	0.1	1.5	9.6
Own/use motors	Yes	255	1882	6247	Yes	2.6	19.3	64.2
	No	26	130	1198	No	0.3	1.3	12.3
Government regions	NE	10	65	392	NE	0.1	0.7	4.0
	NW	35	201	911	NW	0.4	2.1	9.4
	Yorks/Humber	30	157	634	Yorks/Humber	0.3	1.6	6.5
	E.Midlands	16	137	561	E.Midlands	0.2	1.4	5.8
	W.Midlands	17	158	670	W.Midlands	0.2	1.6	6.9
	East of England	15	210	700	East of England	0.2	2.2	7.2
	London	26	234	802	London	0.3	2.4	8.2
	SE	48	365	1104	SE	0.5	3.7	11.3
	SW	38	212	632	SW	0.4	2.2	6.5
	Wales	15	85	423	Wales	0.2	0.9	4.3
	Scotland	31	188	616	Scotland	0.3	1.9	6.3
Weekly unpaid work	Mean	1.05	0	0.01				
	less 1 SD	0	0	0				
	plus 1 SD	8.5	0.02	0.252				
New socio-economic group	Employers large	1	6	9	Employers large	0.0	0.1	0.1
	Employers small	12	43	132	Employers small	0.1	0.4	0.4
	Managers large	10	166	252	Managers large	0.1	1.7	2.6
	Managers small	21	135	475	Managers small	0.2	1.4	4.9
	Prof. self-employed	6	41	55	Prof. self-employed	0.1	0.4	0.6
	Prof. employee	23	133	243	Prof. employee	0.2	1.4	2.5
	Int non-man Anc	59	519	1074	Int non-man Anc	0.6	5.3	11.0
	Int non-man Foreman	12	98	261	Int non-man Foreman	0.1	1.0	2.7
	Junior non-man	42	324	1452	Junior non-man	0.4	3.3	14.9
	Personal service	7	58	258	Personal service	0.1	0.6	2.6
	Manual foreman	17	112	557	Manual foreman	0.2	1.2	5.7
	Skilled manual	27	138	710	Skilled manual	0.3	1.4	7.3
	Semi-skilled manual	20	95	958	Semi-skilled manual	0.2	1.0	9.8
	Unskilled manual	14	34	442	Unskilled manual	0.1	0.3	4.5
	Own-acc non-prof	8	96	481	Own-acc non prof	0.1	1.0	4.9
	Farm employer/mgt	1	2	4	Farm employer/mgt	0.0	0.0	0.0
	Farm own acc	0	5	31	Farm own acc	0.0	0.1	0.3
	Agriculture workers	1	7	51	Agriculture workers	0.0	0.1	0.5
Activity status	Keeping house	3	69	589	Keeping house	0.0	0.7	6.0
	Student	1	2	21	Student	0.0	0.0	0.2
	Other inactive	3	18	88	Other inactive	0.0	0.2	0.9

Table 23.9 Disaggregated results for each cluster

Variable	Cluster Profiles	1	2	3	Descriptors	1(%)	2(%)	3(%)
Highest education	Higher degree	34	232	368	Higher degree	5	37	58
	First degree	60	467	879	First degree	4	33	63
	Teaching qual.	6	37	102	Teaching qual.	4	25.5	71
	Other higher qual.	26	184	553	Other higher qual.	3.5	24	73
	Nursing qual.	2	27	108	Nursing qual.	1.5	20	79
	A levels (2+)	37	271	843	A levels (2+)	3	23.5	74
	A levels (1)	4	61	144	A levels (1)	2	29	69
	GCSE/O (5+)	28	197	808	GCSE/O (5+)	3	19	78
	GCSE/O (<5)	22	169	538	GCSE/O (<5)	3	23	74
	Sub C/1 GCSE/CSE	14	126	687	Sub C/1 GCSE/CSE	2	15	83
	Apprenticeship	4	18	132	Apprenticeship	2.5	12	86
	Other qual.	9	54	375	Other qual.	2	12	85
	Non qual.	35	169	1908	Non qual.	1.5	8	91
White/non-white	Yes	255	1837	6802	Yes	3	20.5	77
	No	26	175	643	No	3	21	76
Health (last 12mths)	Not good	10	100	1052	Not good	1	8.5	91
	Fairly good	54	461	2191	Fairly good	2	17	81
	Good	217	1451	4202	Good	3.5	25	72
Longstanding illness	Yes	66	580	2847	Yes	2	16.5	82
	No	215	1432	4598	No	3.5	23	74
Illness limits activity	Yes	31	265	1754	Yes	1.5	13	86
	No	250	1747	5691	No	3.5	22.5	74
Smoking	Yes	80	409	2278	Yes	3	15	82
	No	201	1603	5167	No	3	23	74
	Cigar yes	10	74	178	Cigar yes	4	28	68
	Cigar no	271	1938	7267	Cigar no	3	20.5	77
	Pipe yes	2	9	40	Pipe yes	4	17.5	79
	Pipe no	279	2003	7405	Pipe no	3	20.5	77
Drink nowadays	Yes	263	1893	6435	Yes	3	22	75
	No	18	119	1010	No	1.5	10.5	88

some regional differences in the results, but of more significance to note is that employers owning large and small businesses, in contrast to skilled and unskilled non-management, have higher levels of participation in sport through being associated with Cluster 1 than other workers, whilst demonstrating a relatively low participation rate in leisure. Most participation of unskilled manual labour is in the leisure cluster (Cluster 3). Only 7% of these cases were in the recreation cluster (Cluster 2).

Attention now turns to investigating the extent of multiple participation, the responses of cases belonging to: (1) sports clubs; and (2) other clubs. *A priori*, one might expect that members of a sports club would be more likely

to participate in other competitive activities that are organised institutionally. The results are presented in Table 23.10.

The table reveals that club-based participation increases for recreational and specialist team or competitive sporting activities, with sports clubs of particular relevance for the sports related activities. The activities are described in column 1. Column 2 identifies the modal cluster associated with the particular activity in the analysis in Table 23.6. The third column provides the percentage of cases assigned to Cluster 1 in column 8 of Table 23.6. The fourth column of Table 23.10 shows the percentage of assigned cases of other clubs to Cluster 1 (OC1). The fifth column shows the percentage of cases of

Table 23.10 The extent of multiple participation

Four-week activity	Mode	Cluster 1(%)	OC1[1]	SC1[2]	Cluster 2(%)	OC2[3]	SC2[4]	Cluster 3(%)	OC3[5]	SC3[6]
Walk of 2+ miles	3	3.77			27.64			68.59		
Snooker past	3	7.86	10.3	7	39.65	36.5	39.5	52.49	53.2	52.5
Watched TV	3	2.89			20.66			76.45		
Listened to Radio	3	3.01			21.77			75.23		
Listened to records/tapes	3	3.10			22.10			74.58		
Read books	3	3.00			23.73			73.27		
Sung/played instrument	3	4.11			30.88			65.01		
Performed in Play	3	5.36			36.90			57.74		
Painting	3	3.55			28.95			67.51		
Dancing	3	3.84			30.15			66.01		
Enrolled on Course	3	3.96			27.97			68.08		
Attending leisure class	3	5.63			43.38			50.99		
Written stories/poetry	3	5.21			33.44			61.35		
Running of Arts events	3	2.84			18.93			78.23		
Swimming diving	2	5.41	5.3	4.9	48.33	7.15	58.5	46.26	23.2	36.6
Swimming diving outdoors	2	9.77	8.3	16.7	65.80	81.7	83.3	24.43	0	0
Cycling	2	7.15	5.3	8.3	47.56	78.9	41.7	45.28	15.8	50
Indoor bowls	2	0.00	0	0	70.67	56.3	86.1	29.33	43.8	13.9
Outdoor bowls	2	10.00	15	7.7	67.50	55	92.3	22.50	30	0
Tenpin bowling	2	7.76	0	33.3	46.84	100	44.4	45.40	0	22.2
Keepfit/aerobics	2	4.37	4.4	8.2	52.80	72.5	55.1	42.82	23	36.7
Martial arts	2	42.39	56.7	35.3	42.39	40	47.1	15.22	3.3	17.6
Weight training	2	12.38	9.7	4.2	73.94	85.3	79.2	13.68	5	16.7
Weight lifting sport	2	13.85	10.4	0	74.62	81.3	0	11.54	8.3	0
Gymnastics	2	0.00	0	16.7	90.48	0	83.3	9.52	0	0
Football indoors	2	22.87	31.3	29	65.43	68.8	66.7	11.70	0	4.2
Football outdoors	2	18.21	24.1	18.2	54.05	59.3	62.3	27.75	16.7	19.5
Cricket	2	3.45	0	3.7	82.76	100	81.5	13.79	0	14.8
Tennis	2	10.98	13.6	6.7	76.88	86.4	91.1	12.14	0	2.2
Badminton	2	10.33	5.3	6.9	78.80	94.7	89.7	10.87	0	3.4
Squash	2	20.14	20.7	34.6	68.35	72.4	50	11.51	6.9	15.4
Table tennis	2	16.36	14.3	0	67.27	85.7	100	16.36	0	0
Jogging/running	2	13.77	11.6	25	68.64	83.7	60	17.59	4.7	15
Angling	2	10.58	4.9	9.1	53.44	65.9	72.7	35.98	29.3	18.2
Ice skating	2	4.88	0	0	95.12	0	0	0	0	0
Golf past	2	5.37	4.1	1.8	57.22	70.1	66.9	37.41	25.8	31.4
Skiing past	2	18.18	0	0	75.00	0	100	6.82	0	0
Horse riding	2	7.62	10	0	67.62	90	100	24.76	0	0
Climbing	2	32.39	57.1	25	63.38	42.9	75	4.23	0	0
Motor sports	2	18.03	6.7	25	40.98	33.3	25	40.98	60	50
Shooting	2	27.62	50	16.7	44.76	37.5	55.6	27.62	12.5	27.8
Rugby	1	80.00	100	80	11.43	0	10	8.57	0	10
American football	1	100.00	2.9	100	0.00	20.7	0	0	76.6	0
Gaelic sports	1	100.00	0	100	0.00	0	0	0	0	0
Hockey	1	89.47	100	85.7	0.00	0	0	10.53	0	14.3
Netball	1	76.47	0	100	11.76	0	0	11.76	0	0
Basketball	1	53.85	100	100	35.90	0	0	10.26	0	0
Athletics	1	70.59	100	85.7	17.65	0	0	11.76	0	14.3
Sailing	1	52.24	90	44.4	29.85	10	44.4	17.91	0	11.1
Canoeing	1	74.07	100	100	25.93	0	100	0	0	0
Windsurfing	1	82.35	100	100	17.65	0	100	0	0	0
Curling	1	100.00	0	100	0.00	0	100	0	0	0
Volleyball	1	90.48	0	100	9.52	0	100	0	0	0

[1] OC1 represents the members of clubs other than sports clubs taking part in a particular activity in a competitive sporting context.

[2] OC2 represents the members of clubs other than sports clubs taking part in a particular activity in a recreation context.

[3] OC3 represents the members of clubs other than sports clubs taking part in a particular activity in a leisure context.

[4] SC1 represents the members of a sports club taking part in a particular activity in a competitive sporting context.

[5] SC2 represents the members of a sports club taking part in a particular activity in a recreation context.

[6] SC3 represents the members of a sports club taking part in a particular activity in a leisure context.

sports clubs members assigned to Cluster 1 for a particular activity (SC1). This process is repeated for the other clusters across the table.

Most of the cases support the interpretation of the modal pattern of cluster membership, established in Table 23.6 and thus add some credibility to the labels given to the clusters. The main results to note are that the sports club and other club memberships are most prevalent for the activities that we have described as sport or recreation. Not surprisingly, therefore, sports clubs are important for activities such as football and golf, whereas other club membership is important for activities such as swimming indoors, keep fit, weight training, snooker and golf across the clusters. A possible explanation for this could be that these people are members of sport and leisure clubs, which offer keep fit, weight-training and swimming facilities under one roof.

Summary of key findings

The cluster analysis identifies that 67% of the GHS sample of 14,827 cases aged over 16 years demonstrated distinct classification profiles that can be identified with their individual and socioeconomic, and sporting, characteristics. In terms of sports participation generally, it is identified that majority of cases are non-active. Of those who did participate, only 3% were active in competitive, institutionalised sport, compared with 20% in recreation activities, with an overwhelming 76% in leisure activities.

On balance, the former, is found to be described as a gendered, youthful activity. Men were twice as likely to participate in sport as women, and the typical age range was 24 to 28. This compares to 28 to 54 years for recreation participants and 32 to 59 years for leisure participants. Access to a motor vehicle increases the likelihood of participation in both sport and recreation eight-fold. Increases are also associated with employment and social-class status. Thus, the mean weekly household wage for sports cases category is £1,690 per week, compared with £888 for the recreation cluster and £612 for

leisure. In all, 3.5% of workers were active in sport, with 23.8% active in recreation. There was no significant sporting activity amongst the unemployed. No ethnic differences were discernable in the results.

The structure of the household and location is also connected with the level of participation. Married couples with no children are likely to withdraw from sporting activity as family size grows, or when the family splits up. Those in the South East, South West and North West are more likely to be involved in sport and recreation than those elsewhere in the country. Education effects are also present. Those with a higher degree are more than three times more likely to be involved in sport than those with no qualifications.

There is also evidence of portfolios of sport and recreation activity. Those in the sporting cluster reported participation in five sporting activities, compared with three for those in recreation and one for those in leisure. There was evidence of portfolios of leisure activity though, with each group reporting activity in four different leisure pastimes.

Health also appears to be important in profiling sport and leisure participation. Cases reporting their health to be good were three and a half times more likely to be in the sport cluster. By contrast, longstanding illness reduces sport participation by one and a half times, and illness limiting activity does so by two-fold. Smoking a pipe and a cigar were both associated with higher participation in sport than non-smokers (4% compared to 3%). Drinkers were also seen to be twice as likely to participate in sport as non-drinkers. Membership of sports or other clubs are also connected with the level of participation in sport in certain cases.

Commentary

The results clearly indicate that the individual and socioeconomic characteristics of cases in the sample are structured in definable and intelligible clusters and that these structures can be linked to sports participation decisions. Although this was an exploratory study, therefore, it provides support for the sorts of mechanism identified as social interactions in the various economic theories of choice discussed above. The key question, of course, is which, if any, of these mechanisms dominates? Ultimately, it can be argued that the choice between them would depend on methodological preference and deliberation. The neoclassical approach is built upon assumptions that describe rational individual choice. The patterns of structured characteristics discussed above would consequently reflect optimal-choice scenarios. This interpretation would mitigate against, for example, the policy activism currently being articulated from the UK government and various sports-related agencies over concern to promote more active lifestyles. By contrast, a heterodox view would identify these scenarios as snapshots of emergent processes in which agents and their structures interact in a non-optimal way. In this regard, scope for such policy activism could become logically grounded. It is in this sense that the above empirical work may aid economic policy making, by providing some general parameters around which more detailed analysis proceed, and specific causal mechanisms investigated further.

How might further analysis proceed? A possible starting point for future study would be to undertake longitudinal study. The British Household Panel provides some limited opportunity here in that some sports and leisure activities are identified. The Taking Part Survey commissioned by the Department of Culture Media and Sport, which was first undertaken in 2006 and will be repeated in 2009, is another opportunity. Such longitudinal data would allow cases to be followed, to an extent, through time. This would allow a more thorough investigation of the interactions and cluster membership.

In addition, the data partitions by cluster could be explored through the role of particular variables and thus begin to say something about causal mechanisms (Byrne 2003, p. 103). This is because the interpretation and assessment of the robustness of clusters are linked. Deleting variables and applying the analysis to sub-samples may

help to indicate capturing elements of real structures. Significantly, however, the cause and effect are not linked to the presence of single factors:

> Rather cause is a property of complex and contingent mechanisms in reality and such mechanisms, moreover, are not universal but only relatively permanent – inherently local. Traditionally causes have been understood as variables. In this text the very expression variable has been rejected and replaced by variate trace of complex and evolutionary system. (Byrne 2003, p. 106)

It is by comparing cases, therefore, that we might be able to say something about causes. Finally, regression analysis could also be used to investigate if cluster membership affects individual choices to participate.

CONCLUSIONS

This chapter has explored the use of cluster analysis in economics by examining the case of sport participation. Two competing traditions of economics have been outlined and argued to stress the need to explore social interactions in examining individual behaviour. It has been argued that cluster analysis can help to elucidate these processes and an application to the GHS (2002) has been presented. It is argued that the evidence is supportive of choice being reflected in limited combinations of individual and socioeconomic characteristics as indicative of social interaction yielding lifestyles. However, it is argued that the implications and refinement of such analysis will hinge on the methodological presuppositions of either the neoclassical or heterodox economic approaches being used to interpret the results.

NOTES

1. Respondents indicated if they had participated or not in the activity over the previous four weeks prior to the interview. The same approach is adopted in the GHS.

2. It is important to recognise that the definitions of sport and leisure are provided by the survey, the

analysis that follows places a different categorisation on them, as implied in Rodgers (1978).

3. Whereas football and cricket are identified as associated with Cluster 2, along with motor racing, both of these activities have large recreational constituencies as well as organised, club-based competitive forms of activity in contrast, say, to rugby and netball.

REFERENCES

Becker, G. 1965 'A theory of the allocation of time' *Economic Journal* 75(299): 493–517.

Becker, G. 1974 'A theory of social interactions' *Journal of Political Economy* 82(6): 1063–1091.

Bourdieu, P. 1990 *The Logic of Practice*. Cambridge: Polity Press.

Burton, T.L. 1971 *Experiments in Recreation Research*. London: George Allen and Unwin Ltd.

Byrne, D. 2003 *Interpreting Quantitative Data*. London: Sage.

Council of Europe 1980 *European Sport for All Charter*. Strasbourg: Council of Europe.

Council of Europe 1993 *European Sports Charter*. Strasbourg: Council of Europe.

Downward, P.M. 2007 'Exploring the economic choice to participate in sport: results from the 2002 general household survey' *International Review of Applied Economics* 21(5): 633–653.

Downward, P.M. and Kay, T. 2007 *Sport and the Family*. London: Sport England. Online. Available: http://www.sportengland.org/index/get_resources/research/tracking/generalhouseholdsurvey_2002.htm.

Downward, P.M. and Riordan, J. 2007 'Social interactions and the demand for sports: an economic analysis' *Contemporary Economic Policy* 25(4): 518–537.

Earl, P.E. 1986 *Lifestyle Economics*. Brighton, UK: Wheatsheaf.

Friedman, M. 1953 'The methodology of positive economics' in *World Health Organization Essays in Positive Economics*. Chicago: University of Chicago Press.

Galbraith, J.K. 1958 *The Affluent Society*. Harmondsworth, UK: Penguin.

General Household Survey 2000 Online. Available from the ESRC data archive: http://www.data-archive.ac.uk/findingData/majorstudies.asp.

Gratton, C. and Taylor, P. 2000 *The Economics of Sport and Recreation*. London: E and F.N. Spon.

Gravelle, H. and Rees, R. 2004 *Microeconomics*. London: Prentice Hall.

Kay, T. 2004 'The family factor in sport: a review of family factors affecting sports participation' in Sport England *Driving up Participation: The Challenge for Sport*. London: Sport England: pp. 37–58.

Lavoie, M. 1994 'A post Keynesian approach to consumer choice' *Journal of Post Keynesian Economics* 16(4): 539–562.

Lawson, T. 1997 *Economics and Reality*. London: Routledge.

Lawson, T. 2003 *Reorienting Economics*. London: Routledge.

Lawson, T. 2006 'The nature of heterodox economics' *Cambridge Journal of Economics* 30(2): 483–507.

Lewis, P. (Ed) 2004 *Transforming Economics*. London: Routledge.

Nell, E.J. 1992 'Demand, pricing and investment' in *World Health Organization Transformational Growth and Effective Demand: Economics After the Capital Critique*. London: Macmillan, pp. 381–451.

Putnam, H. 2002 *The Collapse of the Fact/Value Dichotomy and Other Essays*. Cambridge, MA: Harvard University Press.

Roberts, K. 1999 *Leisure in Contemporary Society*. Wallingford, UK: CABI Publications.

Robbins, L. 1966 Cited T. Lawson 2003 *Reorienting Economics*. London: Routledge.

Robinson, J. 1956 *The Accumulation of Capital*. London: Macmillan.

Rodgers, B. 1978 *Rationalising Sports Policies; Sport in Its Social Context: Technical Supplement*. Strasbourg: Council of Europe.

Romesburg, H.C. 2004 *Cluster Analysis for Researchers*. North Carolina: Lulu Press.

Shackle, G. 1966 *The Nature of Economic Thought*. Cambridge: Cambridge University Press.

Stempel, K. 2005 'Adult participation sports as cultural capital: a test of Bourdieu's theory of the field of sports' *International Review of the Sociology of Sport* 40(4): 411–412.

Sturgis, P. and Jackson, J. 2003 *Examining Participation in Sporting and Cultural Activities: Analysis of the UK 2000 Time Use Survey*. London: Department for Culture, Media and Sport.

Veblen, T. 1899/1931 *The Theory of the Leisure Class*. New York: Modern Library.

24

The Proper Relationship of Comparative-Historical Analysis to Statistical Analysis: Subordination, Integration, or Separation?

James Mahoney and P. Larkin Terrie

'Comparative-historical analysis has claimed its proud place as one of the most fruitful approaches in modern social science,' declares Theda Skocpol (2003, p. 424). It is hard to disagree. In the 1960s and 1970s, comparative-historical research recaptured attention through a series of stunningly successful works (e.g., Moore 1966, Lipset and Rokkan 1968, Bendix 1974, Tilly 1975, Skocpol 1979). Then, in more recent decades, the tradition gathered further momentum through the publication of major new studies and the codification of its methods. Important substantive works can be found in fields as diverse as social provision and welfare-state development (e.g., Esping-Anderson 1990, Skocpol 1992, Steinmo 1993, Pierson

1994, Hicks 1999, Huber and Stephens 2001); state formation and state restructuring (Bensel 1990, Tilly 1990, Ekiert 1996, Ertman 1997, Waldner 1999); economic development and market-oriented adjustment (Haggard 1990, Sikkink 1991, Evans 1995, Karl 1997, Bunce 1999, Kohli 2004); racial, ethnic, and national identities (Lustick 1993, Marx 1998, Yashar 2005); revolutionary change (e.g., Goldstone 1991, Wickham-Crowley 1992, Goodwin 2001); and democratic and authoritarian regimes (Collier and Collier 1991, Luebbert 1991, Downing 1992, Linz and Stepan 1996, Collier 1999, Mahoney 2001, Rueschemeyer et al. 1992). Methodological contributions have come both from those scholars writing self-consciously on comparative-historical analysis (Skocpol and Somers 1980, Mahoney 1999, Mahoney and Rueschemeyer 2003) and those framing their work more generally as contributions to the methodology of qualitative or case-study research (Brady and Collier 2004, George and Bennett 2005).

Yet, while comparative-historical analysis currently stands as a leading approach, two trends could be seen as casting some doubt over its future. The first trend concerns the methodological debate in the social sciences. Despite the proliferation of writings on comparative-historical methods, this mode of research is still received skeptically in some quarters. Perhaps most notably, scholars who pursue the statistical testing of hypotheses with large numbers of cases continue to raise concerns. And as statistical methodologists refine their own tools in ever more technically sophisticated ways, these concerns could be seen as carrying great weight, for statistical analysis continues to enjoy the upper hand – rightly or wrongly – in positioning itself *vis-à-vis* the idea of a rigorous science. Statistical methodologists thus cannot be ignored when they contend that comparative-historical analysis violates well-known aspects of good scientific research design and procedure (e.g., Geddes 1990, 2003, Lieberson 1991, 1994, 1998, King et al. 1994, Goldthorpe 1997, Coppedge 2008). And they carry legitimacy when they use their methodological criticisms as a basis for questioning whether the influential substantive findings produced in this field are, in fact, valid.

Meanwhile, a second trend is at work in substantive research. Recent years have seen a proliferation of multi-method approaches and the appearance of successful multi-method studies. Work that reports on this literature not surprisingly emphasizes the potentially strong complementarities between comparative-historical and statistical methods (Collier et al. 2004a, pp. 256–258, George and Bennett 2005, pp. 34–35, Lieberman 2005). Advocates of multi-method analysis generally do not accept the criticisms of comparative-historical work made by statistical methodologists, instead emphasizing that each tradition

has distinctive strengths and weaknesses and that there are methodological advantages to be gained by combining methods from each tradition. In sharp contrast to the notion of convergence on a singular approach shared by all, the message here is one of trade-offs across alternative designs and the idea that one approach might compensate for weaknesses in the other.

Given these recent developments, how should we think about the emerging place of comparative-historical research in modern social science? The literature seems to suggest one of two conclusions. On the one hand, it suggests that comparative-historical analysis must move in the direction of statistical inference or risk losing prestige and influence within the social sciences. This conclusion points toward a more universal adoption of the tools of statistical analysis. On the other hand, however, the trend toward multi-method research suggests that we will see the integration of comparative-historical and statistical analysis. The logical outcome here is a thoroughly pluralistic social science in which individual studies simultaneously and perhaps equally embody both approaches.

In this chapter, by contrast, we propose an alternative view. Consistent with the advocates of multi-method research, we argue that the methods employed by the two traditions are equally legitimate because each tradition adopts distinct research goals and uses tools that are specifically tailored to achieving its goals. In consequence, advice and criticisms aimed at comparative-historical work that are derived solely from a statistical template are not appropriate (Brady and Collier 2004, Mahoney and Goertz 2006). However, these same differences in research orientation also suggest limits on the extent to which it is possible to integrate the two traditions in single studies. Although the recent emphasis on the complementarities between the two traditions has provided a useful step forward, we instead emphasize the complementarities *within* each tradition, particularly between research goals and methods. As a result of these within-tradition complementarities, specific multi-method studies will tend to be either predominantly statistical or comparative-historical.

CONTRASTING COMPARATIVE-HISTORICAL AND STATISTICAL ANALYSIS

The comparative-historical and statistical traditions are each extremely heterogeneous fields. Within each field, there are substantially different approaches and competing tools. Nevertheless, we follow many others in believing that it is possible and useful to speak of general practices in these whole traditions. In particular, we believe the approaches can be defined and contrasted across a small number of critical dimensions. Here we emphasize three such dimensions: (1) goal of explanation; (2) conception of causation; and (3) mode of hypothesis testing.

In terms of these dimensions, we characterize comparative-historical analysis in the following way: (1) it asks questions about the causes of effects (i.e., why particular dependent variable values occurred in specific cases); (2) it relies on a conception of causation built around necessary and sufficient causes and their derivatives (e.g., INUS causes); and (3) it tests theories with a combination of comparative set-theoretic methods and process tracing. By contrast, we characterize statistical analysis as follows: (1) it asks questions about the effects of causes (i.e., the causal influence of particular independent variables); (2) it uses an average effects conception of causation; and (3) it tests theories with regression techniques. We have demonstrated elsewhere that each set of traits has a strong tendency to cluster together (Mahoney and Terrie 2008). Here our goal is to explore why these traits tend to complement one another. We suggest that the very different kinds of research goal pursued by studies in each tradition leads naturally and appropriately to other methodological differences.

To show how these methodological traits fit together in practice, the discussion is grounded in an examination of two influential studies from the social policy literature – Ann Shola Orloff and Theda Skocpol's 'Why Not Equal Protection? Explaining the Politics of Public Social Spending in Britain, 1900–1911, and the United States, 1880s–1920' (1984), and Evelyne Huber, Charles Ragin, and John D. Stephens' 'Social Democracy, Constitutional Structure, and the Welfare State' (1993). We chose these two classic studies because they are quite well known, very highly regarded, and focus on similar subject matter. Their clarity in approach, explanation, and presentation of findings also allows us to make our central points in an expedient manner.

Orloff and Skocpol

In their study, Orloff and Skocpol (1984) take a clear causes-of-effects approach, seeking to explain divergent social policy outcomes in Britain and the United States in the early twentieth century. As they put it, 'This article aims to explain why Great Britain was among the world's pioneers in launching social insurance, while the early twentieth-century United States failed to adopt old-age pensions and health and unemployment insurance, settling only for workers' compensation and mothers' pensions' (Orloff and Skocpol 1984, p. 727). Their argument focuses on patterns of nineteenth century state formation, particularly whether each country had a national poor law and an independent civil service and whether its political parties were programmatic or patronage-oriented. They find that Britain had a favorable combination of factors for the passage of social insurance as its poor law created a national debate over government policy toward the poor, parties competed for working-class support through programmatic competition, and civil service bureaucrats took the initiative in designing new policies (pp. 739–741). By contrast, the US faced a highly unfavorable combination of factors as it had no national poor law to spur a debate on social policy, it had no independent civil service to formulate and lobby for reforms, and, given the importance of patronage politics, many reform-minded elites were highly reluctant to accept new social spending because they feared it would create new opportunities for patronage-based corruption (pp. 741–743).

Orloff and Skocpol's concern with accounting for dependent variable values in specific cases leads them to apply the criterion of causal sufficiency to potential explanations.[1] They criticize several alternative explanations of welfare-state development – the emergence of the working class, level of socioeconomic development, and strength of liberal values – on the basis that they 'cannot sufficiently explain' the contrast between Britain and the US (p. 745). Furthermore, concern with accounting for a particular outcome also has an affinity with emphasizing necessary causes – factors without which the outcome of interest could not have occurred. A focus on causal necessity comes across most clearly in Orloff and Skocpol's discussion of Massachusetts (included in their study because of its similarity to Britain in terms of urbanization and industrialization). They argue that the concern among Massachusetts' elites that increased social spending would heighten the corruption associated with patronage politics effectively blocked passage of old-age pensions, unemployment insurance, and health insurance by the state legislature (pp. 743–744). The implied counterfactual is that without this blocking mechanism created by patronage politics these social programs would have been far more likely to pass – leading to an outcome different from the observed one.

In terms of theory testing, Orloff and Skocpol rely heavily on process tracing. This method is discussed in more depth below, but, most centrally, process tracing involves the search for evidence that the causal mechanism posited to be linking the independent variable(s) and the outcome of interest is in fact operating in a given case. In their effort to explain the weakness of the American welfare state in the early twentieth century, Orloff and Skocpol show that fear of creating more opportunities for patronage-based corruption blocked the expansion of social protection. The authors

draw in particular on statements by prominent reformers denouncing the already existing Civil War pension system to demonstrate that such fears were widespread (p. 743). In the British case, they establish the importance of the national poor law by using evidence from secondary sources that show how, in the early twentieth century, national politicians became concerned with the way the 'worthy poor' were treated under this law (p. 740).

It is important to note that Orloff and Skocpol do not base their causal inferences solely on process tracing. As is typical of studies that attempt to explain specific outcomes in a small number of cases, they also draw on Mill's methods to assess rival explanations. The methods of agreement and difference have a strong affinity with a necessary and sufficient conception of causation given that they are logically designed to eliminate necessary and sufficient causes. These methods can complement process tracing by providing an additional basis for causal inference (Mahoney 2003). Orloff and Skocpol implicitly use the method of difference when they evaluate and reject several potential causes, including level of industrialization, liberal values, and working class strength. By demonstrating that the US and Britain had similar high scores on these variables, they establish that none of these factors can be said to have generated by itself the contrast between the cases.

Huber, Ragin, and Stephens

The research goal of Huber, Ragin, and Stephens (1993) provides a sharp contrast with that pursued by Orloff and Skocpol, even though the two studies share a common interest in explaining cross-country variation in social protection. Huber et al. take a clear effects-of-causes approach, as they are concerned with 'why various independent variables should have different effects on different operationalizations of "welfare state effort"' (p. 713). Instead of attempting to develop a comprehensive explanation of why certain countries have particular kinds of welfare states, these authors investigate the extent to which their independent variables of interest, primarily Christian Democratic and Social Democratic party strength and constitutional structure, are associated with different kinds of welfare states across 17 industrialized countries. They find that both social democracy and Christian democracy are associated with high expenditure levels but that Social Democratic party strength is more strongly associated with decommodifying and redistributive effects than is Christian Democratic party strength. They also find that to the extent that constitutional structures create multiple possibilities for policy veto, countries tend to have lower scores on various measures of welfare-state effort (pp. 733–738).

Whereas a causes-of-effects approach leads Orloff and Skocpol to gather evidence regarding the causal processes taking place within each of their cases, Huber et al.'s concern with the effects of causes leads them to use regression analysis to estimate the individual causal effects of their independent variables across their full population of cases. With regression analysis it is not necessary to fully account for the dependent variable values in all of one's cases in order to arrive at estimates of the effects of the independent variables of interest. Some methodologists even argue that attempting to build regression models that account for as much variation in the dependent variable as possible can interfere with the goal of estimating causal effects (King 1991, p. 1048). In consequence, statistical researchers who investigate the effects of causes tend to conceptualize causation in terms of the average effects of an independent variable over a large number of cases rather than in terms of necessity or sufficiency. Indeed, as is the norm for statistical social scientific studies, Huber et al. do not discuss their independent variables in terms of their ability to fully account for the types of welfare states in their cases, or the necessity of particular independent variable values for particular welfare-state features, but rather focus on the effects of their independent variables on average across all of their cases.

These two studies came to qualitatively different kinds of findings. Orloff and Skocpol found that a complex configuration of independent variable values accounted for the different outcomes in their cases, while Huber et al. found that their targeted independent variables had incremental effects on particular dimensions of the welfare state. Nonetheless, each study made an important contribution to our understanding of cross-country variation in welfare-state outcomes. These different types of findings were products of the different, though equally legitimate, research goals pursued by each study.

CONCERNS ABOUT METHODOLOGICAL PRACTICES

All observational studies in the social sciences confront important obstacles and potentially are subject to error. However, some analysts have argued that comparative-historical research faces especially grave problems that can often be easily avoided in statistical research (for a recent statement, see Coppedge 2008). The implicit or explicit implication is often that social scientists should pursue statistical research when possible (see also Lijphart 1971). In this section, by contrast, we argue that comparative-historical analysis and statistical analysis pursue different research goals, and that while they both face methodological challenges, they both play an essential role in generating knowledge in social science.

Selection bias

Several methodologists have sounded alarm bells about the tendency of qualitative researchers to select cases based on their value on the dependent variable (Achen and Snidal 1989, Geddes 1991, 2003, King et al. 1994). These stern warnings about deliberately selecting cases because they exhibit certain outcomes are especially applicable to comparative-historical studies, which quite explicitly engage in the practice. On the one hand, of course, selection on the dependent variable in this field is hardly surprising, given that the research goal is precisely the explanation of particular outcomes. If one wishes to explain certain outcomes, it seems natural to choose cases that exhibit those outcomes. On the other hand, however, selecting cases based on their value on the dependent variable will bias findings in statistical research. From this standpoint, the practice seems to violate a basic norm of good research.

To evaluate this concern, when applied to comparative-historical analysis, we need to recognize that the statistical literature on bias deriving from selection on the dependent variable assumes that one wishes to generalize about average causal effects from a sample to a well-defined larger population. In comparative-historical research, by contrast, one seeks to identify realized causal effects in particular cases; generalizing about averages from a sample to a larger population may be a secondary goal or not a goal at all. And insofar as comparative-historical researchers select what can be considered the entire universe of cases, standard issues of selection bias simply do not arise, regardless of whether the cases were chosen for their values on the dependent variable (for more extensive discussions, see Collier and Mahoney 1996, Collier et al. 2004b).[2]

Scope and generalization

These observations raise questions about generalization. Obviously, comparative-historical researchers cannot simply make-up whatever definition of the universe of cases they so choose; the decision to limit a theory's applicability to a particular set of cases should not be arbitrary. One needs to ask, therefore, about the methodological basis for adopting a restrictive understanding of scope. This question is critical because the practice of restricting generalizations to a limited set of cases – not issues of selection bias, as conventionally understood – is often the real source of concern held by statistical methodologists about case selection in comparative-historical analysis. In particular, given the expansive definition of scope often employed in statistical research, the findings of comparative-historical researchers appear to be derived from a potentially unrepresentative sample of cases that is arbitrarily treated as the full population. Let us then explore these issues of scope and generalization.

Social scientists commonly impose scope restrictions on their findings to avoid problems associated with causal heterogeneity, which generates instability in estimates of causal effects. Indeed, primarily because of causal heterogeneity, social scientists of all traditions rarely develop theories that are intended to apply to all places and times. In addition to issues of causal heterogeneity, the need for stable concepts and measurement lead to the use of scope restrictions in which the analyst excludes cases where conceptual and measurement validity cannot be maintained.

In comparative-historical research, analysts adopt a narrow scope because they believe that causal and conceptual heterogeneity are the norm for their theories when assessed across large populations (Mahoney and Rueschemeyer 2003). But is this belief justified? Here we need to recognize that causal heterogeneity is not an ontological property inherent to a population of cases, but rather a feature of the *relationship* between a specific theory and a population of cases (Seawright and Collier 2004, p. 276; and see Chapter 17 by Goertz and Mahoney). A given population of cases may be heterogeneous *vis-à-vis* one theory but not another. The same is true of conceptual heterogeneity: cases may be heterogeneous *vis-à-vis* some concepts but not others. One key implication is that some types of theories (or concepts) might be more likely than others to produce heterogeneity as the size of the population of cases increases.

There are very good reasons for believing that the type of theories evaluated in comparative-historical analysis are especially likely to generate causal heterogeneity in response to even modest increases in population size. To understand why, we need to compare the problem of missing variables in comparative-historical analysis and statistical analysis. This discussion, in turn, will take us back to the contrasting research goals of the two traditions.

In the comparative-historical tradition, the exclusion of one or more important explanatory variables from a theory is appropriately regarded as a major problem (Ragin 2004, pp. 135–138). This is true because the very goal of this kind of work is to explain particular outcomes in specific cases as completely and adequately as possible. All relevant evidence pertaining to the cases should be gathered and assessed. If theories are missing key variables, or have misspecified key relationships among the variables that are included, these facts count significantly against the arguments posited by the researcher. The failure of previous investigators to consider one or more critical variables in fact provides a common basis for analysts to criticize existing work and build new explanatory theories. Missing variables are thus a constant potential source of causal heterogeneity in this field. Similar arguments can be extended to measurement error, which needs to be addressed and eliminated completely for each specific case, if possible (Ragin 2004). Otherwise, the goal of adequately explaining an outcome in particular cases is compromised. In comparative-historical analysis, indeed, theory falsification often occurs with the change in value of one or a small number of variables. Accordingly, in this mode of research, one needs to strive to avoid measurement error for the cases analyzed, otherwise conceptual heterogeneity problems will likely arise.

There are thus good methodological reasons related to the need to avoid causal and conceptual heterogeneity that explain why comparative-historical researchers restrict the scope of their analysis to a limited number of cases. Given the kind of explanatory theory that these analysts pursue, built around the idea of realized causal effects for particular outcomes, they must quite carefully and deliberately define their population of cases to try to avoid all heterogeneity problems. Once the population is defined, even a modest increase in the number of cases runs the risk of excluding key causal factors relevant to the new cases or introducing measurement problems for the variables that are already

included in the theory. Because significant modifications to the theoretical model are often required as new cases are added, the best solution may be to impose restrictive scope conditions that limit generalization.

In statistical analysis, by contrast, the goal of research is typically to estimate the average effects of one or more independent variables. Given this goal, missing variables are not necessarily a problem as long as key assumptions, especially that of conditional independence, still hold. Independent variables that are important for only a small subset of cases might be appropriately considered 'unsystematic' and relegated to the error term of a regression model. Indeed, even missing independent variables that are systematically related to the outcome of interest will not necessarily bias estimates of average effects, as long as conditional independence still applies. Likewise, measurement error in statistical analysis does not raise the kinds of problems that it does in comparative-historical analysis. With a large number of cases, measurement error is always present and cannot be completely eliminated. However, if one seeks to identify average effects, as statistical analysts do, measurement error is not a devastating problem as long as it is non-systematic or at least can be adequately modeled in the event that it is systematic. Unbiased estimates of average effects are quite possible in the presence of measurement error.

The fact that statistical analysis can maintain causal homogeneity even in the presence of missing variables and measurement error allows this kind of research to embrace a more expansive understanding of scope and generalization than the comparative-historical approach. For example, the inclusion of new cases with outcomes that were partially caused by idiosyncratic factors will not necessarily raise any special heterogeneity problems in statistical analysis. As long as assumptions such as conditional independence are valid and measurement error can be modeled, the extension of the scope to include new cases is usually not a problem in statistical research. Not surprisingly, therefore, statistical researchers worry less about issues of heterogeneity as they extend their arguments to new cases.

An important issue arises at this point: if comparative-historical explanations are highly fragile when new cases are introduced, but statistical explanations are much less fragile, does it not also follow that statistical explanations are 'superior'? There are two reasons why this conclusion is not correct. The first is that the ability of statistical analysis to adopt a wide scope of generalization is dependent on the validity of key assumptions, especially conditional independence. In contemporary social science, many empirical researchers feel quite comfortable making this assumption with little elaboration. Yet methodologists and statisticians often suggest that the assumption is an unrealistic leap of faith in much of the observational research pursued in the social sciences (Lieberson 1985, Freedman 1991). Insofar as the assumption of conditional independence cannot be sustained, statistical research suffers from unrecognized and unmodeled causal heterogeneity. In other words, it is possible that the expansive understanding of scope adopted in statistical analysis is often not appropriate.

Second, and more important for our purposes, it is essential to remember that comparative-historical researchers and statistical researchers have distinct research goals. If one wishes to explain particular outcomes in specific cases, as comparative-historical researchers do, then one must formulate theories in which it is not possible to easily extend the scope of generalization. The alternative is to reject the research goals of comparative-historical work; that is, to prohibit studies that seek to explain particular outcomes in specific cases and encourage scholars only to ask questions about average effects across large populations. For reasons that we discuss below, this kind of prohibition against asking comparative-historical questions would be extremely costly for social science knowledge. In short, if one is going to remain open to different forms of knowledge accumulation, and to ask causes-of-effects questions, then one must be willing to live with the restricted scope that accompanies comparative-historical analysis.

Assessing causation with a small N

Even if the limited scope of comparative-historical inquiry makes good sense, some analysts are still concerned that the small number of cases that fall within this scope does not permit the scientific testing of hypotheses. From a statistical standpoint, a small population poses a degrees of freedom problem and insurmountable obstacles for hypothesis testing. How can researchers ever hope to adjudicate among rival explanations if they select so few cases?

The answer to this question again requires appreciating differences between statistical analysis and comparative-historical analysis. In statistical research, where the goal is to estimate average causal effects, one needs to have enough cases to control for relevant variables and still achieve specified confidence levels. However, with comparative-historical research, the goal is not to generalize about typical effects for a large population. Rather, the goal is to determine whether a given variable *did exert* a causal effect on an outcome in a particular set of cases. Given this goal, researchers need to embrace a distinct understanding of causation and indeed of explanation, which – as we shall now see – obviates the need for a large number of cases to achieve valid causal assessment.

Comparative-historical researchers ask the following question about any potential causal factor: 'Did it exert an effect (alone or in combination with other variables) on the specific outcomes of interest in the particular set of cases that comprise the population?' Sometimes, even a cursory examination will allow one to dispose of certain causal factors that might be generally relevant across a large population of cases. For example, when explaining the emergence of democracy in economically poor India or Costa Rica, the variable of development is clearly not useful (at least in the usual way), even though it is positively related to democracy in a large sample of cases. In other instances, however, plausible causal factors cannot be so quickly dismissed. Many potential causal factors are 'correlated' with the specific outcome of interest. How do researchers adjudicate among these rival explanations that are matched with the outcome of interest?

Researchers in the comparative-historical tradition use the method of process tracing – which involves marshalling 'within-case' data – to pass judgment on the validity of rival explanations emphasizing factors that cannot be eliminated through comparative matching techniques. Although here is not the place to discuss at length the mechanics of process tracing (see George and Bennett 2005), a few words are in order. Most basically, process tracing helps one to assess whether a posited causal factor actually exerts a causal effect on a specific outcome. This is done by exploring the mechanisms through which the potential causal factor is hypothesized to contribute to the outcome. If intervening mechanisms cannot be located, then doubt is cast upon the causal efficacy of the factor in question. By contrast, if appropriate intervening mechanisms are found, then one has grounds for believing that the factor in question did exert the effect. Beyond this, process tracing allows one to evaluate hypotheses by considering 'sub-hypotheses' that do not necessarily refer to intervening mechanisms but that should be true if the main hypothesis of interest is valid (Mahoney and Villegas 2007).

It bears emphasis that this mode of hypothesis assessment does not require a large number of cases. Rather, like a detective solving a crime, the comparative-historical researcher who uses process tracing draws on particularly important facts from individual cases (see Goldstone 1997, McKeown 1999). Not all pieces of evidence count equally. Some forms of evidence are 'smoking guns' that strongly suggest a theory is correct; others are 'air-tight alibis' that strongly suggest a theory is not correct (Collier et al. 2004a). For these researchers, a theory is often only one key observation away from being falsified. Yet, they may have certain kinds of evidence that suggest that the likelihood of theory falsification ever occurring is small.

Another relevant consideration is that to assess hypotheses about necessary and sufficient causes, including combinations of causes that are jointly sufficient, a large number of cases is usually not needed. One or two cases may be enough for the simple purpose of eliminating (although not confirming) an explanation about necessary and sufficient causation. A medium number of cases is normally needed to achieve statistical confidence about the validity of an explanation that invokes necessary and/or sufficient causation solely by using cross-case matching techniques.[3] In some comparative-historical studies, this medium number of cases is analyzed. However, in small-N studies (e.g., N = 3), cross-case analysis is generally combined with process tracing. Because the N needed for necessary and sufficient causation is relatively modest, the 'burden' that process tracing must carry in such studies is not overwhelming. Rather, the small-N comparison does some of the work, with process tracing contributing the rest.

IMPLICATIONS OF THE DIFFERENCES

Our discussion has called attention to fundamental differences between comparative-historical analysis and statistical analysis. On the one hand, an awareness of these differences provides a basis for appreciating their distinctive contributions in social science. On the other hand, these differences are relevant for deciding the extent to which the two research traditions might be meaningfully combined. This final section addresses these implications.

The kinds of knowledge generated by comparative-historical research and statistical research are clearly different. Comparative-historical studies tell us why particular outcomes happened in specific cases – this is one important sense in which these studies are 'historical,' though there are others (see Skocpol 1984, Mahoney and Rueschemeyer 2003, Pierson 2004). This historical knowledge, in turn, is relevant for policy and practical reasons. By teaching us about the genesis of outcomes in certain specific cases, the knowledge provides a critical foundation for hypothesizing about the effects of subsequent developments in these cases. Here, a comparison with physicians who seek the medical history of their patients is useful. A cardiologist can offer better advice to a patient if the causes of the patient's earlier heart attack are well understood. Analogously, policy makers can pursue better interventions and offer more helpful suggestions if they understand well the causes of prior relevant outcomes in the cases of interest. Indeed, if one understands a particular pattern of causation in a given case, one would seem especially well situated to explore whether the causal pattern might apply to another similar case. These points will be obvious to some, but the tendency for many in the social sciences is nevertheless to assume that comparative-historical studies are of mostly historical relevance alone.

The strengths and pay-offs of statistical research are different. Whereas comparative-historical analysis is excellent at engaging complex theories with fine-grained overtime evidence, statistical research has the virtue of allowing for the testing of hypotheses about the average effects of particular variables (or specified interactions of variables) within large populations in a way that mimics aspects of a controlled experiment. Findings from large populations may or may not be relevant for thinking about particular cases. For example, a causal variable that promotes a given outcome in the population as a whole might have the opposite effect in a particular case of interest. But statistical findings certainly are relevant for generalizing. Indeed, if one wishes to offer policy advice or recommendations that are intended to – on average – make changes across a large population, the findings generated from statistical methods would seem especially appropriate.

This discussion is not intended to suggest that statistical work is irrelevant for thinking about particular cases. Nor is it meant to suggest that comparative-historical works cannot arrive at quite general findings. Rather, the point is that comparative-historical

and statistical studies have different goals, produce different kinds of information, and thus *tend to be* useful for different (although equally valid) purposes.

Given that each tradition has its own distinctive contributions to make, it is not surprising that there would be interest in combining the two, which perhaps could allow for a 'best of both worlds' synthesis. While contemporary social scientists often value multi-method research, we nevertheless wish to raise here some cautionary notes about combining comparative-historical analysis and statistical analysis. We believe that the combination is more difficult to achieve than is sometimes suggested, and that multi-method research is not always an improvement over work that is exclusively comparative-historical or exclusively statistical.

When they engage in multi-method research, most analysts still pursue either a causes-of-effects approach or an effects-of-causes approach. In this sense, much multi-method research can be considered *primarily* comparative-historical or *primarily* statistical in orientation. With multi-method work that is primarily comparative-historical, the main goal remains the explanation of specific outcomes in particular cases. The statistical analysis is subservient to this goal. By contrast, with multi-method work that is primarily statistical, the main goal is to estimate average causal effects for a large population. Here one or more case studies are used to service this larger goal. Occasionally, of course, some studies will pursue both goals equally and thus truly cross the divide. However, such studies are rare.[4]

How is statistical analysis used in multi-method studies that are primarily comparative-historical in orientation? In the most basic way, generalizations from prior statistical research represent background knowledge that comparative-historical analysts must consider as they formulate their own explanatory hypotheses for their case studies. All comparative-historical analysts react to prior general theories relevant to their outcomes, which often entails situating one's argument in relationship to existing statistical knowledge. Beyond this, comparative-historical researchers also may use statistical findings – including findings they generate themselves – in conjunction with process tracing. Much as a detective draws on knowledge of general causal principles to establish a link between suspect and crime, so too a comparative-historical researcher may use existing or newly discovered statistical findings when attempting to establish the mechanisms that connect cause and effect. For example, one might hypothesize that slow increases in grain prices in eighteenth-century France contributed to peasant revolts by deflating rural wages (i.e., the impact of declining grain prices on overall revolts worked through lower wages at the individual level). To develop this idea, a comparative-historical researcher might wish to carry out regression analysis to assess the effects of prices on wages in France – to make sure that the two are, in fact, statistically linked net of other factors (see Goldstone 1991, pp. 188–189). In doing this, the researcher collects a large number of observations from what is, given the perspective of the comparative-historical research design, a single case. Comparative-historical researchers thus may be especially likely to turn to statistical analysis when macro hypotheses in the small-N research design suggest mechanisms that work at lower levels of analysis. The statistical confirmation of these hypotheses serves the larger goal of validating the small-N argument.

For their part, statistical researchers may draw on the findings from comparative-historical analysis to develop their own hypotheses; comparative-historical work can inspire new ideas about causally relevant factors that can be tested in a statistical model. Statistical researchers may also turn to case studies to determine whether findings make sense when assessed in light of an intensive analysis of specific cases. Through such analyses, statistical researchers can evaluate whether the statistical model is adequate, needs refining and retesting, or is deeply problematic and cannot be salvaged. Although

in the course of the case analyses the researcher could potentially seek to develop fully adequate explanations of the particular cases, the overarching goal typically remains estimating the average effects of independent variables of interest for the population as a whole. For instance, in Lieberman's (2005) nested analysis approach, cases are selected not because their outcomes are inherently interesting, but rather because their location with respect to the regression line makes them good candidates for further assessing the validity of the statistical model. The goal of the nested analysis is generating valid knowledge about effects of causes; the comparative-historical evidence is mostly subordinated to the larger statistical design.

Our purpose in noting that one approach typically is subordinated to the other in multi-method research is not intended as a criticism. Rather, we emphasize the point to make it clear that most multi-method research is not equal parts quantitative and qualitative – it is, rather, primarily driven by the goals and orientations of one side or the other. When this point is acknowledged, it becomes clear that multi-method research is an advantage only to the extent that the use of the secondary method actually and effectively supplements the main method of investigation. Statistical studies that offer superficial case studies as supporting evidence do not contribute to the explanation of particular outcomes in those cases. And if the case studies are carried out without attention to good methodological practice, they will not provide a reliable basis for evaluating the statistical model either. By the same token, comparative-historical studies that use regression analysis in the course of process tracing are not necessarily more powerful than comparative-historical studies that do not use any statistical testing. The value added by statistical testing simply depends on what kind of evidence is needed for successful process tracing to be carried out. And the use of regression analysis with process tracing will not be fruitful if the regression analysis is poorly executed.

The message of this discussion is that there is nothing inherently wrong with conducting comparative-historical work that does not include a statistical component (and vice versa). Indeed, for many research projects, an additional secondary analysis using an alternative methodology is unnecessary or inappropriate. Hence, as social science increasingly moves toward and celebrates multi-method research, we believe that some of the best work that is produced will eschew this trend and remain squarely centered in one field or the other. In short, we believe that the proper relationship of comparative-historical analysis to statistical analysis is both integration and separation while thoroughly avoiding subordination.

NOTES

1. Quite often, researchers treat individual causes as parts of a larger combination of causes that are together *jointly sufficient* for the outcome of interest (Mackie 1980). In fact, in this field, distinct combinations of causes may each be sufficient, such that there are multiple causal paths to the same outcome (see Ragin 1987).

2. Problems of selection bias, as conventionally understood in the statistical literature, arise in comparative-historical studies primarily when analysts seek to generalize their theories beyond the initial cases investigated.

3. Using Bayesian assumptions, for example, Dion (1998) shows that only five cases may be enough to yield 95 per cent confidence about necessary causes. Using a simple binomial probability test, Ragin (2000, pp. 113–115) shows that if one works with 'usually necessary' or 'usually sufficient' causes, seven consistent cases are enough to meet this level of significance. Braumoeller and Goertz (2000) offer many examples of case-oriented studies that pass such significance tests.

4. In a sample of articles from leading journals, we found that only 8.7 per cent of articles pursued this kind of multi-method research (Mahoney and Terrie 2008).

REFERENCES

Achen, C.H. and Snidal, D. 1989 'Rational deterrence theory and comparative case studies' *World Politics* 41: 143–169.

Bendix, R. 1974 *Work and Authority in Industry: Ideologies of Management in the Course of Industrialization.* Berkeley, CA: University of California Press.

Bensel, R.F. 1990 *Yankee Leviathan: The Origins of Central State Authority in America, 1859–1877.* New York: Cambridge University Press.

Brady, H.E. and Collier, D. (Eds) 2004 *Rethinking Social Inquiry: Diverse Tools, Shared Standards.* Lanham, MD: Rowman and Littlefield.

Braumoeller, B.F. and Goertz, G. 2000 'The methodology of necessary conditions' *America Journal of Political Science* 44: 844–858.

Bunce, V. 1999 *Subversive Institutions: The Design and the Destruction of Socialism and the State.* Cambridge: Cambridge University Press.

Collier, D. and Mahoney, J. 1996 'Insights and pitfalls: selection bias in qualitative research' *World Politics* 49: 56–91.

Collier, D., Brady, H.E. and Seawright, J. 2004a 'Sources of leverage in causal inference: toward an alternative view of methodology' in H.E. Brady and D. Collier (Eds) *Rethinking Social Inquiry: Diverse Tools, Shared Standards.* Lanham, MD: Rowman and Littlefield, pp. 229–266.

Collier, D., Mahoney, J. and Seawright, J. 2004b 'Claiming too much: warnings about selection bias' in H.E. Brady and D. Collier (Eds) *Rethinking Social Inquiry: Diverse Tools, Shared Standards.* Lanham, MD: Rowman and Littlefield, pp. 85–102.

Collier, R.B. 1999 *Paths toward Democracy.* New York: Cambridge University Press.

Collier, R.B. and Collier, D. 1991 *Shaping the Political Arena: Critical Junctures, the Labor Movement, and Regime Dynamics in Latin America.* Princeton, NJ: Princeton University Press.

Coppedge, M. 2008 *Approaching Democracy: Research Methods in Comparative Politics.* New York: Cambridge University Press.

Dion, D. 1998 'Evidence and inference in comparative case study' *Comparative Politics* 30: 127–146.

Downing, B.M. 1992 *The Military Revolution and Political Change: Origins of Democracy and Autocracy in Early Modern Europe.* Princeton, NJ: Princeton University Press.

Ekiert, G. 1996 *The State against Society: Political Crises and Their Aftermath in East Central Europe.* Princeton, NJ: Princeton University Press.

Ertman, T. 1997 *Birth of the Leviathan: Building States and Regimes in Medieval and Early Modern Europe.* Cambridge: Cambridge University Press.

Esping-Anderson, G. 1990 *The Three Worlds of Welfare Capitalism.* Princeton, NJ: Princeton University Press.

Evans, P. 1995 *Embedded Autonomy: States and Industrial Transformation.* Princeton, NJ: Princeton University Press.

Freedman, D.A. 1991 'Statistical models and shoe leather' in P. Marsden (Ed.) *Sociological Methodology*. San Francisco: Jossey-Bass.

Geddes, B. 1990 'How the cases you choose affect the answers you get: selection bias in comparative politics' in J.A. Stimson (Ed.) *Political Analysis*. Volume 2. Ann Arbor, MI: University of Michigan Press, pp. 131–150.

Geddes, B. 1991 'Paradigms and sand castles in comparative politics of developing areas' in W. Crotty (Ed.) *Comparative Politics, Policy, and International Relations*. Evanston, IL: Northwestern University Press, pp. 45–75.

Geddes, B. 2003 *Paradigms and Sand Castles: Theory Building in Comparative Politics*. Ann Arbor, MI: University of Michigan Press.

George, A.L. and Bennett, A. 2005 *Case Studies and Theory Development in the Social Sciences*. Cambridge, MA: MIT Press.

Goldstone, J.A. 1991 *Revolution and Rebellion in the Early Modern World*. Berkeley, CA: University of California Press.

Goldstone, J.A. 1997 'Methodological issues in comparative macrosociology' *Comparative Social Research* 16: 107–120.

Goldthorpe, J.H. 1997 'Current issues in comparative macrosociology: a debate on methodological issues' *Comparative Social Research* 16: 1–26.

Goodwin, J. 2001 *No Other Way Out: States and Revolutionary Movements, 1945–1991*. Cambridge: Cambridge University Press.

Haggard, S. 1990 *Pathways from the Periphery: The Politics of Growth in the Newly Industrializing Countries*. Princeton, NJ: Princeton University Press.

Hicks, A. 1999 *Social Democracy and Welfare Capitalism: A Century of Income Security Politics*. Ithaca, NY: Cornell University Press.

Huber, E. and Stephens, J.D. 2001 *Development and Crisis of the Welfare State: Parties and Policies in Global Markets*. Chicago: University of Chicago Press.

Huber, E. Ragin, C. and Stephens, J.D. 1993 'Social democracy, constitutional structure, and the welfare state' *The American Journal of Sociology* 99: 711–749.

Karl, T.L. 1997 *The Paradox of Plenty: Oil Booms and Petro-States*. Berkeley, CA: University of California Press.

King, G. 1991 ' "Truth" is stranger than fiction, more questionable than causal inference' *American Journal of Political Science* 35: 1047–1053.

King, G., Keohane, R. and Verba, S. 1994 *Designing Social Inquiry: Scientific Inference in Qualitative Research*. Princeton, NJ: Princeton University Press.

Kohli, A. 2004 *State-Directed Development: Political Power and Industrialization in the Global Periphery*. New York: Cambridge University Press.

Lieberman, E.S. 2005 'Nested analysis as a mixed method strategy for comparative research' *American Political Science Review* 99: 435–452.

Lieberson, S. 1985 *Making It Count: The Improvement of Social Research and Theory*. Berkeley, CA: University of California Press.

Lieberson, S. 1991 'Small N's and big conclusions: an examination of the reasoning in comparative studies based on a small number of cases' *Social Forces* 70: 307–320.

Lieberson, S. 1994 'More on the uneasy case for using Mill-type methods in small-N comparative studies' *Social Forces* 72: 1225–1237.

Lieberson, S. 1998 'Causal analysis and comparative research: what can we learn from studies based on a small number of cases' in H-P. Blossfeld and G. Prein (Eds) *Rational Choice Theory and Large-Scale Data Analysis*. Boulder, CO: Westview, pp. 129–415.

Lijphart, A. 1971 'Comparative politics and the comparative method' *American Political Science Review* 65: 682–693.

Linz, J.J. and Stepan, A. 1996 *Problems of Democratic Transition and Consolidation: Southern Europe, South America, and Post-Communist Europe*. Baltimore: Johns Hopkins University Press.

Lipset, S.M. and Rokkan, S. (Eds) 1968 *Party Systems and Voter Alignments: Cross-National Perspectives*. New York: Free Press.

Luebbert, G.M. 1991 *Liberalism, Fascism, or Social Democracy: Social Classes and the Political Origins of Regimes in Interwar Europe*. New York: Oxford University Press.

Lustick, I. 1993 *Unsettled States, Disputed Lands: Britain and Ireland, France and Algeria, Israel and the West Bank-Gaza*. Ithaca, NY: Cornell University Press.

Mackie, J.L. 1980 *The Cement of the Universe: A Study of Causation*. Oxford: Oxford University Press.

Mahoney, J. 1999 'Nominal, ordinal, and narrative appraisal in macro-causal analysis' *American Journal of Sociology* 104: 1154–1196.

Mahoney, J. 2001 '*The Legacies of Liberalism: Path Dependence and Political Regimes in Central America*' Baltimore: Johns Hopkins University Press.

Mahoney, J. 2003 'Long-run development and the legacy of colonialism in Spanish America' *American Journal of Sociology* 109(1): 51–106.

Mahoney, J. and Goertz, G. 2006 'A tale of two cultures: contrasting qualitative and quantitative research' *Political Analysis* 14: 227–249.

Mahoney, J. and Larkin Terrie, P. 2008 'Comparative-historical analysis in contemporary political science' in J.M. Box-Steffensmeier, H.E. Brady and D. Collier (Eds) *The Oxford Handbook of Political Methodology*. New York: Oxford University Press, pp. 737–755.

Mahoney, J. and Rueschemeyer, D. 2003 'Comparative historical analysis: achievements and agendas' in J. Mahoney and D. Rueschemeyer (Eds) *Comparative Historical Analysis in the Social Sciences*. New York: Cambridge University Press, pp. 3–38.

Mahoney, J. and Villegas, C. 2007 'Historical enquiry and comparative politics' in C. Boix and S.C. Stokes (Eds) *The Oxford Handbook of Comparative Politics*. Oxford: Oxford University Press, pp. 73–89.

Marx, A.W. 1998 *Making Race and Nation: A Comparison of South Africa, the United States, and Brazil*. Cambridge: Cambridge University Press.

McKeown, T.J. 1999 'Case studies and the statistical worldview' *International Organization* 53: 161–190.

Moore, B. Jr 1966 *Social Origins of Dictatorship and Democracy: Lord and Peasant in the Making of the Modern World*. Boston: Beacon Press.

Orloff, A.S. and Skocpol, T. 1984 'Why not equal protection? Explaining the politics of public social spending in Britain, 1900–1911, and the United States, 1880s–1920' *American Sociological Review* 49: 726–750.

Pierson, P. 1994 *Dismantling the Welfare State? Reagan, Thatcher, and the Politics of Retrenchment*. Cambridge: Cambridge University Press.

Pierson, P. 2004 *Politics in Time: History, Institutions, and Social Analysis*. Princeton, NJ: Princeton University Press.

Ragin, C.C. 1987 *The Comparative Method: Moving beyond Qualitative and Quantitative Strategies*. Berkeley, CA: University of California Press.

Ragin, C.C. 2000 *Fuzzy-Set Social Science*. Chicago: University of Chicago Press.

Ragin, C.C. 2004 'Turning the tables: how case-oriented research challenges variable-oriented research' in H.E. Brady and D. Collier (Eds) *Rethinking Social Inquiry: Diverse Tools, Shared Standards*. Lanham, MD: Rowman and Littlefield, pp. 123–138.

Rueschemeyer, D., Stephens, E.H. and Stephens, J.D. 1992 *Capitalist Development and Democracy*. Chicago: University of Chicago Press.

Seawright, J. and Collier, D. 2004 'Glossary' in H.E. Brady and D. Collier (Eds) *Rethinking Social Inquiry: Diverse Tools, Shared Standards*. Lanham, MD: Rowman and Littlefield, pp. 273–313.

Sikkink, K. 1991 *Ideas and Institutions: Developmentalism in Brazil and Argentina*. Ithaca, NY: Cornell University Press.

Skocpol, T. 1979 *States and Social Revolutions: A Comparative Analysis of France, Russia, and China*. Cambridge: Cambridge University Press.

Skocpol, T. 1984 'Sociology's historical imagination' in T. Skocpol (Ed.) *Vision and Method in Historical Sociology*. Cambridge: Cambridge University Press, pp. 1–21.

Skocpol, T. 1992 *Protecting Soldiers and Mothers: The Political Origins of Social Policy in the United States*. Cambridge, MA: Belknap Press of Harvard University Press.

Skocpol, T. 2003 'Doubly engaged social science: the promise of comparative historical analysis' in J. Mahoney and D. Rueschemeyer (Eds) *Comparative-Historical Analysis in the Social Sciences*. New York: Cambridge University Press, pp. 407–428.

Skocpol, T. and Somers, M. 1980 'The uses of comparative history in macrosocial inquiry' *Comparative Studies in Society and History* 22: 174–197.

Steinmo, S. 1993 *Taxation and Democracy: Swedish, British and America Approaches to Financing the Modern State*. New Haven, CT: Yale University Press.

Tilly, C. (Ed) 1975 *The Formation of National States in Western Europe*. Princeton, NJ: Princeton University Press.

Tilly, C. 1990 *Coercion, Capital, and European States, AD 990–1990*. Cambridge, MA: Basil Blackwell.

Waldner, D. 1999 *State-Building and Late Development*. Ithaca, NY: Cornell University Press.

Wickham-Crowley, T. 1992 *Guerrillas and Revolution in Latin America: A Comparative Study of Insurgents and Regimes since 1956*. Princeton, NJ: Princeton University Press.

Yashar, D.J. 2005 *Contesting Citizenship in Latin America: The Rise of Indigenous Movements and the Postliberal Challenge*. New York: Cambridge University Press.

25

Case Studies and the Configurational Analysis of Organizational Phenomena

Peer C. Fiss

Within the organization and management literatures, the case study has traditionally occupied a somewhat peculiar position. On the one hand, case studies have a long and distinguished history in the study of organizations. They have featured prominently in academic research on organizations, and many of the most highly regarded and influential studies in the organization and management literature have employed a case study approach (cf. Gephart, 2004). Some of the most well-known examples include Selznick's (1949) study of the Tennessee Valley Authority, Blau's (1955) and Crozier's (1964) research on the dynamics of bureaucracy, Allison's (1971) study of governmental action around the 1962 Cuban missile crisis, and Dalton's (1959) and Kanter's (1977) work on life within the modern corporation, to name but a few. In fact, one might well argue that case studies form the cornerstone on which modern organization theory has been built, providing rich insights into the workings of modern organizations

and ample opportunities for theory building. Furthermore, case studies occupy a central role in the curricula of most business schools, where cases are used extensively as a pedagogical tool. Case studies are attractive in the classroom because they simulate real-world experiences, allowing the students to take on the roles of specific decision makers in actual organizations (Mauffette-Leenders et al. 2001). Their closeness to the experience of life in organizations and their appreciation for the complexities of organizational phenomena thus makes case studies attractive to academics and practitioners alike.

On the other hand, there has been a considerable debate over the scientific nature of case studies and the ways in which they are to be conducted. This debate over the case study approach goes back to at least 1940. Back then – as is largely true today – the ability of the case study to generate new ideas and thus contribute to theory development was uncontested, but controversy focused on whether the case study could be used to derive generalizable insights (e.g. Lundberg 1941, Stouffer 1941, Foreman 1948). Even today, the case study remains probably the least understood and least formalized methodology in the study of organizations (Ragin and Becker 1992). Despite a number of works on the use of the case study methodology (e.g. Yin 1981, Eisenhardt 1989), there is still relatively little agreement on how to write a memorable and publishable case study, particularly if this involves the use of qualitative evidence (Van Maanen 1998).

Unfortunately, the classic case studies tend to be of little help in clarifying how an exemplary case study is to be conducted and written up. Most offer no separate section on methodology at all, presenting instead the polished product without the guidelines as to how it was created. A few do offer more detailed insights into how the data was collected, how many interviews were conducted, and what sources were used, with some even offering summary tables of descriptive statistics regarding the context (e.g. Kanter 1977). However, the hermeneutic process of inference – how all these interviews, archival records, and notes were assembled into a coherent whole, what was counted and what was discounted – remains usually hidden from the reader. This is especially true for case studies relying primarily on qualitative field-work methods. Acknowledging the fact that 'there are probably as many "methods" as there are fieldworkers,' Kunda calls the methods section of his influential ethnography of life in US high-tech corporation 'A Confessional of Sorts' (1992, p. 229). Other authors have quite forcefully attacked current case study practices as essentially 'free-form research where everything goes' (Maoz 2002, p. 164). As a result of the questions and perhaps the mystique surrounding it, the case study thus still presents a probably more risky research (and career) strategy, and the majority of published research on organizations tends follows a variable-oriented approach using standard statistical estimation.

In the following, I examine the logic of the case study as it applies to the study of organizations. I take the position that the case study is distinguished from other organizational research strategies by a configurational understanding of organizational phenomena within a specific spatial and temporal context. This configurational nature of the case study presents both an advantage and a challenge vis-à-vis other research strategies, as it raises particular methodological demands. Perhaps most importantly, many of the quantitative methods commonly used to formally examine organizational configurations – such as cluster analysis, interaction effects, and hierarchical linear modeling – are not well suited to grasping the fundamentally configurational nature of the case study approach. As I have argued elsewhere (Fiss 2007), I will suggest that set-theoretic methods such as qualitative comparative analysis (QCA) provide a viable alternative much better suited to the configurational nature of the case study approach.

I begin by discussing the nature of cases and case studies and of organizational configurations as well as how configurations may occur at the intra-organizational, organizational, and supra-organizational levels, and across such levels. I further focus on the methods commonly used to examine organizational configurations – both qualitative and quantitative – and examine the ability of these methods to account for the configurational nature of the case study. I conclude by considering the implications of employing QCA for both the case study methods and the theory of organizational configurations and lay out an agenda for future research on a configurational understanding of organizational phenomena.

OF CASES AND CASE STUDIES

A serious treatment of the case study approach has to come to terms with the entity that the approach takes its name from, that is, the case. As Ragin (1992a) and others have pointed out, despite its widespread use and centrality in scientific discourse, the concept of the case is frequently not well defined and the term 'case' is used in a variety of different ways. Cases, for example, can be understood as theoretical constructs or as empirical units, and their relationship to the underlying phenomena may be conceptualized in a formative or reflective way (e.g. Ragin 1992a). What complicates the situation is that many of the various definitions of cases have considerable merit on their own, making a consensus definition that is both rigorous and encompassing hard to come by.

Rather than attempting a formal definition of a case here, I will focus on the underlying aspect of cases that is most relevant to the questions at hand, namely that cases and the process of 'casing' delimit the real world phenomena of interest within time and space (Ragin 1992b). In order to examine something as a case – whatever that may involve in more detail – one has to be able to identify and thus delimit the case from the multitude of phenomena and aspects that will be not be studied. This process of establishing boundaries around a phenomenon is what reduces complexity to manageable proportions and turns the potentially limitless possibilities into concrete 'cases,' usually by first defining the theoretical category of the case, narrowing it down to a subset of cases within this category, and then selecting specific empirical instances of this subset.[1] Indeed, at an abstract level, 'every study is a case study because it is an analysis of social phenomena specific to time and place' (Ragin 1992a, p. 2). While time and space offer intuitively appealing boundaries around a case, other conceptualizations are of course conceivable, such as cases of mechanisms (e.g. Hedström and Swedberg 1998) or sequences (e.g. Abbott 1992, Heise 1989). However, time and space are usually the most commonly used dimensions, and I will simply follow that convention here.

The process of delimiting or 'casing' is a necessary undertaking because it goes along with a fundamentally *contextual* understanding of cases, which holds that a case combines certain characteristics or features that appear together within it and give the case its essential character. As Walton notes, 'cases come wrapped in theories' (1992, p. 122). More specifically, cases come wrapped in theories about what matters, where boundaries ought to be set, and what may be disregarded as either unimportant or of a different kind. The process of 'casing' is part and parcel of the normal conduct of social science research and often disguised by the ways in which we encounter our phenomena. Much of the social world comes to us in 'chunky' form, and frequently the boundaries of a case will be intuitively plausible and useful due to social convention (e.g. the nation state, an organization, a subunit, a team). However, it is important to remember that not everything that comes in a naturally consumable form is also best understood in that form. Frequently, social phenomena are perhaps better unwrapped, taken apart, and then reassembled in order to form a more analytically useful 'case'.

As noted above, I will argue here that one can distinguish the case study from other organizational research strategies by its configurational understanding of organizational phenomena within a specific spatial and temporal context. As the notion of 'casing' implies, a case is a holistic entity. In order to understand it, we have to study it in its entirety; a mere focus on parts of the case will lead to partial insight, potentially taken out of context. The research strategy of the case study must take account of this configurational character of the case. As Eisenhardt suggests, the case study 'is a research strategy which focuses on understanding the dynamics present within a single setting' (1989, p. 534). Instead of disaggregating the case into its features, operationalizing such features as variables, and then testing for correlations between these variables while controlling for as many other features as possible or relevant, the case study approach aims to preserve the integrity of the case and understand it as a particular configuration of features embedded in a specific context and time. This configurational nature makes problematic any research strategy that focuses on one feature while 'controlling' for the effect of other features. As in the classic Indian fable about the blind men examining an elephant, with each one reporting on a different part of the animal, the challenge lies in comprehending the case in its entirety rather than merely its parts.

A configurational understanding of the case also clarifies the nature of the case study. The case study is fundamentally a *research strategy*, 'to be likened to an experiment, a history, or a simulation, which may be considered alternative research strategies' (Yin 1981, p. 59). As Yin notes, this understanding also helps to remove the frequent confusion between the case study as a research strategy and the types of evidence used in it (e.g. qualitative vs. quantitative data) or the types of data collection methods employed to gather this data (e.g. ethnography vs. survey collection). Because the case study approach is a research strategy that aims to maintain the configurational, holistic nature of the case or cases, it is not limited to any particular form of evidence or data collection, and it can involve single or multiple cases, various methods of data collection and several types and levels of analysis (cf. Eisenhardt 1989). In fact, combining evidence from multiple sources, such as interviews, archival data, and surveys frequently leads to the most successful organizational case studies. An essential feature of the case study approach is therefore its propensity to foster triangulation across different data sources (Eisenhardt 1989, Yin 1984). Clearly not all situations and phenomena will lend themselves to a case study approach. Yet, a case study approach will frequently be a very desirable, if also demanding approach because it requires an in-depth understanding of the case rather than a superficial understanding that goes little beyond the operationalization of variables.

Although the view of the case study I employ here emphasizes the configurational nature of the case as delimited in time and space, it is important to note that this view does not imply an inability to make comparisons. Whereas the case study is a useful research strategy when engaging unique phenomena, most research on organizations is not concerned with such one-of-a-kind entities or events, but instead aims to develop an understanding of organizations that has broader implications. The case study approach thus tends to be comparative in nature, if only in the way in which observations from a case may inform knowledge about organizations and life in them more broadly by elucidating the features of a larger class of similar phenomena (Gerring 2004, 2007). In this sense, the case study approach does frequently resemble more variable-oriented approaches in that the researcher tends to make typological reductions. However, as Stouffer (1941) notes, the case study researcher differs from the statistician in that he can do what the variable-oriented researcher frequently cannot do, namely conduct an intensive, detailed analysis that can be adjusted during the course of the research project. The case study approach is thus more dynamic in nature, and the researchers will constantly compare theory and data in order to achieve a fit between both (Eisenhardt 1989, Ragin 1994).

Furthermore, because the logic of the case study is not built around average tendencies in large samples, the selection of the case or cases takes on a critical role. This selection is usually informed by theoretical, not statistical reasons (Eisenhardt 1989). For example, Pettigrew (1990) argues that the selection of empirical sites for organizational case studies should focus on: (1) extreme situations, critical incidents, and social dramas; (2) polar types that allow for stronger contrasts; and (3) sites with a relatively high experience levels of the phenomena under study, that is, the phenomenon under study should manifest itself clearly and there should be easy to access this manifestation. Case selection is of course probably the most obvious example of the process of 'casing,' and again points to the importance of drawing boundaries around the organizational phenomenon of interest as essential to the case study.

THE NATURE OF ORGANIZATIONAL CONFIGURATIONS

I have argued that the case study approach is unique as a research strategy in its configurational approach, that is, in its focus on the relative arrangement of parts or elements that can only be fully understood in their entirety. To develop these arguments more fully and see how they apply to the study of organizations specifically, it is also necessary to clarify what is meant by a configuration and how configurational reasoning is reflected in current research on organizations. A useful starting point is offered by Meyer et al., who define organizational configurations as 'any multidimensional constellation of conceptually distinct characteristics that commonly occur together' (1993, p. 1175). Two things are particularly notable about this definition. First, it is empirically oriented in that it points to the presence of multiple instances of a constellation, be they across entities or time. Second, the definition emphasizes the co-occurrence of distinct characteristics, thus using commonality as a reference point, but leaving open what this commonality is based on.

The definition of Meyer et al. (1993) can thus be used with both typological and taxonomic approaches to understanding the nature of configurations. Whereas both approaches share the idea that a configuration is marked by some characteristic emerging from the constellation of its elements, they present different ways of arriving at this characteristic. Typological approaches of configurations are essentially reflective in that they conceive of configurations as containing an internal logic that exists independent of concrete instances and is merely reflected in the empirical manifestations. Accordingly, the typological approach is deductive and causality flows from the construct to the empirical manifestations; the empirical manifestations only take on meaning because of the construct (MacKenzie 2003). This approach has been used very successfully in research on organizational configurations, and examples include works by Delery and Doty (1996), Doty et al. (1993) and Drazin and Van de Ven (1985). By contrast, taxonomical approaches to organizational configurations take a more inductive, empirically based approach. Here, the construct is formative in that causality flows from the empirical manifestations to the construct; the construct does not exist independently of its manifestations. Taxonomic approaches to organizational configurations were used more often in the past and include the works of Hambrick (1984) and Miller and Friesen (1978, 1980). However, they have recently become less popular as compared to typological approaches, which are more aligned with an emphasis on theory testing.

Regardless of whether configurations are derived deductively or inductively, researchers are usually interested in identifying the specific constellation of relations between the different parts that make up the organizational configuration (McPhee and Scott Poole 2001). Usually, the internal 'logic' of such organizational configurations is one of consistency that can be achieved by a variety of mechanisms. For example, the 'fit' characterizing configurations may be the result of internal, adaptive learning about how the various elements of the organization are best configured to achieve more efficient outcomes. As such, configurations are most likely to be observed where experimentation is encouraged and indeed feasible, where high levels of interdependence between different organizational elements exist, and where this interdependence is marked by complementarity, that is, if the interdependence is of such a form that engaging in one type of activity will increase returns from another one (Miller 1990, Milgrom and Roberts 1995). A classic example of organizational complementarity is found in manufacturing plants, where the flexibility of production equipment is related to the breadth of the product line. As Milgrom and Roberts (1995, p. 193) show, having more flexible production lines that can be easily switched over to a different product makes it less costly (and thus more valuable) to produce many small batches of customized products that can be matched to customer preferences. Conversely, a diverse product portfolio increases the value of a flexible production line that does not rely on economies of scale and can be quickly shifted over, leading to less downtime while the line is retooled. In practice, it will therefore be rare to see either flexible production equipment or a diverse product portfolio without the other; both are complements in that each increases the value of the other; as organizational components, they are 'sticky.'

Complementary configurations frequently are made up of multiple components commonly found together. For instance, the modern manufacturing process tends to be marked by a number of components such as flexible machines, short production runs, highly skilled workers, horizontal communications, and targeted markets, which tend to make it quite different from the traditional, mass-production system that relied on specialized machinery, long production runs, low worker skills, hierarchical controls, and mass markets (Milgrom and Roberts 1995). Although the examples I have given here come from the field of industrial manufacturing, complementarities can, of course, relate to any number of organizational characteristics, including the classic ones of organizational structure and environment where small, agile organizations are usually considered to perform better in turbulent environments while large, lumbering organizations tend to do better in stable environments.

Alternatively, instead of learning and fit, the logic may be based on an external, environmental selection mechanism such as organizational birth and death due to market competition. Here, some kind of mechanisms is needed to generate variation in organizational configurations, and efficiency pressures then operate to narrow down this variety into a smaller number of viable forms.

Many of the arguments regarding organizational configurations thus take on a functional logic in tying empirically observed configurations to some form of fit based on pressures towards efficiency and consistency. However, arguments relating to the emergence of configurations need not be restricted to efficiency-based responses to either internal consistency demands or external pressures on organizations. Organizational configurations may also be formed around sociocultural or political factors. For example, Peteraf and Shanley (1997) argue that strategic groups may form around a shared identity rather than efficient forms of organizing. Alternatively, organizational configurations may reflect social logics of appropriateness that suggest certain forms of organizing as associated with specific economic activities, logics that might furthermore exhibit considerable differences, for instance across cultural contexts (e.g. Scott 1995).

It is important to note, however, that the assumption of an internal logic to configurations may frequently be too strong. For example, particular configurations of circumstances may be the result of historical constellations following now discernable internal logic yet resulting in particular and identifiable effects. As such, functionally oriented arguments that configurations are based on a logic of consistency may not be warranted. As McPhee and Poole (2001) note the idea that a configuration reflects an underlying logic may to some extent present a problem for configurational theories, and by extension also for the case study approach. Specifically, 'most configurational theories are what Althusser (1972) called "expressive totalities" – they are supposed to be consistent because each part reflects the underlying logic of the whole' (McPhee and Poole 2001, p. 515). However, a good theory should question the assumption of consistency, that is, the assumption that all parts of the configuration are equally necessary or important. For instance, one might alternatively conceive of configurations as consisting of a core and periphery, where core elements are essential whereas more peripheral elements are less important and perhaps expendable. Furthermore, most research on configurations emphasizes the internal consistency of the configuration's underlying logic. Yet there may frequently be inconsistencies within configurations, where 'a better configuration might balance off conflicting logics, or list the necessary conditions for success and make sure that the configuration meets them' (McPhee and Poole 2001, p. 515).

What emerges, then, is a picture of configurations as embedded in space and time and involving varying levels of complexity, dynamism, and analysis. Simple configurations may involve only few and linear interdependencies. In contrast, complex configurations may involve multiple interdependencies that are furthermore characterized by interactions such as complementarity or substitution effects leading to synergies and trade-offs between the different elements. Furthermore, configurations need not be static, but may be dynamically changing, suggesting that organizations follow dynamic constellations that change over their life cycles (e.g. Moores and Yuen 2001). Finally, configurations may be cutting across several levels of analysis. For example, organizational configurations may involve elements at the organizational, intra-organizational, and supra-organizational level.

While the number of conceivable organizational configurations is thus staggering, taxonomic studies of organizations have shown a relatively small number of configurations account for a relatively large share of all organizations in the samples studied (Miller 1990). This phenomenon, which is known as *limited diversity* (e.g. Ragin 1987), presents an important issue for the study of organizational configuration. Table 25.1 demonstrates such

a situation of limited diversity by means of a truth table – an analytical tool for listing all possible combinations of causal conditions. The truth table here lists four organizational characteristics (A, B, C, and D) and one outcome (Z). As a truth table uses binary values, there are sixteen possible combinations here. However, not all conceivable configurations of organizational characteristics also show empirical instances. In Table 25.1, combinations 7, 12, 14, and 15 show a question mark in the outcome column, indicating there may be no empirical instance of this combination, indicating a situation of limited diversity.

Limited diversity stems from a number of reasons. First, as Stouffer (1941) points out for configurational approaches more generally, even relatively few elements can lead to an astronomically large number of different possible complex dynamic configurations, so there will frequently be very few or no empirical instances of any particular configuration. The number of rows in a truth table is calculated as 2^k, with k indicating the number of causal conditions. For Table 25.1, the number of possible combinations is thus 2^4, or 16, but if one was to double the number of causal conditions to 8, the number of possible configurations would jump to 256.

Beyond the issues of manifested versus hypothetical configurations, Miller (1986) points to three reasons why there should be relatively few kinds of organizational configurations. First, competitive pressures from the environment are likely to weed out unsustainable models, an argument that connects to the external selection perspective. Second, organizations should be drawn to certain configurations that are internally harmonious and mutually reinforcing, an argument that connects to an internal selection mechanism, usually based on experience of what works in any given context. And finally, Miller (1990) points out that organizational change tends to be non-continuous and episodic, suggesting that hybrid forms are less likely to be explored and that preference will usually be given to ideal types presenting mutually exclusive positions.

Table 25.1   Truth table exhibiting limited diversity

Configuration	Organizational characteristics				Outcome
	A	B	C	D	Z
1	Yes	Yes	Yes	Yes	Yes
2	Yes	Yes	Yes	No	No
3	Yes	Yes	No	Yes	Yes
4	Yes	Yes	No	No	Yes
5	Yes	No	Yes	Yes	No
6	Yes	No	Yes	No	No
7	Yes	No	No	Yes	?
8	Yes	No	No	No	No
9	No	Yes	Yes	Yes	Yes
10	No	Yes	Yes	No	Yes
11	No	Yes	No	Yes	No
12	No	Yes	No	No	?
13	No	No	Yes	Yes	No
14	No	No	Yes	No	?
15	No	No	No	Yes	?
16	No	No	No	No	Yes

ORGANIZATIONS AND CONFIGURATIONS ACROSS LEVELS OF ANALYSIS

While configurations lie at the heart of the case study approach, not all studies that examine organizational configurations can properly be classified as case studies. Case studies and studies of organizational configurations thus form partially overlapping sets. In the following, I examine studies from the union of those sets rather than the intersection, to provide an overview of the various forms of addressing organizational configurations either explicitly or implicitly. Configurations can occur at the intra-organizational, organizational, and the supra- and inter-organizational levels, as well as across such levels. Because of the extensive literature, it is necessary to note that the studies I use here are for the purpose of illustration rather than for providing an exhaustive overview of work on configurational thinking in organization and management studies.

Intra-organization level

The study of intra-organizational phenomena has been at the focus of a number of the classic case studies. Gouldner's (1954) *Patterns of Industrial Bureaucracy* focuses almost exclusively on intra-organizational phenomena as he described three configurations of 'mock,' 'representative,' and 'punishment-centered' bureaucracy that emerge from rule creation and enforcement. Similarly, Kanter's (1977) *Men and Women of the Corporation* examines how the power structure of a large corporation shapes both the behavior and personalities of its employees, while Dalton's earlier (1959) *Men Who Manage* likewise focused on issues of formal and informal power relations within corporations. More recently, Kunda's *Engineering Culture* (1992) focused on the organizational culture in the engineering department of a large American high-tech corporation. Other research has taken an even more micro-level approach, focusing on configurations at the group level such as the demographic composition of

teams (e.g. Tsui and O'Reilly 1989) and even individual-level configurations such as the fit between the individual and the organization (e.g. Chatman 1989).

Organization level

A considerable number of case studies, as well as studies of organizational configurations more generally, have focused on the organization level, and particularly the relationships between strategy, structure, and processes. Much of the literature on strategic groups operates at this level (e.g. Dess and Davis 1984, Cool and Schendel 1987, Ketchen et al. 1997, McNamara et al. 2003). While many of the studies at this level have employed quantitative methods, there are also a number of case studies using mainly qualitative methods, such as work on organizational activity systems (e.g. Siggelkow 2001, 2002) or Chandler's (1962) *Strategy and Structure*, which examined strategic and organizational change in the United States. Likewise, Philip Selznick's (1949) *T.V.A. and the Grass Roots* is also largely located at this level of analysis, although not exclusively.

Supra-organization level

A smaller number of studies have examined configurations at the inter-organizational level. Examples here include Bensaou and Venkatraman's (1995) study of inter-organizational relationships in the automobile industry, or Malhotra et al.'s (2005) research on supply-chain partnership configurations. Child (2002) likewise uses a configurational approach to examine twenty cases of international joint venture formation, whereas Dubbs et al. (2004) examine configurations at the organizational network and system level in the health care industry. At an even more macro-level, research on Business Systems and the Varieties of Capitalism approach have suggested that economic systems are likewise best understood from a configurational perspective (e.g. Whitley 1999, Hall and Soskice 2001) and analyzed using configurational methods (e.g. Kogut and Ragin 2006).

Cross-level configurations

While the studies I have discussed so far mainly inhabit a single level of analysis, this classification is not a very rigid one, and effects located at different levels frequently impinge upon the configurations at the main level of analysis. However, a number of studies have moved towards a truly multi-level examination of configurations. For examples, Crozier's (1964) classic work on *The Bureaucratic Phenomenon* explicitly connects the bureaucratic control system to the cultural environment in which French administrative organizations are embedded. Similarly, the Miles and Snow (1978) typology of firms as Defenders, Prospectors, Analyzers, and Reactors explicitly theorizes configurations of structure, strategy, and environment, thus spanning the organization and supra-organizational levels. Extending the Miles and Snow framework in a different direction, Moores and Yuen (2001) examine configurations of strategy, structure, leadership style, and decision making style, thus combining characteristics at the organization and individual levels. Furthermore, Greckhamer et al. (2008) use QCA to examine how industry, corporate, and business-unit effects combine, leading to truly multi-level analyses.

METHODOLOGICAL CHALLENGES OF ORGANIZATIONAL CASE STUDIES

Because the case study approach is marked by a configurational understanding of organizational phenomena within a specific spatial and temporal context, it faces a particular challenge, namely analyzing and understanding complex interdependencies between various factors and causal conditions that in combination characterize the case in question. To address this challenge, a variety of different methodological approaches have been employed, each of which offers certain advantages while also carrying certain liabilities.

The most prevalent method for analyzing cases still relies on qualitative research methods such as interviews with members of an organization, observation of life in organizations such as ethnography and participant observation, the use of focus groups, or the examination of various archival records regarding an organization and life around it. Such qualitative methods for the analysis of organizations are grounded in the hermeneutic tradition of the humanities (e.g. Gephart 2004) and usually involve the researcher's inductive and interpretive treatment of the evidence (Van Maanen 1998). The flexibility of these methods makes them very attractive for the case study approach, as they can be applied where quantification is problematic or has to be deferred until a later point in the analysis. However, this very flexibility also presents a challenge in the generally more positivistically oriented field of organization and management studies. Although there are a number of guides as to how qualitative research might proceed in a systematic manner (e.g. Miles and Huberman 1984, Yin 1984, Van Maanen 1988, King et al. 1994, Emerson et al. 1995), as well as advice on how to get this research published in top flight research journals (e.g. Gephart 2004, Suddaby 2006), the typical case study still relies to a considerable extent on the persuasiveness of its narrative. While good qualitative research is systematic and disciplined, there is are few agreed-on rules for drawing conclusions and verifying their robustness (Miles and Huberman 1984). Due to this lack of standardization the analysis still largely resembles an art rather than a science, and as a result 'one cannot ordinarily follow how a researcher got from 3600 pages of field notes to the final conclusions, sprinkled with vivid quotes though they may be'(Miles and Huberman 1984, p. 16).

However, even the most hermeneutic of approaches has to start with observing differences and similarities and likely with either counting their commonness or assigning some weight to their importance. At the most general level, the actual analysis of the collected evidence will thus usually involve a search for similarities and dissimilarities within the data that eventually leads to empirical generalizations, frequently along the lines of inquiry presented by Mill in his *A System of Logic* (1843), and particularly as incorporated in the methods of agreement and difference (e.g. Stouffer 1941, Ragin 1987). Consider, for example, Eisenhardt's (1989) influential work on how organizational researchers can employ case studies to build better theories. Eisenhardt describes two forms of analysis: that of within-case data and the search for cross-case patterns. Among these, the analysis of within-case data presents the first step and is clearly the less formalized approach. Eisenhardt suggests that it is imperative for the researcher to become intimately familiar with the case as a stand-alone entity, for example by writing case histories, examining transcripts, or by collecting and tabulating quantitative data on a variety of relevant aspects. Whatever approach the researcher chooses, the goal of this process is to 'allow the unique pattern of each case to emerge before investigators push to generalize patterns across cases' (Eisenhardt 1989, p. 540). Connected to within-case analysis is the search for patterns across cases to identify similarities and differences. This analysis can take various forms, such as looking for within-group similarity and inter-group differences, examining pairs of phenomena, or comparing the evidence by data sources. Regardless of which particular form is chosen at this time, however, the general approach remains the search for agreement and difference within pattern of the evidence.

While the advantage of a purely qualitative, hermeneutic analysis of the evidence lies in its ability to provide insights that are difficult to achieve using quantitative, statistically oriented methods, the disadvantage of this approach is equally evident and in large part stems from the researcher's cognitive limitations. Purely qualitative analysis quickly exhausts the levels of complexity in patterns it can process (e.g. Stouffer 1941), particularly if the concepts of interest are graded rather than binary in nature. Even if our cognitive capabilities would allow us to consider the exponentially growing number of configurations that emerge quickly even from only a few binary concepts, we would still be

subject to all sorts of cognitive biases, such as the tendency to search for information in a way that confirms our preconceptions (e.g. Wason 1960) or our propensity to neglect the base rate of events (e.g. Kahneman and Tversky 1973). The recognition of how quickly the organizational researcher is overwhelmed by the amounts of data and how difficult it is to identify patterns and draw inferences has led to an increased usage of qualitative data analysis software packages that aim to assist the researcher in sorting, coding, and analyzing the data their data. While these software packages facilitate the process of drawing inferences and tend to make it more systematic, they present but a partial solution to the underlying problem of dealing with the complexity that configurations of factors present.

At the other end of the methodological spectrum lie quantitative methods for identifying and examining configurations. Among these, cluster analysis is probably the most popular one for distinguishing configurations, and has enjoyed a certain revival in the recent literature on organizational configurations, particularly in the field of business studies (e.g. Corso et al. 2003, Uhl-Bien and Maslyn 2003, Desarbo et al. 2005, Malhotra et al. 2005, Lim et al. 2006, Marlin et al. 2007). Cluster analysis is attractive for the study of configurations because it offers various algorithms for grouping cases that share similar features into respective clusters. As an exploratory tool for the analysis of quantitative data, cluster analysis can be used to discover structures in the data without specifying *a priori* what those structures might be. As a result, a number of researchers have used cluster analysis to examine organizational configurations across a variety of levels of analysis (e.g. Hambrick 1983, Cool and Schendel 1987, Ketchen et al. 1993, Bensaou and Venkatraman 1995, Dubbs et al. 2004, Moores and Yuen 2001; for reviews, see Ketchen and Shook 1996, Ketchen et al. 1997).

However, although cluster analysis allows the discovery of configurations of characteristics that commonly occur together, it also has significant weaknesses. Perhaps most importantly, the exploratory nature of cluster analysis makes it unsuitable for testing theory. While it would of course be possible to hypothesize the existence of different types of clusters before actually conducting the analysis, it is not possible to test these hypotheses because there is currently no test statistic for cluster membership. Although one might compare the results of different clustering algorithms or assess performance differences between different clusters, the basic issue remains that cluster analysis will *always* result in some clustering and there is not test statistic to guide the analysis. The fact that even with for the most part randomly distributed data some kind of cluster solution is likely to emerge has led a number of researchers to question the existence of true underlying configurations, suggesting that, for example strategic groups may be merely statistical artifacts (e.g. Hatten and Hatten 1987, Thomas and Venkatraman 1988, Barney and Hoskisson 1990).

Another problematic aspect of cluster analysis is that its assignment of cases to clusters is based on all the characteristics included regardless of the relationship between these characteristics and outcomes of interest, such as performance, reputation, deviance, or some other construct. Consider for example a situation where not all characteristics included in the analysis are in fact causally important regarding the outcome (a situation that is likely to be the rule rather than the exception). Here, cluster analysis is insensitive to the fact that some cases may be *identical* regarding a few causally important characteristics, but may be *different* along a large number of characteristics that are irrelevant. From a causal point of view, such cases belong into the same category since they share the same causally important characteristics. However, cluster analysis would usually place them in different clusters because they differ on many (irrelevant) characteristics. While cluster analysis thus allows the researcher quickly to determine configurations in a dataset, the nature of these configurations and the relationships between

the various characteristics included remains largely unexamined. Although it is possible to use regression analysis with dummy variables for different configurations to examine the relationship between these configurations and an outcome of interest, the issue remains that these configurations need to be identified first, and the usual methods such as cluster analysis show significant weaknesses here. Furthermore, clustering combined with correlational analysis would still not allow a researcher to examine the effect of different levels of the variables that are joined in the dummy for cluster membership. Such an approach would also not be able to address issues of equifinality, that is, situations where 'a system can reach the same final state, from different initial conditions and by a variety of different paths' (Katz and Kahn 1978, p. 30). Equifinality und thus equal effectiveness of different configurations presents an important theoretical issue for configurational thinking on organizations, and methods that cannot address this issue thus do not adequately match up with the theory (Fiss 2007).

Similar critiques also apply to approaches using deviation scores to determine the fit between a hypothesized ideal and empirically observed configuration. While such approaches tend to be deductive in nature and thus are theoretically more attractive than the largely inductive cluster analysis, deviation score approaches hold related problems such as limited insight into the relationship between the different characteristics of the configuration and a considerable sample dependence in how profiles are derived (e.g. Drazin and Van de Ven 1985), thus making them quite sensitive to errors in estimating the 'ideal' configuration and reliability issues (Gupta and Govindarajan 1993).

The recognition that organizational configurations can be nested across multiple levels of analysis has led some researchers towards statistical modeling techniques that allow assessing such multi-level effects. In particular the study of educational organizations has employed hierarchical linear modeling (HLM) to take into account that the achievement of individual students also depends on effects at the school and state level, thus leading to three-level hierarchies (e.g. Raudenbusch et al. 1999). Similarly, HLM can be used to examine multi-level effects of organizational work groups, departments, organizations, and environments (e.g. Hoffman 1997, Hoffman and Gavin 1998). However, while HLM presents a better methodological fit for multi-level theories of organizations and allow the testing of more complex effects, such modeling still has significant shortcomings regarding a truly configurational understanding of cases and organizations.

Specifically, as linear models, HLM equations are based on a number of assumptions that stand in contrast to configurational thinking. For instance, while configurational approaches point to nonlinear, synergistic effects that can lead to equifinal configurations, the econometric model that underlies HLM and regression methods more broadly assumes linear, additive effects that are unifinal. While ordinary regression analysis estimates one average net effect across a whole population, HLM presents an improvement as it allows the net effect to be separated into level-specific effects. However, HLM still treats different variables as competing in explaining the variation of the outcome of interest, with a focus on the unique contribution of each variable while holding all other effects constant. In contrast, configurational thinking emphasizes that one has to consider how causes combine rather than compete to create outcomes, and that the goal should be estimating this very relationship between different parts rather than aiming to statistically control for such effects.

Interaction effects present one way to take these relationships into account and include them into the statistical model, but for all practical purposes such effects have been largely restricted to two-way interactions, as three way interactions are exceedingly hard to interpret and rarely appear in published research. Such a limitation to interaction effects between only two causal factors places an undue burden on the modeling of configurational effects that can easily include four

or more relevant factors. And finally, because they estimate a single equation, regression-based models are problematic when the goal is to examine equifinal outcomes, that is, situations where there are several path to an outcome of interest, thus blocking the empirical investigation of equifinal configurations (e.g. Gresov and Drazin 1997, Fiss 2007). One might consider using ANOVA or regression with dummy variables to examine the relationship between for example, membership in a configuration and performance, but this of course does not address the main issue of how configurations and the relationships between their different characteristics were identified in the first place. A possible approach to estimating these relationships would be the use of log-linear models (e.g. Knoke and Burke 1980), but these make no distinction between dependent and independent variables and thus cannot determine the direction of causality within a relationship. In addition, log-linear models are useful for categorical but not continuous variables, making them again rather unwieldy tools.

Some researchers have aimed to combine qualitative and quantitative analysis as a promising way to better capture the complex nature of configurations that marks case studies. For example, Siggelkow's (2002) study of the configurations of a large US corporation combined in-depth qualitative interviews and the analysis of archival records with network analysis methods. After estimating qualitatively the existence and strength of relationships between the different activities that the corporation engaged in, Siggelkow then used network measures to determine the centrality or 'coreness' of various organizational elements as well as identify the various patterns in the evolution of the organization. Similarly, Black and Boal (1994) suggest the use of network analysis to capture the complex interdependencies between firm resources. Treating the configuration as a network of interdependent characteristics thus offers intriguing possibilities for future case study research.

Both purely qualitative and quantitative approaches thus have considerable difficulties regarding the configurational nature of the case study. Whereas qualitative approaches are flexible, they quickly exhaust the levels of complexity they can handle in a rigorous way. Quantitative approaches allow for the analysis of a large number of data points, but they either allow little insight into how configurations emerge or are rooted in the linear model that is frequently not useful in examining configurational arguments. As I have argued elsewhere (Fiss 2007), this disconnect between configurational arguments and empirical methods in organization and management theory has emerged as significant hindrance to the further development of a configurational understanding of organizations. In a similar manner, the case study approach, with its configurational nature, would likewise benefit from employing more frequently a methodology better in line with its assumptions of complex causal interdependencies. Specifically, set-theoretic methods such as QCA (e.g. Ragin 1987, 2000) provide an attractive alternative here. Rooted in the comparative methods between qualitative and variable-based approaches, QCA is deeply configurational in its understanding of how causes combine to create outcomes, making it a particularly useful tool for the case study approach. QCA is able to handle considerable amounts of causal complexity while retaining the holistic quality of the phenomenon under study – two issues that are essential for the case study approach.

AN AGENDA FOR FUTURE RESEARCH ON CONFIGURATIONAL PHENOMENA

The case study still presents one of the most attractive research strategies for understanding life in and around organizations. The configurational nature of the case study in particular aligns well with the configurational thinking that underlies much of management and organization theory and is typical of the social world more broadly. As I have argued, however, many of the current data analysis approaches used with a case study do not fully speak to this configurational nature of the

case study approach, and the potential for significant methodological improvements along these traditional lines of inquiry seems limited at this time. However, due its configurational nature, set-theoretic methods in general and QCA in particular offer a way to conduct case study research that is both methodologically rigorous and able to offer new and different insights than traditional methods. These methods can be used in a variety of ways. For example, they can be used to analyze quantitative data on organizational structure, strategy, and the environment. However, set-theoretic methods can also be used to examine qualitative evidence contained in the narratives that commonly accompany case studies, allowing for a more rigorous examination than is usually feasible with purely qualitative approaches. Additionally, QCA can be used as a meta-analysis tool to examine case studies. An intriguing example of this approach is offered by Hodson and Roscigno (2004), who combine a content analysis of 204 organizational ethnographies with QCA analysis to determine the causal configurations that lead to organizational success such as employee involvement and competent management. Furthermore, while QCA can now be successfully applied to large-N analyses (e.g. Ragin and Fiss 2007), it was originally designed to handle small-N situations, making it particularly attractive to a case study approach that requires considerable in-depth knowledge about cases and thus places certain constraints on the number of cases that can be explored in sufficient detail.

Beyond the use of tools that speak to the configurational nature of the case study, an important way forward lies with the study of configurations across levels of analysis. While a number of studies have already explored configurations reaching across the individual, organizational, and supra-organizational levels, such research is still the exception rather than the norm. Given the interconnectedness of many organizational phenomena, much more research is needed along these lines. Furthermore, such analyses need not be restricted to the traditional constructs of, for example, strategy, structure, and environment. For example, Fombrun (1989) suggests three levels of constraints that are likely to affect organizational configurations: the infrastructure of interdependencies, the sociostructure of exchange relations, and the superstructure of symbolic representations. However, while most studies have so far focused on the infrastructure of largely economic and technological interdependencies, much remains to be explored regarding the sociopolitical and symbolic-cultural side of configurations. The processes creating organizational configurations operate at many levels, including competitive and evolutionary processes, but also sociopolitical and cultural-symbolic ones, as suggested by the institutional theory (e.g. Lounsbury and Ventresca 2002). Industry-level 'recipes' about how to compete and what is successful in organizing may be powerful scripts leading to specific organizational forms that either are configurations or lead to the formation of specific configurations because of ensuing economic and technical inderdependencies. Accordingly, a true understanding of organizational configurations must go beyond merely technical interdependencies to include the interaction between these and sociopolitical and cultural-symbolic factors.

The goal of extending case study approaches to examine phenomena across more levels of analysis and phenomena furthermore points to the fact that many organizational phenomena are essentially constituted by configurations of configurations. This phenomenon – where the whole takes the same shape or form as its parts – is known as self-similarity in complexity theory. While some researchers have argued that organization theory has much to gain from connecting more closely to the insights of complexity theory (e.g. Brown and Eisenhardt 1997, Levinthal 1997, Rivkin and Siggelkow 2003), so far these connections have not been explored in detail. Furthermore, most of the research in this vein has employed computational modeling as a research strategy, suggesting that much could be gained by connecting to more empirically oriented research such as the case study approach.

Finally, the majority of prior research on organizational configurations has focused on static rather than dynamic configurations. Again, a case study approach can contribute here by allowing for a more dynamic understanding of organizational configurations. Tracking configurations over time is methodological challenging, but certainly not infeasible and would significantly enhance our way of thinking about configurational phenomena in and around organizations.

NOTES

1. For an example of this process, see Ragin's (1992) analysis of Wieviorka's (1992) 'casing' as evidenced in treatment of terrorist groups as social movements.

REFERENCES

Abbott, A. 1992 'What do cases do? Some notes on activity in sociological analysis' in C. Ragin and H. Becker (Eds) *What Is a Case? Exploring the Foundations of Social Inquiry.* Cambridge: Cambridge University Press, pp. 53–82.

Allison, G.T. 1971 *Essence of Decision: Explaining the Cuban Missile Crisis.* Boston: Little, Brown.

Althusser, L.K. 1972 *For Marx.* London: NLB.

Barney, J.E. and Hoskisson, R.E. 1990 'Strategic groups: untested assertions and research proposals' *Managerial and Decision Economics* 11: 187–198.

Bensaou, M. and Venkatraman, N. 1995 'Configurations of interorganizational relationships: A comparison between US and Japanese automakers' *Management Science* 41: 1471–1492.

Black, J.A. and Boal, K. 1994 'Strategic resources: traits, configurations and paths to sustainable competitive advantage' *Strategic Management Journal* 15: 131–148.

Blau, P. 1955 *The Dynamics of Bureaucracy.* Chicago: Chicago University Press.

Brown, S.L. and Eisenhardt, K.M. 1997 'The art of continuous change: linking complexity theory and time-paced evolution in relentlessly shifting organizations' *Administrative Science Quarterly* 42: 1–34.

Chandler, A.D. 1962 *Strategy and Structure: Chapters in the History of the Industrial Enterprise.* Cambridge, MA: MIT Press.

Chatman, J.A. 1989 'Improving Interactional Organizational Research: A Model of Person-Organization Fit' *Academy of Management Review* 14: 333–439.

Child, J. 2002 'A Configurational Analysis of International Joint Ventures' *Organization Studies* 23: 781–815.

Cool, K. and Schendel, D.E. 1987 'Strategic group formation and performance: The case of the US pharmaceutical industry, 1963–1982' *Management Science* 33: 1102–1124.

Corso, M., Martini, A., Pellegrini, L. and Paolucci, E. 2003 'Technological and organizational tools for knowledge management: in search of configurations' *Small Business Economics* 21: 397–408.

Crozier, M. 1964 *The Bureaucratic Phenomenon.* London: Tavistock Publications.

Dalton, Melville. 1959 *Men Who Manage.* New York: Wiley.

Delery, J. E. and Doty, D.H. 1996 'Modes of theorizing in strategic human resource management: tests of universalistic, contingency, and configurational performance predictions' *Academy of Management Journal* 39: 802–835.

Desarbo, W.S., Di Benedetto, C.A., Song, M. and Sinha, I. 2005 'Revisiting the miles and snow strategic framework: uncovering interrelationships between strategic types, capabilities, environmental uncertainty, and firm performance' *Strategic Management Journal* 26: 47–74.

Dess, G.G. and Davis, P.S. 1984 'Porter's (1980) generic strategies as determinants of strategic group membership and organizational performance' *Academy of Management Journal* 27: 467–488.

Doty, D.H., Glick, W.H. and Huber, G.P. 1993 'Fit, equifinality, and organizational effectiveness: a test of two configurational theories' *Academy of Management Journal* 36: 1196–1250.

Drazin, R. and Van de Ven, A.H. 1985 'Alternative forms of fit in contingency theory' *Administrative Science Quarterly* 30: 514–539.

Dubbs, N.L., Bazzoli, G.J., Shortell, S.M. and Kralovec, P.D. 2004 'Reexamining organizational configurations: an update, validation, and expansion of the taxonomy of health networks and systems' *Health Services Research* 39: 207–220.

Eisenhardt, K.M. 1989 'Building theories from case-study research' *Academy of Management Review* 14: 532–550.

Emerson, R.M., Fretz, R.I. and Shaw, L.L. 1995 *Writing Ethnographic Fieldnotes.* Chicago: University of Chicago Press.

Fiss, P.C. 2007 'A set-theoretic approach to organizational configurations' *Academy of Management Review* 32: 1180–1198.

Fombrun, C.J. 1989 'Convergent dynamics in the production of organizational configurations' *Journal of Management Studies* 26: 439–458.

Foreman, P.B. 1948 'The theory of case studies' *Social Forces* 26: 408–419.

Gephart, R.P. 2004 'Qualitative research and the academy of management journal' *Academy of Management Journal* 47: 454–462.

Gerring, J. 2004 'What is a case study and what is it good for?' *American Political Science Review* 98: 341–354.

Gerring, J. 2007 *Case Study Research: Principles and Practices.* Cambridge: Cambridge University Press.

Gouldner, A.W. 1954 *Patterns of Industrial Bureaucracy.* Glencoe, IL: Free Press.

Greckhamer, T., Misangyi, V.F., Elms, H. and Lacey, R. 2008 'Using qualitative comparative analysis in strategic management research: an examination of combinations of industry, corporate, and business-unit effects' *Organizational Research Methods* Special Issue on Research Methods in Strategic Management.

Gresov, C. and Drazin, R. 1997 'Equifinality: Functional equivalence in organization design' *Academy of Management Review* 22: 403–428.

Gupta, A.K. and Govindarajan, V. 1993 'Methodological issues in testing contingency theories: an assessment of alternative approaches' in Y. Ijiri (Ed.) *Creative and Innovative Approaches to the Science of Management.* Westport, CT: Quorum Books, pp. 453–471.

Hall, P.A. and Soskice, D. (Eds) 2001 *Varieties of Capitalism: The Institutional Foundations of Competitive Advantage.* Oxford: Oxford University Press.

Hambrick, D.C. 1983 'An empirical typology of mature industrial-product environments' *Academy of Management Journal* 26: 213–230.

Hambrick, D.C. 1984 'Taxonomic approaches to studying strategy: Some conceptual and methodological issues' *Journal of Management* 10: 27–41.

Hatten, K.J. and Hatten, M.L. 1987 'Strategic groups, asymmetrical mobility barriers and contestability' *Strategic Management Journal* 8: 329–342.

Hedström, P. and Swedberg, R. 1998 *Social Mechanisms: An Analytical Approach to Social Theory.* Cambridge: Cambridge University Press.

Heise, D. 1989 'Modeling event structures' *Journal of Mathematical Sociology* 14: 139–169.

Hodson, R. and Roscigno, V.J. 2004 'Organizational success and worker dignity: complementary or contradictory?' *American Journal of Sociology* 110: 672–708.

Hoffman, D.A. 1997 'An overview of the logic and rationale of hierarchical linear models' *Journal of Management* 23: 723–744.

Hoffman, D.A. and Gavin, M.B. 1998 'Centering decisions in hierarchical linear models: implications for research in organizations' *Journal of Management* 24: 623–641.

Kahneman, D. and Tversky, A. 1973 'On the psychology of prediction' *Psychological Review* 80: 237–251.

Kanter, R.M. 1977 *Men and Women of the Corporation.* New York: Basic Books.

Katz, D. and Kahn, R.L. 1978 *The social psychology of organizations* (second edition). New York: Wiley.

Ketchen, D.J. and Shook, C.L. 1996 'The application of cluster analysis in strategic management research: an analysis and critique' *Strategic Management Journal* 17: 441–485.

Ketchen, D.J., Thomas, J.B. and Snow, C.C. 1993 'Organizational configurations and performance: a comparison of theoretical approaches' *Academy of Management Journal* 36: 1278–1313.

Ketchen, D.J., Combs, J.G., Russel, C.J., Shook, C., Dean, M.A., Runge, J., Lohrke, F., Naumann, S., Haptonstahl, D.E., Baker, R., Beckstein, B.A., Handlers, C., Honig, H. and Lamoureux, S. 1997 'Organizational configurations and performance: a meta-analysis' *Academy of Management Journal* 40: 223–240.

King, G., Keohane, R.O. and Verba, S. 1994 *Designing Social Inquiry: Scientific Inference in Qualitative Research.* Princeton, NJ: Princeton University Press.

Knoke, D. and Burke, P.J. 1980 *Log-Linear Models.* Beverly Hills, CA: Sage.

Kogut, B. and Ragin, C.C. 2006 'Exploring complexity when diversity is limited: institutional complementarity in theories of rule of law and national systems revisited' *European Management Review* 3: 44–59.

Kunda, G. 1992 *Engineering Culture: Control and Commitment in a High-Tech Corporation.* Philadelphia: Temple University Press.

Levinthal, D. 1997 'Adaptation on rugged landscapes' *Management Science* 43: 34–950.

Lim, L.K.S., Acito, F. and Rusetski, A. 2006 'Development of archetypes of international marketing strategy' *Journal of International Business Studies* 37: 499–524.

Lounsbury, M. and Ventresca, M.J. 2002 'Social structure and organizations revisited' *Research in the Sociology of Organizations* 19: 3–36.

Lundberg, G.A. 1941 'Case-studies vs. statistical methods: an issue based on misunderstanding' *Sociometry* 4: 379–383.

MacKenzie, S.B. 2003 'The dangers of poor construct conceptualization' *Journal of the Academy of Marketing Science* 31: 323–326.

Malhotra, A., Gosain, S. and ElSawy, O.A. 2005 'Absorptive capacity configurations in supply chains: gearing for partner-enabled market knowledge creation' *MIS Quarterly* 29: 145–187.

Maoz, Z. 2002 'Case study methodology in international studies: from storytelling to hypothesis testing' in F.P. Harvey and M. Brecher (Eds) *Evaluating Methodology in International Studies: Millennial Reflections on International Studies.* Ann Arbor, MI: University of Michigan Press.

Marlin, D., Ketchen, D.J. and Lamont, B. 2007 'Equifinality and the strategic group-performance relationship' *Journal of Managerial Issues* 19: 208–232.

Mauffette-Leender, L.A., Erskine, J.A. and Leender, M.R. 2001 *Learning with Cases* (second edition). London, Ontario: Ivey Publishing.

McNamara, G., Deephouse, D.L. and Luce, R.A. 2003 'Competitive positioning witching and across strategic groups: the performance of core, subsidiary, and solitary firms' *Strategic Management Journal* 24: 161–181.

McPhee, R.D. and Poole, M.S. 2001 'Organizational structures and configurations' in F. Jablin and L. Putnam (Eds) *The New Handbook of Organizational Communication: Advances in Theory, Research, and Methods.* Thousand Oaks, CA: Sage, pp. 503–543.

Meyer, A.D., Tsui, A.S. and Hinings, C.R. 1993 'Configurational approaches to organizational analysis' *Academy of Management Journal* 36: 1175–1195.

Miles, M.B. and Huberman, M. 1984 *Qualitative Data Analysis: A Sourcebook of New Methods.* Beverly Hills, CA: Sage.

Miles, R.E. and Snow, C.C. 1978 *Organization Strategy, Structure, and Process.* New York: McGraw-Hill.

Milgrom, P. and Roberts, J. 1995 'Complementarities and fit: strategy, structure, and organizational change in manufacturing' *Journal of Accounting and Economics* 19: 179–208.

Mill, J.S. 1843/2002 *A System of Logic: Ratiocinative and Inductive.* Honolulu, HI: University Press of the Pacific.

Miller, D. 1986 'Configurations of strategy and structure: a synthesis' *Strategic Management Journal* 7: 233–249.

Miller, D. 1990 'Organizational configurations: cohesion, change, and prediction' *Human Relations* 43: 771–789.

Miller, D. and Friesen, P.H. 1978 'Archetypes of strategy formulation' *Management Science* 24: 921–933.

Miller, D. and Friesen, P.H. 1980 'Archetypes of organizational transition' *Administrative Science Quarterly* 25: 268–299.

Moores, K. and Yuen, S. 2001 'Management accounting systems and organizational configurations: a life-cycle perspective' *Accounting, Organizations, and Society* 26: 351–389.

Peteraf, M. and Shanley, M. 1997 'Getting to know you: a theory of strategic group identity' *Strategic Management Journal* Summer Special Issue 18: 165–186.

Pettigrew, A. 1990 'Longitudinal field research on change: theory and practice' *Organization Science* 1: 267–292.

Ragin, C.C. 1987 *The Comparative Method: Moving beyond Qualitative and Quantitative Strategies.* Berkeley, CA: University of California Press.

Ragin, C.C. 1992a 'Introduction: cases of "what is a case?"' in C. Ragin and H. Becker (Eds) *What Is a Case? Exploring the Foundations of Social Inquiry.* Cambridge: Cambridge University Press, pp. 1–17.

Ragin, C.C. 1992b '"Casing" and the process of social inquiry' in C. Ragin and H. Becker (Eds) *What Is a Case? Exploring the Foundations of Social Inquiry.* Cambridge: Cambridge University Press, pp. 217–226.

Ragin, C.C. 1994 *Constructing Social Research: The Unity and Diversity of Method.* Thousand Oaks, CA: Pine Forge Press.

Ragin, C.C. 2000 *Fuzzy Set Social Science.* Chicago: University of Chicago Press.

Ragin, C.C. and Becker, H.S. (Eds) 1992 *What Is a Case? Exploring the Foundations of Social Inquiry.* Cambridge: Cambridge University Press.

Ragin, C.C. and Fiss, P.C. 2007 *Fuzzy Set Policy Analysis.* Manuscript. University of Arizona, Tucson, Arizona.

Raudenbush, S.W., Fotiu, R.P. and Cheong, Y.F. 1999 'Synthesizing results from the trial state assessment' *Journal of Educational and Behavioral Statistics* 24(4): 413–438.

Rivkin, J. and Siggelkow, N. 2003 'Balancing search and stability: interdependencies among elements of organizational design' *Management Science* 49: 290–311.

Scott, W.R. 1995 *Institutions and Organizations.* Thousand Oaks, CA: Sage.

Selznick, P. 1949 *T.V.A. and the Grass Roots.* Berkeley, CA: University of California Press.

Siggelkow, N. 2001 'Change in the presence of fit: the rise, the fall, and the renaissance of Liz Claiborne' *Academy of Management Journal* 49: 838–857.

Siggelkow, N. 2002 'Evolution towards fit' *Administrative Science Quarterly* 47: 25–159.

Stouffer, S.A. 1941 'Notes on the case-study and the unique case' *Sociometry* 4: 349–357.

Suddaby, R. 2006 'What grounded theory is not' *Academy of Management Journal* 49: 633–642.

Thomas, H. and Venkatraman, N. 1988 'Research on strategic groups: Progress and prognosis' *Journal of Management Studies* 25: 537–555.

Tsui, A.S. and O'Reilly, C.A. 1989 'Beyond simple demographic effects: the importance of relational demography in superior-subordinate dyads' *Academy of Management Journal* 32: 402–423.

Uhl-Bien, M. and Maslyn, J.M. 2003 'Reciprocity in manager-subordinate relationships: components, configurations, and outcomes' *Journal of Management* 29: 511–532.

Van Maanen, J. 1988 *Tales of the Field: On Writing Ethnography.* Chicago: University of Chicago Press.

Van Maanen, J. 1998 'Different strokes: qualitative research in the administrative science quarterly from 1956–1996' in J. Van Maanen (Ed.) *Qualitative Studies of Organizations.* Thousand Oakes: CA: Sage, pp. ix–xxxii.

Walton, J. 1992 'Making the theoretical case' in C. Ragin and H. Becker (Eds) *What Is a Case? Exploring the Foundations of Social Inquiry.* Cambridge: Cambridge University Press, pp. 121–137.

Wason, P.C. 1960 'On the failure to eliminate hypotheses in a conceptual task' *Quarterly Journal of Experimental Psychology* 12: 129–140.

Whitley, R. 1999 *Divergent Capitalisms: The Social Structuring and Change of Business Systems.* Oxford: Oxford University Press.

Wieviorka, M. 1992 'Case studies: history or sociology?' in C. Ragin and H. Becker (Eds) *What Is a Case? Exploring the Foundations of Social Inquiry.* Cambridge: Cambridge University Press, pp. 159–172.

Yin, R.K. 1981 'The case study crisis: some answers' *Administrative Science Quarterly* 26: 58–65.

Yin, R. 1984 *Case Study Research: Design and Methods.* Thousand Oaks: CA: Sage.

26

The Case in Medicine

Frances Griffiths

The case in medicine has meaning that varies in sometimes quite subtle ways. This can depend on the perspective of the person defining the case, on the current state of knowledge, on the time and place the definition is made and on the reasons for defining the case. This chapter will examine the case in medicine in its various forms as cases are defined in the process of what Ragin (1992) calls 'casing'. Although Ragin uses the expression 'casing' as a process within social research, in this chapter I use the term to include 'casing' for research, for clinical practice and for living with health and illness. 'Casing' is concerned with how a case is cut out of space and time, placing a boundary around the case to delineate it from its relationships with its context (Wieviorka 1992). It might seem obvious that the case in medicine refers to an individual person and, in a sense, this is so, as many medical interventions are designed for individual people to take, use or have done to them. However, this is only a crude approximation in time and space. For example, is an individual person always and in all places a medical case? Is the boundary of an individual at the surface of their skin or are aspects of what makes them who they are bound up in the relationships they

have with the people around them and their environment? In a qualitative study, I found that people with diabetes – a condition that demands their attention many times a day – spend relatively little time attending to their diabetes compared with the rest of life, and that there was no clear boundary between what is them as individuals and how they relate to their world (Griffiths et al. 2007).

This chapter considers different conceptions of 'what is a case' in medicine. Historically, describing patterns of illness symptoms as cases was important in the establishment of clinical sciences. For example, diabetes has been known to physicians since ancient times from their observation of patients and noting the pattern of symptoms. In the eighteenth century, chemists were able to show that people with this pattern of symptoms known as diabetes had a lot of sugar in their urine. In the nineteenth century, anatomists showed that people with symptoms of diabetes had changes in their pancreas at post mortem. As medical science has developed, more detail has been discovered about the differences between people with and without diabetes. Definition of disease as a case also underpins epidemiology, the study of disease in populations. Understanding the transmission of

infectious disease was one of the early successes of epidemiology, where the presence of
the micro-organisms thought to cause the disease was part of the definition of the case. For
example, the presence of the tubercle bacillus
was part of defining a case of tuberculosis.
However, it is possible for an individual to be
infected with the micro-organism and not get
the disease; this person cannot be defined as a
case in terms of illness but is a case in terms
of the transmission of infection.

How a case of a disease in medicine is
defined is constantly changing as the presentation of disease changes and as the methods of
assessment change with new technology and
new understanding of disease mechanisms.
In the last decade the definition of diabetes
(type 2 or late-onset diabetes) has changed
as research has shown that levels of blood
sugar previously though to be normal can
have a damaging effect on body organs in the
long term. When screening for breast cancer
with mammography (X-rays of the breast)
became available, very early changes in the
breast tissue that would previously have gone
unnoticed were then defined as breast cancer.
In the prevention of cardiovascular disease
(e.g. heart attacks) lowering blood cholesterol
was thought to prevent further build up of
atheroma in blood vessels so any narrowing
of the arteries did not get worse. In the last
decade it has been found that if the blood
cholesterol level is brought down very low,
the atheroma actually reduces and so the
narrowing of the arteries is reversed. Having
'cardiovascular disease' used to be considered
a health problem for the rest of an individual's
life, so the individual remained a case of the
disease; this is now less certain.

The definition of the case in medicine
underpins the epidemiological research that
tests new medical interventions for their cost-
effectiveness in clinical trials. These trials are
conducted at a later stage in the development
and testing of new interventions. They are
designed to give precise estimates of the proportion of people likely to benefit from the
interventions expressed as numbers needed to
treat for one case to benefit. Clinical trials
recruit people with a particular condition so

the definition of the condition is a key aspect
of the trial. The tightness of the definition
depends on the type of condition, and our
ability to define it. For example, low back
pain is difficult to define because it fluctua-
tes over time, is perceived very differently
by different people and there is as yet no
definition based on anatomy, physiology, or
medical imaging (imaging is used to look for
causes that can benefit from surgical treatment
or injections but this is a small proportion
of all cases of low back pain). In contrast,
for a trial of a drug treatment for early-stage
cancer, the definition of 'early-stage cancer'
would be very precise and would include the
microscopic appearance of the cancer and
adjoining lymph nodes.

The definition of the case in medicine has
perhaps been most refined for the purposes
of clinical research and the application of
this research to clinical practice. However,
the concept of the case is also important in
medical education, as considered in a classic
study of medical students by Becker (1993).
This observational study describes how medical students defined cases based on their
usefulness for learning about medical conditions as required of them by their teachers
and the medical curriculum. The medical
students classified patients with illness that
was difficult to define or with multiple illness
as 'crocks' because they perceived them as not
useful for their learning.

Individuals living with illness have a
perspective on whether they are a case, as do
their doctors, and this conception may change
with time and place in quite subtle ways.
In this chapter I further explore the case in
medicine in its various forms for research,
teaching, clinical practice and living with
illness, drawing on my experience of working
as a clinician.

I trained and worked in medicine before
becoming an academic and so have the privilege of continuing to see patients in clinical
practice for part of my week. As a doctor
working in general practice,[1] people come to
see me in the role of patient, bringing their
health concerns. In the UK, people attend
their general practitioner (GP) for nearly all

their health concerns and cannot access a specialist without a referral from a GP.[2] Over time I often get to know them quite well as people and they get to know me. In this chapter, I introduce you to people who came to see me during one day in general practice.[3] I have chosen three people to describe in detail as their stories help us tease out issues about the case in medicine, but I want to emphasise that these are three people I happened to see on one day; they are not three unusual cases. Two of the three I had seen before about the same health issue. That same day I saw a further 29 people in the surgery[4] and two in their own homes, seven of whom I had seen for the same health issue before. Two of the three people I describe I have chosen partly because I had seen them before and so I know quite a lot about them. However, perhaps more importantly, for the three people I describe – to differing degrees – their role as patient was currently an important aspect of their life, more so than the other people who consulted that day. The stories also illustrate various aspects of case-ness. The others I saw included a 14-year-old boy with two verrucas whose main concern was what his peers would say about them, a 52-year-old woman needing a sick note because her employer needed more time to adjust the workplace for her return to work, a 38-year-old with knee pain who I know struggles with alcoholism, and five people attending with cough and fever, all with a very similar pattern of onset and progression almost certainly due to the same virus circulating in the community. Their contact with me as patients was brief and it seemed that their health issue was a relatively small part of the overall scheme of their lives. Thus, in choosing the three people to describe I have begun to define case-ness in medicine: people who have attended a doctor, who have health issues that are having considerable impact on their lives.

THE CASE OF MR JONES

Mr Jones entered my consulting room with a younger women assisting him to walk and sit down. I had never met him before. All I knew was his name and that he was living only temporarily in the locality. Introductions established that the younger woman was his daughter. He had been staying with her for the last 6 weeks so he could see his grandson, but his home was in Wales. I was struck by the length of the visit to see his grandson and that Mr Jones was tending to turn his head away from me and fidget about in his seat. I did not comment on this, waiting to hear more. My initial impression was that Mr Jones was in his 70s (this proved to be 20 years out) and I wondered if he was a recovering alcoholic, mentally ill and suffering side effects of the medication or that he felt anxious and uncomfortable with me. Mr Jones' daughter did most of the talking so I wondered if Mr Jones had trouble with speech, but when I spoke directly to Mr Jones he was able to respond clearly and coherently, but quietly. The problem they had come to talk about was back pain, which was an ongoing problem but much worse in the last week. The pain had eased a little since the previous day, and the patient was using a number of pain killers. However, they were concerned as to whether Mr Jones would be well enough to travel back to Wales the following week.

As the conversation continued the daughter mentioned that Mr Jones had Huntington's disease, to which I responded that this was useful to know, and on we went with talking about back pain, pain relief and travel plans. That piece of information immediately told me why Mr Jones was turning his head and fidgeting about as one of the symptoms of Huntington's disease is uncontrollable muscle movements. It also suggested to me an explanation as to why he was having a long visit to see his grandson: Huntingdon's disease is a progressive and terminal illness and Mr Jones would know he would not live to see his grandson grow to adulthood.

I learnt that Mr Jones was cared for by his sister in Wales but about three times a year comes for a long visit to his daughter. This gives his sister a break as well as giving Mr Jones time with his only grandson. As his daughter put it, the arrangement 'works well for everyone and my husband doesn't seem to mind'.

I had not met someone with Huntington's disease in my medical practice for many years. The disease is inherited, with an incidence of 4–7 per 100,000 people, although the incidence varies geographically. Anyone with a parent who has suffered Huntingdon's disease is born with a 50 : 50 chance of inheriting the faulty gene.

The condition was first described in 1872 by George Huntington when aged 21. His father and grandfather had been general practitioners so George Huntington had first encountered the patients he described when he was a child accompanying them on their medical rounds (Durbach and Hayden 1993). George Huntington worked as a general practitioner throughout his life but his description of the patients he encountered was taken up and investigated further by physicians such as William Osler and Alios Alzheimer later in the nineteenth century. Over the years, living in a locality with several families in which the disease occurred, George Huntington was able to observe the condition of each patient and compare it with the others he had seen, refining his description of the characteristics of the disease. When he wrote up the characteristics for publication in a medical journal (Huntington 1872), he focused on the features the patients had in common and so which seemed to indicate the patients suffered from the same condition. This characterisation of cases of Huntington's disease was crucial for investigating the biological causation of the disease. For example, at post mortem, atrophy of the part of the brain called the caudate nucleus was found in people with this particular form of neurological disease, as distinct from other neurological diseases that also caused chorea (uncontrollable muscle movements). As medical technology developed, this atrophy could be identified radiologically in those living with the disease. As biochemistry and medical genetics developed, the faulty gene leading to the development of Huntington's disease was identified along with some of the biochemical processes that lead to atrophy in the brain.

When I first met Mr Jones I didn't think of Huntingdon's disease because it is not very common and I haven't seen anyone with it recently. I was making comparisons between what I saw of Mr Jones and other people I had seen in general practice and linking this with my knowledge of what health problems are common and what causes them. Research on clinical reasoning describes this process of case comparison aided and informed by knowledge of causes of disease and such case characterisation and comparison is a common method for teaching medical students the skills of diagnosis (Norman 2005).

In my consultation with Mr Jones, having Huntington's disease was an important piece of information for me but as soon as I had gained it, this aspect of his life became background to his immediate health problem, the back pain. The Huntington's disease might have contributed to his back pain, but he could also have developed back pain in the way most people at some time develop back pain, for example lifting something or moving awkwardly. If I was teaching a group of medical students about back pain I would not ask Mr Jones to be a case of back pain for the medical students to talk to and examine as there would be too much interference from the Huntingdon's disease for the students to tease out issues about back pain. A neurologist might well ask Mr Jones to see medical students as a case of Huntington's disease. If I was asking patients to talk to medical students about living with a disabling health condition, I could ask Mr Jones to be a case and I would expect the medical students to learn from him about his back pain, his Huntingdon's disease and any other health issues, and how he lives with these conditions. In this learning context, Mr Jones becomes a case of having a disabling medical condition and the emphasis is not only on his medical case-ness but of a person living through life. As a GP, I may focus on a number of different aspects of a person's heath, trying to clarify what the pressing concerns are, what is new and what is not new and what I should remember as important context. In general practice, patients are more people than medical cases because as GPs we work close to the patient's lived reality, we are there to hear about any health concerns and we are trained to deal with people when their illnesses have not yet been well defined, and with people living with multiple illness.

Huntington's disease is an unusual medical problem in being due to the expression of one faulty gene. There are other diseases of this nature but when considered within the whole raft of health problems encountered in society, these diseases are relatively rare. Until the last decade, it was thought that Huntington's disease hardly ever occurred as a spontaneous mutation (the gene changing its nature) so almost all people with Huntington's disease had inherited it from a parent. It was also thought that if you had the abnormal gene you got Huntington's disease and if you didn't have the gene you didn't get the disease. However, the development of the science of genetics and its new understanding of the disease raises some interesting issues for our consideration of the case in medicine. It is possible to test a person for the gene that causes Huntington's disease. Most people with the gene will develop the symptoms of the disease later adult life, usually by the time they are 50, but sometimes later. Is the person with the abnormal gene a case of Huntington's disease before they get the symptoms? This issue has ethical implications as these genetic tests can be undertaken at any stage of life, including during pregnancy. It has become clear that the characterisation of the gene as faulty or not faulty is also not as clear cut as once thought. There is a gene called *huntingtin*, which in people with Huntington's disease has an increased number of CAG triplet repeats (i.e. the CAG pattern of amino acids at this point in the DNA is repeated more often). At this point in the DNA, most people have 15–20 repeats of the CAG sequence. It seems that almost everyone with more than 41 repeats develop the symptoms of Huntington's disease, but for those with fewer excessive repeats the disease might start later and be less severe. It is also likely that people can have excess repeats of CAG and never be diagnosed with Huntington's disease as for

a borderline number of repeats (over 20 but less than 41) the genetic penetrance may be low enough for any effects to go undetected, in the sense of not being characterised as Huntington's disease.

By considering the case of Mr Jones, I have explored how diagnosis defines a medical case, its use in teaching in medicine and its importance in providing a starting point for research into the biological causation of disease. I have described the fluid nature of the patient as a case of an illness when considered in general medical practice. The discussion of Mr Jones also alerts us to how increased understanding of a disease through medical research and the use of medical technology changes the boundary of what is a medical case, making it less clear and potentially bringing people under the medical gaze who previously would have gone unnoticed by medicine.

THE CASE OF MRS GARDENER

As Mrs Gardener walked in to my consulting room I recognised her as someone I had seen recently but I could not recall what about. She was purposeful as she walked in so it seemed that she was clear why she was here. She opened the conversation by reminding me she had seen me 2 weeks earlier and she had come back to discuss the effects of her antidepressants. She went on to tell me that she was still not sleeping well although in the last 7 days she had slept through on two nights, which was an improvement. By this point I had enough information from Mrs Gardener to know she had been depressed so I asked her how she was feeling generally. As patients talk about themselves I begin to access my memory of them and their story. As she told me that she is feeling a whole lot better and her husband said she is a different woman, I recalled seeing her for the first time about 4 weeks earlier when she attended with her mother. At that time, Mrs Gardener had looked sad and was in tears, looking down a great deal and moving slowly. Her mother had brought her because she was so worried about her and so was her husband. Mrs Gardener had described feeling very low, that she was no good at anything, was irritable and cried at anything. She had told me about the suicide of an aunt a few years earlier that had greatly affected her as, although an aunt, she was almost the same age as Mrs Gardener and they had grown up together. She had said she felt a failure as she had been depressed before and she didn't want to go back to that. Mrs Gardener's mother was a striking contrast to her daughter, animated, direct in her communication, fashionably dressed with eye-catching impact and giving an impression of being someone who battles and wins in life. I had wondered if she rather dominated her daughter's life. As the conversation continued she had told me that she herself was from a large extended family that had experienced many traumas and was in her words 'dysfunctional'. This family was part of one of the larger economic migrant groups within the locality. The communication between the mother and daughter had been easy and caring. It had transpired that Mrs Gardener's husband and mother had put some pressure on Mrs Gardener to come and see me and they had decided one of them would accompany her to make sure she came. I recalled that at that first consultation, Mrs Gardener's biggest worry had been that she was not able to look after her own young children and was 'taking it out on them'. With a couple of questions I had clarified that the children were well cared for and I was then able to use this difference between Mrs Gardener's perception and the reality to start turning her very negative story into a more positive one. Mrs Gardener had taken antidepressants for her previous episode of depression and had found them helpful. However, she had felt she should be able to get herself out of feeling how she did and didn't want to rely on antidepressants. After some discussion she had decided to try antidepressants and see a counsellor. We had arranged to meet again so I could review with her how she was feeling. Thus she had returned as planned for review.

Mrs Gardener was resistant to considering herself a case of depression, and viewed taking antidepressants as a marker of being a case. Carrying the label of depression was frightening for her because she perceived it as a permanent characteristic of a person: once a case of depression always a case of depression. My reassurance focused on the nature of depression as a temporary condition, from which people move on.

When Mrs Gardener left my consulting room after her first attendance I recorded the diagnosis of depression. As GPs we write a diagnosis for nearly every attendance although sometimes it may be little more than a description of symptoms, for example, 'headache'. The main reason for writing a diagnosis is as a record of the health issue for the patient so over time we can use the record to help us review progress with particular health issues and to provide background to understanding new health issues. However, recording a diagnosis also enables us to gain an overview of the health conditions we are seeing in general practice and what actions we take. Computerisation has made this easier. For example, we can identify all the cases of depression recorded in the last year, review which antidepressants we prescribed and compare this with national guidance. The diagnostic data can also be used to get an overview of population health. For example, my practice is in a network of sentinel practices in the UK. These are general practices that send their diagnosis data to a central repository every few days. One of the functions of the central repository is to look out for trends in diagnosis. For example, they monitor for early indications of an increase in cases of influenza so those responsible for public health can be alerted to the possibility of an epidemic. I recorded Mrs Gardener as a case of depression for our computerised clinical records and so this diagnosis would have been sent as anonymised data to the central repository. With computerisation there are a growing number of databases of anonymised general practice data for use in epidemiological research with various methods of checking the validity of the data. This type of data is used to inform policy. For example, the

World Health Organization has identified depression as a leading cause of disability worldwide[5] and that health policy should address this issue. The use of clinical data for epidemiology seems to change the diagnosis or case-ness of Mrs Gardener from something rather tentative and temporary to something precise and definite. How important this is when considered over a large population is debatable. There is a danger that the diagnosis becomes what Ragin describes as a conventional casing (Ragin 1992), loosing its tentative and temporary nature and as we discuss below, its contestable nature.

The diagnosis of depression makes an interesting contrast to the diagnosis of Huntington's disease about which, at least until recently, there has been a high degree of agreement in medicine. Depression is a highly contested diagnosis within medicine with a spectrum of views from depression being a biochemical disorder to it not being a diagnosis at all (Dowrick 2004). The latter position does not deny the distress of the patient but questions whether depression is a medical diagnosis. The medicalisation debate generated and developed by sociologists is important for reflecting on and refining the role of medicine in society and will need to continue as society, illness and medicine change. I want to stay focused on the case in medicine and explore medicalisation from this perspective. As a GP, I was trained to use a bio/psycho/social model for understanding patients (Royal College of General Practitioners 1996). This has much in common with understanding patients as complex with many interacting factors affecting health, as illustrated by Mrs Gardener. We have heard that difficulties in her extended family might be influencing her, the loss of her aunt was traumatic, but currently she appears to be in a caring and stable relationship with her husband, mother and children. Mrs Gardener is from the third-generation of a family who came to the locality for work and maintains family connections in their country of origin. Economic migration is a major upheaval for an individual or family, with implications for their health. Mrs Gardener herself tends

to underestimate her ability to cope and, at least at present, perceives herself and the world in a negative way. Her previous experience with antidepressants suggests they can help her. This is not to assume that the cause of her depression is biochemical but that when she is depressed there are changes in the biochemistry of the brain that antidepressants can influence. By resisting assumptions about the level of analysis for causation we can develop an understanding of multiple factors from different levels of analysis, biological, psychological, family, community, nation state, that interact resulting in the emergence of the distress that has been labelled depression. We can also see that factors from a similar level of analysis such as 'family' can have both positive and negative effects. The definitions of common forms of depression that are most widely accepted in medicine are basically descriptions of how a patient says they feel, including low mood, difficulty sleeping and feeling life is not worth living. If depression is a state of health that emerges from the interaction of many factors then this type of definition is the most precise that is possible. This is uncomfortable for branches of medicine that are accustomed to disease definition based on biological features but is the definition that seems to work in day-to-day general medical practice and much of psychiatry, and perhaps benefits from remaining contested.

As a GP, my professional focus is on the patients who come to see me with their concerns. The help I have to offer is focused on the patient: counselling, drugs and providing some continuity of support, including acknowledgement of wider issues affecting the patient. We widen our focus to the immediate family or carers, particularly where they are very involved with the patient's health for example in palliative care. If we have concern about the family, particularly the welfare of the children, we would ask for input from a social worker. For GPs, the diagnosis and its definition focuses on the individual person and their health concerns because that is our job as it has developed in our society. Most societies have developed a role for a person-centred 'healer' although it takes very different forms in different places. On a recent visit to Bolivia to explore the role of primary health care I found that 'traditional healers' in rural areas fulfilled most of the functions of a UK GP, and like us referred on to hospital those patients who could benefit from hospital treatment. The government was in the process of integrating traditional healers into their health service (Meads et al. 2007). However, the experience of depression for individuals can be changed through interventions at other levels of analysis, for example through the family, the local community, the socio-economic locality or the national economy. Each of these can be studied as a case. For example, in an industrial or post-industrial community people present to their GPs with depression precipitated by redundancy through closure of their industry. In a case study of these communities, these individuals become part of the case under study, and an understanding of these communities as cases increases our understanding of the experience of depression.

By examining the case of Mrs Gardener I have explored further the definition of a case of illness through the use of a diagnostic label for which there is no medical consensus on causation. I have considered how the definition of cases is used in the study of the health of populations and through this, impacts on healthcare policy. As a GP, I perceive depression as emerging from the interaction of many factors from many levels of analysis, resulting in a case of depression. As a GP in clinical practice, I am only able to influence factors close to or integral to the patient consulting me, so focusing on the individual as the case. However, an individual with depression may be studied as one of many people in a case study of a community.

THE CASE OF MR CUMBERBATCH

Mr Cumberbatch came briskly into my consulting room, smiling, and greeted me. This indicated to me I had seen him recently so again my mind started working on clues

to spark off my memory of him. I could have glanced through my notes about him in the clinical record displayed on my computer screen. However, I don't like to glance away from the patient initially as I can miss important clues and cues (and it can be perceived as unwelcoming). I can always look at the notes later in the consultation. As Mr Cumberbatch sat down I said 'How can I help?' He touched his nose saying he had been noticing that his nose had been a bit blocked, not completely but it was usually a bit moist and sometimes one nostril was completely blocked and it varied as to which one. He indicated in the way he talked that he had been observing himself since he last saw me and was acknowledging I might have been right about something. By this point I had remembered at least some of his story from our last encounter. He had come to see me because he was snoring and this was causing some friction between himself and his partner. I had gone through the factors that can aggravate snoring: he didn't smoke, he didn't drink a great deal of alcohol, and he was obviously not very overweight. He had described having a dry mouth especially at night. As this is commonly caused by breathing through the mouth because of a blocked nose, I had asked him about his nose but he denied any problem with it. I recalled feeling rather puzzled and uncomfortable at this point because I was facing a moment of incongruity. Mr Cumberbatch was confident he did not get a blocked nose nor that he breathed through his mouth at night, so to account for the dry mouth I had to think of other causes such as diabetes, but nothing else about him pointed me in this direction. My 'rule of thumb' in this situation is to put my initial impression to one side in my mind and reconsider the patient and their story. I may ask the patient to go over their concerns again or I may move on to examination. With Mr Cumberbatch, I recalled examining him including looking at his nose, listening to his chest and doing a breathing test (peak flow), not expecting to find much of interest but to give me time for thought. To my surprise, the peak flow was lower than I expected so I asked him if he had asthma and if he had noticed any problems with his breathing. He responded that he did not have asthma and participated in a great deal of sport. He commented that he had noticed some shortness of breath on starting his sports but this usually passed after some minutes of activity. I moved the consultation to focus on his breathing, unsure if this had any relevance for his snoring. He left with an inhaler to use before sport to see it if improved his breathing and an agreement he would return to tell me whether it helped or not.

The week before seeing Mr Cumberbatch I had seen a woman who denied any problem with her breathing although her breathing tests indicated she had severe chronic obstructive pulmonary disease (COPD, often known as chronic bronchitis), which is a progressive and disabling condition. Over many years she had adapted her lifestyle to her low breathing capacity limiting the amount she walked by 'always using the car' and developing sedentary hobbies because she 'wasn't interested in sport and never had been even at school'. She hadn't really noticed or perhaps acknowledged how much her breathing affected her. Her lack of exercise masked the poor breathing and probably contributed to it as people with COPD can improve their breathing with exercise. She smoked although was trying to give up. Many factors seem to have influenced this patient's development of COPD. She may have had an inherent tendency to get more breathless than her peers at school, which had the effect of discouraging her participation in sport. Social pressure and social context would have influenced her lifestyle including her smoking. The interaction of many factors seemed to have led to her current situation. There is epidemiological evidence that for many people with COPD, stopping smoking improves their breathing. However, there is uncertainty when applying such evidence to an individual patient, intrinsic to the nature of the evidence as it is about probability within populations not about individuals (Fox 2002, Griffiths et al. 2006). Smoking seems to be a major factor in COPD for many people, but not everyone.

I mention this patient with COPD as I might have been over-influenced by her when assessing Mr Cumberbatch, something GPs try to avoid. However, when he mentioned to me the second time I saw him that he used to work in dusty atmospheres and sometimes with asbestos when 'the breathing gear didn't work as well as it does now' I was glad to have followed this up. The inhaler had not helped but Mr Cumberbatch was happy to make an appointment for a more sophisticated assessment of his breathing undertaken by the specially trained COPD nurse to help clarify whether his lungs are a cause for concern or not.

Between the two consultations, Mr Cumberbatch had monitored himself, both his breathing after using the inhaler and his ability to breath through his nose, so at that time he perceived himself as a case for observation. His first consultation had also changed the situation at home. He described the snoring as 'less of an issue because I am trying to do something about it'. Mr Cumberbatch was unusual in being very clear about his self-monitoring. His work involves various types of monitoring in the field of engineering so he was able to use these skills. It is not uncommon for patients to find it difficult to report back on their progress. For example, a patient with pain when asked 'Did the pain-killer help?' may reply 'I don't know'. Many patients don't like taking pills and may have not taken them, or feared they would be masking something serious by taking them. Even if the patient has taken the pain-killer, many other factors can influence pain so it is difficult to know what was the effect of the pain-killer and what the effect of other things. For example, with back pain, the pain can ease with a change in pace of work or be made worse by anxiety. Pain can also ease for no apparent reason or have a fluctuating pattern. The same problem is faced in medical research when trying to demonstrate that a medical intervention has made a difference in a particular case. If the treatment effect is considered the 'signal' and the expected prognosis of the condition is considered the 'noise' then a 'treatment effect is inferred most confidently when the signal to noise ratio is large and its timing is rapid compared with the natural course of the condition' (Glasziou et al. 2007). In the example of low back pain, the 'noise' is high. An intervention would need to cause a very large change in the pain for it to be clear that the intervention was the cause of the change in pain level. However, if a skin blemish that has not changed for years is then treated with a medical laser and fades considerably within a few weeks of the treatment, then it is very likely the treatment caused the blemish to fade.

With this in mind, let us return to Mr Cumberbatch and his problem with snoring. I was interested in his account of what he had noticed about his ability to breath through his nose, as a common cause of snoring is having a blocked nose. I checked his nose for internal polyps that could partially block the nose then we discussed using a steroid nasal spray to reduce any inflammation of the lining of the nose as this can contribute to having clearer nasal passages. I explained the full effect of the spray takes a week or two to build up so he should use it for about a month then report back. If there was no improvement then we would consider other interventions, but these involved referral to a specialist. As his nose was only blocked sometimes and it varied as to how much, Mr Cumberbatch will need quite a dramatic effect from the nasal spray to be sure it has an effect so I advised him to take the highest recommended dose for this trial period. When I reflected on the consultation, what I thought would happen was that he would try the nasal spray and conclude it may be helping a bit. He may be quite impressed with the effect initially but as the rhinitis changed he would become less impressed. However, I think the snoring will slip off his agenda, at least for a while. He has defused the tension at home by seeking help and he knows there are other possible interventions if the snoring does persist. This may result in himself and his wife sleeping better so they are less disturbed by noise and each other's anxiety. The nasal spray may help a bit reducing the snoring. Even if the spray is not used all the

time, he can restart it if the snoring becomes an issue again. If this was what happened could we conclude the nasal spray 'worked'? Using the statistical assessment described above it is very doubtful we could. However, the nasal spray may have changed enough about Mr Cumberbatch to initiate positive feedback effects so the problem becomes not a problem. I didn't expect to see Mr Cumberbatch again even though I suggested he return for review. The nasal spray can be obtained directly from a pharmacy.

If Mr Cumberbatch had talked about himself differently, being tired during the day, waking with a headache most mornings and his wife reporting that he snores and seems to stop breathing frequently during the night (wives tend to notice this as it is frightening for them), then I would have discussed the possibility of sleep apnoea (this is when a person stops breathing for a brief time while asleep; over time, it can be detrimental to the person's general health) and having tests for this with a specialist. The specialist would have the advantage of having seen many patients with sleep apnoea and so be more tuned in to the features that distinguish sleep apnoea from ordinary snoring, and if necessary could arrange for tests to try to demonstrate the apnoea. We tend to expect a specialist to be able to give a definite answer, such as confirming sleep apnoea. Sometimes they can but often this is not possible as a diagnosis of sleep apnoea is a refined conceptual medical case with many people only partially matching the criteria for being a case. If an individual responds to treatment they may be considered a case, but as we have seen, assessing the effect of an intervention for each individual is not easy.

I was very surprised to meet Mr Cumberbatch again about 6 weeks later, after his visit to the nurse. Following national guidelines for the assessment of COPD, the nurse had arranged a blood test for a relatively uncommon genetic predisposition to COPD. For Mr Cumberbatch the test was positive, with the implication that he might find his breathing gradually deteriorates despite his healthy lifestyle.

THE CASE IN MEDICINE

By exploring the case of Mr Cumberbatch I have explored further how a patient is assessed in clinical practice and what influences the focus of clinical assessment. I have considered the difficulty patients and their doctors face in assessing the effect of health interventions and the many inter-relating factors influencing them as medical cases.

CONCLUSION

This chapter has considered the case in medicine by exploring the stories of three individuals who brought their health concerns to general practice in the UK. This exploration may have felt like a meander through these stories, looking at the case in medicine from various perspectives. This reflects to some extent the lived reality of living with a health problem or working as a health professional or researcher in medicine. Case-ness changes depending on who we are, where we are and who or what we are looking at. Defining the case in medicine, cutting out the case from its time and space to study it or to intervene has been important throughout the history of medicine. Defining an illness in terms of the characteristics of a case forms the basis for clinical research both biological and epidemiological. Cases in medicine underpin clinical teaching and can be defined in various ways according to the focus of the teaching. Individuals living with illness may at times perceive themselves as a case in medicine to varying degrees as does the clinician they consult for health care. Medicine mostly responds to health problems brought to the attention of clinicians by individuals. The case in medicine has thus been defined in terms of abnormal function or ill health rather than in terms of health. This is now being challenged by the experience of people living with long-term health conditions who are well and able to function normally although needing to pay particular attention to an aspect of their health such as asthma or diabetes.

There is no clear, consistent boundary to the case in medicine both in space and time. Case-ness can fluctuate very rapidly or be very stable in time. It is difficult to know where to draw the boundary of a case in medicine, even though medicine tends to focus on individual people, as the nature of each person and their health is at least in part formed through their relationships with their social and physical environment. Our understanding of what is a case also changes with our changing understanding of health and illness and changing technology. Medicine also works with what can be considered conceptual cases or an ideal type against which other cases are compared and may match to varying degrees. The definition of how closely an individual matches the concept of a case of a disease will depend on symptoms and medical diagnostic tests but also on their response to treatment.

Conventional casing as suggested by Ragin (1992), such as gender and social class, can be useful and allow researchers to undertake other tasks. Where medicine has a technical skill, such as opening up blocked coronary arteries or providing a complicated chemotherapy regime, it may benefit an individual with the relevant health problem to, at least in part, be identified as a case of a particular disease. The health professionals providing the technical intervention should be aware of the person as individual too, but the technical focus on the case is important to ensure a technically competent intervention. Where there is less certainty about the health problem and the best intervention, a provisional identification of a person as a case of a particular disease can be useful in the process of considering possibilities and potential treatments. As explored in this chapter, a provisional identification of a person as having asthma or depression is one step in exploring what may help solve the health problem presented. The use of definitions of a case in medicine is also useful in epidemiology for understanding disease in populations and the cost-effectiveness of health care interventions. The use of relatively conventional casing in medicine can become problematic if their transient and context dependent nature are forgotten.

Medical sciences are constantly redefining the case in medicine in an iterative way

(Ragin 1992), using both theory and empirical evidence to define and refine case-ness. Medical research using this definition may then itself challenge this definition of case-ness and lead to a critique of the theory and new empirical evidence. The past decade of medical research has been dominated by the desire to produce evidence of cost-effectiveness of clinical interventions through clinical trials, a desire arising from the lack of evidence that existed previously for the effectiveness of many interventions widely used in medicine. However, as expertise in clinical trails has developed so has the realisation of the importance of clarity about the definition of a case and how it is defined, leading to a greater attention to these issues prior to undertaking clinical trials (Campbell et al. 2007).

In clinical practice, case-ness as considered by people living with a health condition and by clinicians also develops iteratively through considering empirical evidence and testing this against concepts of illness. There is a danger of case-ness becoming a fixed idea for individuals through using this comparative process, as the illness concept might appear fixed. However, understanding case-ness as emergent from the interaction of many biological, social and environmental factors highlights the provisional and conditional nature of case-ness and provides a framework for understanding how a similar health problem can emerge for people with very varied bio-social lives and so for whom different interventions may be appropriate. A healthy state for individuals may be where their case-ness is changing, and is perceived as something that changes in relationship with their social context and environment. Being stuck as a particular type of case in medicine may well be an unhealthy state for an individual.

NOTES

1. Known as 'family medicine' in many countries.
2. There are a few exceptions, including accidents and emergencies, but the UK is fairly unusual in the

world for this very full gatekeeper role of general practice.
3. I have changed personal details of the individuals.
4. In the UK, we quaintly and confusingly refer to the building where we see patients as GPs as 'surgery' and we refer to a session of appointments as 'surgery'. We only occasionally do minor surgery such as removing toe nails.
5. http://www.who.int/mental_health/management/depression/definition/en/

REFERENCES

Becker, H.S. 1993 'How I learned what a crock was' *Journal of Contemporary Ethnography* 22: 283–285.
Campbell, N. Murray, E., Darbyshire, J., Emery, J., Farmer, A., Griffiths, F.E., Guthrie, B., Lester, H.E., Wilson, P. and Kinmouth, A.L. 2007 'Designing and evaluating complex interventions to improve health care' *British Medical Journal* 334: 455–459 doi:10.1136/bmj.39108.379965.BE.
Dowrick, C. 2004 *Beyond Depression: A New Approach to Understanding and Management.* Oxford: Oxford University Press.
Durbach, N. and Hayden, M. 1993 'George Huntington: the man behind the eponym' *Journal of Medical Genetics* 30(5): 406–409.
Fox, R.C. 2002 'Gender, health and healing: the public/private divide' in G. Bendelow, M. Carpenter, C. Vautier and S. Williams (Eds) *Medical Uncertainty Revisited* London: Routledge, pp. 236–253.
Glasziou, P., Chalmers, I. et al., 2007 'When are randomised trials unnecessary? Picking signal from noise' *British Medical Journal* 334: 349–351.
Griffiths, F., Green, E. and Bendelow, G. 2006 'Health professionals, their medical interventions and uncertainty: a study focusing on women at midlife' *Social Science and Medicine* 62(5): 1078–1090.
Griffiths, F.M.U., Anton, N., Chow, E., Van Royen, P. and Bastiaens, H. 2007 'Understanding the diversity and dynamics of living with diabetes: a feasibility study focusing on the case' *Chronic Illness* 3: 29–45.
Huntington, G. 1872 'On chorea' *Medical and Surgical Reporter* 26: 317–321.
Meads, G., Griffiths, F.E., Goode, S. and Iwami, M. 2007 'Lessons from local engagement in Latin American health systems' *Health Expectations* 10(4): 407–418.

Norman, G. 2005 'Research in clinical reasoning: past history and current trends' *Medical Education* 39: 418–427.

Ragin, C.C. 1992 '"Casing" and the process of social inquiry' in C. Ragin and H. Becker (Eds) *What Is a Case? Exploring the Foundations of Social Inquiry.* Cambridge: Cambridge University Press.

Royal College of General Practitioners 1996 *The Nature of General Medical Practice.* London: Royal College of General Practitioners.

Wieviorka, M. 1992 'Case studies: history or sociology?' in C. Ragin and H. Becker (Eds) *What Is a Case? Exploring the Foundations of Social Inquiry.* Cambridge: Cambridge University Press.

27

Team-Based Aggregation of Qualitative Case Study Data in Health Care Contexts: Challenges and Learning

Sue Dopson, Ewan Ferlie, Louise
Fitzgerald and Louise Locock

This chapter reflects on our recent experience of undertaking a team-based aggregation of qualitative process data derived from a case study methodology. Our motivation was to explore the question: would 'pooling' results across a family of related studies produce more generalisable findings and increase external validity? We describe the process we went through in some detail and claim that it has certain distinctive features compared with other attempts at aggregation in that we are using our empirical material and not peer-reviewed articles. We also brought together two teams of investigators who had done the research and finally there is the issue of scale: 49 case studies and 1400 interviews all carried out in health care contexts. We draw a number of lessons from this exercise,

most particularly in relation to the varying theoretical approaches and values of team members, the importance of trust and an awareness of team processes.

INTRODUCTION

This chapter reflects on a team of researchers' recent experience of undertaking a aggregation of qualitative process data derived from a case study methodology (Yin 1994). The case study methodology has a long tradition within organisational studies (Thomas and Znaniecki 1918–20, Becker 1968), yet one significant criticism hurled at qualitative methods in general and case study research in particular is a low level of external validity and failure to generate theory. From the point of view of policy makers, evidence from single-case studies is frequently dismissed as 'irrelevant' because of its narrow and contextually particular base. Managers, on the other hand, may find case study research data more accessible and comprehensible.

Yin (1999) has recently discussed how the methodological quality of case studies might be improved. He suggests that an appropriate response to the need to build external validity through theory is not to select cases through a sampling logic, but through a replication logic and he argues that each case study, as a unit, can be considered as a single experiment; and multiple case studies can be considered as multiple experiments. This view has been echoed by other distinguished researchers. Golden-Biddle et al. (2005) argue, for example, that what case studies miss in detailed nuances of each change situation, they gain in access to comparison across multiple change situations. As a team of researchers, we were keen to explore whether it would be additive to aggregate analyses of multiple case studies by taking an overview across a suite of seven related and recently completed studies that considered the diffusion of innovations into use in clinical practice. It is important to be clear that the work constitutes an aggregation of qualitative work, and not a synthesis; 'synthesis' implies the creation of something new, whereas 'aggregation' implies an additive effect. In the literature we briefly review in this chapter, these terms are not precisely defined and are often seen as having the same meaning.

Our question at the beginning of our work together was: would 'pooling' results across this family of related studies, produce more generalisable and applicable findings? If so, how could this be achieved? The chapter is organised as follows. First, and by way of background, we discuss the increase in the work of aggregation in qualitative studies. Second, we reflect on our experiences of a novel team-based[1] exploration of process data collected in health care settings and outline the methodological challenges we met in undertaking this work. Finally, we discuss the implications of our experience.

AGGREGATION IN QUALITATIVE STUDIES

The question of generalization more generally provokes radically different responses amongst social scientists. Flyvberg (2001) argues that generalisation is overvalued and represents an attempt by social science to emulate natural science. This does not mean he precludes generalisation altogether. Indeed, he states that it can be appropriate and valuable in some cases, but is at pains to stress that it is not the only way to work. He also argues that despite the difficulties of summarising qualitative research, case studies can still contribute to cumulative development of knowledge, not least through hypothesis testing and falsification, which is possible from single cases, let alone multiple cases. Nonetheless, he concludes that 'if we want to recover social science from its current role as loser in the Science Wars ... we must drop the fruitless efforts to emulate natural science's success in producing cumulative and predictive theory' (p. 116).

The extreme radical social constructionist position is that generalisation is neither desirable nor feasible. Campbell et al. (2003, p. 673), for example, note that:

... synthesizing qualitative research is a contentious issue for the qualitative research community because it rests on a number of contested assumptions about the nature and purpose of qualitative research. In particular, it presupposes that it is reasonable to generalize beyond individual qualitative studies. Post-modernists reject outright any form of generalization and so will not regard qualitative research synthesis as a legitimate approach. Others, although not rejecting generalization altogether will be concerned that in synthesizing across different studies important differences will be downplayed and that the real value of qualitative research, in terms of its emphasis on context and holism, will be lost.

Even the authors of one of the central texts on qualitative synthesis or 'meta-ethnography', Noblit and Hare (1988), make no claim to generalisation on the basis of a comparative approach to case studies. Whilst positivists see accumulation of knowledge as a means to develop predictions, 'anticipation, rather than prediction, is the more reasonable result of qualitative research' (p. 25). An accumulation of qualitative studies in a particular field may simply reflect the fact that it is an enduring area of concern – 'it may or may not reflect a substantive improvement in how well we understand something' (p. 25).

However, there may be other reasons, beyond generalisation, for attempting aggregation of case study data. Accessing a larger database for analysis also enables the nuances of differences and similarities between contexts to be more thoroughly comprehended. This may potentially have a pragmatic and a theoretical use. Pragmatically, it may enable managers and others to identify the probable key influencers in a situation in advance, and critically it may inform and facilitate theory development.

Those working within an interpretive paradigm stress the importance of context in determining what we can extract in the way of generalisation. Noblit and Hare (1988), for example, note the tendency of quantitative aggregation and synthesis to ignore 'meaning in context' because it is seen to get in the way of producing generalisable findings. It is treated as a confounding variable, which must be controlled for or stripped out of the equation, rather than understood as an important explanatory variable. Context-stripping may help focus on commonalities, but it impedes proper interpretive aggregation or synthesis. In our work, we were acutely aware of the critical role of context in influencing the social processes we were studying. For example, we have argued for a reconceptualisation of context as an active part of the innovation process and to move away from viewing context as a backcloth to action (Dopson and Fitzgerald 2005). Equally, the social context that we as researchers are a part of, crucially mediates our approach to research and writing, points we reflect on later.

Sandelowski et al. (1997, p. 367) identify three further kinds of qualitative meta-synthesis:

(1) The integration of findings from individual pieces of research carried out by the same investigator; for example, the work of Eliot

Rogers (1995), or the work of a team of investigators led by a single director in the case of Van der Ven et al. (1999).

(2) Synthesis of findings across studies carried out by different investigators (used by Sandelowski herself in a recent article; Sandelowski and Barroso 2003).

(3) The use of quantitative methods to aggregate qualitative findings; for example, the case survey method, using highly structured questions to collect information from separate case studies on a particular theme, which can then be turned into a dataset for statistical analysis.

As the above discussion begins to suggest, not only is there debate about what are feasible goals for qualitative aggregation or synthesis, and the extent to which generalisation and accumulation are possible, but there is also a welter of different terms and techniques in use. There is no doubt that aggregation of qualitative research is attracting increased academic interest, stimulated at least partly by the development of quantitative meta-analysis. In addition to the terms 'qualitative synthesis' and 'qualitative aggregation', we have already encountered above the terms 'meta-ethnography', 'narrative review', 'realist synthesis', 'narrative (meta)-synthesis', 'meta-synthesis', 'qualitative systematic review', 'data synthesis of qualitative research' and doubtless many other terms abound in what has been aptly described as a 'lexiconic mess'!

Our work as described below is a further attempt to scale up qualitative and case study-based empirical data and test how this can be done in a methodologically rigorous way. Although it has much in common with other attempts at aggregation described above, we argue it has certain distinctive features. The literature on the aggregation of qualitative work tends to focus on the analysis of secondary, published data, often by researchers who were not involved in any of the original studies. Our own approach is perhaps a step further back in the chain than that, in that we are using our final research reports, which are much longer and more detailed than the findings presented in a peer-review article. Furthermore, we have the advantage of being able to go back to the primary data when needed (e.g. to check for further quotations) and we have the primary data in our shared memory.

Unlike the type of aggregation noted by Sandelowski et al. (1997), which involves the integration of findings from individual pieces of research carried out by the same investigator, we have brought together two teams of investigators and pooled our separately conducted studies which we believe meet the tests of rigour in qualitative research (see Murphy et al. 1998, Popay et al. 1998). Finally, there is the question of sheer scale – for example, Campbell et al. (2003) synthesise findings from 7 studies comprising 193 interviews, and Sandelowski and Barroso (2003) used 45 studies with a total sample size of 925. We have sought to aggregate via discussion and debate over a period of some 6 years the findings of 49 individual case studies of attempts at innovation in health care settings and 1400 interviews of key actors in these contexts (see Table 27.1 for details).

We have found that there are a number of contributions the case study method can make to improving our understanding of the complex social processes involved in health care studies. For example, case studies can:

- Enable us to experience vicariously social processes within a variety of cultural settings.
- Allow us to see the complexity of the social world through the researchers' and respondents' eyes thus prompting new insights and questions.
- Enable us to consider behaviour in a social context.
- Shed light on complex interdependencies between groups and complex social processes.
- Uncover underlying patterns.
- Help tease out aspects of receptive and non-receptive contexts for change.
- Assist in understanding the unanticipated outcomes of change.

Fulfilling such promise, as well as contributing to theory and policy development, requires researchers to meet some important standards for good-quality case study research, these include:

- Using and developing organisational theory.
- Using multiple methods.

- Ensuring that analysis is informed by previous studies/literature/findings.
- As part of the analysis strategy, considering the importance of looking at the objects of one's research historically and in the wider system of social interdependencies (social context) in which they are embedded.
- Seeking where possible to compare the case results with other similar cases improving the basis for generalisation (Dopson 2005).

OUR ATTEMPT AT AGGREGATION

A guiding principle for aggregation is the need to compare like with like: the greater the similarity, the more methodologically appropriate such work becomes. Cross-study comparison is easiest where there is a purposefully designed and prospective replication of an earlier design. It is therefore encouraging that four of the set of studies form two replicated 'pairs': the Ferlie and Fitzgerald team undertook an early study analyzing evidence-based health care[2] (EBHC) implementation in the acute sector (Wood et al. 1998); this was followed deliberately by a replication by the same team in the primary-care sector (Fitzgerald et al. 1999). Dopson and colleagues conducted an evaluation of clinical effectiveness projects in Wales (Locock et al. 1999) explicitly as a continuation of the evaluation methods used in the Promoting Action on Clinical Effectiveness (PACE) project (Dopson et al. 1999).

The other three studies (Dawson et al. 1998, Dopson and Gabbay 1995, CSAG 1998) did not take the form of purpose-designed replications and pose more complexity for what is a retrospective overview. What methodological guidance do we have in this situation? Yin (1999) notes that an increasingly common situation in case study-based research is for cases to be undertaken by multiple teams, in order to meet the tight project deadlines often found in organisational studies. His advice is that such teams need to display a common orientation and training and to follow similar field protocols. Without such common features,

Table 27.1 An overview of the research design and methods across the seven sites. All interviews were in-depth and semi-structured

	Design	No. of case studies	Face-to-face interviews	Telephone interviews*	Written questionnaires	Document analysis	Dates
Dopson and Gabbay 1995	Single-stage case studies on four clinical topics	4	58 (RHA and purchasing managers, clinicians and public health)			✓	2 years, 1993–4
Wood et al. 1998	Two stages: 1. Overview survey across whole region	4	71 (mainly front-line clinicians)			✓	2 years, 1995–7
	2. Case studies, one per clinical topic, selected on evidence of clinical change elicited from first stage		48 (mainly clinicians and clinical managers)			✓	2 years, 1995–7
Dawson et al. 1998	Embedded case studies, two clinical topics in each of four hospitals	8	256 (clinical staff of various professions and grades) plus 20 informal interviews with trust and HA managers		256 (same group as interviews)	✓	2 years, 1995–7
CSAG 1998	Single-stage case study design, full in seven sites, telephone and questionnaire only in six	13 (7 + 6)	250 (front-line clinicians and managers)	321	1317 GPs 256 hospital clinicians	✓	6 months, 1996–7
Fitzgerald et al. 1999	Three stages: 1. Overview across four health authorities on diffusion of innovation	4	38 (senior HA managers and GPs)			✓	2 years, 1997–9
	2. Overview with same group, concentrated on particular innovations		35				2 years, 1997–9
	3. Case studies on four innovations in primary care		40 (GPs and other primary care and physiotherapy staff)			✓	2 years, 1997–9
Dopson et al. 1999	Two stages: 1. Initial round of interviews half-way through project	16	7 (staff from King's Fund and DoH)	51 (project team members, managers and clinicians)		✓	2 years, 1997–8
	2. Second round at end of project, using themes elicited during first stage			122 (project team members, other senior managers and clinicians)	150 (front-line clinicians)	✓	2 years, 1997–9
Locock et al. 1999	Single-stage case studies, after project completion	6	18 (front-line clinicians)	65 (project team members, other senior managers and clinicians, Welsh Office reps)	238 (front-line clinicians)	✓	6 months, 1998–9

it is impossible to be clear whether any differences found between the cases are 'real' or artrefactual due to inter team differences. We discuss later the process we went through in order for us to achieve a common orientation.

In many respects, there are, however, important similarities between the studies. The seven studies were all undertaken within the same national health care system (the English Natinoal Health Service; NHS), during the same period (the late 1990s), so that two very important aspects of context (time period and geographical/organisational setting) are held constant. They were also undertaken by two teams of researchers who displayed similar theoretical and disciplinary bases, that is, they shared an organisational behaviour (OB) perspective and concepts. Both groups used similar – although not identical – comparative case study designs (there are no single-case studies in the set and the number of cases in any study varies from four to sixteen) rather than experimental, observational or indeed post modernist or action research methods. All studies focused on the organisational and group levels of analysis rather than single individuals. There was a common unit of analysis across the studies, namely a social analysis of the career of innovations in real-world health care settings. The material generated and analysed in the studies was verbal and literary (rather than numeric) in nature, typically taking the form of case studies, which are compared and contrasted within the individual study first of all to identify trends and tendencies. Cross-study pooling continues this comparative logic, which is already apparent in the individual studies. All the studies used documentary analyses and in-depth and semi-structured interviews as important data collection methods. The analysis strategy used in all cases was an inductive process of content analysis, and in one study NUDIST qualitative software was used.

Taken as a whole, we conclude that the studies represent a related family of studies, which share important core features so that cross study pooling is methodologically appropriate. There are some particular methodological problems in comparing the results from the studies: the studies are similar but not identical in nature, and we need to be alert to these differences. Resource constraints help explain the decision to use telephone interviews rather than face-to-face interviews in four studies. Four studies used written questionnaires as part of data collection and three did not. Besides these relatively obvious differences, a number of deeper methodological challenges faced us in comparing results across the seven studies.

The process we have gone through for some 6 years has been an iterative one involving several stages; during and after each stage we reflected critically on the methodological experience and recorded our reflections. This was carried out both through collective discussion at meetings and individual written reflections which were shared with the rest of the group. The main stages are described below.

Stage 1 – initial overview

We made a decision early on that we would use the final published reports of each research project as the basis for our work together (Dopson and Gabbay 1995, CSAG 1998, Dawson et al. 1998, Wood et al. 1998, Dopson et al. 1999, Fitzgerald et al. 1999, Locock et al. 1999). Given the number of interviews and case studies involved, we did not feel it was practical to go back to these original sources, although we did – on occasions – go back to the original data to assist clarification. The final reports alone contain approximately 200,000 words when added together.

The initial process of familiarisation entailed every member of both research teams reading all the detailed final project reports, some of which they were not involved. In addition, each individual produced a summary of what they felt were the key points arising from each final report. These were then debated collectively and a deeper understanding of the material and individual perspectives emerged. Each team member brought different 'pre-knowledge' to the debate. This pre-knowledge consisted of two relevant points: first, detailed knowledge of the studies they had conducted, and second, knowledge gained from prior academic work, knowledge of the literature and relevant theory. This open debate proved critical to the taking of the next steps of aggregation.

An important point to note is that to some extent the final reports were already cumulative or comparative, given that each team was building on its past research and that both teams were already in communication with each other and citing each other's findings in some of the later reports. For example, reflections on the socially constructed nature of scientific research evidence and the existence of competing bodies of evidence formed a prominent part of the Warwick Acute Study report (Wood et al. 1998), and influenced the Wales report (Locock et al. 1999). Meanwhile Dawson et al.'s (1998) analysis of how the subjective understandings of clinicians mediate the flow of evidence into practice is cited in the Warwick Primary Care study (Fitzgerald et al. 1999).

After this in-depth debate of the studies, we developed an initial overview of the 'common' findings, identifying common themes emerging from our discussions. The major headings identified at this stage were: evidence, context, professionals/opinion leaders, translation/interpretation, and management/organisation.

Stage 2 – pilot analysis of one theme by one researcher

As a pilot, one researcher undertook to draw together their version of all the data across the studies relevant to the theme of the impact of professional opinion leaders in encouraging or blocking clinical behaviour change. This constituted a detailed re-analysis of the work done in stage 1 and was therefore an extension of the analysis. This was then commented on by the other researchers in the group, and we assessed the feasibility of pursuing

this method for other themes. Following this exercise, we were concerned that we were too reliant on one researchers view of the data. It was therefore decided that for the next stage, each researcher should undertake their own independent analysis of each theme to avoid reliance on one researcher's perceptions and to ensure that we were integrating the data with a shared understanding of the categories in mind.

Stage 3 – analysis of one theme by all researchers

To support the next stage systematically we prepared a draft coding structure of themes and sub-headings, which each team member (total five) independently then applied to one common theme identified in stage 1, the nature of the research evidence. Table 27.2 provides an extract from the draft coding structure relating to this theme for illustration. We used individual field notes to argue about meaning, and questioned the theoretical origins of ideas and framework in use. We then applied the agreed coding framework on 'evidence' to all the studies. We reconvened after this work and debated our efforts and this led to a deeper understanding of the topic.

Stage 4 – analysis of all themes by all five researchers

At the next stage, each researcher individually applied the coding structures developed for all the themes across reports, looking for points of difference as well as convergence, and reflecting on the use of different terms to define similar areas and the use of similar terms but meaning different things. For example, we found uncertainties about definitions of product champions versus opinion leaders between the two research teams, and found differing layers of understanding of what we meant by the term context. Again, the individual outputs generated by all five researchers were debated collectively. This process was important yet time consuming. For example, the analysis of one

Table 27.2 Extract from draft coding structure

Hierarchies of research evidence	Differential acceptance by professional groups
	Different sources with greater or lesser credibility/authority
Availability/accessibility of sources of evidence	Existence or otherwise of 'good' sources (libraries, CRD, etc.)
	How far were there sources for raw evidence or summaries/reviews?
	Skills needed to access them
	Equipment needed to access them
	Presence or absence of effective national and local dissemination strategies
'Strength' of evidence	What is regarded as strong by different groups?
	Is it necessary to achieve change?
	Is it sufficient to achieve change?
	Strong evidence may be strong evidence which does not support change
	Strong evidence may not tell you *how* best to organise care
Weaker evidence	Less likely to achieve change?
	How is weak evidence or gaps in evidence handled?
Other kinds of 'evidence'	Experience/tacit knowledge
	Early training
	Continuing development training
	Expert opinion
	Peer opinion
	Norms of practice (local, national)
	Existing guidelines
	Royal colleges
	Patient views
	Awareness of other reasons to change, e.g. poor quality, need to save money, need to make processes more efficient
	Others

report for all five general themes (evidence, context, professionals/opinion leaders translation/interpretation and management and organisation) took around 20 hours. As this stage proceeded, a more nuanced understanding of themes began to crystallise, and we developed a table assessing the comparative strength and importance of these themes in each study.

The approach we have piloted cannot be described as a systematic review or a meta-analysis in any formal sense, although it has some elements in common with those approaches and goes beyond the usual limited focus on one project. A more accurate characterisation draws on the familiar technique in qualitative data analysis of pattern detection through constant comparison, but on a grand scale. Pattern detection was of course an essential element of each separate research project; the research teams looked for patterns

both amongst respondents within each case study and then across the case studies in each piece of research. Our subsequent aggregation experiment has essentially continued this process across the final reports of each research project, and the result is somewhere between the second-order and third-order constructs noted by Campbell et al. (2003).

METHODOLOGICAL CHALLENGES IN CASE STUDY AGGREGATION

The complexity of process data

As Langley (1999) reminds us, the analysis of process data such as that generated by our research poses many challenges. Such data often include data related to the study of events; data that cross multiple units and levels of analysis; data of variable temporal embeddedness and eclectic data. For all these reasons, developing theory from case study-based process data is complex (Fitzgerald et al. 2001). The data generated by qualitative case studies are themselves relatively loose and difficult to bound. Organisational process research in health care settings, such as we have undertaken, often seeks to analyse patterns in streams of events. But how is an 'event' defined, bounded and analysed? What are the important events on which the researcher wishes to gather data? As Langley (1999) states: 'The analysis of process data requires a means of conceptualising events and of detecting patterns among them' (p. 692). So even if the overall methodology used in our different studies is similar (that is, comparative case studies), the focus of the individual study may determine the particular events to which researchers pay most attention. The nature of the evidence-based health care innovations examined varied subtly across the studies. While all the studies focused on the events generated by the career of evidence-based innovations, three projects (Dopson and Gabbay 1995, Dopson et al. 1999, Locock et al. 1999) concentrated on evidence-based innovations deliberately funded as part of a specific government or regional initiative. The studies by Ferlie and Fitzgerald (Wood et al. 1998, Fitzgerald et al. 1999) focused on evidence-based innovations as they occurred naturally within the normal operation of health care organisations, but sites were selected which were known to have already taken some action on implementing these pieces of evidence. Clinical Standards Advisory Group (CSAG 1998) and Relating Research to Practice (Dawson et al. 1998) also studied naturally occurring innovation.

Our experience of working with process data leads us to the view that to develop theory via aggregation of case study data, two things have to occur: First, it is critical to create the opportunity to debate why and on what basis, with what evidence events are classified as 'important'. Second, detecting patterns is arguably easier to do and easier to test when you have larger volumes of data and more variations in contexts.

Aggregating data on multiple units and levels of analysis with ambiguous boundaries

Within case studies of any complexity, data will probably be collected from a number of units, organisational levels and stakeholders. There are potentially few limits to the data that might be collected. In comparing across cases, we need to be aware of the factors that impinge on the data-collection choices made by researchers, particularly where data are thinner or more contained in some cases than others. Funding constraints may well mean than there is pressure on researchers to use less resource-intensive methods. Compare, for example, the reliance on telephone interviews in the evaluations of the PACE project (Dopson et al. 1999) and the Welsh National Demonstration projects (Locock et al. 1999), with the multiple methods, including on-site 'inspections' of the CSAG project (CSAG 1998), which inevitably affect the depth and quality of data collection. Such constraints may be imposed on researchers undertaking short-term, policy relevant, research, usually commissioned by institutional funders seeking a clear, pragmatic and timely message from the results. This leads to a relatively pragmatic methodology within highly applied projects. Debating the impact of the data collection choices on data analysis is an important aspect of aggregation.

The influence of the theoretical assumptions of researchers and issues of interpretation

Critically, all researchers come with implicit (if not explicit) theoretical frameworks, and this would include positivistic, biomedical researchers as well as those such as ourselves operating from more interpretive, sociological perspectives. We stress this point, given the tendency to see the clinical research paradigm as value-free and objective. In the reflexive world of qualitative and ethnographic research, the subjectivity of researchers needs careful thought and explicit discussion.

Our two teams included researchers whose academic backgrounds are in organisational analysis, medical sociology, social policy and public health. The intellectual similarities within the team were much greater than the differences. None of us would subscribe to a rationalist model of organisational behaviour and we would generally adopt a more processual political perspective, but would place varying emphasis on the importance, for instance, of notions of culture, power and structure in explaining what we find. Indeed, we would probably use all of those factors at different times, depending on the context we are researching. However, we found we had not always been explicit in stating our theoretical perspectives at the outset, either to each other within the team, or when publishing our results. They formed part of a taken for granted assumption that we were close enough theoretically to be able to work together. Yet these differences in conceptual and theoretical viewpoints did cause researchers to pay more attention to some types of data than others, even though as researchers we did attempt to provide cross checks in the research process. Again finding time and space to debate these issues is crucial to ensuring high quality aggregation is achieved.

At an inter study level, the question emerged of how far we mean the same thing when we use the same terms in our analysis. When both teams describe scientific evidence as socially constructed, do we share the same understanding of what this term means? Even when we attempted to clarify our definitions more explicitly as part of the process of aggregation, we tended to use yet more subjective language to explain the definition and found it difficult to come up with precise definitions. This need to build a common use of concepts across the two teams has also been apparent in our joint work on opinion leaders (Ferlie et al. 2001), where the two teams initially operationalised the concept in slightly different ways. Our two research teams adopted different terms, with the Ferlie and Fitzgerald team preferring champions or product champions, and the team led by

Dopson preferring opinion leaders. This gives rise to a number of observations:

- First, it implies that we started with somewhat different theoretical perspectives. The term 'product champion' is rooted more firmly in management studies, especially diffusion of innovation studies, whereas the term 'opinion leader' reflects a more mixed approach stemming from both innovation studies and social influence theory. However, these different perspectives were implicit, and we had probably not been aware of this difference between the two teams until we started to examine the topic in detail across the studies and debated the underlying conceptual framework in use. Had we not uncovered this difference, it is likely that our conclusions from the aggregation would have been distorted.
- Second, both research teams had in practice explored the issue of hostile reactions to innovations among key players. However, the team led by Dopson had explicitly encompassed these within their definition of opinion leaders (reaction could be negative as well as positive), whereas the Ferlie and Fitzgerald team had preferred the term product champion and dealt with hostile stakeholders as a separate issue. This perhaps raises a question about how far one can systematically review material when such different terms and definitions are in use, and the reviewer is in part acting as a translator. Different subjective understandings of these terms on the part of each research team (let alone each individual researcher) will have affected the way that questions about opinion leaders were constructed and asked, and the way in which responses were interpreted and categorised. Discussion enabled us to look at data gathered about opinion leaders, product champions and hostile shareholders together and more thoughtful reflection on the data occurred.
- Third, respondents will also have brought their own subjective understandings to bear. At a broader level, a review of the literature on opinion leaders undertaken by a team led by Dopson has revealed that the problem of inconsistent definitions is widespread and is not confined to health care research (Locock et al. 2001). It is unlikely that the goal of a single replicable description is realistically achievable; the best we can strive for is to make our definitions more explicit both in designing and reporting our research. And of course, the task was made easier in the present overview as the teams

were able to discuss and explore their differing assumptions – which could only be tentatively inferred if one were simply reviewing the written data. An important implication here is that reports of such studies should aim to be more explicit about their theoretical basis than they usually are at present.

MAJOR LESSONS DRAWN

Four main lessons have emerged from our attempt at aggregation documented above. The first lesson highlights some of the hazards in doing this kind of work and relates to the varying theoretical approaches and values of the team members. There is a temptation to assume that we are all sensitive to the need to be self-aware, so we do not need to discuss what we are thinking, how we are conceiving of concepts, how are significant patterns in the data arrived at by each researcher formally as a team. As researchers, we are working with viscous knowledge, which is data rich, qualitative and ambiguous. Knowledge can easily stick because of cognitive and epistemological boundaries between researchers. Knowledge flows slowly, if at all. It therefore requires overt systems for sharing data and underlying rationales. If this does not happen then significant misunderstandings can occur. One critical phase, which we have identified, is the sharing of epistemological viewpoints, which underpin research design and data analysis. Our experience suggests that in order to progress, it is necessary to agree analytic frameworks and what counts as catergories for analysis to allow independent but comparable analysis of the data, and that this is a time consuming but valuable exercise.

A second and related lesson is the importance of recognizing and discussing the possible variation in interpretation of key terms used in research. At a more micro level, individual researchers may attach subtly different meanings to the questions and terms used in, for example, interview schedules, even though we are superficially using the same questions. The way we conduct interviews and how far we pursue particular aspects of the interview schedule will also vary.

The third lesson to be discussed here is the importance of trust among researchers. To share the data and its meaning requires time and a transparent process of open questioning and debate. This presupposes motivation, commitment, trust and shared conceptual understanding. These are not simple to achieve given people have different histories, knowledge and skills. The generation of trust may start from a respect for another's prior work, but trust has to be continually nurtured. The aggregation processes undertaken involve experimentation, trial and therefore a degree of risk taking and can only succeed in high trust relationships.

Organising conversations that facilitate such work in qualitative case-based research also need planning, nurturing and sustaining. The current UK academic system does not constitute a facilitative architecture for such activity to occur. The creation of trust and openness between researchers has to occur against a background of competitiveness within the academic system now shaped by a research and development quasi market. Here we refer to the shrinking of the tenured core of academics and the growth of the contract periphery; the replacement of research grants with research contracts; the increased pressure for researchers to be involved in the policy process and the move from the lone scholar model to research increasingly being carried out in inter-institutional teams. What gets measured is what gets done. Our team contained people who were established in their careers and in a relatively privileged position to do this kind of work. It is questionable whether researchers at other career stages would have the motivation or incentive to engage in such processes. This raises important questions regarding the nature of the structures and processes in higher education designed to facilitate the production of high-quality social research from which theory can be developed and which is of use to policy makers.

A final lesson speaks more specifically to the additional insights we gleaned from our large-scale comparative database with respect to health care contexts that the case study method is well placed to study. The process also generated three additional themes:

1. The key role of context in understanding the context-specific nature of innovation

We suggest that context should not be seen as the backcloth to action, but as an interacting element in the diffusion processes. For innovations to diffuse into use, certain features of the context are perceived as core participating influences:

- The availability and engagement of local, credible and skilled opinion leaders.
- The foundation of prior relationships, especially between different clinical professional groups and between clinicians and managers.
- The historical development of the services, which influences current organisation.
- The structural characteristics of the location; the complexity, volume and configuration of the various organisational components.
- The skills available; the change management and project management capacity within stakeholder groups.
- The support of the senior management, though this may be at a distance.

2. The critical social role played by communities of practice in interpreting and translating evidence into contexts

We note that local professional groups work together in communities of practice, which are frequently uniprofessional. There are complex interactions between and across professional boundaries, both at this most local level and at the level of the whole institution (and indeed at societal level). These boundaries affect the motivations for seeking improvement and upgrading, and the way evidence and knowledge are perceived and interpreted. Our empirical data stress the need to understand the social and cognitive nature of these boundaries.

3. The complex nature of knowledge itself

Knowledge is ambiguous, uncertain, indeed dynamic over time, and interpretable. We reformulate the nature of 'adoption decisions'; that is, empirically we demonstrate that these do not solely focus on an 'accept/reject' of the innovation itself. Deciding to use knowledge is a social and political process, which nearly always involves debate and reference to others views. Hence, the choice of group with which people engage in these debates is also significant. Other research payoffs included a better understanding of cross case differences and patterns and the role of contextual factors in generating those patterns.

CONCLUSION

In conclusion, we have outlined our attempt to improve the external validity of our research by undertaking the case study data aggregation exercise described above. We have found that, as a result of this exercise, we were able to identify patterns in the processes studied and isolate critical generative mechanisms and therefore underlying tendencies that emerged. A number of additional themes were generated constructively as a result of this exercise (see above). Furthermore, across a large number of cases, the similarities and variations are more strongly displayed. Where similarities emerged across seven studies, they confirm the validity of the findings and increase confidence in the profitability of general findings.

We offer our experience of undertaking an aggregation of case study data as a source of refection.

NOTES

1. Team refers to Ferlie and Fitzgerald who worked as one team. Dopson worked with two colleagues, John Gabbay and Louise Locock.
2. The evidence-based health care movement centres on a great deal of research that suggests a significant gap between what research is available and what is done in clinical practice.

REFERENCES

Becker, H.S. 1968 'Social observation and case studies' in D.L. Sills (Ed.) *International Encyclopaedia of the Social Sciences, 14.* New York: Collier and Macmillan. Reprinted in Becker H.S. 1971 *Sociological Work.* Chicago: Aldine.

Campbell, R., Pound, P., Pope, C., Britten, N., Pill, R., Morgan, M. and Donovan, J. 2003 'Evaluating meta-ethnography: a synthesis of qualitative research on lay experiences of diabetes case' *Social Science and Medicine* 56: 6716–6784.

Clinical Standards Advisory Group (CSAG) 1998 *Clinical Effectiveness.* London: Clinical Standards Advisory Group.

Dawson, S., Sutherland, K., Dopson, S., Miller, R. and Law, S. 1998 *The Relationship between R&D and Clinical Practice in Primary and Secondary Care: Cases of Adult Asthma and Glue Ear in Children: Final Report.* Cambridge: Judge Institute of Management.

Dopson, S. 2005 'The diffusion of medical innovations: can figurational sociology contribute?' *Organization Studies 2* 6(8): 1125–1144.

Dopson, S. and Fitzgerald, L. 2005 *Knowledge for Action? Evidence Based Health Care in Context.* Oxford: Oxford University Press.

Dopson, S. and Gabbay, J. 1995 *Evaluation of the National Initiative Getting Research into Practice and Policy.* Oxford: Oxford Regional Health Authority/Department of Health.

Dopson, S., Gabbay, J., Locock, L. and Chambers, D. 1999 *Evaluation of the PACE Programme: Final Report.* Oxford: University of Oxford, Templeton College; Southampton, UK: University of Southampton: Wessex Institute for Health Research and Development.

Ferlie, E., Gabbay, J., Fitzgerald, L., Locock, L. and Dopson, S. 2001 'Evidence based medicine and organisational change: an overview of some recent qualitative studies' in L. Ashburner (Ed.) *Organizational Behaviour and Organizational Studies in Health Care.* Basingstoke, UK: Palgrave.

Fitzgerald, L., Hawkins, C. and Ferlie, E. 1999 *Achieving Change within Primary Care: Final Report.* Warwick, UK: University of Warwick, CCSC.

Fitzgerald, L., Dopson, S., Ferlie, E., Gabbay, J. and Locock, L. 2001 'Producing an overview from qualitative research: the credibility of evidence as an issue of knowledge utilisation' (Working Paper). Leicester: De Montfort University.

Flyvberg, B. 2001 *Making Social Science Matter.* Cambridge: Cambridge University Press.

Golden-Biddle, K., Weibe, E. and Locke, L. 2005 'Using qualitative methodology to study the dynamics of organisations' in R. Lines, G. Stensaker and A. Langley (Eds) *Handbook of Change and Learning.* New York: Oxford University Press.

Langley, A. 1999 'Strategies for theorising from process data' *Academy of Management Review* 24(4): 691–710.

Locock, L., Chambers, D., Surender, R., Dopson, S. and Gabbay, J. 1999 *Evaluation of the Welsh Clinical Effectiveness Initiative National Demonstration Projects: Final Report.* Oxford: University of Oxford, Templeton College; Southampton, UK: University of Southampton: the Wessex Institute for Health Research and Development.

Locock, L., Dopson, S., Chambers, D. and Gabbay, J. 2001 'Understanding the role of opinion leaders in improving clinical effectiveness' *Social Science and Medicine* 53(6): 745–757.

Murphy, E., Dingwall, R., Greatbatch, D., Parker, S. and Watson, P. 1998 'Qualitative research methods in health technology assessment: a review of the literature' Southampton, UK: University of Southampton, NCC *Health Technology Assessment* 2(16).

Noblit, G.W. and Hare, R.D. 1988 *Meta-Ethnography: Synthesising Qualitative Studies.* London: Sage.

Popay, J., Rogers, A. and William, G. 1998 'Rationale and standards for the systematic review of qualitative literature in health services research' *Qualitative Health Research* 8: 341–351.

Rogers, E. 1995 *The Diffusion of Innovations* (4th edition). New York: The Free Press.

Sandelowski, M. and Barroso, J. 2003 'Classifying the findings in qualitative studies' *Qualitative Health Research* 13(7): 905–923.

Sandelowski, M., Docherty, S. and Emden, C. 1997 'Qualitative metasynthesis: issues and techniques' *Research in Nursing and Health Journal* 20: 365–371.

Thomas, W.I. and Znaniecki, F. 1918–20 *The Polish Peasant in Europe and America* (5 volumes). Chicago: University of Chicago Press; Boston: Badger Press.

Van der Ven, A., Polley, D. and Venkataramans, G.R. 1999 *The Innovation Journey.* Oxford: Oxford University Press.

Wood, M., Ferlie, E. and Fitzgerald, L. 1998 *Achieving Change in Clinical Practice: Scientific, Organisational and Behavioural Processes.* Warwick, UK: University of Warwick: CCSC.

Yin, R. 1994 *Case-Study Research – Design and Methods* (2nd edition). London: Sage.

Yin, R. 1999 'Enhancing the quality of case studies in health services research' *Health Services Research* 34(5): 12091–12224.

Working with Cases in Development Contexts: Some Insights from an Outlier

Philippa Bevan

Realistic, methodical plans for social change – even makeshift ones – drawn up with the help of scientific models of development, are an innovation of recent origin. Often the developmental models themselves are plainly still very imperfect, and do not correspond closely enough to the changing social structures to which they refer.

(Elias 1978, p. 28)

DEVELOPMENT RESEARCH IN THE 2000s

All empirical social science research depends, in one way or another, on 'fieldwork'. In the first instance, 'data' are not given or 'collected'; they are *made* by researchers more or less well-connected to the reality they are studying through conceptual and methodological frameworks, and the detailed design of a related programme involving research instruments and/or activities. This chapter is about 'the "dialogue" between ideas and evidence' (Ragin 2000, p. 4) in development studies and development economics,[1] with a particular focus on the relations between development research frameworks, field realities and practice-relevant conclusions. I use the case of a case-based research programme in Ethiopia conducted between 2002 and 2007 to identify some issues of relevance to social scientists engaging in case-based research, particularly in applied fields.[2]

Development research is associated with planned attempts to produce modernising change in poorer areas of the world. Development interventions, in the form of funded policies, programmes and projects, technical assistance, and in recent years 'direct budget support' have been delivered by international and national donors and non-governmental organisations (NGOs) to 'less developed countries' (LDCs[3]) since the middle of the twentieth century. Considerable evidence that aid rarely works in the ways intended has accumulated over the last decades (e.g. Lancaster 1999, Sundberg and Gelb 2006) but development researchers have not widely accepted, theoretically based and empirically supported explanations of why and under what conditions development interventions do or do not achieve their stated goals.

> After nearly six decades of attempts to socially engineer development, the various efforts cannot be judged a success. Where development has been most successful in the East Asian countries, the standard model (e.g. 'Washington Consensus') has not been followed and outside observers do not credit the development agencies with a key role (e.g. Wade 1990). Where the international agencies have had the freest hand to try to impose solutions, e.g. in Africa and Latin America, there has been the least success (e.g. Van de Walle 2001 on Africa). This was the conclusion of even the World Bank's own respected researcher William Easterly (2001). (Ellerman 2005, p. 6)

One[4] reason for this failure is the current state of mainstream policy-related development research, which, thoroughly dominated by a neoclassical economics framework committed to 'the restrictive, homogenising assumptions of conventional variable-oriented analysis' (Ragin 2000, p. 35), seeks to generalise across abstractly-defined cases ('LDCs', 'households', 'firms' and 'individuals'), ignoring the diverse configurations of variables which constitute different types of 'LDC', 'household', 'firm' and 'person', and fails to recognise a range of very important 'real' cases such as kin networks, livelihood systems, ideologies and Big Men.

The domination of economics in development research is almost complete in the World Bank.

> The World Bank's research was recently evaluated by a committee – consisting entirely of academic economists – that provided several important and timely recommendations in its assessment of the World Bank's research. However, it did not make what we consider a more fundamental critique. Namely, that development is about a lot more than economics, and that, accordingly, economics should not have (as it currently does at the Bank) a near-monopoly on determining the content and validity of development research. (Rao and Woolcock 2007)

Development economists have had privileged and direct access to development policy makers in donor organisations and LDC governments.

> The status of economics as a practising profession stands in stark contrast to the SAPG '(Sociology, Anthropology, Political Science, Geography)' disciplines. Until relatively recently[5] they had to rely on influencing public debates and policy through 'enlightenment' – letting their knowledge filter through to public agencies and policy makers through the media (lectures, books, newspaper commentaries) and NGOs – rather, than being able to transfer it directly through the 'engineering' approach that is available to economists and scientists. (Hulme and Toye 2006)

The 'knowledge' that economists transfer to development policymakers derives from a positivist and 'quantitative' stance whose claim to scientific rigour rests on its use of mathematical models to produce the 'ideas' and statistical procedures and techniques, particularly regression analyses applied to survey data or 'brute facts' (Kanbur and Shaffer 2006), to produce the 'evidence'.[6] 'Causation' is seen as 'a contest between independent variables to explain variation in an outcome' (Ragin 2000, p. 15). The techniques attributed to SAPG researchers by Toye and Hulme are 'qualitative': 'ethnographic (conversation, semi-structured interviews, life histories, oral histories and observation) and participatory (focus group discussions, community mapping and institutional analysis, participatory problem/opportunity analysis etc) methods' that produce data 'much of which is non-numeric and which comes from relatively small "n" datasets that make it difficult to infer being representative of a broader population' (Hulme 2007, p. 6).[7] 'Participatory poverty assessments' using participatory methods have become increasingly institutionalised as part of the data-collection process required for the preparation for PRSPs.

In the last few years this bifurcated approach to development research has become increasingly institutionalised in academic[8] and policy-related[9] development research and international development studies teaching.[10]

This split between economists and 'non-economists' seen as a split between quantitative and qualitative research is also reflected at the 'cutting edge' of research into poverty in poor countries as exemplified by the 'Q-squared' approach (Kanbur 2005; www.q-squared.ca); a brief critique appears below.

Case-based approaches of the sort described in this book offer another way of relating ideas to evidence, but have rarely been used as a basis for advice to donors and LDC governments.[11] However, research funders in the UK have recently been looking for innovative policy-relevant approaches to development research, and in 2001 the Economics and Social Research Council (ESRC) invited proposals relating to 'poverty, inequality and quality of life' in developing countries, providing an opportunity for the research described in this chapter. Between 2002 and 2007 they funded a four-country,[12] multi-disciplinary research programme whose goal was the iterative development and use of a conceptual and methodological framework for 'understanding the social and cultural construction of wellbeing in developing countries', which became known as the Wellbeing in Developing Countries (WeD) research programme.

In 2002, I became the Country Coordinator for the Ethiopia WeD programme and started looking for a research strategy to underpin the development of the promised conceptual and methodological framework. We needed a framework that could respond to the rapid change processes linked with 'globalisation' currently affecting LDCs in similar and diverse ways about which not much is known. I came to appreciate the potential value for practical, solution-oriented development research of an approach which recognises the importance of discovery in social science (Ragin 2000), that 'time matters' (Abbott 2001a), that the world is complex and frequently non-linear (Byrne 1998), that this complexity is structured and energised by the interactivities through time of social actors differently located in unequal social and cultural structures (Archer 1995, 1996, 2000), and that it is a complexity which is mostly qualitative (Smith and Jenks 2006) and 'postmodern' (Cilliers 1998) in the sense that social researchers increasingly know that they are themselves embroiled in complex and dynamic systems, or a 'chaos of disciplines' (Abbott 2001b), and recognise that there are 'no epistemological ultimates' (Blackwell 1976, quoted in Cilliers 1998, p. 130). Through participation in the ESRC Research Methods Training Programme, 'Focusing on the Case in Quantitative and Qualitative Research' (Chapter 30), I was introduced to the idea that complex systems are best imagined as 'cases', that '(t)he dynamic systems which are our cases leave traces for us' (Byrne 2002, p. 36), which may be recorded as observations, measures or narratives, and that there are a number of case-based methods through which quantitative and qualitative research instruments and data can be integrated. Here seemed to be a theoretically grounded, empirically-promising and policy-relevant alternative to the Q-squared approach.

THE FOUNDATIONS OF KNOWLEDGE FRAMEWORK

A sound empirical research framework requires clarity in a number of dimensions and in the remainder of the chapter I make use of a conceptual framework used in an earlier exploration of the intellectual[13] barriers to cross-disciplinary collaboration in the study of poverty (Bevan 2005) and wellbeing (Bevan 2007) in LDCs. The Foundations of Knowledge Framework (FoKF) identifies nine sets of 'knowledge assumptions' explicit or implicit in choices made by researchers. These relate to research domain and questions; values; ontology; epistemology; theory; research strategies; type of empirical conclusion; rhetoric; and praxis.

The linkages between the elements of this framework are depicted in Figure 28.1. The framework is used in the remainder of the chapter to explore knowledge assumptions lying behind the Q-squared approach to poverty research, to compare knowledge

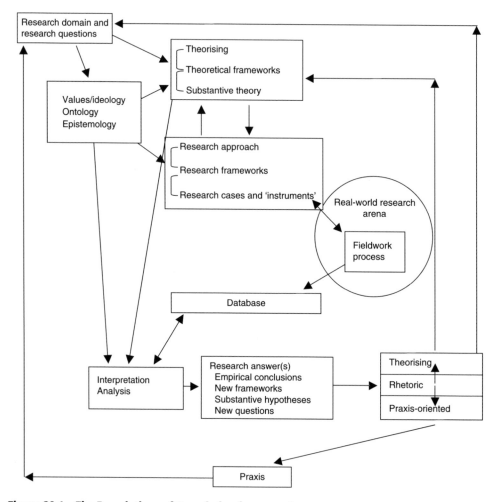

Figure 28.1   The Foundations of Knowledge framework.

assumptions across the five disciplinary 'ideal types' brought together in the multi-disciplinary WeD programme and to identify the knowledge assumptions deliberately made by the Ethiopia WeD team as it developed the case-based approach described below.

THE KNOWLEDGE FOUNDATIONS OF THE Q-SQUARED APPROACH

The term 'Q-squared' was invented by prominent academic and one-time senior World Bank development economist Ravi Kanbur for a project to bring together invited development-oriented poverty researchers in the quantitative and qualitative 'traditions', which was launched at a workshop at Cornell in 2001 (Kanbur 2005) and has continued as a programme based at the University of Toronto (www.q-squared.ca). Table 28.1 reproduces a table (from Bevan 2005) with origins in Kanbur's introductory contribution to the workshop, which identifies differences in the knowledge assumptions behind the two traditions. Kanbur identifies two types of poverty research framework: neoclassical economics, which is 'quantitative' in approach, and what he calls 'broad social sciences', which are 'qualitative' in approach, qualitative meaning participatory methods at community level used inductively.

Table 28.1 The knowledge foundations of the Q-squared approaches to poverty research

Constituents of social science knowledge	Dominant development policy research models: Q-squared	
	'Quantitative'	*'Qualitative'*
Domain or focus of study *What are we interested in?*	Poverty = what is measured in *household* surveys	Poverty = what some *people* in some *communities* say it is
Values/ideology *Why are we interested?*	To reduce it through economic modernisation	To reduce it through empowering the powerless
Ontology *What is the 'reality' of what we are interested in?*	One reality exists independent of our thoughts. People are rational and pursue self-interest, they have preferences revealed in what they do	There are many 'realities' depending on the perspective of the person experiencing and interpreting 'it'
Epistemology *How can we 'know' about that 'reality'?*	'Deductive': use logic to develop models and observe reality ('brute facts') using 'scientific methods'. Using these together it is possible to establish truths/laws	'Inductive': generalize from experience
Theory *How can we explain / understand poverty?*	Causal conjunction: identify the variables which correlate with household consumption/income	Hermeneutics: establish local meanings and explanations
Research strategies *How can we establish what is 'really' happening?*	Statistical analysis of household surveys	'Participatory' methods
Empirical conclusions *What conclusions can be drawn about what is really happening?*	Descriptive statistical conclusions Analytical statistical conclusions depending on regression models; levels of dependent variable are related to levels of 'significant' independent variables	Descriptions/interpretations: what poor people say about their poverty
Rhetoric *How can we inform 'others' about our conclusions?*	Equations, regression analyses, and descriptions in words	Translations and interpretations from local languages
Praxis *What to do? Who should do it?*	Various modernizations; 'sound' economic policies. Assumption that acting to change independent variables will produce measurable change in the dependent variable Donors and poor country governments	Participatory researchers/ practitioners to 'advocate' on behalf of poor people and/or empower them to make and demand changes

Here once more we find the familiar nomothetic–ideographic distinction with the added implication that economics is not really a *social* science, that the other social sciences do not use quantitative data, and that, within the broad social sciences, there is little distinctive about the disciplines. As a picture of poverty research for development policy in most countries it is depressingly accurate. Importantly, such research treats its 'cases' (chiefly 'households' and 'countries') as identically structured units, and ignores other key levels of organisation, such as communities, persons, livelihood systems, kin networks and political hierarchies.

A discourse analysis of the contributions to the first Q-squared workshop (Bevan 2005) led to two main conclusions: both models offer a de-politicised view of poverty in LDCs, and there is a need for a serious engagement in this area by researchers in the 'broad social sciences'. One of the goals of the Wellbeing in Developing Countries (WeD) Research Programme was to bring together the research skills of sociologists, social anthropologists, political theorists, psychologists and development economics.

AN EXPERIMENT IN CROSS-DISCIPLINARITY:[14] THE WELLBEING IN DEVELOPING COUNTRIES PROGRAMME

The programme began with a conceptual development stage, which brought together four research frameworks: (1) from political theory the 'Theory of Human Need' (Doyal and Gough 1991); (2) from psychology a quality of life measure, known as the 'WHOQOL' (Skevington et al. 2004); (3) from development studies the Resource Profiles Framework (Lewis et al. 1991), which 'conceives of individuals and households constructing livelihoods using a range of social and cultural resources alongside familiar material, human and environmental resources' (Gough et al. 2007, p. 20); and (4) from international social policy a country-level welfare regime framework (Bevan 2004b, 2004c, Gough et al. 2004).

> To study the social and cultural construction of wellbeing in developing countries the research group identified four countries in which to carry out the research: Bangladesh, Ethiopia, Peru and Thailand. These span three continents, four dominant religions, and include two middle-income and two low-income countries. Within each country six or seven research sites were selected to cover a spectrum of rural to urban communities. (McGregor 2007, p. 339)

Four common research components were conducted across all the countries. An adapted welfare regime framework was the basis for the collection and analysis of secondary country-level quantitative and qualitative data relating wellbeing outcomes and processes to national and sub-national systems. Data for community profiles were made and accumulated over the fieldwork period, which lasted over a year in each country. Within larger communities, 250 households were randomly selected for a Resources and Needs Survey (RANS); all households were surveyed in communities of less than 250 households. Following an exploratory qualitative phase a psychological instrument for measuring individual quality of life was developed

(the WeD-QoL) and administered as a pilot across the communities in each country to over 350 people mostly selected from RANS households. There was also a qualitative component, which country teams were free to design. In Bangladesh, Peru and Thailand, reports of people's experiences of locally salient 'wellbeing' issues or themes were produced. In Ethiopia a 'core-case' and topic approach was adopted and a programme for making protocol data at community, household and individual levels was developed through the fieldwork period.

Table 28.2 (see p. 473), which is reproduced from a piece on researching across the disciplines written early on for the WeD research programme (Bevan 2007), presents an ideal-typical representation of the research models identified as being most important to the development of the WeD framework, and shows the knowledge assumptions made within them. At that time, it seemed possible that we might be able to negotiate a way towards an interdisciplinary Q-integrated position, but time constraints and disciplinary cultures and habituses proved too strong. There was some dialogue and interaction over the design and implementation of the research instruments used commonly across the countries. For example, questions in the RANS were abstract enough to be asked anywhere (e.g. a question about livestock), but the codes were sensitised to local contexts (e.g. lamas for Peru, camels for Ethiopia) and the items in the WeD-QoL pilot were produced following an exploratory phase in each of the countries. However, we did not confront the contradictions found along rows 3 and 4 in Table 28.2, which contain descriptions of ontologies and epistemologies associated with at least three metatheoretical stances: post-modernism (social anthropology), critical realism (sociology) and positivism (political theory, psychology and economics). It has not proved possible to get agreement on one conceptual framework, and for analysis and writing researchers have retreated to the comfort of their disciplinary homes. In Bangladesh, Peru and Thailand, where there was a mix of researchers from

Table 28.2 An ideal-type depiction of the some of the research models with which the WeD team is negotiating

Questions	From social anthropology	From sociology	From political theory	From psychology	From economics
Focus: What are we interested in?	Local cultures and meanings; use of resources. Local cultural repertoires	Unequal social structures, power, actors, and dynamics; access to resources. Social mechanisms and processes	Universal human needs and intermediate needs satisfiers. Country poverty	Values, goals, resources to meet goals, satisfaction with resources and with life in general	Household poverty; individual functionings; global happiness/satisfaction
Values: Why?	The agency of poor people should be recognised and respected	Social and human suffering should be eradicated	Human needs ought to be met and capabilities expanded	Subjective evaluations of wellbeing ought to be respected	Household poverty should be eradicated and human resources improved
Ontology: What is the 'reality' of what we are interested in?	There are different realities associated with different standpoints or habituses	Reality exists independent of our thoughts, is complexly constituted of things, people, relationships, structures, energy, and time, and much of it is unobservable	One observable reality exists independent of our thoughts	One reality exists independent of our thoughts and only what is observable is real	One reality exists independent of our thoughts and only what is observable is real
Epistemology: How can we know about reality?	Through the interpretation of local meanings in an *abductive* research approach	Truth should be understood as practical adequacy. Develop models of mechanisms/processes (*retroduction*) through an iterative process of conceptualising and fieldwork	We can observe it using scientific methods (*deduction/ induction*) and we can establish truths/generalisations about human beings	We can observe it using scientific methods (*deduction/ induction*) and we can establish truths/generalisations about human beings	Think about it using mathematical logic – *deductive*; observe it using surveys – *inductive*
Theorising	Hermeneutic interpretations and reflexive theorising	Conceptual frameworks to guide exploratory research; explanatory middle range theories out of research results	Normative theories/critical theories. Conceptual frameworks for taxonomising cases	Causal theorising through statistical techniques	Causal theorising via mathematical modelling and statistical techniques

(Continued)

Table 28.2 Continued

Questions	From social anthropology	From sociology	From political theory	From psychology	From economics
Research strategies: How can we establish what is really happening?	*Data:* Ethnography: a range of research instruments *Analysis:* interpretation and comparison	*Data:* Integrated use of surveys, participant observation, and protocols *Analysis:* retroductive; four strategies of comparison; also discourse analysis of key documents	*Data:* secondary sources or 'codified knowledge' and 'experiential knowledge' *Analysis:* inductive	A psychological instrument for country cultures *Data:* exploratory, validation, use phases *Analysis:* statistical	*Data:* household surveys *Analysis:* econometric analysis of household survey data
Theoretical and empirical conclusions: What (kind of) conclusions can we draw?	Understanding of people's actions, and relationships in cultural context *Focus:* community	Identify universal mechanisms/processes and show how they work in different local contexts *Focus:* (interactive) person, household, community, country	Mapping objective wellbeing and analysing the contribution of different structures and institutions to it *Focus:* country and person	Descriptions of subjective quality of lives in the research countries. Regularities with other non-psychological variables *Focus:* person	Descriptive statistics using economic variables. Explanatory: identification of regularities through regression analyses *Focus:* household
Rhetoric: How can we inform others about these?	Interpret local cultures in academic writings; advise practitioners; feedback to research communities	Academic papers and books; research and briefing papers for donors and other practitioners	Academic papers and books and networking through conferences etc with people influential in social policy decision making	Academic papers; networking with relevant practitioners	Academic papers; policy advice to donors; inputs to PRSPs
Praxis: What to do?	Constructive criticism of development approaches which are oblivious to local culture; suggestions of better ways of doing things	Constructive criticism of development approaches which are oblivious to local power structures and how things actually work in local contexts; suggestions of better ways of doing things	Good research helps combine top-down and bottom-up knowledges	Understanding of subjective QoL has implications for policy and practice	Identify the causes of household poverty in particular contexts and the contributing variables. Draw out policy implications
Praxis: Who to do it?	Local inhabitants, NGOs, donors, and government	Sympathetic national mega and meso actors, local inhabitants, Governments, donors, and NGOs	International and national donors, governments		International and national donors, governments

NGO, non-governmental organization; QoL, quality of life; PRSP, (Poverty Reduction Strategy Papers).

economics, psychology, social anthropology and sociology, most of the written outputs (to date) use data produced by one of the research components and are produced within one of the disciplinary frameworks.[15]

In Ethiopia, the economist and psychologist left the project before the data were available for analysis and this constraint turned into an opportunity for the remaining sociologists and social anthropologists to explore, interpret and analyse the (linked) survey, WeD-QoL and protocol data using a theoretically grounded Q-integrated approach (Bevan 2005). In the text below, I describe our meta-theoretical assumptions, the case-based conceptual and methodological framework under construction, the making of the multi-level database, the interpretation/analysis process that is still under way, some of the research answers to date, and how the framework has been used with appropriate data to produce research papers and policy briefs for donor and government policymakers in Ethiopia.

FROM META THEORY TO CONCEPTUAL AND METHODOLOGICAL FRAMEWORKS

Figure 28.2 summarises the meta-theoretical assumptions underpinning our Q-integrated case-based approach.

Research questions

The overarching research goal was to develop 'a conceptual and methodological framework for understanding the social and cultural construction of wellbeing' for use in a range of empirical 'development contexts', and to demonstrate its value by using it in an empirical study of Ethiopia. We interpreted the 'cultural construction' of wellbeing as referring to *ideas* about what 'wellbeing' and 'illbeing' are and the 'social construction' of (well- to ill-) being or life quality to refer to the social and cultural structures, actors and social interactions involved in the reproduction or change of patterns of individual and

collective life quality in particular social contexts.

Values

The underlying goal of the research programme is to change the way in which 'development' is conceptualised within the development industry and consequently: (1) the ways in which it is understood and explained, and assessed and evaluated; and (2) the ways in which development policies, programmes and projects are designed and implemented. In the dominant discourse development is understood as an economic process, its absence explained in terms of 'missing modernisation', and it is evaluated and assessed predominantly in terms of (the variables of) economic output per capita, household income poverty and the quality of 'human' resources defined and measured in terms of illness and deaths, health service use and education levels. In the Ethiopia WeD programme, development is understood as a process of reduction of social suffering and improvement in collective and individual life quality, which has objective/universal, relative/local, and subjective/personal dimensions, and its absence explained in terms of the dynamics and histories of global, country, community and household power structures.

Ontology

The ontology is realist assuming a world constituted of mass and energy involved in an evolutionary process in space and time that has generated the complexly structured and systemised materio-social world we currently inhabit (Smith and Jenks 2006). 'Time' is also complexly structured (Bevan 2004a). Our human ontology recognises that 'being' involves three interactive aspects: physical (Harré 1994), social (Harré 1979) and personal (Harré 1983). The fact that people are born as gendered babies, grow up in a cultural context, age and die has important implications for researching universal, local and subjective life quality, which is reflected

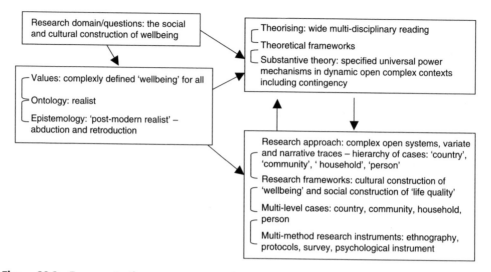

Figure 28.2   From meta theory to conceptual and methodological framework.

in our use of the concept of 'genderage' (Bevan and Pankhurst 2007, Bevan et al. forthcoming). In any place and time the role-related interactivities of genderaged people involve four inter-penetrating types of structure: natural material, manmade material, cultural and social, which are the path-dependent outcome of social interactions and material events in earlier times. These structures have mechanisms (powers and liabilities) that cause things to happen 'by motivating or discouraging, constraining and enabling certain sorts of human action ... although the causal power of structures require the actions of people to work, nevertheless they bring things about that, if they were different, would not occur in the same way' (Carter and New 2004, p. 12). The inter-activities of social actors may reproduce, elaborate or markedly change social structures and systems.

Epistemology

While there is a real world separate from our thoughts about it, perspectives are necessarily partial and relative; they come from the social position of knowers and the theories and concepts on which they draw (Carter and New 2004). Actors involved in social systems have

limited and distorted comprehensions of the nature of the system as a whole. The promise of social science is the use of reflexivity, a range of knowledge rules and techniques, and argument with other social scientists to establish understanding and explanations of social phenomena, which are vulnerable to logical argumentation and contradictory research evidence.

Given our ontology and approach to causation we are not looking for general laws or 'truths' and therefore are not working in 'deductive' or 'inductive' modes. Interplay between existing structures with causal powers and properties and people with distinctive causal powers and properties of their own results in contingent yet explicable outcomes. We are relying on 'abduction' for understanding (how things are or happen) and 'retroduction' for explanation (why things are or happened). Abduction is 'interpretation within a framework' and we are concerned with two types: local frameworks and social science frameworks. One element of the programme is research into values, reasons, beliefs, intentions and the meanings people attribute to local actions and interactions. However to identify the type of act through its meaning is not to explain what brought it about (Carter and New 2004, p. 12) and we need conceptual and methodological frameworks to select and order data in order to produce social scientific understanding and explanations.

Theory

Mouzelis usefully distinguished three types of theory using Althusserian categories: 'Generalities I involves the analysis of the theories of other scholars here described as *theorising*; Generalities II is theory as a tool in social inquiry here described as *theoretical frameworks*; Generalities III is *substantive theory* as a provisional end product' (Mouzelis 1995, pp. 1–3). Theoretical frameworks contain assumptions about the mechanisms implicit in 'cases' and are used to make, order and interpret data to identify the important mechanisms at work in producing the outcomes of interest in the case under consideration. This may involve data interpretation and case analysis in relation to one case, in generalising and diversifying comparisons across two or more cases, or in locating a case in its wider context (Tilly 1984). 'Variables' are understood as 'traces' (Byrne 2002, p. 36) of complex systems produced by generative mechanisms (Pawson 1989, p. 324) whose significance has to be interpreted.

Research approach and research frameworks

The aim was to develop the research framework iteratively through the study of a hierarchy of cases – 'country', 'community', 'household', 'person' – imagined as nested complex open systems, using research methods that picked up directly observable, variate and narrative traces of the systems as they moved through time. We are towards the end of the process of developing and using frameworks for making and organising data on the cultural construction of wellbeing and the social construction of life quality at country and community levels; as the time of writing the household and person frameworks are less well developed.

The cultural construction of wellbeing at macro levels

This framework responds to the question how is 'wellbeing' conceived of in the different ideologies and more diffuse cultural repertoires widely[16] promulgated or available in the country? What kind of repertoires are they and what is their purpose? What do they have to say about illbeing and wellbeing for different kinds of people and their causes and remedies? Who leads the design and dissemination of the content? How and to whom are they disseminated? In what ways are they involved in the social construction of life quality?

The social construction of life quality at macro levels

The current framework[17] for organising data on the social construction of life quality at country level is an adapted welfare regime framework that goes beyond objective 'welfare', defined as income security, health and education, to include relative and subjective aspects of life quality.[18] A recent adaptation (Gough et al. 2004) of the welfare-state regime approach (Esping-Anderson 1990) postulates three ideal-types of welfare or in/security[19] regime: formal welfare regimes relating to commodification, informal security regimes related to clientelisation, and insecurity regimes related to political contention. 'These are ideal-type constructs at a high level of abstraction: adopting the biological hierarchy they are *family* ideal types. Within them we may then go on to identify *genus* and *species*' (Gough 2004, p. 34).

Members of ideal-type formal welfare regimes can reasonably expect to meet their security and human development needs via participation in national or international markets and/or through state finance, services and regulation. They have economic and social rights and opportunities of a formal kind that can be upheld in law. Members of informal security regimes mainly rely on family and community networks and organisations for social protection and human development; insofar as they are included in these networks they have 'informal rights' (Wood 2004). They also have related 'informal duties' to family and other community members. People caught up in insecurity regimes find themselves in situations of collective insecurity often involving famine and/or violent conflict. Family and community networks and organisations are undermined or destroyed as material resources are damaged or stolen and people die or flee their homes.

Ethiopia, like most African countries, has a 'quadrifurcated' regime mix (Bevan 2006). The few urban-based very rich and political elites rely on the burgeoning international liberal market-based welfare regime, using private hospitals, education and financial institutions in richer countries. The next tier, who are mostly urban-based and formally employed or self-employed, use a mix of government and domestic market provision. Members of the third category, by far the largest in Ethiopia, are dependent on local informal security regimes with varying access to patchy, unreliable and aid-financed government services. Those in the fourth category, who inhabit the Ethiopian peripheries, are frequently embroiled in violent crisis situations involving the failure of state, market, community and often family welfare institutions. All members of the rural communities in our study, and most in the urban sites, seek social protection and human development in informal security regimes; some wealthy urban residents have regular access to formal insurance and services.

The cultural construction of wellbeing in informal security regimes

There are three frameworks for exploring the cultural construction of wellbeing in the research communities: for person, household and community life quality. The individual framework has three elements: (1) an objective genderaged 'needs'-based life-quality framework developed through the theorising process; (2) a relative life-quality

framework to identify the local mix of cultural wellbeing repertoires; and (3) a subjective life-quality framework for interpreting people's longer and shorter-term life course experiences. The collective frameworks have two elements: objective and relative.

The social construction of life quality in informal security regimes

The framework for understanding and explaining the social construction of life-quality patterns at local levels is still in process of development. The current version has recently been used in a paper on power and agency for the World Bank (Bevan and Pankhurst 2007). This framework models Ethiopia's rural[20] communities as unequally structured complex, dynamic and adaptive open social systems energised by the interactions of internal and external social actors and reproduced and/or changed through a historical process of iterative interactions between agents and structures. Power and life quality in each rural community are affected by its location in the wider Ethiopian and global context. In these rural community systems four important inter-penetrating fields of action, each with its own structures of opportunity/constraint, can be identified: (1) livelihood production; (2) human, household and kin re/production; (3) community governance; and (4) cultural manipulation or the reproduction and change of local cultural repertoires. Changes in one field of action are likely to impact on other fields leading to complex interactions, which may reverse or divert the original change. Such processes contribute to the reproduction or elaboration of community systems.

Household 'sub-systems' and the networks between them are the key organisations for livelihood production and human reproduction, while other community organisations also have sub-systemic properties. The relationship of individual social actors to the community is mediated through participation in sub-systems, particularly household membership. Each social actor has a gender, an age, a wealth status, and a social origin status, which, *taken together*, underpin the particular opportunities/constraints governing the ability to act in the four fields of action. The power a 'genderaged', 'wealthed' and 'social-origined' person exerts in a particular episode of action depends on an interaction between her current embodied personal agency and the structures of opportunity/constraint she faces, which she will experience as: (1) *resources* she can use, (2) *rules* she should follow and *relationships* or the actions of other people which support, divert or oppose what she is trying to do.

The framework identifies four kinds of data as necessary to understand the social construction of life quality in each community: (1) a community profile to locate the community in its wider context and provide a description of the political economy and local cultural structures including the boxing of households in terms of wealth and position in relation to the ideal household cycle to establish the shape of the social structure; (2) a mapping of household and personal life quality outcomes across class, genderage and other relevant local social statuses and household type; (3) information on events and 'naturo-social' processes; (4) survey and protocol process data enabling the identification of variate and narrative traces of the operation of controlling, collaborative and collective power mechanisms at community and household levels; and (5) data about social interactions between people of different statuses and their potential consequences for community reproduction or elaboration.

Research cases and instruments

We were aware that the conventional categories of country, community, household and individual used to launch the fieldwork process would have to be interrogated in the light of results, and that the data made using ethnography, protocols, survey and the psychological instrument designed for one of the levels would also tell us things about other levels.

FROM RESEARCH FRAMEWORKS TO DATABASE

Identifying and characterising the hierarchy of 'cases'

The first step in the move from early research frameworks to fieldwork was to decide what were 'the cases' in terms of time periods as well as entity. For the country study, we chose the period from 1991, when the current EPRDF regime came to power, to the time when the final draft of the macro chapter in the book is drawing to its end. For process research on topics where the history of the government was relevant we identified three phases, the later Imperial regime (1960s to 1974), the military socialist Derg regime (1974–1991) and the EPRDF regime from 1991 to October 2005, which was when the fieldwork period ended. Some topics (e.g. life histories) required exploration of events and experiences before 1991 (e.g. the 1984–1985 famine). Other 'case-times', such as agricultural seasons and the monthly community, household and member diaries reported over a year, were contained within the main fieldwork period between July 2004 and November 2005.

Each of the multi-level cases presented some fuzziness (Ragin 2000). Although Ethiopia is recognised as a nation-state by the 'international community' there are problems with conceptualising it as a 'country'. One is the fact that in 1993 Eritrea, which had been a province of Ethiopia since 1961, became an independent country; Ethiopia in 1991 was not the same as Ethiopia in 2005. Second, the territory contains diverse cultural groups speaking over eighty languages. Third, in the peripheries the borders cut their way through a set of nomadic or semi-nomadic pastoralist populations with singular cultural identities. Time, in the form of local government reorganisation, with changing regional divisions under the three successive regimes, also affected three of the rural communities studied in depth in 2004–2005. In 1994 they were peasant associations (PAs) in their own right; by 2004 they had been merged with other PAs into larger *kebele* administrations.

There were three issues in relation to households. First, the discourse context within which households were selected for the survey was economics; for theoretical purposes households are defined as organisations in which members share production and consumption indicated by shared dwelling place, income and food. Our analysis of the 'anatomies' of households who responded to the survey showed that, in all sites, a substantial number of 'households' did not operate as independent livelihood units. Second, in practice local government lists were used which in most sites only included households where the head was registered as a land-'owner' and/or taxpayer. This led to the exclusion of 'informal' and some destitute households. Third, it is not clear in what ways a household that has moved years through the household life cycle losing and gaining different members can be considered as the 'same' household at the two points in time.

There were two main issues in relation to the cases of people. The first was to ensure that they were not implicitly imagined either as 'cultural dopes' enacting social roles or as individuals with universal needs making rational choices in their own interest. In this regard, we conceptualised people as physical, personal and social beings with universal and abstract internal needs for meaning, relation, autonomy and competence. 'The specific meaning or form of these "needs" in particular societies is socially constructed' (McGregor 2007, p. 332). The second was to ensure that due respect was paid to the effects of universal and socially constructed differences in genderage on the content of internal needs and external needs-satisfiers.

Selecting the cases

The four rural communities were selected from fifteen that were studied in six rounds of the ERHS[21] panel economics household survey between 1994 and 2004 and a community profiling exercise in 1995 (Bevan and Pankhurst 1996a, 1996b) (Figure 28.3). The fifteen communities were selected to exemplify the major agricultural livelihood systems in Ethiopia in 1994; in 2000 three new cash-crop livelihood systems were added. In 2003, we conducted a month's protocol research in these eighteen sites plus two pastoralist sites (WIDE2[22]). From these twenty sites, four 'exemplar' sites from the

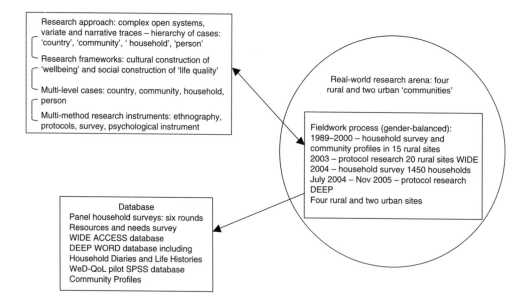

Figure 28.3   FoKF – from Research Frameworks to Database.

Table 28.3 The case-study sites

	Amhara region	Oromia region
Food-surplus and relatively integrated	Yetmen homogenous	Turufe Kecheme ethnic mix
Remote, drought-prone and food-deficit	Dinki ethnic mix	Korodegaga homogenous

two largest regions were selected for the DEEP[23] research to enable the comparisons shown in Table 28.3.

Urban sites around markets were identified in the capital, Addis Ababa, and in Shashemene – the major town for southern migrants. These are not 'communities' in the sense of socially and culturally integrated settlements; people of different ethnic origins and/or wealths tend to occupy different urban spaces and not to mix socially.

All ERHS households (up to 100 in each site), which were randomly selected in 1994, were included in the Resources and Needs Survey (RANS) so that we could use the historic information. As the surviving heads of these households were 10 years older in 2004,

the randomly selected sample of households that was added to bring the total to 250 was age-stratified to compensate. Households and people were purposively selected for the protocol research according to criteria depending on topic, in some cases using RANS results; in all selections genderage and wealth were 'breaking variables'. Figure 28.4 maps the core cases and related instruments at the different research levels.

The research instruments

The research instruments were a household and member survey, the piloting of a psychological instrument whose items were constructed out of exploratory research using focus groups and individual interviews, participant observation, conversations and protocol research which included reported monthly household and member diaries, semi-structured interviews with key informants on a range of topics and life histories. Each protocol had a section on the purpose of the research, a brief description of underlying concepts or theory, instructions as to the kinds of people to be interviewed, protocol

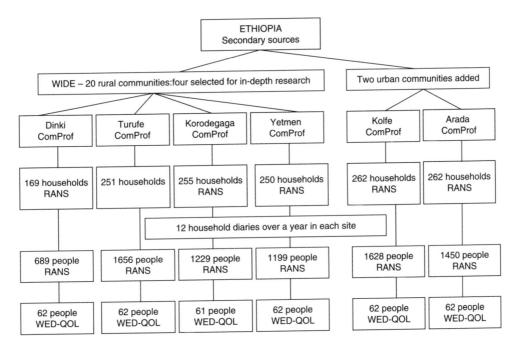

Figure 28.4 Core cases.

questions to guide a conversation about the topic and a list of expected outputs.[24]

Table 28.4 links the two research frameworks to core case and topic-related research instruments.

The fieldwork process

A male and female research officer was recruited for each site; all were graduates of Addis Ababa University, a majority had a

Table 28.4   From research frameworks to research instruments

Research frameworks	Research domains	Research instruments
Cultural construction of 'wellbeing'	Community wellbeing: cultural repertoires	WIDE1 1995 WIDE 2 2003 Module 6 WeD-QoL Pilot
	Household wellbeing: cultural repertoires	WIDE2 2003 WeD-QoL Pilot DEEP Exploratory QoL Household development cycle

	Genderaged and other statused personal wellbeing: cultural repertoires	WIDE 2 2003 Module 6
		WeD-QoL Pilot
		DEEP Exploratory QoL
		    Young lives1
		    Old lives1
		    Elites/Destitutes

Cross-cutting both frameworks		*Participant observation*

Social construction of life quality	Community context	WIDE1 1995; WIDE2 2003
		DEEP Community events
		    Community organisations
		    Community diary
		    Migration and linkages – community

	Objective outcomes	RANS DEEP Community diary Household and person diaries
	Relative outcomes	WeD-QoL Pilot DEEP Community diaries Household and person diaries
	Subjective outcomes	WeD-QoL Pilot DEEP Household and person diaries

	Internalised power mechanisms	DEEP Adult lives
		    Young Lives 2
		    Old lives 2
		    Person Diaries

	Relational power mechanisms	DEEP Collective action
		    Disputes
		    Diaries
		    Inter-generational relations
		    Migration – household

	Collective power mechanisms	DEEP Collective action Diaries

	Events and naturo-social processes	DEEP Household histories
		    Household dynamics: shocks
		    Adult lives
		    Diaries

	Actions and social interactions	DEEP Migration – individual
		    Disputes
		    Community diaries
		    Household diaries

Masters degree and a majority of these had studied social anthropology with the Ethiopia teamleader Alula Pankhurst. Each 'research month' began with a workshop where the topic and protocols for the next month's research were discussed and finalised and training was given. After the first month, there was also a feedback workshop where the previous month's experiences were shared and ideas for follow-up topics discussed. Time was allocated for writing up of the month's finding according to the instructions in the topic protocol. In the two urban and two of the rural sites respondents could speak Amharic. In two of the rural sites, the first language of all or a majority was Oromiffa, but for one site we could not find fluent Oromiffa speakers so local translators were involved. The researchers made notes in Amharic and had to translate these into English, which some found more difficult than others. At two sites, we managed to keep the same two researchers throughout the period, apart from a month's maternity leave. At two other sites, the same researchers were there most of the time, whereas in the other two there was some turnover.

During the training workshops there was discussion of how key concepts should be translated into local languages and during the feedback workshops there were discussions of how local terms should be rendered in English. The research instrument that revealed how distorting translation might be was the psychological instrument that was administered in all six countries as the WeD-QoL Pilot. For example, one element of the instrument was the PANAS, which is a measure of mood originating in America and which has been 'validated' in a number of other cultural contexts. There was considerable difficulty in translating a number of the items, for example 'jittery', with the Amharic and Oromiffa versions often containing a large number of words. The research officers reported some problems in getting people to understand a number of the items. When we added some Amharic mood words there was a parallel difficulty in translating them into English.

Making the database

Most of the research officers did not have access to computers and provided their outputs in written form, which were typed up by secretaries. As the research process unfolded, a male and female research manager were appointed to manage the research officers and their outputs and to send them to Bath to be stored in a Microsoft Word®-based database. Each household and respondent has an identifier number to enable us to locate people in households in the communities about which we have survey and other information.

Table 28.5 shows an extract from the DEEP database, which contains all the research reports from male and female research officers individually accessible for each community via hyperlinks under the headings community level, community diaries by month, household level; household diaries by month; and individual level. There are three ACCESS/SPSS databases: the RANS, Household Diary Income and Expenditure and WeD-QoL. The WIDE data have mostly been entered in an ACCESS database and the WIDE data for the DEEP sites has been added to the DEEP database.

FROM DATABASE TO RESEARCH ANSWERS

The DEEP data (Figure 28.5) can be used in range of ways, for example: (1) to explore individual community cases in depth; (2) to compare one or more communities in relation to selected topics; (3) to explore individual household cases in depth; (4) to classify and compare households, for example by stage in the life cycle, household structure, wealth status and gender of household head; (5) to explore intra-household and cross-household relationships; (6) to explore individual lives in depth; (7) to compare the lives of children, adults and old people within and across gender, wealth and other statuses; (8) and to explore community, household, and person topics in order to generate new questions or

Table 28.5   WeD Ethiopia Database

Click on the file you want individual level

Protocol	Yetmen	Dinki	Turufe K	Korodegaga	Addis Kolfe	Shashemene
Adult Lives: Male	M Yet ALives	M Din ALives	M Tur ALives	M Kor ALives	M Kol ALives	M Sha ALives
Adult Lives: Female	F Yet ALives	F Din ALives	F Tur ALives	F Kor ALives	F Kol ALives	F Sha ALives
Etc.						

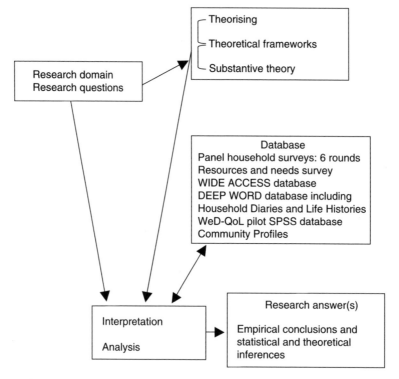

Figure 28.5   The DEEP database.

hypotheses. At the time of writing, we have used the first four approaches as follows:

(1) We developed community profiles for each site in three stages. In the rural sites, we began by updating the profiles researched in 1995 (CPIs) to produce CPIIs (www.wed-ethiopia.org) mainly in the words of the research officers. In the urban sites, there was a two-stage research process to produce CPIIs. We then re-structured the CPIIs in the light of the emerging conceptual framework and added quantitative and narrative data from the WIDE and DEEP research phases to produce CPIIIs as a basis for community case studies and comparative analysis in the book that we are in the process

of writing (Bevan et al. forthcoming). This re-structuring involved 'analysis protocols' to ensure consistency among the three researchers each writing on two of the communities.

(2) We have used the WIDE2 data from twenty sites for comparisons of 'famine' and food aid, and the consequences for the mother-infant couple, and understandings of HIV/AIDS, and the DEEP data for a comparative analysis of community power structures and life quality in the four rural sites.

(3) There are 72 diary households across the sites; the 12 in each site were selected to reflect wealth and household size differences and to ensure that female-headed households were included. We have developed an analysis

protocol for exploring the cases in depth, and for the first cut on the data selected 12 households across the four rural sites with one from each of the differentiated categories. The urban households vary considerably across ethnicity and livelihood activity so we are doing a rapid interpreto-analysis of all of them. There is the potential for using qualitative comparative analysis on this set of medium-N cases.

(4) We have used the RANS data to 'wealth-box' each household into seven productive wealth categories using local criteria derived from the exploratory quality of life research in each site. Households can be allocated to each category through more than one 'route', for example, in Korodegaga the very rich category includes one household specialising in keeping camels, while the others have combinations of rain-fed land, irrigated land, livestock and in one case a job (which is very rare). We have also used the data to describe ideal household lifecycles, which vary by religion/ethnicity, and to identify where each household stands in relation to the local ideal.

FROM RESEARCH ANSWERS TO SCHOLASTIC CONCLUSIONS

One purpose of the programme was the development of a conceptual and methodological framework for understanding the social and cultural construction of wellbeing (Figure 28.6). The current conceptual frameworks have been described above but we have not yet paid attention to what we have learned through designing and fielding the set of research instruments and using the resulting data.

The second purpose was to demonstrate the value of using such a framework in the Ethiopian context. The main output in this connection is the book, which has four major data-based parts covering the social construction of life quality at country, local, household and person levels. A number of background papers related to different substantive research questions have already appeared: on power and social policy at country level (Bevan 2006); on gender policy (Newton 2007); at community level on power and agency (Bevan and Pankhurst 2006, 2007), local cultural repertoires (Bevan forthcoming), HIV/AIDS (Pankhurst 2004), 'famine' and food aid (Pankhurst and Bevan 2004) and the mother/baby couple (Bevan 2004d); on household wealth/poverty and individual life quality dynamics (Pankhurst 2006, 2007a); and on various aspects of individual life quality (Bethlehem 2005, Bevan 2005, Lavers 2007, Pankhurst 2007b, Yisak 2006). Selections from the data have

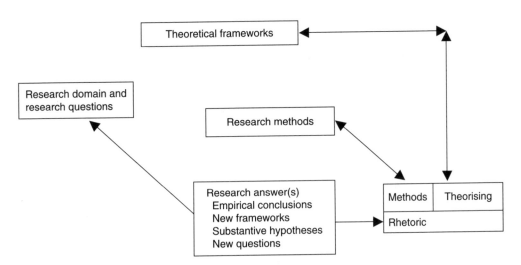

Figure 28.6   Framework for understanding the social and cultural construction of wellbeing.

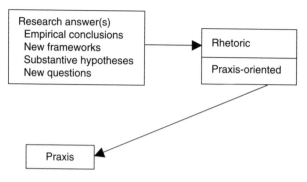

Figure 28.7   Drawing conclusions.

also been used by a number of Masters and PhD students approaching it with different substantive questions. We are also developing new substantive hypotheses and questions (Figure 28.7).

FROM SCHOLASTIC TO PRAXIS-ORIENTED CONCLUSIONS

We have so far used the research approach and database to produce research papers on migration and the informal sector for the World Bank (Feleke et al. 2005), and on migration and rural-urban linkages for Irish Aid (Feleke et al. 2006). We have completed a paper on 'destitution' and poverty dynamics for the World Bank (Pankhurst and Bevan 2007). We have completed a paper for the World Bank on power structures, agency and community dynamics commissioned by the 'Empowerment team' (Bevan and Pankhurst 2007), which is used as an example here. In that paper we posed three substantive questions in relation to the four rural case communities:

(1) In these communities, how do local power structures affect the personal and collective power of rural people of different genders, ages, household wealth, ethnicity and religion?
(2) How does the functioning of, and interactions among, the four fields of action contribute to the collective achievements and failures of the community system?

(3) What have been the trajectories of the community systems in the longer run?

We used the data to construct an 'evidence base' for our conclusions in relation to each question which we presented under three headings: for Ethiopian policymakers, for World Bank empowerment thinkers and for development researchers. Given that policy-makers are busy people,[25] we also wrote an executive summary of ten pages and a policy brief of four pages, in which we explained why power matters, how power matters, gave simple answers to the three research questions, provided a number of key policy messages related to the four fields of action, and drew some conclusions about the potential of different kinds of 'empowerment' interventions. We are hoping that we are beginning to establish a case-based 'engineering' relation with development policy makers.[26]

However, this might not be the most important route for the dissemination of the approach and its conclusions. The fieldwork process involved a long dialogue between researchers and residents, which has affected the ways in which local people think. More than fifty Ethiopian researchers have been involved in different aspects of the research, most of them in the field. Many of these are working in further research projects in which the research experience they gained is proving useful. We have also disseminated regularly to a network of Ethiopian academics and government and NGO employees through conference presentations and an e-mail network.

WORKING WITH CASES IN DEVELOPMENT CONTEXTS: SOME INSIGHTS FROM AN OUTLIER

This was an exploratory research project aimed at producing new concepts and conceptual frameworks and some related and integrated multi-methods of relevance to development research. In order to convince other social scientists and development practitioners of its rigour and relevance it was necessary to be clear about the knowledge foundations underpinning the frameworks. The need to think and read in the areas of normative theory, ontology and epistemology led us to new ways of thinking about concepts, frameworks and the relation between ideas and evidence, frameworks and field research, data and conclusions, and conclusions and practice, all dependent for execution on a 'focus on the case'. The focus in the ontological framework on historically situated open systems and sub-systems contextualised in, and interacting with, a dynamic structure of surrounding and encompassing systems opens up new ways of thinking about development and the design, implementation and monitoring of planned interventions. There is a shift from a focus on measured variables – consumption poverty, asset vulnerability, years of schooling, risk and growth – to a focus on the interactions of people of different genderages and cultural histories located in roles in unequal household, community and country structures whose actions and interactions reproduce or change structures, cultures and people. Policy is no longer a 'technical issue' but embedded in politics and culture. We believe that, in the development research field this complex dynamic system Q-integrated approach offers a strong scholastic and praxis alternative to Q-squared, and also that some of the insights which emerged during the process of developing it are relevant for social science more broadly.

Development research is an outlier in the social science field in at least five spaces of interest for case-based researchers. First, the focus on a *diverse* set of *foreign* political economies, social systems and cultures poses universal conceptual and methodological problems in such extreme forms that they cannot be ignored. Second, the research objects in LDCs are experiencing unprecedented changes linked to globalisation processes; as time passes multi-level 'cases' fuzz, merge, split and evaporate, with big implications for the question 'what is a case?' Third, compared with accumulated and available social science knowledge about rich 'developed' countries, little is known about LDCs, putting a premium on exploratory research. Fourth, much of what is known about LDCs remains confined within disciplines, even though research frameworks and methods from all the social science disciplines are potentially relevant. Fifth, the 20-year dominance of development policy by the neoclassical economics research approach provides evidence that total reliance on 'quantitative' mathematical models and econometric regression analyses is not a good idea; they have not produced understandings and explanations which donors and LDC governments have been able to translate into effective policies and practices.

The cultural gap between ideas and realities

The cultural gap between: (1) social science concepts and frameworks developed in Euro-American or 'Western' contexts; and (2) the diverse local concepts, frameworks and realities found in LDCs is recognised and reflected in the design of the conceptual and methodological framework described above, particularly the ideas and methods related to objective/universal, relative/local and subjective/personal aspects of life quality. However, we have taken only a small step towards institutionalising respect for the local in development research frameworks and development policy recommendations. Neither contributor to the Q-squared tradition recognises that the gap is problematic. The development economics solution is to claim universality for abstract economic cases such as 'households', and processes, such as 'markets' which, when compared with field realities, turn out to be 'fictions' (Hedstrom 2005, p. 3). The participatory solution is to relate to local people through a set of instruments such as mapping, wealth-ranking and focus groups, which bypass their local concepts and frameworks.

There is always a cultural gap between researcher and researched; this can be reduced if: first, the dimensions of the problem it might cause in the particular research context are identified and solutions developed; and, second, data are made through iterations between frameworks and field. Assumptions in empiricist/positivist epistemologies which assume that universal laws or truths can be established by making inferences on the basis of statistical procedures applied to 'brute facts' does not 'mind the gap'.

Researching cases in times of change

Researchers working in areas of applied social science are regularly called on to make recommendations for action in a particular context. Such recommendations depend on assumptions about what might happen in the future. These are easier to make in relation to stable social systems about which there is an up-to-date bank of knowledge when predictions are often 'more of the same'. Researchers working in current development contexts cannot assume stable social systems and must develop frameworks to deal with non-linearity.

Most writing on comparative case-based methods (e.g. King et al. 1994, Ragin 2000, Brady and Collier 2004) are theory- or classification-oriented rather than praxis-oriented, adopting a synchronic approach in a search for conclusions about the world in general rather than about the trajectory of the case(s) under consideration. While attention may be paid to the question 'what Is a case?' (Ragin and Becker 1992) or to what extent is this a case (Ragin 2000)? I have not been able to find any discussion of the implications for data-making and interpreto-analysis of the question 'to what extent is this the same case as it was at time 1?', although

such discussions may exist somewhere in the chaos of disciplines.[27] There are lessons here for all social research; social change over longer and shorter periods is ubiquitous and challenges both linear models and attempts to generalise.

Why social research should always have an exploratory dimension

We have not solved the problem of how to conduct case-based empirical research in contexts which are or may be undergoing rapid social change, and, although we believe a complex dynamic system approach is a way forward, we have not done much more than use the term as a metaphor. One of the characteristics of complex systems described by Cilliers is relevant here:

> It is often difficult to define the border of a complex system. Instead of being a characteristic of the system itself, the scope of the system is usually determined by the purpose of the *description* of the system, and is thus often influenced by the position of the observer. (Cilliers 1998, p. 4)

This chimes with Ragin's argument that social research is 'heavily knowledge- and theory-dependent' and '[i]t is impossible for social scientists to talk about social life in a way that frees them from their immersion in it' (Ragin 2000, pp. 332, 333). Our experience in the field in Ethiopia convinced us that social scientists undertaking comparative research in foreign contexts, especially if there is little or nothing in the relevant knowledge bank, must continually reflect on the appropriateness of their assumptions, concepts and methods, and adjust them as they engage empirically with the complex system cases which are their research objects. This requires a 'relatively open or permissive stance towards epistemology' (Sayer 2000, p. 32) in which knowledge is seen as resulting from a negotiation between the position of the observer and the characteristics of the complex system cases. In exploratory projects, these characteristics are best identified through the sequenced use of multi-method research instruments.

When challenged development economists use an outdated empiricist/positivist epistemology to justify their methods and conclusions (Kanbur and Shaffer 2006), although most take little interest in the nature of their claims to knowledge.

> Discussions of method and methodology leave most economists queasy – among the younger bloods it is a common enough jibe that those who can, do; those who cannot, do methodology. Indeed, this lack of curiosity about the nature of their method is, in my view, the strength of economists as well as their weakness. (Kanbur and Shaffer 2006, p. 8)

Those 'who do' are caught up in a world of visible variables and hidden cases, which are assumed to be similar in structure and function. Relatively few design their own household surveys and those who do rarely take time to explore the appropriateness of their concepts and methods to the cases interrogated during the survey, a process that is undertaken by enumerators trained to ask each identical question in the same way, which is a condition for the production of 'brute facts' (Kanbur and Shaffer 2006).

Again there is an insight for social scientists engaged elsewhere in survey and comparative protocol research in contexts which are less foreign and more densely researched, which is that the validity of data depends on explication of concepts, the identification and selection of real rather than fictional cases and the detailed design of appropriate research instruments. These tasks require an initial exploratory research phase.

Researching within and across disciplines

Despite frequent calls for cross-disciplinarity in development research it is hard to find a successful example. The WeD experiment in inter-disciplinarity foundered partly because people from different disciplines were committed to meta-theoretical assumptions and related research methods that were incompatible. After a period of trying to work in a cross-disciplinary way with development economists, which began in 1993, I have become convinced that the way forward must be 'post-disciplinary', involving agreement on ontologies based on currently accepted (social) science findings, 'postmodern realist' epistemologies and a comparative case-based approach making use of technical expertises developed within disciplinary frameworks but adapted for the purpose in hand.

Integrating quantitative and qualitative research

In applied area academic fields such as development research there is a need to understand what is going on, or how the policy object *works* as a whole in its space–time and social/economic/cultural/political context. Most scholastic approaches, including development economics, are not designed to produce this kind of knowledge, and, from the perspective of those looking for solutions to real and horrible practical problems, the range of research expertises that has been developed within twentieth-century disciplinary confines is not being used as it should. Given recent developments in philosophy there is an opportunity to provide a meta-theoretical grounding for post-disciplinary approaches that, through iterative dialogues between frameworks and reality, develop models that correspond well enough to 'the changing social structures to which they refer' (Elias 1978, p. 28). Given recent developments in computing technology there is an opportunity to use the frameworks and models to make, and interpret data, and compare classify cases and develop understandings and explanations through 'systematically structured qualitative interpretation' (Byrne and Ragin 2006), which can be used to produce locally appropriate 'realistic, methodical plans for social change' (Elias 1978, p. 28).

NOTES

1. In the UK Development Studies in 2007 is an applied multi-disciplinary field within which mainstream (neo classical) development economists rarely work.

2. The research on which this chapter draws was funded by the UK Economic and Social Research Council (ESRC), whose support is gratefully acknowledged. Funds were provided as part of the programme of the ESRC Research Group on Wellbeing in Developing Countries, based at the University of Bath, and by an individual ESRC research grant 'Towards a Post-Disciplinary Approach to Global Poverty'. The research was conducted by the Ethiopia WeD team, which, over the life of the project, involved more than fifty dedicated researchers (see www.wed-ethiopia.org) led by Alula Pankhurst. He and I have worked very closely on the ideas and evidence described here. I am grateful for comments on an earlier draft of the chapter from David Byrne, Andries du Toit, Alula Pankhurst and Charles Ragin.

3. 'LDC' is now a formal UN category with its own High Commissioner. The criteria for the identification of LDCs are three: a low-income criterion, a human resource weakness criterion and an economic vulnerability criterion. The list of LDCs is ratified by the General Assembly of the UN. There are currently 50 LDCs: 32 in Africa, 10 non-African small islands, 7 in Asia and 1 in the Middle East. Aid is not confined to these countries.

4. Other (linked) reasons are to be found in international and LDC political economy structures.

5. Since 2000, the UK Department for International Development has funded a number of multi-disciplinary research centres, which currently include: the Chronic Poverty Research Centre; the Crisis States Programme; the Centre for the Future State; the Centre on Citizenship, Participation and Accountability; and the Centre for Research on Inequality, Ethnicity and Human Security. However, although these centres include research organisations based in LDCs, produce Working Papers, and hold workshops and conferences, they do not have an 'engineering' relationship with DFID, other donors or LDC governments.

6. Although in many such research outputs there is no connection between the model and the data analysis.

7. Toye and Hulme do not mention the increasing involvement of political scientists in policy-focused development research associated with the recent donor interest in 'good governance'.

8. See, for example, the two types of working paper produced by the UK ESRC-funded Growth and Poverty Reduction Group www.gprg.org/pubs/workingpapers/default.htm

9. See, for example, the two types of working paper produced for a workshop at the UK DFID-funded Chronic Poverty Research Centre www.chronicpoverty.org/news_events/ConceptsWorkshop-Oct2006.htm

10. See, for example, Desai and Potter (2006).

11. Although donors have recently started using development consultants to conduct multiple-case evaluations of aid instruments such as 'General Budget Support' (www.oecd.org) and single-case evaluations of country aid programmes over the longer term. For example, the Danish Aid Ministry has recently commissioned evaluations of its long-term programmes in Uganda www.mokoro.co.uk/Danidafp.html, Ghana and Mozambique.

12. Bangladesh, Ethiopia, Peru and Thailand.

13. There are other barriers: disciplinary cultures, disciplinary habituses and the histories and political economies of: (1) the social sciences disciplines; and (2) donor-related poverty research and policy (Bevan 2007).

14. Cross-disciplinarity refers to any work across one or more disciplines. Multi-disciplinarity refers to work done within disciplines by researchers who collaborate to develop together an overall analytical synthesis and conclusions. Inter-disciplinarity refers to research that integrates two or more disciplinary approaches throughout the research exercise (Kanbur 2002).

15. However, the data are in the public domain and there is potential for combining it in various cross-disciplinary combinations. For more information on the research conducted in the other three countries, see: www.welldev.org.uk.

16. In line with Mouzelis' characterisation of 'macro' as reaching far in space and time (1995).

17. This was used in a paper on power and social policy in Ethiopia (Bevan 2006); it will be revised in the light of the subsequent decision to adopt a complex systems approach.

18. There are five spaces of comparison in the regime framework: in/security outcomes; the mechanisms generating insecurity; political settlements and the 'welfare mix; mobilisations by regime actors; stratification outcomes.

19. The concept of 'in/security' is neutral and more appropriate than 'welfare' for regimes that produce suffering for many.

20. We have not yet brought this framework to the urban data.

21. The Ethiopian Rural Household Survey (www.ifpri.org).

22. Wellbeing and Illbeing Dynamics in Ethiopia.

23. In-Depth Exploration of Ethiopian Poverty.

24. At the time of writing all the protocols are available on www.wed-ethiopia.org

25. For those with more time, the evidence base also provides a detailed picture of lives in these communities and gives a voice to some of the residents.

26. On 2 October 2007, my colleague made a presentation at the retreat of the World Bank office in Ethiopia, which one listener described as the most interesting hour he had spent in his $3\frac{1}{2}$ years in the country.

27. That being said, comparative classification at different time-periods is useful in approaching such questions.

REFERENCES

Abbott, A. 2001a *Time Matters: On Theory and Method.* London: University of Chicago Press.

Abbott, A. 2001b *Chaos of Disciplines.* London: University of Chicago Press.

Archer, M.S. 1995 *Realist Social Theory: The Morphogenetic Approach.* Cambridge: Cambridge University Press.

Archer, M.S. 1996 *Culture and Agency: The Place of Culture in Social Theory* (revised edition). Cambridge: Cambridge University Press.

Archer, M.S. 2000 *Being Human: The Problem of Agency.* Cambridge: Cambridge University Press.

Bethlehem, T. 2005 'Integrating adult and child worlds: children's work and play in three Ethiopia WeD research sites' Proceedings of Third Ethiopian Economics Association International Conference, Addis Ababa.

Bevan, P. 2004a 'Exploring the structured dynamics of chronic poverty: a sociological approach' WeD Working Paper No 6. Online Available: http://www.welldev.org.uk.

Bevan, P. 2004b 'Conceptualising in/security regimes' in I. Gough et al. (Eds) *Insecurity and Welfare Regimes in Asia, Africa and Latin America.* Cambridge: Cambridge University Press, Chapter 3.

Bevan, P. 2004c 'The dynamics of African insecurity regimes' in I. Gough et al. (Eds) *Insecurity and Welfare Regimes in Asia, Africa and Latin America.* Cambridge: Cambridge University Press, Chapter 6.

Bevan, P. 2004d 'Hunger, poverty and famine in Ethiopia: mothers and babies under stress' WeD Ethiopia Working Paper No 4. Online Available: http://www.wed-ethiopia.org.

Bevan, P. 2005 'Studying multi-dimensional poverty in Ethiopia: towards a Q-integrated approach'. Online Available: http://www.q-squared.ca.

Bevan, P. 2006 'Poverty and social policy in development contexts: Ethiopia's in/security regime'. Paper presented at the APSA Conference Philadelphia, September 2006. Online Available: http://64.112.226.77/one/apsa/apsa06/index.php?click_key=2.

Bevan, P. 2007 'Researching wellbeing across the disciplines: some key intellectual problems and ways forward' in I. Gough and J.A. McGregor (Eds) *Well-Being in Developing Countries: From Theory to Research.* Cambridge: Cambridge University Press. Also available as WeD Working Paper No 25. Online Available: http://www.welldev.org.uk.

Bevan, P. forthcoming 'Cultural constructions of "wellbeing" in rural Ethiopia: competing local models under pressure'. Paper presented at the Wellbeing in International Development Conference, Bath, July 2007. Online Available: www.welldev.org.uk.

Bevan, P. and Pankhurst, A. 1996a *A Social Analysis of Fifteen Rural Economies in Ethiopia.* A Report for the Overseas Development Administration, UK. Online Available: http://www.wed-ethiopia.org.

Bevan, P. and Pankhurst, A. (Eds) 1996b *Fifteen Ethiopian Village Studies.* CSAE/Department of Sociology, Addis Ababa University. Online Available: http://www.csae.ox.ac.uk.

Bevan, P. and Pankhurst, A. 2006 'Power and poverty in Ethiopia: lessons from four rural case studies' Proceedings of the Fourth Ethiopian Economics Association International Conference, Addis Ababa.

Bevan, P. and Pankhurst, A. 2007 'Power structures, agency and community dynamics in rural Ethiopia'. Paper prepared for the Empowerment team in the World Bank. Online Available: http://www.wed-ethiopia.org.

Bevan, P. Pankhurst, A. et al. forthcoming *Power and Life Quality in Ethiopia: the Social and Cultural Construction of 'Wellbeing'.*

Blackwell, R.J. 1976 'A structuralist account of scientific theories' International philosophical Quaterly, Vol 16, pp. 263–274.

Brady, H.E. and Collier, D. (Eds) 2004 *Rethinking Social Inquiry: Diverse Tools, Shared Standards.* Oxford: Rowman and Littlefield.

Byrne, D. 1998 *Complexity Theory and the Social Sciences: an Introduction.* London: Routledge.

Byrne, D. 2002 *Interpreting Quantitative Data.* London: Sage.

Byrne, D. and Ragin, C. 2006 'Handbook of case centred methods – rationale and draft contents'. Mimeograph: instructions to authors.

Carter, B. and New, C. 2004 'Introduction: realist social theory and empirical research' in B. Carter and C. New (Eds) *Making Realism Work.* London: Routledge.

Chronic Poverty Research Centre. Online Available: http://www.chronicpoverty.org.

Cilliers, P. 1998 *Complexity and Postmodernism: Understanding Complex Systems.* London: Routledge.

Desai, V. and Potter, R. (Eds) 2006 *Doing Development Research.* London: Sage.

Doyal, L. and Gough, I. 1991 *The Theory of Human Need.* Basingstoke, UK: Macmillan.

Easterly, W. 2001 *The Elusive Quest for Growth: Economists' Adventures and Misadventures in the Tropics.* Cambridge MA: MIT Press.

Elias, N. 1978 *What is Sociology?* London: Hutchinson.

Ellerman, D. 2005 'Can the world bank be fixed?' *Post-Autistic Economics Review* 13: 2–16.

Esping-Andersen, G. 1990 *Three Worlds of Welfare Capitalism* Cambridge: Polity Press.

Feleke, T., Pankhurst, A. and Bevan, P. 2005 'Migration, labour markets and the informal sector: an exploratory study in Ethiopia'. Paper prepared for the World Bank. Online Available: http://www.wed-ethiopia.org.

Gough, I. 2004 'Welfare regimes in development contexts: a global and regional analysis' in I. Gough et al. (Eds) *Insecurity and Welfare Regimes in Asia, Africa and Latin America.* Cambridge: Cambridge University Press, Chapter 1.

Gough I., McGregor, J.A. and Camfield, L. 2007 'Theorising wellbeing in international development' in I. Gough and J.A. McGregor (Eds) *Wellbeing in Developing Countries: from Theory to Research.* Cambridge: Cambridge University Press.

Gough. I, and Wood, G. with Barrientos, A., Bevan, P., Davis, P. and Room, G. 2004 *Insecurity and Welfare Regimes in Asia, Africa and Latin America.* Cambridge: Cambridge University Press.

Harré, R. 1979 *Social Being.* Oxford: Blackwell.

Harré, R .1983 *Personal Being.* Oxford: Blackwell.

Harré, R. 1994 *Physical Being.* Oxford: Blackwell.

Hedstrom, P. 2005 *Dissecting the Social.* Cambridge: Cambridge University Press.

Hulme, D. 2007 'Integrating quantitative and qualitative research for country case studies of development'. GPRG-WPS-063. Online Available: http://www.gprg.org.

Hulme, D. and Toye, J. 2006 'The case for cross-disciplinary social science research on poverty, inequality and well-being' Q-squared Working Paper No 19. Online Available: http://www.q-squared.ca.

Kanbur, R. 2002 'Economics, social science and development' *World Development* 30(3): 477–486.

Kanbur, R. (Ed) 2005 'Q-squared: qualitative and quantitative poverty appraisal: complementarities, tensions and the way forward' Q-squared Working Paper No 1. Online Available: http://www.q-squared.ca.

Kanbur, R. and Shaffer, P. 2006 'Epistemology, normative theory and poverty analysis: implications for Q-squared in practice' *World Development* 35(2): 183–196.

King, G., Keohane, R. and Verba, S. 1994 *Designing Social Inquiry: Scientific Inference in Qualitative Research.* Princeton, NJ: Princeton University Press.

Lancaster, C. 1999 *Aid to Africa: So Much to Do, So Little Done.* London: University of Chicago Press.

Lavers, T. 2007 'Asking people what they want or telling them what they need? Contrasting a theory of human need with local expressions of goals' WeD Working Paper No 28. Online Available: http://www.welldev.org.uk.

Lewis,D., Glaser, M., McGregor, J.A., White, S. and Wood , G. 1991 'Going it alone: Female headed households in Bangladesh' CDS Occasional Paper

Bath: Centre for Development Studies, University of Bath.

McGregor, J.A. 2007 'Researching wellbeing: from concepts to methodology' in I. Gough and J.A. McGregor (Eds) *Wellbeing in Developing Countries: From Theory to Research.* Cambridge: Cambridge University Press.

Mouzelis, N. 1995 *Back to Sociological Theory: the Construction of Social Orders.* London: Macmillan.

Pankhurst, A. 2004 'Conceptions of and responses to HIV/AIDS: responses from twenty Ethiopian rural villages' WeD Ethiopia Working Paper No 2. Online Available: http://www.wed-ethiopia.org.

Pankhurst, A. 2006 'Wealth, poverty and life quality dynamics: objective and subjective measurement and interpretation based on a case-study approach from Dinki'. Proceedings of Fourth Ethiopian Economics Association International Conference, Addis Ababa.

Pankhurst, A. 2007a 'Destitution in Dinki, Amhara region: conceptions, comparisons, processes and shocks'. Paper Presented at the WeD Conference, Bath, UK. Online Available: http://www.welldev.org.uk.

Pankhurst, A. 2007b 'Destitution and life quality: objective, subjective and dynamic measures and interpretation based on household cases from Dinki, Amhara region'. Paper presented at the XVI International Conference of Ethiopian Studies, Trondheim, Norway. Online Available: http://www.wed-ethiopia.org.

Pankhurst, A. and Bevan, P. 2004 'Hunger, poverty and "famine" in Ethiopia: some evidence from twenty rural sites in Amhara, Tigray, Oromia and SNNP regions' Ethiopia WeD Working Paper No 1. Online Available: http://www.wed-ethiopia.org.

Pankhurst, A. and Bevan, P. 2007 'Unequal structures, unbuffered shocks and undesirable strategies'. Paper prepared for the Social Protection Department of the World Bank. Online Available: http://www.wed-ethiopia.org.

Pawson, R. 1989 *A Measure for Measures.* London: Routledge.

Ragin, C. 2000 *Fuzzy-Set Social Science.* London: University of Chicago Press.

Ragin, C. and Becker, H. (Eds) 1992 *What Is a Case? Exploring the Foundations of Social Inquiry.* Cambridge: Cambridge University Press.

Rao, V. and Woolcock , M. 2007 *Disciplinary Monopolies in Development Research: A Response to the Research Evaluation Process.* Washington, DC: World Bank.

Sayer, A. 2000 *Realism and Social Science.* London: Sage.

Skevington, S., Lotfy, M. and O'Connell, K.A. 2004 'The World Health Organisation's WHOQOL-BREF Quality of Life Assessment' *Quality of Life Research* 13: 299--310.

Smith, J. and Jenks, C. 2006 *Qualitative Complexity Ecology: Cognitive Processes and the Re-Emergence of Structures in Post-Humanist Social Theory*. London: Routledge.

Sundberg, M. and Gelb, A. 2006 'Making aid work' IMF: Finance and Development.

Tadele, F., Pankhurst, A., Bevan, P. and Lavers, T. 2006 'Migration and rural-urban linkages in Ethiopia'. Paper prepared for Irish Aid Ethiopia. Online Available: http://www.wed-ethiopia.org.

Tilly, C. 1984 *Big Structures, Large Processes, Huge Comparisons*. New York: Russell Sage Foundation.

Van de Walle, N. 2001 *African Economies and the Politics of Permanent Crisis*. New York: Cambridge University Press, 1979–1999.

Wade, R. 1990 *Governing the Market: Economic Theory and the Role of Government in East Asian Industrialization*. Princeton, NJ: Princeton University Press.

Wood, G. 2004 'Informal security regimes; the strength of relationships' *Insecurity and Welfare Regimes in Asia, Africa and Latin America*. Cambridge: Cambridge University Press, Chapter 2.

Yisak, T., 2006 'Intergenerational transfer of poverty/wealth in Ethiopia: evidence from four communities'. Proceedings of Fourth Ethiopian Economics Association International Conference, Addis Ababa.

29

Non-nested and Nested Cases in a Socioeconomic Village Study

Wendy Olsen

INTRODUCTION

In this chapter, several data-management issues are brought to the foreground in a study of social class and workers' behaviour in south India. This case-study-based research project used a variety of local face-to-face means to explore a complex rural situation. Both classes in terms of employment relations and asset hierarchies in a place riddled with high economic inequality were part of the background of the study. In this section, I define social class and the aims of the chapter; the next section gives a more detailed review of the data and methods used in the study. The following two sections explore causality in this context. They look specifically at the outcome variable 'resistance' measured as a fuzzy set in a village using 39 household cases. The complexity of the relationship between persons and households is so great that some people give up using the case-study method and prefer, instead, the two extremes of 'qual' and 'quant' research: either a smaller number of personal investigations, or a secondary

statistical analysis of survey data. But the case-study method sits nicely in between these two extremes and I will show that a lot has been learned through our case-study research. I then discuss the methodology further, stressing that the findings for classes and villages illustrate non-nested cases with very small N (two villages and five classes). By contrast, the household and individual relationships offer us nested cases with N = 39 households. This research is also grounded in a larger random-sample study of 187 households in the same two villages. Overall, in this chapter, both the challenges and the advantages of the mixed-methods case-study approach are exposed.

Social class is usually defined in Western countries in terms of how an individual's occupation or employment fits into a status hierarchy. In India, social-class studies are rooted in the Marxian analysis of bourgeois, petit-bourgeois and worker classes in mixed agrarian–capitalist societies (Patnaik 1976). Based on these grounding principles, social-class studies usually take into account assets, employment relations and the status or stability of employment. The unit of analysis is the individual. For adapting this framework to a rural Indian situation, I would stress that the unit of ownership for assets is traditionally the household and indeed the wider patriarchal extended family (Agarwal 1994). In India, women are widely excluded from personal ownership of land (Swaminathan 2002, Jejeebhoy and Sathar 2001). Social class can be defined at the household level using (again) a mixture of assets, employment relations and the status or stability of employment of the dominant occupation or highest-earning employment in the household. This method tends to mask women's labouring experiences and is andro-centric. In short, class can be operationalised either at the individual level or at the household level. Conceptually, the work is similar, but empirically the results are very different. Change over time is also differentiated because of the very different sex-sterotyped patterns of occupations whether we are considering a Western country scene or south Indian rural scene.

To handle the class and nested class issues, we decided to use Microsoft Excel® to hold survey data on persons and on households, notebooks to contain fieldnotes and family history notes, NVivo to hold interview transcripts from MP3 sound recordings, and other software – fsQCA – to study the patterns in some of the data. The case-study method did not restrict us to a single level (persons, households, classes or villages). Instead, with this range of software it enabled us to make connections and get a deeper understanding across the levels. Indeed, the use of the word 'levels' is mainly metaphorical here (Heil 2003). A higher level builds upon a lower level, but each level also suffuses and constitutes the other level so it is never clear – even where there is a hierarchy – that there is an 'up' or a 'down'. Thus, it is not only true that classes consist of persons, but also that class relations are more than just a sum of persons. Classes have their own properties, history, tendencies and liabilities. I treat the farmer class, worker-with-land class and worker class in some detail in the paper. Is class 'above' the worker? Or is it a

fundamental grounding social structure upon which the worker glides through life? I do not see class as dictating or deterministic. However, it represents a set of powerful causal mechanisms that are embedded into many social relationships. So although the 'levels' metaphor fails as a literal description of where class sits *vis-à-vis* the person, it is useful in data management. We create serial numbers for each person and then carry these through into the household data and various other lists. We also have household serial numbers 1–39 in this instance. Although there are lots of people, there are only a few classes (here five for the village context).

To complete my overview of the nested and non-nested aspects of this case-study research, consider two other sets of cases: local self-help groups and villages. We used Excel® spreadsheets to hold background data such as a list of all the women members of the microfinance self-help groups for the two villages we were working in. This list had the women's real names and their household addresses. We then matched up members to the other data we have in questionnaires. We soon found a few errors in the microfinance self-help group lists, such as women of high caste status who were listed in the membership lists as being Dalit. A Dalit person is one who comes from the families who, according to traditional Hindu thought, were considered very low status, beneath the caste set-up and ritually polluting to the touch. In the nineteenth century, many Hindus used to avoid contact with Dalits, but Gandhi (1869–1948) called them Harijans (God's People) and worked to free them from casteism. In 1947, the newly created Indian state banned all caste-based discrimination. However, today, whereas high-caste people sometimes try to pretend to be Dalit, or "backward caste", to get benefits that are part of reverse discrimination policies, Dalits cannot successfully pretend to be high-caste because there is still intimate, implicit and widespread caste discrimination. The phrase "forward caste" is sometimes used to group together some of the "higher" castes, such as Brahmins and landlord castes, into a supposedly structurally privileged group. The data on self-help groups revealed that caste is a live issue in ways not mentioned during our interviews.

The second spreadsheet lists data horizontally for each of 187 households randomly chosen from the two villages. Call the villages Smallville and Bigville for simplicity (*Chinnapalli* and *Peddapalli* being their pseudonyms). They lie in the Western Chittoor district of southern Andhra Pradesh. The state has 76 million people, of whom about 7% are Muslim. We need random samples to get good estimates of the local proportions who are Muslim (also 7%), proportion having membership in a self-help group (around 40%) and other important socioeconomic variables.

The 39 households and couples who are reported on in the case-study research are a sub-set of the 187 households in the survey questionnaire dataset. Within the SPSS data for 187 households, all individuals are listed and their education and health is recorded. Thus persons are nested all neat and tidy within households. But classes cut across households and, in a sense (taking gender into account), households cut across classes. For example, this arises if you have a woman with a salaried job in a farming household. The man's 'class' is F (Farmer) but the woman's class is S (Salaried). It is hard to classify such a household's social class. Ontologically the classes are distinct. Households are non-nested with (individualised) social classes.

Nested case relationships have a 1-to-N format when notated mathematically. They are easy to record in database software such as ACCESS, but we have preferred to use the much simpler Excel® software to manage the households-and-persons data. Non-nested case relationships have an N-to-N format. In QCA we have techniques for studying both nested and non-nested cases at the same time.

DATA AND METHODS

The analysis of case-study data with small or medium 'N' cannot test hypotheses using statistical inference because there are not enough cases. Indeed, as a realist, I am sceptical of hypothesis testing because it does not sufficiently allow for the exploration of data, the discovery of new themes through insight or the existence of dialectics in society (Danermark 2001, Byrne 2002). However, if one wants to do hypothesis testing, it might take the form of testing whether a factor X is causal for an outcome Y, in various configurational contexts, using QCA. I tend to test a hypothesis within a wider context of retroduction and exploration. The three are summarised below:

(1) *Hypothesis*: Resistance to employers' demands is strongly associated with having a lot of assets, high social class, high education and specific assets. This hypothesis was rejected for the two villages.

(2) *Exploration*: Using interview data, what factors emerge as important aspects of the relationships between land-owners and workers in the land and labour markets? The answer in these villages includes resistance, exiting to migrate, conformity and secret sources of power of workers.

(3) *Retroduction*: What factors seem to have occurred that were either necessary or sufficient to cause resistance among workers? No particular single factor was consistently either necessary or sufficient. However, among non-workers, resistance was absent due to the absence of the exploitative wage–labour relationship; so class was very important. Among workers, those with some land or other assets were more commonly able to resist landlords' demands. However, they also conformed to landlord demands.

The data for this study arise from a study involving data triangulation: a survey and interviews. I reviewed literature from five schools of thought and then set up the topics of semi-structured interviews for piloting. The questions were adapted after piloting and can be found online (see www.ruralvisits.org/ TenantsStudyResearchDesign.htm). I held survey data from 1994 for the two selected Indian villages, using a sample of 115 households drawn randomly from lists of village households (Olsen 1997). From this sample, 26 households were relocated during 2006, and for these, plus 13 more, a new questionnaire was completed in 2006 using face-to-face structured interviewing. The questionnaires covered land and other assets, land tenancy, the household members' education, usual work and secondary work if any. The 1994 set of questionnaires had also covered labour, land tenancy and credit extensively (available from ESRC Data Archive along with 1994 interviews with 20 women). The 2006 questionnaire survey also included ten Likert scale attitude questions about their views on different forms of agricultural labouring such as exchange labour, casual labour, child labour. Data about the previous year's crops were also recorded in the questionnaire.

The respondent in the 2006 survey was an adult *person*. Male and female 'respondents' were randomly sampled from among the random-sample list of households, but data on all household members were collected. Thus the individuals are nested inside the households. A serial number identifying households was used alongside a number and a name indicating each individual. Pseudonyms were added for each individual adult in the 39 households selected for interviews.

From the 1994 survey, the household social class in 1994 was worked out and compared with social class of household in 2006. We (the research team) used the social classes of worker, worker with land, small farmer, landlord, salaried household and self-employed trader. A worker with land may either own or rent that land, and their employment is not restricted to casual wage labour. Instead, the people in worker-with-land households also worked as 'farmer', *ryot* in Telugu. They like to perceive themselves as peasants. However, the 'farmer' class are those who not only class themselves as *ryots* but also do not do any paid wage-labour. When selecting 39 households in 2006, salaried and merchant households were avoided because the study was focused on labouring and land rental. However, a few households were later found to have regular salaries coming in. In practice, the boundaries between these three agrarian classes were fluid

and permeable. For the 26 households that can be traced from 1994 to 2006, mobility by social class is very low (Kendall's Tau-a 0.27, significance 1.9%, showing an ordinal association). There are signs of increasing poverty due to the bad conditions for agriculture in the years 1996–2006. The distribution of the five main social classes among the quota sample interviewed in 2006 appears in Figure 29.1 and Table 29.1.

In Figure 29.1, vertically we have a fuzzy set of household education (see Ragin 2000, Ragin et al. 2006). If all adults of a household had high school education or higher, and the children were in school, the fuzzy set was 1.0, and if all were illiterate and not in school the fuzzy set was 0.0. In between, we use the numbers 0.17 or 0.33 to indicate that some adults were illiterate but that either the children were in school or at least one adult had primary school education (more for the 0.33 level). Completing the ordinal variate, we set the markers at 0.67 and 0.87 if all children of school age were in school but not all the adults had any education – this fuzzy set method is described in broad terms in Ragin (2008) and Rihoux and Ragin (2008); education sharing by proximity is described by Basu and Narayan (2001). This vertical axis represents the household's overall access to human capital (formal education). Meanwhile, the horizontal axis represents the assets of the household. Again, an ordinal fuzzy set was arranged: 0 for no assets, 1 for having land and 3 for the following: bulls/cows, a well, a tractor, buffaloes. In between, 0.17 reflected having sheep or goats only; 0.33 for a radio, TV or bicycle, as well as a small animal; 0.5 for any cow, bullock or buffalo; 0.67 for any land possessed (besides the house plot); and 0.87 for land plus at least two of the other possible assets. The horizontal and vertical rankings are strongly associated with social class itself (Kendall's tau-a 0.41 for class by assets, p = 0.0001; and Kendall's tau-a 0.29 for class by education at household level, p = 0.0044). In each case n = 39 and we have 99% confidence in a pattern of association. Education is only weakly associated with class itself in

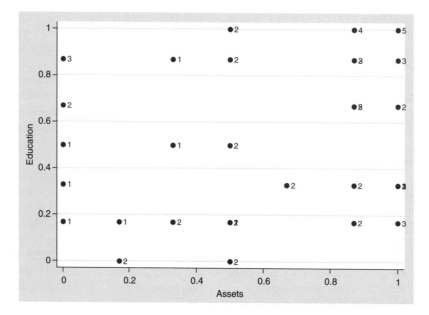

Figure 29.1   Social class, education and assets of 39 households. The annotated number is the social class as in Table 29.1. Key: the horizontal axis is a fuzzy set of assets, the vertical axis is a fuzzy set of education; both are at household level. The annotation numbers indicate the social class. Household class: 1, worker; 2, worker with land; 3, farmer; 4, landlord. In two cases, two households overlap on one point.

this non-random sample. The non-randomly selected sample of 39 households is biased towards class 2, the workers with a little land. Further details of the sampling and class structure can be found in Olsen (2008a). Quota sampling was used to get strong contrasts between types of household including a range of farmers and workers in both villages.

The interviews were coded in NVivo software, and a 'casebook' of household attributes was created. During our analysis, we studied whether strategies could be read off from – and were caused by – the structural location of a household in the caste-class system. This proved impossible because strategies themselves are so complex (Olsen 2008a). The actions embedded in a strategy mean different things depending on whether the household wanted to leave agriculture, or expand their farming. Some families tried to diversify within agriculture, too. Thus even the renting of land proved to have several meanings ranging from a desperately poorly paid form of agricultural work to a source of

self-confidence and autonomy and finally to exciting investment plans (e.g. new silk or sugar producers).

I coded within each interview a series of types of acts that are typically either 'conformist' or 'resistant' within the local social milieu, with respect to casual daily paid work (known as '*kuulie*' work in Telugu, the local language; *kuulie* often has a negative connotation). The conformist acts include doing unpaid labour for the employer at their house; accepting late payment for casual-paid wage labour; acting respectfully towards employers; and accepting work from several different employers. The resistant acts reported included refusing to do the unpaid work when asked to by a landlord, renting land in order to avoid *kuulie* work, and picking a preferred employer over one whose behaviour is considered bad. Arguing with the landlord was coded as resistant, whereas criticising the landlord's behaviour but accepting that one must get on with them was coded as conforming. A variety of other conformist

Table 29.1 Calibrated data for household caste and landholding (crisp and fuzzy sets) along with qualitative variates for resistance, conformity, etc (Microsoft product screen shot(s) reprinted with permission from Microsoft Corporation).

Microsoft Excel - Questionnaire data Yetavakili-Miniki.xls

File Edit View Insert Format Tools Data Window Help Adobe PDF

AD3 — resistf

	tenancy	rentinwet	rentindry	wataccess	havecows	totoland	NonKuulie	ConformN	AvoidN	ExitN	ResistN	InnovateN	JoinN	resistf
4	1	2	0	1	1	2	0	1	2	1	0	0	0	0.17
5	1	0	2	0										
6	0	0	0	1	1	3	0	3	3	1	1	1	1	1
7	0	0	0	0	0	0.5	0	1	1	0	0	0	1	0
8	1	0.5	0.5	0.87	0	0	0	3	1	1	0	1	0	0.17
9	1	1	0	1	1	1	0	2	1	1	1	0	0	0.17
10	0	0	0	0	1	0	0	2	2	0	2	1	1	1
11	0	0	0	0.87	1	2	0	0	0	1	0	1	1	0.17
12		0	0		0	30	1	0		0		0	1	2	0.87
13	0	0	0	1	1	18	1	0	0	0	1	0	2	0.87
14	1	1.5	0	1	1	3	0	2	0	0	1	0	0	0
15	1	0.75	0	1	1	6.5	0	0	0	0	0	1	2	1
16	1	1.5	0	1	1	3	1	0	1	1	0	1	0	0.87
17	1	0	1	0	1	0	0	1	1	0	4	0	0	0
18	0	0	0	0	0	0.75	0	0	0	1	1	0	0	0.17
19	0	0	0	0	1	0	0	1	1	1	1	2	1	1
20	0	0	0	1	0	45	1	0	0	0	0	0	0	0.87
21	1	0	2	0	1	0.5	0	2	1	0	3	3	3	1
22	0	0	0	0	0	0	0	2	1	1	0	1	0	0.17
23	1	0.5	0	0.87	1	1	0	3	0	1	1	2	0	1
24	1	0	2.5	0	1	0	0	1	0	0	0	2	0	0.87
25	0	0	0	0	0	7	1	0	0	0	0	2	0	0.17
26	0	0	0	0	0	0	0	0	1	0	0	0	0	0
27	0	0	0	0	0	0	0	2	1	0	1	0	0	0.17
28	0	0	0	1	0	12	0	0	0	1	0	0	1	0.17
29	0	0	0		1	3	0	0	1	1	0	1	0	0
30	0	0	0	0	1	0	3	1	0	0	1	0	0	0
31	1	0.5	1.5	1	1	1	0	4	0	0	3	0	0	0
32	1	0	3	1	1	4.5	0	1	1	0	1	0	0	0
33	1	1	0	1	1	1	0	0	1	0	0	0	0	0.17
34	0	0	0	0	0	0	0	0	0	0	1	0	0	0.17
35	0	0	0	0	0	0	1	5	0	0	1	0	0	0.87
36	0	0	0	0	0	0	0	0	0	0	1	3	0	1
37	1	1	0	1	1	0.75	0	5	1	1	1	3	0	0.17
38	0	0	0	0	0	0	0	0	1	1	1	0		0.17

Respondents \ PreparingFairQCASheet \ IndivData \ FairCopyConformity \

Ready

ConformN, number of incidents of conformity described in a one-hour interview; ResistN, number of different incidents of resistance described in a one-hour interview, etc.

and resistant acts were found, too. 'Exit' was another strategy used by many labourers who had (or had a wife or son) migrated to a nearby town or city for work. These are still workers but they exit the *kuulie* labour market. Notable also were innovative acts like growing silk or renting land with tamarind trees, precisely to get revenue without doing *kuulie* wage labour. Another category, 'Avoiding', was used to code those who perceived that they had arranged to evade the labour market altogether through self-employment or a salaried job.

Joining local women's groups was coded as 'Joining'. In each case, the number of different *types* or *incidents* of an act, within a category, were counted up. Incidents were not counted twice and repetitions (which were rare) were ignored.

The act types are summarised in Table 29.1, along with some structural fuzzy sets during the calibration process. Owning cows was reduced to a 0/1 binary (a crisp set). Owning land (measured in acres) was calibrated as the assets fuzzy set. However, the wetland component of owned land was combined with renting in wetland in order to create a fuzzy-set 'wetaccess'. This is operational irrigated land and takes the values 0 if none, 0.87 if up to 1 acre, and 1 if ≥ 1 acre. For me as a sociologist, the assets and education variables represented background structural factors that were likely to be causal mechanisms for labour-market outcomes. Assets would be associated with the class structure, and education would reflect the background class structure as well as recent opportunities for developing human capital and cultural capital. The idea of these two 'variates' existing at household level reflects the widespread sharing of such resources within the family group. Thus, individual ownership is nested and hidden within these two fuzzy sets. A third fuzzy set of 'wetland access' also reflected a type of asset that has recently grown in importance due to predominant groundwater shortage and strong rain fluctuations from year to year.

In Table 29.2 you see a variety of variables used in this study. The website http://www.ruralvisits.org contains more details about the study.

To simplify the outcomes from six to one, I expected to be able to create a fuzzy set ranging from 'very resistant to landlords' to 'very conformist with landlord expectations'. The data reduction stage utilised all the six variates from the 39 interviews. A cluster analysis method for ordinal variables is described further below. After clustering to get

an outcome variate (i.e. a dependent variable), a fuzzy set was created so that 'resisted landlord or employer' took the value 1 and 'did not resist the landlord or employer' took the value 0. In between are some intermediate situations. This method follows the advice of Byrne (Chapter 5).

Having created the dependent variable and introduced the pseudonyms for the main adult man and woman of each household, the fuzzy-set raw data table began to take shape. Figure 29.2 illustrates part of this table.

In Figure 29.2, you can trace the Muslim case of Syed and Farhana, the Dalit cases of Govinda and Laxmamma (and five others), and so on. The fsQCA software can create X–Y plots of variables, e.g. Assets by Education, for the 39 cases. However, in Figure 29.1 I used STATA software in order to benefit from slightly more flexible case labelling. In STATA scatterplots, the 'jigger' function can also allow multiple dots to be grouped around the ordinal point, e.g. {1.0, 0.33}, where several households overlap. Jiggering is useful for larger studies with medium N.

Thus, the study was a mixed-methods study that integrated the analysis of labour markets with the awareness of microfinance, land tenancy, gender and class relations. Mixed-methods research of this kind has been recommended in development studies by Grootaert et al. (2004), Olsen (2004) and Jones and Woolcock (2007). The ambitious scope of the research is interdisciplinary.

Table 29.2 Conformist and resistant actions *vis-à-vis* the local employers, as mentioned in one interview (per household)

Social class	Number of households	% which acted to conform to landlord's wishes	Examples of conforming	% which acted to resist landlord's wishes	Examples of resistance
1 = worker	10	60%	Accept given constraints, ask landlord for help, accept given employment terms and conditions, negotiate within given parameters	40%	Negotiate, shame, criticise, bargain with the employer; buy or otherwise obtain a bullock or cow pair to enable self to do more highly paid *kuulie* work
2 = worker with land	18	11/18, i.e. 61%		56%	
3 = farmer	5	20%		40%	
4 = landlord	3	Not applicable		Not applicable	
5 = salaried	3	0		0	
All	39	50%		41%	

The number of different reported actions of each type was measured by studying the transcripts from 39 household interviews in two Indian villages 2006–2007.

FS/QCA Data Sheet

File Variables Cases Analyze Graphs

Case	hhid	resistf	class	assets	education	pseudman	pseudfem	classlab	dalit
1	1	0.17	2	0.87	0.17	Venkatramana	Laxmi	W+	0
2	2	1	2	0.5	0.5	Khaleed	Pathima	W+	0
3	3	1	2	0.5	1	Kistappa	Kumari	W+	0
4	4	0	2	0.67	0.33	Pullayya	Nagamani	W+	1
5	5	0.17	2	0.33	0.17	Chinnayappa	Uma	W+	1
6	6	0.17	2	1	0.67	Khaleel	Hajbee	W+	0
7	7	1	2	0.5	0.87	Chandran	Sita	W+	1
8	8	0.17	2	0.87	0.67	Sridhar	Padmavathi	W+	1
9	9	0.87	4	0.87	1	Ramaiah	Lakshmidevi	L	0
10	10	0.87	5	1	1	Vasanth Reddy	Jayasri	S	0
11	11	0	2	0.87	0.17	Chitram	Swati	W+	0
12	12	1	3	1	0.17	Narayana	Parvatha	F	0
13	13	0.87	3	1	0.33	Manju		F	0
14	14	0	2	0.17	0	Akbar	Nagamani	W+	0
15	15	0.17	5	0.87	0.67	Syed	Farhana	S	0
16	16	1	1	0.33	0.87	Jayanth	Yasmeen	W	0
17	17	0.87	4	0.87	1	Venkateswaralu	Savita	L	0
18	18	1	2	0.87	0.33	Ranga	Mangamma/Manju	W+	1
19	19	0.17	1	0	0.33	Govinda	Laxmamma	W	1

File: FairQCAFuzzySheet39Cases.csv

Figure 29.2 Qualitative comparative analysis (fsQCA) spreadsheet. Class labels: W, worker; W+, worker with land; F, farmer; L, landlord; S, salaried. These are also numbered 1 to 5, respectively. (Microsoft product screen shot(s) reprinted with permission from Microsoft Corporation).

RESISTANCE TO EMPLOYERS' EXPLOITATION IS NOT THE OPPOSITE OF CONFORMITY

In setting up the outcome variate for fuzzy-set QCA, we used cluster analysis to reduce the data. Cluster analysis can use continuous variables or a mixture of categorical and continuous variables. The measurement metric in the 'continuous' variables will influence the way cases fall into types in the outcome. Another important factor is the number of types (clusters) that the user specifies should be produced by the cluster analysis software. Using SPSS, two-way cluster analysis reduces the data even when there is a mixture of continuous and categorical data. This method was used since the measurement of 'types of incidents of resistance described' and the other variables are counts and hence more ordinal than cardinal in their level of measurement. The cluster analysis was conducted in stages. Figure A1, a brief appendix, shows in detail for all 39 cases an interim stage of clustering (VAR00014) and the final four clusters (TSC_6084). Two raw counts are also graphed in Figure 29.3. The cluster analysis sought to divide the cases into four or five types, which have maximum homogeneity within clusters while having strong heterogeneity between clusters. SPSS gives detailed measures of the contribution of each variable to each cluster. The resulting multinomial variable can be simplified to a fuzzy set.

The cluster analysis results did not meet my expectation that resistance and conformity would be mutually exclusive characteristics of households. As seen in Figure 29.3, they were co-associated for a few households, absent for a larger group of non-labour households and generally not associated with each other at all. The hypothesis of a negative association is rejected through Figure 29.3. By inspecting Figure A1, and re-running cluster analysis using six variates, I obtained four coherent clusters. These could be roughly characterised as fully resistant, strongly but not fully resistant, not very resistant and not

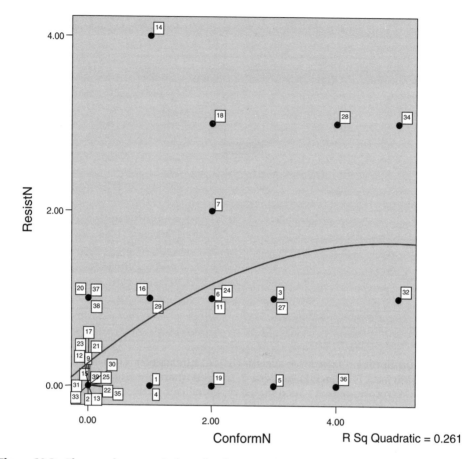

Figure 29.3 The very low association of resistance with conformity. Markers indicate the household ID number for the scattergram of two ordinal variates. In this figure, the absolute number of recorded instances of types of resistance and conformity in a one-hour interview are shown. These range from 0 to 5 for each scale and are shown in the dataset as variates ResistN and ConformN.

resistant. Fuzzy-set values were set at 1 and 0.87 for the first groups (types 4 and 2 in Figure A1, right-hand column), 0.17 for a group that combined innovation with exiting and avoidance behaviour, and 0.00 for the non-workers who did not resist at all because the concept was inapplicable to them. Please note that the inapplicability of a concept to a group was not an *a priori* assumption. In the rural farming scene with growing groundwater shortage, landlords and many people who were previously employers are taking up paid wage labour work. Therefore, we cannot assume that class maps directly onto the labour relations in the villages that we are studying here. But having looked at

the clusters, it did appear that class was the mechanism that stopped the last group (type 3) from resisting. The annotation in the column VAR00014 shows my thoughts while iterating from qualitative to cluster and towards fuzzy sets. Iteration is advised by both Kent (2008) and Rihoux and Ragin (2008). Iteration is also recommended by Danermark et al. (2001) in their overview textbook about methods of post-positivist research.

Further research could investigate the frequency of these behaviours, some of which are seasonal or take place at holiday times, in more detail. The interviews caused these categories to come up without explicit prompting. Thus, this is an exploratory stage of the research. It offers an ordinal variate for resistance which embeds other aspects of strategic labour market behaviour, such as seasonal migration ('Exit'), which we had thought of as alternatives to resistance.

The fuzzy set (RESISTFZ) seen in Figures 29.2 and 29.3 is not strongly associated with class or assets. Qualitative study of individual household cases suggested that exit of one family member from the local labour market was often accompanied by one of several other ways that workers can avoid doing casual wage labour. These ways included: (1) going into self-employment, e.g. rolling cigarettes; (2) joining a women's microfinance self-help group; (3) renting land. Tenancy emerged as an important tool of bargaining power in the local labour market. Those who rent land in (or have cows or grow silkworms) can afford to reject undesirable wage offers. They can offend an employer who exhibits irksome or unacceptable behaviour towards the workers. Those without a plot of land to rent in were less able to object when they felt insulted. Some very poor workers said that they felt insulted but also felt they must not offend the employers. The tenants were in a relatively stronger position in the labour market whether they had a lot of assets or not (Olsen and Neff 2007).

We began to retroduce why these data patterns had unexpectedly turned up. There was some precedent in the literature, e.g. Kapadia (1995) notes that local labour groups bargain with employers in locally situated ways. Nadkarni (2002) points out that land reforms could give more power to the poor. Srivastava (1989) noted the importance of tenancy in the changing class structure of Indian agriculture. It has long been known that farming, tenancy and labouring are linked for the poor and especially for poor women (Agarwal 2003a). Studies of microfinance have shown that it has impacts in the labour market (Mayoux 1993) and yet is not a panacea for all the problems of poverty in south India (Roesch 2005). Agarwal (2003b) comments that there are a range of other empowering changes in the land market, and that microfinance is just part of a package if structural change is desired. In particular, our fieldwork interviews suggested that owning cows can be a risky and expensive business, which may exceed some poor workers' capacity over a period of years, in spite of cheap credit to buy the cows. If a cow gets sick, the family's prospects are seriously damaged. The labouring, investment and earnings decisions are all interlinked (Olsen 2008b).

We soon realised, looking at the data with retroduction in mind, that many resisters were also conformers. One reason is apparently that for other households being expected to conform is simply unimaginable. Some forms of conformity are aspects of debt bondage or labour tying. For example, doing symbolic work at the landlord's house on a holiday morning prior to a feast is a way of indicating that one is tied to that employer. An example of debt bondage is where the worker must work without pay (e.g. cleaning dishes or cleaning up after cows, sweeping and gathering water), since the worker's household owes money to the landlord and indeed depends on their willingness to continue to rent them land and employ them in the busy season.

In some instances, avoiding 'conformity' is due to the high caste of the worker. Indeed, no non-workers reported conforming behaviours. A class mechanism is behind this pattern: landlord and salaried class people would never do *kuulie* daily wage work so they do not fit easily into the labour bargaining scenario. For those who do fit into that scenario as workers, those who reported resisting were no less likely than the rest to report sometimes conforming. Many people do both.

Our dependent variable was therefore set up to focus on 'resistance' and did not have an opposite extreme of 'conformity'. Instead, the fuzzy set is stipulated to represent 'resist' and 'do not resist'.

CAUSAL ANALYSIS AT THE HOUSEHOLD OR COUPLE LEVEL

The causal analysis of factors leading to resistance reflected a return to structuralist

Table 29.3   The truth table for fuzzy-set analysis, final model

resistfz Fuzzy	assets Fuzzy	education Fuzzy	dalit Crisp	smallville Crisp	wetaccess Fuzzy	havecows Crisp	Number, i.e. Case Count	Config'n Number
0	0	0	1	0	1	0	1	1
0	0	0	1	1	0	0	4	2
0	0	1	0	0	0	1	1	3
0	0	1	1	0	0	0	2	4
0	1	0	0	0	1	1	3	5
0	1	1	0	0	0	0	1	6
0	1	1	0	1	1	0	1	7
0	1	1	1	1	1	1	1	8
1	0	0	0	0	0	1	1	9
1	1	0	0	1	1	1	4	10
1	1	0	1	0	0	0	1	11
1	1	0	1	0	1	1	1	12
1	1	0	1	1	0	1	1	13
1	1	0	1	1	1	1	1	14
1	1	1	0	0	1	0	2	15
1	1	1	0	0	1	1	4	16
1	1	1	0	1	0	0	1	17
1	1	1	0	1	1	1	1	18
						SUM:	31	

At this point, the remainders had been omitted. This left 31 cases in 18 configurations.

hypotheses. In Table 29.3, the fuzzy-set data are shown to include both structural and other factors. A structuralist argues that class relations and other major social structures *cause* people to act in specific ways. 'The class structure is just such that these outcomes are inevitable' would be a deterministic way of phrasing this hypothesis (see Sayer 1997 for an alternative approach). In fuzzy-set causal analysis, we asked, would class or caste emerge as predicting resistance? Specifically, if one is above the poorest workers and more of a 'farmer' (peasant), or of high caste, are they more likely to resist? If one is a worker but has a lot of capital (assets) or education, then is one more likely to resist?

I tested large, medium and small models that embedded this hypothesis. Purely structural models (with assets, caste and class variates, k = 1, 2 or 3) did not perform well for RESIST fuzzy outcome; mixed models were better (k = 4 or 5). Large models (k = 6 or more) showed extremely diverse outcomes. The resist crisp set (coded 0 for no resistance and 1 for some resistance) was not a useful way to avoid the complexity that was seen in the fuzzy-set analysis. Several crisp-set

models were tested – each using fuzzy sets among the conditions – but they did not have good coverage or consistency. Figure 29.4 provides details of the interim calculations.

To test whether structuralist Marxism has any explanatory power at all in the villages, I then paused to test the effect of assets on education. With the random sample survey data (N = 187) a regression model showed strong class effects. T-statistics had 1% significance in models that have the household education level as the dependent variable. (The sum of years of schooling for two adults was the outcome variable.) In these regressions, there was no effect for respondent's gender or for 'village', but age was a significant factor. Young people tend to have more education and I controlled for this. Thus, the surrounding social scene is one in which class has massive positive, morphostatic effects on social and economic mobility through education. Fuzzy-set analysis of N = 39 cases also shows strong associations of class, assets and education (see classes 4 and 5 in Figure 29.2 for evidence).

However, the study of resistance in the villages is in part the study of agency, not

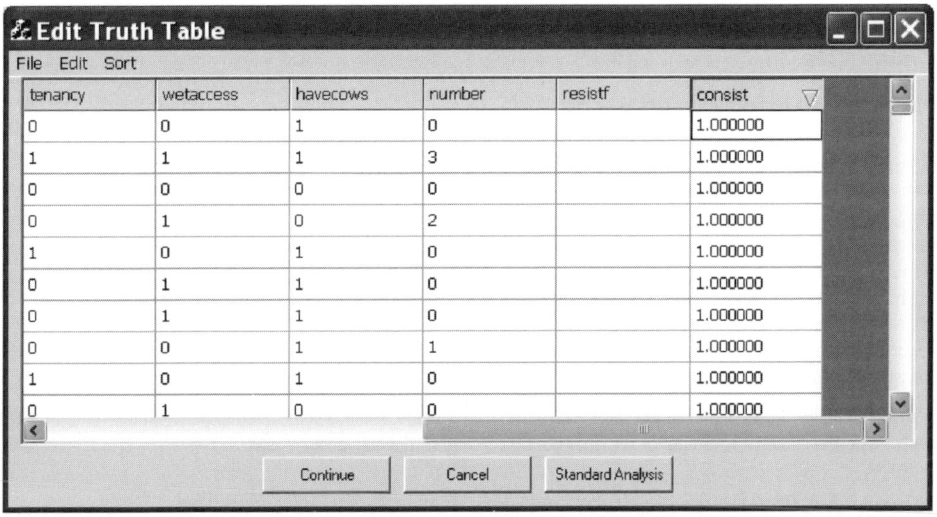

tenancy	wetaccess	havecows	number	resistf	consist
0	0	1	0		1.000000
1	1	1	3		1.000000
0	0	0	0		1.000000
0	1	0	2		1.000000
1	0	1	0		1.000000
0	1	1	0		1.000000
0	1	1	0		1.000000
0	0	1	1		1.000000
1	0	1	0		1.000000
0	1	0	0		1.000000

Figure 29.4 The truth table while deciding on model form. In this truth table, a fuzzy set and two crisp sets are visible. Consistency is 1 for the visible cases, but the table needs to be cleaned yet by: (1) removing configurations which have no cases; and (2) sorting by consistency and then filling in the empty column which is the resistance fuzzy set. After cleaning, fewer rows will exist and some will be 'positive' configuration, marked 1, whereas many others will be 'negative' configurations, marked 0. My consistency cutoff point for a positive configuration varied from model to model but was around 0.77 in the final models. (Microsoft product screen shot(s) reprinted with permission from Microsoft Corporation).

of structure. Here the patterns were more varied. Agency takes many forms and involves complex strategies. Pacifying an employer one month would be followed by an assertive bargaining stance or an argument the next month. Those who had arguments turning into court cases might still behave submissively with the next employer. Mies's observation that women are submissive and exploited in Andhra Pradesh rural labour markets can still be applied to some women and men of the working class today (Mies 1982). Unfortunately, the bad farming conditions and rapid modernisation are also causing a wave of farmer suicides which has been well documented (Chindarkar 2007). It is widely thought that men are predominantly the ones committing suicide due to agrarian crisis (Mohanty 2005). In such conditions, the workers told us that they bide their time and choose their arguments carefully. They were cautious about being interviewed and like the idea of using pseudonyms (aliases). Many chose their own aliases such as 'Gold Man' (*Bangarappa),* which has very positive connotations of dignity. Many women had bought cows and this added to their dignity as well as their bargaining power. Having cows was considered to be a household characteristic. Family members shared the work of the cow management. However, women are now more frequently considered personally the owner of the cows because the cows are for milk production and not for ploughing. Less than 5% of local cattle were for pulling ploughs (based on random sample survey data, N = 187).

The results from the fuzzy-set analysis are summarised in Table 29.4. Table 29.4A shows the initial results, and Table 29.4B shows a simplified result after weakening the assumptions that go into the analysis. The only assumption made here in 29.4B is that we are agnostic about predicting what outcome might have occurred for the absent combinations of conditions.

In this table, coverage measures the proportion of cases that are within the group

Table 29.4   Fuzzy-set QCA results for resistance (N = 39)

A. Unreduced form

Sufficient conditions for resistance fuzzy to be high:

	Raw Coverage	Consistency
ASSETS*EDUCATION*dalit*smallville*WETACCESS+	0.240	0.836
ASSETS*education*DALIT*SMALLVILLE*HAVECOWS+	0.075	0.831
ASSETS*education*DALIT*WETACCESS*HAVECOWS+	0.077	0.834
ASSETS*dalit*SMALLVILLE*WETACCESS*HAVECOWS+	0.161	0.734
assets*education*dalit*smallville*wetaccess*HAVECOWS+	0.061	0.910
ASSETS*education*DALIT*smallville*wetaccess*havecows+	0.031	0.837
ASSETS*EDUCATION*dalit*SMALLVILLE*wetaccess*havecows	0.040	1.000

solution coverage: 0.650
solution consistency: 0.830

The coverage figures for each part of the solution are the raw coverage. There is some overlap between the configurations covered here. The cutoff of coverage for the fuzzy-set outcome to be deemed positive was 0.77.

B. Reduced form in which the contradictory configurations are specified as 'don't cares' rather than 'removed'

Sufficient conditions for resistance fuzzy to be high:

	Raw Coverage	Consistency
ASSETS*DALIT*smallville+	0.110	0.877
ASSETS*SMALLVILLE*wetaccess+	0.133	0.905
EDUCATION*smallville*WETACCESS+	0.271	0.802
dalit*SMALLVILLE*HAVECOWS+	0.208	0.746

solution coverage: 0.686
solution consistency: 0.812

The cutoff of coverage for the fuzzy-set outcome to be deemed positive was 0.77.

represented by the configuration. This proportion is calculated using Boolean algebra to get a ratio. Boolean algebra for fuzzy sets is an algebra that uses 'AND' and 'OR' for fuzzy sets; AND means intersection, and OR means union. (See Ragin [2008] for a bivariate explanation and Smithson and Verkuilen [2006] for the multivariate algebra.) The coverage ratio is the intersection of the cases in the configuration to the total number of cases. Consistency, on the other hand, is a ratio that shows how accurately the configuration is sufficient for the outcome to have occurred, within that configuration only.

In Rihoux and Ragin (2008), an algebraic definition of both ratios is provided. For the study of sufficient causes, the minimum of $\{X_i, Y_i\}$ is very important because it allows us to calculate the proportion of cases in which the outcome, Y_i, is lower than the causal variate X_i. ('Lower' in ordinal, not cardinal, measurement terms.) This ratio can be represented as Coverage $(Y_i \leq X_i) = \sum(\min(X_i, Y_i)) / \sum(Y_i)$. As X_i can be a vector of conditions (i.e. a mixture of fuzzy sets), this algebra can be extended to the multivariate case (Rihoux and Ragin 2008, chapter 3, p. 11). The numerator of coverage is visible in an X–Y plot as the horizontal distance from the axis to each point in the graph. For sufficiency to be strongly supported by the data, most points should lie in the upper left, not the lower right diagonal. We are measuring how close the cases lie to the diagonal line, relative to the average.

However, consistency is defined by using a different denominator (Rihoux and Ragin 2008, chapter 3, p. 17). X_i consistency is the relative scale of the sum of the $\min\{X_i, Y_i\}$ to the sum of all the cases. Here, counting the $\min\{X_i, Y_i\}$ focuses on those cases whose ordinal Y value exceeds the X value – again the upper left triangle. In other words, outcomes only give a high value of Consistency (for sufficiency) if the outcome is ordinally higher than the causal factor. This is where QCA becomes non-symmetrical in Y. If we reverse the procedure and study not-Y, we would get different results. The specific ratio that is used to measure consistency is represented as Consistency $(Y_i \leq X_i) = \sum(\min(X_i, Y_i)) / \sum(X_i)$.

Ragin defines consistency as follows: (1) for crisp sets: 'A straightforward measure of the consistency of set relations using crisp sets: the proportion of cases with a given cause or combination of causes that also display the outcome' (Ragin 2008, chapter 3, p. 5); (2) for fuzzy sets: 'One straightforward measure of set-theoretic consistency using the fuzzy membership scores is simply the sum of the consistent membership scores in a causal condition or combination of causal conditions divided by the sum of all the membership scores in a cause or causal combination' (Ragin 2008, chapter 3, p. 5).

Causal necessity is measured using the same concepts with different measurement equations. Specifically the Boolean denominators are switched around (see Rihoux and Ragin 2008, chapter 3 for details). In the fsQCA software, the causal analysis of sufficiency is found in the 'analyse ≪fuzzy set≫ truth table algorithm' menu option, but the causal analysis of necessity is found separately under 'analyse ≪necessary conditions≫'.

DISCUSSION: THE MIXED-METHODS QCA APPROACH USES VARIATES, NOT VARIABLES

In this chapter, I have examined social data using an iterative realist methodology based on mixed-methods data collection. The chapter began by noting that hypothesis testing, exploration and retroduction were all going to be carried out. In the middle of the chapter I even conducted a statistical regression to test or 'check out' a hypothesis

that was expected to hold in the study area. This hypothesis was a structuralist one arising from Marxian class theory. It found support in the larger dataset (N = 187) for an education outcome, but class was not found in the smaller dataset (N = 39) to influence resistance in the labour market very much. The main effect of class was simply that if one is not working class then one does not 'resist' as workers may do. However, among the three working classes: 'worker', 'worker with land' and 'farmer', resistance was spread out in ways not directly predictable by assets. Exploring the structuralist hypothesis more might involve further research on individuals and group resistance. Thus instead of 'falsifying' the hypothesis, I moved on to exploring the situation and retroducing what has caused the data to follow the patterns that it does follow. For this, QCA was useful.

The fuzzy-set analysis seemed to be testing hypotheses, because it had a cause-and-effect interpretation in my research, but in fact I was trying out different models to develop a deeper understanding of causal relationships, not in the *whole sample* but in different groups of configurations. Looking closely at Table 29.4B, we find that overall consistency was 0.81 (quite good) and coverage 0.69 (not as wide as we might have found if class structure determined agency). The intriguing finding is that causality varies between configurations. Specifically, the first two lines of the result read:

RESISTFZ = ASSETS*DALIT*smallville

+ ASSETS*SMALLVILLE*wetaccess

In other words, having a lot of assets was sufficient to cause resisting if a household of Dalit caste group was in the smaller village, and did not have access to wetland. (Recall that + means 'or', and * means 'and' in Boolean notation.) These two configurations only covered a small proportion of the cases, though. The rest of the solution reads:

RESISTFZ = EDUCATION*smallville

*WETACCESS + dalit*SMALLVILLE

*HAVECOWS

Each of these two configuration covers about 20% of the cases. One situation where formal education is high and there is wetland; and another sufficient set of conditions is where the non-Dalit household in the small village has cows. In a broad sense, economic resources matter for all the sufficient combinations (wetland, cows, etc.). However, land ownership or tenancy in itself was not sufficient to cause someone to resist the demands made by employers.

This summary ignores the other cases, each falling into smaller groups of negative or unique configurations. However, I have studied all the configurations in detail. I have also written qualitative analyses of seven of the case households (see several Global Poverty Research Group working papers and Olsen, 2008). Thus my qualitative, interpretive and exploratory work is more central here than the testing of hypotheses. I felt that I was understanding the effects of structure better, as well as learning about other factors in the village, while I studied the case-study data.

Thus the research methodology was not just hypothesis testing. Even in so far as I did test hypotheses, my grounding assumption was that causality was not going to be universal within the 39 cases. Therefore the correct word for RESISTFZ, ASSETS and the other causal conditions is not 'variables', but 'variates' (Byrne 2002; and see chapter 5). The variates may not apply across all cases. They cannot really be called variables in social statisticians' usual sense.

CONCLUSION

This chapter has illustrated a case-study research method in a pair of Indian villages. The data were organised both at the person level and at the household level using Excel® and NVivo. The persons were nested in households. Other levels that were studied included social classes and villages. These were non-nested with households and with

each other. Non-nested cases are in an N-to-N relation to each other, whereas nested cases are in a 1-to-N relation to each other. The data were in this particular instance not held in Access, but in a series of different software packages that enabled the use of cluster analysis in SPSS (Figure 29.5) and of qualitative comparative analysis in fsQCA. Random sampling played a role at an early stage of the research, where N = 187, yet the 39 main household cases were not randomly sampled, but instead were a quota sample that was embedded within a larger random sample. The methodology included some realist assumptions about the kind of outcome that was of interest – here, how workers and small farmers relate to the landlord class – and included doing retroduction (asking why) not only on this outcome but on the data themselves. An iterative process began with qualitative enquiry in re-analysing semi-structured interviews, then moved to a QCA stage where configurations and patterns were explored, next moved to cluster analysis to simplify the outcome variable and finally concluded with a causal analysis (see Byrne 2005; see also Chapter 5).

The findings based on the causal analysis gave new insights into class relations in the area. For example, structures of access to land – especially wetland – proved important as factors enabling resistance to landlords' exploitative and tying behaviours. Whereas class was initially specified in terms of employment relations and assets, the QCA indicates that wetland is a different kind of asset from dryland. Owning wetland with water was a very important differentiating factor among the workers and small farmers. Other important factors included having a person migrate to the city; and education. We allowed education to be a fuzzy set at household level because of proximate sharing of school-based skills. This enabled the causal relationship with resistance to show through in some configurations. Conformity with landlord demands was also widespread but especially among the poorest house-holds.

*IndiaTenancy39Cases7vars.sav [DataSet2] - SPSS Data Editor

File Edit View Data Transform Analyze Graphs Utilities Window Help

31 : VAR00014   non-kuulie class

	Nonkuulie	conform	avoid	exit	resist	innovate	join	TSC 6792	TSC 1079	VAR00014	TSC 6084	var	var	var	var	var
1	.00	1.00	2.00	1.00	.00	.00	.00	1	1	migrants, exiters	1					
2	.00	3.00	1.00	1.00	.00	1.00	1.00	2	1		1					
3	.00	2.00	1.00	1.00	1.00	.00	.00	1	1		1					
4	.00	.00	.00	1.00	.00	1.00	1.00	1	1		1					
5	.00	.00	.00	1.00	.00	.00	.00	1	1		1					
6	.00	2.00	1.00	1.00	.00	1.00	.00	1	1		1					
7	.00	.00	.00	1.00	.00	.00	.00	1	1		1					
8	.00	.00	.00	1.00	.00	1.00	.00	1	1		1					
9	.00	.00	.00	1.00	.00	.00	.00	1	1		1					
10	.00	.00	1.00	1.00	.00	.00	.00	1	1		1					
11	.00	.00	1.00	1.00	1.00	1.00	.00	1	1		1					
12	.00	.00	1.00	1.00	.00	3.00	.00	2	2	joiners and resisters	4					
13	.00	3.00	3.00	1.00	1.00	1.00	1.00	2	2		4					
14	.00	2.00	2.00	.00	2.00	1.00	1.00	2	2		4					
15	.00	.00	.00	.00	.00	1.00	2.00	2	2		4					
16	.00	1.00	1.00	1.00	1.00	2.00	1.00	2	2		4					
17	.00	.00	3.00	.00	1.00	1.00	2.00	2	2		4					
18	.00	.00	1.00	.00	.00	2.00	.00	2	2		4					
19	.00	.00	1.00	1.00	1.00	1.00	2.00	2	2		4					
20	.00	1.00	1.00	.00	.00	.00	.00	1	3	conformers	2					
21	.00	2.00	.00	.00	1.00	.00	.00	1	3		2					
22	.00	1.00	1.00	.00	4.00	.00	.00	1	3		2					
23	.00	2.00	1.00	.00	1.00	.00	.00	1	3		2					
24	.00	1.00	.00	.00	1.00	.00	1.00	1	3		2					
25	.00	3.00	1.00	.00	1.00	.00	.00	1	3		2					
26	.00	4.00	.00	.00	3.00	.00	.00	1	3		2					
27	.00	1.00	1.00	.00	1.00	.00	.00	1	3		2					
28	.00	.00	1.00	.00	.00	.00	.00	1	3		2					
29	.00	5.00	.00	.00	1.00	.00	.00	1	3		2					
30	.00	4.00	.00	.00	.00	.00	.00	1	3		2					
31	1.00	.00	1.00	.00	.00	.00	.00	3	4	non-kuulie class	3					
32	1.00	.00	.00	.00	.00	1.00	2.00	3	4		3					
33	1.00	.00	1.00	1.00	.00	1.00	.00	3	4		3					
34	1.00	.00	.00	.00	.00	.00	.00	3	4		3					
35	1.00	.00	.00	.00	.00	2.00	.00	3	4		3					
36	1.00	.00	.00	1.00	.00	.00	.00	3	4		3					
37	1.00	.00	.00	.00	.00	.00	.00	3	4		3					
38	.00	2.00	1.00	.00	3.00	3.00	3.00	2	5	/ mixalso conformed.	4					
39	.00	5.00	1.00	1.00	3.00	3.00	.00	2	5	/ mixed/ conformedjoi	4					
40																
41																
42																
43																

Data View / Variable View

SPSS Processor is ready

Figure 29.5 SPSS data for 39 household interviews during cluster analysis. The data are sorted here by the early cluster analysis in column 9. The final cluster analysis used shows here in column 11 and some labels in column 10 that correspond to the findings in column 9. (Microsoft product screen shot(s) reprinted with permission from Microsoft Corporation).

REFERENCES

Agarwal, B. 2003a 'Gender and land rights revisited: exploring new prospects via the state, family and market' *Journal of Agrarian Change* 3: 184–224.

Agarwal, B. 2003b 'Women's land rights and the trap of neo-conservatism: a response to Jackson' *Journal of Agrarian Change* 3(4): 571–585.

Basu, K.A., Narayan, D. and Ravallion, M. 2001 'Is literacy shared within households? Theory and evidence for Bangladesh' *Labour Economics* 8(6): 649–665.

Byrne, D. 2002 *Interpreting Quantitative Data.* London: Sage.

Byrne, D. 2005 'Complexity, configuration and cases' *Theory, Culture and Society* 22(10): 95–111.

Byrne, D. 2008 'Using cluster analysis, QCA and NVIVO in relation to the establishment of causal configurations with pre-existing large N datasets – machining hermeneutics' in D. Byrne and C. Ragin (Eds) *Handbook of Case-Study Research Methods.* London: Sage, Chapter 14.

Chindarkar, N. 2007 'A comparative analysis of farmers' suicides in Andhra Pradesh, India' *Methodological Innovations Online* 2(2).

Danermark, B. 2001 *Explaining Society: An Introduction to Critical Realism in the Social Sciences.* London, New York: Routledge.

Grootaert, C., Narayan, D. et al., 2004 'Measuring social capital: an integrated questionnaire'. World Bank Working Paper No 18.

Heil, J. 2003 'Levels of reality' *Ratio (new series)* XVI(3): 204–221.

Jackson, C. 2003 'Gender analysis of land: beyond land rights for women?' *Journal of Agrarian Change* 3(4): 453–480.

Jejeebhoy, S.J. and Sathar, Z.A. 2001 'Women's autonomy in India and Pakistan: the influence of religion and region' *Population and Development Review* 27(4): 687.

Jones, V.N. and Woolcock, M. 2007 'Using mixed methods to assess social capital in low income countries: a practical guide'. Online. Available: http://

www.bwpi.manchester.ac.uk/resources/Working-Papers/12jones-woolcock-mixedmethods.pdf.

Kapadia, K. 1995 *Siva and Her Sisters: Gender, Caste and Class in Rural South India*. Boulder, CO: Westview Press.

Kent, R. 2008 'Using fsQCA: a brief guide and workshop for fuzzy-set qualitative comparative analysis'. Teaching Paper No 3. Manchester: The Cathie Marsh Centre, University of Manchester. Online. Available: http://www.ccsr.ac.uk/publications.

Mayoux, L. 1993 'A development success story: low caste entrepreneurship and inequality – an Indian case-study' *Development and Change* 24(3): 541–568.

Mies, M. 1982 *The Lace Makers of Narsapur: Indian Housewives Produce for the World Market*. London: Zed Books.

Mohanty, B.B. 2005 'We are like the living dead': farmer suicides in Maharashtra, western India' *Journal of Peasant Studies* 32(2): 243–276.

Nadkarni, M.V. 2002 'Review article: land reforms: a bus that India missed which may never come again' *Indian Journal of Agricultural Economics* 57(4): 750–761.

Olsen, W.K. 1997 'Crops, debt and labour in two South Indian villages 1994–1995' ESRC *Data Archive Study* Number 3927.

Olsen, W.K. 2004 'Methodological triangulation and realist research: an Indian exemplar' in B. Carter and C. New (Eds) *Realism and Empirical Research*. London: Routledge Taylor & Francis, Chapter 6.

Olsen, W.K. 2006 'Pluralism, poverty, and sharecropping: cultivating open-mindedness in poverty studies' *Journal of Development Studies* 42(7): 1130–1157.

Olsen, W.K. 2008a 'Beyond sociology: structure, agency, and strategy among tenants in India' *Asian Journal of Social Sciences* (in press).

Olsen, W.K. 2008b 'Aspiration paradox in Indian micro-finance: a difficulty and an opportunity for debate'. Brooks Working Papers Series. Online. Available: http://www.bwpi.manchester.ac.uk/resources/Working-Papers/.

Olsen, W.K. and Neff, D. 2007 'Informal agricultural work habits and practices in an Indian context'

Global Poverty Research Group Working Paper No 79. Online. Available: http://www.gprg.org [accessed December 2007].

Patnaik, U. 1976 'Class differentiation within the peasantry: an approach to analysis of Indian agriculture' *Review of Agriculture Economic and Political Weekly*: A81–A101.

Ragin, C. 2008 *Redesigning Social Inquiry: Fuzzy Sets and Beyond*. Chicago: University of Chicago Press.

Ragin, C., Rubinson, C., Schaefer, D., Anderson, S., Williams, E. and Giesel, H. 2006 'User's guide to fuzzy-set/qualitative comparative analysis'. Department of Sociology, University of Arizona. Online. Available: http://www.compasss.org/Softwares.htm.

Rihoux, B. and Ragin, C. (Eds) 2008 *Configurational Comparative Analysis*. London: Sage Publications.

Roesch, M. 2005 'Année de la microfinance: l'over_dose ou changer de concept' *Revue Dialogue* 35: 53–57.

Sayer, A. 1997 'Essentialism, social constructionism, and beyond' *The Sociological Review* 24(3): 453–487.

Sharma, H.R. 2000 'Tenancy relations in rural India: a temporal and cross-sectional analysis' *Indian Journal of Agricultural Economics* 55(3).

Singh, S. 2003 *Contract Farming in India: Impacts on Women and Child Workers*. London: International Institute for Environment and Development (SIDA).

Smithson, M. and Verkuilen, J. 2006 *Fuzzy Set Theory: Applications in the Social Sciences*. Thousand Oaks, CA: Sage Publications.

Srivastava, R. 1989 'Tenancy contracts during transition: a study based on fieldwork in Uttar-Pradesh (India)' *Journal of Peasant Studies* 16(3): 339–395.

Swaminathan, P. 2002 'The violence of gender-biased development: going beyond social and demographic indicators' in K. Kapadia (Ed.) *The Violence of Development: The Politics of Identity, Gender and Social Inequalities in India*. London: Kali Books and Zed Press, pp. 69–141.

Venkateswarlu, D. 2003 'Female child bonded labour in hybrid cottonseed production in Andhra Pradesh' Hyderabad: Global Consultancy and Research Services. Online. Available: http://www.indianet.nl/sob.html#contents [accessed January 2008].

30

Causality and Interpretation in Qualitative Policy-Related Research

David Byrne, Wendy Olsen
and Sandra Duggan

The state in contemporary Britain is increasingly characterized by new kinds of reflexivity, mediated through systems and institutions of technical expertise – in which policy rooted in *evidence* [original emphasis] is central to its strategic practices, and thus to political discourse. These are expressed in many ways, but involve a central shift towards the primacy of (largely quantitative) knowledge as the foundation for an increasingly active and managerial model of state intervention across a range of policy fields. The emergence of this imperative towards *evidence-based* [original emphasis] policy in the final decades of the twentieth century is one important ideological feature of the apparently post-ideological character of contemporary British politics. In the British case this has involved the rapid development of policy mechanisms and agencies through which this work can be effectively delegated to the Academy. ... One outcome of this is that sociologists might now find themselves among the outsourced civil servants of the evidence based state. This is why political contests about methods are important.

(May 2005, pp. 526–527)

Amen to that. The point is of enormous significance for all social scientists. In an evidence-based polity, disputes about the character of methods move beyond academic politics – and any Sociology of Science must pay attention to claims for resources and status within the academy itself – into the political and administrative process as a whole. Here, the phrase 'as a whole' means not only into processes of policy formation at a high, for example national level but also into the detailed practices of implementation. Despite the rhetoric of the postmodernists, the evidence-based system of governance – because these developments extend beyond what is traditionally conceived of as the state – is explicitly modernist in terms of the justification it seeks in science for its policies and practices. This means that debates about method have profound general importance.

May was responding to an article by Payne et al. (2004), which reflected on the character of the methods employed by contributors to a set of mainstream sociology journals in the UK. The primary conclusion, of what was recognized by those authors to be an exploratory study, was that qualitative work predominated. There is an interesting issue about the tendency towards qualitative sociological work in the domain of the academy itself. However, the qualitative is not confined to the academy. Despite the recent assertion (in an otherwise quite useful piece) by the Chief Economist and Director of Analytical (interesting word) Services at the Department for Education and Skills that:

> Both government and social science fail too often in the only rare use of experimental evaluation and randomized control trials. From these comes the knowledge most valuable to policy makers. (Payne et al. 2004, p. 26)

there has been a massive turn towards qualitative work across the policy arena, precisely because quantitative approaches have proved inadequate in addressing the issues of context and complex causation that underlie social intervention at all stages, but particularly in relation to actual implementation. Put crudely but directly, experimental methods can never tell us 'what works' in complex systems. Let alone, this crucial methodological issue, it seems as if both policy makers and practitioners are primarily persuaded by grounded accounts that can illustrate by instantiation. In this context, it is really rather important to understand what policy researchers using qualitative methods think they are doing. In particular is their objective the demonstration of causality – however complex – as a basis for prediction – after all saying what works is to predict – or is it the establishment of thick descriptions which enable social actors – policy makers and practitioners – to transfer understanding of complex social processes in context from one locale of social action to another? Of course, in practice it may – in best Copenhagen tradition – be both things at once. However, the heuristic value of raising the question is considerable.

We were led to a belief in the nature and importance of this issue in a particular way. During 2004–2005 we ran a series of four workshops funded under the ESRC Research Methods Initiative that were concerned with research methods that emphasized the significance of cases rather than variables: 'Focusing on the Case'. Some fifty people participated in these workshops, most of them throughout the whole series. The workshops dealt with numerical taxonomy techniques – cluster analyses, configurational approaches – qualitative comparative analysis, qualitative statistical modelling and traditional field work based qualitative case studies. The participants were drawn from varied backgrounds and stages of their careers. Most were social scientists but some were biomedical or environmental scientists who worked in areas that brought them into contact with social processes. The great majority of participants were people who were 'applied social scientists' in that they had a clear view of the necessity for translating the findings of research into the development and improvement of policies and practices. As Weinstein (2000, p. 1) puts it they tended: '… to embrace an essentially pragmatic philosophy of science in which the ultimate test of a theory is the extent to which it can produce knowledge "that works"'.

The workshops combined demonstration of techniques with focus-group discussions in which participants discussed the implications of the techniques for their own understanding, practice and applied work. The programme was explicitly based on a dialogical approach to pedagogy. The organizers were both concerned to draw on the knowledge of participants and to respond to participants' views as to how the series should develop. The groups were 'unstructured' in terms of organization. The stimulus for discussion was a combination of documentary (including web page), lecture and demonstration introduction to a technique set in its methodological context. In the groups, people were simply asked to respond to these stimuli. The organizers participated in the groups as full members and there was a very clear development of discussion in which people drew both on the presented material and on previous discussions in the development of perspective and understanding. In proper dialogical fashion this was just as much the case for the workshop organizers as for other participants.

A variety of themes emerged in discussion but one that became immediately apparent, and that continued to be central to our discussions, was the contrast between research as a process of establishing causality, however complex and contingent that causality – and research as a process of interpretation in which the objective is to generate what Geertz calls 'thick description'. This is an ongoing issue in social research in general but what we noted in our discussions is that it is a central tension for applied social researchers who increasingly work in an environment that emphasizes the significance of systematic evidence as a basis for practice. Indeed, the development of schemata for evidence bases in the form of the Cochrane and Campbell collaborations privileges techniques that focus on simple causation alone. As Harrison (1998, p. 20) puts it:

> The pinnacle of the hierarchy is occupied by the RCT ... Other research methods are ranked lower in the hierarchy, with other types of *controlled* study second to the RCT and uncontrolled methods a poor third. In practice advocates of RCTs tend to regard uncontrolled methods as suitable only for hypothesis building with a view to an eventual controlled study.

Even in the quantitative tradition, this emphasis on the RCT is rather primitive. There is a developed literature on complex causal modelling that does try to address issues of complex causation and the implications of interaction, but the continued emphasis on single causation is central to the construction of hierarchies of evidential procedures.

Applicants for the workshop series were asked to write short notes outlining their reasons for wishing to participate in the exercise. Even at this initial stage, the centrality of the issue of just how research that went beyond the programme of simple causality established through a reductionist programme

was explicitly stated by several of them. Four extracts from these notes illustrate this:

> Policy-makers want researchers to tell them 'what works', and this usually means wanting to know whether or not *x* will cause *y*. I believe that the workshops will help me in my work at the Centre by investigating what a variety of qualitative and quantitative methods can achieve and exploring how the two types of research can be integrated. Causality and 'what works' have traditionally been the domain of quantitative research. Qualitative methods are increasingly being recognized as providing important information for policy development, but are confined to the area of explaining why policies work (rather than if they work) and are still often considered suspiciously unscientific. And yet qualitative methods, by being able to escape the positivistic framework of quantitative methods, have great potential for exploring social complexity. Can qualitative methods be 'hard' enough to be credible whilst still being 'soft' enough to have rich explanatory power? Can quantitative and qualitative methods, often resting on competing epistemological and ontological foundations, be truly integrated? (P39 – a policy researcher with a first degree in Maths and Philosophy)

> I am interested in case-based methods as a means of understanding policy in terms of the complexity of the setting. In much policy-oriented research it seems that the attempt is to understand the impact of an 'initiative' by abstracting it from its setting. My early experience in researching health services pointed our how inappropriate this approach was because national policy cannot be applied uniformly, but interacts with local context to create very different sets of conditions and, therefore, services. The unit of the case therefore allows the researcher to pay full attention to the significance of context, to understand interaction and the intended and unintended consequences of policy implementation. (P9 – a sociologist working in health and related areas)

> One is that I have been doing some research for the Department of Health in my last job, which was about intermediate care for older people but it was using a case-study method, and I thought that was a really valuable way of trying to get hold of the complexity of a whole set of policy interventions. Because there is no way which you can identify a policy intervention in absence of its context. So to look at a health services or social services intervention in the absence of understanding the way that housing and other policies within health work in that locality is a fairly pointless exercise. So that was the value of the approach. (P9 – as above)

> Like many other social scientists, I have been torn between the dual demands of identifying both patterns and mechanisms in social life. The difficulty

is related to the contentious issue of quantity versus quality because quantitative methods such as statistical modelling and network analysis are good at displaying the patterns in a large population but they have been accused of only scratching the surface. Even though many researchers are aware of the caveat that statistical associations should not be taken as evidence of causality, they still tend to do so, consciously or unconsciously. *On the other hand, others rely on case studies in order to find 'deeper' meanings and causes, without worrying very much about the cases that are not covered by a particular investigation* [our emphasis]. Similarly to the situation for quantitative methods, although these social scientists know that conclusions based on a few cases may lose their validity if applied to other cases, very often they derive statements in a general manner. Of course, we should not make the distinction in a too restrictive way, as it depends on the definition of a case. However, we cannot avoid such annoying issue if we talk about the unit of empirical investigation or if we compare two projects with the same empirical design. (P46 – a sociologist with a background in statistics)

The issue of complexity of causation is plainly evident in these remarks and this continued to be of significance throughout our discussions. It is important to note that the idea of complex causation was simply agreed by all participants in all discussions. No one at all argued for the primacy of a reductionist programme in which causal patterns could be decomposed into components that could be addressed by controlled experiment, (although some participants did support experimentation as part of the repertoire of techniques). This understanding of complex cause was inherently linked to the idea of local specificity. However, participants generally did not endorse the notion that knowledge was completely idiographic. Instead, they were anxious to find some way in which cases studies could be generalized beyond the specific instances that are the locales of particular research projects. Three passages illustrate this concern:

Trying to find out how it works you can say how it works in one authority we want to know how it works overall because if you say this is how it works for us and this is how it works for another authority that doesn't neither of those necessarily in itself mean anything for the next authority. And what we don't want to do everything is contingent

everything depends on context then you can't learn any lessons for the next one and so you want to look at some of those processes and changes I suppose. I am not sure. (P24 – a health scientist with a background in psychology now working on policy research)

Can I ask the question – just going back one conversation that you were saying in a sense you know case studies – how can they be used, who are we trying to influence and thinking about trying to influence policy makers. And you know there is all these buzz words that come out but, at the moment, people are saying it is evidence-based policy and we are going to get that from participatory methods etc. So, to what extent and what are the limitations of focusing on the case or the case studies? When do case studies actually offer evidence which is meaningful? When would we all feel comfortable or when is it just, as how I describe it, as an insight? Because we have talked about the fact that it could be a unique situation, may not be replicable, could only be found in that certain set of circumstances. Obviously, the policy maker will be saying ok that's fine but I am not going to take a risk to make an investment just on a singular case. Or would they, if there was a number of cases and that represented a body of evidence? So my question from your own experiences and potentially for people who have got to design projects to provide that evidence, to give that security – how do you overcome that or to what level – how do you answer that question? (P40 – an ecologist with a background both in ecology and in business and management)

I don't think people can use one case to show the evidence. A single case study is always done for illustration purposes to me, to demonstrate how things work within one case. You gain insight in that way – all the details – you know how it works, you know the dynamics, the process. You cannot gain that detailed information with hundreds or thousands of cases – you cannot do that. You cannot do it one by one and then come together. Because you have got to simplify things when you have a lot of cases. To me the strategy, we can categorize the context of the subject of the population of your study - you can categorize, for example, different neighbourhoods, different cities or different people. And then you select some cases from each context or each group to show that we have something and then I think you can talk about evidence. Because then we are talking about something that represents the larger population or the larger object. Otherwise any single case study can never show any evidence, to me. (P46 – a sociologist with a statistical background)

Here, it is important to consider the distinctive character of comparison of cases that we would argue should be central to policy-based case studies in contrast to the approach adopted by academic work concerned with 'theory building'.[1] Systematic comparative analysis is neither: '… the integrative case method [which] regards the micro-context as a setting in which a particular "macro" principle … reveals itself' nor the single site 'extended case method' (Burawoy 1991, p. 6) although it can employ the procedures of both approaches in the construction of its account. Indeed, it might best be understood as a multi-site version of the extended case method in which, to use the terminology of critical realism, complex and contingent generative mechanisms are expressed in local contexts in accordance with Byrne's (2002) modification of Pawson and Tilly's (1997) formula:

Context @ Mechanism → Outcome

That is, context in interaction with mechanism generates outcome.

Perhaps the key phrase here is 'systematic comparison'. Lots of case-study work has been ideographic – demonstrative on the basis of single account – or at best comparison has been simply part of a narrative without either a clear understanding of complex and contingent causality or a systematic underpinning procedure for exploring the range of potential complex causes.

Interestingly, Pawson and Tilley's work was explicitly cited by one workshop participant as illustrative of this point in policy application:

I think that is really interesting what you have just said and quite sobering. I don't know how many are familiar with the Pawson and Tilley book, *Realistic Evaluation*, but there is an argument in there that criminological research went through a very negative phase where all the studies seemed to be suggesting nothing works and they developed a critique of that by saying nothing worked because these studies were based on large-scale data exercises where it was the average all the time. They argue for a case-based approach on the basis that things work sometimes for some people, and sometimes in some places, but sometimes not for some people, and sometimes not in some other places. That was the message to policy makers that that book makes: that things are very context

dependent and you cannot say that something doesn't work, or something does work – it's that some things work in certain circumstances. And that's where I think there is a danger in the case-study approach, which is the sort of pen portrait of good practice, 'cos I think they can lack rigour and actually can send quite misleading messages but, where it's case study as part of a planned research design that's looking for the influence of context as well as the influence of the intervention, sort of the intervention and how it works out in different contexts – I think that's really important. It's getting that round the head of policy makers though is really difficult – partly because of what a centralized state we are – it has to be national policy. And probably the most receptive audience for this type of stuff, is for example local authorities or community organizations that know the context. (P5 a geographer working in policy-related areas)

Configurational approaches in the form of qualitative comparative analysis (QCA) (Ragin 1987, 2000) are particularly suited to small-N comparisons of cases in which there is a movement through from detailed qualitative interpretation of traditional qualitative material in the form of documents, observational field notes and intereview/focus-group transcripts to the specification of components that can be entered into QCA procedures in order to establish multiple causal configurations. In other words, such approaches can offer *multiple* answers to the question 'what works?' Moreover, they can do so in relation to specification of type. To exemplify, local authorities can compare themselves with other authorities that have mostly the same configurations of characteristics/processes but differ in one or more respects, and do better by some criterion. The factors that might have a beneficial effect for that type of local authority – cases with similar configurations – can be identified. This technique inherently addresses the issues that derive from path dependency. We might have a set of authorities that are in the same sets with regard to population size, resource base, ethnic composition of populations and spatial distribution of population. Some may do well by Audit Commission measurement criteria; others may do less well. QCA techniques might identify that some combination of administrative management and political leadership is the distinguishing element between those that do well and those that don't. In essence, this amounts to a systematic and IT-based development of the method of differences with differences allowed to be multiple rather than single.

It is important to note that this approach to causality has much more in common with general philosophical discussion, which focuses on cause in relation to events – to effects understood as qualitative changes of kind – in contrast with statistical modelling, which sees effects as incremental changes in the value of a dependent variable as caused by changes in a set of independent variables (see Spirtes et al. 2004, p. 448). Whereas many policy indicators are continuous in form, in actual administrative practice they are combined in 'starring systems' to produce differentiated and ordered categories. In such approaches, there is an implicit understanding of membership of a category as an event. QCA outcomes are events, in the form of current stable situation of a system's trajectory.

However, a key issue for several participants was that QCA and related approaches seemed to represent a reversion from a qualitative and interpretative mode of reasoning to a causal and quantitative approach. The component of the last preliminary statement that we have underlined outlines the background to this issue very clearly. This participant, without endorsing the position, recognized that for many researchers the search for causality was inappropriate. What they were interested in was deeper meaning. This is of course a strongly held position in the interpretive social sciences and is perhaps most coherently expressed in Geertz's advocacy of 'thick description'. However, it is extremely important to recognize that it is not just a view held explicitly by social scientists but also, essentially implicitly, by practitioners – despite the apparent hegemony of reductionist causal reasoning as a foundation for evidence-based practice.

Of course, this dilemma is general in applied social research. The organizers of a recent ESRC seminar series posed the question precisely – albeit as one among a wider set relating primarily to the relationship between researchers and participants: 'How does thick description and the rich social interpretation it affords relate to the need for precise methods of explanation and generalizable conclusions?'

Their description of the current marginality of this crucial issue despite its central importance is one with which we would wholly accord:

> Exploring these questions is a priority within the larger project of making what social scientists do more meaningful, more useful and more accountable. At present, however, such understanding is partial: pursued at the margins of research projects when time and resources allow, and rarely shared. Moreover, theoretical debates about problems of method have become dissociated from practical questions of research design, delivery and dissemination. (Methods in Dialogue: http://www.uel.ac.uk/cnr/mid/whatis.htm)

In an abstract for that series, Greenhalgh repeated the common assertion that researchers and policy makers inhabit different worlds. However, evidence in relation to the use practitioners, if not necessarily policy makers, make of research findings suggests that this might not be the case. As one workshop participant put it:

> We had a discussion about this about the power of numbers but there is also a power of words perhaps you don't kind of appreciate or maybe it's not appreciated by your power structures but certainly once you move out into the practice world, the snippet that comes form a qualitative study can be just as powerful and lasting even though it like one snippet one quote that somebody said like a table of numbers. (P28 – a health scientist working in health research)

The reflection by another participant on the way in which educational practitioners tend to reject 'non-located' generalization but want to understand practices in specific contexts, illustrates this. In essence, educational practitioners want 'thick description' rather than the abstracted 'thin description'. Indeed their approach seems to be an intuitive version of what Bourdieu (2003) has called participant objectification – they want to know the other and its context in relation to that which they know about themselves and their own context:

> Qualitatively based case studies aim to interpret and make assertions from their investigations, rather than make statistical generalizations. Even so, by exploring phenomena within one undergraduate nursing programme from an instrumental case-study perspective, other similar programmes are likely to benefit. For example, in comparing urban and rural schools, Stake showed that although the different groups frequently reject examples from each other's practices, this becomes much less common once they have examined their case studies. He suggested instead that they find commonalities in process and situation that become useful to inform educational practice. (P29 – a nurse educator with postgraduate qualifications in management working in health-related areas)

Another participant who had a quantitative background made a set of observations, over several discussions, which commanded general support from other participants to the effect that in the policy formation process as well, context and narrative matter far more in influencing policy makers. Indeed, quantitative studies may have status precisely because policy makers do not understand them.

> Ultimately, everything that we do has to convince some policy maker either to make some policy changes or to give us money to do things. In a sense, that's what you are trying to do – to convince people that you have got a way of changing the situation which is the effect of something else. So all research must start with the effects thing – saying this is what's happening, there is deprivation or someone is ill or something – which is an effect of something else and that is what you want to change and then you start working backwards. And what you said about policy makers not being able to add up three and four, I think this is partly the explanation of why they give so much more value to numbers because they don't understand them and therefore if you can write them a story which they will understand and they think why do I pay scientist to do all that. (P24 – a policy researcher with a background in health science and psychology)
> The way they feed in to policy process, the Minister picks out one snippet because they like snippets and so we do this ginormous report

an all-side report and presentation and all the contextualization that we can think of is within there and then it goes through up to the ranks of the policy makers and then it is fed into the Minister and the Minister asks 'can you give me some highlights' and they ask for four sentences which they like. (P24 – as above)

It is interesting to compare this account with one of the surprisingly few studies in the formal policy literature that has utilized the idea of 'thick description'. Thompson (2001, p. 65) argues for thick description asserting that it has two major benefits:

> As ethnography, it privileges the subject, and because of its 'thickness' it makes policy analysis accessible to members of the general public so that they can understand the issues at stake.

This is an interesting fix on thick description but it is a perfectly reasonable one. Geertz has always rejected any post-modernist relativism and argued to the effect that thick description is a realist project – without using that particular terminology.[2] Thompson, whilst arguing clearly for a social science, is arguing for thick description because it generates accessible and understandable science. Compare this with Bourdieu in a piece of exceptional clarity, which might almost be taken as his valedictory engagement with English speaking social science:

> Participant objectivation undertakes to explore not the 'lived experience' of the knowing subject but the social conditions of possibility – and therefore the effects and limits – of that experience and, more precisely, of the act of objectivation itself. It aims at objectivizing the subjective relation to the object, which, far from leading to a relativistic and more-or-less antiscientific subjectivism, is one of the conditions of genuine scientific objectivity. (Bourdieu 2003, p. 282)

This is radically different from Freire's conception of dialogical engagement in participatory research, precisely because Bourdieu does privilege the social scientist – and yet, in a revealing and touching passage in this piece, he remarks on the way in which a key informant in his Bearn study – who happened to be his mother – provided him with a central clue as to the way in which marriage and familial arrangements were constructed in relation to domains of economic and cultural capital. Of course, this was a one-way conversation in terms of interpretation where Freire would insist on the raising the scientific account in dialogue with the informant. For Freire Burawoy's distinction between: '... the perspective of the participant who calls for understanding and the perspective of the observer who seeks causal explanation' (1991, p. 3) does not exist. What Thompson raises is the issue of the genuine accessibility of the meaning centred interpretive account although as our participant noted, this can have the dual disadvantage of appearing to be inherently non-scientific and at the same time being easily reduced to a simplistic and erroneous summary.

This raises the interesting question of the nature of the audience for this work. Plainly, Thompson wants to influence general democratic debate and Bourdieu's whole political engagement demonstrates that he had an essentially similar view of the role social science could play in informing political discussion and processes. Here, the actual character of contemporary politics matters. One participant remarked:

> The issue there is that what happens is the politicians or the policy makers or whoever it is they go out and talk to social scientists broadly social scientists from sociologists, economists, health researchers whatever and they want some kind of evidence and some kind of research done. But the politicians would like to have hard and fast answers, as if we are in the age of physics pre-Heisenberg. This is sort of roughly what is happening and these kinds of conditions ... what we do ... gets misread or misused because it doesn't work because nobody is willing to engage, so to speak, the social sciences that far to develop alternative scenarios and you talk about possible intended effects or unintended consequences and you see what kind of and to acknowledge that in this sense you have strategic choices. Of course, partly it is the political system that has the problem there because politicians – because of the nature of the political system – will tend to say that there is no alternative to what we are doing and so on. So you can't really open up this thing of 'are there different strategic choices – whether you need to do a, b, c, d'. And then it looks like we are supposed to provide the

> hard and fast answers which will undoubtedly – and it doesn't. (P2 – a sociologist working as an academic)

The interesting thing about this statement is that it describes the politics of governance in an era when the notion of ideological bases for politics has been abandoned. Alternative futures do exist and do depend on social action. What is done makes what will be. However, alternative futures are the futures that serve different interests in a deeply divided social order. In what Crouch (2000) has called 'post-democracy', the actual processes of governance have been rendered apolitical and technical. It is not so much that there is no alternative to the present – much of governance is directed at achieving various kinds of social change particularly in relation to the mantra of 'inclusion' – but rather that the notion of different and irreconcilable interest based conceptions of what change should be, cannot be admitted into the policy debate. If science does not provide one path to the future but rather offers different outcomes depending on actions now – the central implication of 'complexity science' in the social world – then social research necessarily becomes political rather than technical. Discussion of real strategic choice is dangerous and disturbing.

The same participant made a very similar point with formal reference to methodological debates in science:

> I have a critical realist intervention to this problem of effects-/cause-/policy-/evidence-informed, based or whatever. It seems to be from a critical realist point of view there seems to be fundamental flaw in the idea that if you do any research you can afterwards go and tell the policy maker what to do in the future. This is because any critical realist will need to acknowledge that the future is open and the best thing you can do is you can develop scenarios. You can say what the logic of the situation is at the present and you might be able to say something about the possible choices. You can develop scenarios about certain causes of actions and, if you are very good, you might be able to say that if you went down that road or you went down that road, those are the most likely intended outcomes that you will have. But what do we know about the unintended consequences that you might

get hit by? Therefore, so to speak, to ask anybody on the basis of research about the effects that is known now and then looks into the past to say what do in the future.... (P2 – as above)

CONCLUSION

Three themes emerge from the experience of the workshops – which in essence were a dialogical exercise in researching the researchers – taken in the context so well expressed by May in the epigraph to this chapter. The first is about the nature of meaningful evidence when we are dealing with complex systems. May notes that '... the primacy of (largely quantitative) knowledge as the foundation for an increasingly active and managerial model of state intervention across a range of policy fields'. And yet the experience of the researchers is that quantitative knowledge cannot work without a narrative. There is a major turn to qualitative work in part because it provides narratives. Of course, this is partly a matter of context. Although health, and indeed medical researchers were quite strongly represented in the workshop groups, even those who were clinicians were working with difficult, multi-character conditions, indeed with cases in the form of people who presented with lots of things all at once. For the clinical researchers, the issue was that the RCT breaks down when there is significant and complex interaction.

Most of the applied researchers, including health researchers, were working in areas of policy development and implementation. The large-N linear-modelling-based methods of traditional statistics were generally inappropriate for most of them because they were not working with large samples from theoretically infinite populations. There is, for example, no infinite population of English local authorities[3] and the actual 'data' about them are constructed in the process of qualitative research. The issue for these researchers was about how knowledge generated in field research – perhaps a better term than 'qualitative research' because numbers were used even if only in the form

of descriptive statistics although embedded in narrative accounts – could inform social action. This is usually understood in terms of generalizability but the argument between that approach and thick description moved far beyond its usual academic locale into a developed discussion about the way in which the audience for applied research actually thinks about what it is hearing and seeing.

The second theme is about the necessity for a politics not so much of method, as May puts it, but of methodology. There is a long history in the philosophy of social science of the perhaps uneasy but nonetheless real co-existence of a brute positivist approach to the use of the products of social research, especially but not exclusively the quantitative products, alongside an essentially relativist understanding of the epistemological status of those products and the methods used to construct them. The 'conventionalism' of sophisticated positivism is a pertinent example. This will not do! There is a politics to methodology. Both the grant-holders for the research project are card-carrying critical realists. Whilst making our position clear to workshop participants we did not seek to impose it, nor would the participants have stood for such imposition! However, the experience of the workshop discussions absolutely reinforced our commitment to the general explanatory logic of what Harvey (1996) has called 'complex realism'.[4]

It is worth reflecting a little more on these issues. In fact, when we use the phrase 'the politics of methodology' we are referring to two inter-linked domains. One is the academy and to use the word 'politics' in relation to academic debate is to go beyond the usual and formal account of academic work as taking the form of disputation founded on reason. In other words, we recognize that academics are organized into gangs with a different set of weapons but a no less vicious commitment to the defence of territory than the street gangs of the inner city. There are different discourses of research practice and methodology and these discourse are, in best Foucauldian style, sources of power and reward. So to challenge variable centred approaches to social research is to challenge a whole power structure in the academy based on the promotion of these methods as *the* answer to adequate causal explanation of the social world. That power structure has powerful allies in that its nomothetic project corresponds to the 'scientism', which, although now under serious challenge, still dominates 'the sciences' as a great estate of the academic realm. We agree partially with the conclusion of the report by the Gulbenkian Commission on the Restructuring of the Social Sciences on the future of the social sciences:

> In taking the natural sciences as a model they [the nomothetic social sciences] nurtured three kinds of expectations that have proved impossible to fulfil as stated in universalist form: and expectation of prediction; an expectation of management; both in turn premised on an expectation of quantifiable accuracy. Whereas matters of debate in the domain carved by the humanities were sometimes thought to rest on the subjective preferences of the researcher, the nomothetic social sciences built themselves on the premises that social achievement can be measured, and that measurements themselves can be agreed upon universally. (Gulbenkian Commission on the Restructuring of the Social Sciences 1996, p. 50)

Certainly, nomothetic scientist approaches based on transferring the language of variables to the social world has – in brutal summary – been largely useless. That said a different conception of measurement, basically a return to classification which allows for the exploration of the changes that matter, changes of kind, can help us to understand 'what works' provided we always add to the phrase 'what works' the other for phrase 'and for whom'. However, saying this is a fundamental challenge to powerful academic empires and great academic nobles. It is a revolutionary challenge and revolutions are not made without breaking eggs or egos or power bases.

The other domain of the politics of methodology is politics itself. Few politicians – the late Harold Wilson, a greatly distinguished economic statistician being the marked exception – have any real competence in relation

to the interpretation of quantitative data. Its role for them has, to a considerable extent, been magical. In practice most of the data with which they engage is either simple counts or the same counts turned into the numerator of a fraction with the denominator being the count, or supposed count, of some population. This is particularly the case in relation to the whole set of discrete indicator targets that dominate all areas of governance in the UK and increasingly are spreading like a rash across national and international governance systems. So we have enormous emphasis on crime rates, education success rates, waiting list times for operations and on composite indices of, for example multiple deprivation, constructed from sets of such indicators. Given that they are rates, they generally take the form of continuous variables and therefore can be 'handled' using linear methods, which deal with proportionate change in continuous variables. Although most (but perhaps not all) politicians can count, there is little evidence that they understand the output and limitations of, for example a logistic regression. Nonetheless, this looks like 'science', can be taken to be proof and serves as magic to underpin stories of progress on the basis of policy initiatives.

Case-based methods are much messier but that is exactly because they correspond to messy reality itself *and* they require narratives of difference, which include – necessarily – narratives of differential, indeed differentiated, outcomes. Some benefit and some lose but the story of universalism in contemporary governance does not work well if that differentiation is clearly identified. Universalist nomothetic models that 'fit the data' also fit rather well the requirements of a system of governance that asserts its universalist objectives and ignores the reality of social differentiation and consequence social conflict. In other words, case-based methods, precisely because they do represent complex and conflict-ridden social reality, are disturbing and difficult for governance processes that deny that conflict. Thus the politics of methodology has important consequences for the politics of politics itself.

Finally, there is a message both about pedagogy and research. The whole experience was dialogical; this reflected the 'status' of workshop participants. They were informed and articulate social (and other) scientists. We would not have worked with them in any other way but on the basis of explicit dialogue that respected their knowledge and ability to express it. In terms of pedagogy, this raises some interesting issues. Certainly, we would not engage with teaching first year students in the same way, although those with experience of adult education know that any adult participant does bring something to the dialogue. However, it does perhaps provide something of a model for advanced training. The ESRC tends to see advanced quantitative methods in terms very much of, to use Freire's phrase, banking education in which deficits in technique are deposited in minds which passively receive them. Well that won't do. We have to argue here.

There is also a message for research although this is more complex in terms of its implications. Social scientists do have understanding and technical abilities that are different from the subjects of our research. But – and reflecting the dialectical character of that word 'subject' – subjects of research are also subjects of verbs in action. They do things. These issues emerge most centrally in action-research and we will return to them in subsequent work. Here we can do no more than assert that they are crucial to engaged social research and cannot be handled without careful attention to the politics of methodology in theory and in practice.

NOTES

1. Again, of course, this is a heuristic distinction or rather a dichotomizing of what is essentially a continuum of purposes. Some work is wholly 'academic'. Some is wholly applied. A lot mixes both.

2. Although Burawoy (1991, p. 302) argues that Geertz's position abandons a notion of explanation external to the system under consideration.

3. Draper (1996) makes this point in an important and clear way in relation to studies of school

performance. The traditional basis of frequentist statistics is irrelevant when we have data about all the cases.

4. Neither of the quoted critical realist statements came from a workshop organizer.

REFERENCES

Bourdieu, R. 2003 'Participant objectification' *Journal of the Royal Anthropoligical Institution* 9(2): 281–294.

Burawoy, M. 1991 *Ethnography Unbound*. Berkley, CA: University of California Press.

Byrne, D.S. 2002 *Interpreting Quantitative Data*. London: Sage.

Crouch, C. 2000 *Coping with Post-democracy*. London: Fabian Society.

Draper, D. 1996 'Discussion of Goldstein and Spiegelhalter' *Journal of the Royal Statistical Society – Series A* 3: 416–418.

Gulbenkian Commission on the Restructuring of the Social Sciences 1996 *Open the Social Sciences*. Stanford, CA: Stanford University Press.

Harrison, S. 1998 'The politics of evidence based medicine in the UK' *Policy and Politics* 26(1): 15–31.

Harvey, D.L. and Reed, M.H. 1994 'The evolution of dissipative social systems' *Journal for the Theory of Social Behavior* 17(4): 371–411.

May, C. 2005 'Methodological pluralism, British sociology and the evidence-based state: a reply to Payne et al' *Sociology* 39(3): 519–528.

Pawson, R. and Tilly, N. 1997 *Realistic Evaluation*. London: Sage.

Payne, G., Williams, M. and Chamberlain, S. 2004 'Methodological pluralism in British sociology' *Sociology* 38: 153–163.

Ragin, C. 1987 *The Comparative Method*. Berkley, CA: University of California Press.

Ragin, C. 2000 *Fuzzy-Set Social Science*. Chicago: University of Chicago Press.

Spirtes, P., Scheines, R., Glymour, C., Richardson, T. and Meek, C. 2004 'Causal inference' in D. Kaplan (Ed.) *Sage Handbook of Quantitative Methodology for the Social Sciences*. London: Sage, pp. 447–478.

Thompson, W.B. 2001 'Policy making through thick and thin: Thick description as a methodology for communication and democracy' *Policy Sciences* 34: 63–77.

Weinstein, J. 2000 'The place of theory in applied sociology' *Theory and Science*. Online. Available: http://theoryandscience.icaap.org/content/vol001.001/01weinstein_revised.html.

31

Reflections on Casing and Case-Oriented Research

Charles C. Ragin

INTRODUCTION

'What Is a case?' was originally a conference that Howard Becker and I organized
almost two decades ago (Ragin and Becker
1992). The basic idea was to invite eight
distinguished scholars to offer their answers
to a question that seemed both foundational
and largely ignored. The eight were chosen
to yield a variety of answers, and vary they
did. One thing we found was that the 'case
question' was a Rorschach: a stimulus that
provoked diverse and revealing responses.
Just as the Rorschach test can reveal subtle
aspects of a person's personality, answers
to 'What Is a case?' reveal social scientists' varied methodological commitments and
their diverse epistemological and ontological
positions.

My co-editor for this Handbook, David
Byrne, shares with me the conviction that
the case concept is central to social research
and proposed that we do this Handbook in
part as a way to revisit core methodological
issues raised, but certainly not resolved, in

Ragin and Becker (1992). However, this book
goes far beyond its predecessor in several
important respects. First, it takes as its starting
point the centrality of case-oriented research
to contemporary social science and seeks to
improve its practice. One implicit goal of
Ragin and Becker (1992) was to make the
case for case-oriented research by bringing
the case concept to the foreground of social
science discourse (see also Feagin et al. 1991).
Comparing today with the early 1990s, it is
clear that the status of case-oriented work
has improved, and scholars can describe their
work as case-oriented without feeling awk-
ward or vulnerable to attack. Second, unlike
its predecessor, which was short on practical
advice, this Handbook is both conceptually
oriented and practically oriented. It not only
revisits conceptual issues addressed in the
previous work but also raises an array of
new issues, packaged around discussions of
a variety of case-oriented techniques. The
practical advice offered in the present book
spans the entire spectrum of case-oriented
inquiry, with a special emphasis on analytic

techniques that maintain the integrity of cases through the research process and also provide ways of viewing cases as coherent bundles of aspects and attributes (e.g. cluster analysis, correspondence analysis, single-case probabilities, qualitative comparative analysis). Third, many of the contributions to this Handbook explicitly engage the realist perspective in some way. In essence, to posit *cases* is to engage in ontological speculation regarding what is obdurately real but only partially and indirectly accessible through social science. Bringing a realist perspective to the case question deepens and enriches the dialogue, clarifying some key issues while sweeping others aside. For example, while it is clear that cases, at their very best, are invoked by researchers, it is also true that some case constructions are vastly and demonstrably superior to others, especially in terms of their degree of resonance with the objects of study.

This Handbook documents the considerable progress of the last two decades, both in case-based analytic procedures and in the discussion of conceptual issues linked to the case concept. The contributions to this Handbook – like the contributions to 'What is a case?' – underscore the importance of the case concept to social research and also its Rorschach nature. The case concept gets at the heart of what social scientists do and how they think about what they do. It is difficult to imagine an empirical social science that is also 'caseless.'

In this chapter, I offer several reflections on key issues raised in this handbook. First, I revisit the concept of 'casing' that I first elaborated in Ragin and Becker (1992). Then, I turn to several issues in applying this concept. I explore the issue of casing across several research design, with special attention to the issue of 'negative cases' and the relation of casing to another core but rarely questioned foundational concept, the idea that social scientists study (and make inferences about) 'populations.' At various points in this essay, I challenge practices that are central to conventional quantitative social science and elaborate

approaches that are more compatible with the realist perspective, especially its synthesis with complexity theory. For example, there is a clear tension between what I call 'casing by outcome,' an approach that is more compatible with the realist perspective, and the more conventional 'casing by population,' which usually posits more cross-case homogeneity or comparability than may be warranted. A taken-for-granted or 'given' population may contain several distinct types of cases. Treating heterogeneous cases in a taken-for-granted population as comparable instances of 'the same thing' is little more than asserting comparability by fiat and runs the risk or relegating important case differences to the error vector of linear models. As one alternative to simply assuming comparability, I offer 'possibility analysis,' a method that directly examines the degree to which the members of a given set of cases are candidates for the outcome under investigation (see also Mahoney and Goertz 2004).

CASING AND THE REALIST PERSPECTIVE

In Ragin (1992), I proposed an approach to the issue of cases that I hoped would make it more tractable. The approach I suggested was to shift the discussion from its primarily ontological focus (Can cases be specified in some universally coherent and valid manner?) to more practical concerns, especially research practices (How, when, and why do researchers invoke cases?). In this formulation, 'casing' is a more-or-less routine research act, especially in the social sciences. Researchers 'case' their evidence in order to bring closure to difficult issues in conceptualization and research design and thus allow analysis to proceed. Empirical evidence is infinite in its complexity, specificity, and contextuality. Casing focuses attention on specific aspects of that infinity, highlighting some aspects as relevant and obscuring others. For example, it matters greatly whether a set of actions by a group of individuals is characterized as 'dissonance reduction,' 'collective behavior,' 'collective action,' 'resource expenditure' by a 'social movement organization,' or 'incipient institutionalization.' Different casings provide different blinders, different findings, and different connections to theory, research literatures, and research communities. Casing locates research in the vast domain of social science, linking it to the efforts of some researchers and severing its connections with others.

The idea of casing resonates with the realist perspective in several ways. First, the realist perspective keeps the case concept in the foreground. Rather than assuming that cases are mere observations, much like coin tosses, contained within given populations, the realist perspective supports the idea that cases are real entities and reflect the operation of actual causal mechanisms and processes. Of course, these entities and mechanisms are shrouded, even by our conceptions of them as cases, but still they discipline both our casings and our attempts to conceptualize and understand. Second, the realist perspective resonates strongly with the central idea that casing is a tentative and iterative process. The casing that inspires an investigation is always open to refinement and revision. By the time the research is complete, both the cases and their casing may have shifted substantially. Finally, it is clear that the realist perspective accepts that social phenomena are basically unknowable in a way that many social scientists would like. These phenomena do not arrive at our doorsteps in neat packages, ready to be opened and admired. Rather social phenomena and inordinately complex, contingent, and context specific. When we case social phenomena we gain brief glimpses of the possibility that social phenomena are ordered in some way that we can grasp.

Complex realism (see especially the chapters by my co-editor David Byrne [Chapter 5] and David Harvey [Chapter 1], in Part 1 of this handbook) also brings important insights to casing, in part explaining why it so often seems fluid and tentative. Complex realism views cases in social research as 'complex' as opposed to 'simple' systems. Simple systems generally conform to the expectations of linear models, which means that researchers can simply sum the impact of the relevant causal vectors in order to make predictions regarding a system's behavior. Complex systems, by contrast, are composed internally of bundles of interrelated aspects that can be understood only in these terms, as mutually reciprocal influences that together constitute the complex whole. Furthermore, complex systems have the capacity for qualitative, case-wide change, which can follow from routine, small-scale changes that accumulate and cascade through the system as a whole. In part, phase shifts (qualitative changes) occur due to the interconnectedness of system aspects and their reciprocal determination. The complex realist perspective provides important tools for social scientists when confronted with the difficult task of casing, with its emphasis on phase shifts and qualitative change providing clues as to how aspects are interconnected. Cilliers' (1998, 2001) notion that the boundaries of a system (and its 'caseness') are analytically inseparable from the processes that constitute the system is very useful here, as well, suggesting that the processes that produce phase shifts are central to the constitution of the system as whole.

It is always possible to push casing too far – to homogenize social phenomena in ways that contradict their specificity and their integrity. Complex realism offers an important caution not to betray social phenomena, by making comparable cases of things that are not. Casings are invoked; they also can be revoked. Complex realism recognizes the necessity of their invocation, but also celebrates their refinement, their revision, and even their revocation.

CASING OUTCOMES VERSUS POPULATIONS

One enduring source of confusion in the discussion of casing in the social sciences is that it has a dual nature, for the casing of a study can be based on either the outcome of a larger population of candidates for the outcome. For example, a researcher might study multiple instances of ethnic political mobilization and describe his or her cases in these terms, explicitly casing the study according to the outcome shared by the cases included in the study. However, a second researcher might conduct a study of ethnic political mobilization that includes countries with politically relevant ethnic differences, regardless of whether ethnic political mobilization actually occurred. Thus, the second study incorporates 'negative cases' of ethnic political mobilization. In this second framing, the cases of the study are not countries with ethnic political mobilization, but the larger population of countries in which ethnic political mobilization is thought to be possible (which, of course, includes both positive and negative cases). Thus, the question 'What Is the case?' can have different answers in studies that might appear, at first glance, to have identical casings. In the first study, casing is centered on the phenomenon in question – the set of cases with the outcome. In the second study, casing is centered on a larger population embracing both positive and negative instances.

Before discussing casings as outcomes versus populations further, it is important to address a common misunderstanding in the social sciences regarding the so-called error of 'selecting on the dependent variable.' Many case-oriented studies examine only positive cases (e.g. only actual instances of ethnic political mobilization, with negative cases excluded). In fact, the first step in much case-oriented inquiry is to identify the best possible instances of the phenomenon to be explained and then to study these instances in great depth. This research strategy is consistent not only with the realist perspective, but also with Lars Mjøset's 'contextualist' definition of cases, which he describes in Chapter 2: an outcome, the processes leading to the outcome, and the enabling features of the setting in which it occurred. Implicit in this formulation is the idea that casing is outcome driven and that instances of the outcome, on the one hand, and the population of relevant cases, on the other, are one and the same. The logic of this approach is straightforward,

for it is very difficult, if not impossible, to 'process trace' phenomena that do not exist or have yet to occur. Imagine, for example, trying to process trace the emergence of publicly funded paternity leave programs in poor countries.

Despite the obvious value of studying good instances of the phenomenon of interest, this practice is routinely castigated by conventional quantitative researchers. In *Designing Social Inquiry*, a book hailed by some as a handbook on how to conduct good qualitative research, King et al. (1994) are unabashedly hostile to this practice. Their reasoning is that studies that select on values of the dependent variable attenuate correlations between causal conditions and outcomes. In various publications, I have explained why this critique, while sound enough from a strictly correlational point of view, is fundamentally misguided (Ragin 1997, 2000, 2008). Of course, negative cases are often quite useful, especially when they offer theoretically decisive contrasts with positive cases. The search for negative cases is also important when researchers seek to establish the sufficiency of a given set of causal conditions for an outcome, because all (or virtually all) of the cases that display this set of conditions should also display the outcome (see Ragin 2000). The key point, however, is that it is wrong to label a study flawed simply because it omits negative cases, for there are many good reasons to study positive cases in isolation from negative cases. One obvious justification is the simple fact that it is very difficult to identify 'candidates' for an outcome – as any good negative case should be – without first knowing a lot about positive cases (Ragin 1997).

More pertinent to the topic of casing than the so-called error of selecting on the dependent variable is the tension that exists between casing outcomes and casing populations. The issue can be highlighted by examining the practice of casing across a range of research designs.

First, consider the single case study, which is almost always cased according to the outcome in question. For example, a researcher might conduct a case study of the

US Civil War as a 'modernizing revolution,' using the conceptual framework Barrington Moore, Jr (1966) elaborated in *Social Origins of Dictatorship and Democracy*. This researcher would probably argue that findings from her study are relevant to modernizing revolutions in general. Of course, this same set of events could be cased in other ways, for example, as part of a worldwide struggle against slavery, as an attempt to purge the US political economy of its neocolonial vestiges, or in some other manner. The point is not the choice of casing; rather, the point is that when researchers case a collection of processes and events, tied to a specific setting, they tend to focus on the outcome. The fact that multiple casings can be applied to a single case makes it a 'rich' case and also illustrates one of the central purposes of casing, which is to provide necessary blinders. Different casings highlight different case aspects and downplay or obscure others. Casing makes it possible for researchers to deal with the inherent complexity, specificity, uniqueness, and contextuality of social phenomena – to conduct social science despite all the obvious obstacles.

Next up in the hierarchy of research designs is the study of a set of cases with the same outcome, such as the one mentioned above – the study of positive instances of ethnic political mobilization. Again, casing in this design is primarily in terms of the outcome. However, the notion of casing by population is more in play, because the researcher in this example must cope with the diversity of cases in a well-defined set (e.g. the set of cases with ethnic political mobilization). Note that because there are multiple instances, the casing of the outcome is, in effect, constrained by observable commonalities in the outcome across relevant cases. In other words, the conceptualization of the outcome, and thus the casing, is more empirically constrained in this design than it is in the single case study. Despite the absence of negative cases, this design can be put to a lot of different uses. Is there a single set of causal conditions linked to the outcome? Do they make sense as necessary conditions?

Or are there different sets of causal conditions linked to different subsets of cases with the outcome? Might these different sets of causal conditions signal the existence of subtypes of the outcome? Finally, are there meaningful differences across cases in the outcome, linked to differences in causal conditions? A simple example: are there differences in the success of ethnic political mobilization linked to differences in the political strategies adopted by these movements?

Consider next the addition of purposefully selected negative cases to the design just described. The casing of 'outcomes versus populations' now shifts even more in the direction of populations. With the addition of explicitly selected negative cases, the focus is on the larger population of candidates for the outcome, whether or not the outcome has occurred. This set is inherently more difficult to define than the set of cases with the outcome. The definition of this set is heavily knowledge and theory dependent, for it is impossible to know where something might have happened without explicit guidance. Note also that any definition of candidacy for the outcome that a researcher might propose could be contested. For example, one researcher might claim that any country with ethnic diversity is a candidate for ethnic political mobilization; another might claim that there must also be ethnic inequality; another might claim that in addition to ethnic inequality the political system must be non-repressive; and so on. In short, the question of candidacy concerns the kinds of settings capable of sustaining a process that could lead, potentially, to the outcome in question.

Finally, consider a research design where the casing is almost entirely by population. This design goes well beyond the previous, which involves careful specification of relevant negative cases based on their candidacy for the outcome in question. Instead, the researcher relies on a generic casing and uses a given, preconstituted population of cases. The central goal of research of this type is to construct generalizations about that population. For example, researchers studying ethnic political mobilization might argue that their cases include 'all formally constituted nation states,' a generic population, and that the research goal is to construct generalizations about that population. In much research of this type, the question of candidacy for the outcome is bypassed altogether. Researchers instead assume that the cases found in generic populations constitute the proper basis for constructing social scientific generalizations. Notice, however, that the outcome may not be possible for many members of a generic population. For example, ethnic political mobilization may not be even a remote possibility in many 'formally constituted nation states.' Because the researcher's focus is on the population as a whole, however, this issue is veiled.[1]

Some variable-oriented quantitative researchers who favor using generic populations would argue additionally that outcomes should be seen simply as dependent variables and not as emergent phenomena. For example, these researchers might substitute the dependent variable 'level of ethnic political mobilization' for the qualitative outcome, 'emergence of political mobilization along ethnic lines.' In this view, no mobilization (i.e. a score of zero on level of ethnic political mobilization) is simply one of many possible scores on the dependent variable, and the difference between a score of zero and a score of one is the same as the difference between a score of nineteen and a score of twenty. After all, in this view the goal of empirical analysis is to identify the independent variables that are the best predictors of variation in the dependent variable in a given population. It is clear that in this final step of the progression from the case study to the variable-oriented study, the possibility that the qualitative outcome, 'ethnic political mobilization,' might constitute a proper way of casing the study has been eliminated. Instead, casing is constituted by the boundaries of a generic population of substitutable observations. These observations, in turn, display the required variation-to-be-explained in the dependent variable, which in turn is now conceived as a variable aspect of members of the designated population. The possibility

that a score of zero on the dependent variable might signal that the outcome is impossible for some cases is now veiled by the assumption that the key research question concerns the properties of a population.[2]

Whereas focusing on the properties of taken-for-granted populations seems to relieve researchers of the problem of identifying relevant negative cases (via inclusion by fiat), this design merely sidesteps the issue without addressing it. The idea that the central goal of research is to study the properties of populations trumps even the concept of cases, downgrading them to the status of mere 'observations.' Below, I sketch an alternative approach to negative cases centered on the systematic identification of cases for which the outcome is possible (i.e. the identification of candidates for the outcome). Before elaborating this approach, I establish important groundwork showing how multi-dimensional state spaces and truth tables can be used to identify kinds of cases.

CASING AND MULTI-DIMENSIONAL VARIATE SPACES

In Chapter 5, my co-editor, David Byrne, describes complex systems (i.e. cases) in terms of their 'co-ordinates … in a multi-dimensional state space, the dimensions of which are the variate measures describing the system.' Whereas cases have different trajectories in this multi-dimensional space, they tend to cluster in specific locations. Furthermore, cases are capable of qualitative change, which means that they can move from one location in the variate space to another, even though the second location may be relatively distant from the first. Most regions of the variate space are devoid of cases, and only a relatively small number of well-populated locations or sectors exist. The variate space contains only a small number of well-populated locations (yielding clusters of cases) because of the way case aspects fit together. That is, aspects of cases cohere in meaningful packages that have a syndrome-like (and thus mutually reinforcing) character. These 'coherencies' reflect the interconnectedness of case aspects and the fact that only a limited number of combinations of aspects go together well.

This understanding of complex systems resonates well with the concept of 'limited diversity' in qualitative comparative analysis (QCA). In both its crisp set and fuzzy set versions, QCA relies on truth tables, which list all logically possible combinations of causally relevant conditions. With crisp sets, there are 2^k logically possible combinations of presence/absence of dichotomies (where k is the number of conditions). With fuzzy sets, a truth table can be used to summarize a k-dimensional vector space, with each row of the truth table corresponding to a specific corner of the k-dimensional space. (There are 2^k corners of the multi-dimensional space defined by the k fuzzy-set causal conditions and thus 2^k corresponding truth table rows; see Ragin 2000, 2008.) In essence, a truth table lists the different sectors of a 'multi-dimensional state space' and shows the number of cases in each sector.

In the typical application of the truth table approach, researchers find that most cases are captured by a relatively small subset of truth table rows, which correspond, in turn, to the most populated sectors of the multi-dimensional state space. In other words, a common finding in truth table analysis is that case diversity is profoundly limited. Often, only a minority of the logically possible combinations of conditions can claim empirical instances. The examination of limited diversity (i.e. the distribution of cases across truth table rows) shows which 'coherencies' are empirically common and which combinations of attributes are uncommon (perhaps even impossible).

For an illustration of these principles, consider Table 31.1, which shows a truth-table summary of a variate space for black males in the United States. The data are from the National Longitudinal Survey of Youth, which documents the connections between various background characteristics, especially educational experiences, and socioeconomic status as an adult. The variate traces used to construct the table are married versus not married, children versus no children, degree of membership in the set of cases with high income parents, degree of membership in the set of cases with college education, and degree of membership in the set of cases with low test scores (the Armed Forces Qualifying Test; AFQT).

Consider the distribution of the cases across the thirty-two sectors of the five-dimensional variate space defined by the causal conditions (see columns 1–5 of Table 31.1). The sectors (locations) are ranked according to their case counts, with the most common combination of conditions listed first. Column 6 shows the number of cases in each sector; column 7 shows the cumulative percentage of cases, moving down the table from the most frequent combination, to the second most frequent, and so on. As the table clearly shows, cases are distributed unevenly. In fact, the five most populated sectors of the thirty-two-sector, five-dimensional variate space capture nearly 65% of the cases. The ten most populated sectors embrace more than 80% of the cases, and the eighteen sectors with at least ten cases each account for almost 95% of the cases. Viewed from the opposite end of the table, the fourteen least populated sectors together snare only about 5% of the cases. In other words, nearly half of the thirty-two sectors of the five-dimensional state space are virtually void of cases.

From the perspective of 'coherencies,' it is clear that the most populated sectors combine conditions that are linked to poor prospects for socioeconomic advancement. The five most populated sectors (nearly 65% of the cases), for example, all combine low membership in both high parental income and college education. Three of these five also include high membership in low test scores, and none of the five displays the family configuration most often linked to avoiding poverty – married without children. In short, when viewing black males in the US in terms of the characteristics they most often combine, that is, the aspects that most often 'cohere,' it is clear that they face substantial obstacles to advance their socioeconomic status.

Table 31.1 Distribution of cases across sectors of five-dimensional state space (black males, National Longitudinal Survey of Youth)

Married	Children	Low test score	College educated	High parental income	Frequency	Cumulative percentage
0	0	1	0	0	212	28.0
0	0	0	0	0	89	39.8
1	1	1	0	0	82	50.6
1	1	0	0	0	60	58.5
0	1	1	0	0	48	64.9
0	0	0	1	0	37	69.7
0	0	1	0	1	22	72.7
0	0	0	0	1	19	75.2
1	0	1	0	0	19	77.7
1	1	0	1	0	19	80.2
0	0	0	1	1	17	82.4
0	0	1	1	0	16	84.6
1	0	0	0	0	16	86.7
0	1	0	0	0	15	88.6
1	0	0	1	1	12	90.2
1	1	0	0	1	12	91.8
1	1	0	1	1	11	93.3
1	1	1	0	1	11	94.7
1	0	0	1	0	8	95.8
1	0	0	0	1	6	96.64
1	0	1	0	1	5	97.2
1	1	1	1	0	5	97.9
0	0	1	1	1	4	98.4
0	1	0	1	0	4	98.9
0	1	0	0	1	3	99.3
0	1	1	1	0	3	99.7
0	1	1	0	1	1	99.9
1	0	1	1	0	1	1
0	1	0	1	1	0	1
0	1	1	1	1	0	1
1	0	1	1	1	0	1
1	1	1	1	1	0	1

Married, 1 = yes; children, 1 = yes; low test scores, 1 = strong membership; college educated, 1 = strong membership; high parental income, 1 = strong membership.

Using truth tables it is also possible to differentiate combinations of conditions that clearly 'exist' in the data from those that do not. The key concern here is *not* the difference between having at least one case versus having no cases, which simply differentiates the bottom four rows of Table 31.1 from the rest. Rather, the interest is in combinations of conditions registering *non-trivial* counts of cases versus those registering *trivial* counts. With a large N and individual-level data, it is important to consider the possibility that measurement error generates assignment error and that some combinations may have cases only as a result of such errors. Thus, in an analysis of this type it is useful to specify a frequency threshold that signals which combinations are non-trivial. The cumulative percentage data shown in column 7 of Table 31.1 are useful for establishing such a threshold. For example, defining rows with frequencies of at least ten cases as non-trivial differentiates the eighteen most populated sectors (containing 94.7% of the cases) from the fourteen least populated sectors (containing 5.3% of the cases). Of course, other frequency thresholds are reasonable, within obvious limits. For example, a threshold of at least fifteen cases captures 88.6% of the cases distributed across fourteen of the thirty-two sectors.

The larger point is that multi-dimensional state spaces, and by implication truth tables, provide a good starting point for thinking about and analyzing the 'kinds' of cases that exist in a given collection. This way of approaching the question of kinds differs from some of the more inductive approaches discussed in this handbook (e.g. cluster analysis and correspondence analysis) because it starts with a specification of the key dimensions, rather than arriving at them through a bottom-up analysis of case-level similarities and differences. Specifying kinds of cases, based on an encompassing view of their key attributes, is central to the larger process of casing, addressing the question: 'What are these cases, cases of?'

The identification of the kinds of cases in a given set is an important gateway to possibility analysis. In essence, the specification of a frequency threshold defines which locations in the multi-dimensional state space are well-populated 'coherencies' and therefore worthy of further analysis. Using 'at least ten cases' as the threshold identifies eighteen kinds of cases. Using 'at least fifteen cases' as the threshold identifies fourteen kinds of cases. The choice of threshold depends ultimately on whether the researcher is more interested in a fine-grained representation (using a lower frequency threshold) or a coarse-grained representation (using a higher frequency threshold). After establishing different kinds of cases, the next step is to evaluate each type with respect to the outcome, determining for each type whether the outcome is possible.

POSSIBILITY ANALYSIS

A key issue in the study of case outcomes, such as ethnic political mobilization, is the question of candidacy, as discussed previously. Does it make sense to include in a study the analysis of cases that cannot be considered candidates for the outcome? In general, the answer is that it is not sensible, except in those situations where the stated goal of the research is to generalize to a given population, that is, to estimate some population-wide effect or property. Furthermore, that population must be known, uncontested, and relatively well bounded. Absent this goal, researchers must address the issue of candidacy when identifying potential negative cases. Should the UK in the twentieth century be included in the set of countries vulnerable to peasant revolution? Certainly not, and it would be a monumental waste of intellectual labor to pursue this question through in-depth study.

Related to the idea of candidacy is the analysis of possibility (Mahoney and Goertz 2004). The key focus in possibility analysis is determining which cases have a possibility of displaying the outcome. For some cases, an outcome may be virtually certain. For example, children of the rich who attend the top prep schools and universities, earn high marks, and score well on achievement tests are almost certain to achieve a middle class life style, or better, as adults. Cases below these, say those from solidly middle class families, have a decent probability of achieving a middle class lifestyle, but this outcome is far from certain or even nearly certain. Instead, depending on the specific circumstances, the outcome is reached in a probabilistic manner; some cases have a higher probability, and some cases have a lower probability. Finally, at the opposite end of the distribution of causal conditions, there may be those for whom a middle class lifestyle is only a dream. They are the flipside of the first group, because their outcome is completely opposite: they are almost certain not to achieve a middle class lifestyle. In effect, the probabilistic range is sandwiched in between two kinds of quasi-uniformity – those who are almost certain to succeed, on the one hand, and those who are almost certain not to, on the other.

Conventional quantitative social science focuses exclusively on the realm of probability. That is, the extremely high probabilities of the outcome at one end (i.e. those who are almost certain to display the outcome) and the extremely low probability of the outcome at the other end are viewed simply as part of the range of probabilities (i.e. as mere quantitative variation) and not as signaling possible qualitative discontinuities or breaks in the range of probabilities. By contrast, set theoretic analysis focuses explicitly on such qualitative breaks. When cases with a specific combination of characteristics (e.g. those displayed by the offspring of the rich) are almost certain to display an outcome (e.g. high socioeconomic status as adults), they constitute a near-perfect subset of the cases with the outcome. Furthermore, the combination of characteristics they share can be considered sufficient for the outcome (that is, assuming this connection resonates with theoretical and substantive knowledge). Likewise, if the cases at the opposite end of the distribution are almost certain not to display the outcome, then these cases constitute a near-perfect subset of those with an absence of the outcome, and the characteristics they share may be considered sufficient for its absence.

The qualitative break between 'almost certain not to display the outcome' and 'a non-trivial probability of displaying the outcome' is an important and vastly under-explored divide in the analysis of social phenomena. Cases with a non-trivial probability of the outcome (which includes those cases for which the outcome is almost certain) are those for whom the outcome is 'possible.' Cases with a null or trivial probability of the outcome are those for whom the outcome is virtually impossible.

For illustration of these ideas, consider again the cases presented in Table 31.1. The analysis of these data, using degree of membership in the set of cases achieving a middle class income (or better) as the outcome, reveals that two of the listed combinations (among the eighteen rows that pass the frequency threshold mentioned above) have truly trivial probabilities of displaying the outcome. Cases in these two rows combine the following four characteristics: they are unmarried with children, and they have low membership in college educated and low membership in high parental income. (They may or may not have low AFQT scores.) The results suggests that there is a chasm

separating cases in these two truth table rows from those in the other sixteen combinations of conditions, for the row with the next highest probability of the outcome displays a value well above those registered by these two rows. From a purely probabilistic point of view, cases in these two rows are simply those with a very low probability of the outcome, and a conventional statistical analysis might predict these low probabilities with reasonable accuracy. From a set theoretic point of view, however, the combination of these four conditions is sufficient for virtual exclusion from the outcome. That is, the set-theoretic view differentiates between these cases and the rest in a qualitative manner by focusing on the substantively meaningful difference between trivial and non-trivial probabilities of the outcome.

Expressed as a logical equation, the set-theoretic formulation for exclusion from the outcome is:

$$\sim \text{possible} = \sim \text{married} \bullet \text{children} \bullet \sim \text{high\_income\_parents} \bullet \sim \text{college}$$

where '$\sim$' signals negation or not, '$\bullet$' signals combined conditions (set intersection – logical *and*), 'possible' is the set of cases for whom the outcome is possible, 'married' is the set of married individuals, 'high_income_parents' is the set of cases with high income parents, and 'college' is the set of cases with college education. By applying De Morgan's Law (see Ragin 1987) to this logical equation, a set-theoretic formulation describing the conditions linked to the *possibility* of the outcome can be derived:

$$\text{possible} = \text{married} + \sim \text{children} + \text{high\_income\_parents} + \text{college}$$

where '$+$' signals alternate conditions (set union – logical *or*). The equation indicates that the possession of any one of these four advantages makes a black male in the US a candidate for inclusion in the set of cases with at least middle-class incomes. This conclusion cannot be derived statistically, but follows instead from a set-theoretic analysis of the evidence. The main point of this exercise, however, is not its substantive conclusion, but rather to demonstrate that researchers can exploit the qualitative break between trivial and non-trivial probabilities and thereby explore conditions of possibility. This exploration relies on the understanding of this qualitative break as a basis for conducting set theoretic analysis.

The 'possibility analysis' just presented has a direct bearing on the issue of casing. In the absence of an explicit interest in deriving population-specific properties or estimates, possibility analysis shows which cases are *not* candidates for the outcome and thus are implausible negative cases. In a conventional quantitative analysis, the inclusion of implausible cases simply inflates theory-confirming correlations. Correlations are strong when there are many cases displaying both the cause and the outcome and, simultaneously, there are many cases displaying the absence of both the cause and the outcome. Both kinds of cases contribute equally to the strength of a correlation, for its calculation is completely symmetrical. The inclusion of cases that are not plausible candidates for the outcome in a correlational analysis simply pads the number of cases in the null-null category or sector, and thus also pads the correlation, for such cases lack both the relevant causal conditions and the outcome.

It is important to point out that many data sets used by social scientists are not true populations or even samples drawn from true populations, but instead are simply convenient collections of cases. Furthermore, most researchers are not that interested in inferring population properties, *per se*. More commonly, they are interested in looking at patterns across their cases, usually via the application of correlational analysis or some technique based on correlational analysis (e.g. multiple regression, logistic regression, structural equations models, and so on). Researchers routinely subject these convenient collections of cases to conventional statistical analysis as a way to identify important patterns and relationships. When these analyses include a substantial

number of cases that are not candidates for the outcome in question, researchers risk inflating correlations and thereby distorting their results. Thus, while it may seem that reliance on given populations offers a safe haven from the problem of identifying valid negative cases, in fact, given populations are often laden with results-distorting irrelevant cases.

CONCLUSION

Lurking behind my discussion of negative case, populations, and possibility analysis is the implication that treating cases as members of given (and fixed) populations and seeking to infer the properties of populations may be a largely illusory exercise. While demographers have made good use of the concept of population, and continue to do so, it is not clear how much the utility of the concept extends beyond their domain. In case-oriented work, the notion of fixed populations of cases (observations) has much less analytic utility than simply 'the set of relevant cases,' a grouping that must be specified or constructed by the researcher. The demarcation of this set, as the work of case-oriented researchers illustrates, is always tentative, fluid, and open to debate. It is only by casing social phenomena that social scientists perceive the homogeneity that allows analysis to proceed.

My critique of the idea of given populations also has policy implications. Conventional quantitative researchers largely focus on the estimation of the net causal effect of independent variables across a large, encompassing, given population of observations. Case-oriented researchers, by contrast, are more focused on kinds of cases and their different fates. As I have noted elsewhere (Ragin and Rihoux 2004), elaborating kinds of cases and studying their different fates is more relevant to policy than the estimation of the net effects of causal variables across a broad population (often containing unknown and unacknowledged heterogeneity). After all, a common goal of social policy is to make decisive interventions, not to move average levels or rates up or down by some small increment. A social policy is most capable of decisive intervention when it is grounded in explicit case-oriented knowledge about specific sets of cases. The idea of population and the notion that the goal of social science is to estimate the properties of populations undermine fine-grained attention to types and kind, and to context and contingency.

CODA

This handbook illustrates the substantial progress that has occurred over the past two decades in the field of case-based social research. There have been many important practical advances, and there is now available an array of techniques that address cases as bundles of connected attributes. Today, these techniques can be viewed properly as members of a family of related techniques, all case-centered. Without the 'case-centered' label, they appear as separate attempts to analyze social phenomena in ways that diverge from conventional 'net effects' approaches (Ragin 2008), where the focus is on parsing each independent variable's unique effect. By joining the different case-centered techniques together, as we have in this handbook, it is possible to see their connections, as well as to imagine new ways of combining them.

Cases are obviously at the foundation of case-centered methods. It is impossible to address case-centered methods without also addressing what is meant by *case*. Many of the contributions to this handbook address the issue of casing in one way or another, often with the aid of some version of the realist perspective. As I have indicated in this chapter, the process of casing is as varied as the research designs that social scientists contrive. The important underlying commonality is that the process of casing offers a way of seeing, with different casings offering different, though selective and limited, views of the same infinite body

of evidence. Casing has the potential to offer glimpses of the underlying processes and entities that are the central focus of any social science that seeks to go beyond the immediate.

NOTES

1. In many quantitative studies, conditions that might be viewed by case-oriented researchers as those that define the set of relevant cases (e.g. scope conditions; see Goertz and Mahoney, Chapter 17) become independent variables in multivariate analyses and are used to predict variation in the dependent variable. This practice is very common; it is also fundamentally flawed. Suppose, for example, that a quantitative researcher studying variation in ethnic political mobilization in all formally constituted nation states uses 'degree of ethnic diversity' as an independent variable, estimating its net effect on the dependent variable. Superficially, this practice appears perfectly reasonable, for there should be a non-trivial correlation between ethnic diversity and ethnic political mobilization across formally constituted nation states. The problem with this approach is that all other predictors of ethnic political mobilization in this analysis should have their effect only when country scores on 'ethnic diversity' are non-trivial. In effect, a non-trivial level of ethnic diversity, in this hypothetical analysis, is a necessary condition for ethnic political mobilization and thus should be understood as a condition that must be substantially present for the other causal conditions to have any impact (or at least for the researcher to be able to properly estimate their impact). In practical terms, the implication of this understanding is that ethnic diversity should be included in the model only in multiplicative interaction terms, with ethnic diversity paired with most, if not all, of the other predictors. Of course, a simpler and more straightforward way to address this issue is simply to exclude irrelevant cases (i.e. those with low levels of ethnic diversity). However, quantitative researchers are often reluctant to exclude cases because successful statistical analysis often hinges on having a large number of cases – the larger the N, the better.

2. Of course, there are techniques that address the qualitative break between a score of zero on the dependent variable and a non-zero score, for example, Tobit analysis (see, e.g., Walton and Ragin 1990). In effect, these techniques estimate a model that addresses the differences between zero and a non-zero case and then controls for these effects when estimating the impact of causal conditions on variation in the level of the outcome across the non-zero cases. Although these techniques do address differences between the two basic kinds of cases, the issue is viewed primarily as a data problem and focuses on

the technical challenge of estimating the true level of the dependent variable for cases that have zero scores on the outcome, as though these scores have been censored in some way. These techniques do not address the problem of defining the set of relevant cases.

REFERENCES

Cilliers, P. 1998 *Complexity and Postmodernism*. London: Routledge.

Cilliers, P. 2001 'Boundaries, hierarchies and networks in complex systems' *International Journal of Innovation Management* 5(2):135–147.

Feagin, J.R., Orum, A.M. and Sjoberg, G. (Eds) 1991 *A Case for the Case Study*. Chapel Hill, NC: University of North Carolina Press.

King, G., Keohane, R.O. and Verba, S. 1994 *Designing Social Inquiry: Scientific Inference in Qualitative Research*. Princeton, NJ: Princeton University Press.

Mahoney, J. and Goertz, G. 2004 'The possibility principle: choosing negative cases in comparative research' *American Political Science Review* 98: 653–669.

Moore, Barrington, Jr 1966 *The Social Origins of Dictatorship and Democracy: Lord and Peasant in the Making of the Modern World*. Boston: Beacon.

Ragin, C.C. 1992 '"Casing" and the process of social inquiry' in C.C. Ragin and H.S. Becker (Eds) *What Is a Case? Exploring the Foundations of Social Inquiry*. Cambridge: Cambridge University Press, pp. 217–226.

Ragin, C.C. 1997 'Turning the tables: how case-oriented methods challenge variable-oriented methods' *Comparative Social Research* 16: 27–42.

Ragin, C.C. 2000 *Fuzzy-Set Social Science*. Chicago: University of Chicago Press.

Ragin, C.C. 2008 *Redesigning Social Inquiry: Fuzzy Sets and Beyond*. Chicago: University of Chicago Press.

Ragin, C.C. and Becker, H.S. (Eds) 1992 *What Is a Case? Exploring the Foundations of Social Inquiry*. Cambridge: Cambridge University Press.

Ragin, C.C. and Rihoux, B. 2004 'Qualitative comparative analysis (QCA): state of the art and prospects' *Qualitative Methods* 2(2): 3–13.

Walton, J. and Ragin, C.C. 1990 'Global and national sources of political protest: third world responses to the debt crisis' *American Sociological Review* 55(6): 876–890.

Author Index

Subject Index